THE GREAT COMBAT PICTURES:

Twentieth-Century Warfare on the Screen

by
JAMES ROBERT PARISH

The Scarecrow Press, Inc.
Metuchen, N.J., & London
1990

British Library Cataloguing-in-Publication data available

Library of Congress Cataloging-in-Publication Data

Parish, James Robert.
  The great combat pictures : twentieth-century warfare on the
screen / by James Robert Parish.
    p.   cm.
  ISBN 0-8108-2315-2 (alk. paper)
  1. War films—Catalogs.   I. Title.
PN1995.9.W3P37   1990
016.79143'658—dc20   90-8457

Dedicated to the memory of

DeWITT BODEEN

a true friend and a fine cinema historian.

CONTENTS

Acknowledgments   vii
Introduction   ix

THE GREAT COMBAT PICTURES   1

Filmography   463
Combat Programs on Television,
    compiled by Vincent Terrace   473
About the Author   476

v

ACKNOWLEDGMENTS

John Cocchi

Howard Davis

Alex Gildzen

Kim Holston

Doug McClelland

Alvin H. Marill

Jim Meyer

Peter Miglierini

Movie Poster Service (Bob Smith, Charles Smith)

Michael R. Pitts

Vincent Terrace

Editorial Consultant: T. Allan Taylor

INTRODUCTION

There are many solid reasons why combat films have been such an enduring staple of filmmakers, long before PLATOON (1986) made the waning genre big commercial box-office once again and television began offering such weekly Vietnam series as "Tour of Duty" and "China Beach." There are so many varied ways persons react to the rigors and horrors of combat that screenwriters are drawn by the dramatic potentials. Then too, the sundry acts of warfare allow for a full spectrum of special effects to depict the exploding violence as man kills man in a host of ways—all staple ingredients for rousing action feature films. And, of course, because motion pictures are such a powerful propaganda tool, what better way than producing a carefully crafted patriotic tribute to arouse viewers to a particular cause and to train them how to think of the "enemy."

The focus of this book is on the combat feature film and, in particular, English-language theatrical releases and telefeatures dealing with twentieth-century wars, especially World War I, World War II, the Korean War, and the Indo-China/Vietnam War.

As such, this volume does not cover service comedies (e.g., SEE HERE, PRIVATE HARGROVE, 1944; DON'T GO NEAR THE WATER, 1957); training service dramas (e.g., DEVIL DOGS OF THE AIR, 1935; WINGED VICTORY, 1944; TAKE THE HIGH GROUND, 1953; BILOXI BLUES, 1988); war tales that are primarily espionage studies (e.g., ASSIGNMENT IN BRITANNY, 1943; THE HEROES OF TELEMARK, 1965); patriotic dramas of life on the homefront either during a major war (e.g. SINCE YOU WENT AWAY, 1944) or after (e.g., THE BEST YEARS OF OUR LIVES, 1946; COMING HOME, 1978); documentaries (e.g., THE BATTLE OF MIDWAY, 1942; DEAR AMERICA, LETTERS HOME FROM VIETNAM, 1987); fantasies about war (e.g., WORLD WAR III, 1982-TV; RED DAWN, 1984); or in general, films about the resistance movement (e.g.,THE NORTH STAR, 1943, EDGE OF DARKNESS, 1943).

As always the author would appreciate readers' comments.

James Robert Parish
4338 Gentry Avenue #1
Studio City, CA 91604

THE GREAT COMBAT PICTURES

ABOVE AND BEYOND (Metro-Goldwyn-Mayer, 1952) 121 mins.

Producers/directors, Melvin Frank, Norman Panama; story, Beirne Lay, Jr.; screenplay, Frank Panama, Lay; art directors, Cedric Gibbons, Malcolm Brown; set decorators, Edwin B. Willis, Ralph Hurst; music, Hugo Friedhofer; music conductor, Andre Previn; sound, Douglas Shearer; montages, Peter Ballbusch; special effects, A. Arnold Gillespie, Warren Newcombe; camera, Ray June; editor, Cotton Warburton.

Robert Taylor (Colonel Paul Tibbets); Eleanor Parker (Lucy Tibbets); James Whitmore (Major Uanna); Larry Keating (Major General Vernon C. Brent); Larry Gates (Captain Parsons); Marilyn Erskine (Marge Bratton); Stephen Dunne (Major Harry Bratton); Robert Burton (General Samuel E. Roberts); Hayden Rorke (Dr. Ramsey); Larry Dobkins (Dr. Van Dyke); Jack Raine (Dr. Fiske); Jonathan Cott (Dutch Van Krik); Jeff Richards (Thomas Ferebee); Dick Simmons (Bob Lewis); John McKee (Wyatt E. Duzenbury); Patrick Conway (Radio Operator); Christie Olson (Paul Tibbets, Jr.); William Lester (Driver); Barbara Ruick (Mary Malone); Jim Backus (General Curtis E. LeMay); G. Pat Collins (Major General Creston); Harlan Warde (Chaplain Downey); Crane Whittey (General Corlane); Don Gibson (Dexter); John W. Baer (Captain); John Close (Co-Pilot); Lee MacGregor (General Roberts' Aide); Ewing Mitchell (General Wolfe); Dorothy Kennedy (Nurse); Sam McKim (Captain); Robert Forrest (Military Police Officer); Dabbs Greer (Haddock); John Hedloe (Lieutenant Malone); Frank Gerstle (Sergeant Wilson); John Pickard (Miller); Gregory Walcott (Burns); Roger McGee (Johnson); and: Roger Fuller.

At 8:15 A.M. on August 6, 1945, a United States B-29 long-range bomber plane dropped a four-ton atomic bomb on Hiroshima, Japan. This atomic attack which killed 150,000 and destroyed about 60% of the city, along with the subsequent bomb dropped on Nagasaki (August 9, 1945), is credited with bringing about the end of the Pacific Theatre of War in World War II.

The dramatic events leading up to this cataclysmic event provide the backdrop for ABOVE AND BEYOND, MGM's

1

Eleanor Parker and James Whitmore in ABOVE AND BEYOND (1952).

second excursion into dealing with the devastating event. (The studio's earlier THE BEGINNING OR THE END, 1947, dealt in elaborate detail with the development of the atomic bomb.)

U.S. Air Force Colonel Paul Tibbets (Robert Taylor), with two years of action in the European theatre of the War, is dispatched back to the States to begin testing an experimental long-range bomber and training its crew. The mission is cloaked in utmost secrecy, which means that neither Tibbets nor his men can reveal the least detail of their activities even to their families. Those breaking the code of silence are removed immediately from the project. The strain on duty and especially on the home front provides the backdrop for this very long feature.

At a very long 121 minutes, ABOVE AND BEYOND suffers from its too meticulous detail-by-detail presentation. The contrived interweaving of the tense domestic relationship between Tibbets and his overwrought wife (Eleanor Parker) is not enough to maintain viewer interest. Not even the climactic mission of the B-29 bomber *Enola Gay** over enemy territory makes this a compelling film.

---

*Tibbets named the aircraft after his mother. (Much was made of the fact that Enola spelled backward is alone.) Accompanying aircraft on the mission were the *Great Artiste* and *#44-27291.*

Production values are extremely high and there is the expected ushering in and out of historically key military and political personnel. This was the first of three pictures Robert Taylor and Eleanor Parker made together, and at the time of the release of ABOVE AND BEYOND the co-stars were rumored to be romantically interested in one another offscreen, all of which helped initial box-office grosses. Actually James Whitmore as the jocular Major Uanna, security head of the project, gives the film's best performance. ABOVE AND BEYOND was named one of the year's ten best films by the National Board of Review and Louella O. Parsons chose the film as "Best Drama of the Month" in her *Cosmopolitan* magazine column.

The story would later be retold in the made-for-television feature, ENOLA GAY: THE MEN, THE MISSION, THE ATOMIC BOMB (1980), q.v.

ABOVE US THE WAVES (Republic, 1955) 92 mins.

Producer, J. Arthur Rank; director, Ralph Thomas; story, C. E. T. Warren, James Benson; screenplay, Robin Estridge; art director, George Provis; music, Arthur Benjamin; music director, Muir Mathieson; camera, Ernest Steward; editor, Gerald Thomas.

John Mills (Commander Frazer); John Gregson (Duffy); Donald Sinden (Corbett); James Robertson Justice (Admiral Ryder); Michael Medwin (Smart); James Kenney (Abercrombie); O. E. Hasse (*Tirpitz* Captain); Lee Patterson (Cox); Lyndon Brook (*X2* Diver Navigator); William Russell (Ramsey); Theodore Bikel (German Patrol Boat Officer); Thomas Heathcote (Hutchins); Harry Towb (McCleery); Anthony Newley (*X2* Engineer); Cyril Chamberlain (Chubb); John Horsley (Andersen); Anthony Wager (George); William Franklyn (*X2* #1); Leslie Weston (Winley); Guido Lorraine (Officer Interpreter).

". . . ABOVE US THE WAVES has that near-documentary quality which has been the hallmark of its type of British film. . . . Acting maintains a high all-round standard . . ." (*Variety*).

In mid-World War II the German battleship *Tirpitz* is keeping half the British Home Fleet preoccupied, guarding against the vessel leaving the shelter of the Norwegian fjords and attacking Allied ships heading to or from England. This diversionary tactic results in other Allied vessels being insufficiently protected and they are being sunk by Axis destroyers. The Royal Navy concocts a wild scheme of sending midget submarines to plant underwater explosives on the hulk of the *Tirpitz*. British Naval Commander Frazer (John Mills) is in charge of the desperate operation. The two attempts to accomplish the mission provide the tension, and in September 1943 the *Tirpitz* is put out of action for the duration of the war. The cost of victory: two of the three British mini-subs are captured by the Germans and the third is blown up with the *Tirpitz*.

This production was released originally in April 1955 in England by General Film Distributors with a 99-minute running time. While the film has an unfortunate studio-bound look, the superior performances and well constructed script give it substance.

ACES HIGH (Cine Artists, 1976) Color 114 mins.

Producer, S. Benjamin Fisz; associate producer, Basil Keys; director, Jack Gold; suggested by the play *Journey's End* by R. C. Sherriff; screenplay, Howard Barker; set decorator, Syd Caine; music, Richard Hartley; assistant director, Derek Cracknell; technical advisers, Air Commodore Alan Wheeler, Group Captain Dennis David; special effects, Derek Meddings; camera, Gerry Fisher; aerial camera, Peter Allwork; editor, Anne Coates.

Malcolm McDowell (Squadron Leader Gresham); Christopher Plummer (Sinclair); Simon Ward (Crawford); Peter Firth (Croft); John Gielgud (Headmaster); Trevor Howard (Lieutenant Colonel Silkin); Richard Johnson (Colonel Lyle); Ray Milland (Brigadier Whale); David Wood (Thompson); David Daker (Bennett); Elliott

ACES HIGH (1976).

Cooper (Wade); Pascale Christophe (Croft's Girlfriend); Jeanne Patou (Chanteuse).

R. C. Sherriff's highly-regarded play, *Journey's End* (1929), about the harrowing effect of World War I trench warfare on soldiers, made an equally effective feature film, JOURNEY'S END (1930), q.v. Both had become genre classics in their mediums. In this Anglo-French co-production, Sherriff's story is reworked to focus on the stress Allied pilots underwent during the First World War. The glossy results provide admirable aerial gymnastics, while on the ground the action is unabashedly clichéd.

Youngish Squadron Leader Gresham (Malcolm McDowell) is responsible for the welfare of the young British airmen of 76 Squadron, including enthusiastic newcomer Croft (Peter Firth), emotionally susceptible Sinclair (Christopher Plummer), and frightened Crawford (Simon Ward). Pressure-driven Gresham appreciates the futility of war but knows his duty to country and to his charges; the grueling conflict leads him to hide behind drink. During the story Crawford hopes to finagle a military discharge; Firth romances a tempting French girl (Pascale Christophe) but is later killed in aerial combat; and avuncular second-in-command Sinclair also dies for England.

Much is made of brief "special guest appearances" by John Gielgud as the pompous school headmaster and by Ray Milland, Trevor Howard, and Richard Johnson as General Headquarters brass safely tucked away in a French chateau eating and drinking to excess while toying unfeelingly with the lives of their men.

The highlight of ACES HIGH remains the aerial sequences, as vintage aircraft zoom through their war maneuvers, creating a vivid ballet in the sky. These scenes almost make it worthwhile for the viewer to endure the hackneyed retelling of Sherriff's strong dramatic original.

ACTION IN THE NORTH ATLANTIC (Warner Bros., 1943) 126 mins.*

Producer, Jerry Wald; director, Lloyd Bacon; based on the novel by Guy Gilpatrick; screenplay, John Howard Lawson; additional dialogue, A. I. Bezzerides, W. R. Burnett; art director, Ted Smith; set decorator, Clarence Steensen; assistant director, Elmer Decker; dialogue director, Harold Winston; music, Adolph Deutsch; music director, Leo F. Forbstein; sound, C. A. Riggs; montages, Don Siegel, James Leicester; special effects, Jack Cosgrove; camera, Ted McCord; editors, Thomas Pratt, George Amy.

---

*Computerized color version now available.

Humphrey Bogart (Joe Rossi); Raymond Massey (Captain Steve Jarvis); Alan Hale (Boats O'Hara); Julie Bishop (Pearl); Ruth Gordon (Sarah Jarvis); Sam Levene (Chips Abrams); Dane Clark (Johnnie Pulaski); Peter Whitney (Whitey Lara); Minor Watson (Rear Admiral Hartridge); J. M. Kerrigan (Caviar Jinks); Dick Hogan (Cadet Robert Parker); Kane Richmond (Ensign Wright); Chick Chandler (Goldberg); George Offerman, Jr. (Cecil); Don Douglas (Lieutenant Commander); Art Foster (Pete Larson); Ray Montgomery (Ahern); Creighton Hale (Sparks); Elliott Sullivan (Hennessy); Alec Craig (McGonigle); Ludwig Stossel (Captain Ziemer); Dick Wessel (Cherub); Frank Puglia (Captain Carpolis); Iris Adrian (Jenny O'Hara); Irving Bacon (Bartender); James Flavin (Lieutenant O'Hara).

When an American tanker carrying highly volatile gas is torpedoed and sunk by a Nazi submarine, its lifeboat is rammed by the sub, forcing the survivors into the water. The few remaining men endure eleven days at sea on a raft before they are rescued. While awaiting reassignment, Captain Steve Jarvis (Raymond Massey) recuperates at home with his wife (Ruth Gordon), while first mate Joe Rossi (Humphrey Bogart) meets and marries a club singer (Julie Bishop). Jarvis is assigned a new ship, the *Sea Witch*, and makes Rossi his executive officer. Their assignment as part of the Merchant Marines is to join a convoy carrying valuable cargo to the Soviet allies in Murmansk. In the North Atlantic, German submarines assault the convoy and the *Sea Witch* is separated from the others. Although hunted by a sub, the *Sea Witch* holds off the attack with its guns, and in the cover of night steals away. However, the sub alerts the Luftwaffe and the next day two Axis planes attack the vessel. Several seaman are killed and Captain Jarvis is wounded before the planes are shot down. Rossi assumes command and in a tactical maneuver rams the surfaced pursuing German submarine. Later, a squadron of Russian planes escorts the damaged *Sea Witch* and its unharmed cargo into Murmansk where it receives a cheering welcome.

The two-hour-plus feature is both a rousing patriotic salute to the generally unheralded U.S. Merchant Marine* during World War II and an exciting action picture. "It is, in fact, one of the most efficient manifestations of the Warner Bros. adventure-drama formulas, in which the action is piled up in great layers. Like other

---

*When the feature debuted at Manhattan's Strand Theater on May 19, 1943, several hundred sailors from the Maritime Service Academy accompanied by the Merchant Marine Band trooped into the theatre to present beaming and proud Warner Bros. studio head Jack L. Warner with the Merchant Marine Victory Flag.

Warner Bros. wartime dramas, ACTION IN THE NORTH ATLANTIC is constructed on the theory that solid subject matter eliminates the necessity of a devious or complicated plot. . . . The story moves along without a hitch, and the audience knows what to expect—fast-moving drama, excellent character portrayals, and realistic dialogue" (Stephen L. Hansen, *Magill's American Film Guide*, 1983).

What makes the formula of brave Americans versus heartless Germans work so effectively in this film is the expert mixture of (stereo)types: brusque but heart-of-gold Rossi, the idealistic Captain Jarvis, blarney-laden rogue Boats O'Hara (Alan Hale), the introspective Jewish Chips Abrams (Sam Levene), the Brooklyn powderkeg Johnnie Pulaski (Dane Clark) and the edgy newcomer (Dick Hogan). Especially engaging is former screen bad guy Humphrey Bogart, here immersed in his new era of celluloid heroics, as the second-in-charge who gains a new sense of maturity when he takes over the command from fatherly Captain Jarvis. (The latter had shown his mettle early in the film when, in the choppy icy water with his surviving crew, he screams at the German sub crew, "We'll get ya!")

AIR FORCE (Warner Bros., 1943) 124 mins.

Executive producer, Jack L. Warner; producers, Hal B. Wallis, Howard Hawks; director, Hawks; screenplay, Dudley Nichols; (uncredited) William Faulkner; art director, John Hughes; music, Franz Waxman; music director, Leo F. Forbstein; orchestrator, Jack Sullivan; chief pilot, Paul Mantz; assistant director, Jack Sullivan; sound, Oliver B. Garretson; special effects, Roy Davidson, Rex Wimpy, H. F. Koenekamp; camera, James Wong Howe; aerial camera, Elmer Dyer, Charles Marshall; editor, George Amy.

John Ridgely (Captain Michael Quincannon, the Pilot); Gig Young (Lieutenant Bill Williams, the Co-Pilot); Arthur Kennedy (Lieutenant Tommy McMartin, the Bombardier); Charles Drake (Lieutenant Monk Hauser, the Navigator); Harry Carey (Sergeant Robbie White, the Crew Chief); George Tobias (Corporal B. B. Weinberg, the Assistant Crew Chief); Ward Wood (Corporal Gus Peterson, the Radio Operator); Ray Montgomery (Private Henry Chester, the Assistant Radio Operator); John Garfield (Sergeant Joe Winocki, the Aerial Gunner); James Brown (Lieutenant Tex Rader, the Pursuit Pilot); Stanley Ridges (Major Mallory); Willard Robertson (Colonel); Moroni Olsen (Commanding Officer); Edward S. Brophy (Sergeant J. J. Callahan); Richard Lane (Major W. G. Roberts); Bill Crago (Lieutenant P. T. Moran); Faye Emerson

(Susan McMartin); Addison Richards (Major Daniels); James Flavin (Major A. M. Bagley); Ann Doran (Mary Quincannon); Dorothy Peterson (Mrs. Chester); James Millican (Marine with Dog); William Forrest (Jack Harper); Murray Alper (Demolition Squad Corporal); George Neise (Hickam Field Officer); Tom Neal (Marine); Henry Blair (Quincannon's Son); Warren Douglas (Control Officer); Ruth Ford (Nurse); William Hopper (Sergeant); Walter Sande (Joe); and: Lynne Baggett, Leah Baird, Rand Brooks, James Bush, Ross Ford, Sol Gorss, George Offerman, Jr., Theodore von Eltz.

Opening with a quotation from Abraham Lincoln's Gettysburg Address, AIR FORCE is a magnificently integrated study of military teamwork under the stress of combat. As the film's Captain Michael Quincannon (John Ridgely) informs surly aerial gunner Joe Winocki (John Garfield), ". . . We all belong to this airplane. We're a single *team*. Each one of us has got to rely on every other man doing the right thing at the right time. Teamwork is all that counts."

It is December 1941 and the U.S. is still not officially in World War II. Nine Flying Fortress aircraft embark from San Francisco for a destination unknown, with the crews' families seeing them off.

John Garfield, Harry Carey, George Tobias, and Ward Wood in AIR FORCE (1943).

Once airborne, Captain Quincannon, pilot of the Boeing B-17 *Mary Anne,* opens his orders: his craft is bound for Hawaii. Just before arrival time, Pearl Harbor is bombarded by the Japanese and the *Mary Anne* is re-routed to a nearby island where it is attacked by fifth columnist Japanese-Hawaiians. Escaping, the crew chances a landing at badly damaged Hickman Field. Bombardier Tommy McMartin (Arthur Kennedy) learns that his sister Susan (Faye Emerson) has been injured in the surprise raid on Pearl Harbor and he blames her date, Lieutenant Tex Rader (James Brown), but learns later that his sister had been reckless while Rader had been heroic. Once refueled, the *Mary Anne* commences a hazardous 7,000-mile trek to the Philippines, with pilot Brown aboard. Stopping at Wake Island to refuel, the crew admires the doomed Marine detachment fighting overwhelming odds against the invading Japanese. The Marines persuade Corporal B. B. Weinberg (George Tobias) to take their mascot, a mongrel dog named Tripoli, aboard. At their destination, the Flying Fortress has several dangerous missions, one of which causes the Captain's death and the craft's near destruction. Just as the Japanese reach the airfield, the crew completes makeshift repairs to the *Mary Anne* and it takes off for Australia. En route it encounters the Japanese fleet and radios for air support from the Americans based in Australia. With the *Mary Anne* leading the strike force, the enemy vessels are vanquished. Once in Australia the *Mary Anne* and its crew prepare to join in the future bombing attacks against Japan.

As the film concludes, President Franklin D. Roosevelt is heard enunciating one of his famous war messages: "We shall carry the attack against the enemy. We shall hit him, and hit him again, wherever and whenever we can reach him, for we intend to bring this battle to him on his own home grounds!" The postscript informs viewers: "This story has a conclusion but not an end—for the real end will be the victory for which Americans, on land, on sea and in the air have fought, are fighting now, and will continue to fight until peace has been won."

Beyond the strikingly effective aerial combat scenes, the film boasts several compelling emotional sequences. There is the moment when Sergeant Robbie White (Harry Carey), the veteran Crew Chief, learns that his twenty-year-old aviator son has been killed. As he is handed his son's effects in a tiny handkerchief, he says, "He didn't even get into the air!" While Captain Quincannon lies dying in the hospital, he is surrounded by his loyal crew who promise they will repair the mutilated *Mary Anne* and that it will somehow fly again. As he dies, Quincannon hallucinates that he is on another mission and his crew fall into step. When asked their direction, Lieutenant Monk Hauser (Charles Drake), the navigator, says, "Due east . . . into the sunrise," and then the Captain dies. Another memorable sequence occurs during the refurbishing of the mangled *Mary Anne*, with audience tension mounting as the enemy approaches the airfield. The crew members are determined to keep their word to Quincannon by getting the craft airborne, and they do so with the once non-team player Rader at the controls.

Nothing highlights the need and effectiveness of military service teamwork more than the transformation of iconoclastic Winocki, played by Warner Bros.' resident rebel, John Garfield. Roughneck Winocki, who was washed out of flight school by Quincannon, intended to quit the service before Pearl Harbor. As Robin Wood says in *Howard Hawks* (1981), "Winocki's individualism is at first aggressive and destructive, we trace the process, not of its suppression, but of its conversion into a positive force. . . . The integration which follows carries for Winocki a sense of fulfillment: far from losing integrity, he gains it." When Winocki, against orders, assumes command of the hit plane after the crew has bailed out, he has achieved his goal of becoming a pilot. As Wood explains further in his book on director Hawks, ". . . The personal ambition has been assimilated into something nobler: it is the triumph of individualism placed at the service of something beyond itself, plane and Captain constituting the focal point of group unity."

Not only did AIR FORCE* become one of the top ten grossing films** of 1943, but it enjoyed substantial critical endorsements. "The action is so furious, the scope so comprehensive, the horizon so limitless, that one sees and still one cannot grasp in full the racing, roaring, ripping rush of drama, almost unadorned by emotion other than a passion to win the war" (*New York Daily Mirror*). Bosley Crowther (*New York Times*) enthused that it is a ". . . picture which tingles with the passion of spirits aglow."

ALBERT, R.N. (Eros, 1953) 88 mins.

Producer, Daniel M. Angel; director, Lewis Gilbert; based on the play by Guy Morgan, Edward Sammis; screenplay, Vernon

---

*For a detailed account of the (pre)production complexities of filming (with location shooting near Tampa, Florida) and rushing AIR FORCE into release before it became untopical, see Lawrence Howard Suid's introduction to the published screenplay of *Air Force* (1983).

**The advertisements for AIR FORCE read: "130 MILLION AMERICAN HEARTS FLY WITH IT. . . . THE PICTURE THAT REMEMBERS PEARL HARBOR. . . . COURAGE YOU CAN'T HELP CHEERING, IN MEN YOU CAN'T HELP LOVING!"

Harris, Morgan; music, Malcolm Arnold; camera, Jack Asher; editor, Charles Hesse.

Anthony Steel (Lieutenant Geoffrey Ainsworth); Jack Warner (Captain Maddox); Robert Beatty (Lieutenant Jim Reid); William Sylvester (Lieutenant "Texas" Norton); Michael Balfour (Lieutenant Henry Adams); Guy Middleton (Captain Barton); Paul Carpenter (Lieutenant Erickson); Moultrie Kelsall (Commander Dawson); Eddie Byrne (Commander Brennan); Geoffrey Hibbert (Lieutenant Craig); Peter Jones (Lieutenant Browne); Frederick Valk (Camp Kommandant); Anton Diffring (Hauptmann Schultz); Frederick Schiller (Hermann); Walter Cotell (Feldwebel); Peter Swanwick (Obergefreiter).

Coming in the same year as Hollywood's much-acclaimed STALAG 17, q.v., the overshadowed British-made ALBERT, R.N. is nevertheless a well-constructed prisoner-of-war drama, bolstered by an effective cast and a script which makes the mundane seem almost original.

The setting is a German prison camp for allied naval officers, and the time is late in 1944. Utilizing a lifelike papier maché dummy named Albert, R.N. to substitute for missing prisoners, Allied prisoners begin slipping out from the stronghold. The dummy's creator Lieutenant Geoffrey Ainsworth (Anthony Steel), allows others to try escaping before him, for he fears a future encounter with the female pen pal he has never met. But when a fellow serviceman dies in an escape attempt, Ainsworth realizes he must take his own turn. Before he sneaks away, he kills an odious German captor, Hauptmann Schultz (Anton Diffring). Jack Warner is resolute as the understanding senior British officer who maintains control over the other camp prisoners.

ALL QUIET ON THE WESTERN FRONT (Universal, 1930) 140 mins.

Presenter, Carl Laemmle; producer, Carl Laemmle, Jr.; director, Lewis Milestone; based on the novel *Im Westen Nichts Neues* by Erich Maria Remarque; screenplay, Del Andrews, Maxwell Anderson, George Abbott, (uncredited) Milestone; dialogue, Anderson, Abbott; titles, Walter Anthony; art directors, Charles D. Hall, William R. Schmidt; dialogue director, George Cukor; assistant director, Nate Watt; music/synchronization, David Broekman; sound, C. Roy Hunter; sound technician, William W. Hedgecock; special camera effects, Frank H. Booth; camera, Arthur Edeson, (uncredited) Karl Freund; editors, Edgar Adams, Milton Carruth.

Louis Wolheim (Sergeant Stanislaus Katczinsky); Lew Ayres (Paul Baumer); John Wray (Himmelstoss, the Postman); Raymond Griffith (Gerard Duval); George "Slim" Summerville (Tjaden); Russell Gleason (Muller); William Bakewell (Albert); Scott Kolk (Leer); Walter Rogers (Josef Behm); Ben Alexander (Franz Kemmerich); Owen Davis, Jr. (Peter Leer); Beryl Mercer (Mrs. Baumer);* Edwin Maxwell (Mr. Baumer); Harold Goodwin (Detering); Marion Clayton (Miss Baumer); Richard Alexander (Westhus); G. Pat Collins (Lieutenant Bertinck); Yola D'Avril (Suzanne); Poupée Andriot, Renée Damonde (French Girls); Arnold Lucy (Professor Kantorek); William Irving (Ginger); Edmund Breese (Herr Meyer); Heinie Conklin (Mammacher); Bertha Mann (Sister Libertine); Bodil Rosing (Wachter); Joan Marsh (Poster Girl); Tom London (Orderly); Vincent Barnett (Cool); Fred Zinnemann (Man).

ALL QUIET ON THE WESTERN FRONT (CBS-TV, 11/14/79) Color 158 mins.

Executive producer, Martin Starger; producer, Norman Rosemont; associate producer, Ron Carr; director, Delbert Mann; based on the novel *Im Westen Nichts Neues* by Erich Maria Remarque; teleplay, Paul Monash; production designer, John Stoll; art director, Karl Varcek; costumes, Jimmy Smith; makeup, Yvonne Coppard; music/music director, Allyn Ferguson; second unit director, Ernie Day; assistant directors, Pat Clayton, Kieron Phipps, Don French, Milos Kohut, Vladimir Blazek; technical adviser, Gunter Pfau; sound, Derek Ball; supervising sound editor, Don Sharpe; special effects, Roy Whybrow; camera, John Coquillon; supervising editor, Bill Bluenden; editor, Alan Pattilo.

Richard Thomas (Paul Baumer); Ernest Borgnine (Sergeant Stanislaus Katczinsky); Ian Holm (Himmelstoss); Donald Pleasence (Professor Kantorek); Patricia Neal (Paul's Mother); Mark Drewry (Tjaden); Mark Elliott (Josef Behm); Dai Bradley (Albert Kropp); Mathew Evans (Friedrich Muller); George Winter (Franz Kemmerich); Deonic Dephcott (Peter Leer); Colin Mayes (Westhus); Ewan Stewart (Detering); Simon Haywood (Gessler); Kevin Stoney (Hollerstein); Ken Hutchison (Hammacher); Stephen Reynolds

---

*After the first preview of the completed film during which audiences, used to seeing ZaSu Pitts in comedy roles, laughed when she came onscreen as Paul's mother, the studio had those scenes reshot with more dramatic (if saccharine) Beryl Mercer as Mrs. Baumer. However, some of the already completed silent prints with Pitts's role intact had been shipped abroad for distribution.

(Franz); Ian Hastings (Kewandowski); Denys Graham (Kaiser); Mary Miller (Kemmerich's Mother); Michael Sheard (Paul's Father); Marie Noelle-Barre (French Brunette); Dominique Varda (French Blonde); Arda Brokmenn (French Girl); Drahomira Fialkova (Sister Libertine); Katrina Lirova (Paul's Sister); Veronika Jenikova (Anna); Mark Roemmich (Gerard Duval) Andrew Burleigh, Tomas Juricka (Recruits); Bruce Purchase (Cook).

"This is what we must do. Strike with all our power to win victory before the end of the year. You are the life of the fatherland, you boys. . . . You are the iron men of Germany. . . . "

Warming to his subject, the speaker continues, "Perhaps some will say you should not be allowed to go yet, that you are too young. . . . Are your mothers so weak they cannot send their sons to defend the land which gave them birth?"

Reaching a crescendo, he concludes "Our country calls! The fatherland needs leaders!. . . Here is a glorious beginning for your lives. . . . What has kept you back? . . . You know how much you are needed. I see you look to your leader, Paul Baumer. I wonder what you are going to do?"

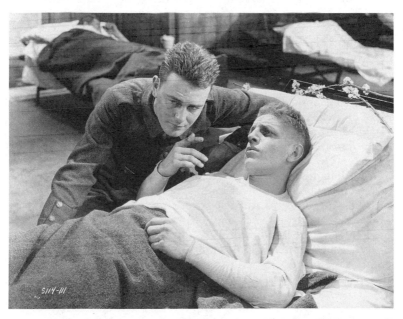

Lew Ayres and Ben Alexander in ALL QUIET ON THE WESTERN FRONT (1930).

It is World War I Germany and the lecturer is war-mongering Professor Kantorek (Arnold Lucy). En masse, his fired-up high school charges, led by young Paul Baumer (Lew Ayres), rush off naively to join the Kaiser's military service. In training camp the once gentle postman (John Wray), turned martinet corporal, transforms the novices into "soldiers" ready to fight. At the western front Paul is befriended by veteran soldier Sergeant Katczinsky (Louis Wolheim) who teaches him how to survive in battle. One by one Paul's comrades become "cannon fodder." Tension and disillusionment mount as the Kaiser's troops realize the final victory will not be theirs. The brief liaison Paul and his comrades experience with French girls, who trade sexual favors for food, is only a momentary diversion.

Having survived a near fatal wound, Paul returns home on leave, but he is a man out of step with time. He tries to soothe his ailing, frightened mother (Beryl Mercer), but to no avail. He visits his old school and is exhorted by jingoistic Professor Kantorek to tell the new crop of students about the glories of war. "I can't tell you anything you don't know," sighs the war-weary Paul. "We live in the trenches out there, we fight . . . we try not to be killed. Sometimes we are. That's all!" Then throwing aside his mask of caution, he adds, "When it comes to dying for your country, it's better not to die at all. There are millions out there dying for their country. What good is it?" He is booed and hissed from the classroom.

Paul realizes he should not have come home. He reasons, "Up at the front you are alive or you're dead and that's all and you can't fool anyone about that for very long . . . every day a year, every night a century." Now a cynic, he understands, "Our bodies are earth, our thoughts are clay and we eat and sleep with death and we're done for because you can't live that way and keep anything inside you."

Back in the trenches Paul finds that the few remaining members of his company are now intermingled with a bunch of raw young recruits. He locates Katczinsky, but his friend is soon killed by bomb shrapnel from a passing enemy plane. Later, on a lyrically peaceful day, the last day of war, Paul reaches out from his trench post to catch a butterfly and is killed by an enemy sniper. Quiet has come to the front.

As superb viewing today as when it was initially released, ALL QUIET ON THE WESTERN FRONT is a monumental screen translation of Erich Maria Remarque's incisive pacifist novel (1929). Produced at a cost of $1,250,000, with a 200-acre southern California ranch (in Irvine) serving as the battlefields for the 2,000 ex-servicemen extras, ALL QUIET was begun originally as a silent film, and then after a few weeks of shooting restarted as a sound feature.

There are many unforgettable and visually remarkable sequences: fluid tracking shots along the embattled trenches and the barbed wire fencing leading to the no man's land between the two forces; a montage of combat scenes focusing just on the boots of the soldiers; grim images depicting the human carnage of war.

And there are several memorable exchanges. Tjaden (George "Slim" Summerville) and Katczinsky philosophize about war.

> *Tjaden*: "Me and the Kaiser feel just alike about this war. Neither of us didn't want any war, so I'm going home. He's there already."

> *Katczinsky*: "Whenever there is a big war coming on you should rope off a big field . . . and on the big day you should take all the kings and their cabinets and their generals, put them in the center dressed in their underpants and put them in the center with clubs and let the best country win."

The hospital scene in which Kemmerich (Ben Alexander) learns that his leg has been amputated and shrieks in disbelief and anguish is riveting.

There is the horrifying moment where Baumer seeks refuge in a shell crater and finds a French soldier whom he stabs. Afraid to leave the shelter, Baumer must keep company with the dying man. Filled with remorse and near the breaking point, Baumer carries on a "conversation" with the dead enemy. "You're better off than I am. They can't do anything more to you now. Oh God, why did they do this to us? We only wanted to live, you and I. Why should they send us out to fight each other? If we threw away these uniforms and rifles, you could be my brother. You'll have to forgive me, brother comrade. Forgive me. Forgive me. Forgive me!"

Most haunting of all are the film's final screen moments after Baumer's ironic death on the final day of fighting. There are glimpses of many dark hillsides covered with the crosses of the war dead, and there, superimposed on the screen, is a passing profile of Baumer and all his dead classmates/fellow soldiers, looking back accusingly at the audience.

This strongly realistic anti-war film, showing that many of the German troops were sensitive human beings and not beasts, received tremendous acclaim in the United States (the *New York Times* judged it "pulsating and harrowing"). It won Academy Awards for Best Picture and for Best Director (Lewis Milestone). Unexpectedly, abroad the film was denounced in Nazi-infested

Germany as American propaganda, and other nations condemned the picture as a distortion of reality.

Remarque wrote a sequel, *The Road Back*, which Universal filmed in 1937 under the direction of James Whale. It dealt with the returning soldiers in post-war Germany, with Slim Summerville repeating his screen assignment as Tjaden. It made little box-office impact in a world growing to fear and/or hate the newly aggrandizing Germany. In 1939, ALL QUIET ON THE WESTERN FRONT, cut by several minutes, would be reissued with a special new prologue exhorting viewers to avoid having the horror of war occur again.

In 1979 ALL QUIET ON THE WESTERN FRONT was elaborately staged for television at a reputed cost of $6,000,000. For anyone who has seen the original, this new rendition leaves a lot to be desired. "It attempts to bring back all the horrors of World War I, but even the great detail issued to this film can't hide its TV mentality and melodramatic characters" (*Video Movie Guide 1988*, 1987). Nevertheless, the remake was nominated for seven Emmy Awards and won two Emmy trophies: for editing and special effects. When it was released in England in the spring of 1980 as a theatrical feature, the running time had been chopped to 129 minutes. The reaction was not favorable. "This ploddingly expensive film is as redundant a remake as one could conceive. Any sense of the horror or futility of the First World War proves persistently elusive . . . the movie remains at heart a gaudy costume drama—the essential unbelievability of the enterprise encapsulated in the casting of Ernest Borgnine as the cheerfully avuncular 'Kat'. . ." (John Pym, British *Monthly Film Bulletin*)

ALL THE YOUNG MEN (Columbia, 1960) 86 mins.

Producer/director/screenplay, Hall Bartlett; art director, Carl Anderson; assistant director, Lee Lukather; sound, James Flaster; camera, Daniel Fapp; editor, Al Clark.

Alan Ladd (Kincaid); Sidney Poitier (Sergeant Towler); James Darren (Cotton); Glenn Corbett (Wade); Mort Sahl (Crane); Ana St. Clair (Maya); Paul Richards (Bracken); Dick Davalos (Casey); Lee Kinsolving (Dean); Joe Gallison (Jackson); Paul Baxley (Lazitech); Charles Quinlivan (Lieutenant); Michael Davis (Cho); Mario Alcaide (Hunter); Maria Tsien (Korean Woman); Ingemar Johansson (Torgil).

In the winter of 1951 during the Korean War, a detachment of Marines is ambushed, with only a dozen surviving. The dying commanding officer puts black Sergeant Towler (Sidney Poitier) in charge. This causes resentment among several of the Marines:

veteran soldier Kincaid (Alan Ladd), who, although recently demoted, feels he should be the successor; southern redneck Bracken (Paul Richards); wise-cracking Crane (Mort Sahl); street-rough but sweet kid Cotton (James Darren), and pressured Wade (Glenn Corbett). Only the introspective Swedish Torgil (Ingemar Johansson) doesn't seem to mind the new commander's color.

It is Towler's decision to follow out the C.O.'s dying order that they should occupy a nearby farmhouse and await help. While enemy snipers outside begin picking off the Marines, within the farmhouse the racial tension mounts. When one of the men tries to rape the young Eurasian woman Maya (Ana St. Clair) there, Towler saves her and earns more scorn from the others. Towler and Kincaid put a North Korean tank out of commission, but in the fray Kincaid's leg is mangled and must be amputated. Towler provides his blood for the transfusion. Ordering Maya, her family, and the others to higher ground, he and the crippled Kincaid prepare to hold off the enemy assault as long as possible.

Treading heavily on the box-office popularity of rising star Sidney Poitier, the picture's major thrust was to milk the uniqueness of the racial theme. ("It crashes the boldest boundary line ever stretched across the screen!" exclaimed the film's ad copy.) As far as the study of racial prejudice at the front went, Variety opined, "The examination is neither dramatically plausible nor philosophically stimulating, at least one of which it ought to be."

Of minor note were the screen debut (and finale) of Ingemar Johannson, the former World Heavyweight boxing champion, the appearance of stand-up comic Mort Sahl, and the presence of teen-age idol Jimmy Darren, who sang the film's forgettable theme tune.

AMBUSH BAY (United Artists, 1966) Color 109 mins.

Executive producer, Aubrey Schenck; producer, Hal Klein; director, Ron Winston; screenplay, Marve Feinberg, Ib Melchior; music/music conductor, Richard La Salle; music editor, Edna Bullock; assistant director, Read Killgore; makeup, Charles Blackman; technical adviser, Lieutenant Colonel Clement J. Stadler; sound, Burdick S. Trask; sound effects editor, Del Harris; special effects, Charles Schuthies; camera effects, Butler-Glouner, Inc.; camera, Emmanuel Rojas; editor, John Schreyer.

Hugh O'Brian (First Sergeant Steve Corey); Mickey Rooney (Sergeant Ernest Wartell); James Mitchum (Private First Class James Grenier); Tisa Chang (Mijazaki); Pete Masterson (Sergeant William Maccone); Harry Lauter (Corporal Alvin Ross); Gregg Amsterdam (Corporal Stanley Parrish); Jim Anauo (Private Henry

Reynolds); Tony Smith (Private George George); Clem Stadler (Captain Alonzo Davis); Amado Abello (Amado); Juris Sulit (Midori); Max Quismundo (Max); Bruno Punzalan (Ramon); Buff Fernandez (Lieutenant Tokuzo); Joaquin Farjado (Captain Kayamatsu); Limbo Lagdameo (Man); Nong Arceo (Soldier).

Nine marines land on a Philippines isle in 1944 to contact an agent with information to pass along regarding General MacArthur's intended invasion of the islands. When their captain is killed, First Sergeant Steve Corey (Hugh O'Brian) takes charge. Rescuing their contact, Mijazaki (Tisa Chang), Sergeant Ernest Wartell (Mickey Rooney) sacrifices himself so that the remaining Marines can continue onward. Later they detonate the mines in the bay where MacArthur will land. Private First Class James Grenier (James Mitchum) is the sole survivor and lives to hear MacArthur's radio broadcast, "People of the Philippines, I have returned."

This film is definitely one of the better of the ilk of Philippines-lensed (Luzon) action pictures that glutted the 1960s movie theatres.

AN AMERICAN GUERRILLA IN THE PHILIPPINES (Twentieth Century-Fox, 1950) Color 105 mins.

Producer, Lamar Trotti; director, Fritz Lang; based on the novel by Ira Wolfert; screenplay, Trotti; art directors, Lyle Wheeler, J. Russell Spencer; set decorators, Thomas Little, Stuart Reiss; costumes, Travilla, Charles LeMaire; makeup, Ben Nye, Ernst Park; music, Cyril J. Mockridge; second unit director, Robert D. Webb; assistant director, Horace Hough; sound, Bernard Freerick, Harry M. Leonard; special effects, Fred Sersen; camera, Harry Jackson; editor, Robert Simpson.

Tyrone Power (Ensign Chuck Palmer); Micheline Presle (Jeanne Martinez); Tom Ewell (Jim Mitchell); Bob Patten (Lovejoy); Tommy Cook (Miguel); Juan Torena (Juan Martinez); Jack Elam (The Speaker); Robert Barrat (General Douglas MacArthur); Carleton Young (Colonel Phillips); Maria Del Val (Senora Martinez); Eddie Infante (Colonel Dimalanta); Orlando Martin (Colonel Benson); Miguel Anzures (Native Traitor); Chris de Varga, Eduardo Rivera (Japanese Officers); Arling Gonzales, Fred Gonzales (Radio Operators); Sabu Camacho (Bo); Rosa del Rosano, Kathy Ruby, Erlinda Cortez (Partisans).

Bataan is a peninsula guarding the entrance to Manila Bay in the Philippines. On April 9, 1942, 75,000 surviving American military surrendered to the Japanese. However, Navy Ensign Chuck Palmer (Tyrone Power) and his fellow seamen hide out in the jungle, hoping to reach Leyte and acquire a boat to take them to Australia and on to more war action. En route they are joined by Jeanne (Micheline

Presle), the comely wife of a sympathetic planter Juan Martinez (Juan Torena). She and Palmer fall in love, a romance which is consummated after Martinez' death. The group finds a small craft but it flounders at sea and the survivors return to shore where Filipino partisans hide them in the jungle. Palmer, Jim Mitchell (Tom Ewell), and the others work to free Leyte, supporting the guerrilla warfare in any way possible. Later, when the Japanese close in on Palmer's operation, most of his contingent are killed, but Palmer survives to be on hand to greet General Douglas MacArthur (Robert Barrat) and receive his commendation for bravery.

Based on the real life exploits of Navy Lieutenant I. D. Richardson, this film was disavowed by German director Fritz Lang who claimed, "It was . . . offered me—and even a director has to make a living! . . . a director has to eat." Shot entirely on location in the Philippines, the heroics exhibit a gritty earnestness, and the too-frequently-phlegmatic Tyrone Power seems enlivened by his role as the inventive, brave American naval officer. As so many better war films depict, soldiers under pressure to survive and to overcome overwhelming odds can be tremendously resourceful and seem to enjoy those proverbial nine lives.

British release title: I SHALL RETURN.

THE AMERICANIZATION OF EMILY (Metro-Goldwyn-Mayer, 1964) 115 mins.

Producer, Martin Ransohoff; associate producer, John Calley; director, Arthur Hiller; based on the novel by William Bradford Huie; screenplay, Paddy Chayefsky; art directors, George W. Davis, Hans Peters, Elliott Scott; set decorators, Henry Grace, Robert R. Benton; makeup, William Tuttle; costume designer, Bill Thomas; music, Johnny Mandel; song, Johnny Mercer and Mandel; music conductor, Robert Armbruster; assistant director, Al Shenberg; sound, Franklin Milton; special visual effects, J. McMillan Johnson; camera, Philip Lathrop; additional camera, Christopher Challis; editor, Tom McAdoo.

James Garner (Lieutenant Commander Charles E. Madison); Julie Andrews (Emily Barham); Melvyn Douglas (Rear Admiral William Jessup); James Coburn (Lieutenant Commander "Bus" Cummings); Joyce Grenfell (Mrs. Barham); Edward Binns (Admiral Thomas Healy); Liz Fraser (Sheila); Keenan Wynn (Old Sailor); William Windom (Captain Harry Spaulding); John Crawford (C.P.O. Paul Adams); Douglas Henderson (Captain Marvin Ellender); Edmon Ryan (Admiral Hoyle); Steve Franken (Young Sailor); Paul Newlan (General William Hallerton); Gary Cockrell (Lieutenant Victor Wade); Alan Sues (Enright); Bill Fraser (Port Commander); Lou Bryne (Nurse Captain); Alan Howard (Port Ensign); Linda Marlowe (Pat); Janine Gray, Judy Carne, Kathy Kersh ("Nameless Broads"); and: Sharon Tate.

This is one of those films that can not decide whether they are comedy or drama. The subject matter, when not diverting into romantic and sexual episodes, is a grim study of inter-branch fighting among the commanders of the American forces out to gain glory and fame no matter what the expense to their troops.

Lieutenant Commander Charles E. Madison (James Garner) is an aide to eccentric Rear Admiral William Jessup (Melvyn Douglas) in wartime London shortly before D-Day. Crafty Madison's specialty is supplying top Navy brass with treats ranging from exotic foodstuffs to party girls. It is Madison's theory that in wartime cowardice is more virtuous than heroics because the latter leads to more wars. Meanwhile Madison falls in love with Emily Barham (Julie Andrews) his pert British motorpool driver who has lost both her husband and brother in the war. The singular Admiral Jessup is convinced that the Army is overshadowing the Navy in publicity and his cure calls for the first dead man on Omaha Beach on D-Day to be a sailor. Madison is ordered to photograph the

Julie Andrews and James Garner in THE AMERICANIZATION OF EMILY (1964).

D-Day landing and later, at gunpoint, is made to be the first man ashore. When he trips a land mine, he is reported to be the first serviceman killed in the invasion. Dead he is a hero and Jessup is jubilant. But Madison turns up alive and threatens to reveal the cowardice which saved his life. Upon pressure from Emily who won't marry him if he tells the truth, Madison agrees to quietly accept a hero's welcome.

Highly touted for its adult themes, much maligned for its super cynicism and especially for its puerile sexual romp interludes, this "major" feature was generally ignored by the public, despite its star cast. The best performance is provided by Joyce Grenfell as the grief-stricken Mrs. Barham who has lost so much in the war.

Reissue title: EMILY.

ANGELS ONE FIVE (Stradford, 1954) 98 mins.

Director, George More O'Ferrall; screenplay, Derek Twist; music, John Woodridge; camera, Christopher Challis; editor, Daniel Birt.

Jack Hawkins (Group Captain "Tiger" Small); Michael Denison (Peter Moon); Andrew Osborn (Bill Ponsford); Cyril Raymond (Barry Clinton) Humphrey Lestocq ("Batchy" Salter); John Gregson ("Septic" Baird); Ronald Adam (Group Controller): Dulcie Gray (Nadine Clinton); Veronica Hurst (Betty Carfax); Amy Veness (Aunt Tabitha); Philip Stainton (Police Constable); and: Anthony Moore, Gordon Bell, Thorp Devereaux, Neil Wilson, Vida Hope, Richard Dunn, Russell Hunter, Donald McLisky, Harold Siddons, Rosemary Lomax, Ewan Roberts, John Harvey, Sam Kydd, Karen Grayson, Gillian Maude, Ann Lancaster, Harry Fowler, Victor Maddern, Russell Waters.

"No heroics, downbeat, but exciting and very successful war film" (*British Sound Films*, David Quinlan, 1984).

A no-nonsense study of the military maxim that individualism must always be sacrificed for the good of military teamwork. "Septic" Baird (John Gregson) is a rambunctious volunteer reserve pilot in 1940 England, who meets an insurmountable obstacle: stern Group Captain "Tiger" Small (Jack Hawkins), a man driven by the book rather than by wartime experience. "Septic" is attracted to ambulance driver Betty Carfax (Veronica Hurst) and adapts to squadron discipline. In the air he demonstrates that he is a sharp fighter pilot, but is later shot down by a German ace.

Working around budgetary restrictions, the film has more action taking place on the ground than in the air, and too much of the combat is talked about and not seen.

ANGELS ONE FIVE was released originally in England in 1952 by Associated British-Pathé with a 98-minute running time.

ANZIO (Columbia, 1968) Color 117 mins.

Producer, Dino De Laurentiis; director (English version), Edward Dmytryk; (Italian version) Duilio Coletti; based on the book by Wynford Vaughan-Thomas; adaptors, Frank DeFelitta, Coletti, Giuseppe Mangione, Canestri; screenplay (English), Harry A. L. Craig; art directors, Luigi Scaccianoce, Dante Ferretti; set decorators, Francesco Bronzi, Emilio D'Andria; costumes, Ugo Pericoli; makeup, Amato Garbini; music/music conductor, Riz Ortolani; song, Ortolani and Jerome "Doc" Pomus; assistant directors, Giorgio Gentili, Gianni Cozzo; sound, Aldo De Martinez; sound editor, Norman Schwartz; special effects, Walfrido Traversari; camera, Giuseppe Rotunno; editors, Peter Taylor, Alberto Gallitti.

Robert Mitchum (Dick Ennis); Peter Falk (Corporal Rabinoff); Arthur Kennedy (General Lesly); Robert Ryan (General Carson); Earl Holliman (Sergeant Stimler); Mark Damon (Richardson); Reni Santoni (Movie); Joseph Walsh (Doyle); Thomas Hunter (Andy); Giancarlo Giannini (Cellini); Anthony Steel (General Mash); Patrick Magee (General Starkey); Arthur Franz (General Howard); Elsa Albani (Emilia); Wayde Preston (Colonel Hendricks); Venantino Venantini (Captain Burns); Annabella Andreoli (Anna); Wolfgang Preiss (Marshal Kesselring); Tonio Selwart (General Von Mackensen); Stefanella Giovannini (Diana); Marcella Valeri (Assunta); Enzo Turco (Pepe); Elisabeth Tompson (Raffaella); Wolfgang Hillinger (Hans); Dante Maggio (Neapolitan Street Hawker); Tiberio Mitri (British Member of Parliament); Vittoria Dal Verme, Giorgia Della Giusta, Carmen Scarpitta (Neapolitan Girls).

The June 22, 1944 Allied invasion of Italy at Anzio beach was structured to cut off German forces in the lower portion of the Italian peninsula. Due to military misaction on the part of the Allied forces such was not the case.

Cynical American war correspondent Dick Ennis (Robert Mitchum) who has covered the battlefield "for seven years, from China to Italy," drives into Rome with Movie (Reni Santoni), a ranger, and Corporal Rabinoff (Peter Falk), a commando. They are astounded that General Lesly (Arthur Kennedy) refuses to move his troops onward, instead remaining frozen to reinforce the position. This gives the Germans time to reorganize their defense and a subsequent Allied attack on a crucial village site leads to the loss of countless Allied lives. Ennis, Movie, and Sergeant Stimler (Earl

Holliman) survive behind enemy lines and return eventually to Anzio with information about the Nazi trap being set up around the Anzio beachhead. After four months of a stalemate and many bloody battles, the Nazis are shellacked and the Allies march into Rome. The incompetent General Carson (Robert Ryan) acts the glorious hero, leaving Ennis more disillusioned than ever.

Superficially geared as a why-must-there-be-a-war movie, ANZIO thrives on "meaningful" dialogue interchanges:

General Lesly (Arthur Kennedy): You think this is a game?

Ennis: Isn't it the ultimate game? Men kill each other because they like to.

Lesly: You found the answer then. . . . It's a hell of a condemnation of mankind.

Ennis: Maybe if we admit it, recognize it, we might be able to live with each other.

Lesly: We hope.

At the finale, world-weary Ennis in Rome snipes out the comment, "Nothing changes except the uniforms and the transportation. . . . Well, we've seen the conquering heroes, let's go home."

Any seasoned moviegoer watching this Italian co-production knew that problems lay ahead as soon as Jack Jones began crooning the insipid title song. "ANZIO suffers from flat writing, stock performances, uninspired direction and dull pacing . . . film would seem to be large scale war epic, but it really is a pale tale of a small group of men trapped behind German lines" (*Variety*).

British release title: BATTLE FOR ANZIO.

APOCALYPSE NOW (United Artists, 1979) Color 153 mins.*

Producer, Francis [Ford] Coppola, co-producers, Fred Roos, Gray Frederickson, Tom Sternberg; associate producer, Mona Skager; director, Francis [Ford] Coppola; based on the novella *Heart of Darkness* by Joseph Conrad; screenplay, John Milius, Francis [Ford] Coppola; commentary written by Michael Herr; production designer, Dean Tavoularis; art director, Angelo Graham; set decorator, George E. Nelson; costumes, Charles E. James; assistant directors, Jerry Ziesmer, Larry J. Franco, Tony Brandt;

---

*APOCALYPSE NOW was released originally at 141 minutes in its 70mm widescreen "roadshow" engagements; in later playdates in the 35mm version it ran 153 minutes with an end title sequence appended.

music, Carmine Coppola, Francis [Ford] Coppola; stunt coordinator, Terry Leonard; aerial co-ordinator, Dick White, David Jones; marine coordinators, Pete Cooper, Dennis Murphy, Sam Edwards; sound montage/designer, Walter Murch; sound, Jacob Jacobsen; sound editor, Richard Cirincione; special effects, Joseph Lombardi, A. D. Flowers; camera, Vittorio Storaro; supervising editor, Richard Marks; editors, Murch, Gerald B. Greenberg, Lisa Fruchtman.

Marlon Brando (Colonel Walter E. Kurtz); Robert Duvall (Lieutenant Colonel Bill Kilgore); Martin Sheen (Captain Benjamin

Robert Duvall, Albert Hall, and Martin Sheen in APOCALYPSE NOW (1979).

Willard); Frederic Forrest ("Chef" Hicks); Albert Hall (Chief Phillips); Sam Bottoms (Lance B. Johnson); Larry Fishburne ("Clean"); Dennis Hopper (Photo Journalist); G. D. Spradlin (General Corman); Harrison Ford (Colonel Lucas); Scott Glenn (Captain Richard Colby); Jerry Ziesmer (Civilian); Bo Byers, Larry Carney (Military Police Sergeants); James Keane (Kilgore's Gunner); Kerry Rossall (Mike from San Diego); Ron McQueen (Injured Soldier); Tom Mason (Supply Sergeant); Glenn Walken (Lieutenant

Carlsen); Bill Graham (Agent); Cyndi Wood, Colleen Camp, Linda Carpenter (Playmates); George Cantero (Soldier with Suitcase); Damien Leake (Machine Gunner); Herb Rice (Roach); William Upton (Aircraft Spotter); Marc Coppola (Radio Announcer); Daniel Kiewet (Major from New Jersey); Father Elias (Catholic Priest); Hattie James (Voice of Clean's Mother); Francis [Ford] Coppola (Television Combat Director); Jerry Ross (Johnny from Laibu); Dick White (Helicopter Pilot); Hugao People of Banaue, Philippine Islands (Montagnard Tribesmen).

Director Francis [Ford] Coppola once described the thrust of APOCALYPSE NOW as ". . . a film experience that would give its audience a sense of the horror, the madness, the sensuousness, and the moral dilemma of the Vietnam war." Originating in a 1969 screenplay by John Milius, the much-publicized production underwent a 238-day shooting schedule—with many delays caused by the rainy season in the Philippines and co-star Martin Sheen suffering a heart attack—and emerged after four years in the making at $31 million-plus over its original $12 million budget. It remains today a bold anti-war statement filled with cinematic greatness and flawed by many excesses, the least of which is the ambiguous script.

"It was a real choice mission," drones burned-out Captain Benjamin Willard (Martin Sheen) in one of his many voice-over commentaries, "and when it was over I would never want another." Willard, of the 505th Battalion, 173rd Airborne, is back in Saigon to fulfill yet another covert assassination assignment. This one is ordered by the military brass who have determined that renegade Green Beret Colonel Walter E. Kurtz (Marlon Brando), who is conducting his own ferocious war from a Cambodian temple neighboring the Vietnam frontier, must be terminated "with extreme prejudice." Willard puzzles at his assignment ("What do you call it when an assassin calls an assassin an assassin?") but accepts that he must do the job and wants to obey orders. He appreciates that "In this war things get confused out there. Power, ideas, the old morality and the practical military necessity."

Willard journeys up the Mekong River on a patrol boat with a four-man crew headed by the black Chief Phillips (Albert Hall), and including the mute California surfer, Lance B. Johnson (Sam Bottoms), the New Orleans ex-saucier, "Chef" Hicks (Frederic Forrest); and the black ghetto youth, "Clean" (Larry Fishburne), who thrives on listening to rock music on his tape player. "I was going to the worst place in the world," Willard insists, ". . . hundreds of miles up a river that snaked through the war like a main circuit cable and plugged straight into Kurtz. I really didn't know what I'd do when I faced him." Surviving enemy fire, the boat reaches an American helicopter base. There Willard encounters the crazed Lieutenant Colonel Bill Kilgore (Robert Duvall) of the Ninth Air Cavalry, who always wears his black Stetson cavalry hat. The deranged Kilgore, "who loves the smell of napalm in the morning . . . the smell of victory," orders a senseless attack on a Vietcong village. With the "Ride of the Valkyries" blaring away from their choppers ("to scare the shit out of the slopes"), the Americans devastate the village below, while the killer-mad Kilgore (whose helicopter is painted with the motto "Death From Above") thrives on watching Lance riding the surf waves at the peak of battle.

Further upstream at a supply depot at Hau Phat, Willard and his boat crew visit a USO show featuring three talentless Playboy Bunnies who arouse the GI audience to a sexual frenzy. After passing the besieged Do Lung bridge, the boat moves across the Cambodian border into the heart of darkness. "Clean" is killed during a Vietcong attack and as they approach the temple fortress, Chief Phillips dies in a skirmish with Kurtz's primitive Montagnard warriors. At Kurtz's camp Willard is greeted by a frenetic, spaced-out freelance photographer (Dennis Hopper) who extolls the greatness of this jungle lord. Finally Willard meets his prey, the enigmatic, crazed Kurtz and Willard is subjected to rambling monologues about the necessities of brutality. Willard witnesses ferocity at first hand when Chef's decapitated head is presented to him by Kurtz's minions. "Horror has a face and you must make a friend of it," insists the bulbous Kurtz. "Horror and moral terror are your friends and if not, then they are enemies to be feared. They are truly enemies." Kurtz recounts that the turning point in his life occurred when, a few years earlier, the Vietcong charged into a native village and hacked off the arms of any child inoculated against polio by the preceding Americans. Kurtz found this act of atrocity a revelation. It made him respect the strength of men who could have love of family but the commitment to perform such monstrous deeds.

The depressed Kurtz understands Willard's mission and his chief concern is that his son back home won't know what he was about. "Nothing I detest more than the stench of lies," Kurtz insists. He charges Willard with preserving the truth about him. Willard terminates Kurtz with a machete and he and Lance escape as the natives gain on the retreating gunboat.

Winning Academy Awards for Best Cinematography and Best Sound, APOCALYPSE NOW remains a muddled mystery to many viewers, not helped by the various editing and differing release versions as Coppola labored over the "final cut" at showings in 1978 and 1979. *Variety* labeled it "Alternately a brilliant and bizarre film" but the baffled public, confused by Coppola's muddled symbolic theme of "war is hell" and the fuzzy artiness of the production, only contributed $37,957,000 in United States-Canadian net theater rentals, not a remarkable sum considering the cost and ballyhoo surrounding the production. (In the wake of the PLATOON movie mega success, APOCALYPSE NOW was reissued in August 1987 in six U.S. cities, but made no noticeable impact.)

Perhaps the ultimate reason for the commercial (and artistic) misfire of APOCALYPSE NOW was enunciated by Gilbert Adair in *Vietnam on Film* (1981). "The Indochina war, however, was an incontrovertible defeat for the United States, a defeat rendered all the more poisonous by the hindsight realization that its advent had been written on the wall (often literally) as early as LBJ's [President Lyndon B. Johnson] 'abdication' in 1968 and that hostilities had been prolonged for principally electoral reasons. How then could a spectacular movie be made out of that defeat which would mobilize the public in sufficient numbers to recoup a colossal investment."

If one is distracted and distressed by the flat-voiced narrative snatches uttered by Willard, the same can be said for the last third of the film, which owes its literary origins to Joseph Conrad's 1899 novella, *The Heart of Darkness.* Just as Kurtz's figure never emerges from the shadows of his temple headquarters, neither do the character's ramblings add up to sufficiently meaningful dialogue. Too many of Coppola's points in this film remain hidden in elusive suggestion and misdirection. What remains in the filmgoer's memory are fleeting, striking moments: the visual/audio assault on the senses as the Vietcong village is decimated; the scene where the gunboat encounters a sampan and in a moment of jitteriness the Vietnamese passengers are strafed with machine gun fire; and the entrance into Kurtz's dank compound, as the newcomers pass through a litter of mutilated bodies, heads on pikes, dead enemies hanging from trees.

The flawed APOCALYPSE NOW, with all its technological proficiencies, remains a nagging milestone in the war film genre. It eschews most of the traditional trappings of combat action pictures, while still focusing on the causes and effects of war—that heart of darkness that is in every man.

ATTACK! (United Artists, 1956) 107 mins.

Producer/director, Robert Aldrich; based on the play *The Fragile Fox* by Norman Brooks; screenplay, James Poe; music, Frank DeVol; camera, Joseph Biroc; editor, Michael Luciano.

Jack Palance (Lieutenant Costa); Eddie Albert (Captain Cooney); Lee Marvin (Colonel Bartlett); Robert Strauss (Private First Class Bernstein); Richard Jaeckel (Private First Class Snowden); Buddy Ebsen (Sergeant Tolliver); William Smithers (Lieutenant Woodruff); Jon Shepodd (Corporal Jackson); James Goodwin (Private First Class Ricks); Peter Van Eyck (Tall German); Steven Geray (Short German); Judson Taylor (Private First Class Abramowitz); Louis Mercier (Old Frenchman); Strother Martin (Sergeant Ingersol).

"ATTACK! . . . pulls no punches about combat. Based on a [short-running 1954] stage play, it is nevertheless one of the great films about World War II combat. Mean and tough, cynical and despairing, it clearly shows how genre works. Keeping strictly to the basic ideas of hero, group, and objective, it begins the demolition of the wholesomeness of the tradition" (Jeanine Basinger, *The World War II Combat Film*, 1986).

During the Battle of the Bulge in Belgium, cowardly Captain Cooney (Eddie Albert) is a thorn in the side of Lieutenants Costa (Jack Palance) and Woodruff (William Smithers), who receive no troop support from their despicable military chief. Costa swears he

Buddy Ebsen, Eddie Albert, and Jimmy Goodwin in ATTACK! (1956).

will kill Cooney if he causes one more mishap. In a strategic blunder, Cooney orders his troops forward, leaving Costa and his men surrounded by the enemy. As his men are killed off one by one, Costa begs via radio for help, but Cooney will chance none. (Cooney's actions are backed by Colonel Bartlett [Lee Marvin], who thinks that Cooney may have political usefulness after the war.) With his men dead, Costa vows to murder Cooney, but is run over by a tank. However, Woodruff kills his superior who has by now gone off the deep end. Later, other GIs shoot into Cooney's corpse to cover over the matter and Colonel Bartlett pretends not to know what has happened. Woodruff calls the general to tell the truth.

Acknowledging the power and realism of ATTACK!, Norman Kagan judged in his study *The War Film* (1974), ". . . ATTACK! is a great watershed: the Cold War themes of the brutality of war, command levels, social responsibility, the nature of the enemy in a shifting moral world are all transformed and transfigured. AT-TACK! is the first postwar film to connect the new brutality of war with confusion, corruption, and incompetence of American leadership and American motives. . . . ATTACK! shows us the other side of the coin—the criminals, lunatics, and idiots in our ranks, integrated with the system."

ATTACK ON THE IRON COAST (United Artists, 1968) Color 89 mins.

Executive producer, Irving Temaner; producer, John C. Champion; associate producer, Ted Lloyd; director, Paul Wendkos; story, Champion; screenplay, Herman Hoffman; art director, Bill Andrews; set decorator, Ken Ryan; wardrobe, John Briggs; makeup, George Blackler; music, Gerard Schurmann; sound, Cyril Sern; special effects, Bowie Films; camera, Paul Beeson; second unit camera, Desmond Dickinson; editor, Ernest Hosler.

Lloyd Bridges (Major James Wilson); Andrew Keir (Captain Owen Franklin); Sue Lloyd (Sue Wilson); Mark Eden (Lieutenant Commander Donald Kimberley); Maurice Denham (Sir Frederick Grafton); Glyn Owen (Lieutenant Forrester); Howard Pays (Lieutenant Graham); George Mikell (Captain Strasser); Simon Prebble (Lieutenant Smythe); Keith Buckley, Bill Henderson, Gavin Breck (Commandos); Walter Gotell (Von Horst); Michael Wolf (Lieutenant Kramer); John Welsh (Cansley); Joan Crane (Wren Officer); Ernest Clark (Air Vice Marshal Woodbridge); Richard Shaw (German Infantry Sergeant); Victor Beaumont (German Battery Commander); John Albineri (German Gunnery Sergeant); John

Kelland (Flag Lieutenant); Mark Ward (Timmy Wilson); Dick Haydon (Pringle); John Golighty (Helmsman); Murray Evans (Bosun's Mate); Robin Hawdon (Radar Man); Sean Barrett (Radio Man).

During World War II, American commando leader Major James Wilson (Lloyd Bridges) is determined to raid a German naval installation on the coast of France (called "The Iron Coast" by the Nazis). He is opposed by Captain Owen Franklin (Andrew Keir) because the latter's son was killed in a mission headed by Wilson. However, the British Admiralty insists that the mission proceed and Franklin is ordered to assist Wilson. While training, Lieutenant Commander Donald Kimberley (Mark Eden) is blinded accidentally and Wilson wants to call off the objective, but Kimberley convinces him otherwise. Using a British minesweeper loaded with explosives, the commandos reach the French coast and ram the loading dock where the Nazi command is based. As the others go ashore to destroy other targets, the injured Wilson detonates the charges, sacrificing himself to complete the demolition of the Iron Coast.

This too conventional war action was filmed on location in England.

AWAY ALL BOATS (Universal, 1956) Color 114 mins.

Producer, Howard Christie; director, Joseph Pevney; based on the novel by Kenneth M. Dodson; screenplay, Ted Sherdeman; art directors, Alexander Golitzen, Richard H. Ridel; music, Frank Skinner; music director, Joseph Gershenson; special action scenes director, James C. Havens; camera, William Daniels; special effects camera, Clifford Stine; editor, Ted J. Kent.

Jeff Chandler (Captain Jeb Hawks); George Nader (Lieutenant Dave MacDougall); Julie Adams (Nadine MacDougall); Lex Barker (Commander Quigley); Keith Andes (Dr. Bell); Richard Boone (Lieutenant Fraser); William Reynolds (Ensign Kruger); Charles McGraw (Lieutenant Mike O'Bannion); Jock Mahoney (Alvick); John McIntire (Old Man); Frank Faylen (Chief "Pappy" Moran); Grant Williams (Lieutenant Sherwood); Floyd Simmons (Lieutenant Robinson); Don Keefer (Ensign Twitchell); Sam Gilman (Lieutenant Randall).

Naval Captain Jeb Hawks (Jeff Chandler) has the unenviable World War II duty of training rookie sailors for action in the South Pacific. He is the moody loner whose strategy is to focus all the frustration of his charges aboard the USS *Belinda* against him, so they will pull together as a team. His second-in-charge (George Nader) understands the tactic and convinces the men to work in unison with Hawks. Eventually the shakedown cruise leads to confrontations with the enemy, including Japanese kamikaze attacks, and the crew of the USS *Belinda* proves itself in battle.

Bosley Crowther (*New York Times*) was unimpressed with the "standard ingredients" of this "efficient Universal service film," but then this VistaVision, Technicolor release was not geared for the intelligentsia.

Of minor note is that the cast boasts of two screen Tarzans: Lex Barker and Jock Mahoney.

BACK TO BATAAN (RKO, 1945) 97 mins.

Producer, Robert Fellows; associate producer, Theron Warth; director, Edward Dmytryk; story, Aeneas MacKenzie, William Gordon; screenplay, Ben Barzman, Richard H. Landau; art directors, Albert S. D'Agostino, Ralph Berger; set decorators, Darrell Silvera, Charles Nields; music, Roy Webb; music director, C. Bakaleinikoff; technical adviser, Colonel George S. Clarke (U.S. Army); assistant director, Ruby Rosenberg; sound, Earl A. Wolcott, James G. Stewart; special effects, Vernon L. Walker; camera, Nicolas Masura; editor, Marston Fay.

John Wayne (Colonel Joseph Madden); Anthony Quinn (Captain Andres Bonifacio); Beulah Bondi (Miss Bertha Barnes); Fely Franquelli (Dalisay Delgado); Richard Loo (Major Hasko); Philip Ahn (Colonel Kuroki); J. Alex Havier (Sergeant Biernesa); "Ducky" Louie (Maximo); Lawrence Tierney (Lieutenant Commander Waite); Leonard Strong (General Masaharu Homma); Paul Fix (Jackson); Abner Biberman (Japanese Captain); Vladimir Sokoloff (Señor Buenaventura J. Bello); Benson Fong (Japanese Announcer); John Miljan (General Jonathan M. "Skinny" Wainwright); Kenneth McDonald (Major McKinley); Ray Teal (Lieutenant Colonel Roberts); Angel Cruz (Corporal Cruz); Bill Williams, Edmund Glover (Aides); Erville Alderson (Teacher); *actual American Soldiers at Cambanatuan prison camp:* Lieutenant Emmett L. Manson (U.S. Navy); Lieutenant Earl G. Baumgardner (U.S. Navy); Corporal Dennis D. Rainwater (U.S. Marine Corps); Sergeant Eugene C. Commander (U.S. Marine Corps); Private Jesus Santos (U.S. Army); Lieutenant George W. Greene (U.S. Naval Reserves); Sergeant Kenneth W. Mize (U.S. Marine Corps); Corporal Max M. Greenberg (U.S. Army); Private Alfred C. Jolley (U.S. Army); Private Virgil H. Greenaway (U.S. Army); Private First Class Lawrence C. Hall (U.S. Army); Corporal Neil P. Iovnio (U.S. Marine Corps)

From start to finish this is a carefully calculated wartime paean, filled with all the necessary ingredients of action and patriotism to arouse viewers. It succeeds magnificently.

The narrative opens in January 1945 with the freeing of American prisoners from the Philippines jungle prisoner-of-war camp at Cabanatuan, Luzon during World War II. The story then flashes back to 1942.

Colonel Joseph Madden (John Wayne) commands a group of Filipino Scouts on Bataan. His second-in-command is Captain Andres Bonifacio (Anthony Quinn) who is distraught that his sweetheart, Dalisay Delgado (Fely Franquelli), is part of a radio team operating from Japanese-held Manila, begging her countrymen to surrender. Madden is ordered by U.S. General Jonathan M. "Skinny" Wainwright (John Miljan) to build up the insurgent forces among the Filipino partisans. Later Madden rescues the embittered Bonifacio from the Japanese, hoping that this grandson of a well-known Filipino patriot can become a unifying symbol of the resistance. When Bonifacio learns from Madden that Dalisay is really helping the Allies by sending coded messages in her radio broadcasts, he agrees to take an active role in the warfare. As the Filipinos push harder against the Japanese, General Masaharu Homma (Leonard Strong) demands that his senior officers (Philip Ahn, Richard Loo) tighten their control over the local villagers. The Japanese try vainly to woo the Filipinos over to their side, claiming that as part of the "greater East Asia co-propensity sphere" they are true brethren. After the school principal (Vladimir Sokoloff) is hung by the Japanese soldiers, Bertha Barnes (Beulah Bondi), an American teacher, gives up her school. One of her pupils, Maximo ("Ducky" Louie) is arrested and tortured by the Japanese, who insist he lead them to the resistance headquarters. However, he manages to steer the truck in which he, the Japanese officers and many soldiers are riding over a cliff, and all die. Two years pass and with the return of General MacArthur and the Allied landing on Leyte, the Filipino guerrillas overwhelm the Japanese defenses. With the American Rangers, they free the prisoners at Cabanatuan.

While John Wayne's Colonel Madden is certainly the focal point of the nearly non-stop action, there are other vivid ingredients: scenes of the horrific Bataan Death March in which 25,000 Allied prisoners died along the sixty-five-mile trek to the Japanese-held Camp O'Donnell; the onslaught of battle as the screaming Japanese troops advance, wave after wave, against the Allies; the feisty courage of schoolmarm Miss Barnes; the pluckiness of young Maximo in the face of torture; and, especially, the cathartic opening and closing scenes of freeing the prisoners.

According to Jay Hyams in *War Films* (1984), "BACK TO BATAAN shows the maturing of Hollywood war movies . . . [the battle scenes] are noticeably more realistic. . . . There is also some of the introspective philosophizing that characterizes later films. The [frequent] farewell 'I'll be seeing you' is . . . made touching by frequent discussions of how in wartime people meet and then soon separate, never to see one another again. Victory celebrations were accompanied by memories of the dead."

BATAAN (Metro-Goldwyn-Mayer, 1943) 113 mins.*
    Producer, Irving Starr; director, Tay Garnett; screenplay, Robert D. Andrews; art directors, Cedric Gibbons, Lyle Wheeler; set decorators, Edwin B. Willis, Glen Barner; makeup, Jack Dawn; music, Bronislau Kaper; technical adviser, Captain L. S. Chappalear; assistant director, William Lewis; sound, Douglas Shearer; special camera effects, A. Arnold Gillespie, Warren Newcombe; camera, Sidney Wagner; editor, George White.
    Robert Taylor (Sergeant Bill Dane); George Murphy (Lieutenant Steve Bentley); Thomas Mitchell (Corporal Jake Feingold); Lloyd Nolan (Corporal Barney Todd/Danny Burns); Lee Bowman (Captain Henry Lassiter); Robert Walker (Leonard Purckett); Desi Arnaz (Private Felix Ramirez); Barry Nelson (Private F. X. Matowski); Phillip Terry (Private Matthew Hardy); Roque Espiritu (Corporal Juan Katigbak); Kenneth Spencer (Private Wesley Eeps); J. Alex Havier (Private Yankee Salazar); Tom Dugan (Private Sam Malloy); Donald Curtis (Lieutenant), Lynne Carver, Mary McLeod, Dorothy Morris (Nurses); Bud Geary (Infantry Officer); Ernie Alexander (Wounded Soldier); Phil Schumacher (Machine Gunner).
    Advertised as "The story America will never forget!" and "The story of a patrol of 13 heroes!", BATAAN is a special milestone in American cinema. Following in the trail of Wake Island (1942), q.v., it was one of the first 1940s Hollywood motion pictures to depict the brutalities of combat as they really were. It boasted an integrated cast (with black actor Kenneth Spencer playing a private) and it showed that ordinary Americans were the backbone of the U.S. Army. The Office of War Information was enthused by the cinematic results, praising the film for showing superior officers willing to accept suggestions from subordinates. "Thus, the army reflects the democratic way of life. . . . this is a people's army, fighting a people's war." (The film features an amalgam of ethnic stereotypes: a Mexican from California [Desi Arnaz], a Pole from Pittsburgh [Barry Nelson], a Filipino ex-boxer [Roque Espiritu], a black [Spencer], an Irish-accented Jew [Thomas Mitchell]; as well as assorted WASPS.)

---

*Computerized color version now available.

It is early in 1942* and the Americans under General Mac-Arthur are in full retreat following the evacuation of Manila. Japanese planes appear suddenly and attack a Red Cross ambulance, firing into the crowd indiscriminately. The ground rules are set for the viewer: the cruel Imperial Army does *not* fight by humane rules.** To slow down the enemy, a group of men remains behind to prevent the Japanese troops from crossing a crucial bridge.

The film focuses on this diverse group of Americans and their fellow Filipinos. At first they argue among themselves, but soon they realize they have one common enemy and must stand together as a team. When Captain Lassiter (Lee Bowman), a West Point graduate, is killed by a sniper, veteran Sergeant Bill Dane (Robert Taylor) takes command. He tells the men, "It doesn't matter where a man dies so long as he dies for freedom!" Meanwhile Lieutenant Steve Bentley (George Murphy), who has hidden his disabled plane in the jungle, attempts emergency repairs. Wisecracking, cynical Corporal Barney Todd (Lloyd Nolan) is using a phony name because of a scuffle years ago when he killed another soldier. Dane knows of this but says nothing. Naive gum-chewing Naval Band musician Leonard Purckett (Robert Walker) cannot conceive that they will not come out alive. Grizzled Corporal Jake Feingold (Thomas Mitchell), a chemical engineer, appreciates fully the seriousness of the situation. The camp cook (Tom Dugan) is the butt of many jokes, but has untapped resiliency. Private Matthew Hardy (Phillip Terry) is a pacifist in the Medical Corps. As time passes, their number dwindles and finally the Japanese begin a full-fledged assault. Bentley's plane is revved up but in the take-off he is wounded fatally. He crashes his plane into the bridge the Japanese are repairing, and the structure is destroyed. One of the Filipinos tries to sneak through the Japanese lines at night, but the next morning his mutilated body is found hung from a tree. Three men remain: one is picked off by a sniper, another stabbed in the back by a enemy soldier feigning death. As the Japanese troops rush out of the jungle cover, Dane jumps into his already dug grave (the rest

---

*The film opens with the following prologue: "When Japan struck—our desperate need was time—time to marshal our new armies. Ninety-six priceless days were bought for us—with their lives—by the defenders of Bataan, the Philippine Army which formed the bulk of MacArthur's infantry fighting shoulder to shoulder with Americans. To those immortal dead, who heroically stayed the wave of barbaric conquest, this picture is reverently dedicated."

**There are many references in BATAAN to how the Americans were (supposed) to regard the inhuman enemy. At one point Corporal Jake Feingold (Thomas Mitchell) is shooting off rounds into the jungle and spots a monkey capering through the trees, "I'd hate to hit him by mistake for a Jap."

have already been buried) and as the assault advances through the mist and gunsmoke, shouts over his blaring machine gun, "Come on suckers. Come and get me. We're still here—we'll always be here—come and get it." At the finale, a narrator assures the audience, "So fought the heroes of Bataan. Their sacrifice made possible our victories in the Coral and Bismarck Seas, at Midway, on New Guinea and Guadalcanal. Their spirit will lead us back to Bataan!"

It was no secret, even at the time of release, that BATAAN was structured as a loose retelling of John Ford's classic THE LOST PATROL (1934), q.v., but that did nothing to lessen the impact of this stellar MGM production filled with fine vignettes by its diverse cast.

One of the most demanding contemporary reviewers was James Agee, who wrote in *The Nation*, ". . . I think it [BATAAN] much less shallow than most of the more ambitious war pictures. . . . It is essentially, I think, not a drama but a certain kind of native ritual dance. As such its message of war is not only naive, coarse-grained, primitive; it is also honest, accomplished in terms of its aesthetic, and true."

BATTLE CIRCUS (Metro-Goldwyn-Mayer, 1953) 89 mins.

Producer, Pandro S. Berman; director, Richard Brooks; story, Allen Rivkin, Laura Kerr; screenplay, Brooks; art directors, Cedric Gibbons, James Basevi; music, Lennie Hayton; camera, John Alton; editor, George Boemler.

Humphrey Bogart (Major Jed Webbe); June Allyson (Lieutenant Ruth McCara); Keenan Wynn (Sergeant Orvill Statt); Robert Keith (Lieutenant Colonel Hillary Whalters); William Campbell (Captain John Rustford); Perry Sheehan (Lieutenant Laurence); Patricia Tiernan (Lieutenant Rose Ashland); Adele Longmire (Lieutenant Jane Franklin); Jonathan Cott (Adjutant); Ann Morrison (Lieutenant Edith Edwards); Helen Winston (Lieutenant Graciano); Sarah Selby (Captain Dobbs); Danny Chang (Korean Child); Philip Ahn (Korean Prisoner); Steve Forrest (Sergeant); Jeff Richards (Lieutenant); Dick Simmons (Captain Norson).

Army relief nurses reach Major Jed Webbe's (Humphrey Bogart) mobile field hospital behind the front lines in Korea. One of them, starry-eyed Lieutenant Ruth McCara (June Allyson), intent on self-sacrifice, draws his attention and they begin an on-again, off-again romance, hindered/abetted by her screwball impetuousness which alternately gets her in danger or in trouble. Sergeant Orvill Statt (Keenan Wynn) is the ex-circus man in charge of pulling up stakes as Webbe's unit moves to avoid the enemy and doctor the wounded G.I.s. Between bouts of hard drinking and heavy philoso-phizing ("Three world wars in one lifetime. Maybe whisky's as much a part of our life as war"), Webbe draws closer to Ruth and they eventually agree to marry.

While in its day BATTLE CIRCUS was passed off as a well-mounted but jumbled concoction featuring two mismatched co-stars, it has gained stature in reevaluation over the decades. Since it features the Mobile Army Surgical Corps it is a direct predecessor to M*A*S*H (1970), q.v., and on that note worthy of a place in cinema history. With its screwball comedy, romance, hospital scenes, and moments of combat and war, it is an uneven but interesting mixture of several genres.

BATTLE CRY (Warner Bros., 1955) Color 147 mins.

Director, Raoul Walsh; based on the novel by Leon M. Uris; screenplay, Uris; music, Max Steiner; technical adviser, Colonel H. P. "Jim" Crowe, U.S. Marine Corps; camera, Sid Hickox; editor, William Ziegler.

Van Heflin (Major Huxley); Aldo Ray (Andy); Mona Freeman (Kathy); Nancy Olson (Pat); James Whitmore (Sergeant Mac); Raymond Massey (General Snipes); Tab Hunter (Danny); Dorothy Malone (Elaine); Anne Francis (Rae); William Campbell (Ski); John Lupton (Marion); Justus E. McQueen (L. Q. Jones); Perry Lopez (Joe Gomez); Fess Parker (Speedy); Jonas Applegarth (Light-tower); Tommy Cook (Ziltch); Felix Noriego (Crazy Horse); Susan Morrow (Susan); Carleton Young (Major Wellman); Rhys Williams (Enoch Rogers); Allyn [Ann] McLerie (Waitress); Gregory Walcott (Sergeant Beller); Frank Ferguson (Mr. Walker); Sarah Selby (Mrs. Forrester); Willis Bouchey (Mr. Forrester).

"Amatory, rather than military, action is the mainstay of this saga of the United States Marines. . . . Technically, however, the film is not as realistic as is desirable for this type of subject" (*Variety*).

Novelist Leon Uris only had himself to blame for the over-stuffed screen version of his pungent, best-selling novel (1953). He wrote the scenario!

This widescreen war film follows several World War II servicemen from their induction at the Marine Corps boot camp in San Diego, through training on Saipan, and on to New Zealand where they head into combat. Interspersed with the military action are several overdrawn romantic pairings: ex-logger Andy (Aldo Ray) finds love with Pat (Nancy Olson), a New Zealander who has already lost a husband and brother in the war; young Marine Danny (Tab Hunter) must choose between lonely San Diego married

James Whitmore and Van Heflin in BATTLE CRY (1955).

woman Elaine (Dorothy Malone) and his girl back home (Mona Freeman); while bookwormish Marion (John Lupton) finds happiness with prostitute Rae (Anne Francis). Major Huxley (Van Heflin) is the tough officer charged with turning his men into fighting machines, with sympathetic top sergeant Mac (James Whitmore) on tap to mother his boys. In the course of battle, the Major and Marion are killed, but both Andy and Danny (despite earlier scenes that seem to the contrary) survive the warfare. Danny decides to go back to his hometown sweetheart, while the girl-chasing Andy weds Pat.

While this celluloid tribute to the Marines was popular with filmgoers, it received few critical endorsements. "No one can say that Mr. Uris and Director Raoul Walsh have missed many tricks in splashing a long, episodic, Rover Boyish service story on the screen. . . . It is amazing how neatly and patly the whole thing has been designed to follow an unswerving pattern of convention and rectitude" (Bosley Crowther, *New York Times*).

Max Steiner's rousing score was Oscar-nominated and BATTLE CRY grossed $5,100,000 in domestic film rentals.

BATTLE FOR ANZIO *see*: ANZIO.

BATTLE HYMN (Universal, 1956) Color 108 mins.

Producer, Ross Hunter; director, Douglas Sirk; screenplay, Charles Grayson, Vincent B. Evans; art directors, Alexander Golitzen, Emrich Nicholson; set decorators, Russell A. Gausman, Oliver Emert; gowns, Bill Thomas; makeup, Bud Westmore; music, Frank Skinner; music supervisor, Joseph Gershenson; assistant director, Marshall Green; technical adviser, Colonel Dean Hess; sound, Leslie I. Carey, Corson Jewett; camera, Russell Metty; special camera, Clifford Stein; editor, Russell Schoengarth.

Rock Hudson (Colonel Dean Hess); Martha Hyer (Mary Hess); Dan Duryea (Sergeant Herman); Don DeFore (Captain Skidmore); Anna Kashfi (Miss Yang); Jock Mahoney (Major Moore); Alan Hale (Mess Sergeant); Carl Benton Reid (Deacon Edwards); Richard Loo (General Kim); James Edwards (Lieutenant Maples); Philip Ahn (Old Man); Bartlett Robinson (General Timberidge); Simon Scott (Lieutenant Hollis); Teru Shimada (Korean Official); Carleton Young (Major Harrison); Jung Kyoo Pyo (Chu); Art Millan (Captain Reardon); William Hudson (Navy Lieutenant); Paul Sorensen (Sentry); Children from the Orphan Homes of Korea (Themselves); General Earle E. Partridge, U.S. Air Force (Himself).

Based on the true life story of Colonel Dean Hess, "the Flying Parson," BATTLE HYMN reflects more on the emotional price of war than on combat itself. As General Earle E. Partridge, U.S. Air Force, Fifth Airforce, states in his on-camera preface, Hess's story is about "courage, resourcefulness, and sacrifice . . . [the] poignant and often secret struggle with the problem peculiarly his own."

During World War II U.S. fighter pilot Hess (Rock Hudson), known as "Killer Hess," is on an attack mission over Germany and accidentally bombs an orphanage, killing 37 children. After the war the guilt-ridden man becomes a parson in West Hampden, Ohio. While a man of God he finds he is still not necessarily *with* god. When the Korean Conflict breaks out, he rejoins the Air Force, leaving his understanding but concerned wife (Martha Hyer) at home. On the new battlefront where he is assigned to train the ROK Air Force as well as flying 250 missions in ground support, he comes to terms slowly with himself, helping to save 1,000 orphans whom he airlifts to safety, and organizing an orphanage for them on Cheju Island.

Among the supporting cast are Dan Duryea in a change-of-pace role as the cocky, carefree Air Force Sergeant Herman, Anna Kashfi as the real-life Miss Yang, who silently loves the married clergyman and sacrifices her life on behalf of the orphanage; Philip Ahn as the Old Man who helps with the orphans, and Don DeFore, the pudgy devil-may-care pilot who dies in combat.

Colonel Dean Hess served as technical adviser on this inspirational film in which Rock Hudson provides one of his more able performances and filmgoers were treated to a reverential mixture of "piety and pugnacity" (*New York Times*) so standard in service films.

Interspersed in the story are several speeches about the quality of war. Captain Skidmore (Don DeFore) expresses his practical viewpoint to the agog Hess: "I thought you knew what war was about. Just keep this one thing in mind. All that counts is who wins, not how nice a guy you are. You win or you die. You go soft and you're one step from being dead."

Hess admits in a moment of revelation, "Perhaps through the agony of war, I have finally done what I never before was able to do. In reaching beyond myself I have found myself." He is enunciating the same tenet that many combat films would evoke: through war man can redeem his soul. This identical message is a prime theme of THE DIRTY DOZEN (1967), q.v.

THE BATTLE OF BRITAIN (United Artists, 1969) Color 132 mins.

Producers, Harry Saltzman, S. Benjamin Fisz; associate producer, John Palmer; director, Guy Hamilton; based on the book *The Narrow Margin* by Derek Wood, Derek Dempster; screenplay, James Kennaway, Wilfred Greatorex; supervising art director, Maurice Carter; art directors, Bert Davey, Jack Maxsted, William Hutchinson, Gil Parrondo; wardrobe supervisor, John Wilson-Apperson; makeup, George Frost, Eric Allright; British technical/tactical advisers, Hamish Mahaddie (Group Captain), Tom Gleave (Group Captain), Robert Stanford-Tuck (Wing Commander), Robert Wright (Wing Commander), Ginger Lacey (Squadron Leader), B. Drobinski (Squadron Leader), Claire Legge (Wing Commander); German technical/tactical advisers, Adolf Galland (Lieutenant General), Hans Brustellin (Colonel), Franz Frodl (Major); dialogue director, Carl Duering; main title, Maurice Binder; music/music conductor, Ron Goodwin; "Battle in the Air" by William Walton and conducted by Malcolm Arnold; assistant director, Cracknell; sound, Gordon Everett, Gordon McCallum; sound editors, James Shields, Ted Mason; special effects, Cliff Richardson, Glen Robinson, Wally Veevers, Ray Caple; camera, Freddie Young; second unit camera, Bob Huke; aerial camera, Skeets Kelly, John Jordan; editor, Bert Bates.

Laurence Olivier (Air Chief Marshal Sir Hugh Dowding); Robert Shaw (Squadron Leader Skipper); Christopher Plummer (Squadron Leader Colin Harvey); Susannah York (Section Officer Maggie Harvey); Ian McShane (Sergeant Pilot Andy); Michael Caine (Squadron Leader Canfield); Kenneth More (Group Captain Baker); Trevor Howard (Air Vice Marshal Keith Parks); Patrick Wymark (Air Vice Marshal Trafford Leigh-Mallory); Ralph Richardson (British Minister in Switzerland); Curt Jurgens (Baron von Richter); Harry Andrews (Sir Francis Stokes); Michael Redgrave (Air Vice Marshal Evill); Nigel Patrick (Group Captain Hope); Michael Bates (Warrant Officer Warrick); Isla Blair (Andy's Wife); John Baskcomb (Farmer); Tom Chatto (Willoughby's Assistant); James Cosmo (Jamie); Robert Flemyng (Wing Commander Willoughby); Barry Foster (Squadron Leader Edwards); Edward Fox (Pilot Officer Archie); W. G. Foxley (Squadron Leader Evans); David Griffin (Sergeant Pilot Chris); Jack Gwillim (Senior Air Staff Officer); Myles Hoyle (Peter); Duncan Lamont (Flight Sergeant Arthur); Sarah Lawson (Skipper's Wife); Mark Malicz (André Maranne, French N.C.O.); Anthony Nicholls (Minister); Nicholas Pennell (Simon); Andrzej Scibor (Ox); Jean Waldon (Jean-Jacques); Wilfried van Aacken (General Osterkamp); Karl Otto Alberty (Jeschonnek); Alexander Allerson (Major Brandt); Dietrich Frauboes (Field Marshal Milch); Alf Jungermann (Brandt's Navigator); Peter Hager (Field Marshal Kesselring); Wolf Harnisch (General Fink); Reinhard Horras (Bruno); Helmut Kircher (Boehm); Paul Neuhaus (Major Foehn); Malte Petzel (Colonel Beppo Schmid); Manfred Reddemann (Major Falke); Heinz Reiss (Reichs Marshal Goering); Rolf Stiefel (Hitler).

"A film of this size is always difficult to cast because there are so many vital roles; because of the nature of important roles it becomes extremely hard to schedule, to slot in an actor's availability. This was our problem. Now we have succeeded. These are the best actors for the roles. Their names enhance our film, although the real star of the film is the story itself. Five units are working simultaneously to encompass the scope of the story: more than a hundred Spitfires, Hurricanes, Messerschmitts and Heinkels of the period have been assembled for the film" (Harry Saltzmann, producer).

Following the evacuation of Dunkirk (May 27 to June 4, 1940) and England's refusal of Adolf Hitler's (Rolf Stiefel) armistice offer, the British struggle to gain time to prepare for the pending clash with the Luftwaffe. Reichs Marshal Goering (Heinz Reiss) plans to destroy British air power on the ground, and the Luftwaffe successfully attacks airfields in southern England, inflicting tremendous losses. Nevertheless, the RAF fights diligently, vindicating Air Chief Marshal Hugh Dowding's (Laurence Olivier) decision to retain air strength in England during the battle for France. The relentless German assaults take their toll on the RAF, and its best pilots, including Squadron Leaders Skipper (Robert Shaw) and Harvey (Christopher Plummer), show the strain. (The life expectancy of a fighter pilot was 87 hours of air time.) Meanwhile a new crop of inexperienced pilots is rushed into the fray. After a German plane bombs London, the British shell Berlin. Hitler orders the destruction of London and other key British cities. During the blitzkrieg, the RAF rebuilds its airfields and, now relying on the assistance of the Polish Freedom Fighters, regroups. Goering's major attack (September 15, 1940) is countered by a strong RAF, and the order to invade Britain is cancelled.* The film concludes with the words of Prime Minister Winston Churchill: "Never in the field of human conflict was so much owed by so many to so few."

"The twelve million dollars spent on BATTLE OF BRITAIN was nearly as much as the cost of the actual battle, and neither was much fun. . . . It was rather extravagant to pay for so many famous faces, when they were indistinguishable behind pilot's masks" (Ronald Bergen, *The United Artists Story*, 1986).

In the air THE BATTLE OF BRITAIN is a magnificent celluoid recreation of those decisive sixteen weeks in the summer of 1940. The aerial scenes are vivid, authentic, mesmerizing, as is the "Battle in the Air" music composed by William Walton. But on the ground, the film is a mixed matter. Olivier is efficient, unobtrusive, and effective as the Air Chief Marshal who tells his confrères early on, "We are fighting for survival . . . losing . . . we need pilots . . . and a miracle. Goodnight gentlemen." But the romantic interludes—mostly in hotel bedrooms—between Christopher Plummer and his section officer wife (Susannah York) are embarrassing. ("No," she says, "it's not just bed. It's us, you . . . me.") There is an attempt to be objective in presenting both the British and German

---

*Statistics for the Battle of Britain include the participation of 2365 Allied pilots (of whom 433 were killed), versus the Germans who suffered 1644 pilots killed, with another 1445 missing and believed killed).

points of views, but it is clear on which side the production's loyalties lie.

THE BATTLE OF BRITAIN lost over $10,000,000 at the box-office.

BATTLE OF RIVER PLATE *see:* PURSUIT OF THE GRAF SPEE.

THE BATTLE OF THE BULGE (Warner Bros., 1965) Color 162 mins.

Producers, Milton Sperling, Philip Yordan; director, Ken Annakin; screenplay, Yordan, Sperling, John Melson; art director, Eugene Lourie; music/music conductor, Benjamin Frankel; song, Kurt Wiehle and Frankel; costume designer, Laurie de Zarate; makeup, Trevor Crole-Rees, Jose Maria Sanchez; advisors, Meinrad von Lauchert (Major General), Luis Martin Pozuelo (Lieutenant Colonel), Sherman Joff (Lieutenant Colonel), Edward King; assistant directors, Jose Lopez Rodero, Martin Sacristan, Luis Garcia; sound, David Hildyard, Gordon McCallum; sound editors, Kurt Herrnfeld, Alban Streeter; special effects, Richard Parker, Kit West, Basilio Cortijo; camera, Jack Hildyard; second unit camera, John Cabrera; special effects camera, Alex Weldon; supervising editor, Derek Parsons.

Henry Fonda (Lieutenant Colonel Kiley); Robert Shaw (Colonel Hessler); Robert Ryan (General Grey); Dana Andrews (Colonel Pritchard); George Montgomery (Sergeant Duquesne); Ty Hardin (Schumacher); Pier Angeli (Louise); Barbara Werle (Elena); Charles Bronson (Wolenski); Hans Christian Blech (Conrad); Werner Peters (General Kohler); James MacArthur (Lieutenant Weaver); Telly Savalas (Sergeant Guffy); Karl Otto Alberty (Von Diepel); William Conrad (Narrator); and: Steve Rowland, Robert Woods, Charles Stalnaker, David Thomson, Sebastian Cavalieri, Raoul Perez, Jack Gaskins, Janet Grandt, Max Slaten, Carl Rapp, Axel Anderson, Donald Pickering, Bud Strait, Peter Herendeen, Ben Tatar, Paul Eshelman, Richard Zeidman, John Schereschewsky, Victor Brandt, Richard Baxter, William Boone, John Clarke, Ward Maule, Paul Polansky, Freddie Toehl, Leland Wyler, Quinn Donoghue, John Friess, Reginald Gillam, Peter Grzeegorczyk, Richard Laver, Harry Van Der Linden, Derek Robertson, Martin Rolin, Robert Royal, Russ Stoddard.

At the conclusion of THE BATTLE OF THE BULGE a final credit card informs: "This picture is dedicated to the one million men who fought in this great battle of World War II. To encompass the whole of the heroic contributions of all the participants, names, places, and characters have been generalized and action has been synthesized in order to convey the spirit and essence of the battles." This alerts the audience belatedly to what it—or a greater portion— already knew; the film was a conglomerate fabrication more concerned with cashing in on the cycle of epic war films than in presenting true or dramatic reality.

By December 1944 the Allies foresee victory in Europe. However, Lieutenant Colonel Kiley (Henry Fonda), an intelligence officer, is convinced the Germans intend to launch a desperate, gigantic offense somewhere in the Ardennes Forest of Belgium. General Grey (Robert Ryan) and Colonel Pritchard (Dana Andrews) disagree. Meanwhile, heroic German Panzer tank commander Colonel Hessler (Robert Shaw) has returned from the Russian front to spearhead the attack, utilizing the latest Tiger tanks and massive troop detachments. When foul weather puts the Allied Air Force temporarily out of commission, the Germans launch their offensive, leading to the massacre at Malmedy. Watching the Allies retreat, Kiley realizes the enemy tanks will soon be out of fuel. Helped by Lieutenant Weaver (James MacArthur) and others, they regain control of the largest fuel depot from the English-speaking German infiltrators. As the Nazi tanks reach the dump, Weaver and his team roll drums of gasoline towards them, setting the vehicles ablaze, including that of hard-pressing Hessler. The last serious threat from the German army is over.

Appearing in one-dimensional characterization are: Sergeant Guffy (Telly Savalas), the flippant black marketeer who realizes he loves his cohort (Pier Angeli); Sergeant Duquesne (George Montgomery), the professional non-commissioned officer; Wolenski (Charles Bronson), whose life is sacrificed for the sake of strategy; precise Third Reich General Kohler (Werner Peters) who has alluring Elena (Barbara Werle) in his array of tactical tricks; and Conrad (Hans Christian Blech), Hessler's battle-weary aide.

Filmed in Spain, THE BATTLE OF THE BULGE was roadshown in the Cinerama widescreen process, grossing a rather modest $5,100,000 in domestic theater rentals. For later engagements, the running time was reduced to 140 mins. The fabrication was a distant cry from the far superior THE LONGEST DAY (1962), q.v., also directed by Ken Annakin.

BATTLE OF THE CORAL SEA (Columbia, 1959) 80 mins.

Producer, Charles H. Schneer; director, Paul Wendkos; story, Stephen Kandel; screenplay, Daniel Ullmann, Kandel; music, Ernest Gold; camera, Wilfrid Cline; editor, Chester W. Schaeffer.

Cliff Robertson (Lieutenant Commander Jeff Conway); Gia Scala (Karen Philips); Teru Shimada (Commander Mori); Patricia Cutts (Lieutenant Peg Whitcomb); Rian Garrick (Al Schechter); Gene Blakely (Lieutenant Len Ross); L. Q. Jones (Yeoman Halliday); Robin Hughes (Major Jammy Harris); Tom Laughlin (Ensign Franklin); Eiji Yamashiro (Oshikawa); James T. Goto (Captain Yamazaki); K. L. Smith (Chief Petty Officer Connors); Carlyle Mitchell (Admiral McCabe); Larry Thor (Army Major); Patrick Westwood (Simes)

Most of the action takes place before the decisive May 7-8, 1942 conflict known as the Battle of Coral Sea (which actually occurred in the Solomon Sea).

Lieutenant Commander Jeff Conway (Cliff Robertson) heads a submarine crew charged with reconnoitering the enemy's position

Advertisement for BATTLE OF THE CORAL SEA (1959).

prior to the battle. Having photographed their objective, the sub is returning to base when it is captured and the men imprisoned on a Japanese isle. Aided by a Eurasian neutral (Gia Scala), three of the officers escape and provide the Navy with needed information to wreck the enemy.

Far more effective than the staunch and overly stern Cliff Robertson is Teru Shimada as the unyielding Commander Mori.

BATTLE OF THE RIVER PLATE *see*: PURSUIT OF THE GRAF SPEE.

BATTLE STATIONS (Columbia, 1956) 81 mins.

Producer, Bryan Foy; director, Lewis Seiler; story, Charles S. Goul; screenplay, Crane Wilbur; art director, Cary Odell; music, Mischa Bakaleinikoff; camera, Burnett Guffey; editor, Jerome Thorns.

John Lund (Father Joe McIntyre); William Bendix (Chief Bosun Buck Fitzpatrick); Keefe Brasselle (Chris Jordan); Richard Boone (The Captain); William Leslie (Ensign Pete Kelly); John Craven (Commander James Matthews); James Lydon (Squawk Hewitt); Claude Akins (Marty Brennan); George O'Hanlon (Patrick Mosher); Eddie Foy, III (Tom Short); Jack Diamond (William Halsey); Chris G. Randall (Archie Golder); Robert Forrest (John Moody); Dick Cathcart (Eddie); Gordon Howard (Lieutenant Hanson); James Lilburn (Williams); Eric Bond, Frank Connors (Bosuns).

BATTLE STATIONS spans the World War II period between a carrier leaving Alameda Naval Air Station after battle repairs to the time it returns to Brooklyn for more patching after fighting in Japanese territory. Too much footage is devoted to the training of the men, a tour of the enormous carrier, and unsubtle attempts at shipboard humor. Along for the ride are: the Captain (Richard Boone); Father McIntyre (John Lund), newly posted to the carrier; roughneck Chief Bosun Buck Fitzpatrick (William Bendix); cocky gob Chris Jordan (Keefe Brasselle), and Ensign Pete Kelly (William Leslie) who wants to live to see his child born. The bits of combat action are all stock footage.

BATTLE TAXI (United Artists, 1955) 82 mins.

Producers, Ivan Tors, Art Arthur; director, Herbert L. Strock; story, Malvin Wald, Arthur; screenplay, Wald; art director, William Ferrari; music director, Herman Sukman; camera, Lothrop B. Worth; editor, Jodie Copelan.

Sterling Hayden (Captain Russ Edwards); Arthur Franz (Lieutenant Pete Stacy); Marshall Thompson (Second Lieutenant Tim

Sterling Hayden (Captain Russ Edwards); Arthur Franz (Lieutenant Pete Stacy); Marshall Thompson (Second Lieutenant Tim Vernon); Leo Needham (Supply Sergeant Slats Klein); Jay Barney (Lieutenant Colonel Stoneham); John Goddard (Wounded G.I.); Robert Sherman (Lieutenant Joe Kirk); Joel Marston (Lieutenant Marty Staple); John Dennis (Master Sergeant Joe Murdock); Dale Hitchinson (Blue Boy Three-Gene); Andy Andrews (Lazy Joker Two); Vance Skarsted (Lieutenant Smiley Jackson); Michael Colgan (Medic Captain Larsen); Captain Vincent McGovern (Co-Pilot Harry).

Between June 1950, when the Communists invaded South Korea, and the final cease fire which concluded the fighting on July 27, 1953, 1,319,000 Americans had served in the Korean arena; 33,629 died, and a further 115,785 were injured.*

It is a strong reflection on American culture and political climate that so few significant films were made about "the century's nastiest little war," in contrast to the motion pictures that have been produced, albeit belatedly, about the Vietnam War horror.

BATTLE TAXI refers to the U.S. Air Rescue Service in action during the Korean War. Captain Russ Edwards (Sterling Hayden) is in charge of the squadron. A good deal of his effort is devoted to convincing his men, especially overzealous Lieutenant Pete Stacy (Arthur Franz), that their job is to save lives, not to engage the enemy in action. "There are old pilots and there are bold pilots, but there are no old, bold pilots" he tells the men.

Made with the cooperation of the Department of Defense and using a good deal of poorly integrated stock footage, this low-budget entry hardly made a dent on the public. ". . . [T]he requisite combat wallop is in short supply." complained *Variety*.

BATTLE ZONE (Allied Artists, 1952) 82 mins.

Producer, Walter Wanger; associate producer, William A. Calihan, Jr.; director, Lesley Selander; screenplay, Steve Fisher; art director, David Milton; assistant director, Henry Hartman; music, Marlin Skiles; camera, Ernest Miller; editor, Jack Ogilvie.

John Hodiak (Danny); Linda Christian (Jeanne); Stephen McNally (Mitch); Martin Milner (Andy); Dave Willock (Smitty); Jack Larson (O'Doole); Richard Emory (Lieutenant Orlin); Philip

---

*The South Korean Army suffered 415,000 casualities and 429,000 wounded; the British Commonwealth lost 1,263 with 7,000 wounded. An estimated 500,000 to 1,500,000 North Koreans and Chinese gave their lives during this "military action."

Ahn (Korean); Carleton Young (Colonel); John Fontaine (Lieutenant Pilot); Todd Karnes (Officer); Gil Stratton, Jr. (Runner).

Focusing on Marine combat photographers in the Korean War, the action opens at the Marine Corps base in Camp Pendleton, California, where Danny (John Hodiak) has reenlisted in the combat photographic division. There he encounters his old pal Mitch (Stephen McNally) and finds the latter is engaged to Jeanne (Linda Christian), a Red Cross nurse whom Danny once loved. The Marines and the Red Cross unit are shipped to Korea. When not vying with each other over the affections of Jeanne, Danny and Mitch are on assignment at the Yalu River, the border between North Korea and Chinese Manchuria, where they are photographing enemy installations.

The obvious parallels to the Quirt-Flagg characters of WHAT PRICE GLORY? (1926, 1952), qq.v., were not lost on astute moviegoers. This low-budget entry had little new to offer to the war film genre.

BATTLEGROUND (Metro-Goldwyn-Mayer, 1949) 118 mins.

Producer, Dore Schary; associate producer, Robert Pirosh; director, William Wellman; story/screenplay, Pirosh; art directors, Cedric Gibbons, Hans Peters; set decorators, Edwin B. Willis, Alfred E. Spencer; makeup, Jack Dawn; music, Lennie Hayton; assistant director, Sid Sidman; sound, Douglas Shearer, Conrad Kahn; montage, Peter Ballbusch; camera, Paul C. Vogel; editor, John Dunning.

Van Johnson (Holley); John Hodiak (Jarvess); Ricardo Montalban (Roderiguez); George Murphy ("Pop" Starzak); Marshall Thompson (Jim Layton); Jerome Courtland ("Little" Abner Spudler); Don Taylor (Standiferd); Bruce Cowling (Wolowicz); James Whitmore (Kinnie); Douglas Fowley ("Kipp" Kippton); Leon Ames (The Chaplain); Guy Anderson (Hanson); Thomas E. Breen (Doc); Denise Darcel (Denise); Richard Jaeckel (Bettis); Jim Arness (Garby); Scotty Beckett (William J. Hooper); Brett King (Lieutenant Teiss); Roland Varno (German Lieutenant); George Offerman, Jr., William Self (G.I.s); Dewey Martin, Tommy Noonan, David Holt (G.I. Stragglers); Michael Browne (Levenstein); Jim Drum (Supply Sergeant); Jerry Paris (German Sergeant); Nan Boardman (Belgian Woman Volunteer); John Mylong (German Major); Ivan Triesault (German Captain); George Chandler (Mess Sergeant); Dick Jones (Tanker); Tommy Kelly (Casualty); Ian MacDonald (General George McAuliffe); Screaming Eagles of the 101st Airborne Division (Themselves).

"The guts, gags, and glory of a lot of wonderful guys!" blazed the advertising copy for MGM's BATTLEGROUND, the first significant post-World War II Hollywood film to deal with that war. It had a more dramatic and commercial impact than the studio's earlier combat reenactment, BATAAN (1943), q.v., made at the height of war.

BATTLEGROUND opens with the audience told the following quote from German General Henrich von Luttwitz (47th Panzer Corps): "Bastogne must be taken. Otherwise it will remain an abscess on our lines of communication. We must clean out Bastogne and then march on." Next on screen is a title card: "This story is about, and dedicated to, those Americans who met General Henrich von Luttwitz and his 47 Panzer Corps and earned for themselves the honored and immortal name Battered Bastards of Bastogne."

On December 17, 1944, the 101st Airborne Division (the "Screaming Eagles") dreams of a long-hoped for rest in Paris, complete with showers, clean sheets, gals, food and wine. Their dreams evaporate when they are assigned to the German-surrounded Belgian town of Bastogne.

Among the 101st's "Screaming Eagles" are: girl-chasing, opportunist Holley (Van Johnson), who romances Denise (Denise Darcel) the willing French girl with whom they are billeted; "Pop" Ernest Stazak (George Murphy), arthritic, thirty-five years old and awaiting discharge to look after the kids his sick wife can't tend; Jarvess (John Hodiak), the midwestern small town newspaper editor who was inspired to enlist by his own writings; Roderiguez (Ricardo Montalban), a Mexican from southern California who experiences his first snowfall in Belgium; "Kipp" Kippton (Douglas Fowley), the cynic who desperately wants out of the war and who is either constantly misplacing his false teeth or using them like a chattering telegraph; "Little" Abner Spudler (Jerome Courtland), the Kentucky hills recruit who because of his foot size can't find boots to fit, which eventually will cause his downfall; Standiferd (Don Taylor), the blue-blood who learns about democracy in combat; the introspective Lutheran Chaplain (Leon Ames), who questions why they are there; the two youngsters, Bettis (Richard Jaeckel), who is detailed to KP and dies in the "soft" assignment, and Joe Layton (Marshall Thompson), the green kid who is stuck digging trenches he never occupies; the laconic squad leader Wolowicz (Bruce Cowling); Hanson (Guy Anderson), whose heart is always home with his wife and baby; and the tough tobacco-chewing sergeant Kinnie (James Whitmore), who can never get his feet warm.

I Company, 3rd Platoon, 2nd Squad of the "Screaming Eagles" endures a history-making week in Bastogne during the "Rundstedt offensive" as they fight to hold their ground against the Nazis, despite being surrounded and outnumbered. At one juncture the Germans don G.I. uniforms and blow up bridges behind them to further entrap the 101st. Each day becomes more grim as the field hospital is captured, tanks run short of gas, and gunners run out of ammunition. The bewildered men fight to survive; their victories are confined to gaining a little strip of snowy ground. When the Germans demand an unconditional American surrender, General George McAuliffe's (Ian MacDonald) response is "Nuts!" Just as all seems lost, Allied tanks rumble into view and the sky fills with Allied planes and parachuted supplies: ammunition, gasoline, and rations. The battered 101st is saved. At the finale, what remains of the platoon is deployed to the back lines. They pass a group of green recruits moving up to the front lines. The "Screaming Eagles" fall into step as much as their battered situation allows, and begin their famous Jody chant, "You won't get home till the end of the war . . . Sound off! One, two. . . . "

While the focal point of BATTLEGROUND is quick-dealing Holley, who experiences his own horrific moments of fear and cowardice, the storyline development traces the maturation of new recruit Joe Layton as he becomes seasoned in warfare, learning to survive and to help his comrades in arms. The film contains its own political message. When the Chaplain is asked the real reason behind this war trek he responds, "Was this trip necessary? Thousands died because they thought it wasn't; till there was nothing left to do but fight. We must never let any kind of force dedicated to a super race or a super idea or a super anything get strong enough to impose itself on a free world. We have to be smart enough and tough enough in the beginning to put out the fire before it starts spreading."

The bulk of BATTLEGROUND was filmed on the MGM soundstages and backlot (including using the reassembled French village set from THE STORY OF G.I. JOE, 1945, q.v., also directed by William A. Wellman), but the picture is remarkably realistic. It captures the mood, look, and the damnable cold of that December 1944 in the Ardennes Forest. Twenty of the original 101st Airborne paratroopers, stationed then at Fort Bragg, North Carolina, were detailed to join the actors in retelling this uncompromising battle story. No background music was used in the picture because "They had no eighty-piece orchestra in the foxholes" (Robert Pirosh).

Screenwriter and associate producer Robert Pirosh, who had

served in the 320th Regiment, 35th Infantry Division at the Battle of the Bulge, was uniquely equipped to write this Academy Award-winning scenario. He would boast later, "I avoided at least three clichés in writing the script for BATTLEGROUND. There is no character from Brooklyn in the story. Nobody gets a letter from his wife or girl saying she has found a new love, and nobody sweats out the news of the arrival of a newborn baby back home."

The critical reaction to BATTLEGROUND was far more enthusiastic than producer Dore Schary* could have anticipated. "BATTLEGROUND emerges as a super entry. There will be the inevitable comparison to post-World War I's BIG PARADE and ALL QUIET ON THE WESTERN FRONT and, while not without justification, perhaps it should suffice that BATTLE-GROUND sets its own standard circa 1949" (Abel Green, *Variety*). Bosley Crowther (*New York Times*) endorsed, "For here, without bluff or bluster or the usual distracting clichés . . . is a smashing pictorial re-creation of the way that this last one was for the dirty and frightened foot-soldier who got caught in a filthy deal. Here is the unadorned image of the misery, the agony, the grief and the still irrepressible humor and dauntless mockery of the American GI."

BATTLEGROUND earned $5,060,000 in theater rentals at the United States-Canadian box-office, won *Photoplay* Magazine's Gold Medal as Best Picture of the Year, and was Oscar-nominated for Best Picture and Best Supporting Actor (James Whitmore).

For many BATTLEGROUND represented a new trend in the combat film genre. "This film is on the side of survival, since it is aimed at an audience of survivors," points outs Jeanine Basinger in *The World War II Combat Film* (1986). "No beardless youth dies here. On the contrary, Marshall Thompson, who represents the type, learns to survive by studying the ultimate in survivors, the character played by Van Johnson."

BEACH RED (United Artists, 1967) Color 105 mins.

Producer/director, Cornel Wilde; based on the book *Sunday Red Beach* by Peter Bowman; screenplay, Clint Johnston, Donald A. Peters, Jefferson Pascal; art director, Francisco Balangue; wardrobe, Vicente Cabrera; makeup, Neville Smallwood; technical

---

*For a detailed account of the years-in-the-brewing of BATTLEGROUND when scriptwriter Robert Pirosh and executive Dore Schary were both at RKO and Robert Ryan, Robert Mitchum, and Bill Williams were to play the lead roles, see Steven Jay Rubin's *Combat Films: 1945–1970* (1981).

adviser, James C. Murray; music arranger/conductor, Antonio Buenaventura; song, Elbey Vid; assistant directors, Derek Cracknell, Francisco MacLang; sound, James Chapman; special effects, Paul Pollard; camera, Cecil Cooney; editor, Frank P. Keller.

Cornel Wilde (Captain MacDonald); Rip Torn (Sergeant Honeywell); Burr De Benning (Egan); Patrick Wolfe (Cliff); Jean Wallace (Julia MacDonald); Jaime Sanchez (Colombo); Genki Koyama (Captain Sugiyama); Gene Blakely (Goldberg); Norman Pak (Nakano); Dewey Stringer (Mouse); Fred Galang (Lieutenant Domingo); Hiroshi Kiyama (Michio); Michael Parsons (Sergeant Lindstrom); Dale Ishimoto (Captain Tanaka); Linda Albertano (Egan's Girl Friend); Jan Garrison (Susie); Michio Hazama (Captain Kondo); Masako Otsuki (Colonel's Wife); Kiyoma Takezawa (Japanese Soldier); and: John Allen, George Bayot, Phil Beinke, Juan Bona, Bill Dunbar, Ed Finlan, Ernie Holt, Mike McMichael, Rod Meir, Charles Weaver, Pat Whitlock, Dennis Ullmann.

"In contrast to many professedly anti-war films, BEACH RED is indisputably sincere in its war-is-hell message. . . . Its pacifist plea might conceivably draw favorable editorial comment from those willing to overlook its faults" (Lee Beaupre, *Variety*).

During the height of World War II, a U.S. Marines battalion headed by Captain MacDonald (Cornel Wilde) and sadistic Sergeant Honeywell (Rip Torn) lands on the beach of a Japanese-held island near the Philippines. The Americans suffer tremendous casualties but reach a forest shelter where they encamp. Youngster Cliff (Patrick Wolfe) and hillbilly Egan (Burr De Benning) scout out the Japanese's position. They radio back the information, but Cliff is killed and Egan and a young Japanese soldier are seriously wounded. Egan and his "enemy" exchange a water canteen and a cigarette. Honeywell comes onto the scene and kills the young Japanese. Captain MacDonald arrives and, shocked by the carnage about him, ponders the ultimate futility of war.

Based on a 1945 novel and filmed in the Philippines and Japan, this very personal production for producer/director/actor Cornel Wilde received tremendous publicity when released, due to its unrelenting, ironic depiction of the bloodiness of war (made even more graphic by the garish De Luxe color hues). There is next to no plotline in the production, and there are very few genre stereotypes; mostly it is a grueling, highly gory depiction of bloody warfare with wrenching visions of torn flesh and maimed souls. Throughout the staccato narrative, there are frequent nostalgic flashbacks as both American and Japanese combatants recall their home lives (allowing for the real life Mrs. Wilde, Jean Wallace, to appear as Captain MacDonald's wife—she also sings the title tune!).

BEACHHEAD (Universal, 1954) Color 89 mins.
    Producer, Howard W. Koch; director, Stuart Heisler; based on
the novel *I've Got Mine* by Richard G. Hubler; screenplay, Richard
Alan Simmons; music, Emil Newman and Arthur Lange; camera,
Gordon Avil; editor, John F. Schreyer.
    Tony Curtis (Burke); Frank Lovejoy (Sergeant Fletcher); Mary
Murphy (Nina); Eduard Franz (Bouchard); Skip Homeier (Rey-
nolds); John Doucette (Major Scott); Alan Wells (Biggerman);
Sunshine Akira Fukunaga (Japanese Sailor); Dan Aoki (Sniper);
Steamboat Mokuahi (Melanesian).
    A Marine platoon during World War II storms a Japanese-held
island to rescue Bouchard (Eduard Franz), a plantation owner/spy.
Most of the men are killed, with only Burke (Tony Curtis), Sergeant
Fletcher (Frank Lovejoy), and Bouchard's daughter Nina (Mary
Murphy) escaping. Handsomely filmed in Hawaii with lots of
muscular chasing and pursuing, the plot tension exceeds the combat
special effects.

BEHIND THE FRONT (Paramount, 1926) 5,555'
    Presenters, Adolph Zukor, Jesse L. Lasky; director, Edward
Sutherland; based on the story "The Spoils of War" by Hugh Wiley;
adaptor, Monte Brice; screenplay, Ethel Doherty; camera, Charles
Boye.
    Wallace Beery (Riff Swanson); Raymond Hatton (Shorty
McGee); Mary Brian (Betty Bartlett-Cooper); Richard Arlen (Percy
Brown); Hayden Stevenson (Captain Bartlett-Cooper); Chester
Conklin (Scottie); Tom Kennedy (Sergeant); Frances Raymond
(Mrs. Bartlett-Cooper); Melbourne MacDowell (Mr. Bartlett-
Cooper).
    When detective Riff Swanson (Wallace Beery) has his pocket
picked by Shorty McGee (Raymond Hatton), the resultant chase
ends at Betty Bartlett-Cooper's (Mary Brian) mansion where she is
hostessing an Army enlistment party. During the festivities she
inveigles both men to join up. Enduring the horrors of basic training
under their no-nonsense sergeant (Tom Kennedy), they are shipped
to the front lines in France. More often in the guardhouse than on
patrol in no man's land, they survive the war and return home only
to find Betty is marrying wealthy Percy Brown (Richard Arlen).
    "There are long intervals between really good humorous points
in BEHIND THE FRONT . . . which strike some as a burlesque of
THE BIG PARADE. Most of the fun . . . is wrought with a mailed
fist . . . " (Mordaunt Hall, *New York Times*).
    One of the few Hollywood features to deal with the war, it was
felt that audiences would accept its subject matter only under the

Raymond Hatton and Jack Pennick in BEHIND THE FRONT (1926).

guise of comedy.* It was the first of seven silent features for Wallace
Beery and Raymond Hatton at Paramount.
  A.k.a.: BEHIND THE DOOR.

THE BEST OF ENEMIES (Columbia, 1962) 104 mins.

  Producer, Dino De Laurentiis; associate producer, Luigi Lu-
raschi; assistant producer, Ralph Serpe; director, Guy Hamilton;
story, Luciano Vicenzoni; adaptors, Age & Scarpelli, Suso Cecchi
D'Amico; screenplay, Jack Pulman; art director, Mario Garbuglia;
set decorator, Giorgio Herman; costumes, Ezio Frigerio, Dario
Cecchi; music, Nino Rota; assistant director, Mario Maffei; dialogue director, Manuel Del Campo; sound, Piero Cavazutti, Bruno
Brunacci; camera, Giuseppe Rotunno; editor, Bert Bates.

---

*Others of the period included: PRIVATE IZZY MURPHY (1927), with George
Jessel; SPUDS! (1927), with Larry Semons; and ROOKIES (1927), with the team
of Karl Dane and George K. Arthur.

David Niven (Major Richardson); Alberto Sordi (Captain Blasi); Michael Wilding (Lieutenant Burke); Amedeo Nazzari (Major Fornari); Harry Andrews (Captain Rootes); David Opatoshu (Captain Bernasconi); Aldo Giuffre (Sergeant Todini); Tiberio Mitri (Corporal Moccaia); Kenneth Fortescue (Lieutenant Thomlinson); Duncan Macrae (Sergeant Trevethan); Noel Harrison (Lieutenant Hilary); Robert Desmond (Private Slinger); Michael Trubshawe (Colonel Brownslow); Bernard Cribbins (Private Tanner); Ronald Fraser (Prefect); Pietro Marescalchi (Corporal Brotolin); Alessandro Ninchi (Lieutenant Del Pra); Pippo Fazio (Sergeant Spadoni); Bruno Cattaneo (Private Mattone); Luigi Bracale (Guddu).

In 1941 British Major Richardson (David Niven) and RAF reconnaissance pilot Lieutenant Burke (Michael Wilding) crash land in the Abyssinian desert and are captured by an Italian patrol. Italian Captain Blasi (Alberto Sordi) wants to save rations and permits the duo to escape, after they agree not to let the British pursue the Italian patrol. Later, Richardson is forced to retract his word. Richardson captures Blasi and his men and they hole up at a deserted fort, where the common enemy becomes native tribesmen. Eventually they reach Addis Ababa, now held by the British. Blasi and his group are shipped off to a prisoner of war camp; before they go, Richardson and his men salute the defeated enemy.

THE BEST OF ENEMIES was well received internationally ("Wryly witty, offbeat wartime comedy with serious undertones," exclaimed *Variety*), but this comedy of errors never found its audience at the American box-office.

The picture was filmed on location in Israel and released in Italy in 1961 as I DUE NEMICI.

BETWEEN HEAVEN AND HELL (Twentieth Century-Fox, 1956) Color 94 mins.

Producer, David Weisbart; director, Richard Fleischer; based on the novel *The Day the Century Ended* by Francis Gwaltney; screenplay, Harry Brown; art directors, Lyle R. Wheeler, Addison Hehr; music, Hugo Friedhofer; music conductor, Lionel Newman; orchestrator, Edward B. Powell; camera, Leo Tover; editor, James B. Clark.

Robert Wagner (Sam Gifford); Terry Moore (Jenny); Broderick Crawford (Colonel "Waco"); Buddy Ebsen (Willie); Robert Keith (Colonel Gozzens); Brad Dexter (Joe Johnson); Mark Damon (Terry); Ken Clark (Morgan); Harvey Lembeck (Bernard Meleski); Skip Homeier (Swanson); L. Q. Jones (Kenny); Tod Andrews (Ray Mosby); Biff Elliot (Tom Thumb); Bart Burns

(Raker); Frank Gertle (Colonel Miles); Carl Switzer (Savage); Gregg Martell (Sellers); Frank Gorshin (Millard); Darlene Fields (Mrs. Raker); Ilene Brown, Scotty Morrow, Pixie Parkhurst, Grad Morrow (Raker Children); Scat Man Crothers (George); Tom Edwards (Soames).

"As the memory of the last war recedes, the stories to come out of that war are getting a sharper and more critical perspective. . . . [This film is] a good, hard-hitting action film, replete with the usual heroics but also full with the ugly realization that the men who fought the war were far from perfect" (*Variety*).

What makes this CinemaScope color production so intriguing is its depiction of social/racial bigotry during World War II. Southern aristocrat Sam Gifford (Robert Wagner) is inducted in the army shortly after the outbreak of World War II, along with the Dixie National Guard unit from his area, including several share-croppers such as Willie (Buddy Ebsen), as well as Chicago boy

Broderick Crawford and Skip Homeier in BETWEEN HEAVEN AND HELL (1956).

Bernard Meleski (Harvey Lembeck). Despite the presence of fatherly Colonel Gozzens (Robert Keith), unyielding Gifford is guilty of insubordination to another officer and as a penalty is demoted to a nearby suicide unit of misfits commanded by Colonel "Waco" (Broderick Crawford), a crude psychopath despised by his men, except for Millard (Frank Gorshin) and Swanson (Skip Homeier). It is Willie who gives Gifford a new slant on democracy, and to save his pal, Gifford makes a dangerous run through Japanese patrols.

With plenty of war action there was little widescreen on-camera time allotted to shapely Terry Moore as Wagner's love interest.

BEYOND VICTORY (RKO-Pathé, 1931) 70 mins.
    Producer, E. D. Derr; director, John Robertson; story/ adaptors, Horace Jackson, James Gleason; sound, Charles O'Loughlin, T. Carmen, B. Winkler, H. Stine; camera, Norbert Brodine; editor, Daniel Mandell.

    William Boyd (Bill); Zasu Pitts (Fritzie); Lew Cody (Lew); Marion Shilling (Ina); James Gleason (Jim); Lissi Arna (Katherine);* Theodore Von Eltz (Major Sparks); Mary Carr (Mother); Russell Gleason (Russell); and: Fred Scott, Frank Reicher, Wade Boteler, E. H. Calvert, Charles Coleman, Max Barwin, Hedwig Reicher.

    At the front during World War I, four soldiers, pondering what caused them to enlist, relate their pre-war amours back home. Youngster Russell (Russell Gleason) and playboy Lew (Lew Cody) are soon killed, while Jim (James Gleason) and the commander, Bill (William Boyd), survive. Jim has a wife (Zasu Pitts) back in the States and Bill has found romance with German girl Katherine (Lissi Arna).

    "Film will suffer . . . because its action is incidental to the dialog. It's a frank lecture against war. . . . In pointing out that national prejudices are wrong this picture, perhaps, has gone further in exploiting the point than others" (*Variety*).

THE BIG PARADE (Metro-Goldwyn-Mayer, 1925) 150 mins.**
    Director, King Vidor; story, Laurence Stallings; screenplay, Harry Behn; titles, Joseph W. Farnham; art directors, Cedric Gibbons, James Basevi; wardrobe, Ethel P. Chaffin; music score, William Axt, David Mendoza; camera, John Arnold; editor, Hugh Wynn.

    John Gilbert (James Apperson); Renee Adoree (Melisande); Hobart Bosworth (Mr. Apperson); Claire McDowell (Mrs. Apper-

---

*Replaced Thelma Todd in the role of Katherine.
**Technicolor sequences.

son); Claire Adams (Justyn Reed); Robert Ober (Harry); Tom O'Brien (Bull); Karl Dane (Slim); Rosita Marstini (French Mother).

"A man walks through the war and looks at it, neither a pacifist nor a soldier, he simply goes through, and has a look, and is pulled into these experiences" (King Vidor, director of THE BIG PARADE).

Based on wartime experiences by writer Laurence Stallings (who also co-authored the hit war play/film, WHAT PRICE GLORY?, q.v.) the silent film THE BIG PARADE is a massive panorama of the First World War. It focuses on the (mis)adventures, combat traumas and romances of a trio of Americans: James Apperson (John Gilbert), the unambitious son of a wealthy southern mill owner (Hobart Bosworth); steelworker/riveter Slim (Karl Dane) and bartender Bull O'Hara (Tom O'Brien). The three enlistees become good friends by the time they have passed through basic training and reached France. The three meet a willful farmer's daughter, Melisande (Renee Adoree), with whom they all fall in love. However, it is handsome Apperson who wins her affection and, in the process, forgets about

Renee Adoree and John Gilbert in THE BIG PARADE (1925).

his American sweetheart, Justyn Reed (Claire Adams). (There is a marvelous scene in which Apperson teaches Melisande how to chew gum.)

When the men are ordered to the front lines, Melisande goes to bid farewell to Apperson, desperate in her love for him. At Belleau Woods the Allies meet the Germans and the battle wages furiously as the ranks of Apperson and his comrades are thinned. The company commander orders that one go forth to clean out a machine gun nest. They spit for the honor and Slim, a tobacco chewer, wins. He wipes out the German nest, but is wounded on the way back. Apperson and Bull rush to rescue Slim. Bull is killed and Slim dies as Apperson reaches him. Crawling back through no-man's land, Apperson is wounded by a sniper and in return shoots him. Apperson follows his victim to a shell hole where the dying youth asks for a cigarette. He gives him one and the boy expires. Rescued, Apperson is hospitalized, but when he hears the town his sweetheart lives in has been bombed, he escapes and goes there. He cannot locate her. When the enemy shells the area, Apperson is hit and once more hospitalized; his leg is amputated. Back in America he is greeted as a hero and finds his brother and sweetheart are in love. His mother (Claire McDowell) urges Apperson to return to France, and there he and Melisande reunite.

"Everything one can expect from real war is in this picture. One sees the various branches of artillery in action, plenty of hand-grenade and machine-gun warfare, gas attacks, tractors, etc. Also men marching over the dead in the fields and men dropping right and left. There are air attacks and maneuvers, and not a detail lacking that occurred in the big affray" (*Variety*).

Romanticists have long cherished this film's lengthy screen sequence in which the parade of soldiers and trucks depart for the front, with a highly emotional Melisande searching frantically for her loved one. She finds him boarding a truck and does not want to let go, even to grabbing onto a truck chain and dragging herself after the procession till she falls off. Most vivid are the well-orchestrated battle scenes, a harrowing symphony of death and destruction. Images that remain in the mind most are the flanks of soldiers pushing into battle and being mowed down by machine-gun fire; the moment when Jim finishes the cigarette he has pulled from the dead German's mouth; the helmet trophies gathered like scalps by Slim; and the hysterical soldier in the midst of the battle crying out, "They cheered us when we went away, and they'll cheer us when we return. But who the hell cares after this?"

Made at a cost of $250,000, THE BIG PARADE would gross over $15,000,000 worldwide and would be reissued several times over the years with a sound effects/music background track added. It became the standard by which all later war films would be judged.

"Because it depicts death, mutilation, and separation in wartime, THE BIG PARADE was advertised as an antiwar film. It is not; at least not in the manner in which later films would attack war as an institution. Jim loses a leg in the war, but he also finds a lover and himself in the process. The theme of the film is maturation through conflict and testing, with war representing the ultimate test. War is horrible, but inevitable, and the men who survive it fulfill the rites of passage" (Don K. Thompson, *Magill's Survey of Cinema, Silent Films*, 1982).

THE BIG RED ONE (United Artists, 1980) Color 111 mins.

Executive producers, Merv Adelson, Lee Rich; producer, Gene Corman; director/screenplay, Samuel Fuller; art director, Peter Jamison; assistant director, Arne Schmidt; second unit director, Lewis Teague; music, Dana Kaproff; camera, Adam Greenberg; supervising editor, David Breatherton; editor, Morton Tubor.

Lee Marvin (Sergeant); Mark Hamill (Griff); Robert Carradine (Zab); Bobby DiCicco (Vinci); Kelly Ward (Johnson); Stephane Audran (Walloon); Siegfried Rauch (Schroeder); Serge Marquand (Rensonnet); Charles Macaulay (General/Captain); Alain Doutey (Broban); Maurice Marsac (Vichy Colonel); Colin Gilbert (Dog Face Prisoner of War); Joseph Clark (Shep); Ken Campbell (Lemchek); Doug Werner (Switolski); Perry Lang (Kaiser); Howard Delman (Smith); Marthe Villalonga (Madame Marbaise); Giovanna Galetti (Woman in Sicilian Village); Gregori Buimistre (The Hun); Shimon Barr (German Male Nurse); Matteo Zoffoli (Sicilian Boy); Avrahan Ronai (German Field Marshal); Galit Rotman (Pregnant French-woman).

Writer/producer/director Samuel Fuller, who served in World War II is the creator of several highly-regarded war films: FIXED BAYONETS (1951), THE STEEL HELMET(1951), CHINA GATE (1957), and MERRILL'S MARAUDERS (1962), qq.v. His most recent genre entry is the extremely personal, autobiographical THE BIG RED ONE,* which *Variety* endorsed as "... a terrific war yarn, a picture of palpable raw power which manages both intense

*Fuller had been planning and attempting to make this film since the early 1950s; in 1957 it was announced that John Wayne would star in the picture for Warner Bros. When it was finally finished, Fuller had a four-hour long picture which he was ordered to cut severely. When the producers were still dissatisfied with the director's re-edited version done with Morton Tubor, David Bretherton was brought in and narration was added and other restructuring to the film done.

intimacy and great scope at the same time." Perhaps if it had been produced at a different time, with a far greater budget, and with a star *not* past his prime, its overall effect would have matched the epic conception of auteur Fuller. As Howard H. Prouty observes in *Magill's American Film Guide* (1983), ". . . [The] cinema has changed since Fuller's heyday, and he has remained much the same: wild and obsessive, striving for clarity at the expense of subtlety. . . . Fuller has more to say than many of today's filmmakers, but he has no interest in obscuring his ideas with new cinematic techniques; consequently, there are moments in THE BIG RED ONE that may seem awkward and simpleminded for a 'modern' film."

In the closing days of World War I, Sergeant (Lee Marvin) kills a German, unaware that the armistice had been declared four hours earlier. The action jumps to November 1942 and North Africa and to the 1st Squad, 1st Platoon, I Company, 16th Infantry. Sergeant is back in action and has four "wet noses" to whip quickly into shape: Griff (Mark Hamill), the left-handed sharpshooter who likes to draw cartoons; Johnson (Kelly Ward), the farmboy with hemorrhoids; Vinci (Bobby DeCicco), the street kid who plays jazz on the saxophone; and Zab (Robert Carradine), the cigar chomping Hemingway of the Bronx who keeps a diary. Through these five, World War II from 1942 to 1945 is traced. The focus is not on the war as a whole, but on the scattered events in the day-to-day lives of these men. Their goal is to survive—no matter the terrain, no matter who else dies, no matter who their latest fellow soldiers may be. The narrative moves from the defense of the beach at Algeria to the confrontation between the Americans and Rommel's Afrika Korps at Kasserine Pass, to the Allied landing at Sicily, and, then, on to Czechoslovakia in May 1945. Once again Sergeant, unaware the war is over, fights a German, but this time he saves his enemy.

Accomplished with a full sense of what a combat film is all about, but told in Fuller's distinctly personal terms, THE BIG RED ONE presents a ripely cynical view of war. "Surviving is the only glory in war," Sergeant intones. At another point he explains, "We don't murder, we kill." "I suppose horses have as much right to go crazy in this war as men do," he decides. Jaded by the inexperienced military command so often found in war, he explains snidely to one of his charges, "How do you smoke out a sniper? Send a guy into the open and see if he gets shot. They thought that one up at West Point." Ever practical, he and the men use G.I.-issued condoms to keep their rifles dry. In the film's most bizarre interlude, there is a confrontation between American and Nazi soldiers in an insane asylum. One inmate grabs a machine gun and as he begins firing it at random, shouts out, "I am one of you. I am sane!"

There are many de rigeur war scenes: a group of soldiers hiding in a cave, powerless as Nazi tanks rumble by; during the D-Day invasion at Omaha Beach, G.I.s. scaling the cliffs in the midst of overwhelming enemy gunfire; the moment where the battle-frightened Griff finds a Nazi soldier hiding in the oven of a liberated concentration camp and, finally understanding war's horror, blasts away at the enemy mercilessly; the GI farmboy delivering a baby in the pit of a tank.

For the record, the film's oblique title refers to the insignia of the Fighting First Infantry Division.

THE BLUE MAX (Twentieth Century-Fox, 1966) Color 156 mins.

Executive producer, Elmo Williams; producer, Christian Ferry; director, John Guillermin; based on the novel by Jack D. Hunter; adaptors, Ben Barzman, Basilio Franchina; screenplay, David Pursall, Jack Seddon, Gerald Hanley; production designer, Wilfrid Shingleton; art director, Fred Carter; wardrobe supervisor, Elsa Fennell; makeup, Charles Parker, Tony Sforzini, John O'Gorman; air super-

George Peppard in THE BLUE MAX (1966).

visor, Allen Wheeler (Commodore); music/music conductor, Jerry Goldsmith; assistant directors, Jack Causey, Derek Cracknell; sound, Claude Hitchcock, John Cox, Bob Jones; sound editor, Chris Greeham; special effects, Karl Baumgartner, Maurice Ayers, Ron Ballanger; camera, Douglas Slocombe; aerial camera, Skeets Kelly; editor, Max Benedict; assistant editor, Elizabeth Thoyts.

George Peppard (Bruno Stachel); James Mason (Count von Klugermann); Ursula Andress (Countess Kaeti von Klugermann); Jeremy Kemp (Willi von Klugermann); Karl Michael Vogler (Heidemann); Anton Diffring (Holbach); Harry Towb (Kettering); Peter Woodthorpe (Rupp); Derek Newark (Ziegel); Derren Nesbitt (Fabian); Loni von Friedl (Elfi von Friedl); Friedrich Ledebur (Field Marshal von Lenndorf); Carl Schell (Baron von Richthofen); Hugo Schuster (Hans); Alex Scott (Orator); Roger Ostime (Crown Prince); Ray Browne, Timothy Parkes, Ian Kingsley (Pilots); and: John Harvey.

Visually this is one of the most stunning war films, its crisp CinemaScope cinematography (re)capturing World War I in the air, and the spectacular one-on-one dogfights between the Allies and Germans. Equally superior is Jerry Goldsmith's soaring soundtrack music. Unfortunately the ironic, sardonic tone of the book original does not come across onscreen.

"The Blue Max" is a medal bestowed on German flying aces for shooting down at least 20 enemy planes. Towards the end of World War I, newly-trained German fighter pilot Bruno Stachel (George Peppard), overjoyed at having escaped being an infantry soldier, becomes obsessed with winning this recognition. For his single-mindness, he is at odds with his fellow pilots. His chief rival is Willi von Klugermann (Jeremy Kemp), who is one "kill" away from winning the prized medal himself. Meanwhile Willi's uncle, Count von Klugermann (James Mason), arrives with his beautiful young wife Kaeti (Ursula Andress). She not only has an affair with Willi, but starts one with Stachel. Returning from a mission, Willi is killed and Stachel twists the situation to claim Willi's final "kill" and to win the medal. The squadron commander, Heidemann (Karl Michael Vogler), suspects the truth, but the Count plans to award Stachel "The Blue Max" at a ceremony launching a new plane Stachel is testing. Angered that Stachel will not run away with her to Switzerland, petulant Kaeti confesses to her husband that Heidemann's suspicions about Stachel are true. In the meantime a court-martial is being prepared to investigate Stachel's acts of inhumanity in the air. The Count, knowing Germany needs a new working class hero, does not want Stachel disgraced. (He also is aware of Stachel's affair with his wife.)

He finds a ready solution when he learns that Stachel's test plane has a structural fault and should not be flown. He does not tell Stachel about the danger and the young pilot takes off in the plane to do his daring maneuvers, his ironic fate sealed.

Putting aside James Mason's expertise in depicting the overbearing, manipulative Prussian Count, Ursula Andress' blatant sexuality, and the extravagantly well-mounted trappings, THE BLUE MAX comes alive only in the sky. "A Sunday supplement picture of a war, but not the war itself . . . the film never gets a bite on the period" (London *Observer*). *Time* magazine labeled it a "synthetic melodrama" and added, "Diffuse and emotionally flat despite its expert airborne excitement. . . ." In *The War Film* (1974) Norman Kagan offers his own idea of what might have salvaged the terra firma action: "Perhaps it would have been best if Stachel stayed the hateful, murderous, alcoholic, blackmailing, class-climbing bad hat of the novel, instead of having the adapters follow the Hollywood rule that a hero-heel must be boyish, winning, and a terror abed." THE BLUE MAX earned $7,725,000 in film rentals at U.S.-Canadian theaters.

THE BOLD AND THE BRAVE (RKO, 1956) 87 mins.

Producer, Hal E. Chester; director, Lewis R. Foster; screenplay, Robert Lewin; music, Herschel Burke Gilbert; song, Ross Bagdasarian and Mickey Rooney; costumes, Dick Chaney; camera, Samuel Leavitt; editor, Aaron Stell.

Wendell Corey (Fairchild); Mickey Rooney (Dooley); Don Taylor (Preacher); Nicole Maurey (Fiamma); Race Gentry (Hendricks); Ralph Votrian (Wilbur); Wright King (Technician); Stanley Adams (Master Sergeant); Bobs Watson (Bob); Tara Summers (Tina).

It was the year of alliterative titles such as THE PROUD AND PROFANE, q.v., and THE BOLD AND THE BRAVE.

Filmed on a modest budget, this independently produced entry distributed by RKO focuses on a disparate G.I. trio on the World War II Italian front. Fairchild (Wendell Corey) is the pacifist; Preacher (Don Taylor), the sergeant, is the religious bigot who gains insight from a local girl (Nicole Maurey); and there is exuberant Dooley (Mickey Rooney) who wins $30,000 in a crap game—enough to open a restaurant in New Jersey—and then is killed on patrol attempting to guard his cache.

Multi-talented Mickey Rooney, who co-wrote the film's song, was Oscar-nominated for his performance in THE BOLD AND THE BRAVE.

Advertisement for THE BOLD AND THE BRAVE (1956).

BOMBARDIER (RKO, 1943) 97 mins.

Producer, Robert Fellows; director, Richard Wallace; story, John Twist, Martin Rackin; screenplay, Twist; art directors, Albert S. D'Agostino, Al Herman; set decorators, Darrell Silvera, Claude

Carpenter; song, M. K. Jerome and Jack Scholl; music, Roy Webb; music director, C. Bakaleinikoff; assistant director, Edward Killy; sound, Baily Fester, James G. Stewart; montages, Douglas Travers; special effects, Vernon L. Walker; camera, Nicholas Musuraca; editor, Robert Wise.

Pat O'Brien (Major Chick Davis); Randolph Scott (Captain Buck Oliver); Anne Shirley (Burt Hughes); Eddie Albert (Tom Hughes); Walter Reed (Jim Carter); Robert Ryan (Joe Conner); Barton MacLane (Sergeant Dixon); Richard Martin (Chito Rafferty); Russell Wade (Paul Harris); James Newill (Captain Rand); Bruce Edwards (Lieutenant Ellis); John Miljan (Chaplain Craig); Harold Landon (Pete Jordan); Margie Stewart (Mamie); Joe King (General Barnes); Leonard Strong (Japanese Officer); Abner Biberman (Japanese Sergeant); Russell Hoyt (Photographer); Wayne McCoy, Charles Russell (Instructors); Bud Geary (Sergeant); Warren Mace, George Ford, Mike Lally (Co-Pilots); Kirby Grant, Eddie Dew (Pilots); Erford Gage (Mayer); Charles Flynn (Radio Operator); Neil Hamilton, Lloyd Ingraham (Colonels); Stanley Andrews, John Sheehan, Walter Fenner, Bert Moorhouse (Congressmen); Lee Shumway, Ed Peil, Robert Middlemass (Officers); Paul Parry (Captain Driscoll); James Craven (Major Morris); Cy Ring (Captain Randall); Larry Wheat (Doctor); Joey Ray, Dick Winslow (Navigators); Paul Fix (Big Guy); John Calvert (Illusionist); Hugh Beaumont (Soldier); Allen Wood (Army Clerk); and: Joan Barclay, Marty Faust.

BOMBARDIER was churned out as war propaganda to explain precision bombing as handled by the U.S. Army Air Force. It had been started in pre-Pearl Harbor 1941 but its release was delayed as events made the initial version obsolete. It had contemporary combat footage tacked on for topical value, particularly relevant after General Doolittle's 1942 raid over Japan.

Major Chick Davis (Pat O'Brien) is a by-the-books man who is developing the modern bombsight, while Captain Buck Oliver (Randolph Scott) is the daring, unconventional pilot type. They are at odds over procedural methods at bombardier school and their rivalry for the affection of Burt Hughes (Anne Shirley), sister of cadet Tom Hughes (Eddie Albert). The film traces the U.S.'s entry into World War II and a bomber raid over Tokyo. Buck's plane is downed while trying to explode an ammunition dump and he and his crew are tortured by the Japanese under the direction of an extremely sadistic officer (Leonard Strong). Buck escapes but is badly wounded. He drives a burning gas truck through a supply dump, destroying the camouflage. Chick's plane arrives, and using

BORN FOR GLORY (Gaumont British, 1935) 70 mins.
Director, Walter Forde; based on the novel by C. S. Forester;
screenplay, J. O. C. Orton; dialogue, Michael Hogan, Gerald Fairlie;
second unit director, Anthony Asquith; camera, Bernard Knowles;
editor, Otto Ludwig.

Betty Balfour (Elizabeth Brown); John Mills (Albert Brown);
Barry Mackay (Lieutenant Sommerville); Jimmy Hanley (Ginger); H.
Marion-Crawford (Max); H. G. Stoker (Captain Holt); Percy Walsh
(Kapitan von Lutz); George Merritt (William Brown); Cyril Smith
(William Brown, Jr.).

Several years before its official entry into World War II, England
was preparing its people for the patriotic challenge ahead.

Out of a brief affair in 1893 between a London grocer's daughter
(Betty Balfour) and Naval Lieutenant Sommerville (Barry Mackay),
Albert Brown (John Mills) is born. Albert grows up and becomes a
sailor. During World War I his ship is torpedoed and he is saved by
the enemy. The cruiser docks at a remote island named Resolution to
make repairs and there Brown escapes with a gun. He opens fire on
the Germans, hoping to delay the vessel's departure till the British
arrive. He is successful, but at the cost of his life. The British cruiser
destroys the German ship and later the English captain, examining the
dead hero's effects, finds a pocket watch. He realizes this was the son
he never knew about.

This film was released originally in England by Gaumont British
at an 80-minute running time.

A.k.a. FOR EVER ENGLAND

THE BOYS IN COMPANY C (Columbia, 1978) Color 125 mins.
Executive producer, Raymond Chow; producer, Andre Mor-
gan; associate producer, Dennis Joban; director, Sidney J. Furie;
screenplay, Rich Natkin, Furie; production designer, Robert Lang;
art director, Laida Perez; costumes/ wardrobe, Erwin Arenas; music,
Jaime Mendoza-Nova; song, Craig Wasson; assistant directors, Fred
Slark, Herman Robles, Ulysses Formanzes, Madalena Chan; sound,
Bob Litt, Danny Daniel; camera, Godfrey A. Godar; editors, Michael
Berman, Frank J. Urioste, Allan Pattillo, James Benson.

Stan Shaw (Tyrone Washington); Andrew Stevens (Billy Ray
Pike); James Canning (Alvin Foster); Michael Lembeck (Vinnie
Fazio); Craig Wasson (Dave Bisbee); Scott Hylands (Captain Col-
lins); James Whitmore, Jr. (Lieutenant Archer); Noble Willingham
(Sergeant Curry); Lee Ermey (Sergeant Loyce); Santos Morales
(Sergeant Aquilla); Drew Michaels (Colonel Metcalfe); Karen Hilger
(Betsy); Peggy O'Neal (Nancy Bisbee); Claude Wilson (Roy Foster);
Chuck Doherty (George Pike); Cisco Oliver (Spoon); Stan Johns

(Receiving Sergeant); Don Bell (Junior Drill Instructor); Bob Mallett (Hank); Parris Hicks (Oates); and: Frederick Matthews, Logan Clarke, Ray Wagner, Duane Mercier, Noel Kramer, Fred Smithson, Eazy Black, Rick Natkin, Helen McNeely, Charles Waters, Ken Metcalfe, Vic Diaz, Jose Mari Avellana, Victor Pinzon, Michael Cohen.

Timing is everything and 1978 was still too early in the intellectual and emotional reevaluation of the Vietnam War for moviegoers to appreciate this film's strong anti-war message. Had it come seven or eight years later, this Philippines-lensed war movie would have had far more commercial impact.

On one level THE BOYS IN COMPANY C is a more than acceptable study of diverse young men coming to grips with maturity, aided by their camaraderie. On another plane it is a well-intentioned indictment of senseless killing in a bewildering world controlled by incompetent military officers and an unyielding enemy (Viet Cong), rarely seen but always felt.

It is August 1967 and five new recruits arrive at a Marine Corps induction center: Tyrone Washington (Stan Shaw), a hardened drug pusher from Chicago's black ghetto; Billy Ray Pike (Andrew Stevens), a professional football player from Galveston, Texas; Vinnie Fazio (Michael Lembeck), a sex-obsessed young man from Brooklyn; guitar-playing draft dodger Dave Bisbee (Craig Wasson) from Seattle, escorted to the center in handcuffs by the FBI; and Alvin Foster (James Canning), the would-be writer from Emporia, Kansas. It is Alvin who chronicles the five's military (mis)adventures for the book that will never be written.

"From now on," Drill Instructor Sergeant Loyce (Lee Ermey) snarls, "you will not eat, sleep, blow your nose or scratch your ass until someone tells you to do so. . . . You better give your soul to God because your ass is mine." With that, the five begin the grueling training that shapes them physically and mentally to be a team. But they are still individuals who fear the unknown of battle, and who are aware constantly that death can lie ahead. (They are told the casualty rate for young Marines in Vietnam is 50% and they learn that a body bag is "a nice convenient little package.")

Aboard the troop carrier taking them to Vietnam in early 1968 they learn to play soccer, the "theory" being that understanding the agile sport will give them a sense of the enemy's rhythm. No sooner do they land in Vietnam than they experience a skirmish with the enemy. They are assigned to the driven and obviously unstable Captain Collins (Scott Hylands) whose only concern is that the monthly body count be very high—no matter whose body makes up the count. The five are soon part of a squad escorting a trailer through enemy terrain; along the way two of their number are killed. Bisbee discovers that the truck contains not essential combat supplies but goodies for a general's birthday party. In protest he blows up the vehicle. Alvin continues to write of the boys' experiences, including that at a Da Nang brothel; Tyrone, who has become the group's

Andrew Stevens in THE BOYS IN COMPANY C (1978).

leader, investigates ways to smuggle drugs back to the States; Pike, who learns his girlfriend back home has given birth to a child, is coping with a drug habit induced by the crazed Captain.

The five are ordered that they must lose an upcoming soccer game with the South Vietnamese in order to give their allies moral support. The reward for losing will be a withdrawal for them from active duty and they will be sent on an extended soccer playing tour of safe non-combat bases in the Far East. The boys agree reluctantly, but midway through the game they rebel and win the match. In the midst of victory the Viet Cong attack the stadium and Alvin is killed as he throws himself down on a grenade to protect nearby children.

As would be expected in a coming-of-age combat film, much of THE BOYS IN COMPANY C deals with the shock of coping with death. One green recruit recoils in horror, "I never saw a dead body before. They look real small." However, this film was done in 1978 and a new moral consciousness has impinged on the genre to add a different message. No longer is there talk of the war being a righteous one or a good war, or a war to end all wars— as in World Wars I and II. Now both the top brass and the soldiers have their doubts. Victory is no longer the key issue. One Marine officer says in the film, "Maybe there's just one thing we can accomplish. Just get these little peckerheads out of here in one piece." Alvin writes in his journal, "We'll just keep on walking into one bloody mess after another until somebody figures out that living has got to be more important than winning."

The time was not yet ripe on-screen to denounce overtly the Vietnam War as a bad war, but the point had come where the competency of the military command down the line could be questioned directly. "You," says Shaw to an officer, "are the enemy."

BRADDOCK: MISSING IN ACTION III (Cannon, 1988) Color 96 mins.

Producers, Menahem Golan, Yoram Globus; associate producers, Michael Hartman, Michael R. Sloan; director, Aaron Norris; based on characters created by Arthur Silver, Larry Levinson, Steve Bing; screenplay, James Bruner, Chuck Norris; production designer, Ladislav Wilhelm; second unit art director, Rodell Cruz; second unit set decorator, Pia Fernandez; costume designer, Tamy Mor; second unit director/stunt coordinator, Dean Ferandini; sound, Paul Le-Mare, Eli Yarkoni; second unit sound, Nity Clemente; music, Jay Chattaway; camera, Joao Ferandes; editor, Michael J. Duthie.

Chuck Norris (Colonel James Braddock); Aki Aleong (General Quoc); Roland Harrah, III (Van Tan Cang); Miki Kim (Lin Tan Cang); Yehuda Efroni (Reverend Rolansk); Ron Barker (Mik).

Given the hefty box-office receipts for MISSING IN ACTION I (1984) and to a lesser degree from MISSING IN ACTION II (1985), q.v., there was no question that a third installment of the vengeance-prone good guy would reach the marketplace. But the marketplace was changing and the film only drew in $2,065,000 in theater rentals in the U.S. and Canada, having cost $9,000,000 to make during a sixteen-week production schedule.

Having exhausted any other reason for Colonel James Braddock (Chuck Norris) to return to celluloid Vietnam, this entry uses as background the 15,000 Amerasian children still held in Vietnam today. These offspring of American soldiers and Vietnamese women have been ignored by the Americans and treated very badly by the Vietnamese.

Braddock learns his wife (Miki Kim) did not die in the fall of Saigon in 1975 but lives in a rural Vietnamese shack with the boy (Roland Harrah, III) he never knew existed. His mission established, the loner flies to Thailand where, after shaking his CIA shadows, he organizes an attack force for his foray into Vietnam. He is stalked by sadistic General Quoc (Aki Aleong). Before long, Braddock's wife has been killed, he has been tortured, and he has earned finally the respect of his solemn son. He has also destroyed at least two Viet Cong bases through a combination of martial arts and weaponry, and led the Amerasian orphans into Thailand in the midst of a helicopter attack.

As expected, the critics were unimpressed. "Apart from better than competent production values and pyrotechnics, the Norris gung-ho forays are cheap imitations of more serious explorations on the scars of war. . . . [It] is a by-the numbers filmed atrocity" (Sheila Benson, *Los Angeles Times*). "The story of Braddock is strictly for comic-book fans . . . sharp production work can't save this violent throwaway" (Ed Kaufman, *The Hollywood Reporter*). In contrast, filmmaker Norris told the *LA Reader*'s Gary L. Wosk, "I think it's one of the best I've done."

BREAKOUT (Continental Distributing, 1959) 101 mins.

Producer, Colin Lesslie; director, Don Chaffey; based on the novel by Michael Gilbert; screenplay, Bryan Forbes, Frank Harvey; music, Francis Chagrin; camera, Arthur Grant; editor, John Trumper.

Richard Todd (Lieutenant Colonel David Baird, M.C.); Bernard Lee (Lieutenant Colonel Huxley); Michael Wilding (Major Charles Marquand); Richard Attenborough (Captain "Buster" Phillips); Dennis Price (Captain Roger Byford); William Franklyn (Captain Tony Long); Vincent Ball (Captain Pat Foster); Peter Arne (Capitano Benucci); Peter Jones (Captain Alfred Piker); Ronnie Stevens (Lieutenant Coutoules); Harold Siddons (Captain "Tag" Burchnall); Ian Whittaker (Second Lieutenant Betts-Hanger).

". . . [BREAKOUT] is a smooth, alert prisoner-of-war film which may have lost some impact by lagging a long time behind several other pix of similar setting" (*Variety*).

Over 400 British officers in an Italian prisoner-of-war camp are plotting their escape, hampered by an informer. Lieutenant Colonel David Baird, M.C. (Richard Todd) is heartily behind the effort, but the senior British leader, Lieutenant Colonel Huxley (Bernard Lee), is slow to join the plan. Having discovered the enemy in their midst, the men dash for freedom on the day the Italians surrender and just before the Nazis are due to take over.

Released in England by British-Lion as DANGER WITHIN.

BREAKTHROUGH (Warner Bros., 1950) 91 mins.

Producer, Bryan Foy; director, Lewis Seiler; story, Joseph I. Breen, Jr.; screenplay, Bernard Girard, Ted Sherdeman; art director, Stanley Fleischer; set decorator, J. Kissill; music, William Lava; assistant director, Don Page; camera, Edwin DuPar; editor, Folmar Blangsted.

David Brian (Captain Hale); John Agar (Lieutenant Joe Mallory); Frank Lovejoy (Sergeant Bell); Bill Campbell (Dominick); Paul Picerni (Private Ed Rojeck); Greg McClure (Private Frank Finley); Richard Monahan ("Four-Eff" Nelson); Eddie Norris (Sergeant Roy Henderson); Matt Willis (Private Jumbo Hollis); Dick Wesson (Hansen); Suzanne Dalbert (Collette); William Self (Private George Glasheen); Danny Arnold (Private Rothman); Dani Sue Nolan (Lieutenant Janis King); Howard Negley (Lieutenant Colonel Lewis).

During the Allied forces' fight through Normandy in World War II, the narrative follows one company of infantry. Joe Mallory (John Agar) is the unseasoned lieutenant, Sergeant Bell (Frank Lovejoy) the all-knowing veteran sergeant, and Captain Hale (David Brian) the hardheaded company commander who proves unstable emotionally as the war pressure mounts. Collette (Suzanne Dalbert) is the attractive village girl.

"The best way to take this picture is as an obvious glamorization of war, mixed with abundant scenes of battle and some starkly realistic news footage. . . . Those who were in the Normandy campaign may be a little surprised at the manner in which Director Lewis Seiler has deployed (or *not* deployed his troops). A whole platoon grouped behind one hedgerow, which is what we often see here, would have been a fatal concentration" (Bosley Crowther, *New York Times*).

BREAKTHROUGH (1979) see: CROSS OF IRON.

THE BRIDGE AT REMAGEN (United Artists, 1969) Color 116 mins.

Producer, David L. Wolper; associate producers, Julian Ludwig, Theodore Strauss; director, John Guillermin; based on the book by

Kenneth William Hechler; story, Roger Hirson; screenplay, Richard Yates, William Roberts, Ray Rigby; art director, Alfred Sweeney; makeup, Milan Jandera; costumes, Frank Balchus; music, Elmer Bernstein; second unit director, William Kroenick; assistant director, Reggie Callow; advisers, Cecil E. Roberts (Colonel, U.S. Army Retired), Hechler; stunt supervisor, Hal Needham; sound, Don Wortham, Al Overton; special effects, Logan Frazee; camera, Stanley Cortez; editor, William Cartwright.

George Segal (Lieutenant Phil Hartman); Robert Vaughn (Major Paul Kreuger); Ben Gazzara (Sergeant Angelo); Bradford Dillman (Major Barnes); E. G. Marshall (Brigadier General Shinner); Peter Van Eyck (General von Brock); Matt Clark (Corporal Jellicoe); Fritz Ford (Colonel Dent); Tom Heaton (Lieutenant Pattison); Bo Hopkins (Corporal Grebs); Robert Logan (Private Bissell); Paul Prokop (Captain Colt); Steve Sandor (Private Slavek); Frank Webb (Private Glover); Hans Christian Blech (Captain Carl Schmidt); Joachim Hansen (Captain Otto Baumann); Gunter Meisner (SS General Gerlach); Richard Munch (Field Marshal von Sturmer); Heinz Reincke (Emil Holzgang); Sonja Ziemann (Greta Holzgang); Vit Olmer (Lieutenant Zimring); Rudolf Jelinek (Private Manfred); Anna Gael (Girl).

In early 1945 the Allies' objective is to capture the Ludendorff railway bridge at Remagen, twelve miles south of Bonn on the Rhine River. It is the final barrier keeping the Allies from reaching the heart of Germany. The German High Command orders General von Brock (Peter Van Eyck) to demolish the span. He has second thoughts, because it would cut off 50,000 of his men from retreating back into the homeland. Von Brock in turn orders aristocratic Major Paul Kreuger (Robert Vaughn) to hold the bridge as long as possible. Meanwhile, U.S. Brigadier General Shinner (E. G. Marshall) is pushing the drive across the Rhine. He orders an armored infantry division under Major Barnes (Bradford Dillman) to stop the Germans, even if they destroy the bridge. Overly ambitious Barnes is disliked by his men, especially by his platoon leader, Lieutenant Phil Hartman (George Segal) and the opportunistic Sergeant Angelo (Ben Gazzara), who scavenges for valuables among the enemy corpses. The Americans reach Remagen. Kreuger delays dynamiting the bridge, waiting for a German troop train to cross. When he does set off the explosives, he finds they are defective. By night the Allies cross the bridge. Kreuger is shot by the SS for having failed to raze the bridge. In March 1945 the bridge collapses on its own, making the American "victory" meaningless.

One of the late 1960s cycle of *big* war movies, THE BRIDGE

OF REMAGEN was generally overlooked. It boasted explosive action sequences and tried to present impartially both sides' thinking about this battle, but it never made its military/political overview sharp enough for viewers to absorb.

Based on the 1957 book, it was filmed in Czechoslovakia, Italy, and West Germany.

THE BRIDGE ON THE RIVER KWAI (Columbia, 1957) Color 161 mins.

Producer, Sam Spiegel; director, David Lean; based on the novel by Pierre Boulle; screenplay, Boulle, (uncredited) Michael Wilson, Carl Foreman; music, Malcolm Arnold; assistant directors, Gus Agosti, Ted Sturgis; camera, Jack Hildyard; editor, Peter Taylor.

William Holden (Shears); Alec Guinness (Colonel Nicholson); Jack Hawkins (Major Warden); Sessue Hayakawa (Colonel Saito); James Donald (Major Clipton); Geoffrey Horne (Lieutenant Joyce); Andre Morell (Colonel Green); Peter Williams (Captain Reeves); John Boxer (Major Hughes); Percy Herbert (Grogan); Harold Goodwin (Baker); Ann Sears (Nurse); Henry Okawa (Captain Kanematsu); K. Katsumoto (Lieutenant Miura); M. R. B. Chakra-bandhu (Yai); Vilaiwan Seeboonreaung, Ngamta Suphaphongs, Java-nart Punynchoti, Kannikar Wowklee (Siamese Girls).

"Without law," says Colonel Nicholson (Alec Guinness), "there is no civilization." THE BRIDGE ON THE RIVER KWAI is a perceptive study of the confusion of right and wrong in wartime and the hell it plays on fanatical military leaders straining to obey and interpret orders in the midst of chaos. Beneath its epic trappings, THE BRIDGE ON THE RIVER KWAI is a thoughtful anti-war film.

British Colonel Nicholson and his troops have surrendered to the Japanese in 1943 Burma and are placed in a prisoner-of-war camp in the heart of the jungle. Camp Sixteen is ruled by the excessively proud Colonel Saito (Sessue Hayakawa). The determined Saito advises his captives, "The Japanese army cannot have idle mouths to feed. There is no barbed wire, no stockade, no watch tower. We are an island in the jungle. Escape is impossible." Saito's mission is to get an elaborate railroad bridge built by May across the River Kwai, part of the network that will stretch from Singapore to Malaya and on to Bangkok and Rangoon. Saito's problem is that he needs the British to engineer and build the structure. At first Nicholson, the prim martinet, refuses to cooperate because the Japanese want everyone to assist in the manual labor. "Use of officers for manual labor is expressly forbidden by the Geneva Convention," insists Nicholson. Saito's response is to torture Nicholson, and when that fails, he reaches a compromise because he must deal with the baffling British logic. ("You are defeated, but you have no shame.") Nicholson has gained his point. However he has lost sight of the fact that the completed bridge will be used by the Japanese against the Allies. He embarks enthusiastically and madly on the bridge building, driving his men almost beyond endurance. His rationalization is that constructing a "proper bridge" will unite and distract his demoralized men. It will be a lasting monument to British ingenuity.

Meanwhile, cynical Shears (William Holden), who has escaped from Camp Sixteen, reaches Mount Lavinia Hospital in Ceylon, where Major Warden (Jack Hawkins) advises him that he knows all about Shears' impersonation of an officer and that he has no choice but to join a squad heading back into the jungle to blow up the Kwai River bridge. Shears agrees reluctantly and, along with Warden, Lieutenant Joyce (Geoffrey Horne) and others, parachutes into the Burmese jungle. They reach their objective the night before the Japanese will move troop trains over the completed bridge. The explosive charges are planted along the bridge structure, but the next morning on an inspection tour perfectionist Nicholson spots a detonation wire and it leads him to the British commandos. In the scuffle that follows, Nicholson is wounded. As he dies, he realizes the enormity of his actions ("My God, what have I done?"). He falls (accidentally?) on the plunger and the bridge blows up, destroying the train. Meanwhile Shears and others have been killed, leaving Major Clipton (James Donald) a witness to the grisly spectacle. He concludes, "It's all madness."

"Unlike so many of the multimillion-dollar super-spectacles which seem to equate sheer bulk with entertainment value, KWAI starts out with something important to say, something to prove. 'War is madness' is M. Boulle's central theme—a madness that afflicts conquered and conquerors alike" (Arthur Knight, *Saturday Review*). "[The film] may rank as the most rousing adventure film inspired by the last World War . . . its characters run to a strange variety but they remain valid, seeming to spring out of the background of the picture. Their casual rise to exploits of foolhardy valor makes the deeds seem credible . . ." (Alton Cook, *New York World Telegram*).

THE BRIDGE ON THE RIVER KWAI, which cost $3,000,000 to film on location in Ceylon, earned $17,195,000 in theater rentals in the U.S. and Canada. The adaptation of the "Colonel Bogey March" (composed in 1916) combined with "The River Kwai March" film theme became a standard "pop" favorite. The action epic won seven Academy Awards: Best Picture, Best Director, Best Actor (Alec Guinness), Screenplay, Music, Cinematography, Editing.

A BRIDGE TOO FAR (United Artists, 1977) Color 175 mins. Producers, Joseph E. Levine, Richard P. Levine; co-producer, Michael Stanley-Evans; associate producer, John Palmer; director, Richard Attenborough; based on the book by Cornelius Ryan; screenplay, William Goldman; production designer, Terry Marsh; art directors, Roy Stannard, Stuart Craig; music, John Addison; assistant director, David Tomblin; stunt coordinator, Alf Joint; sound, Simon Kaye; special effects, John Richardson; camera, Geoffrey Unsworth; editor, Anthony Gibbs.

Dirk Bogarde (Lieutenant General Browning); James Caan (Staff Sergeant Eddie Dohun); Michael Caine (Lieutenant Colonel Joe Vandeleur); Sean Connery (Major General Robert Urquhart); Edward Fox (Lieutenant General Brian Horrocks); Elliott Gould (Colonel Bobby Stout); Gene Hackman (Major General Sosabowski); Anthony Hopkins (Lieutenant Colonel John Frost); Hardy Kruger (General Ludwig); Laurence Olivier (Dr. Spaander); Ryan O'Neal (Brigadier General James M. Gavin); Robert Redford (Major Julian Cook); Maximilian Schell (Lieutenant General Bittrich); Liv Ullmann (Kate ter Horst); Arthur Hill (Tough Colonel); Wolfgang Preiss (Field Marshal von Rundstedt); Siem Vroom (Underground Leader); Eric Vant Wout (Kid with Glasses); Mary Smithuysen (Old Dutch Lady); Marlies Van Alcmaer (Wife); Nicholas Campbell (Captain Glass); Christopher Good (Major Carlyle); Keith Drinkel (Lieutenant Cornish); Peter Faber (Captain Harry).

Cornelius Ryan wrote a monumental book (1974) detailing the horrible debacle of "Operation Market Garden" in September 1944, in which Field Marshal Montgomery and General Eisenhower agreed to drop 35,000 Allied troops into eastern Holland to secure six strategic bridges leading into Germany. Next, the British would push through Belgium sixty-four miles to the last bridge at Arnhem, and from there two divisions would crash into the industrial Ruhr area and squash the already damaged factories of the Third Reich. If the bold plan had worked the War in Europe could have been over, but the bridge at Arnhem proved to be "the bridge too far." Everything went wrong, especially for the Allies: the weather, bad judgment, worse luck, and sheer panic. It was a bloody defeat.

As *Variety* assessed this box-office failure, "Futility and frustration are the overriding emotional elements. . . . There is such an overhanging sense of doom that one can never really get behind any of the principals; they all seem either dazed, deceived or otherwise out of touch with events."

Director Richard Attenborough displayed all the meticulous care he lavished on his Oscar-winning GANDHI (1982), but here his costly efforts ($25,000,000) did not pay off (the film "only" earned

$20,298,000 in theater rentals in the U.S. and Canada); especially in the use of scores of star turns for marquee appeal (e.g., Ryan O'Neal as a brigadier general, Laurence Olivier as a Dutch doctor, Liv Ullmann as a housewife, Elliot Gould as a wise-cracking colonel.) Even in a decade where war was no longer popular, the recreation of a stunning Allied defeat did not appeal to filmgoers. "When events begin to overwhelm, director Attenborough loses his design in the smoke and din of a huge confused battle" (Richard Schickel, *Time* magazine). The British press was particularly put off by the production. "I really doubt if one any longer wants movies that turn some horrifying human disaster into the stuff of visceral entertainment or try to celebrate the tens of thousands of unknowns who died and at the same time assign main roles to famous faces who glorify the Hollywood star system" (Alexander Walker, London *Evening Standard*).

Much was made of the fact that the film opens with non-widescreen black and white footage of the actual war in 1944, a startling contrast to the unwieldy color panorama that would follow.

THE BRIDGES AT TOKO-RI (Paramount, 1955) Color 102 mins.

Producer, William Perlberg; director, Mark Robson; based on the novel by James A. Michener; screenplay, Valentine Davies; art directors, Hal Pereira, Henry Bumstead; costumes, Edith Head; makeup, Wally Westmore; music, Lyn Murray; Technicolor consultant, Richard Mueller; technical adviser, Commander M. V. Beebe, U.S. Navy; sound, Hugo Grenzbach, Gene Garvin; camera, Loy Griggs; aerial camera, Charles G. Clarke; second unit camera, Wallace Kelley, Thomas Tutweiler; editor, Alma Macrorie.

William Holden (Lieutenant Harry Brubaker, U.S. Navy Reserve); Grace Kelly (Nancy Brubaker); Fredric March (Rear Admiral George Tarrant); Mickey Rooney (Mike Forney); Robert Strauss (Beer Barrel); Charles McGraw (Commander Wayne Lee); Keike Awaji (Kimiko); Earl Holliman (Nestor Gamidge); Richard Shannon (Lieutenant Second Grade Olds); Willis Bouchey (Captain Evans); Nadene Ashdown (Kathy Brubaker); Cheryl Lynn Callaway (Susie); James Jenkins (Assistant C.I.C. Officer); Marshall V. Beebe (Pilot); Charles Tannen (Military Police Major); Teru Shimada (Japanese Father); Dennis Weaver (Air Intelligence Officer); Jack Roberts (Quartermaster); Robert Kino (Bellboy); James Connell (Bartender); Burton Metcalfe (Military Police Sergeant); Chise Freeman (Setsuko, the Governess); Corey Allen (Enlisted Man); Bill Ash (Talker); Paul Raymond (Spotter); Ayam Ikeda (Japanese Mother); Sharon Munemura, Claudia Satow (Japanese Children).

William Holden and Mickey Rooney in THE BRIDGES AT TOKO-RI (1955).

Thirty-five-year-old Denver lawyer Harry Brubaker (William Holden) of the Naval Reserve is recalled to active duty during the Korean Conflict. Based on a carrier commanded by Rear Admiral George Tarrant (Fredric March), Brubaker is one of several pilots assigned to fly missions over North Korea to destroy strategic bridges. His worried wife (Grace Kelly), based in Tokyo, can only comfort her husband and pray for the best for her family. Having accomplished his goal, Brubaker's plane is downed and oddball helicopter pilot Mike Forney (Mickey Rooney) attempts unsuccessfully to rescue him. They both are killed by Communist troops.

Remarkable for its stirring air and sea sequences, THE BRIDGES AT TOKO-RI combines in measured doses, patriotism, domestic relationships, cultural contrasts, and service loyalties. Just as the preposterously garbed Mike Forney (green top hat and scarf) is a good trooper, so seasoned carrier commander Tarrant takes his responsibilities seriously, agonizing over the imminent dangers for his pilots. (At the end of a particularly eloquent speech eulogizing the death of Harry and the others, he asks, "Where do we find such men?") The film is a recruitment officer's delight. There is Harry Brubaker's character realizing why, at his age and having already served in World War II, he is "needed" in the Korean conflict. His adapting to his situation and becoming one of the men is all a commanding officer could desire of a subordinate. This being 1954 there are no fuzzy edges to anyone's enunciated reasoning about the U.S. involvement in Korea.

"THE BRIDGES AT TOKO-RI takes itself very seriously on the subject of the Korean War. . . . [It] is a conventionally structured war movie. It has a little of everything: . . . [including] the familiar mission briefings complete with baton and visual aids. Special effects provide the film's central attraction and won for THE BRIDGES AT TOKO-RI an Academy Award. The spectacular raid sequence contains excellent model work that intercuts beautifully with shots of real planes" (Glen M. Erickson, *Magill's American Film Guide*, 1983). THE BRIDGES AT TOKO-RI earned $4,295,000 in theater rentals in the U.S. and Canada.

THE CAINE MUTINY (Columbia, 1954) Color 123 mins.

Producer, Stanley Kramer; director, Edward Dmytryk; based on the novel and the play (*The Caine Mutiny Court-Martial*) by Herman Wouk; screenplay, Stanley Roberts; additional dialogue, Michael Blankfort; technical adviser, Commander James C. Shawn (U.S. Navy); color consultant, Francis Cugat; production designer, Rudolph Sternad; art director, Cary Odell; set decorator, Frank Tuttle; costumes, Jean Louis; makeup, Clay Campbell; assistant director, Carter DeHaven, Jr.; music, Max Steiner; songs: Wouk and Fred Karger, Jimmy McHugh and Clarence Gaskill; sound, Lambert Day; special effects, Lawrence Butler; camera, Franz Planer; second unit camera, Ray Cory; editors, William Lyon, Henry Batista.

Humphrey Bogart (Captain Philip Francis Queeg); Jose Ferrer (Lieutenant Barney Greenwald); Van Johnson (Lieutenant Steve Maryk); Fred MacMurray (Lieutenant Tom Keefer); Robert Francis (Ensign Willie Keith); May Wynn (May Wynn); Tom Tully (Captain DeVriess); E. G. Marshall (Lieutenant Commander Challee); Arthur Franz (Lieutenant Paynter); Lee Marvin (Meatball); Warner Anderson (Captain Blakely); Claude Akins (Horrible); Katharine Warren (Mrs. Keith); Jerry Paris (Ensign Harding); Steve Brodie (Chief Budge); Todd Karns (Stilwell); Whit Bissell (Lieutenant Commander Dickson); James Best (Lieutenant Jorgenson); Joe Haworth (Ensign

Carmody); Guy Anderson (Ensign Rabbit); James Edwards (Whittaker); Don Dubbins (Urban); David Alpert (Engstrand); Dayton Lummis (Uncle Lloyd); James Todd (Commodore Kelvey); Don Keefer (Court Stenographer); Patrick Miller (Movie Operator); Tyler McVey, John Tomeck, Kenneth MacDonald, Paul McGuire, Robert Bray, Gaylord (Steve) Pendleton, Richard Norris (Board Members);

Van Johnson in THE CAINE MUTINY (1954).

Don Anderson (Radar Man); Eddie Laguna (Winston); Jay Richards, Frank Losee, John Duncan (Sailors).

It is assumed (or at least used to be) that commanding military officers know what they are doing, especially in wartime, and that they are accountable fully for their actions. Doubting this authority and the rationality of the chain of command is the focal point of

THE CAINE MUTINY, based on the Pulitzer Prize winning novel and the Broadway hit play* by Herman Wouk.

Rebellious Ensign Willie Keith (Robert Francis), a Princeton graduate, is assigned to the shabby destroyer/minesweeper USS *Caine* at Pearl Harbor in 1943. Aboard he meets the executive officer, Lieutenant Steve Maryk (Van Johnson) and the intellectual Lieutenant Tom Keefer (Fred MacMurray) who, before the war, had been a novelist (he even smokes a pipe). A new captain comes aboard to replace the disorganized Captain DeVriess (Tom Tully), Lieutenant Commander Philip Francis Queeg (Humphrey Bogart), who soon proves he has his own set of special problems. During a target-towing exercise, Queeg is too involved in upbraiding a disheveled sailor and permits his vessel to cut its own towline. Later, while guiding Marine landing craft to an island beachhead, Queeg finds the *Caine* under shore attack. He orders a yellow dye marker tossed on the water to show where he is leaving the support group, and then moves out of firing range as quickly as possible. His men regard this as an act of cowardice and begin calling him "Old Yellowstain." Soon the demarcation lines are drawn between those pro-Queeg and those anti-. The latter faction is led by Keefer, who infers that Queeg is paranoid and suggests that Maryk maintain a medical log on the Captain. The climax of the battle of wills occurs when battle-fatigued Queeg discovers strawberries missing from the ship's supplies and conducts an extensive search for an alleged duplicate icebox key. (The mess boys were the actual culprits and Queeg had been so informed, but refused to believe it.) During a major storm when the *Caine* looks to be in danger, Maryk relieves Queeg of his duty. He is backed up in his action by Willie. In San Francisco Maryk is summoned to a court-martial inquiry, where he is defended by acerbic Lieutenant Barney Greenwald (Jose Ferrer). During the hearing Queeg is defended by Lieutenant Commander Challee (E. G. Marshall), which leads the shifty Keefer to alter his position. On the stand Queeg buckles under the pressure of Greenwald's questioning and loses control of himself; rolling the steel balls in his hand, he comes close to babbling insanity. Maryk and Willie are acquitted. At the celebration among the *Caine*'s officers, the sneering Greenwald condemns them for their actions against this veteran captain who has served his

---

*The most recent adaptation of Herman Wouk's play aired on May 9, 1988 on CBS-TV, featuring Brad Davis (Captain Queeg), Jeff Daniels (Lieutenant Maryk), and Eric Bogosian (Lieutenant Greenwald). It was directed by Robert Altman. *People* magazine reported, "The writing remains impressive—a spectacular drama about a complex conflict of ethics and emotions, of power and corruption. The direction is remarkably underdone. . . . "

country for so long. Greenwald tosses a glass of champagne in Keefer's face, claiming he is the real author of the mutiny. Willie is assigned to a new berth, commanded by DeVriess, the original *Caine* captain.

Nominated for Best Picture and Best Actor (Bogart), THE CAINE MUTINY is a resourceful drama of wartime conflict, this time not on the battlefield but within military ranks. An opening credit to the film alerts the audience that there never has been a mutiny in the U.S. Navy nor a trial for one and that this story deals with men reacting to extreme pressure. THE CAINE MUTINY earned an impressive $8,700,000 in theater rentals in the U.S. and Canada.

This drama remains a classic study of motion picture ensemble playing by the cast.

THE CAMP ON BLOOD ISLAND (Hammer, 1958) 82 mins.

Producer, Anthony Hinds; director, Val Guest; screenplay, Jon Manchip White, Guest; music, Gerard Schurmann; camera, Jack Asher; editor, Bill Lenny.

Carl Mohner (Piet Van Elst); Andre Morell (Colonel Lambert); Edward Underdown (Major Dawes); Walter Fitzgerald (Cyril Beattle); Phil Brown (Lieutenant Bellamy); Barbara Shelley (Kate Keiller); Michael Goodliffe (Father Anjou); Michael Gwynn (Tom Shields); Richard Wordsworth (Dr. Keller); Edwin Ritchfield (Sergeant Major); Ronald Radd (Colonel Yamamitasu); Wolfe Morris (Interpreter); Michael Ripper (Jap Driver); Mary Merrall (Mrs. Beattle); Liliane Sottane (Mala); Grace Denbigh Russell (Thin Woman).

When Hammer Films was not turning out Frankenstein and other science fiction/horror entries, it produced such sensational offerings as THE CAMP ON BLOOD ISLAND. Based on a real life event, it deals with British officers in a prisoner-of-war camp who keep the news of the war's end from the sadistic Japanese commandant because he threatens to massacre all the prisoners should Japan lose the war.

"There are as many holes in the film as there are in a fishing net. Yet it holds the attention mainly because of the frightful realization that such things did actually happen in the war" (*Variety*).

CAPTAINS OF THE CLOUDS (Warner Bros., 1942) Color 113 mins.

Producer, Hal B. Wallis; associate producer, William Cagney; director, Michael Curtiz; story, Arthur T. Horman, Roland Gillett; screenplay, Horman, Richard Macaulay, Norman Reilly Raine; art director, Ted Smith; makeup, Perc Westmore; music, Max Steiner; music director, Leo F. Forbstein; song, Harold Arlen and Johnny

Mercer; technical adviser, Squadron Leader O. Cathcart-Jones; dialogue director, Hugh MacMullan; Technicolor consultants, Natalie Kalmus, Henri Jaffa; sound, C. A. Riggs; special effects, Byron Haskin, Rex Wimpy; camera, Sol Polito, Wilfred M. Cline; aerial camera, Elmer Dyer, Charles Marshall, Winton C. Hoch; editor, George Amy.

James Cagney (Brian MacLean); Dennis Morgan (Johnny Dutton); Brenda Marshall (Emily Foster); Alan Hale (Tiny Murphy); George Tobias (Blimp Lebec); Reginald Gardiner (Scrounger Harris); Air Marshal William A. Bishop (Himself); Reginald Denny (Commanding Officer); Russell Arms (Prentiss); Paul Cavanagh (Group Captain); Clem Bevans (Store Teeth Morrison); J. M. Kerrigan (Foster); J. Farrell MacDonald (Dr. Neville); Patrick O'Moore (Fyffo); Morton Lowry (Carmichael); O. Cathcart-Jones (Chief Instructor); Frederic Worlock (President of Court Martial); Roland Drew (Officer); Lucia Carroll (Blonde); George Meeker (Playboy); Benny Baker (Popcorn Kearns); Hardie Albright (Kingsley); Roy Walker (Mason); Charles Halton (Nolan); Louis Jean Heydt (Provost Marshal); Gig Young, Tod Andrews (Student Pilots); Willie Fung (Willie); Frank Lackteen, James Stevens, Bill Wilkerson (Indians); Emmett Vogan (Clerk); Miles Mander (Churchill's Voice); Larry Williams (Duty Officer); Tom Dugan (Bartender); Edward McNamara (Dog Man); Charles Smith (Bellboy); Winifred Harris (Woman); George Offerman, Jr. (Mechanic); Gavin Muir (Orderly).

Set in the period before Pearl Harbor forced the U.S. into World War II, CAPTAINS OF THE CLOUDS is a well-crafted Technicolor blend of high adventure, a semi-documentary pilot's training guide, and unabashed patriotism.

Four carefree Canadian bush pilots—Johnny Dutton (Dennis Morgan), Tiny Murphy (Alan Hale), Blimp Lebec (George Tobias), and Scrounger Harris (Reginald Gardiner)—compete with brash newcomer Brian MacLean (James Cagney) over jobs and women, especially attractive but self-serving Emily Foster (Brenda Marshall). Then comes the evacuation of Dunkirk (May 1940) and in a surge of patriotism, the free-spirited bush pilots join the Royal Canadian Air Force. There they learn a new type of flying and sacrifice individuality for the conformity of teamwork. Overly independent, irascible Brian washes out of the demanding service and lives to regret it, especially when his buddies head overseas. When Tiny is killed in a flight accident, Brian assumes his identity and becomes part of an unarmed squadron ferrying Hudson bombers from Newfoundland to England. Enemy planes appear as they near England, and after co-pilot

Scrounger has been mortally wounded, the regenerated Brian heads straight at the Messerschmitt, dying to save the rest of the bombers. At the time of the film's release much was made of the fact that Air Marshal Bishop, a free-spirited flying ace of World War I, appeared in CAPTAINS OF THE CLOUDS as himself, endorsing the new breed of flyers—those who understand that cool-headed group cooperation is far more essential to the success of the war effort than hot-tempered bravura.

CAPTAINS OF THE CLOUDS was Oscar-nominated for Best Color Cinematography and Best Color Set Direction.

CARGO OF INNOCENTS see: STAND BY FOR ACTION.

CAST A GIANT SHADOW (United Artists, 1966) Color 141 min.

Producer, Melville Shavelson; co-producer, Michael Wayne; director, Shavelson; based on the book by Ted Berkman; screenplay, Shavelson; production designer, Michael Stringer; art director, Arrigo Equini; costumes, Margaret Furse; makeup, David Grayson, Euclide Santoli; music, Elmer Bernstein; orchestrators, Leo Shuken, Jack Hayes; songs: Dov Seltzer; Dan Almagor; assistant directors, Charles Scott, Jr., Tim Zinnemann; sound, David Bowen, Chuck Overhulser; special effects, Sass Bedig; camera, Aldo Tonti; second unit camera, Marko Yakovlevich; editors, Bert Bates, Gene Ruggiero.

Kirk Douglas (Colonel David "Mickey" Marcus); Senta Berger (Magda Simon); Angie Dickinson (Mrs. Emma Marcus); James Donald (Safir); Stathis Giallelis (Ram Oren); Luther Adler (Jacob Zion); Haym Topol (Abou Ibn Kader); Frank Sinatra (Vince); Yul Brynner (Commander Asher Gonen); John Wayne (General Mike Randolph); Gary Merrill (Pentagon Chief of Staff); Ruth White (Mrs. Chaison); Gordon Jackson (James MacAfee); Michael Hordern (British Ambassador); Allan Cuthbertson (British Immigration Officer); Jeremy Kemp (Senior Officer); Sean Barrett (Junior Officer); Michael Shillo (Andre Simon); Rina Ganor (Rona); Roland Bartrop (Bert Harrison); Vera Dolen (Mrs. Martinson); Robert Gardett (General Walsh); Michael Balston, Claude Aliotti (Sentries); Samra Dedes (Belly Dancer); Michael Shagrir (Truck Driver); Frank Latimore, Ken Buckle (United Nations Officers); Rod Dana (Randolph's Aide); Arthur Hansell (Officer); Don Sturkie (Parachute Sergeant); Hilel Raveh (Yaakov); Shlomo Hermon (Yussuff); Robert Ross (Bit).

This film proved to be one of those *big* misguided motion pictures that distort a potentially invigorating message into overblown theatrics.

The British decide to withdraw from Palestine in late 1947 and

Advertisement for CAST A GIANT SHADOW (1966).

the Arabs are rebelling at the United Nations' decision to divide Palestine into separate Jewish and Arab states. Colonel David "Mickey" Marcus (Kirk Douglas), a Jewish West Point graduate, a D-Day participant, a military adviser to President Franklin D. Roosevelt, and a New York lawyer, is asked by the Israeli government to use his American and military know-how to (re)organize the Haganah underground army. Both his wife (Angie Dickinson) and the Pentagon urge him not to go, but he does. He learns that the Haganah is outnumbered 60 to 1 by the enemy and that its offensive capabilities are diluted by internal strife. He becomes involved romantically with Magda Simon (Senta Berger), a freedom fighter. After a short trip back home, he returns to Israel where he is ordered to break through a mountain pass to Jerusalem before the truce occurs and land boundaries become firm. He is victorious. However, one night a few hours before the truce takes effect, he is shot by one of his own sentries because he is unable to understand or speak Hebrew and cannot supply the requisite passwords.

For worse rather than better, there are several star cameos in this overblown melodramatic outing: John Wayne as salty two-star General Mike Randolph, who tries unsuccessfully to convince Marcus not to meddle in the Israeli business; Yul Brynner as Israeli military leader Asher Gonen; and most offensive of all, Frank Sinatra as flippant, devil-may-care pilot Vince, who hurls seltzer bottles at Egyptian tanks below.

As *Variety* decided, "CAST A GIANT SHADOW exemplifies the problems in contemporary film biography, particularly when the subject is less well known than the events which brought him honor." The trade paper added, "Unfortunately . . . it was found necessary to go into World War II flashbacks to establish the Marcus character."

CASTLE KEEP (Columbia, 1969) Color 105 mins.

Producers, Martin Ransohoff, John Calley; associate producer, Edward L. Rissen; director, Sydney Pollack; based on the novel by William Eastlake; screenplay, Daniel Taradash, David Rayfiel; production designer, Rino Mondellin; art directors, Max Douy, Jacques Douy, Mort Rabinowitz; costume designers, Jacques Fonteray, Jack Martell; makeup, Robert J. Schiffer; music/music conductor, Michel Legrand; choreography, Dirk Sanders; assistant director, Marc Maurette; sound, Antoine Petitjean, Yves Dacquay; special effects, Lee Zavitz; camera, Henri Decae; aerial camera, Tyler Camera Systems; editor, Malcolm Cooke; assistant editor, Michele Roberts.

Burt Lancaster (Major Abraham Falconer); Patrick O'Neal (Captain Beckman); Jean-Pierre Aumont (Comte de Maldorais); Peter Falk (Sergeant Rossi); Astrid Heeren (Therese); Scott Wilson

(Corporal Clearboy); Tony Bill (Lieutenant Amberjack); Al Free-
man, Jr. (Private Benjamin); James Patterson (Private Three Ears of
an Elk); Bruce Dern (Billy Bix); Michael Conrad (Sergeant De Vaca);
Caterina Boratto (Red Queen); Bisera Vukotic (Baker's Wife);
Elisabeth Teissier, Marja Allanen, Anne Marie Moskovenko, Eya
Tuli, Elizabeth Darius, Karen Blanguernon, Maria Danube (Red
Queen Girls); Jancika Kovac (David); Ernest Clark (British Colonel);
Harry Baird (Dancing Soldier); Dave Jones (One-Eared Soldier); Jean
Gimello (Puerto Rican).

Based on a 1965 book, CASTLE KEEP is an expensively-
mounted surrealistic allegory of war, peace, and confused cultural
values. For viewers intent on a blood and guts exercise it is a failure;
for intellectuals wanting a stimulating exercise in philosophizing, it
has merit.

In the late winter of 1944 near Bastogne, one-eyed infantry
Major Abraham Falconer (Burt Lancaster), billets his group of
battle-worn soldiers at a tenth-century castle owned by the impotent
aesthete Comte de Maldorais (Jean-Pierre Aumont), who begs
Falconer not to resist the expected German attack because the castle is
filled with valuable art treasures. Falconer's seven men are: Corporal

Burt Lancaster in CASTLE KEEP (1969).

Rossi (Peter Falk), a Brooklyn baker who falls in love with a local baker's widow (Bisera Vukotic); Lieutenant Amberjack (Tony Bill), a one-time clergy student who cannot cope with the goings-on at the local brothel; the liquor-loving Sergeant De Vaca (Michael Conrad); the sour-faced ex-cowboy, Corporal Clearboy (Scott Wilson), who fixates on the virtues of a captured Volkswagen car; the acerbic Indian, Private Henry Three Ears of an Elk (James Patterson); the black intellectual, Private Benjamin (Al Freeman, Jr.), who is writing a novel about his wartime experiences; and art historian Captain Beckman (Patrick O'Neal), who intends to save the castle and its art. Meanwhile the Comte endorses a romance between Falconer and his wife Therese (Astrid Heeren) and hopes it will result in her having a child.

The Nazis march on the castle, blanketed in snow, and the Comte is killed, even while helping the enemy make a peaceful entry. Neither dynamiting the secret passage with its art treasures nor the brothel girls hurling homemade bombs on the Nazi tanks can save the G.I.s. A bloody battle ensues. The only survivor is Private Benjamin, who escapes with Therese. The castle is blown up.

"The stylized battle scenes at the finale are well-engineered but by this point most watchers are anesthetized. CASTLE KEEP is part realism, part fantasy and hovers ridiculously between being serious and being satiric. The dialogue creaks with ponderous epigrams and flippant quips about life and war" (Tony Thomas, *Burt Lancaster*, 1975).

CATCH-22 (Paramount, 1970) Color 122 mins.

Producers, John Calley, Martin Ransohoff; associate producer, Clive Reed; director, Mike Nichols; based on the novel by Joseph Heller; screenplay, Buck Henry; production designer, Richard Sylbert; art director, Harold Michelson, set decorator, Ray Moyer; costume supervisor, Ernest Adler; men's wardrobe, Lambert Marks; makeup supervisor, Del Armstrong; music conductor, Fritz Reiner; assistant directors, Edward A. Teets, Martin Cohan, Ron Grow; technical adviser, Alexander Gerry; flying supervisor, Frank Tallman; sound, Larry Jost, Elden Ruberg; supervising sound effects editor, Gordon Daniel; sound effects editor, Howard Beals; special effects, Lee Vasque; camera, David Watkin; second unit camera, Harold Wellman; helicopter camera, Nelson Tyler; special camera effects, Albert Whitlock; editor, Sam O'Steen.

Alan Arkin (Captain Yossarian); Martin Balsam (Colonel Cathcart); Richard Benjamin (Major Danby); Art Garfunkel (Captain Nately); Jack Gilford (Doc Daneeka); Buck Henry (Lieutenant

Colonel Korn); Bob Newhart (Major Major); Anthony Perkins (Chaplain Tappman); Paula Prentiss (Nurse Duckett); Martin Sheen (Lieutenant Dobbs); Jon Voight (Milo Minderbinder); Orson Welles (General Dreedle); Seth Allen (Hungry Joe); Bob Balaban (Captain Orr); Susanne Benton (General Dreedle's WAC); Peter Bonerz (Captain McWatt); Norman Fell (Sergeant Towser); Charles Grodin (Aarfy Aardvark); Austin Pendleton (Colonel Moodus); Gina Rovere (Nately's Whore); Olympia Carlisi (Luciana); Marcel Dalio (Old Man); Evi Maltagliati (Old Woman); Liam Dunn (Father); Elizabeth Wilson (Mother); Richard Libertini (Brother); Jon Korkes (Gunner Sergeant Snowden); John Brent (Cathcart's Receptionist); Collin Wilcox-Horne (Nurse Cramer); Phil Roth, Bruce Kirby, Jack Riley (Doctors); Felice Orlandi (Man in Black); Wendy D'Olive (Aarfy's Girl); Fernanda Vitobello (Kid Sister).

Stationed on a Mediterranean isle during World War II, Captain Yossarian (Alan Arkin) implores Doc Daneeka (Jack Gilford) to certify him unfit for further air duty. However, the Catch-22 (of the title) is that only a sane person would ask to be relieved of hazardous flight assignment and so. . . .

Demented Colonel Cathcart (Martin Balsam) is determined to coax more missions out of his frazzled flyers, hoping it will lead to a feature article on him in *The Saturday Evening Post*. This pressure on the men causes them to act even more bizarrely. Milo Minderbinder (Jon Voight), head of M & M Enterprises ("what's good for M & M Enterprises is good for the country"), is a mercenary survivor who barters parachutes and drugs from the pilots' kits on the black market. The bureaucratic Major Major (Bob Newhart) allows visitors to his office *only* when he is not there. Visionary Captain Nately (Art Garfunkel) intends to wed an Italian whore, but he dies in a bombing of the airbase instigated by wheeler dealer Milo. Bombastic General Dreedle (Orson Welles) bestows medals on survivors of a mission who dropped all their bombs at sea. Captain McWatt (Peter Bonerz) mangles fellow pilot Hungry Joe (Seth Allen) in his propeller. And meanwhile, the action billows around Captain Yossarian. He fumbles in his attempt to make love with Nurse Duckett (Paula Prentiss); he arrives naked at an award ceremony because a fellow soldier (Jon Korkes) has just died in his arms and bled all over his uniform; he is stabbed by Nately's whore (Gina Rovere). In the hospital he learns from the Chaplain (Tony Perkins) that another crazed pilot (Bob Balaban) has made it to safety in Sweden, so Yossarian leaps from the hospital window, finds a rubber raft and begins paddling—across the Mediterranean.

CATCH-22 was made at a cost of $18,000,000 and earned only $12,250,000 in theater rentals in the U.S. and Canada. It was based on Joseph Heller's best-selling novel of 1961, a black comedy revolving around the theme: war is insane; to survive is sane; anything else is craziness. Unfortunately audiences did not know what to make of this episodic, over-inflated satire. Also the disparate acting styles under Mike Nichols' direction helped little in retaining audience attention. On May 31, 1973, ABC-TV telecast a lackluster pilot derived from the book/film, starring Richard Dreyfuss, Dana Elcar, and Stewart Moss. The projected series never materialized.

THE CHALLENGE (ABC-TV, 2/10/70) Color 78 mins.

Producers, Jay Cipes, Ed Palmer; director, Allen Smithlee [pseudonym for unknown director]; teleplay, Marc Norman; art directors, Jack Martin Smith, Ed Graves; music, Harry Geller; music supervisor, Lionel Newman; camera, John M. Nicholaus; editors, Stanford Tischler, Joe Gluck.

Darren McGavin (Jacob Gallery); Broderick Crawford (General Lewis Meyers); Mako (Yuro); Skip Homeier (Lyman George); Paul Lukas (Dr. Nagy); Sam Elliott (Bryant); Adolph Caesar (Clarence Opano); Andre Philippe (Swiss Official); Arianne Ulmer (Sarah); Davis Roberts (Scientist); Byron Morrow (Defense Secretary); Bill Zuckert (Army Colonel); Joseph Bernard (Doctor); Gene Lebell (Karate Instructor); Lew Brown (Sergeant); Eddie Guardino (Soldier); Garry Walberg (Submarine Captain); Bill Quinn (Marine Colonel); Michael Hinn (Army Captain).

An offbeat made-for-television film with an allegorical premise. Two nations are on the verge of war and decide to resolve the situation with a soldier from each side in a fight to the death on a deserted isle.

CHE! (Twentieth Century-Fox, 1969) Color 96 mins.

Producer, Sy Bartlett; director, Richard Fleischer; story, Bartlett, David Karp; screenplay, Michael Wilson, Bartlett; art directors, Jack Martin Smith, Arthur Lonergan; set decorators, Walter M. Scott, Stuart A. Reiss; makeup supervisor, Dan Striepeke; music/music conductor, Lalo Schifrin; assistant director, Richard Glassman; sound, Don Bassman, David Dockendorf; special camera effects, L. B. Abbott, Art Cruickshank, John C. Caldwell; camera, Charles Wheeler; editor, Marion Rothman.

Omar Sharif (Ernesto Che Guevara); Jack Palance (Fidel Castro); Cesare Danova (Ramon Valdez); Robert Loggia (Faustino Morales); Woody Strode (Guillermo); Barbara Luna (Anita Marquez); Frank Silvera (Goatherd); Albert Paulsen (Captain Vasquez); Linda Marsh (Tania); Tom Troupe (Felipe Munoz); Rudy Diaz

Omar Sharif in CHE! (1969).

(Willy); Perry Lopez (Rolando); Abraham Sofaer (Pablo Rojas); Richard Angarola (Colonel Salazar); Sarita Vara (Celia Sanchez); Paul Bertoya (Raul Castro); Sid Haig (Antonio); Adolph Caesar (Juan Almedia); Paul Picerni (Hector); Ray Martell (Camilo Cienfuegos); Valentin De Vargas (Captain Flores); Miguel Suarez (Guide); Jess Franco (Sergeant Terraza).

Made during Darryl F. Zanuck's final period as a major executive at Twentieth Century-Fox, this film proved to be an embarrassing artistic and commercial misfire. It was quickly withdrawn from theatrical release.

CHE! is loosely based on the facts surrounding the life of the near mythical Ernesto Che Guevara (1920 to 1967) and deals through flashback with the "events" leading to his execution on October 9, 1967.

Among the rebels joining cigar-chomping Fidel Castro (Jack Palance) in combat against the military machine of Cuban President Batista is a young Argentinian doctor, Ernesto Che Guevara (Omar Sharif). Che proves himself in battle as a natural leader and a sharp strategist and Castro makes him his primary adviser. It is Che who is in charge of the reprisals against their enemy when Castro's forces move triumphantly into Havana. A few years later Che, disillusioned with Castro and envisioning a larger revolution encompassing all of South America, goes to Bolivia where he joins with revolutionary Tania (Linda Marsh) and starts a fresh guerrilla war. However, the peasant forces do not rally behind Che and Tania is killed. Che is wounded, captured and summarily shot. It is reported to the press that Che died in hostilities between his men and Bolivian Army rangers.

The hazy and distorted politics to one side, CHE! does far better in depicting the rigors and effects of jungle warfare on partisan troops.

CHE! competed in the international marketplace with the 1968 Italian picture EL CHE GUEVARA, starring Francisco Rabal as Che, John Ireland as a CIA Agent, and Giacomo Rossi Stuart as Prado.

CHINA GATE (Twentieth Century-Fox, 1957) 96 mins.

Producer/director/screenplay, Samuel Fuller; art director, John Mansbridge; music, Victor Young, Max Steiner; song, Young and Harold Adamson; camera, Joseph Biroc; editor, Gene Fowler, Jr.

Gene Barry (Sergeant Brock); Angie Dickinson (Lucky Legs); Nat "King" Cole (Goldie); Paul DuBov (Captain Caumont); Lee Van Cleef (Major Cham); George Givot (Corporal Pigalle); Gerald

Milton (Private Andreades); Neyle Morrow (Leung); Marcel Dalio (Father Paul); Maurice Marsac (Colonel De Sars); Warren Hsieh (The Boy); Paul Busch (Corporal Kruger); Sasha Harden (Private Jaszi); James Hong (Charlie); William Soo Hoo (Moi Leader); Walter Soo Hoo (Guard); Weaver Levy (Khuan).

A deceptively simple black-and-white CinemaScope production that was Hollywood's first motion picture to really deal with Vietnam's political problems and, as such, a watershed mark in the combat film genre. At the time it was passed off as a simple action programmer from the iconoclastic filmmaker Samuel Fuller.

During the waning days of the French influence in Vietnam, a French Legionnaire contingent must locate and destroy a Communist munitions dump. World-weary Sergeant Brock (Gene Barry) is the duty-bound American leading the patrol, and guiding the demolition mission is Eurasian Lucky Legs (Angie Dickinson) who was once wed to Brock and by whom she had a child. Her price for the assignment is to have their child (Warren Hsieh) brought up in America. Reaching their target, Lucky Legs sacrifices her life to detonate the explosives. Brock survives the hazardous expedition.

For Norman Kagan in *The War Film* (1974), CHINA GATE is ". . . an anticipation and allegory of the entire Vietnam War and withdrawal, a tragedy of people following their changing feelings to pain, death, and finally understanding."

Other points of interest about China Gate: the film opens with film clips tracing the history of the French influence and conflicts in Vietnam; not only does singer Nat "King" Cole do well in his acting assignment, but he sings the title song; composer Victor Young died during production and the score was completed by his friend Max Steiner.

COCKLESHELL HEROES (Columbia, 1955) Color 97 mins.

Producers, Irving Allen, Albert R. Broccoli; director, Jose Ferrer; story, George Kent; screenplay, Bryan Forbes, Richard Maibaum; music, John Addison; "Cockleshell Heroes" march, Lieutenant Colonel F. Vivian Dunn; camera, John Wilcox, Ted Moore; editor, Alan Osbiston.

Jose Ferrer (Major Stringer) Trevor Howard (Captain Thompson); Victor Maddern (Sergeant Craig); Anthony Newley (Marine Clarke); David Lodge (Marine Ruddock); Peter Arne (Marine Stevens); Percy Herbert (Marine Lomas); Graham Stewart (Marine Booth); John Fabian (Marine Cooney); John Van Eyssen (Marine Bradley); Robert Desmond (Marine Todd); Walter Fitzgerald (Gestapo Commandant); Karel Stepanek (Gestapo Officer);

Dora Bryan (Myrtle); Beatrice Campbell (Mrs. Ruddock); Sydney Tatler (Policeman); Gladys Henson (Barmaid); Jacques Brunius, Andrea Malendrinos (French Fishermen); Christopher Lee (Submarine Commander).

What makes films such as COCKLESHELL HEROES viable entertainment is their combination of historic fact and superior performances, bolstered by the depiction of amazing, but real, bursts of teamwork and heroism during combat. *Variety* endorsed this Cinemascope Anglo-American co-production: "Ferrer has caught the traditional British touch of understatement in his direction and performance, and has completely avoided the pitfall of false heroics."

To counteract the strength of German shipping in Bordeaux Harbor, British Major Stringer (Jose Ferrer) develops a wild plan for ten Royal Marines to paddle cockleshell canoes into enemy waters and slap limpet exploding mines on Nazi boats. Captain Thompson (Trevor Howard) is the administrative officer bitter about being passed up for advancement and stubborn in his insistence on modifying Stringer's plan. Stringer's heroic tactics work, but at the cost of all but two of the lives; Thompson and several others are captured, tortured and shot by the Germans; others are killed in the fray.

THE COLDITZ STORY (Atlantic, 1955) 97 mins.

Producer, Ivan Foxwell; director, Guy Hamilton; based on the book by Pat Reid; adaptors/screenplay, Hamilton, Ivan Foxwell; sets, Vetchinsky; music, Francis Chagrin; camera, Gordon Dines; editor, Peter Mayhew.

John Mills (Pat Reid); Eric Portman (Colonel Richmond); Christopher Rhodes (Lieutenant Mac); Lionel Jeffries (Harry); Bryan Forbes (Jimmy); Ian Carmichael (Robin); Richard Wattis (Richard); David Yates (Dick); Frederick Valk (Kommandant); Denis Shaw (Priem); Anton Diffring (Fischer); Ludwig Lawinski (Franz Josef); Carl Duering (German Officer); Keith Pyott (French Colonel); Eugene Deckers (La Tour); Rudolf Offenbach (Dutch Colonel); Theodore Bikel (Vandy); Arthur Butcher (Polish Colonel).

The seemingly impregnable Colditz Castle in Saxony houses incorrigible Allied prisoners-of-war who have attempted escapes from other Nazi Germany fortresses. Colonel Richmond (Eric Portman) coordinates the escape plans of the many-nation prisoners incarcerated. However, due to a Polish spy in their midst several freedom plans end in death. It is Scottish Lieutenant Mac (Christo-

Richard Wattis, Ian Carmichael, and Christopher Rhodes in THE COLDITZ STORY (1955).

pher Rhodes) who creates the scheme that succeeds: having four men dress in Gestapo uniforms walk openly through the enemy mess and through the main gates to freedom.

Based on the real life exploits of Pat Reid, played in the film by John Mills, THE COLDITZ STORY was released originally in England by British Lion. *Variety* enthused, "Film is loaded with meaty suspense situation and neatly leavened with good-natured humor. . . . The all-male cast keeps the yarn rolling at a lively pace."

COMMAND DECISION (Metro-Goldwyn-Mayer, 1948) 111 mins.

Producer Sidney Franklin; associate producer, Gottfried Reinhardt; director, Sam Wood; based on the play by William Wister Haines; screenplay, William R. Laidlaw, George Foreschel; art directors, Cedric Gibbons, Urie McLeary; music, Miklos Rozsa; sound, Douglas Shearer; special effects, A. Arnold Gillespie,

Warren Newcombe; camera, Harold Rossen; editor, Harold F. Kress.

Clark Gable (Brigadier General K. C. "Casey" Dennis); Walter Pidgeon (Major General Roland Goodlow Kane); Van Johnson (Technical Sergeant Immanuel T. Evans); Brian Donlevy (Brigadier General Clifton I. Garnet); Charles Bickford (Elmer Brockhurst); John Hodiak (Colonel Edward Rayton Martin); Edward Arnold (Congressman Arthur Malcolm); Marshall Thompson (Captain George Washington Bellpepper Lee); Richard Quine (Major George Rockton); Cameron Mitchell (Lieutenant Ansel Goldberg); Clinton Sundberg (Major Homer V. Prescott); Ray Collins (Major Desmond Lansing); Warner Anderson (Colonel Ernest Haley); John McIntire (Major Belding Davis); Moroni Olsen (Congressman Stone); John Ridgely (James Carwood); Michael Steele (Captain Lucius Malcolm Jenks); Edward Earle (Congressman Watson); Mack Williams (Lieutenant Colonel Virgil Jackson); James Millican (Major Garrett Davenport); John James (Officer); Pete Martin (Command Sergeant); Barry Nelson (Loudspeaker Voice); Wilson Wood, Arthur Walsh, J. Lewis Smith (Photographers); Henry Hall, Sam Flint (Congressmen); William Lester (Parker, the Chauffeur); and: Hank Daniels.

"Heroes, cowards, fighters, braggarts, liars, lovers . . . and what goes on in their hearts." So read the advertising slogan for MGM's stellar COMMAND DECISION, based on William Wister Haines' acclaimed 1947 Broadway hit which ran for 409 performances and was later translated into a novel.

In this post-World War II (re)assessment of the recent global struggle, COMMAND DECISION focuses on the torment of command during combat, and the heavy burden military leaders suffer in choosing their options, knowing whatever they decide will cost lives. In addition, it is a telling depiction of the squabbles between the Pentagon, the military brass, and the people most affected—the fighting troops. Above all, it shows that every command decision has a very heavy price for everyone concerned.

U.S. Air Force Brigadier General K. C. "Casey" Dennis (Clark Gable) commands an American bomber base in 1943 England. He orders a top secret bombing raid under the code name Operation Stitch (in time). The daytime precision bombing mission centers on destroying Third Reich plants manufacturing a new German jet plane. The controversy revolves around the excessive number of lost men and planes required to obliterate the target in daylight. Among those opposing the operation are wheedling Major General Roland Goodlow Kane (Walter Pidgeon), opportunistic

Brigadier General Clifton I. Garnet (Brian Donlevy), and skeptical war correspondent Elmer Brockhurst (Charles Bickford).

With a four-day break in the weather, a first bombing mission is dispatched, with partial success but heavy losses sustained. On the second day of the raid, Dennis has to talk in a bombardier (Cameron Mitchell) whose pilot and co-pilot have been killed. Dennis later convinces Kane that the mission must be completed, but the revelation by Colonel Edward Rayton Martin (John Hodiak) that another town—not Schweinhafen—was hit by mistake causes Kane much hesitancy and agony before ordering another strike, this one costing Martin's life. Still later Kane, who understands politics and says, "This is my kind of war," requests that the officer-nephew (Michael Steele) of blustering Congressman Arthur Malcolm (Edward Arnold) be decorated. But Dennis counters that the man has been arrested for refusing to participate in the last raid. By agreeing to allow the decoration, Dennis is permitted to continue the bombing strikes. The target is destroyed, but at a heavy cost and Malcolm denounces Dennis. Kane replaces him with Garnet who, finally realizing the importance of it all, orders a strike on Fendelhorst. Dennis assumes a Pacific command, knowing his operation will be realized, but wondering ("They can't do this to me") if he is up to the further pressures of his new post.

". . . [It] gives us a most impressive sense of real heroism in high places behind the actual battle scenes. . . . It is rugged. And it makes a point, as well as a most disturbing drama, about the background realities of war" (Bosley Crowther, *New York Times*). *Newsweek* magazine championed the cast, who ". . . contribute to a script that is worthy of their most valiant efforts." *Variety* approved that "There are no phony touches in this drive for drama." Others endorsed the fact that MGM avoided the temptations to open up the film with more visual action and/or to write in scenes for actresses. Miklos Rozsa's rousing film score and Harold Rossen's stark black and white cinematography were equally praised. Among the dissenters were the British and British press who thought it "contemptuous" and "insulting" that this American film gave the impression that they had won the war single-handedly.

Notable scenes include the control tower's "talking down" of a damaged bomber, the magnificent take-off of the Flying Fortresses heading for deadly action in the mist, the think-through of the sounds of aerial combat, and most striking of all, the telling strain of Clark Gable's ultra caring Brigadier General Dennis, a former pilot who realizes all too well that "It's all in the kids' hands now."

CONVOY (Associated British, 1940) 95 mins.

Producer, Michael Balcon; director, Fen Tennyson; screenplay, Patrick Kirwan, Tennyson; camera, Roy Kellino, Gunther Krampf.

Clive Brook (Captain Armitage); John Clements (Lieutenant Crawford); Edward Chapman (Captain Eckersley); Judy Campbell (Lucy Armitage); Penelope Dudley-Ward (Mabel); Edward Rigby (Mr. Matthews); Charles Williams (Shorty Howard); Allan Jeayes (Commander Blount); Michael Wilding (Dot); Stewart Granger (Sutton); Harold Warrender (Lieutenant Commander Martin); David Hutcheson (Captain Standeman); George Carney (Bates); Al Millen (Knowles); Charles Farrell (Walker); John Laurie (Gates); George Benson (Parker); Hay Petrie (Minesweeper Skipper); Albert Lieven (Commander, U-Boat #37); Hans Wangraf (Commander, *Deutschland*); Edward Levy (Merchantman Skipper); Mervyn Johns (Mate).

Captain Armitage (Clive Brook) on the cruiser *Apollo* heads a convoy heading across the North Sea to England. A German mini-battleship locates the convoy and the enemy is engaged. First Officer Crawford (John Clement), with whom Armitage's wife Lucy (Judy Campbell) has been having an affair, sacrifices himself to save the convoy and to keep the *Apollo* afloat.

Dedicated to the "Officers and Men of the Royal and Merchant Navies," CONVOY is a melodramatic contrivance geared to demonstrate that the ship is a miniature community, that the men aboard are important individuals (not part of a machine), and that England could and would hold its own. It was England's first documentary-style war picture.

CORREGIDOR (Producers Releasing Corp., 1943) 74 mins.

Producers, Dixon R. Harwin, Edward Finney; director, William Nigh; screenplay, Doris Malley, Edgar Ulmer; art director, F. Paul Sylos; set decorator, Glenn P. Thompson; music, Leo Erdody; music director, David Chudnow; assistant director, Bart Carre; sound, Corson Jowett; camera, Ira L. Morgan; editor, Charles Henkel.

Otto Kruger (Jan Stockman); Elissa Landi (Dr. Royce Lee); Donald Woods (Michael); Frank Jenks (Sergeant Mahoney); Rick Vallin (Pinky); Wanda McKay (Hey Dutch); Ian Keith (Captain); Ruby Dandridge (Hyacinth); Eddie Hall (Brooklyn); Charles Jordan (Bronx); Ted Hecht (Filipino Lieutenant); Frank Hagney (Lieutenant #2); Frank Jaquet (Priest); Jack Rutherford (General);

John Grant, I. Stanford Jolley (Soldiers); Jimmy Vilan (#1 Boy); Gordon Hayes (Marine).

Because combat films, even using stock footage, are expensive to grind out, few poverty row studios produced such genre entries during World War II. This is one of the exceptions, and a sad one at that.

Corregidor, known as "The Rock," is an island at the wide section of Manila Bay and during the Second World War was used to guard the sea approach to the Philippines' capital. When nearby Bataan surrendered to the Japanese on April 9, 1942, its downfall (May 6, 1942) was unavoidable.

CORREGIDOR focuses on the brave stand of the U.S. Marines on Corregidor, with two doctors (Otto Kruger, Donald Woods) vying for the love of another physician (Elissa Landi). Visually the film has tunnel vision, for the bulk of the action is set in one of the many island caves used as protection from the shelling.

CORVETTE K-225 (Universal, 1943) 99 mins.

Producer, Howard Hawks; director, Richard Rosson; screenplay, John Rhodes Sturdy (R.C.N.V.R.); art directors, John B. Goodman, Robert Boyle; set decorators, Russell A. Gausman, A. J. Gilmore; music, David Buttolph; music director, Charles Previn; assistant director, William Tummell; sound, Bernard Brown; special effects, John Fultes; camera, Tony Gaudio; convoy camera, Harry Perry; editor, Edward Curtiss.

Randolph Scott (Lieutenant Commander MacClain); James Brown (Paul Cartwright); Ella Raines (Joyce Cartwright); Barry Fitzgerald (Stooky O'Meara); Andy Devine (Walsh); Fuzzy Knight (Cricket); Noah Beery, Jr. (Stone); Richard Lane (Admiral); Thomas Gomez (Smithy); David Bruce (Rawlins); Murray Alper (Jones); James Flavin (Gardner); Walter Sande (Evans); Edmund MacDonald (Lieutenant LeBlanc); Matt Willis (Roger); Robert Mitchum (Sheppard); Charles McGraw (E.R.A.); Oscar O'Shea (Captain Smith); Addison Richards (Commander Rowland); Jack Wegman (Naval Captain); James Dodd (Steward); John Diggs (Bailey, the Naval Rating Man); Milburn Stone (Canadian Captain); Lester Matthews (British Captain); Ian Wolfe (Paymaster Commander); Holmes Herbert (Commodore Ramsay); Frank Faylen, Charles Cane (Workmen); Oliver Blake (Cook); William Forrest (Commander Manning); John Mylong (Submarine Commander); Guy Kingsford (Royal Air Force Pilot); John Frederick, Jack Mulhall, Stewart Garner (Officers); Franklin Parker (Captain); Rod Bacon (Naval Academy Graduate); Peter Lawford (Naval Officer); Frank Coghlan, Jr. (Rating); Eddie Dew (Crewman); Jack Luden

(Merchant Marine Officer); Cliff Robertson (Lookout); Richard Crane (Leading Torpedo Man); Michael Kirk (Petty Officer).

Shipboard life in wartime has more hazards than just the enemy. There is also the sea, which in foul weather can be equally detrimental to survival.

Staunch Lieutenant Commander MacClain (Randolph Scott) of the Royal Canadian Navy skippers a corvette (a fast, small craft used to guide and protect convoys of transport ships across the Atlantic). After his vessel is destroyed, MacClain is drydocked until his new craft, Corvette K-225, is launched. Meanwhile he falls in love with reluctant Joyce Cartwright (Ella Raines); she is leery of seamen since her older brother died at sea. When the K-225 is seaworthy, he finds among his 60-man crew Paul Cartwright (James Brown), Joyce's Naval Cadet brother, who has a difficult time adjusting to MacClain's stern rule. Others aboard include irascible seadog Stookey O'Meara (Barry Fitzgerald) and the comedic Walsh (Andy Devine) and Jones (Murray Alper). As K-225 and other corvettes

Barry Fitzgerald, Thomas Gomez, and Robert Mitchum in CORVETTE K-225 (1943).

guide their convoy from Halifax to North Ireland they cope with raging seas, enemy planes and, most deadly, a Nazi submarine pack. In the height of battle, Paul proves himself a real hero.

Much of the highly acclaimed authenticity of this semi-documentary derives from director Richard Rosson's spending months traveling with actual Canadian corvettes across the Atlantic; the cinematographers being aboard such treks and capturing the reality of the sea journey; and John Rhodes Sturdy of the Canadian Navy, who not only provided technical advice during filming but wrote the film's screenplay. It is rumored that producer Howard Hawks helped to direct some sequences in this realistic feature.

British release title: THE NELSON TOUCH.

CRASH DIVE (Twentieth Century-Fox, 1943) Color 105 mins.

Producer, Milton Sperling; director, Archie Mayo; story, W. R. Burnett; screenplay, Jo Swerling; technical adviser, M. K. Kirkpatrick (Commander U.S. Navy); art directors, Richard Day, Wiard B. Ihnen; set decorators, Thomas Little, Paul Fox; music, David Buttolph; music director, Emil Newman; assistant director, John Johnston; sound, Roger Heman; special camera effects, Fred Sersen; camera, Leon Shamroy; editors, Walter Thompson, Ray Curtiss.

Tyrone Power (Lieutenant Ward Stewart); Anne Baxter (Jean Hewlitt); Dana Andrews (Lieutenant Commander Dewey Connors); James Gleason (McDonnell); Dame May Whitty (Grandmother); Henry Morgan (Brownie); Ben Carter (Oliver Cromwell Jones); Frank Conroy (Captain Bryson); Minor Watson (Admiral Bob Stewart); Kathleen Howard (Miss Bromley); Charles Tannen (Harmond); Florence Lake (Doria); John Archer (Curly); Frank Dawson (Henry, the Butler); Edward McWade (Crony); Paul Burns (Simmons, the Clerk); Gene Rizzi (Sailor); Thurston Hall (Texas Senator); Trudy Marshall (Telephone Operator); Chester Gan (Lee Wong); Bruce Wong (Waiter); Cecil Weston (Woman); Lionel Royce (Q Boat Captain); Hans Moebus (German Officer); David Bacon (Lieutenant).

CRASH DIVE is a stylish Technicolor paean to the U.S. Navy submarines in World War II. There are the expected episodes of claustrophobic shipboard life amid the complex submarine machinery, a conventional love triangle, and, most of all, rousing, colorful action sequences as American servicemen combat the Axis both at sea and on shore. The commando raid, with its vivid explosions of the land installation, is the film's combat highlight.

PT (plywood torpedo) mosquito boat Lieutenant Ward Stewart (Tyrone Power), with several successful missions to his credit, is reassigned by his admiral uncle (Minor Watson) to submarine duty. While based at the submarine school at New London, Connecticut he falls in love with local schoolteacher Jean Hewlitt (Anne Baxter), unaware that she is engaged to Lieutenant Commander Dewey Connors (Dana Andrews), his new skipper. Aboard their submarine, the USS *Corsair*, Stewart and Connors, not knowing they both love the same girl, display fine teamwork, and through a clever ruse their sub sinks the most troublesome of the German Q boats in the North Atlantic. Back on shore, Jean finally admits her involvement with Connors and, realizing she loves Stewart, agrees to break off her engagement to Connors. The latter overhears this conversation and, back on board ship, makes life difficult for Stewart. Meanwhile, the sub follows a tanker to a hidden Axis base and the U.S. Naval men manage to explode the ammo and fuel dumps, with McDonnell (James Gleason) killed in the daring escapade. Later Connors is wounded and Stewart assumes command of their vessel. Once more land side, Connors bows out of his relationship with Jean, leaving her and Stewart to plan their wedding.

CRASH DIVE received two Academy Awards for Special Effects: Sound (Roger Heman) and Photographic (Fred Sersen). This was star Tyrone Power's last film for the duration of World War II as he entered the Marine Corps. To be noted is the integrated presence of a black (Ben Carter) aboard the submarine, although he is relegated to mess duty. Many scenes were filmed on location at the submarine base at New London, Connecticut.

CRIMSON ROMANCE (Mascot, 1934) 70 mins.

Producer, Nat Levine; director, David Howard; story, Al Martin, Sherman Lowe; screenplay, Mildred Krims, Doris Schroeder; camera, Ernest Miller; editor, Doris Drought.

Ben Lyon (Bob Wilson); Sari Maritza (Alida Hoffman); Erich von Stroheim (Captain Wolters); Hardie Albright (Hugo); James Bush (Fred von Bergen); William Bakewell (Adolph); Herman Bing (Himmelbaum); Bodil Rosing (Mama von Bergen); Vincent Barnett (The Courier); Arthur Clayton (Baron von Eisenlohr); Oscar Apfel (John Fleming); Purnell Pratt (Franklyn Pierce); Jason Robards (Pierre); William von Brincken (Von Gering); Eric Arnold (Von Muller); Fred Vogeding (German Colonel); Harry Schultz (Drill Sergeant); and: Brandon Hurst.

A singular entry, even in 1934. Two young Americans who love flying, Bob Wilson (Ben Lyon) and Fred von Bergen (James Bush), are induced to join the German Air Force only to see World War I break out. German-born Fred remains with the Kaiser's military while Bob joins the Allies. Fred dies in combat and Bob survives and weds his pal's sweetheart, Alida Hoffman (Sari Maritza). Back in the United States, they visit Fred's pacifist mother (Bodil Rosing).

With its direct, pro-German sympathies CRIMSON RO-MANCE is a Hollywood anomaly, more noted for a brief appearance by Erich von Stroheim as the sadistic German captain and its stock footage of aerial combat.

CROSS OF IRON (Avco Embassy, 1977) Color 133 min.

Producer, Wolf C. Hartwig; director, Sam Peckinpah; based on the book *Das geduldige Fleisch* [Cross of Iron] by Willi Heinrich; screenplay, Herbert Asmodi, Julius J. Epstein; music, Ernest Gold; music editor, Robin Clarke; action coordinator, Peter Brayham; assistant director, Bert Batt; wardrobe supervisors, Kent James, Carol James; makeup supervisor, Colin Arthur; sound, Rodney Holland; special effects, Richard Richtsfeld; camera, John Coquillon; editors, Mike Ellis, Tony Lawson, Herbert Taschner.

James Coburn (Sergeant Steiner); Maximilian Schell (Stransky); James Mason (Colonel Brandt); David Warner (Captain Kiesel); Klaus Lowitsch (Kruger); Vadim Glowna (Kern); Roger Fritz (Triebig); Dieter Schidor (Anselm); Burkhardt Driest (Maag); Fred Stillkraut (Schnurrbart); Michael Nowka (Dietz); Veronique Vendell (Marga); Arthur Brauss (Zoll); Senta Berger (Eva); Slavco Stimac (Mikael).

It is 1943 on the Russian front and the Nazis are retreating. Resolute Colonel Brandt (James Mason) and his cynical staff captain Kiesel (David Warner), who realize the war may not be won after all by the Third Reich, meet arrogant Prussian Stransky (Maximilian Schell). This opportunistic officer has had himself transferred from France ostensibly because he wants to help "destroy the myth of Russian superiority." In actuality, he covets the Iron Cross (the highest medal bestowed by the German Army) and hopes in the midst of chaos to maneuver winning the Cross. He claims he cannot face his family if he does not acquire the medal. To carry out his manipulations he blackmails a homosexual officer (Roger Fritz) and brands the realistic and truthful Sergeant Steiner (James Coburn), a veteran soldier who has won the Iron Cross in battle, as his enemy, especially when the latter refuses to help doctor the facts to verify that Stransky is worthy of the Cross.

In the midst of the battle hysteria, Steiner remains a dedicated soldier ("Your duty is to me and the platoon"), a compassionate man (as when he helps a Russian boy escape his men only to see the youth shot, ironically, by Soviet troops), and a perceptive man

("You think they'll ever forgive us for what we've done or forget us?"). He is an honorable man who accepts the rules of war.

As the film concludes, a title card on the screen quotes from Bertolt Brecht: "Don't rejoice in his defeat, you men. For though the world stood up and stopped the bastard, the bitch that bore him is in heat again." CROSS OF IRON is both a study of the Nazi Army in retreat (defeat), told from the German point of view, and a cutting study of the male camaraderie of warfare.

Director Sam Peckinpah is well known for his extended screen depictions of blood and guts, and CROSS OF IRON (even with edits made for the U.S. release print) is no exception. Jay Hyams notes in *War Movies* (1984), "There is no order or sense to the battles scenes, no way of discerning who is winning or losing, who is in a safe place or who is in danger. It is all one savage horror. The bodies of the dead are everywhere, and the bodies of the still living squirt blood when pierced by bullets or are blasted apart and thrown into the air by artillery shells. Much of this gore takes place in slow motion."

Because of the international (if not American) box-office success of this British-West German co-production, in 1979 BREAKTHROUGH (a.k.a. SERGEANT STEINER), a semi-sequel to CROSS OF IRON, was released. Directed by Andrew McLaglen and set on the western front, it has Richard Burton as Corporal Steiner, involved in the 1944 assassination plot against Adolf Hitler and helping to save the life of an American colonel (Robert Mitchum).

THE CRUEL SEA (Universal-International, 1953) 120 mins.

Producer, Michael Balcon; director, Charles Frend; based on the book by Nicholas Monsarrat; screenplay, Eric Ambler; art director, Jim Morahan; camera, Gordon Dines; editor, Peter Tanner.

Jack Hawkins (Captain Ericson); Donald Sinden (Lockhart); John Stratton (Gerrahy); Denholm Elliott (Morell); Stanley Baker (Bennett); John Warner (Baker); Bruce Seton (Tallow); Liam Redmond (Watts); Virginia McKenna (Julie Hallam); Moira Lister (Elaine Morell); June Thorburn (Doris Ferraby); Megs Jenkins (Tallow's Sister); Meredith Edwards (Yeoman Wells); Glyn Houston (Phillips); Alec McCowan (Tonbridge); Len Phillips (Wainwright); Dafydd Havard (Signalman Rose); Fred Griffiths (Gracey); Laurence Hardy (Sellars); Sam Kydd (Carslake); John Singer (Gray); Barry Steele (Broughton); and: Barry Letts, Gerard Heinz, Gerik Schjelderup, Gaston Richer, Kenn Kennedy, Harold

Goodwin, George Curzon, Anthony Snell, Ronald Simpson, Don Sharp, Herbert C. Walton, Jack Howard, Russell Waters, Harold Jameson, Warwick Ashton.

Based on the best-selling book by Nicholas Monsarrat, this unrelenting war film details the severe life aboard a British corvette in which the heroes are the men, the heroines are the ships, and the villain is the cruel sea.

Ever-reliable Captain Ericson (Jack Hawkins) is the only seasoned seaman aboard the corvette *Compass Rose*, as he trains his men to cope with the tensions of World War II naval warfare. In the course of the years-long Battle of the Atlantic, he almost cracks under the strain of command but manages to pull through. His second-in-command is the sturdy but harshly strict Lockhart (Donald Sinden). The corvette is sunk by the Germans, with only a few of the Britishers surviving on a raft for days. Ericson is given another command, a frigate, and he pursues the Germans on the high waters, determined to have revenge.

"It is an unimpeachable testament to gallantry, but this drama of the tiny armed convoy escorts and their crews, most of whom

Virginia McKenna and Donald Sinden in THE CRUEL SEA (1953).

were either enlisted or drafted landlubbers, is expert documentation rather than high film art" (A. H. Weiler, *New York Times*).

One of the picture's most grueling sequences occurs when harried Captain Ericson chases a submerged German U-boat, even at the unavoidable expense of riding over the adrift survivors of a torpedoed Allied ship.

THE CRUEL SEA was released originally in England by General Film Distributors in a 140-minute print.

CRY HAVOC (Metro-Goldwyn-Mayer, 1943) 97 mins.

Producer, Edwin Knopf; director, Richard Thorpe; based on the play *Proof Thro' the Night* by Allan R. Kenward; screenplay, Paul Osborne; art directors, Cedric Gibbons, Stephen Goosson; set decorators, Edwin B. Willis, Glen Barner; music, Daniele Amfitheatrof; assistant director, Rollie Asher; sound, Frank B. MacKenzie; camera, Karl Freund; editor, Ralph E. Winters.

Margaret Sullavan (Lieutenant Smith); Ann Sothern (Pat); Joan Blondell (Grace); Fay Bainter (Captain Marsh); Marsha Hunt (Flo Norris); Ella Raines (Connie); Frances Gifford (Helen); Diana Lewis (Nydia); Heather Angel (Andra); Dorothy Morris (Sue); Connie Gilchrist (Sadie); Gloria Grafton (Steve); Fely Franquelli (Luisita); Billy Cruzy (Filipino Boy); Allan Byron [Jack Randall] (Lieutenant Holt); William Bishop, Victor Kilian, Jr. (Soldiers); James Warren, Richard Crane, Bill Cartledge, Paul Oman (Men); Robert Mitchum (Groaning Man); Lorin Raker (Voice of Japanese Pilot); Bob Lowell (Dying Soldier); Russ Clark (Doctor); Richard Derr (Marine); Anna Q. Nilsson (Nurse); Morris Ankrum (Chaplain); Joy Louie (Frightened Child).

In the male chauvinist tradition, little was made on-screen of the heroics of women in war; mostly they were confined to being publicly brave and privately weepy on the homefront. Two 1943 films, MGM's CRY HAVOC and Paramount's SO PROUDLY WE HAIL, q.v., did their best to counter this distorted image.

The very stagy CRY HAVOC is based on a Los Angeles little theatre production which opened on Broadway in late 1942 as *Proof Through the Night* for a 12-performance run with Ann Shoemaker and Carol Channing, among others, in the cast. MGM transformed the property into a major distaff patriotic salute. "The popularity that CRY HAVOC should achieve on the screen will stem less from this probably factual record of American nurses serving, sweating, and dying in the beleaguered Filipino jungle than from the impressive all-woman cast which Metro-Goldwyn-Mayer has rounded up for the historic occasion."

Frances Gifford, Connie Gilchrist, Diana Lewis, and Joan Blondell in CRY HAVOC (1943).

In the spring of 1942 Bataan is falling and a group of nurses takes refuge in an outfield hospital tending wounded soldiers. Professional nurse Lieutenant Smith (Margaret Sullavan) is in charge, struggling to keep her team's spirits up and battling a bout of malaria. (She is also secretly wed to an Army lieutenant.) When not listening to advice from motherly Captain Marsh (Fay Bainter), Smith is the strict disciplinarian guiding former waitress Pat (Ann Sothern), ex-burlesque queen Grace (Joan Blondell), southern belle Nydia (Diana Lewis), *et al*. As the situation gets more tense, the nurses carry on, occasionally breaking under the strain.

The end comes when the Japanese surround the bunker. The nurses, with hands held over their heads, file out, resigned to their fate.

The gruesome depiction of American women becoming victims at the mercy of the Imperial Japanese Army was strong medicine for World War II filmgoers. "The production itself is full of horror and the latent bravery that has made our enemies change their opinion about this being a 'soft' nation. CRY HAVOC is an estimable war picture, but it is still reiterative and numbing" (*Variety*).

Had CRY HAVOC amputated some of its theatrical artifices, it would have been a much more powerful essay. To be noted is Robert Mitchum in the bit role of a wounded soldier.

D-DAY, THE SIXTH OF JUNE (Twentieth Century-Fox, 1956) Color 106 mins.

Producer, Charles Brackett; director, Henry Koster; based on the novel by Lionel Shapiro; screenplay, Ivan Moffat, Harry Brown; art directors, Lyle R. Wheeler, Lewis H. Creber; costumes, Charles LeMaire; music, Lyn Murray; music director, Lionel Newman; special effects, Ray Kellogg; camera, Lee Garmes; editor, William Mace.

Robert Taylor (Captain Brad Parker); Richard Todd (Major John Wynter); Dana Wynter (Valerie Russell); Edmond O'Brien

Dana Wynter and Robert Taylor in D-DAY, THE SIXTH OF JUNE (1956).

(Colonel Trimmer); John Williams (Brigadier Russell); Jerry Paris (Raymond Boyce); Robert Gist (Dan Stenick); Richard Stapley (David Archer); Ross Elliott (Major Mills); Alex Finlayson (Colonel Harkens); Marie Brown (Georgina); Rama Bai (Mala); Dabbs Greer (Arkinson); Boyd "Red" Morgan (Sergeant Brooks); Queenie Leonard (Corporal); Geoffrey Steel (Major McEdwen); George Pelling (Captain Waller); Cyril Delevanti (Coat Room Attendant); Conrad Feia (Lieutenant at Party); Richard Aherne (Grainger); Victoria Ward (Mrs. Hamilton); Patricia McMahon (Suzette); John Damier (Lieutenant Colonel Cantrell); Thomas B. Henry (General Bolthouse); Damien O'Flynn (General Pike); Ben Wright (General Millensbeck); Howard Price (American War Correspondent); Reggie Dvorak (Taxi Driver); Chet Marshall (Lieutenant Crawford Binns); Parley Baer (Sergeant Gerbert); Ashley Cowan (Lance Corporal Bailey); June Mitchell (Waitress).

Even in as ambitious a war film as D-DAY, THE SIXTH OF JUNE, shot in CinemaScope, color, and stereophonic sound, the focal point of combat gets displaced by on-screen syrupy romance.

On the eve of the June 1944 landing at Normandy, American Captain Brad Parker (Robert Taylor) and British commando Major John Wynter (Richard Todd) think back on the woman (Dana Wynter) they both love and to happier days in London. Parker, with a wife back in Connecticut, falls in love with the pert daughter (Wynter) of an unhappily retired Brigadier (John Williams). She is engaged to a British commando (Todd), who is on duty in Africa. Parker and Valerie realize their love is wrong, but the affair continues. A wounded Wynter returns from combat and is nursed by Valerie; she tries to give up Parker, but cannot. The scene flashes back to the present and the all-important Normandy offensive. Parker is among the group, headed by Wynter, who will tackle the beachhead ahead of the main force. Each knows the other's story. Ashore Parker is wounded but is returned safely to the task force, while Wynter calmly marches to his death, (deliberately) stepping on a land mine. Back in London a repentant Valerie sends Parker back to his wife.

"What do they think they're proving with this sort of romantic guff. . . . [I]f they think they're kidding the public into believing that this is the way World War II was—wistful love in cozy London apartments and a quick little scramble up a cliff . . . then they'd better watch the box-office figures on this one" (Bosley Crowther, *New York Times*).

A.k.a.: THE SIXTH OF JUNE.

THE DAM BUSTERS (Warner Bros., 1955) 125 mins.

Producers, Robert Clark, W. A. Whittaker; director, Michael Anderson, Sr.; based on the book *Enemy Coast Ahead* by Wing Commander Guy Gibson, and the book *The Dam Busters* by Paul Brickhill; screenplay, R. C. Sherriff; music, Louis Levy; camera, Edwin Hiller; special effects camera, Gilbert Taylor; editor, Richard Best.

Richard Todd (Wing Commander Guy Gibson); Michael Redgrave (Dr. Barnes N. Wallis); Ursula Jeans (Mrs. Wallis); Basil Sydney (Sir Arthur Harris); Derek Farr (Group Captain J. N. H. Whitworth); Patrick Barr (Captain Joseph Summers); Charles Carson (Doctor); Stanley Van Beers (Sir David Pye); Colin Tapley (Dr. W. H. Glanville); Raymond Huntley (Laboratory Official); Ernest Clark (AVM Ralph Cochrane); John Fraser (Flight Lieutenant Hopgood); Nigel Stock (Flight Lieutenant Spofford); Bill Kerr (Flight Lieutenant Martin); George Baker (Flight Lieutenant Maltby); Robert Shaw (Flight Sergeant Pulford); Anthony Doonan

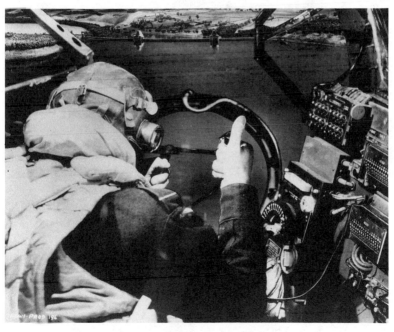

THE DAM BUSTERS (1955).

(Flight Lieutenant Hutchinson); Harold Goodwin (Crosby); Laurence Naismith (Farmer); Frank Phillips (BBC Announcer); and: Ewen Solon, Patrick McGoohan.

"This is a small slice of history, told with painstaking attention to detail and overflowing with the British quality of understatement" (*Variety*).

In 1943 scientist Dr. Barnes N. Wallis (Michael Redgrave) develops a new type of heavy duty "bouncing baby" bomb that, dropped from dangerously low-flying craft, charts an underwater course before exploding against its target. Royal Air Force Commander Guy Gibson (Richard Todd) is charged with the top-secret precision training of the bomber squadron which will carry out the near suicidal mission on the Ruhr Valley dams. By exploding these dams, Nazi industrial power would be crushed. The mission is successful, but at the cost of 56 men.

DANGER WITHOUT *see*: BREAKOUT.

DANGEROUS MOONLIGHT *see*: SUICIDE SQUADRON.

DARBY'S RANGERS (Warner Bros., 1958) 121 mins.

Producer, Martin Rackin; director, William A. Wellman; suggested by the book by Major James Altieri; screenplay, Guy Trosper; art director, William Campbell; set decorator, William A. Kuehl; costumes, Marjorie Best; makeup, Gordon Bau; music, Max Steiner; orchestrator, Murray Cutter; assistant director, George Vieira; project training instructors, 2nd Lieutenant Lee Mize, Sergeant First Class Richard Sandlin; technical advisers, Colonel Roger A. Murray (U.S. Army); sound, Robert B. Lee; camera, William Clothier; editor, Owen Marks.

James Garner (Major William Orlando Darby); Etchika Choureau (Angelina De Lotta); Jack Warden (Master Sergeant Saul Rosen); Edward Byrnes (Lieutenant Arnold Dittman); Venetia Stevenson (Peggy McTavish); Torin Thatcher (Sergeant McTavish); Peter Brown (Rollo Burns); Joan Elan (Wendy Hollister); Corey Allen (Tony Sutherland); Stuart Whitman (Hank Bishop); Murray Hamilton (Sims Delancey); Bill Wellman, Jr. (Eli Clatworthy); Andrea King (Sheila Andrews); Aram Williams ("Heavy" Hall); Frieda Inescort (Lady Hollister); Reginald Owen (Sir Arthur); Philip Tonge (John Andrews); Edward Ashley (Lieutenant Manson); Raymond Bailey (Major General Wise); Willis Bouchey (Brigadier General Truscott).

This war adventure film is based on the real-life exploits of audaciously brave U.S. Army Colonel William Orlando Darby

Jack Warden and James Garner in DARBY'S RANGERS (1958).

(1911-1945), who organized, trained, and led the First American
Ranger Battalion in mid-1942. His special combat force would fight
in North Africa, Sicily and Italy; its amazing war record of daring
landings and bold behind-enemy-lines raids is reflected in the active
duty deaths of most of the Rangers. Darby himself would be killed
on April 16, 1945 in Italy and he would be promoted posthumously
to brigadier general.

Not content with recreating the hard-hitting true life saga of
this gutsy military leader and his rugged team, DARBY'S RANG-
ERS intertwines several romantic interludes as Darby's men intermingle with distaff civilians. Fortunately director William A.
Wellman (WINGS, 1927; THE STORY OF G.I. JOE, 1945;
BATTLEGROUND, 1949, all qq.v.) well knew how to keep the
action rolling and provided James Garner (then at his "Maverick"
TV series peak) a showcase vehicle as the dedicated and resourceful
military leader.

British release title: THE YOUNG INVADERS.

THE DAWN PATROL (First National, 1930) 90 mins.

Producer, Robert North; director, Howard Hawks; based on the story "The Flight Commander" by John Monk Saunders; adaptors/dialogue, Hawks, Dan Totheroh, Seton I. Miller; special effects, Fred Jackman; camera, Ernest Haller; aerial camera, Elmer Dyer; editor, Ray Curtiss.

Richard Barthelmess (Captain Dick Courtney); Douglas Fairbanks, Jr. (Lieutenant Douglas Scott); Neil Hamilton (Major Brand); William Janney (Gordon Scott); James Finlayson (Field Sergeant); Clyde Cook (Bott); Gardner James (Ralph Hollister); Edmund Breon (Lieutenant Bathhurst); Frank McHugh (Flaherty); Jack Ackroyd, Harry Allen (Mechanics); Leo Nomis, Robbie Robinson, Frank Tomick, Clinton E. Herberger (Flyers).

TV title: THE FLIGHT COMMANDER.

DAWN PATROL (Warner Bros., 1938) 103 mins.

Producers, Hal B. Wallis, Robert Lord; director, Edmund Goulding; based on the story "The Flight Commander" by John Monk Saunders; screenplay, Seton I. Miller, Dan Totheroh; art director, John Hughes; technical adviser, Captain L. G. S. Scott; assistant director, Frank Heath; music, Max Steiner; orchestrator, Hugo Freidhofer; sound, C. A. Riggs; special effects, Edwin A. DuPar; camera, Tony Gaudo; editor, Ralph Dawson.

Errol Flynn (Captain Dick Courtney); David Niven (Lieutenant Douglas Scott); Basil Rathbone (Major Brand); Donald Crisp (Phills); Melville Cooper (Watkins); Barry Fitzgerald (Bott); Carl Esmond (Von Mueller); Peter Willes (Hollister); Morton Lowater (Ronny Scott); Michael Brooke (Squires); James Burke (Flaherty, the Motorcycle Driver); Stuart Hall (Bentharn, the Singer); Herbert Evans (Scott's Mechanic); Sidney Bracy (Ransom, the Orderly); John Sutton (Adjutant); George Kirby (Kirby, the Orderly); Tyrone Brereton, Tim Henning, Douglas Gordon (Orderlies); John Rodian (Russell, the Replacement); Norman Willis (German Aviator); Gordon Thorpe (Smythe); Wally Reardon (Cleaver); Gilbert Wilson (Moorehead); Anthony Marsh (Rutherford); Hal Brazeale (Gregory); Tom Seidel (Jones).

HELL'S ANGELS and JOURNEY'S END,* qq.v., were both released prior to THE DAWN PATROL in 1930 and to much

---

* At the time of release, both Howard Hughes (HELL'S ANGELS) and R. C. Sherriff (JOURNEY'S END) sued First National/Warner Bros., claiming that THE DAWN PATROL "borrowed" too much from their individual works. Legal remedies were denied and THE DAWN PATROL benefitted much from the resultant publicity.

greater hoopla. However, it is THE DAWN PATROL and its 1938 remake which remain today the sterling classics of World War I air war.

Both THE DAWN PATROL's story writer John Monk Saunders and director/co-adaptor Howard Hawks (handling his first sound feature) had been First World War Air Service pilots. Their idealized recollections of the Great War gave substance to this virile anti-war film.

It is 1915 France and the Royal Flying Corps' #59 Squadron is suffering tremendous losses in combatting the well-trained German pilots who have better aircraft. The British are sending up inexperienced youths in "canvas coffins" to meet certain death. Yet the Allied group accept their fate and are content to be part of an elite war club whose individual futures are counted in moments and hours. All their frustrations are vented on Major Brand (Neil Hamilton), the senior officer responsible for choosing who will fly the (death) missions dispatched dawn after dawn.

Carefree pilots Captain Dick Courtney (Richard Barthelmess) and Lieutenant Douglas Scott (Douglas Fairbanks, Jr.) have been buddies since before the war. They revel in their friendship, the freedom of the air, and the opportunity to prove that they are special. This is a gentleman's war in the sky, where the enemy is entitled to courtesy and respect, and his death, while necessary, is a time for remorse. Having been taunted by the German Air Corps, Dick and Douglas stage a daring but foolhardy raid on the German airfield, destroying several enemy planes before they can take off to fight in the air. Captain Brand, at the breaking point from the strain of command, lashes out at his two reckless men. At this juncture orders arrive transferring Brand to another command. Now Courtney is in charge. In an about-face, Courtney is the one faced with ordering his men to their certain death. Like his predecessor he becomes morose and drinks heavily. Scott takes Courtney's place as the leader of the men and he now considers his pal the "enemy." When Courtney refuses to play favorites and sends Scott's younger brother—a green recruit pilot—on a death patrol, the two men's friendship is strained to the limit. Scott volunteers for a suicide flight, but at the last moment Courtney gets him drunk and substitutes himself for the assignment. The bombing mission over Soulet is a success, but Courtney dies in the fracas. At the finale, a sobered Scott is now in command. It is his turn to send men out on the fatal dawn patrols.

Much of the film focuses on aerial dogfights, as vintage aircraft (doctored to resemble the real thing) swoop through the sky individually and in formation with the agility of attacking eagles.

The cinematic challenges of combining visuals with sound is obvious in Howard Hawks' structuring of the air clashes. On the ground, the dialogue is sometimes stagy and the performances (especially Neil Hamilton's) stilted, but the overall effect is powerful. War is a waste, even for men caught up in the glory of showing off their very best bravery. Occasionally a man (Gardner James) breaks down in disgust at the carnage, but even he dies courageously saving a flyer buddy. War is nihilistic, says THE DAWN PATROL, but man must do his duty, no matter the consequence. Perhaps, suggests the film, there is meaning to life found in death. THE DAWN PATROL won an Academy Award for Best Original Screen Story.

Eight years passed and a memo circulated from Warner Bros. executive producer Hal B. Wallis to studio head Jack L. Warner: "I wish you would think seriously about the re-making of THE DAWN PATROL. . . . By using our exterior shots from THE DAWN PATROL, and just remaking the interiors, which consists almost entirely of the little headquarters shack, we should be able to re-make the picture for a 'quarter.' . . . [We] could knock out a very good picture in a very short time, and one that I think would bring us a fortune now when the whole world is talking and thinking war and re-armament."

Seton I. Miller on his own, but crediting his earlier screen collaboration with Dan Totheroh, subtly reshaped DAWN PA-TROL (with its abbreviated title) into a more vigorous production. The new cast (Errol Flynn, David Niven, Basil Rathbone, et al.) is more proficient, if more glamorized than their predecessors in the roles and no longer can the story be phrased in a post-war mode. It is now 1938 and World War II is pending. While the aerial combat (using much footage from the original) remains the new version's highlight, there are alterations in the on-ground thematics. The stoic men still play "Poor Butterfly" on the victrola and sing their fatalistic war chant at the headquarters bar: "So stand by your glasses steady. This world is a world of lies. Here's to the dead already. Hurrah for the next man who dies!"

However, it is no longer good enough to face death manly. There is a much bigger picture. Captain Courtney (Errol Flynn) tells inexperienced newcomer Ronny Scott (Morton Lowater) that the war is ". . . a great big, noisy, rather stupid game that doesn't make any sense at all. . . . Here we are going at it hammer and tongs and I bet you those fellows over there feel exactly the same way about it—the enemy. Then one day I suppose it'll end as suddenly as it began and we'll go home." Then he adds, ironically, "Till some other bunch of criminal idiots sitting around a large table shoves us into another war." At the same time, DAWN PATROL condemns war but accepts its necessity when the die is cast.

"It would seem, after all these years and all those wartime aviation films, that time and custom should have inured us to the sight and sound of droning planes. . . . Then along comes DAWN PATROL . . . and we discover to our amazement that we respond to the same old stimuli . . . that we get a hollow feeling in the pit of the stomach when a plane is shot down and exult unashamedly when the dashing hero bombs the enemy munition dump off the map" (Frank S. Nugent, *New York Times*).

THE DEEP SIX (Warner Bros., 1958) Color 105 mins.

Producer, Martin Rackin; director, Rudolph Mate; based on the novel by Martin Dibner; screenplay, John Twist, Harry Brown, Rackin; costumes, Howard Shoup; music, David Buttolph; camera, John Seitz; editor, Roland Gross.

Alan Ladd (Alec Austen); Dianne Foster (Susan Cahill); William Bendix (Frenchy Shapiro); Keenan Wynn (Lieutenant

Alan Ladd in THE DEEP SIX (1958).

Commander Edge); James Whitmore (Commander Meredith); Efrem Zimbalist, Jr. (Lieutenant Blanchard); Joey Bishop (Ski Krakowski); Barbara Eiler (Clair Innes); Ross Bagdasarian (Slobodjian); Jeanette Nolan (Mrs. Austen); Walter Reed (Paul Clemson); Peter Hansen (Lieutenant Dooley); Richard Crane (Lieutenant [j.g.] Swanson); Morris Miller (Collins); Perry Lopez (Al Mendoza); Warren Douglas (Pilot); Nestor Paiva (Pappa Tatos); Robert Whitesides (Eddie Loomis); Robert Clarke (Ensign David Clough); Carol Lee Ladd (Ann); Ann Doran (Elsie); Jerry Mathers (Steve); Franz Roehn (Waiter); and: Officers and Men of the USS Stephen Potter.

By 1958 Alan Ladd's screen career was fast ebbing, as was the combat film genre, if THE DEEP SIX is any indication.

Alec Austen (Alan Ladd), an advertising agency artist, loves co-worker Susan Cahill (Dianne Foster). World War II is declared, and being a Quaker, Austen is unsure how he will react in battle. He is assigned the position of gunnery officer aboard the USS *Poe* where he becomes pals with the Jewish Frenchy Shapiro (William Bendix), a rough-and-tumble enlisted man with a heart of gold. He earns the scorn of the cynical, bigoted Lieutenant Commander Edge (Keenan Wynn), who is convinced (and tells others) that Austen will not hold up under fire. This point is substantiated when a plane heads straight at the ship, and Austen refuses to fire. It is not because he alone knew it was a U.S. plane, but because he froze at his post. Later he and Frenchy dismantle a Japanese bomb and Austen wins the ship's respect, which is deepened when he participates in a dock-side rumble. His true test comes when on a land raid with Frenchy. With machine gun in hand his moment of truth arises. After Frenchy dies from enemy bullets the aroused Austen machine-guns the enemy, firing madly till he collapses from his own wounds. He is rescued and returned state-side, and now has the peace of mind to wed Susan.

There are many parallels between the themes of THE DEEP SIX and the earlier, highly regarded HIGH NOON (1952) and FRIENDLY PERSUASION (1956), the latter two both starring Gary Cooper and both dealing with the subject of Quakers and how they react to violence and bloodshed. However, the lackluster THE DEEP SIX was too conventional in its clichéd dramatization to win any plaudits for its depiction of a moral dilemma during blood-and-guts warfare.

THE DEER HUNTER (Columbia/Warner Bros., 1978) Color 183 mins.

Producers, Barry Spikings, Michael Deeley, Michael Cimino,

John Peverall; associate producers, Marion Rosenberg, Joann Carelli; director, Cimino; story, Cimino, Washburn, Louis Garfinkle, Quinn K. Redeker; screenplay, Deric Washburn; art director, Ron Hobbs, Kim Swados; set decorators, Dick Goddard, Alan Hicks; costumes, Eric Seelig; makeup, Del Acevedo, Ed Butterworth; assistant director, Charles Okun; music, Stanley Myers; special effects, Fred Cramer; sound, Darrin Knight; camera, Vilmos Zsigmond; editor, Peter Zinner.

Robert DeNiro (Michael); John Cazale (Stan); John Savage (Steven); Christopher Walken (Nick); Meryl Streep (Linda); George Dzundza (John); Chuck Aspegren (Axel); Shirley Stoler (Steven's Mother); Rutanya Alda (Angela); Pierre Segul (Julien); Mady Kaplan (Axel's Girl); Amy Wright (Bridesmaid); Mary Ann Haenel (Stan's Girl); Richard Kuss (Linda's Father); Joe Grifasi (Bandleader); Christopher Colombi, Jr. (Wedding Man); Victoria Karnafel (Sad Looking Girl); Jack Scardino (Cold Old Man); Joe Strand (Bingo Caller); Helen Tomko (Helen); Paul D'Amato (Sergeant); and: Dennis Watlington, Charlene Darrow, Jane Colette Disko, Michael Wollet, Robert Beard, Joe Dzizmba, Father Stephen Kopestronsky, John F. Buchmelter, III, Frank Devore, Tom Becker, Lynn Kongkham, Dale Burroughs, Parris Hicks.

More than a decade after its release, the ambitious THE DEER HUNTER remains a powerful, if overextended, cinematic experience. Brutal, shrill, and at times unsophisticated, it is a disturbing study of late twentieth-century western man's reaction to the brutalities of warfare.

THE DEER HUNTER abounds in symbolic ceremonies and rituals. The long opening sequence in Clairton, Pennsylvania details the traditional Russian Orthodox marriage and reception of blue collar steel worker Steven (John Savage) to Angela (Rutanya Alda). He is surrounded by two hometown buddies, Michael (Robert DeNiro) and Nick (Christopher Walken). Then comes a rite of masculinity as the three pals, about to be drafted into the Vietnam War, go on a deer hunt accompanied by bar owner John (George Dzundza), the grunting Axel (Chuck Aspegren), and would-be womanizer Stan (John Cazale). In a rite of male superiority, displaying human power over animals, Michael kills the deer with a single bullet. Soon the three friends are in Vietnam, seasoned fighters who do their grizzly job without question.

The three soldiers are captured by the Viet Cong and placed in a bamboo cage submerged in the disease- and death-infested water under a command shack. Later, along with other prisoners, they are yanked out of the river and forced to play bloody Russian roulette while everyone, including themselves, bets on their odds for survival. The Viet Cong find this great sport, observing the tension-driven prisoners as they reach the brink of insanity. It is crafty Michael who devises an escape plan. He convinces their captors to give him extra bullets for the suicidal roulette game, and in a burst of gunfire kills the V.C. The three friends escape, floating downriver and being spotted by a U.S. Army helicopter. Nick is rescued but Michael and Steven fail to get aboard and Steven breaks his legs on the rocks below. Michael drags him to safety within the South Vietnamese lines.

Back in the United States Michael attempts to push the embittered Steven, whose legs have been amputated, back into communication with his wife; while he himself pursues a romance with Linda (Meryl Streep), the grocery store clerk. In the meanwhile, Nick is still in Saigon with the city about to fall to the Viet Cong. He is an emotional zombie, scarred beyond help by his wartime nightmare. He comes across young Vietnamese playing Russian roulette for money. Nick impulsively joins in the game and before long becomes a professional at the sport. Michael arrives and attempts to awaken his pal to reality through love, shock, or anything else that might work. But Nick cannot be saved. He blows his brains out in a final spin of Russian roulette.

Michael brings Nick's body home for burial. He helps Steven to reconcile with Angela, his romance with Linda deepens, but his life has changed. He tries the ritual of deer hunting again, but he cannot bring himself to kill the deer. After the funeral services, the group gathers in John's bar for a breakfast wake, and haltingly, they break out into "God Bless America," both embarrassed and exhilarated by their singing.

Earning $27,434,806 in theater rentals in the U.S. and Canada, THE DEER HUNTER won Academy Awards for Best Picture, Best Director, Best Supporting Actor (Walken), Sound and Editing. It achieved the financial, critical, and intellectual glory that such Vietnam-themed films as GO TELL THE SPARTANS (1978), q.v., and APOCALYPSE NOW (1979), q.v., strove for but failed to gain.

THE DESERT FOX (Twentieth Century-Fox, 1951) 89 mins.

Producer, Nunnally Johnson; director, Henry Hathaway; based on the book *Rommel* by Brigadier Desmond Young; screenplay, Johnson; art directors, Lyle Wheeler, Maurice Ransford; set decorators, Thomas Little, Stuart Reiss; makeup, Ben Nye; costume designer, Edward Stevenson; wardrobe director, Charles Le Maire; music, Daniele Amfitheatrof; orchestrator, Maurice de Packh; assistant director, Gerd Oswald; sound, Eugene Grossman,

Roger Heman; special camera effects, Fred Sersen, Ray Kellogg; camera, Norbert Brodine; editor, James B. Clark.

James Mason (Field Marshal Erwin Rommel); Cedric Hardwicke (Dr. Karl Strolin); Jessica Tandy (Lucie Maria Rommel); Luther Adler (Adolf Hitler); Everett Sloane (General Burgdorf); Leo G. Carroll (Field Marshal Von Rundstedt); George Macready (General Fritz Bayerlein); Richard Boone (Aldinger); Eduard Franz (Colonel Von Stauffenberg); Desmond Young (Himself); William Reynolds (Manfred Rommel); Charles Evans (General Schultz); Walter Kingsford (Admiral Ruge); John Hoyt (Keitel); Don De Leo (General Moisel); Richard Elmore (Rommel's Driver in Africa); John Vosper (Major Walker); Dan O'Herlihy (Commando Captain); Scott Forbes (Commando Colonel); Victor Wood (British Medic); Lester Matthews (British Officer); Mary Carroll (Maid); Paul Cavanagh (Colonel Von Hofaker); Jack Baston (Jodi); Carleton Young (German Major); Freeman Lusk (German Surgeon); Robert Coote (British Medical Officer); Sean McClory (Jock); Lumsden Hare (Doctor); John Goldsworthy (Stulpnagel); Ivan

Jessica Tandy, James Mason, and Richard Boone in THE DESERT FOX (1951).

Triesault (German Major); Michael Rennie (Desmond Young's Voice); Trevor Ward (General Montgomery); and: Philip Van Zandt.

"This film does as much to revive the discredited legend of an efficient, wise and above all gentlemanly military caste as if it had been made by the Propaganda Department of the Wehrmacht itself . . ." (London *Evening Standard*).

At the time of its release, this intelligent film (based on a best-selling biography) garnered tremendous adverse public reaction for depicting Nazi Field Marshal Rommel (1891-1944) as a civilized, brave, and brilliant general. Its attempt to be "objective" backfired and in many parts of the United States and England the film was picketed.

Told through flashback, THE DESERT FOX focuses on Field Marshal Rommel, known as the Desert Fox, who commands the super-efficient Afrika Korps during World War II. His inspired military tactics against tremendous odds win him the respect of both sides in the war. Because he lacks needed supplies from Hitler, his war efforts are hampered and he makes known his feelings. At the battle of El Alamein he disobeys the Fuehrer's commands for "victory or death" and on October 23, 1942 withdraws his troops. After recuperating from a severe case of jaundice, Rommel tours the Atlantic defenses and is disillusioned to realize that Hitler's battle strategy is flawed. It forces him to balance his sharp military judgment against his loyalty to the German High Command. In the meantime, his friend, Dr. Karl Strolin (Cedric Hardwicke), has subtly suggested that Hitler is damaging the Third Reich and a remedy must be found. Later, Rommel is part of the June 1944 conspiracy to assassinate Hitler, but it fails and Rommel's name is implicated in the treason. Rather than risk danger to his wife (Jessica Tandy) and son (William Reynolds) or discredit his family's name, he commits suicide.

A few years earlier—and even at this time—it was (almost) unheard of to make the hero of an English-language war film, a Nazi general. To depict this great general as a sensitive, loving family man was a shock (and a revelation) to most English-speaking filmgoers. For Norman Kagan in *The War Film* (1974), ". . . This film can be seen as another view of the 1950s obsession with command and responsibility in a world of skimpy loyalties, a metaphor of the Cold War. . . . What are the limits of loyalty? What *do* we do when the moral ground shifts under us?"

For the record, the actual battle scenes shown in this feature are footage from David MacDonald's British documentary, DESERT

VICTORY (1943), and none of the American/British actors playing Nazis use German accents.
British release title: ROMMEL—DESERT FOX.

DESERT PATROL (Universal, 1962) 78 mins.

Presenter, J. Arthur Rank; producers, Robert S. Baker, Monty Berman; director, Guy Green; story, Sean Fielding; screenplay, Robert Westerby; art director, Maurice Pelling; wardrobe, Jack Verity; makeup, Roy Ashton; music, Clifton Parker; music director, Muir Mathieson; assistant director, Denis O'Dell; sound, Bob Jones; special effects, Cliff Richardson, Roy Whybrow; camera, Wilkie Cooper; editor, Gordon Pilkington.

Richard Attenborough (Trooper Brody); John Gregson (Captain Williams); Michael Craig (Captain Cotton); Vincent Ball (Sergeant Nesbitt); Percy Herbert (Trooper White); Barry Foster (Corporal Matheson); Andrew Faulds (Sergeant Parker); George Murcell (Corporal Simms); Ray McAnally (Sergeant Hardy); Harold Goodwin (Road Watch); Tony Thawnton (Captain Giles): Dermot Walsh (Major Jeffries); Wolf Frees (German Sergeant); George Mikell (German Officer).

Four years after its release in England by the Rank Organization as SEA OF SAND, and cut by nineteen minutes, DESERT PATROL debuted in the U.S. "Excellent war film full of incident; familiar types come sweatingly to life" (David Quinlan, *British Sound Films*, 1958).

During the buildup for the Battles of El Alamein in 1942 North Africa, Y Patrol of the Long Range Desert Group is charged with blowing up a pivotal Nazi petrol dump. Accomplishing their task, the nine men fight their way back through pursuing tanks, sandstorms, minefields, etc. to home base. Five survive the ordeal. Among their original number is Desert Rat officer Captain Cotton (Michael Craig), stiff-upper-lip, by-the-book Captain Williams (John Gregson), and individualistic cockney, Trooper Brody (Richard Attenborough).

Variety, while labeling it a "routine war adventure," commended the on-location production because it ". . . splendidly capture[s] the remote loneliness of the vast desert, the heat, the boredom and the sense of pending danger."

THE DESERT RATS (Twentieth Century-Fox, 1953) 88 mins.

Producer, Robert L. Jacks; director, Robert Wise; screenplay, Richard Murphy; art directors, Lyle Wheeler, Addison Hehr;

music, Leigh Harline; special effects, Ray Kellogg; camera, Lucien Ballard; editor, Barbara McLean.

Richard Burton (Captain MacRoberts); Robert Newton (Bartlett); Robert Douglas (General); Torin Thatcher (Barney); Chips Rafferty (Smith); Charles Tingwell (Lieutenant Carstairs); James Mason (Field Marshal Erwin Rommel); Charles Davis (Pete); Ben Wright (Mick); James Lilburn (Communications); John O'Malley (Riley); Ray Harden (Hugh); John Alderson (Corporal); Richard Peel (Rusty); Michael Pate (Captain Currie); Frank Pulaski (Major O'Rourke); Charles Keane (Sergeant Donaldson); Pat O'Moore (Jim); Trevor Constable (Ginger); Albert Taylor (Jensen); John Wengraf (German Doctor); Arno Frey (Kramm); Alfred Ziesler (Von Helmholtz); Charles Fitzsimons (Fire Officer).

As an antidote to the controversial THE DESERT FOX (1951), q.v., yet hoping to duplicate its box-office receipts, Twentieth Century-Fox created the patriotic THE DESERT RATS. The advertising campaign was sufficient to show that this was no intellectual successor to the earlier picture: "The immortal story of THE DESERT RATS, whose heroic stand at Tobruk stopped the Afrika Korps dead in its tracks!"

In 1941 North Africa at Tobruk, British Captain MacRoberts (Richard Burton) is serving with the 9th Australian Division and ordered to train a fresh detachment of inexperienced Aussie troopers. He is a martinet of discipline to everyone save Bartlett (Robert Newton), the alcoholic and cowardly ex-schoolteacher whom MacRoberts knew years ago. As the Germans attack Tobruk, MacRoberts perceives Rommel's battle plan and outmaneuvers the enemy. He is appointed Lieutenant Colonel and leads commando raids on Rommel's Afrika Korps. On one such excursion he is wounded and captured. At a German field hospital he encounters an ailing Rommel and they politely discuss the military value of Tobruk to both sides. Later, MacRoberts escapes and returns to combat. In one deadly skirmish, he orders his men to surrender, but they (including the philosophizing Bartlett) dig in and it is the Panzer tank units which withdraw in the face of the arriving British relief divisions. The battle of Tobruk is over.

For many, the brief "guest appearance" of Field Marshal Rommel (James Mason—this time boasting a German accent) was a needless commercial artifice, better left undone.

DESPERATE JOURNEY (Warner Bros., 1942) 107 mins.

Producer, Hal B. Wallis; associate producer, Jack Saper; director, Raoul Walsh; based on the story "Forced Landing" by Arthur T. Horman; screenplay, Horman; art director, Carl Jules

Alan Hale, Ronald Reagan, Errol Flynn, and Arthur Kennedy in DESPERATE JOURNEY (1942).

Weyl; costumes, Milo Anderson; makeup, Perc Westmore; technical adviser, S/L.O. Cathcart-Jones (Royal Canadian Air Force); music, Max Steiner; orchestrator, Hugo Friedhofer; sound, C. A. Riggs; special effects, Edwin DuPar; camera, Bert Glennon; editor, Rudi Fehr.

Errol Flynn (Flight Lieutenant Terrence Forbes); Ronald Reagan (Flying Officer Johnny Hammond); Nancy Coleman (Kaethe Brahms); Raymond Massey (Major Otto Baumeister); Alan Hale (Flight Sergeant Kirk Edwards); Arthur Kennedy (Flying Officer Jed Forrest); Ronald Sinclair (Flight Sergeant Lloyd Hollis); Albert Basserman (Dr. Mather); Sig Rumann (Preuss); Patrick O'Moore (Squadron Leader Lane Ferris); Felix Basch (Dr. Herman Brahms); Ilka Gruning (Frau Brahms); Elsa Basserman (Frau Raeder); Charles Irwin (Captain Coswick); Robert O. Davis (Kruse); Henry Victor (Henrich Schwartzmuller); Hans Schumm, Robert Stephenson (Gestapo Men); Walter Brooke (Warwick); William Hopper (Aircraftsman); Rolf Lindau (Sergeant); Otto Reichow (Private Koenig); Sigfried Tor (Private Rasek); Philip Van Zandt (Soldier); Roland Varno (Unteroffizier); Sven Hugo Borg (Mechanic); Helmut Dantine (Co-Pilot); Bruce Lester (Assistant

Plotting Officer); Kurt Katch (Hesse); Victor Zimmerman (Captain Eggerstedt); Douglas Walton (British Officer); Harold Daniels (German Soldier); Henry Rowland (Motorcycle Scout); Arno Frey (Private Trecha); Frank Alten (Lieutenant); Gene Garrick (Polish Boy).

World War II action films could be topical; World War II action films could be patriotic; but not all World War II action films took their combat motifs seriously. Such a one was DESPERATE JOURNEY, a rousing Errol Flynn adventure vehicle, directed in high style by veteran Raoul Walsh (his second of seven features with swashbuckling Flynn) and bolstered by Warner Bros.' polished stock company and pulsating film style. Audiences and critics alike were generally enthusiastic about this flag-waving entertainment. "If a handful of guys can do this much, you wonder what an army might do—provided, of course, it had the service of a Warner scriptwriter and cast" (Bosley Crowther, *New York Times*).

After their Royal Air Force bomber plane is shot down on a mission over Poland, the surviving five of an eight-man crew make a dash for the Allied lines through Germany. There is enterprising Flight Lieutenant Terrence Forbes (Errol Flynn), now in command; seasoned Flight Sergeant Kirk Edwards (Alan Hale), who cares as much about food as killing the enemy; very American Flying Officer Johnny Hammond (Ronald Reagan); ever-so-British young Flying Sergeant Lloyd Hollis (Ronald Sinclair); and pragmatic Flying Officer Jed Forrest (Arthur Kennedy). Their chief adversary becomes Major Otto Baumeister (Raymond Massey), a high-ranking Gestapo officer who has a difficult time keeping the Allied quintet prisoners. Kaethe Brahms (Nancy Coleman) is the sympathetic German romantically inclined to Forbes. In the course of their hi-jinks, the men impersonate German officers, blow up an incendiary bomb plant, use a Nazi command vehicle for a jaunt almost into Berlin, etc. By the time they hijack a bomber plane (which is being readied to attack London's hydraulic works), only Forbes and Hammond are still alive. As they take off for England, Forbes enthuses, "Now for Australia and a crack at those Japs!"

There are great structural similarities between this production and the British-made THE FORTY-NINTH PARALLEL (1941) (a.k.a. THE INVADERS).

DESTINATION GOBI (Twentieth Century-Fox, 1953) Color 89 mins.

Producer, Stanley Rubin; director, Robert Wise; based on the story "Sixty Saddles for Gobi" by Edmund G. Love; screenplay, Everett Freeman; art directors, Lyle Wheeler, Lewis Creber; music,

Richard Widmark, Casey Adams [Max Showalter], Leonard Strong, Ross Bagdasarian, Darryl Hickman, and Don Taylor in DESTINATION GOBI (1953).

Sol Kaplan; music director, Alfred Newman; camera, Charles G. Clarke; editor, Robert Fritch.

Richard Widmark (Chief Petty Officer Sam McHale); Don Taylor (Jenkins); Casey Adams [Max Showalter] (Walter Landers); Murvyn Vye (Kengtu); Darryl Hickman (Wilbur Cohen); Martin

Milner (Elwood Halsey); Ross Bagdasarian (Paul Sabatello); Judy
Dann (Nura Satu); Rodolfo Acosta (Tomec); Russell Collins
(Commander Wyatt); Leonard Strong (Wali-Akham); Anthony
Earl Numkena (Kengtu's Son); Earl Holliman (Frank Svenson);
Edgar Barrier (Yin Tang); Alvy Moore (Aide); Stuart Randall
(Captain Briggs); William Forrest (Skipper); Bert Moorhouse
(Naval Captain); Jack Raine (Admiral).

"With the stress on realism, the pic never strains credibility"
(*Variety*).

DESTINATION GOBI is based on an unusual yet factual
chapter in the history of World War II. A U.S. Naval detachment is
ordered to observe weather conditions in the Mongolian desert.
When Commander Wyatt (Russell Collins) is killed in a Japanese air
raid, Chief Petty Officer Sam McHale (Richard Widmark) assumes
leadership; but he is still furious that he is stuck in this desert
outpost instead of at the battle front. Eventually the sailors use a
Chinese junk to sail their patrol through the Japanese lines.

Using Technicolor effectively this offbeat combat film realisti-
cally captures the parched heat and driving winds of the desert, and
the isolated patrol which must rely on teamwork for survival.

DESTINATION TOKYO (Warner Bros., 1944) 135 mins.*

Producer, Jerry Wald; director, Delmer Daves; story, Steve
Fisher; screenplay, Daves, Albert Maltz; art director, Leo K. Kuter;
set decorator, Walter Tilford; makeup, Perc Westmore; technical
adviser, Lieutenant Commander Philip Compton; music, Franz
Waxman; orchestrator, Leon Raab; music director, Leo F. Forbstein; assistant director, Art Lueker; sound, Robert B. Lee; special
effects, Lawrence Butler, Willard Van Enger; montages, James
Leicester; camera, Bert Glennon, editor, Christian Nyby.

Cary Grant (Captain Cassidy); John Garfield (Wolf); Alan
Hale (Cookie); John Ridgely (Reserve Officer Raymond); Dane
Clark (Tin Can); Warner Anderson (Executive Officer Andy);
William Prince (Pills); Robert Hutton (Tommy Adams); Tom Tully
(Mike Connors); Faye Emerson (Mrs. Cassidy); Peter Whitney
(Dakota); Warren Douglas (Larry, a Diving Officer); John For-
sythe (Sparks); John Alvin (Sound Man); Bill Kennedy (Pete, the
Gunnery Officer); William Challee (Quartermaster); Whit Bissell
(Yo Yo); John Whitney (Communications Officer); George Lloyd
(Chief of Boat); Maurice Murphy (Toscanini); John Hudson (Radio
Man); Jimmy Evans, George W. Robotham, Dan Borzage, Bernie
Sell, Paul Parry, "Sailor" Vincent, Charles Sherlock, Warren Cross,

---

*Computer colorized version now available.

Wally Walker, William Hudson, Charles Sullivan, Cy Malis, Bob Creasman, John Sylvester, Duke York, Ted Jacques, Harry Bartell, Jay Ward, John Forrest, Alan Wilson (Crew Members); Joy Barlowe (Wolf's Girl); Bill Hunter (Market Street "Commando"); Hugh Prosser (Pilot); Frank Tang (Japanese Pilot); Angel Cruz (Japanese Bombardier); Pierre Watkin (Admiral); Mark Stevens, Jack Mower (Admiral's Aides); Cliff Clark (Admiral on *Hornet*); Charles Thompson (Rear Admiral); Russ Whiteman (First Class Yeoman); Tony Hughes (Navy Air Officer); Deborah Daves (Debby Cassidy); Michael Daves (Michael Cassidy); Bob Lowell (Radio Operator); George Anderson (Officer); Eddie Lee, Wing Foo (Japanese at Listening Post); Ya Sing Sung (Japanese on Beach); Benson Fong, James B. Leong (Japanese); Bruce Wong (Japanese Antenna Man); Roland Got (Japanese Officer); Mary Landa (Tin Can's Girl) Carlyle Blackwell (Man on Phone); Dorothy Schoemer (Saleslady); Kirby Grant (Captain at Briefing); Herbert Gunn (Lieutenant); Warren Ashe (Major); Lane Chandler (Chief Petty Officer); Lou Marcelle (Narrator).

DESTINATION TOKYO is rightly one of the most celebrated combat motion pictures about World War II. Produced by Warner Bros., the same studio credited with AIR FORCE (1943), q.v., this proved to be the penultimate submarine feature film, focusing entirely on the crew and its vital mission against the enemy.

"PROCEED TO SEA IMMEDIATELY WITH FULL ALLOWANCE TORPEDOES, FUEL AND AMMUNITION ALSO CONFIDENTIAL GEAR AND SEALED ORDERS."

With this decoded directive, DESTINATION TOKYO is underway. Captain Cassidy (Cary Grant) of the submarine USS *Copperfin*, mindful of how much he misses his own wife and two children back in Oklahoma City, is sympathetic to his men, especially in these pre-Christmas days. But it is wartime and he knows his duty. He is bluntly direct as he advises his crew about their unknown but dangerous mission: "I don't believe in fight talks. When a man gives a fight talk, I suspect he needs one himself. For the benefit of the newcomers, you're here because you volunteered. You're well trained, highly selected men and we're glad to have you aboard. You may be infants in the submarine service, but we figure you'll be veterans by the time we make port again. We've had pretty fair luck so far. Let's hope we really smear 'em [the Japanese] this time."

As the *Copperfin* leaves San Francisco, bound for the Aleutians, the crew is introduced, including: Wolf (John Garfield), the girl-chasing gob who wants to even the score for his uncle having been killed in Europe; Cookie (Alan Hale), the hearty scullery mate; Tin Can (Dane Clark), the high-strung gob; nineteen-year-old Tommy Adams (Robert Hutton), who carries a picture of his sister; Pills (William Prince), the pharmacist's mate; Sparks (John Forsythe), in communications; Mike Connors (Tom Tully), the Irish-American torpedoman who listens endlessly to a recording made by his wife back at home. They pick up meteorology specialist Raymond (John Ridgely) and the crew learns more details of its secret mission: to sneak into Tokyo harbor, send Raymond and a landing party ashore, and chart weather conditions so that General Doolittle can launch his bombing raids on Tokyo. The *Copperfin* slithers through the net surrounding the harbor as a Japanese vessel passes above water. The Japanese-speaking Raymond, along with Wolf and Sparks, go ashore and complete their task. They barely make it back to the *Copperfin*. The vital data are radioed to the USS *Hornet* and Doolittle's squadron takes off. In the midst of the chaos of the bombing raid, the *Copperfin* sneaks out of the mine-infested harbor. Next, Cassidy launches torpedoes against a Japanese carrier and sinks it, but soon enemy destroyers are in pursuit, dropping depth charges on the submarine. Almost at the last moment the *Copperfin* sinks its last opponent, and Cassidy heads the submarine back to San Francisco. Approaching the Golden Gate the men each voice how they will spend their shore leave. Cassidy's wife (Faye Emerson) and children (Michael Daves, Deborah Daves) are on the dock waving their greetings to the Captain.

Because there is little energy or screen time devoted to romance, this war film has ample opportunity (within 135 minutes) to present many revealing snippets of life aboard the claustrophobic submarine. There is the defusing of an unexploded bomb aboard; the emergency appendectomy operation on Tommy in which Pills uses a medical book to guide his unknowing hands as the Captain administers ether; the burial at sea of Mike the torpedoman; the abrasive conflict between Wolf and Tin Can; and avuncular Captain Cassidy, always jocular, all-knowing, and resourceful. The men chat, reminisce (with the use of flashbacks), and listen to Japanese propaganda on the radio. Always the pressure of war is there, but it is presented as a given and not something to be feared. The men, for the most part, treat the trek as a lark. "I've always wanted to see one of those geisha up close," admits one crew member. When Cassidy asks Wolf to volunteer for the land mission, he says jokingly, "How would you like a little shore leave?" Almost offhandedly he adds, "This isn't an order. If you go, you go voluntarily. You might not come back." To the crew, being positioned in Tokyo harbor is an exciting adventure, almost a joke to be sitting in "the Nips' bird bath." When asked the ultimate question of why he became a submarine officer, Cassidy tosses off, "I used to get a kick out of swimming underwater."

Above all, DESTINATION TOKYO is a crafty mixture, depicting the Japanese enemy as cruel and heartless (when the rescued Japanese pilot stabs to death the torpedoman Mike), and at the same time suggesting that the Japanese are a misguided race of people led astray by their cultural traditions. As Cassidy and Raymond agree, "Japs do what they're told. They've been sold a swindle and they've swallowed it. . . . Japs don't understand the love we [Americans] have for our women. They don't even have a word for it in their language." Also enunciated is the need to end war: "There's lots of Mikes [the torpedoman] dying now and a lot more Mikes will die till we wipe out the system that puts daggers in the hands of five year old children. You know, if Mike were here to put it into words now, that's just abut what he died for. More rollerskates in this world, including some for the next generation of Japanese kids, because that's the kind of man Mike was." Always mindful that this was 1943 and there was still a war to be won, DESTINATION TOKYO ends with a narrator commending the men of the silent service and wishing them "Good luck and good hunting!"

DESTINATION TOKYO has shown, in somewhat exaggerated heroic terms, that a team of men fighting for what is right and believing in God can pull together in a democratic way and beat almost impossible odds.

DESTROYER (Columbia, 1943) 99 mins.

Producer, Louis F. Edelman; director, William A. Seiter; story, Frank Wead; screenplay, Wead, Lewis Melzer, Borden Chase; art directors, Lionel Banks, Cary Odell; set decorator, Frank Tuttle; music, Anthony Collins; music director, Morris W. Stoloff; assistant director, Milton Carter; sound, Ed Bernds; camera, Franz F. Planer; editor, Gene Havlick.

Edward G. Robinson (Steve Boleslavski); Glenn Ford (Mickey Donohue); Marguerite Chapman (Mary Boleslavski); Edgar Buchanan (Kansas Jackson); Leo Gorcey (Sarecky); Regis Toomey (Lieutenant Commander Clark); Ed Brophy (Casey); Warren Ashe (Lieutenant Morton); Craig Woods (Bigbee); Curt Bois (Yasha); Pierre Watkin (Admiral); Al Hill (Knife Eating Sailor); Bobby Jordan (Sobbing Sailor); Roger Clark (Chief Engineer); Dean Benton (Fireman Moore); David Alison (Fireman Thomas); Paul Perry (Doctor); John Merton (Chief Quartermaster); Don Peters (Helmsman); Virginia Sale (Spinster); Eleanor Counts (Sarecky's Girl); Dale Van Sickel (Sailor); Addison Richards (Ferguson);

Edward G. Robinson, Glenn Ford, and Marguerite Chapman in DESTROYER (1943).

Lester Dorr, Bud Geary (Ship's Fitters); Eddie Drew (Survivor); Tristram Coffin (Doctor); Larry Parks (Ensign Johnson); Eddy Chandler (Chief Gunner's Mate); Lloyd Bridges (Fireman); Dennis Moore (Communications Officer); Charles McGraw (Assistant Chief Engineer); Edmund Cobb (Workman); Eddy Waller (Riveter).

Heroism in wartime is not always exclusively for the young. Welder Steve Boleslavski (Edward G. Robinson) is helping to build the USS *John Paul Jones*, a new warship which will replace the one on which he served in the First World War. After the ship is launched, he re-enlists and finds himself reporting to Lieutenant Commander Clark (Regis Toomey), a reversal of the situation from World War I. Aboard the *John Paul Jones* Boleslavski is considered an old-timer out of step with the new order, especially by boatswain's mate Mickey Donohue (Glenn Ford) who later becomes infatuated with Boleslavski's daughter Mary (Marguerite Chapman). In the course of battle Boleslavski proves himself a hero, winning the respect of all aboard.

"As this indestructible hero, Mr. Robinson utilizes the same tough snarl, the same withering looks and mute sarcasm that made him the scourge of muggs in days gone by. . . . It is a leaky and top-heavy vessel on which Mr. Robinson serves" (Bosley Crowther, *New York Times*).

THE DEVIL'S BRIGADE (United Artists, 1968) Color 130 mins.

Producer, David L. Wolper; associate producers, Theodore Strauss, Julian Ludwig; director, Andrew V. McLaglen; based on the book by Robert H. Adleman and Colonel George Walton; screenplay, William Roberts; art director, Alfred Sweeney; set decorator, Morris Hoffman; makeup, Donald W. Robertson; stunt supervisor, Hal Needham; music/music conductor, Alex North; orchestrator, Henry Brant; assistant directors, Terry Morse, Jr., Newt Arnold, Dennis Donnelly; sound, Al Overton, Clem Portman; special effects supervisor, Logan Frazee; camera, William H. Clothier; editor, William Cartwright.

William Holden (Lieutenant Colonel Robert T. Frederick); Cliff Robertson (Major Alan Crown); Vince Edwards (Major Cliff

William Holden (second from right) and Vince Edwards (fourth from right) in THE DEVIL'S BRIGADE (1968).

Bricker); Andrew Prine (Private Theodore Ransom); Claude Akins (Rocky Rockman); Richard Jaeckel (Omar Greco); Jack Watson (Corporal Wilfred Peacock); Jeremy Slate (Patrick O'Neal); Richard Dawson (Hugh MacDonald); Dana Andrews (Brigadier General Walter Naylor); Michael Rennie (Lieutenant General Mark Clark); Carroll O'Connor (Major General Maxwell Hunter); Gretchen Wyler (A Lady of Joy); Tom Stern (Captain Cardwell); Tom Troupe (Al Manella); Luke Askew (Hubert Hixon); Bill Fletcher (Bronc Guthrie); Jean-Paul Vignon (Henri Laurent); Harry Carey, Jr. (Captain Rose); Norman Alden (Military Police Lieutenant); Paul Hornung (Lumberjack); Gene Fullmer (Bartender); Patrick Knowles (Admiral Lord Louis Mountbatten); Don Megowan (Luke Phelan); David Pritchard (Corporal Coker); Paul Busch (German Captain); James Craig (American Officer).

Yet another distillation of THE DIRTY DOZEN (1967), *infra*, motif which, by this time, was beginning to pale on jaded moviegoers.

As part of its planned assault on enemy strongholds in Europe, the Allies form the First Special Service Force. Its goal is to launch daring commando raids on Nazi-occupied Norway. Lieutenant Colonel Robert T. Frederick (William Holden), who has never experienced field command, is put in charge of disparate troops: G.I. misfits* led by Major Cliff Bricker (Vince Edwards) and an efficient Canadian force headed by Major Alan Crown (Cliff Robertson). By the time the training in Montana is completed, the opposing factions have blended into a homogeneous whole, with Frederick a seasoned and willing leader. Then Frederick learns the Norwegian operation has been cancelled and he appeals to Major General Maxwell Hunter (Carroll O'Connor) to give his task force a new assignment. His mission becomes patrolling the German lines in southern Italy. They are ordered to take Mt. La Difensa, which requires scaling a steep mountainside. Victory proves to be theirs, but at a tremendous human loss. The Germans nickname Frederick's force "The Devil's Brigade."

---

*The film's advertisement had a colorful way of describing the motley crew: Private Theodore Ransom (Andrew Prine)—"Wanted for what he did to an officer's wife"; Omar Greco (Richard Jaeckel)—"Had more tricks for getting out of jail than Houdini"; Rocky Rockman (Claude Akins)—"He'll put lead in your gut"; Major Cliff Bricker (Vince Edwards)—"He keeps rattlesnakes for pets"; Lieutenant Colonel Robert T. Frederick (William Holden)—"Creator of the Brigade—a madman or a genius!"; Major Alan Crown (Cliff Robertson)—"The Loser—He teaches the art of murder while smiling"; Corporal Wilfred Peacock (Jack Watson)— "Laugh at his kilts . . . but don't let him hear you!"; (Richard Dawson)—"The little man with the deadly sting."

The reviewers were not kind to this brawling actioner. "An uneven combination of the worst of THE DIRTY DOZEN and the best of WHAT PRICE GLORY. The irony here is that the story actually happened, as opposed to the somewhat fictitious plot of DOZEN . . ." (*Variety*). "One can, as in the case of THE DIRTY DOZEN, even see a logical truth in the proposition that it takes a psychopath to indulge in the psychopathic activity of war with feeling and gusto. Further, the commando-wartime aspect permits us to see human flesh desecrated by more than shot and shell; what marvelous closeups we can get of garotting, of bashing, of sinking knife and shiv into meat and of the freshest of red stuff thereby released!" (Judith Crist, *New York* magazine). "There is hardly a character, a situation or a line of dialogue that has not served a useful purpose in some earlier movie or television show" (Vincent Canby, *New York Times*).

THE DIRTY DOZEN (Metro-Goldwyn-Mayer, 1967) Color 149 mins.

Producer, Kenneth Hyman; associate producer, Raymond Anzarut; director, Robert Aldrich; based on the novel by E. M. Nathanson; screenplay, Nunnally Johnson, Lukas Heller; art director, William Hutchinson; main title designer, Walter Blake; makeup, Ernest Gasser, Wally Schneiderman; music, Frank De Vol; song, De Vol and Mack David; De Vol and Sibylle Siegfried; assistant director, Bert Batt; sound, Franklin Milton, Claude Hitchcock; sound editor, John Poyner; special effects supervisor, Cliff Richardson; camera, Edward Scaife; editor, Michael Luciano.

Lee Marvin (Major Reisman); Ernest Borgnine (General Worden); Charles Bronson (Joseph Wladislaw); Jim Brown (Robert Jefferson); John Cassavetes (Victor Franko); Richard Jaeckel (Sergeant Bowren); George Kennedy (Major Max Armbruster); Trini Lopez (Pedro Jiminez); Ralph Meeker (Captain Stuart Kinder); Robert Ryan (Colonel Everett Dasher Breed); Telly Savalas (Archer Maggott); Donald Sutherland (Vernon Pinkley); Clint Walker (Samson Posey); Robert Webber (General Denton); Tom Busby (Milo Vladek); Ben Carruthers (Glenn Gilpin); Stuart Cooper (Roscoe Lever); Robert Phillips (Corporal Morgan); Colin Maitland (Seth Sawyer); Al Mancini (Tassos Bravos); George Roubicek (Private Arthur James Gardner); Thick Wilson (General Worden's Aide); Dora Reisser (German Officer's Girl).

DIRTY DOZEN: THE DEADLY MISSION (Metro-Goldwyn-Mayer/United Artists TV/NBC-TV, 3/1/87) Color 100 mins.

Executive producer, David Gerber; producer, Mel Swope;

associate producers, Boris Gregoric, Clive Reed; director, Lee H. Katzin; teleplay, Mark Rodgers; production designer, John Stoll; music, John Cacavas; camera, Tomislav Pinter; editors, Richard E. Rabjohn, Ronald J. Fagan.

Telly Savalas (Major Wright); Ernest Borgnine (General Worden); Randall "Tex" Cobb (Eric "Swede" Wallan); Vincent Edwards (Sergeant Holt); Gary Graham (Joe Stern); Wolf Kahler (Colonel Kreiger); Thom Mathews (Francis Kelly); Emmanuelle Messignac (Marie Valentine); James Van Patten (David Webber); Vincent Van Patten (Ronnie Webber); Bo Svenson (Maurice Fontenac); Paul Picerni (Ernesto Ferucci); and: Pavle Balenovic, Mario Barbaric, Branko Blace, Milan Ristic, Matko Rajuz, David Horovitch, Bernard Woringer, Meg Wynn Owen, Jay Burra, Bozidar Smiljanic, Frederick Barthman, Werner Stocker, David Pullan, Ned Vukovich, Sam Douglas, Vila Matula, Ivo Kristof, Bozena Ruk-Focic, Gus Savalas.

THE DIRTY DOZEN: THE FATAL MISSION (Metro-Goldwyn-Mayer/United Artists/NBC-TV, 2/14/88) Color 100 mins.

Producer, Mel Swope; associate producer, Boris Gregoric; director, Lee H. Katzin; teleplay, Mark Rodgers; music, John Cacavas; camera, Tomislav Pinter; editors, Richard E. Rabjohn, Leon Carrere.

Telly Savalas (Major Wright); Ernest Borgnine (General Worden); Hunt Block (Private Joe Stern); Matthew Burton (SS General Karl Richter); Jeff Conaway (Sergeant Holt); Alex Cord (Dravko Demchuk); Erik Estrada (Carmine D'Agostino); Ernie Hudson (Private Joe Hamilton); James Carroll Jordan (Lonnie Wilson); Ray Mancini (Tom Ricketts); John Matuszak (Fred Collins); Natalia Nogulich (Yelena Vascovic); Heather Thomas (Lieutenant Carol Campbell); Anthony Valentine (Colonel Clark); Richard Yniguez (Roberto Eccevaria); and: Branko Blace, Robert Bobinac, Budimar Sobat, Matko Raguz, Ranko Zidaric, Ray Armstrong, Greg Charles, Drew Lucas, Derek Huxby, Peter Arp, Slavko Juraga, Gus Savalas, Clare Grant, Kaiza Pelka, Richard Garnett, Slavka Knezevic, Tibor Belicza, Sreten Mokrovic, Slobodan Mrovanovic, Kreso Dolencic, Damir Saban, Ivo Kristof, Milan Blecas.

DIRTY DOZEN: THE NEXT MISSION (Metro-Goldwyn-Mayer/United Artists TV/NBC-TV, 2/4/85) Color 100 mins.

Producer, Harry R. Sherman; associate producer, Frederick Muller; director, Andrew V. McLaglen; teleplay, Michael Kane;

production designer, Peter Mullins; music, Richard Harvey; camera, John Stanier; editor, Alan Strachan.

Lee Marvin (Major Reisman); Ernest Borgnine (General Worden); Ken Wahl (Anthony Valentine); Larry Wilcox (Tommy Wells); Sonny Landham (Sam Sixkiller); Richard Jaeckel (Military Police Sergeant Bowren); Wolf Kahler (Colonel Sepp Dietrich); Gavan O'Herlihy (Conrad Perkins); Ricco Ross (Arlen Driggers); Stephen Hattersley (Otto Deutsch); Rolf Saxon (Robert Wright); Jay Benedict (Didier LeClair); Michael John Paliotti (Baxley); Paul Herzberg (Reynolds); Jeff Harding (Sanders); Sam Douglas (Anderson); Russell Somers (Gary Rosen); Michael Sheard (Adolf Hitler); Bruce Boa (Colonel); John Malcolm (Field Marshal); Morgan Sheppard (German General); Crispin DiNys (Schmidt); Denis Holmes (General Pierre Fontaine); Alan Barry (General Bulldog Bardsley); Don Fellows (General Trent Tucker).

DIRTY DOZEN: THE SERIES: DANKO'S DOZEN (Metro-Goldwyn-Mayer/United Artists TV/Fox-TV, 4/30/88) Color 100 mins.

Senior executive producers, John Furia, Jr., Dan Gordon; executive producers, Jonas McCord, Mark Rodgers; director, Kevin Connor; based on the novel by E. M. Nathanson; teleplay, McCord, Rodgers, Gordon; art director, Zelijko Senecic; music, Doug Timm; sound, Tony Jackson; camera, Douglas Milsome; editors, Richard E. Rabjohn, Leon Carrere, Mark Conte.

Ben Murphy (Lieutenant Danko); John Bradley (Jonathan Farrell); John DiAquino (Jean Lebeq); John Slattery (Dylan Leeds); Jon Tenney (Janosz Feke); Mike Jolly (Vern); Glenn Withrow (Roy); Lanny Flaherty (Sergeant Butts); Jamie Koss (Dana Jankowski); Daniel Roebuck (Moskowitz); Pat Skipper (Brody); Michael DeLorenzo (Fuentes); Frank Marth (Major General Worth); and: Paul Glawion, Constantine Gregory, Fred Bryant, Slavko Juraga, Manning Redwood, Dusko Valentic, Aleksander Cvjetkovic, Rob Freeman, Filip Nolan, Pedja Petrovic, Hrvoje Perusic, Boris Svrtan.

"Whoever dreamed up this scheme must have been a lunatic!" muses Major Reisman (Lee Marvin) near the start of THE DIRTY DOZEN. But the filmmakers of this shockingly gutsy, rowdy, anti-human combat film knew exactly the outcome of this star-studded exercise: big box-office dollars! (The original 1967 film would earn $20,300,000 in theater rentals in the U.S. and Canada.)

In the crucial months before the D-Day Invasion of Europe in 1944, U.S. Army Major Reisman, based in England, is ordered by

General Worden (Ernest Borgnine) to train twelve convicted
GIs—viciously corrupt criminals—for a suicide mission. Their goal
is to parachute into Nazi-held France and destroy a chateau filled
with high-ranking German officers. Among the motley crew are:
psychopathic Chicago hoodlum Victor Franko (John Cassavetes);
anti-white black man Robert Jefferson (Jim Brown); idiotic Vernon
Pinkley (Donald Sutherland); confessed murderer Joseph Wladislaw (Charles Bronson), a coal miner's son who (conveniently)
speaks German; American Indian Samson Posey (Clint Walker),
who is full of silent rage; guitar-strumming Mexican Pedro Jiminez
(Trini Lopez); and racial bigot/religious fanatic/sex deviant Archer
Maggott (Telly Savalas) who lives up to his surname. Their reward,
if the mission succeeds and *if* they survive its perils, is a prison
pardon.

At first the felons taunt and test the cool and resourceful
Reisman, but finally, through the combined efforts of Reisman, his
no-nonsense sergeant (Richard Jaeckel) and psychiatrist Captain
Kinder (Ralph Meeker), the ethnically diverse squad is whipped into

John Cassavetes and Lee Marvin in THE DIRTY DOZEN (1967).

a battle frenzy. In the meantime, Reisman and his unorthodox methods in war game maneuvers irritate Colonel Breed (Robert Ryan) as well as Generals Worden and Denton (Robert Webber). "The Dirty Dozen" (nicknamed for the period they are deprived of soap and water) are dropped by parachute into France and reach the chateau. The sabotage mission is almost ruined when Maggott goes crazy, but he is shot by his comrades and the battle royal begins. Victory is insured when the Allies blow the chateau to smithereens. Three of the deadly assault team survive: Wladislaw, Posey, and Sawyer. Later General Worden informs Reisman that the once-criminals killed in combat are now recorded as American soldiers who died honorably in wartime.

THE DIRTY DOZEN, which the public and critics alike endorsed as one of the most violent of violent war pictures, grossed $20,300,000 in domestic film rentals, ranking as 1967's top ranking film and #6 in MGM's all-time box-office winners. John Poyner's explosive sound effects received an Academy Award.

Having combined a cache of genre clichés with a new format in which the real enemy is the military establishment, THE DIRTY DOZEN inspired a lot of imitators, including four, to date, television sequels and a teleseries.

DIRTY DOZEN: THE NEXT MISSION (1985) found Lee Marvin, Ernest Borgnine, and Richard Jaeckel recreating their original big screen roles, as respectively, Major Reisman, General Worden, and MP Sergeant Bowren. Their mission impossible this time around was to stop an assassination plot against Hitler. It was now eighteen years later and the genre forerunner had become trite, especially with its diluted made-for-television production values. However, it enjoyed high audience viewership, and two years later DIRTY DOZEN: THE DEADLY MISSION (1987) appeared. This time Telly Savalas, who had played the bigoted psychopath in the film original, was now elevated to Major Wright, who with the help of his criminal misfit "gang" destroys a cache of poison gas in Nazi-occupied France. In the next outing, THE DIRTY DOZEN: THE FATAL MISSION (1988), filmed in Yugoslavia as was #3, the filmmakers tried a few formula variations. One of the dirty dozen is a woman (Heather Thomas) and there is a spy in their midst. The team's unrealistic objective this time is to destroy a trainload of high-ranking Nazis heading to Istanbul on the Orient Express to establish the Fourth Reich. DIRTY DOZEN: THE SERIES: DANKO'S DOZEN (1988) finds the fearsome group out to destroy a Nazi radar installation located near a children's hospital. Among the commandos is Dana Jankowski (Jamie Koss), who masquerades as a nun to help accomplish their task. Regarding the series, produced on location in Yugoslavia for Fox Television, Terry Atkinson (*Los Angeles Times*) enthused, ". . . The show does throw some of its own nice touches in with the clichés, notably a wry, self-kidding side to Danko—making him considerably less stern than the equivalent role played by Lee Marvin in the picture." *Daily Variety* confirmed that "The American commandos still have life in them, and now, they have the verve of youthfulness; it could easily work to the advantage of the series. . . ." The syndicated series lasted one season.

A DOG OF THE REGIMENT (Warner Bros., 1927) 45 mins.
   Director, Ross Lederman; based on the story by Albert S. Howson; screenplay, Charles R. Condon; assistant director, Joe Barry; camera, Edward Du Par; editor, Clarence Kolster.
   Rin-Tin-Tin (Rinty); Dorothy Gulliver (Marie von Waldorf); Tom Gallery (Richard Harrison); John Peters (Eric von Hager).
   A minor offshoot of the war melodrama, allegedly based on the real-life Rin-Tin-Tin.
   American lawyer Richard Harrison (Tom Gallery), in Germany to settle an estate, opposes attorney Eric von Hager (John Peters) and wins the respect of Marie von Waldorf (Dorothy Gulliver) and her dog Rinty (Rin-Tin-Tin). The First World War breaks out and Richard, now a pilot, is downed behind enemy lines. Rinty pulls him from the wreckage, but he is captured by Eric. Richard and Rinty later escape and after the war reunite with Marie.
   Of this entry in Warner Bros.'s popular dog star series, *Variety* noted, "It is impossible to present naturalism in a picture featuring a dog of pretended human intelligence, but a good attempt has been made here."

DOUGH BOYS (Metro-Goldwyn-Mayer, 1930) 80 mins.
   Director, Edward Sedgwick; story, Al Boasberg, Sidney Lazarus; screenplay, Richard Schayer; dialogue, Boasberg, Schayer; art director, Cedric Gibbons; wardrobe, Vivian Baer; choreography, Sammy Lee; songs: Sedgwick, Howard Johnson, and Joseph Meyer; sound, Karl E. Zint, Douglas Shearer; camera, Leonard Smith; editor, William Le Vanway.
   Buster Keaton (Elmer Stuyvesant); Sally Eilers (Mary); Cliff Edwards (Nescopeck); Edward Brophy (Sergeant Brophy); Victor Potel (Svedenburg); Arnold Korff (Gustave); Frank Mayo (Captain Scott); Pitzy Katz (Abie Cohn); William Steele (Lieutenant Randolph); Sidney Bracy (Recruiter).
   Originally reviewed as THE BIG SHOT, DOUGH BOYS is Buster Keaton's first sound feature. It is a funny movie, but lacks

the impact that Charles Chaplin's SHOULDER ARMS (1918), q.v., had made.

In the midst of a recruitment parade for World War I, rich Elmer Stuyvesant (Buster Keaton) gets himself drafted into the Army and soon finds himself overseas in the trenches, with Sergeant Brophy (Edward Brophy) his tough supervising officer. When not romancing canteen worker Mary (Sally Eilers) he becomes a hero by accident at the front. Back home he forms a new business with his army buddies and their once martinet sergeant is now the company porter.

A Spanish-language version of DOUGH BOYS, entitled DE FRENTE, MARCHEN! was issued in the spring of 1931 with Conchita Montenegra as Keaton's co-star. *Variety* quipped that it ". . . is quite bad enough to start another Spanish-American war."

British release title: FORWARD MARCH.

DUNKIRK (Metro-Goldwyn-Mayer, 1958) 135 mins.

Producer, Michael Balcon; director, Leslie Norman; based on

Sally Eilers, Edward Brophy, and Buster Keaton in DOUGH BOYS (1930).

the novel *The Big Pick-Up* by Elleston Trevor and the book *Dunkirk* by Lieutenant Colonel Ewan Butler; screenplay, David Divine, W. P. Lipscomb; art director, Jim Morahan; music, Malcolm Arnold; music director, Dock Mathieson; camera, Paul Beeson; editor, Gordon Stone.

John Mills (Corporal Binns); Robert Urquhart (Mike); Ray Jackson (Barlow); Meredith Edwards (Dave Bellman); Anthony Nicholls (Military Spokesman); Bernard Lee (Charles Foreman); Michael Shillo (Jouvet); Richard Attenborough (Holden); Sean Barrett (Frankie); Victor Maddern (Merchant Seaman); Maxine Audley (Diana Foreman); Bud Flanagan and Chesney Allen (Themselves); Kenneth Cope (Lieutenant Lumpkin); Denys Graham (Fraser); Ronald Hines (Miles); Ronald Curran (Harper); Patricia Plunkett (Grace Holden); Rodney Diak (Pannet); Eddie Byrne (Commander); Lionel Jeffries (Colonel); Warwick Ashton (Battery Sergeant Major); Peter Halliday (Battery Major); Cyril Raymond (Viscount Gort); Nicholas Hannen (Vice Admiral Ramsey); Michael Gwynn (Commander); Fred Griffiths (Old Sweet); Christopher Rhodes (Sergeant on Beach); John Horsley (Padre); Patrick Allen (Sergeant); Joss Ambler, Frederick Piper (Boat-Owning Volunteers); and: Michael Bates, Bernard Cribbins, Barry Foster, Dan Gressy, Lloyd Lamble, Harry Landis, John Welsh, William Squire.

". . . DUNKIRK is a splendid near-documentary which just fails to reach magnificence. . . . The film throughout is deliberately underplayed, with no false heroics and with dialog which has an almost clinical authenticity. . . . It is an a absorbing rather than an emotion-stirring film" (*Variety*).

Between May 27 and June 4, 1940, some 338,000 military personnel were removed from the beaches of Dunkirk, France, using 1,200 Allied civilian and naval crafts. The event was known as Operation Dynamo. In the midst of defeat, the Allies created a near miracle which proved a great moral boost, particularly in unifying Britain to meet the hellish war years ahead.

DUNKIRK is told through the eyes of three individuals and how they react to and during the Dunkirk evacuation. Perceptive cockney Corporal Binns (John Mills) and a few of his men are separated from the rest of their unit and must reach safety on their own. Acid newspaper reporter Charles Foreman (Bernard Lee) is a loner filled with cynicism. It is he who says, "What a shambles we've made of this whole rotten business." Ironically it is Foreman who dies in the course of helping with the mammoth rescue operation. Civilian Holden (Richard Attenborough) is a complacent soul who is shocked into consciousness by the dramatic events around him. An epilogue voice at the end states that Dunkirk was "a great miracle." "No longer were there fighting men and civilians, there were only people. A nation had been made whole."

DUNKIRK was among the final three film releases for British Ealing Studios which had begun twenty years earlier.

THE EAGLE AND THE HAWK (Paramount, 1933) 72 mins.

Director, Stuart Walker; associate director, Mitchell Leisen; story, John Monk Saunders; screenplay, Bogart Rogers, Seton I. Miller; camera, Harry Fischbeck.

Fredric March (Jerry Young); Cary Grant (Henry Crocker); Jack Oakie (Mike Richards); Carole Lombard (The Beautiful Lady); Sir Guy Standing (Major Dunham); Forrester Harvey (Hogan); Kenneth Howell (John Stevens); Leyland Hodgson (Kinsford); Virginia Hammond (Lady Erskine); Crauford Kent (General); Douglas Scott (Tommy Erskine); Robert Manning (Voss); Adrienne D'Ambricourt (Fifi); Jacques Jou-Jerville (French General's Aide); Russell Scott (Flight Sergeant); Paul Cremonesi (French General); Yorke Sherwood (Taxi Driver); Lane Chandler, Dennis O'Keefe (Flyers); Olaf Hytten (Story-Telling Officer); Edgar C. Anderson, Garland Lincoln (Stunt Flyers).

Passed off as a near-programmer at the time of release, THE EAGLE AND THE HAWK has gained stature over the years. While its dramatics are irritatingly overdone at times, its cynical overtone remains powerful. Because its story was conceived by prolific John Monk Saunders (WINGS) and the screenplay was by Seton I. Miller (DAWN PATROL), the film has many derivative elements from each of these features.*

It is World War I and the British are taking a shellacking in the air. Jerry Young (Fredric March), the bold leader of a British flying squadron, has seen too much death in the skies and is cracking under the strain. Henry Crocker (Cary Grant) arrives at the post and is assigned to be Young's observer/gunner, occupying the rear cockpit of the two-man plane. Crocker is resentful that he is not a pilot and blames Henry for keeping him back. When more of the squadron dies in aerial combat, the strain becomes too much for Young. He is forced to take a ten-day leave, and back in England he meets a "Beautiful Lady" (Carole Lombard) who temporarily renews his

---

*Footage from WINGS (1927), q.v., is used as well as a crash sequence from LILAC TIME (1928), q.v. It is believed that some of the P-1 plane footage is from THE DAWN PATROL (1930), q.v.

spark of life. Meanwhile Crocker uses Young's absence to fly a reckless mission himself, during which fun-loving Mike Richards (Jack Oakie) is killed. Young is distraught at this news. He reaches the breaking point when he shoots down a famed German ace in a dogfight, only to learn shortly thereafter that his adversary was a mere boy. After getting drunk and delivering a hysterical anti-war plea to his fellow pilots denouncing the so-called glories of war, Young leaves them and commits suicide. Rather than have his friend be labeled a coward, Crocker takes his lifeless friend on a final mission. Once in the air, he turns the machine guns on Young's body, so it will appear that he died bravely in combat. Young is given a hero's funeral as the somber Crocker looks on.

EAGLE SQUADRON (Universal, 1942) 105 mins.

Producer, Walter Wanger; director, Arthur Lubin; based on the story by C. S. Forester; screenplay, Norman Reilly Raine; foreword by Quentin Reynolds; art directors, Jack Otterson, Alexander Golitzen; music, Frank Skinner; music director, Charles Previn; technical adviser, Flight Officer John M. Hill (Royal Air Force); assistant director, Gil Vailee; dialogue director, Joan Hathaway; special effects, John Fulton; camera, Stanley Cortez; editor, Philip Kahn.

Robert Stack (Chuck Brewer); Diana Barrymore (Anne Partridge); John Loder (Paddy Carson); Eddie Albert (Leckie); Nigel Bruce (McKinnon); Leif Erikson (Johnny Coe); Edgar Barrier (Wadislaw Borowsky); Jon Hall (Hank Starr); Evelyn Ankers (Nancy Mitchell); Isobel Elsom (Dame Elizabeth Whitby); Gladys Cooper (Aunt Emmeline); Alan Hale, Jr. (Olesen); Don Porter (Ramsey); Edmund Glover (Meeker); Stanley Smith (Bell); Howard Banks (Barker); Richard Crane (Griffith); Clarence Straight (Chandler); Richard Davies (White); Harold Landon (Welch); Todd Karns (Meyers); Charles King, Jr. (Chubby); Donald Stuart (Hoskins); Frederick Worlock (Grenfall); Stanley Ridges (Air Minister); Robert Warwick (Bullock); Richard Fraser (Lieutenant Jefferys); Gavin Muir (Major Severn); Harold de Becker (Private Owen); Rhys Williams (Sergeant Johns); Paul Cavanagh (Sir James Partridge); Gene Reynolds (The Kid); Alan Napier (Black Watch Officer); Jill Esmond (Phyllis); Queenie Leonard (Bridget); Olaf Hytten (Day Controller); Ian Wolfe (Sir Charles Porter); Carl Harbord (Lubbock); Charles Irwin (Sir Benjamin Trask); Mary Carr (A Mother); Simon Olivier (Georgie); William Severn (Billy); Linda Bieber (Little Girl); Peggy Ann Garner (Child); Quentin Reynolds (Narrator); Eugene Tobin, Gregory "Gus" Daymond, C.

W. McColpion, Chesley Peterson, Bill Geiger (Men of #71 Eagle Squadron).

EAGLE SQUADRON opens with a solemn foreword spoken by famed war correspondent Quentin Reynolds: "This is the story of some of our countrymen who did not wait to be stabbed in the back. These boys . . . knew that the security of our country must depend upon our dominating and controlling the air."

Three Americans, Chuck Brewer (Robert Stack), Leckie (Eddie Albert), and Johnny Coe (Leif Erickson), join the #71 (Eagle) Squadron (the all-American branch) of the Royal Air Force in the fall of 1941. Brewer, a former California test pilot, has difficulty understanding the staid British personality, that emotion-hiding reserve which makes them seem cold and heartless, even to death. Having learned to be aggressive combat pilots, the three join their squadron in air attacks on the Germans both over the Channel and in France. It is Coe who breaks the rules, by leaving formation, in an offensive sweep on the Continent. In the midst of his solo attack on an ammunitions truck his plane is shot down and he dies. When the RAF learns that the Germans have a secret new weapon (a detection device that permits pilots to see aircraft in any type of weather or light), Chuck Brewer joins a sea/land commando assault into France to steal one of the new craft. He does so, and after downing several pursuing German planes, returns to home base. He and his squadron listen to a patriotic speech devoted to the Allies' ultimate victory.

When not sidetracked by a sluggish romantic story between Robert Stack and screen newcomer Diane Barrymore (as an understanding British girl), EAGLE SQUADRON is filled with exciting combat footage, much of it provided by the British government. It is a very contrived but effective salute to the Americans fighting against the Germans in the months (and years) before the Pearl Harbor attack brought America into World War II.

One aspect of this production that backfired was its London premiere in July 1941. According to James H. Farmer in *Celluloid Wings* (1984), the Eagle Squadron members in attendance were shocked by what appeared on the screen. "The film," said one of their number, "was so far-fetched from actual combat . . . it was embarrassing." After that unnerving episode, the Eagle Squadron refused cooperation with the press, fearing its criticism could create ruptures in the harmony between the American and British fighter pilots in the Royal Air Force. Before the end of 1942, the three Eagle Squadrons would be incorporated into the United States Army Air Force Fourth Fighter Group.

EMILY *see*: THE AMERICANIZATION OF EMILY.

THE ENEMY BELOW (Twentieth Century-Fox, 1957) Color 98 mins.
Producer/director, Dick Powell; based on the novel by Commander D. A. Rayner; screenplay, Wendell Mayes; art directors, Lyle Wheeler, Albert Hogsett; set decorators, Walter Scott, Fay Babcock; wardrobe designer, Charles Le Maire; music, Leigh Harline; music conductor, Lionel Newman; orchestrator, Edward B. Powell; special effects, Walter Rossi; special camera effects. L. B. Abbott; camera, Harold Rosson; editor, Stuart Gilmore.

Robert Mitchum (Captain Murrell); Curt Jurgens (Von Stolberg); Al [David] Hedison (Lieutenant Ware); Theodore Bikel (Schwaffer); Russell Collins (Doctor); Kurt Kreuger (Von Holem); Frank Albertson (Chief Petty Officer Crain); Biff Elliott (Quartermaster); Alan Dexter (Mackason); Doug McClure (Ensign Merry); Jeff Daley (Corky); David Blair (Ellis); Joe Di Reda (Robbins); Ralph Manza (Lieutenant Bonelli); Ted Perritt (Messenger); Jimmy Bayes (Quiroga); Arthur La Ral (Kunz); Dan Tana, Dale Cummings, Roger Cornwall, Sasha Harden (German Sailors); Michael McHale, Joe Brooks (German Soldiers); Richard Elmore, Ronnie Rondell, Vincent Deadrick, Dan Nelson (American Sailors); Peter Dane (Andrews); Werner Reichow (Mueller); Robert Boon (Chief Engineer); Frank Obershall (Braun); David Post (Lewis); Lee J. Winters (Striker); Jack Kramer (Albert, the German Sailor); Robert Whiteside (Torpedo Petty Officer); Maurice Donner (Cook).

In assessing the structure and impact of this film *Variety* noted, ". . . Perhaps World War II is now safe and remote enough so that it can be viewed through slightly rose-tinted specs."

Just as aerial dogfights are won by pilots with razor-sharp reflexes and a wealth of tactical experience, so sea battles are really cat and mouse chess games between captains of opposing vessels. The victor is nearly always the best man at anticipating his adversary's next moves. Actor-turned-director Dick Powell amply proves this thesis in the sterling THE ENEMY BELOW, a gritty World War II sea chase which has the added dimension of being a superior character study of two top flight combatants who are excellent naval warfare strategists.

The first of the two foes is war-weary, ill Captain Murrell (Robert Mitchum) who has taken charge recently of the USS *Haines*, a destroyer escort. Not only must this veteran win the respect of his new crew, but he must fight a war which is draining his patriotism and inventiveness. His very worthy opponent is seasoned Unterboatenkommandant Von Stolberg (Curt Jurgens), the U-boat submarine captain whose two sons have died in the war and whose belief in Der Fuehrer and the glorious Third Reich has been nearly extinguished. The action is set in the Atlantic Ocean as the *Haines* detects the presence of Von Stolberg's sub, and Captain Murrell determines to sink the enemy no matter how long it takes. The pursuit continues mercilessly as the *Haines* drops depth charges, with the U-boat scurrying to and fro to avoid destruction. At one point, Von Stolberg sets his vessel on the ocean bottom (unmindful of the tremendous pressure that could rip the sub apart), playing possum. Later, having properly judged the *Haines* will do so, Von Stolberg fires torpedoes as the Allied craft turns about, mortally wounding it. Murrell has one further ploy: a pretense that his disabled boat is totally finished. The sub then surfaces, only to be rammed by the American vessel. Murrell, who has remained with the *Haines* after ordering his men to abandon ship, sees Von Stolberg try to save his gravely wounded second-in-command (Theodore Bikel). He goes to his adversary's aid and the trio make it into the water before a timed bomb explodes aboard the sub. The two survivors (Murrell and Von Stolberg) are picked up by an American ship and, once aboard, the two civilized adversaries commend one another for their maritime cunning.

During one lull in the hunt, Captain Murrell admits to a junior officer, "I don't want to know the man I am trying to destroy." This scene says much about the dehumanization of warfare on many levels.

THE ENEMY BELOW won an Academy Award for Best Special Effects.

ENOLA GAY (NBC-TV, 11/23/80) Color 150 mins.

Executive producers, Frank R. Levy, Mike Wise, Richard S. Reisberg; producers, Stanley Kallis, Ted Zachary; director, David Lowell Rich; based on the book by Gordon Thomas, Max Morgan Witts; teleplay, James Poe, Millard Kaufman; art directors, Jack DeShields, John Cartwright; music, Maurice Jarre; camera, Robert L. Morrison; aerial camera, Clay Lacey; editor, Byron Chudnow.

Billy Crystal (Lieutenant Jake Beser); Kim Darby (Lucy Tibbets); Patrick Duffy (Colonel Paul Tibbets); Gary Frank (Major Tom Ferebee); Gregory Harrison (Captain Bob Lewis); Stephen Macht (Major William "Bud" Uanna); Walter Olkewicz (Sergeant Shug Crawford); Robert Pine (Captain William "Deke" Parsons); James Shigeta (Field Marshal Abebata); Robert Walden (J. Robert Oppenheimer); Richard Venture (Alexander Sachs); Richard Herd (General Groves); Henry Wilcoxon (Secretary of War Stimson); Stephen Roberts (President Franklin D. Roosevelt); Michael Tucci

(Captain Claude Eatherly); Stephen Burleigh (Theodore Van Kirk); Than Wyenn (General Curtis LeMay); James Saito (Lieutenant Tatsuo Yamato); Marion Yue (Aya); Bill Morey (General George Marshall); John Fujioka (General Nagain); and: Gary Mike Casper, Michael Currite, Peter Fox, Stanley Grover, Nancy Hamilton, Tony Lucatorto, Devon Nuir.

Eighteen years after MGM's glossy and empty ABOVE AND BEYOND, q.v., ENOLA GAY, subtitled THE MEN, THE MISSION, THE ATOMIC BOMB, debuted. Like its predecessor it depicted the step-by-step build-up to the dropping of the atomic bomb on Hiroshima in 1945. Despite the tremendous promotional build-up given this telefeature, it was strikingly average.

Colonel Paul Tibbets (Patrick Duffy) is the U.S. pilot charged with the fateful mission, and the story interweaves the pressures of the task and its effect on Tibbets' domestic life with his patient spouse (Kim Darby). The most interesting casting in this study of the *Enola Gay* bomber plane crew is comedian Billy Crystal as Lieutenant Jake Beser, the Army Air Force radar officer aboard.

This made-for-television feature is dedicated "to the memory of James Poe," who died before completing the teleplay.

ESCAPE FROM BATAAN *see*: THE LONGEST HUNDRED MILES.

ESCAPE TO MINDANAO (Universal TV/NBC-TV, 12/7/68) Color 100 mins.

Producer, Jack Lewood; director, Don McDougall; story, Orville H. Hampton; teleplay, Harold Livingston; art director, Napoleon Enriquez; costume designer, Grady Hunt; music, Lyn Murray; camera, Ray Flin; editor, Richard G. Wray.

George Maharis (Joe Walden); Nehemiah Persoff (Captain Kramer); James Shigeta (Lieutenant Takahashi); Ronald Remy (Lieutenant Parang); Willi Koopman (Anna Kramer); Vic Diaz (Sokuri); Eddie Arenas (Captain Aquino); Gil Deleon (Zairin); Andres Centenera (Viray); Vic Uematsu (Sergeant Major).

An unconvincing early made-for-television entry in which two American prisoners-of-war break free from a Japanese prison compound with an enemy decoder and head for freedom with the "aid" of a grasping Dutch sea captain (Nehemiah Persoff).

EYE OF THE EAGLE (Concorde, 1986) Color 82 mins.

Producer/director, Cirio H. Santiago; story, Catherine Santiago; screenplay, Joseph Zucchero, Nigel Hogge; production designer, Joe Mari Avellano; music director, Marita Manuel; second unit directors, Avellano, Bobby Santiago; stunt coordinator, Fred

Espiana; sound, Do Bulatano; camera, Ricardo Remias; editor, Gervacio Santos.

Brett Clark (Sergeant Rick Stratton); Robert Patrick (Johnny Ransom); Ed Crick (Sergeant Rattner); William Steis (Captain Carter); Cec Verell (Chris Chandler); Ray Malonzo (Corporal Willy Leung); Mike Monty (Colonel Stark); Vic Diaz (Colonel Trang); Henry Strzalkowski (Colonel Watkins); David Light (Sergeant Maddox).

The intriguing but undeveloped premise of this low-budget feature shot in the Philippines is that G.I.s in Vietnam who were categorized as missing-in-action or prisoners-of-war have actually come together to form a death squadron operating against the Viet Cong. Sergeant Rattner (Ed Crick) is their leader and among their number is Sergeant Rick Stratton (Brett Clark), who has a score to settle with the squad's commander.

The lackluster film was shot in 1986 and was generally not reviewed until its home casette release in early 1988. "Pic consists mainly of mindless machine gun battles, in which shooting and explosions are boring and out of context" (*Variety*).

FIGHTER ATTACK (Allied Artists, 1953) Color 80 mins.

Producer, William Calihan, Jr.; director, Lesley Selander; screenplay, Simon Wincelberg; music, Marlin Skiles; song, Skiles and Sol Meyer; camera, Harry Neumann; editors, Stanley Rabjohn, Lester A. Swanson.

Sterling Hayden (Steve); J. Carrol Naish (Bruno); Joy Page (Nina); Kenneth Tobey (George); Anthony Caruso (Aldo); Frank DeKova (Benedetto); Paul Fierro (Don Gaetano); Maurice Jara (Ettore); Tony Dante (Mario); David Leonard (Father Puola); James Flavin (Colonel Allison); Harry Lauter (Lieutenant Duncan); John Fontaine (Lieutenant Gross); David Bond (Priest); Louis Lettieri (Boy); and: Joel Marston.

FIGHTER ATTACK owes a great deal to Ernest Hemingway's novel *For Whom the Bell Tolls*, which was filmed by Paramount in 1943. Unlike that earlier work, this far lower-budget entry is a direct war adventure in which the leading character is a military officer stuck behind enemy lines.

Steve (Sterling Hayden), part of the U.S. Air Force contingent based in 1944 Corsica, is charged with blasting out a Nazi supply dump. During one air mission his plane is shot down and he parachutes to safety. Nina (Joy Page) of the underground takes him to her mountain hideout where Bruno (J. Carrol Naish) is the guerrilla leader. Before long, the group zeros in on the objective and with the assistance of Steve's flyer pals, the dump is destroyed.

FIGHTER SQUADRON (Warner Bros., 1948) Color 96 mins.
    Producer, Seton I. Miller; director, Raoul Walsh; screenplay, Miller, Martin Rackin; art director, Ted Smith; set decorator, Lyle B. Reifsnider; makeup, Perc Westmore, Norman Pringle; music, Max Steiner; music director, Ray Heindorf; technical adviser, Major Joseph Perry (U.S. Air Force); assistant director, Russell Saunders; sound, Leslie G. Hewett; special effects, John Olden, Roy Davidson, H. F. Koenekamp; camera, Wilfred M. Cline; editor, Chris Nyby.
    Edmond O'Brien (Major Ed Hardin); Robert Stack (Captain Stu Hamilton); John Rodney (Colonel Bill Brickley); Tom D'Andrea (Sergeant Dolan); Henry Hull (Brigadier General Mike McCready); James Holden (Tennessee); Walter Reed (Captain Duke Chappell); Shepperd Strudwick (Brigadier General M. Gilbert); Arthur Space (Major Sanford); Jack Larson (Shorty); William McLean (Wilbur); Mickey McCardle (Jacobs); George Backus, Joel Allen (Sentries); Gilchrist Stuart, Elliott Dare, Guy Kingsford (British Photographers); Bill Cabanne (Control Tower Operator); Robert Manning (Bomber Pilot); John Morgan (Gunner); Dick Paxton (Turret Gunner); George Adrian (German Pilot); Harry McKim (Ball Turret Gunner); Patricia Northrop (Blonde Girl); John McGuire (Major Duncan); Rock Hudson, Don Phillips (Lieutenants); Jack Grant (Projectionist); Carl Harbaugh (Cockney); Willy Wickerhauser, Geza Remy (German Pilots); Charles Lind (Beagle Operator); Jeff Richards (Captain); William Yetter, Jr., John Royce (German Radio Operators); Hallen Hill (Old Lady); Jean Fenwick (Lady Woodbine).
    "All (or most all) of the clichés that one has ever heard (or seen in the movies) about the brave fellows who zoomed and strafed in the boundless blue and then spent their evenings drinking, are in this rowdy film which is, rather significantly, the first of a new crop of war films" (Bosley Crowther, *New York Times*).
    Directed by Raoul Walsh, an experienced hand at war films (WHAT PRICE GLORY?, OBJECTIVE, BURMA!, qq.v.) and written/produced by Seton I. Miller (of THE DAWN PATROL acclaim), this feature was a lengthy 63 days in production. It has many elements of COMMAND DECISION, q.v., then still playing on Broadway and the film version of which would not be released until several weeks after FIGHTER SQUADRON debuted.
    Major Ed Hardin (Edmond O'Brien), a Flying Tiger veteran, is part of the Air Force hammering away at the enemy in 1943-44, during the pre-D-Day buildup. He is one of the undisciplined "Hot Rocks" fighting the deadly war game both in the air against the

Germans and on the ground against his own superior officers—the overworked, war-weary military brass (Henry Hull, Shepperd Strudwick). It is Hardin's flippant contention that using more unorthodox flight procedures will put the odds of survival and success more in their favor. During the D-Day invasion, Hardin's luck runs out; he is shot down and later eulogized by his men, including his protegé/successor, Captain Stu Hamilton (Robert Stack). Also on hand are amorous Sergeant Dolan (Tom D'Andrea); Shorty (Jack Larson), who gets his first taste of battle action; and Tennessee (James Holden), the hillbilly recruit. Making his screen debut is Rock Hudson, seen extremely briefly as a fighter pilot.

THE FIGHTING SEABEES (Republic, 1944) 100 mins.*
    Executive producer, Herbert J. Yates; associate producer, Albert J. Cohen; director, Edward Ludwig; story, Borden Chase; screenplay, Chase, Aeneas MacKenzie; art director, Duncan Cramer; set decorator, Otto Siegel; assistant director, Phil Ford; music, Walter Scharf; song, Peter DeRose and Sam M. Lewis; technical advisers, Lieutenant Commander Hubert Hunter, Lieutenant Commander William A. McManus; special effects, Theodore Lydecker, Howard Lydecker; camera, William Bradford; editor, Richard Van Enger.
    John Wayne (Wedge Donovan); Susan Hayward (Constance Chesley); Dennis O'Keefe (Lieutenant Commander Robert Yarrow); William Frawley (Eddie Powers); Leonid Kinskey (Johnny Novasky); J. M. Kerrigan (Sawyer Collins); Grant Withers (Whanger Spreckles); Paul Fix (Ding Jacobs); Ben Welden (Yump Lumkin); William Forrest (Lieutenant Kerrick); Addison Richards (Captain Joyce); Jay Norris (Joe Brick); Duncan Renaldo (Juan); Al Murphy, Roy Barcroft, Abdullah Abbas, Charles Sullivan (Men); Chief Thundercloud (Indian); William Hall (Swede); Jean Fenwick (Secretary to Captain Joyce); LeRoy Mason (Jonesey); Adele Mara (Twinkles Tucker); Forbes Murray (Navy Surgeon); Bud Geary (Workman); Ben Taggart (Aircraft Carrier Captain); Hal Taliaferro (Lieutenant Commander Hood); Crane Whitley (Lieutenant Commander Hunter).
    This is one of those rousing 1940s feature films that led the American public to "believe" that John Wayne almost won the Second World War single-handedly. While ostensibly a depiction of the forming of the Seabees (the Construction Battalions or C.B.s) it is a dynamic adventure story of men fighting for what they

---

*Computerized color version now available.

believe. Diminishing the picture's message is the presence of red-haired Susan Hayward as the apex of a contrived love triangle.

Wedge Donovan (John Wayne) and his construction crew are employed by the Navy on a remote Pacific island building an airstrip and fortifications. Their liaison is Naval Lieutenant Commander Robert Yarrow (Dennis O'Keefe). Also on hand is news correspondent Constance Chesley (Susan Hayward); she is adored by Yarrow, but she loves the pugnacious Donovan. The Japanese invade the isle and Donovan, angered at seeing his unarmed civilian workers mowed down by strafing Japanese planes, arms his men and they go into combat with the enemy land troops using their trucks, or any other vehicle at hand. Not only are Donovan's men massacred by their more professional opponents, but his interference messes up Yarrow's carefully planned battle strategy. While searching for Donovan on the battlefield, Constance is badly wounded by a Japanese soldier "playing" dead. She recovers in surgery and is convinced now that she can gain wildcat Donovan's affections. Donovan, in the meantime, is more concerned with forming a branch of the Armed Forces for the construction workers, and he and Yarrow fly to Washington to get the new service underway. Now trained, garbed, and armed as soldiers, the Seabees are dispatched to another Pacific atoll, known as X-371. They start building an airstrip but are soon decimated by the surrounding Japanese. The enraged Donovan leads a commando raid against the enemy, killing several in hand-to-hand combat, and he mows down a whole bunch more with a machine gun. To save Yarrow and his contingent from annihilation, Donovan drives a bulldozer stacked with dynamite into an oil tank, blasting both the enemy and himself. Back in the States he is given a posthumous citation while the now reunited Constance and Yarrow look on contentedly, knowing that Donovan died for his country and to help establish the Seabees. (Their creed is: "We build for fighters. We fight for what we build.")

Because for so much of the film Donovan is a rebel hothead, unmindful of rules and regulations, THE FIGHTING SEABEES pushes the traditional combat film format aside and makes its own rules. There is no politeness or understanding of a bigger picture in Donovan's mentality. This is a donnybrook between him and "Tojo and his bug-eyed pals." Even Yarrow, the more civilized, disciplined Naval man, admits, "We're not fighting men anymore, we're fighting animals." After Donovan pushes a Japanese tank over a cliff with a bulldozer, he shouts gleefully, "That'll teach 'em to monkey with construction men."

Susan Hayward, Dennis O'Keefe, and Ernest Golm in THE FIGHTING SEA-
BEES (1944).

Walter Scharf's rousing score for THE FIGHTING SEABEES
was Oscar-nominated, and the specially composed "The Song of the
Seabees" (by Peter DeRose and Sam M. Lewis) is exhilarating.

THE FIGHTING 69TH (Warner Bros., 1940) 90 mins.*
    Executive producer, Jack L. Warner; producer, Hal B. Wallis;
associate producer, Louis F. Edelman; director, William Keighley;
screenplay, Norman Reilly Raine, Fred Niblo, Jr., Dean Franklin;
art director, Ted Smith; makeup, Perc Westmore; technical advisers, Captain John T. Prout, Mark White; music, Adolph Deutsch;
orchestrator, Hugo Friedhofer; music director, Leo F. Forbstein;
special effects, Byron Haskin, Rex Wimpy; sound, Charles Lang;
camera, Tony Gaudio; editor, Owen Marks.

_____

*Computerized color version now available.

James Cagney (Jerry Plunkett); Pat O'Brien (Father Francis P. Duffy); George Brent (Major Wild Bill Donovan); Jeffrey Lynn (Joyce Kilmer); Alan Hale (Sergeant "Big Mike" Wynn); Frank McHugh ("Crepe Hanger" Burke); Dennis Morgan (Lieutenant Ames); Dick Foran (Lieutenant "Long John" Wynn); William Lundigan (Timmy Wynn); Guinn "Big Boy" Williams (Paddy Dolan); Henry O'Neill (The Colonel); John Litel (Captain Mangan); Sammy Cohen (Mike Murphy [Moskowitz]); Harvey Stephens (Major Anderson); De Wolf [William] Hopper (Private Turner); Tom Dugan (Private McManus); George Reeves (Jack O'Keefe); John Ridgely (Moran); Charles Trowbridge (Chaplain Holmes); Frank Wilcox (Lieutenant Norman); Herbert [Guy] Anderson (Casey); J. Anthony Hughes (Healey); Frank Mayo (Captain Bootz); John Harron (Carroll); George Kilgen (Ryan); Richard Clayton (Tierney); Edward Dew (Regan); Wilfred Lucas, Joseph Crehan, Emmett Vogan (Doctors); Frank Sully (Sergeant); James Flavin (Supply Sergeant); George O'Hanlon (Eddie); Jack Perrin (Major); Trevor Bardette, John Arledge, Frank Melton, Edmund Glover (Alabama Men); Edgar Edwards (Engineer Officer); Frank Faylen (Engineer Sergeant); Arno Frey, Roland Varno (German Officers); Robert Layne Ireland (Heferman); Elmo Murray (O'Brien); Jacques Lory (Waiter); Frank Coghlan, Jr. (Jimmy); Jack Boyle, Jr. (Chuck); Sol Gorss, Byron Nelson (Soldiers); and: Eddie Acuff, Nat Carr, Creighton Hale, Jack Mower, Benny Rubin, Jack Wise.

In 1940 many Americans realized that the U.S. could not stay out of the burgeoning World War II for long. As part of this subtle "Be Prepared" and "Pro Patriotism" campaign, Hollywood turned out government-endorsed feature films which succeeded in rousing sentiment for the (pending) war cause.

Unlike the relatively few features of the 1920s and 1930s such as THE BIG PARADE (1925), q.v., ALL QUIET ON THE WESTERN FRONT (1930), q.v., and THE DAWN PATROL (1930, 1938), q.v., which regarded the First World War as a nihilistic catastrophe that must not be repeated, THE FIGHTING 69TH is motivated entirely differently. It is a paean to the Big War. No mention is made that it was supposed to be "The war to end all wars." After all, the United States was gearing up for its inevitable entry into World War II.

The prologue of THE FIGHTING 69th states "In gratitude to all those millions of men who served and fought in the fighting forces of the United States in the last war . . . to the 69th New York Regiment (165th Infantry A.E.F.) which was the average, yet the epitome, of our national courage . . . and to the memory of Father Francis P. Duffy (1871-1932), a beloved Chaplain and a truly great humanitarian . . . Warner Bros. respectfully dedicates this picture."

The action opens at Camp Mills, New York in 1917 as a diverse crew of recruits (including a Jew) are absorbed into the famed all-Irish Regiment. Their leader is Major Wild Bill Donovan (George Brent), a seasoned soldier who knows how to fight a battle and to control his men; their chaplain is Father Francis P. Duffy (Pat O'Brien), a resourceful humanitarian who, although a man of the cloth, is a man's man and a friend to all. Included is Joyce Kilmer (Jeffrey Lynn), the company's famed poet and chronicler. Among the newcomers is pugnacious Jerry Plunkett (James Cagney), a street-tough young Brooklynite. He is the non-conformist who from the start cannot understand the need for regimentation, for teamwork, or for getting along with his fellow soldiers. He has no appreciation for the group's long military tradition. Plunkett's fainting when he is inoculated by the army medic is a foreshadowing that he suffers from that most unforgivable of diseases (in a patriotic film)—he has a cowardly streak.

Meanwhile, the true theme of THE FIGHTING 69th is slammed across to the audience. There is a huge battle royal between the men of The Fighting 69th ("an Irishman never needs a prayer in a fight") and those from the 4th Alabama. They had been enemies during the Civil War, but now, Donovan and Duffy stress, they must be unified. "You're in a common cause. . . . We're all one nation now, a team, the Rainbow Division," they're told over and over. And the men are reminded constantly that "No man has ever let the regiment down—remember that!"

As for what war is all about, Major Donovan intones solemnly, "War is a brutal business. That's why I've been so hard on the men." When he must send his men into certain death, he does not question the wisdom of the top command: "Orders are orders." His rationale is "Our is not to reason why, ours is to do and die." Father Duffy recites a prayer to express his feelings: "Oh father, they're so young and they know so little of life, nothing of all the bloody attacks to which they move, carrying the great sacrifice of their youth. Grant me the strength to keep them steadfast in faith and decency and courage and to the glory of God and their country in the bad times to come. And if in battle you see fit to gather them to your protecting arms thy will be done. Let them die like men, valiant and unafraid." For most of the men, going to France to fight the Krauts is more of a lark. "Quit crabbing," says one, "It's all part of the game." The blarney-laden Sergeant "Big Mike" Wynn (Alan

Hale) enthuses about the battlefield, "Tis a fine bit of a scrimmage."
The men have one motto: "Get the Krauts!"

Of all the recruits, Plunkett has the most difficult time
adjusting overseas. He had been a fearless hooligan back in New
York, but over here life in the trenches where you cannot always see
the enemy is driving him crazy. "I have never been afraid of
anything in my life before but this stuff, seeing what a bursting shell
can do to human flesh and blood, it's made me yella . . . yella."
Later Plunkett's carelessness with a flare causes the death of several
buddies, and still later he turns cowardly in battle. He is court-
martialed and sentenced to be shot. But during an enemy offensive,
Father Duffy frees him from the makeshift prison and suggests he
has two alternatives: find safety behind the battle lines, or go help
rescue his beleaguered fellow soldiers. Plunkett lurches into the
front lines and with the aid of "Big Mike," uses a stokes gun to blast
an opening in the enemy's lines so that the troops can push on to the
offensive. When a grenade lands in their trench, Plunkett falls on it
to save his teammates.

With Plunkett dying, Father Duffy appears to administer the
last rites. The wounded man says to the priest, "I've just been
talking to your boss."

> *Duffy:* You're not afraid, are you Jerry?
>
> *Plunkett:* No Father, not any more.

Plunkett dies and Big Mike, who had been scornful of Plunkett
from the first, admits, "From now on, whenever I hear the name of
Plunkett I'll snap to attention and salute." Through bravery,
Plunkett has redeemed himself. This is the true message of the
trend-setting THE FIGHTING 69th.

The film concludes with a rousing prayer dedication intoned by
Father Duffy as the American Expeditionary Force parades proudly
into Paris, and then the viewer sees close-ups of all the main
characters from the film marching by in a farewell roll call.
". . . [America's lost generation] accepted privation, wounds and
death that an ideal might live. Don't let it be forgotten, Father, amid
turmoil and angry passions when all worthwhile things seem swept
away. Let the tired eyes of a troubled world rise up and see the
shining citadel of which these young lives form the imperishable
stones. America, the citadel of peace. Peace forever more. This I beg
of you through Christ our Lord. Amen."

With its enthusiastic tribute to America, to the Irish, to the
Catholic, and most of all to the bravery that was (or should have
been), it is hard not to like THE FIGHTING 69th. It is full of

clichés and stereotypes, but it is a well-crafted production with just enough action scenes to keep most anyone's interest.

FIRST BLOOD see: RAMBO: FIRST BLOOD PART II.

FIRST TO FIGHT (Warner Bros., 1967) Color 97 mins.
Executive producer, William Conrad; director, Christian Nyby; screenplay, Gene L. Coon; art director, Art Loel; set decorator, Hal Overell; makeup supervisor, Gordon Bau; music, Fred Steiner; assistant director, Victor Vallejo; technical adviser, Fred A. Kraus (Major, U.S. Marine Corps, Retired); dialogue supervisor, Stacy Harris; sound, Robert B. Lee; camera, Harold Wellman; editor, George Rohrs.

Chad Everett (Marine Sergeant Jack Connell); Marilyn Devin (Peggy Sanford); Dean Jagger (Colonel Baseman); Bobby Troup (Lieutenant Overman); Claude Akins (Captain Mason); Gene Hackman (Sergeant Tweed); James Best (Sergeant Carnavan); Norman Alden (Sergeant Schmidtmer); Bobs Watson (Sergeant Maypole); Ken Swofford (O'Brien); Ray Reese (Hawkins); Garry Goodgion (Karl); Robert Austin (Adams); Clint Ritchie (Sergeant Slater); Stephen Roberts (President Franklin D. Roosevelt).

By the late 1960s this flag-waving type of World War II film seemed grossly out of place. *Time* magazine chided it for dragging up "every war cliché except the soldier from Brooklyn."

Marine Sergeant Jack Connell (Chad Everett) meets Marilyn Devin (Peggy Sanford) on a war bond selling tour. She agrees to wed him if he promises *not* to return to active duty, since she lost her last fiancé in the war. The guilt of being on the sidelines proves too much for Jack, and Peggy allows him to return to action. On his first mission he becomes immobilized, fearful of fighting. Eventually his courage returns and he bravely leads his men on a mission against a Japanese stronghold.

Much of the film's nostalgia occurs when Jack and Marilyn go to the movies and see CASABLANCA; and the film's theme song is used as a motif throughout the picture. Battle scenes for FIRST TO FIGHT were lensed at Camp Pendleton Marine Base (Oceanside, California) and in the San Fernando Valley (Los Angeles County, California) at Bell Ranch and Africa U.S.A.

FIXED BAYONETS! (Twentieth Century-Fox, 1951) 92 mins.
Producer, Jules Buck; director, Samuel Fuller; based on the novel by John Brophy; screenplay, Fuller; art directors, Lyle Wheeler, George Patrick; set decorators, Thomas Little, Fred J. Rhode; costumes, Charles Le Maire; makeup, Ben Nye; technical

adviser, Captain Raymond Harvey; music, Roy Webb; music director, Lionel Newman; orchestrator, Maurice de Packh; assistant director, Paul Melnick; special effects, Fred Sersen; camera, Lucien Ballard; editor, Nick De Maggio.

Richard Basehart (Corporal Denno); Gene Evans (Sergeant Rock); Michael O'Shea (Sergeant Lonergan); Richard Hylton (Wheeler); Craig Hill (Lieutenant Gibbs); Skip Homeier (Whitey); Henry Kulky (Vogl); Richard Monohan (Walowicz); Paul Richards (Ramirez); Tony Kent (Mainotes); Don Orlando (Borcellino); Patrick Fitzgibbon (Paddy); Neyle Morrow (Medic); George Wesley (Griff); Mel Pogue (Bulcheck); George Conrad (Zablocki); David Wolfson (Bigmouth); Buddy Thorpe (Husky Doggie); Al Negbo (Lean Doggie); Wyatt Ordung (Fitz); Pat Hogan (Jonesy); James Dean, John Doucette (G.I.s); and: Bill Hickman, Kayne Shew.

It is 1951 Korea and the midst of a snowy winter. A U.S. general decides, "Somebody's got to be left behind and get their bayonets wet." The strategy is that 15,000 GIs will retreat back to safer lines, while 48 men are left in position to confuse the North Koreans into thinking the regiment is still in position. Sergeant Rock (Gene Evans), Sergeant Lonergan (Michael O'Shea) and Lieutenant Gibbs (Craig Hill) are the men in charge of this last-stand mission. They know there's "Nothing dirtier than a rear guard action" and that they are being sacrificed for the greater good.

This is not like in World War I or II; here the Americans are coping with facing military defeat, with no real victory in sight. There is a different moral tone to the infantrymen's feelings about the Korean conflict. They question their reason for being so far from home. "They told me this was goin' to be a police action," one GI snarls. "So why didn't they send cops?" his pal asks.

The snipers' battle continues and slowly, one by one, each of the commanding officers of this "lost platoon" dies, with the next in rank assuming command. "Strip him of everything we can use. Roll him in a blanket and bury him . . . and mark it!" There is no time for mourning the dead. Eventually it is the bookish Corporal Denno's (Richard Basehart) turn to be in charge. It is he who goes into the no-man's land to drag back the fallen Sergeant Lonergan, only to find that he is dead. But the act of bravery has restored the sensitive corporal's courage and now Denno truly takes control of the surviving men. Eventually relief troops come into sight. Denno has learned an important lesson of wartime: "Ain't nobody goes out looking for responsibility. Sometimes you get it whether you're looking for it or not."

FIXED BAYONETS! was made on a low budget with the same drive and deliberate lack of slickness that filmmaker Samuel Fuller employed in his earlier THE STEEL HELMET (1951), q.v. Because it was released at the time of the extended Korean truce talks, it had a topicality that helped it at the box-office. This new entry, with its mythical overtones, intense character studies, and grim depiction of battle as a place of survival not glory, added much to Fuller's reputation as a prime chronicler of the war experience.

THE FLIGHT COMMANDER see: THE DAWN PATROL (1930).

FLY AWAY HOME (Warner Bros. TV/ABC-TV, 9/18/81) Color 100 mins.

Producer, Stirling Silliphant; associate producer, F. A. Miller; director, Paul Krasny; teleplay, Silliphant; art director, George B. Chan; music, Lee Holdridge; song, Silliphant and Johnny Stewart; camera, Isidore Mankofsky; editor, Donald R. Rode.

Bruce Boxleitner (Carl Danton); Tiana Alexandra (Mai); Michael Beck (Lieutenant Mark Wakefield); Randy Brooks (Shenandoah Brookford); Teri Copley (Sabrina); Brian Dennehy (Tim Arnold); Laura Johnson (Chickie Wakefield); Lynne Moody (Mercy); Edward Winters (Lieutenant Colonel Hannibal Pace); Olivia Cole (Sarah Brookford); Louis Giambalvo (Vogel); Michael Alldredge (Jed Holston); Kieu Chinh (Anh); Barry Jenner (Sergeant Downs); Michael Fairman (Hap Andrews); Keye Luke (Duc); Duc Juy (Linh); Wayne Heffley (Maloney); John Berwick (Captain in District 8).

Long before ABC-TV's "Tour of Duty" in 1987 proved that a weekly teleseries about the Vietnam War was viable "entertainment," Academy Award-winning screenwriter Stirling Silliphant wrote and produced this very ambitious pilot film for a potential series. It focused on a combat cameraman (Bruce Boxleitner) in 1968 Vietnam, with Brian Dennehy as his tough bureau chief boss and Tiana Alexandra (Mrs. Silliphant) as the love interest. Because the dramatics were too contrived and the public was not ready to deal on a weekly basis with the defeat (and dishonor) of Vietnam, the series never materialized.

FLYING FORTRESS (Warner Bros., 1942) 110 mins.

Producer, Max Milner; director, Walter Forde; story, Brock Williams; screenplay, Gordon Wellesley, Edward Dryhurst, Williams; art director, Norman Arnold; music director, Jack Beaner;

Bruce Boxleitner in FLY AWAY HOME (1981).

special effects, Henry Harris, George E. Blackwell; camera, Basil
Emmott, Gus Drisse.

Richard Greene (Jim Spence, Jr.); Carla Lehmann (Sydney
Kelly); Betty Stockfield (Lady Deborah Ottershaw); Donald Stew-
art (Sky Kelly); Charles Heslop (Harrington); Sydney King (Lord
Ottershaw); Basil Radford (Captain Wilkenson); Joss Ambler
(Sheepshead); Edward Rigby (Dan Billings); Billy Hartnell (Drunk
Taxi Driver); John Stuart (Captain Harvey); Percy Parsons (Coro-
ner); Gerry Wilmot (Control Tower Operator); Frank Wilcox
(Judge); Robert Beatty (Connor, the Scandal Photographer); John
Slater (Air Raid Warden); and: John Boxter, Peter Croft, Tommy
Duggan, Hubert Gregg, Andrea Malandrinos.

Made by Warner Bros. at its Teddingham, England studio, this
pastiche of a war movie was greeted with few kind words from
contemporary reviewers. The first segment shows dissolute playboy
Jim Spence, Jr. (Richard Greene) causing the death of a passenger in
his private plane, although it is his pilot, Sky Kelly (Donald
Stewart), who is blamed. Jim is guilt-stricken and makes amends by
joining the Air Ferry Service in Canada, where his instructor is
Kelly. Part two is set in London during an air raid and the two men
patch up their quarrel. The third and only lively section of this
patriotic salute is an RAF bombing raid on Berlin, in which Jim
proves both resourceful and successful. (He even climbs out onto
the wing of his plane to patch a hole!)

In later distribution, much of the earlier section of FLYING
FORTRESS was scissored.

FLYING LEATHERNECKS (RKO, 1951) Color 102 mins.

Presenter, Howard Hughes; producer, Edmund Grainger;
director, Nicholas Ray; story, Kenneth Gamet; screenplay, James
Edward Grant; art directors, Albert S. D'Agostino, James W.
Sullivan; set decorators, Darrell Silvera, John Sturtevent; music,
Roy Webb; music director, C. Bakaleinikoff; technical consultant,
Morgan Padelford; sound, Frank McWhorter, Clem Portman;
camera, William E. Snyder; editor, Sherman Todd.

John Wayne (Major Dan Kirby); Robert Ryan (Captain Carl
Griffin); Don Taylor (Lieutenant "Cowboy" Blithe); Janis Carter
(Joan Kirby); Jay C. Flippen (Clancy); William Harrigan (Lieuten-
ant Commander Joe Curan); James Bell (Colonel); Barry Kelley
(General); Maurice Jara (Shorty Vogay); Adam Williams (Lieuten-
ant Malotke); James Dobson (Pudge McCabe); Carleton Young
(Captain McAllister); Steve Flagg (Lieutenant Jorgenson); Brett
King (Lieutenant Ernie Stark); Gordon Gebert (Tommy Kirby);
Lynn Stalmaster (Lieutenant Castle); Brit Norton (Lieutenant

Tanner); John Mallory (Lieutenant Black); Douglas Henderson (Lieutenant Foster); Ralph Cook (Lieutenant Kelvin); Frank Fiumara (Lieutenant Hawkins); Michael Devry (Lieutenant Hoagland); Adam York (Lieutenant Simmons); Don Rockland (Lieutenant Stuart); Hal Bokar (Lieutenant Deal); Tony Layng (Lieutenant Woods); Hugh Sanders (General); Mack Williams (Colonel); Leslie O'Pace (Peter); Milton Kibbee (Clark); Bernard Szold (Papa Malotke); Eda Reis Merin (Mama Malotke); Pat Priest (Greta Malotke); Sheila Fritz, Charles Bruner (Old Indians); Fred Graham (Marine); Gail Davis (Virginia); Inez Cooper (Nurse); Frank Iwanaga, Rollin Moriyama (Japanese Pilots).

Major Dan Kirby (John Wayne) is a no-nonsense kind of a fella, a stern Marine officer who saves his grieving over battle losses for private sessions and the long letters he writes to the men's survivors. It is 1942 and the battle at Guadalcanal (to halt the Japanese advance toward Australia) is underway. Kirby heads a flyer squadron and it is his conviction that they must do everything possible, including flying dangerously low to hit their targets, to give full ground support to the infantrymen. His opponent is individualistic Captain Carl Griffin (Robert Ryan) and the two men debate at length over the virtues of each's theories. There is a touching interlude when Kirby is sent on Stateside leave and stumbles awkwardly in telling his wife (Janis Carter) how much he loves her, and in trying to explain to his son (Gordon Gebert) that there is no glory to war. Once again back in combat, Kirby is wounded in action and sent home. Before he leaves, he and Griffin make peace and Kirby is relieved to know that his one-time adversary has seen the errors of his ways and is ready to take command.

For many viewers, this film proved to be too long, the integrated stock combat footage too obvious, the clichés (including Jay C. Flippen as the opportunistic crew chief) and the ethnic stereotypes (Maurice Jara as an Indian who loses a leg in battle) too much of a distraction. For others, an action-packed John Wayne film can do no wrong. Since FLYING LEATHERNECKS was released in the middle of the Korean Conflict, the topicality of this production increased its box-office receipts.

FLYING TIGERS (Republic, 1942) 102 mins.

Executive producer, Herbert J. Yates; producer, Edmund Grainger; director, David Miller; story, Kenneth Gamet; screenplay, Gamet, Barry Trivers; art director, Russell Kimball; music, Victor Young; music director, Walter Scharf; technical adviser,

William D. Pawley; special effects, Howard Lydecker, Daniel J. Blomberg; camera, Jack Marta; editor, Ernest Nims.

John Wayne (Jim Gordon); John Carroll (Woody Jason); Anna Lee (Brooke Elliott); Paul Kelly (Hap Davis); Gordon Jones (Alabama Smith); Mae Clarke (Verna Bales); Addison Richards (Colonel Lindsay); Edmund MacDonald (Blackie Bales); Bill Shirley (Dale); Tom Neal (Reardon); Malcolm McTaggart (McCurdy); David Bruce (Lieutenant Barton); Chester Gan (Mike); James Dodd (McIntosh); Gregg Barton (Tex Norton); John James (Selby); Charles Lane (Airport Official); Tom Seidel (Barratt); Richard Loo (Doctor); Richard Crane (Airfield Radio Man); Willie Fung (Jim, the Waiter); Paul Mantz (Stunt Flying).

The foreword to this film is supplied by then Generalissimo Chiang Kai-Shek, who pays tribute to the American Volunteer Group, the men who ". . . have become the symbol for the invincible strength of the forces now upholding the cause of humanity and justice." In its own way, the film is a tribute to General Claire J. Chennault (1890-1958) and his American volunteer group in China which shot down many Japanese aircraft in the period before America entered World War II.

Don Taylor and John Wayne in FLYING LEATHERNECKS (1951).

The *New York Times'* Thomas M. Pryor acknowledged FLY-
ING TIGERS as a ". . . first-rate aerial circus chock-full of exciting
dogfights," but noted that ". . . the fictional story, which has a way
of overshadowing factual incidents, follows the well-known Hollywood service-film formula."

Cocky Woody Jason (John Carroll) has joined the American
Volunteer Group for the fun of it and for the $600 reward for each
downed Japanese plane. He is a grandstanding type of pilot, which
goes against the tenets of squadron leader Jim Gordon (John
Wayne) and such other flyers as Gordon's second-in-command,
Hap Davis (Paul Kelly). Another new recruit is Blackie Bales
(Edmund MacDonald), who, Jason insists, was the cause of a
friend's death in an air circus crackup back home. Blackie's wife
(Mae Clarke) begs Gordon to let her husband fly, and in battle he
dies heroically. Brooke Elliott (Anna Lee) is the tireless British Red
Cross worker who loves the solemn Gordon but is wooed by the
reckless, handsome Jason. One day when the egotistic, self-serving
Jason (busily courting Brooke) fails to appear for a scheduled
mission, Hap Davis, who has failing eyesight, takes his place and
dies in the air. Gordon snarls at the late arriving Jason and Brooke,
"I hope you had a good time, because Hap paid the bill!" Jason,
chastised and wanting redemption, is grounded but begs Gordon for
a reprieve. Together they fly a dangerous mission to bomb a railroad
bridge. En route, the Japanese attack the plane and Jason is badly
wounded. He pushes Gordon out of the plane and the latter
parachutes to safety, while the dying Jason crashes his plane into the
railroad bridge as the enemy troop/supply train passes through.

This was the first of several wartime films in which John Wayne
would star. It established all the characteristics of such future
outings. Wayne's character is brave, solemn, and seemingly callous.
When a new pilot (Bill Shirley) dies on his first combat mission,
Wayne's Jim Gordon snarls, "He should have stayed in college
where he came from, but he begged for a chance . . . begged for it
like some kid asking to go to the circus." Wayne must win over a
misguided hothead (here John Carroll's Woody Jason); must suffer
the loss of many fine buddies in battle, and any romantic interludes
must take a decidedly second place to the noble war duty ahead.
Usually the enemy will be vanquished under seemingly impossible
odds, with the battling Wayne overcoming tremendous obstacles.
Always humble, he is never a braggart about his victories, but he is
quick to bark at any breach of his authority and beliefs, or
endangerment of the safety of his men.

In examining the liveliness of FLYING TIGERS, James H.
Farmer wrote in *Celluloid Wings* (1984), ". . . [There is] a

refreshingly energetic, even original visual presentation." In dissecting the opening scene as an example of this, Farmer points out, "Having compressed what appears to be a maximum of raw energy into this initial framing of the film's opening scene, the camera continues to pull back, revealing a remarkably broad scope of dynamic, thoughtfully composed activity. There amid the trees, the dust, and waving Chinese locals, six of the Tigers' P-40s are quickly manned to take their battle to the skies."

For their technical contributions to FLYING TIGERS, Howard Lydecker and Daniel J. Blomberg (department head) received an Academy Award nomination for Best Special Effects.

FOR EVER ENGLAND *see*: BORN FOR GLORY.

FORCE OF ARMS (Warner Bros., 1951) 98 mins.

Producer, Anthony Veiller; director, Michael Curtiz; based on the story "Italian Story" by Richard Tregaskis; screenplay, Orin Jannings; art director, Edward Carrere; music, Max Steiner; camera, Ted McCord; editor, Owen Marks.

William Holden (Sergeant Peterson); Nancy Olson (Eleanor McKay); Frank Lovejoy (Major Blackford); Gene Evans (McFee); Dick Wesson (Klein); Paul Picerni (Sheridan); Katherine Warren (Major Waldron, WAC); Ross Ford (Hooker); Ron Hagerty (Private First Class Minto); Amelia Kova (Lea); Robert Board (Frank); Donald Gordon (Sergeant Weber); Slats Taylor (Private First Class Yost); Ron Hargrave (Remington); Mario Siletti (Signor Maduvalli); Argentina Bruenetti (Signora Maduvalli); Anna Dometrio (Mama Mia); Jay Richards (Guard); Henry Kulky (Sergeant Reiser); Andy Mariani, Francesco Cantania (Barbers); Lea Lamedico (Anna); Adriana Page (Therese); Philip Carey, Bob Ohlen (Military Police); Joan Winfield (Nurse); John McGuire (Doctor).

This black-and-white feature is an uncredited updating of Ernest Hemingway's novel, *A Farewell to Arms* (which Paramount had filmed in 1932). FORCE OF ARMS is "A stark, uncompromising picture of men at war . . . the screenplay depicts with a maturity surprising in a Hollywood film both the savagery of soldiers under fire and their animal enjoyment of a five-day pass" (James S. Barstow, Jr. *New York Herald Tribune*).

Sergeant Peterson (William Holden) is among the GIs participating in the bloody battle of San Pietro, Italy during World War II. His group is pulled out of active duty during a battle lull and while on rest and relaxation he meets WAC Lieutenant Eleanor McKay (Nancy Olson). At first they seem at odds with each other, but then admit their love for one another. More smitten than he realizes, Peterson now has a reason to stay alive and this makes him dangerous in battle—he holds back his aggressiveness and this weakness causes the death of Major Blackford (Frank Lovejoy) and others of his group. Peterson is haunted by these men's sacrifice. He and Eleanor marry, but he returns to the front lines (instead of accepting a less dangerous post) because he must heed his sense of duty and clear his conscience. Later he is reported wounded in a fierce encounter and assumed dead, as the Allied soldiers had had to move on. Eleanor refuses to accept this verdict and searches the battlefields herself. Reaching Rome she finds him with the liberated prisoners-of-war.

Variety endorsed, ". . . The battle footage is among some of the most realistic yet staged for a picture and has the added authenticity of using some brief clips from the actual Italian campaign."

FORCE 10 FROM NAVARONE (American International, 1978) Color 118 mins.

Presenter, Samuel Z. Arkoff; producers, Oliver A. Unger, John R. Sloan, Anthony B. Unger; director, Guy Hamilton; based on the novel by Alistair MacLean and the adaptation by Carl Foreman; screenplay, Robin Chapman; production designer, Geoffrey Drake; costumes, Emma Porteous; music, Ron Goodwin; assistant director, Bert Batt; stunt coordinator, Eddie Stacey; special effects, Rene Albouze; camera, Chris Challis; editor, Ray Poulton.

Robert Shaw (Major Mallory); Harrison Ford (Colonel Barnsby); Edward Fox (Miller); Barbara Bach (Maritza); Franco Nero (Lescovar); Carl Weathers (Weaver); Richard Kiel (Drazac); Angus MacInnes (Reynolds); Michael Byrne (Schroeder); Alan Badel (Petrovich); Christopher Malcolm (Rogers); Nick Ellsworth (Salvone); Jonathan Blake (Oberstein); Michael Sheard (Bauer).

FORCE 10 FROM NAVARONE was part of the motion picture industry's trendy transition from conventional combat films about twentieth-century warfare to extended commando raid activities within the confines of a war (as here) or to the more extreme aftermath of a war (e.g., the RAMBO and MISSING IN ACTION series).

THE GUNS OF NAVARONE (1961), q.v., had been a tremendous box-office hit (earning over $13,000,000 in theater rentals in the U.S. and Canada alone) and it paved the way for this follow-up film (based on another Alistair MacLean novel) which is *not* a sequel to THE GUNS OF NAVARONE.

As a tie in to the earlier entry, this new entry opens during World War II with the closing sequence of its predecessor—the destruction of the guns at Navarone—and then launches into the team's new "impossible" mission. Two hold-over characters are among the ranks of the commandos in the new adventure: British Major Mallory (Robert Shaw; previously played by Gregory Peck) and demolition expert Miller (Edward Fox; previously played by David Niven). They are joined by American Colonel Barnsby (Harrison Ford), and Weaver (Carl Weathers), the black GI. Their objective is to destroy a key bridge separating the Germans and the Yugoslavian partisans. Along the way they interact with Lescovar (Franco Nero), a Nazi double agent; towering Drazac (Richard Kiel), a Chetnik conspirator; and Maritza (Barbara Bach), a patriotic resistance fighter. A good deal of the fighting takes place

Barbara Bach and Robert Shaw in FORCE 10 FROM NAVARONE (1978).

within the group, with Weaver dealing with racial prejudice, Barnsby resentful of being stuck with limeys Miller and Mallory, and Mallory unsure that Lescovar is the traitor in their midst who must be liquidated.

As its own ironic comment that man is not the final destroyer even in wartime, FORCE 10 FROM NAVARONE has the combat team blow up a giant dam; this unleashes a fury of water, bringing down the "indestructible" bridge.

In retrospect, FORCE 10 FROM NAVARONE is neither as inventive nor as star-worthy as THE GUNS OF NAVARONE and it was soon forgotten. (It earned only $3,200,000 in theater rentals in the U.S. and Canada.) Its star, Robert Shaw, was dead of a heart attack before the film debuted.

FOREVER IN LOVE *see:* PRIDE OF THE MARINES.

FORWARD MARCH *see:* DOUGH BOYS.

THE FOUR HORSEMEN OF THE APOCALYPSE (Metro, 1921) 11 reels.

Director, Rex Ingram; based on the novel *Los Cuatros Jinetes del Apocalipsis* [The Four Horsemen of the Apocalypse] by Vicente Blasco-Ibanez; adaptor, June Mathis; art directors, Joseph Calder, Amos Myers; music, Louis F. Gottschalk; assistant director, Walter Mayo; art titles, Jack W. Robson; camera, John F. Seitz; assistant camera, Starret Ford, Walter Mayo; editor, Grant Whytock.

Rudolph Valentino (Julio Desnoyers); Alice Terry (Marguerite Laurier); Pomeroy Cannon (Madariaga, the Centaur); Josef Swickard (Marcelo Desnoyers); Brinsley Shaw (Celendonio); Alan Hale (Karl von Hartrott); Bridgetta Clark (Dona Luisa); Mabel Van Buren (Elena); Nigel De Brulier (Tchernoff); Bowditch Turner (Argensola); John Sainpolis (Laurier); Mark Fenton (Senator Lacour); Virginia Warwick (Chichi); Derek Ghent (Rene Lacour); Stuart Holmes (Captain von Hartrott); Edward Connelly (Lodgekeeper); Georgia Woodthorpe (Lodgekeeper's Wife); Kathleen Key (Georgette); Wallace Beery (Lieutenant-Colonel von Richthofen); Jacques D'Auray (Captain d'Aubrey); Curt Rehfeld (Major Blumhardt); Harry Northrup (The Count); Claire De Lorez (Mademoiselle Lucille); Bull Montana (The Butler); Isabelle Keith (The German Woman); Jacques Lanoe (German Woman's Husband); Nobel Johnson (Conquest); Minnehaha (Old Nurse); Arthur Hoyt (Lieutenant Schnitz); Beatrice Dominguez (Dancer).

THE FOUR HORSEMEN OF THE APOCALYPSE (Metro-Goldwyn-Mayer, 1962) Color 153 mins.
Producer, Julian Blaustein; associate producer, Olallo Rubio, Jr.; director, Vincente Minnelli; based on the novel *Los Cuatro Jinetes del Apocalipsis* [The Four Horsemen of the Apocalypse] by Vicente Blasco-Ibanez; screenplay, Robert Ardrey, John Gay; art directors, George W. Davis, Urie McCleary, Elliot Scott; Four Horsemen figures designer, Tony Duquette; set decorators, Henry Grace, Keogh Gleason; costume designers, Rene Hubert, Walter Plunkett; additional gowns, Orry-Kelly; makeup, Charles Parker, William Tuttle; music, Andre Previn; choreography, Alex Romero; assistant director, Eric Von Stroheim, Jr.; sound, Franklin Milton; special visual effects, A. Arnold Gillespie, Lee Leblanc, Robert R. Hoag; montages, Frank Santillo; camera, Milton Krasner; editors, Adrienne Fazan, Ben Lewis.

Glenn Ford (Julio Desnoyers); Ingrid Thulin (Marguerite Laurier); Charles Boyer (Marcelo Desnoyers); Lee J. Cobb (Julio Madariaga); Paul Henreid (Etienne Laurier); Paul Lukas (Karl von Hartrott); Yvette Mimieux (Chi-Chi Desnoyers); Karlheinz Bohm (Heinrich von Hartrott); Harriett MacGibbon (Dona Luisa Desnoyers); Kathryn Givney (Elena von Hartrott); Marcel Hillaire (Armand Dibie); George Dolenz (General von Kleig); Stephen Bekassy (Colonel Kleinsdorf); Nestor Paiva (Miguel); Albert Remy (Francois); Richard Franchot (Franz von Hartrott); Brian Avery (Gustav von Hartrott); (uncredited) Angela Lansbury (Voice of Marguerite Laurier).

For many the original 1921 THE FOUR HORSEMEN OF THE APOCALYPSE is a lavishly produced love story against the backdrop of World War I. For others it marks the screen ascendancy of new Hollywood star Rudolph Valentino. In cinema history, this silent motion picture epic is a semi-landmark in the emergence of the war film. It is a tale of love, noble actions by noblemen, and a strong sidelight is its implied comments on the inhumanity of war.

When wealthy Argentinian cattle owner Madariaga (Pomeroy Cannon) dies, his rich estate enables his large family to move abroad. The Von Hartrott clan emigrates to Germany and the Desnoyers to Paris. There Julio (Rudolph Valentino) paints, enjoys the good life and falls in love with Marguerite Laurier (Alice Terry), who is married to a lawyer (John Sainpolis). When World War I breaks out, Laurier enlists and Marguerite, now part of the Red Cross, learns he has been blinded in action. She vows from now on to resist Julio's advances. The distraught Julio, inspired by a stranger who calls upon the mystical Four Horsemen (War,

Conquest, Famine, Death), enlists and proves to be a brave soldier. He is later killed in a gunfire exchange with his cousin (Stuart Holmes), a German officer.

"When all is said about THE FOUR HORSEMEN, however, the central fact remains that it is an exceptionally well done adaption of a novel, and an extraordinary motion picture work to boot" (*New York Times*). When not savoring the charismatic Valentino at his peak, moviegoers recall the battle scenes of trench warfare and the depiction of lives brutally cut short. As David Robinson notes in *Hollywood in the Twenties* (1968), "THE FOUR HORSEMEN OF THE APOCALYPSE (1921) got by more on extraneous sources of glamor and on the current fashion for Ibanez novels than as a war subject. The picture it represented in any case reflected the popular home sentiments of vengeance by depicting the conflict in cruelly hard blacks and whites."

Forty-one years later the financially ailing MGM participated in a desperate Hollywood trend of remaking past box-office successes. MGM had the misguided notion of remodeling THE

John Sainpolis, Alice Terry, and Rudolph Valentino in THE FOUR HORSEMEN OF THE APOCALYPSE (1921).

FOUR HORSEMEN OF THE APOCALYPSE, which had been a fantastic box-office success in its day. It was an extremely expensive misjudgment.

The overblown CinemaScope "new" production was directed by Vincente Minnelli (far more attuned to handling colorful, stylish musicals) and its story was updated to World War II times. Now Laurier (Paul Henreid) is a Parisian anti-Nazi broken in the concentration camps. Julio (Glenn Ford) is a playboy who becomes involved in the Resistance and when Marguerite (Ingrid Thulin) leaves him to tend her cuckolded sick husband, he renews his patriotic underground activities. He participates in guiding British bombers to destroy a Nazi headquarter in Normandy. At the finale, knowing they are soon to die, Julio and his German cousin (Karlheinz Bohm) toast each other and the happiness they once knew as a united family. Critics and audiences alike detested the vapid new version which had no style, no point of view, and no credible performances. It was a $6,000,000 fiasco.

THE FROGMEN (Twentieth Century-Fox, 1951) 96 mins.

Producer, Samuel G. Engel; director, Lloyd Bacon; story, Oscar Millard; screenplay, John Tucker Battle; art directors, Lyle Wheeler, Albert Hogsett; set decorators, Thomas Little, Fred J. Rode; makeup, Ben Nye; wardrobe, Charles LeMaire; music, Cyril Mockridge; music director, Lionel Newman; orchestrators, Herbert Spencer, Earl Hagen; assistant director, Dick Mayberry; sound, Winston H. Leveritt, Roger Heman; camera, Norbert Brodine; editor, William Reynolds.

Richard Widmark (Lieutenant Commander Lawrence); Dana Andrews (Flannigan); Gary Merrill (Lieutenant Commander Pete Vincent); Jeffrey Hunter (Creighton); Warren Stevens (Hodges); Robert Wagner (Lieutenant [j.g.] Franklin); Harvey Lembeck (Canarsie); Robert Rockwell (Lieutenant Doyle); Henry Slate (Sleeny); Robert Adler (Chief Ryan); Bob Patten (Lieutenant Klinger); Harry Flowers (Kinsella); William Bishop (Ferrino); Fay Roope (Admiral Dakers); William M. Neil (Commander Miles); James Gregory (Chief Petty Officer Lane); Russell Hardie (Captain Redford); Parley Baer (Dr. Ullman); Peter Leeds (Pharmacist's Mate); Richard Allen, Frank Donahue, Jack Warden (Crew Members); Norman McKay (Captain Phillips); Sydney Smith (General Coleson); Ray Hyke (Repair Man); Rush Williams (Ziegler); George Yoshinga (Swimmer); Harry Hamada (Gunner).

Seemingly every branch of the military service had its day being lauded, depicted, and exploited by Hollywood filmmakers. THE FROGMEN deal with the unique UDT (Underwater Demolition

Team), an elitist branch of approximately 1,000 out of the 3,000,000-member U.S. Navy during World War II.

The film suffers from relying too much on the usual combat picture structure: the new superior officer, Lieutenant Commander Lawrence (Richard Widmark), of a UDT must cope with the group's steadfast devotion to their late commander who died in action saving one of his men. Lawrence is efficient, stern, and unyielding. Most damaging of all to his rapport with the men, he refuses to acknowledge that "the Frogmen" are any more special than any other service group. Flannigan (Dana Andrews) is the non-commissioned officer who is as puzzled as the others by Lawrence's attitude. Lieutenant Commander Pete Vincent (Gary Merrill) is the captain of one of the naval boats used to transport these special commandos to their assignment.

Clichés aside, THE FROGMEN focuses effectively on the dangerous exploits of these underwater warriors, leading to several breathtakingly exciting action scenes and many moments of unique cinematic visuals. Before THE FROGMEN reaches its conclusion, there is the final mission: the UDT, garbed with oxygen masks, explosives, and weapons, swim underwater to a Japanese submarine pen, planting explosives to destroy the enemy vessels. Before the goal is attained, they must combat Japanese frogmen, leading to an aquatic ballet of death struggle.

FULL METAL JACKET (Warner Bros., 1987) Color 116 mins.

Executive producer, Jan Harlan; producer, Stanley Kubrick; co-producer, Philip Hobbs; associate producer, Michael Herr; director, Kubrick; based on the novel *The Short-Timers* by Gustav Hasford; screenplay, Kubrick, Herr, Hasford; production designer, Anton Furst; art directors, Rod Stratford, Les Tomkins, Keith Pain; costume designer, Keith Denny; music, Abigail Mead; technical adviser, Lee Ermey; assistant directors, Terry Needham, Christopher Thomson; sound, Edward Tise; special effects supervisor, John Evans; camera, Douglas Milsome; aerial camera, Ken Arlidge; editor, Martin Hunter.

Matthew Modine (Private Joker); Adam Baldwin (Animal Mother); Vincent D'Onofrio (Leonard Lawrence [Private Gomer Pyle]); Lee Ermey (Gunnery Sergeant Hartman); Dorian Harewood (Eightball); Arliss Howard (Cowboy); Kevyn Major Howard (Rafterman); Ed O'Ross (Walter J. Schinoski [Lieutenant Touchdown]); John Terry (Lieutenant Lockhart); Keiron Jecchinis (Crazy Earl); Kirk Taylor (Payback); Tim Colceri (Doorgunner); John Stafford (Doc Jay); Bruce Boa (Poge Colonel); Ian Tyler (Lieutenant Cleves); Sal Lopez (T.H.E. Rock); Gary Landon Mills

Advertisement for FULL METAL JACKET (1987).

(Donlon); Papillon Soo Soo (Da Nang Hooker); Peter Edmund (Snowball); Ngoc Le (Vietcong Sniper); Leanna Hong (Motorbike Hooker); Tan Hung Francione (Arvn Pimp); Marcus D'Amico (Hand Job); Costas Dino Chimona (Chili); Gil Kopel (Stork); Keith Hodiak (Daddy Da); Peter Merrill (TV Journalist); Herbert Norville (Daytona Dave); Nguyen Hue Phong (Camera Thief); Duc Hu Ta (Dead NVA); Martin Adams, Adrian Bush, Wayne Clark, Chris Cornibert, Danny Cornibert, Nigel Goulding, Bob Hart, Derek Hart, Barry Hayes, Tony Hayes, Liam Hogan, Trevor Hogan, Gary Meyer, John Morrison, Al Simpron, John Wilson, John Wonderling (Parris Island Recruits/Vietnam Platoon).

"Kubrick has largely succeeded in violating the war picture formula. FULL METAL JACKET's story is short on logic, continuity and closure. Its tone is unsentimental to a fault. Its characters remain nondescript or cartoonish . . . and they lack coherent motivation. . . . FULL METAL JACKET makes few concessions to our conventional gratification. It shocks us, alienates us, angers us and (it must be said) occasionally bores us with shapeless scenes" (John Powers, *L.A. Weekly*).

"Part One" opens in 1968 at the U.S. Marine Corps' Parris Island, South Carolina boot camp. Gunnery Sergeant Hartman (Lee Ermey) greets a new batch of recruits. He renames them to suit his whim. There is Private Joker (Matthew Modine), the group comedian; Private Cowboy (Arliss Howard), the youth from Texas; and the soon-to-be brunt of barracks' abuse, Leonard Lawrence (Vincent D'Onofrio) the overweight misfit whom Hartman nicknames Private Gomer Pyle. Nothing is sacred as Hartman drives, taunts, drags, and punishes these young men through their hellish basic training. All along the way, it is the fat bumpkin Gomer Pyle who is the butt of the Drill Instructor's most sadistic indoctrination, including a Hartman-instigated ritualistic beating by the other recruits. Before the regimen is completed, Gomer Pyle has become a sure shot who even talks to his rifle. One night before graduation, the omnipresent Hartman finds Gomer Pyle in the latrine with his rifle loaded. Hartman rebukes the boy, who first shoots the D.I. and then kills himself.

"Part Two" jumps to 1968 Da Nang, Vietnam where Joker is now a reporter for the *Stars and Stripes* military magazine, with Rafterman (Kevyn Major Howard) as his staff photographer. The Viet Cong launch an unexpected offensive during the Tet holiday cease-fire and Joker and Rafterman are dispatched to besieged Hue to cover the event. There Joker encounters Cowboy, now part of the "Lusthog Squad" (First Platoon, H Company, Second Battalion, Fifth Marine Regiment). During the siege, platoon commander

Lieutenant Touchdown (Ed O'Ross) is killed and, later, squad head Crazy Earl (Keiron Jecchinis) dies in a booby-trapped mine explosion. Cowboy is now in charge and in the crossfire Eightball (Dorian Harewood) and Doc Jay (John Stafford) die. During the advance, Cowboy is killed and the Viet Cong sniper, a woman, is trapped by Rafterman just as she is about to kill Joker. Near death, the sniper begs Joker to kill her. He does. Marching back to camp, Joker says, "I live in a world of shit, yes, but I'm alive and I am not afraid."

Having dissected, satirized, exploited, and reflected the world of warfare in such films as FEAR AND DESIRE (1953), PATHS OF GLORY (1958), q.v., SPARTACUS (1960), and DR. STRANGELOVE (1963), much was expected of filmmaker Stanley Kubrick when he transferred Gustav Hasford's 1979 novel to the screen. The fact that the Academy Award-winning PLATOON (1986), q.v., beat FULL METAL JACKET to the screen did not help the latter picture with critics, although the film did reasonably well, considering its production costs, at the box-office. It earned $22,700,000 in theater rentals in the U.S. and Canada.

Perhaps the artistic disappointment engendered by FULL METAL JACKET is best summed up by Richard Corliss (*Time* Magazine) who assessed, "FULL METAL JACKET fails only by the standards the director demands be set for him. By normal movie standards, with whatever reservations one may entertain, the film is a technical knockout."

For many, Kubrick's Vietnam picture (shot entirely in England) is too diffuse in storyline, fuzzy in characterization, and ambivalent in emotional/intellectual comment. By following so closely the book's two-part structure, the film does viewers a disservice. The opening 45-minute segment of boot camp hell has a deja vu flavor,* not helped by the presence of Lee Ermey, the ex-Drill Instructor turned actor/technical adviser who had done similar chores for THE BOYS IN COMPANY C (1978), q.v. (Veteran combat filmmaker Sam Fuller's reaction to Kubrick's barracks episodes, "He's a great film maker, but I don't like training films. I got the first part in five minutes and if it wasn't Kubrick, I'd have left after 10.") Part Two has its own structural problems. It jumps to a new setting (Vietnam), viewers are introduced to a mostly new set of characters (or so it seems for a time), and the storyline has no marked coherency as the helter skelter battle and the dissipation of the squad under fire occurs. (Reportedly this

*Much of the voice over musings/rambling were supplied by co-writer Michael Herr who had done the same for APOCALYPSE NOW (1979), q.v.

apparent unfocused approach was meant as a deliberate reflection of the unstructured chess game of war.)

Several grisly scenes did not survive the script revises for FULL METAL JACKET. There was to be a sequence in which Joker and Rafterman, accompanied by a South Vietnamese officer, are in a chopper with a V.C. prisoner. When the latter refuses to cooperate, he is pushed to his death. When the officer objects to Rafterman taking photos, Joker shoots him. A closing sequence was to have shown Animal Mother (Adam Baldwin) cutting off the head of the woman sniper Joker has just killed.

When the Academy Award race of 1988 began, some strange events occurred. The score for FULL METAL JACKET by Kubrick's daughter, Abigail Mead, was rejected for consideration because it did not contain sufficient original material to qualify. The screenplay by Kubrick, Michael Herr, and Gustav Hasford was Oscar-nominated. However, even this Academy Award nomination backfired because the press played up the Oscar tie-in when writer Gustav Hasford was accused of keeping several hundred books allegedly "borrowed" from libraries around the world. It certainly did not help FULL METAL JACKET's chance of winning in this category. As it happened, the category's award went to John Patrick Shanley for MOONSTRUCK.

G.I. JOE *see*: THE STORY OF G.I. JOE.

THE GALLANT HOURS (United Artists, 1960) 111 mins.

Producer/director, Robert Montgomery; screenplay, Beirne Lay, Jr., Frank D. Gilroy; art director, Wiard Ihnen; set decorator, Frank McKelvey; costumes, Jack Martell; makeup, Lorand Cosand; assistant director, Joseph C. Behm; music/music director, Roger Wagner; music editor, Alfred Perry; technical supervisor, Captain Idris B. Monahan (U.S. Navy); technical consultant, Captain Joseph U. Lademan (U.S. Navy); Japanese naval technical adviser, James T. Goto; camera, Joe MacDonald; editor, Frederick Y. Smith.

James Cagney (Fleet Admiral William F. Halsey, Jr.); Dennis Weaver (Lieutenant Commander Andy Lowe); Ward Costello (Captain Harry Black); Richard Jaeckel (Lieutenant Commander Roy Webb); Les Tremayne (Captain Frank Enright); Robert Burton (Major General Roy Geiger); Raymond Bailey (Major General Archie Vandergrift); Carl Benton Reid (Vice Admiral Robert Ghormley); Walter Sande (Captain Horace Keys); Karl Swenson (Captain Bill Bailey); Vaughan Taylor (Commander Mike Pulaski); Harry Landers (Captain Joe Foss); Richard Carlyle (Father Gehring); Leon Lontoc (Manuel); James T. Goto (Admiral Isoroku Yamamoto); James Yagi (Rear Admiral Jiri Kobe); John McKee (Lieutenant Harrison Ludlum); John Zaremba (Major General Harmon); Carleton Young (Colonel Evans Carlson); William Schallert (Captain Tom Lamphier); Nelson Leigh (Admiral Callaghan); Sydney Smith (Admiral Scott); Herbert Lytton (Admiral Murray); Selmer Jackson (Admiral Chester Nimitz); Tyler McVey (Admiral Ernest J. King); Maggie Magennis (Red Cross Girl); Art Gilmore (Narrator of Japanese Sequences); Robert Montgomery (Narrator); James Cagney, Jr., Robert Montgomery, Jr. (Marines).

The closing words of THE GALLANT HOURS are: "There are no great men. There are only great challenges that by circumstances ordinary men are forced to meet."

This is the tenor of THE GALLANT HOURS, a reverential, low-keyed tribute to U.S. Naval Admiral William F. "Bull" Halsey (1882-1959). The film avoids depicting (costly) battle sequences and focuses on two opposing military strategists, how they think, react, and exist. That producer/director (and former actor and Navy Lieutenant) Robert Montgomery was able to draw such a restrained performance from usually bombastic James Cagney was an accomplishment in itself.

THE GALLANT HOURS opens in 1945 as Halsey (James Cagney) is retiring, and then flashes back to the crucial period of October to December 1942 when the Japanese and U.S. forces were locked in battle at Guadalcanal. Halsey's opponent is Isoroku Yamamoto (James T. Goto), the Japanese Admiral and Chief of the Combined Fleet. Yamamoto, who planned the attacks of Pearl Harbor and Midway and was killed on April 18, 1943 when his plane was shot down by the U.S. Army Air Force. It turned the tide for the Allies in this chapter of the Pacific Theatre of War.

Director Montgomery deliberately makes his black-and-white movie (co-produced with James Cagney) very stylized. An overabundance of facts and details is thrown at the viewer as each historical character is presented in the solemn narrative; with the voiceover acting god-like as he relates what fate lays ahead for each. The Robert Wagner Chorale sings reverently on the soundtrack, giving the unfolding plotline a religious overtone and almost making a deity of Halsey. (Montgomery seeks to counterbalance this by presenting the very human sides of Halsey: his fear of inoculation needles, his love of swimming, his concern for his fighter pilot aide, Andy Lowe [Dennis Weaver], etc.).

More interesting than entertaining, more educational than stimulating, THE GALLANT HOURS is a unique war film. Its reputation is far better than it deserves, but Cagney's performance as the bull-headed tactician who thrived on naval life is quietly captivating.

GALLIPOLI (Paramount, 1981) Color 110 mins.

Executive producer, Francis O'Brien; producers, Robert Stigwood, Patricia Lovell; associate producers, Martin Cooper, Ben Gannon; director/story, Peter Weir; screenplay, David Williamson; production designer, Wendy Weir; art director, Herbert Pinter; makeup, Judy Love; music, Brian May; assistant director, Mark Egerton; sound, Don Connolly; stunt coordinators, Dennis Hunt, Vic Wilson; sports adviser, Jack Giddy; supervising sound editor, Greg Bell; special effects, Chris Murray, Mont Fieguth, David Hardie, Steve Courtley, Bruce Henderson; camera, Russell Boyd; editor, William Anderson.

Mark Lee and Mel Gibson in GALLIPOLI (1981).

Mark Lee (Archy Hamilton); Bill Kerr (Jack); Mel Gibson (Frank Dunne); Ron Graham (Wallace Hamilton); Harold Hopkins (Les McCann); Charles Yunupingu (Zac); Heath Harris (Stockman); Gerda Nicholson (Rose Hamilton); Robert Grubb (Billy); Tim McKenzie (Barney); David Argue (Snowy); Reg Evans, Jack Giddy (Officials); Dane Peterson (Announcer); Paul Linkson (Recruiting Officer); Jenny Lovell (Waitress); Steve Dodd (Billy Snakeskin); Harold Baigent (Stumpy); Robyn Galwey (Mary); Don Quin (Lionel); Phyllis Burford (Laura); Marjorie Irving (Gran); John Murphy (Dan Dunne); Bill Hunter (Major Barton); Peter Ford (Lieutenant Gray); Diane Chamberlain (Anne Barton); Ian Govett (Army Doctor); Geoff Parry (Sergeant Sayers); Clive Bennington, Giles Holland-Martin (English Officers); Moshe Kedern (Egyptian Shopkeeper); John Morris (Colonel Robinson); Don Barker (Non-Commissioned Officer at Ball); Kiwi White (Soldier on Beach); Paul Sonkkila (Sniper); Peter Lawless (Observer); Saltbush Baldock (Sentry); Les Dayman (Artillery Officer); Stan Green (Sergeant Major); Max Wearing (Colonel White); Graham Dow (General Gardner); Peter R. House (Radio Officer).

In the years when Australian films (and rising star Mel Gibson) were becoming international big business, GALLIPOLI emerged as a searing, haunting study of war's futility and in particular of the disastrous Gallipoli campaign of World War I. With its plot revolving around the fighting spirit of runners, many compared this production to CHARIOTS OF FIRE (1981).

It is May 1915 in Australia and Archy Hamilton (Mark Lee) wins a 100-yard dash in Fremantle. He is enthusiastic about enlisting in the service to assist the Anzac war push in the Dardenelles. Because he is under-age, he is rejected initially. However, Frank Dunne (Mel Gibson), a fellow runner, convinces Hamilton to jump a train to Perth to try again. Hamilton is accepted in the Light Horse Regiment, but Dunne's inferior horsemanship keeps him out. Instead, he and others join the infantry. In Egypt the two reunite and Dunne is brought into the Light Horse. From Cairo they go to the Gallipoli peninsula. The unyielding Colonel Robinson (John Morris) insists that the men make a bayonet charge on the Turkish trenches. This is supposed to divert the enemy from the British landing at Suvla Bay. Meanwhile the kindly Major Barton (Bill Hunter) sends Dunne, his personal runner, to headquarters for permission to stop this suicidal charge. Dunne returns as the massacre is in progress, too late to prevent Barton's death.

". . . [We] are . . . encouraged to wonder at the indifference to danger exhibited by the Australian soldiers precariously dug into a cliffside while Turkish shells perpetually explode on the beach below—a beach on which they find time both to work and play. Weir states the case for innocence, but leaves matters there; his film strenuously avoids argument in favour of the creation of mood" (John Pym, British *Monthly Film Bulletin*).

GO FOR BROKE! (Metro-Goldwyn-Mayer, 1951) 92 mins.

Producer, Dore Schary; director/screenplay, Robert Pirosh; art directors, Cedric Gibbons, Eddie Imazu; set decorators, Edwin B. Willis, Alfred E. Spencer; makeup, William Tuttle; music, Alberto Colombo; assistant director, Jerry Thorpe; sound, Douglas Shearer; camera, Paul C. Vogel; editor, James E. Newcom.

Van Johnson (Lieutenant Michael Grayson); Lane Nakano (Sam); George Miki (Chick); Akira Fukunaga (Frank); Ken K. Okamoto (Kaz); Henry Oyassato (O'Hara); Harry Hamada (Masami); Henry Nakamura (Tommy); Warner Anderson (Colonel Charles W. Pence); Don Haggerty (Sergeant Wilson I. Culley); Gianna Canale (Rosina); Dan Riss (Captain Solari).

Having hit paydirt with BATTLEGROUND (1949), writer-turned-director Robert Pirosh devised this earnest study of the Japanese-Americans (Nisei) who served so bravely on the Allied side in World War II. It almost seemed unpatriotic to dislike this contrived but well-meaning morale booster. During its plea for racial tolerance, the film depicts graphically the horrors of war.

Lieutenant Michael Grayson (Van Johnson) is a non-Nisei officer charged with training American Nisei. At first he feels his appointment to the 442nd Regimental Combat Team is a letdown, but as he gets to know the men and they become seasoned in combat in Italy, he comes to appreciate and admire these courageous troopers.

"Go for broke" was the war cry of this unique battalion. Veterans from this much-decorated fighting team were used in the cast. The screenplay for GO FOR BROKE was Oscar-nominated. The film grossed $2,500,000 in domestic box-office receipts, ranking #20 in the twenty top earning films of 1951.

GO TELL THE SPARTANS (Avco Embassy, 1978) Color 114 mins.

Executive producer, Michael Leone; producers, Allan F. Boddoh, Mitchell Cannold; associate producer, Jesse Corallo; director, Ted Post; based on the novel *Incident at Muc Wa* by Daniel Ford; screenplay, Wendell Mayes; art director, Jack Senter; costumes, Ron Dawson; sound, Bill Randall; camera, Harry Stradling, Jr.; editor, Millie Moore.

Burt Lancaster (Major Asa Barker); Craig Wasson (Corporal Stephen Courcey); Jonathan Goldsmith (Sergeant Oleonowski); Marc Singer (Captain Al Olivetti); Joe Unger (Lieutenant Raymond Hamilton); Dennis Howard (Corporal Abraham Lincoln); David Clennon (Lieutenant Finley Wattsberg); Evan Kim (Cowboy); John Megna (Corporal Ackley); Hilly Hicks (Signalman Toffer); Dolph Sweet (General Hornitz); Clyde Kasatsu (Colonel Minh); James Hong (Corporal Oldman); Denice Kumagai (Butterfly); Tad Horino (One-Eyed Charlie); Phong Diep (Minh's Interpreter); Ralph Brannen (Minh's Aide-de-Camp); Mark Carlton (Captain Schlitz).

"A good war film needs heroes. But Vietnam, the most unpopular war in U.S. history, had no heroes in the eyes of most Americans. Commercially then, all Vietnam War films must overcome a handicap, and perhaps it's a losing battle from the start" (*Variety*). While this was written long before PLATOON (1986) and the RAMBO and MISSING IN ACTION film types proved differently, it was prophetically true with the much underrated, much ignored GO TELL THE SPARTANS.

In 1964 Vietnam the French are abandoning their last claim to this troublesome land and the U.S., once just "advisors," are now in charge of helping the South Vietnamese. Major Asa Barker (Burt Lancaster) is a burned-out career soldier who had never seen real glory in any war. A sexual indiscretion with a general's wife cost him good postings, and now he commands the ill-defined American Military Assistance Advisory Group at Penang. General Hornitz (Dolph Sweet) orders him to reconnoiter a town called Muc Wa on the coast. Among Barker's raw command are over-zealous, naive Second Lieutenant Raymond Hamilton (Joe Unger), for whom everything is black and white; an intelligent new draftee named Corporal Stephen Courcey (Craig Wasson), who picked Vietnam service because he insisted on being in "the roughest, toughest unit in the whole U.S. Army"; battle-worn Sergeant Oleonowski (Jonathan Goldsmith), who had been with Barker in Korea; somber Corporal Abraham Lincoln (Dennis Howard); Captain Olivetti (Marc Singer), Barker's helper; and black signalman Toffer (Hilly Hicks). Under Hamilton's command, they reach Muc Wa, which had been abandoned by the French in 1953. They pass by a cemetery for French soldiers and a sign at the entrance states, "Stranger, when you find us lying here, go tell the Spartans that we obeyed their orders."

Despite feeling it a worthless exercise, the discouraged Barker follows orders and has Hamilton and the men rebuild the base at Muc Wa. Thereafter they fight off the Viet Cong, helped by blood-hungry South Vietnamese Cowboy (Evan Kim) and other locals. The cumulative strain is too much on Oleonowski and he commits suicide. Courcey befriends a group of Vietnamese peasants, only to have them later proven to be Viet Cong sympathizers who must be massacred. As the Viet Cong build-up intensifies, the higher echelon of command decides to evacuate the base. Barker arrives via helicopter to supervise the evacuation. When Courcey refuses to leave Cowboy and the other stragglers, Barker impulsively decides to remain behind too. The enemy closes in. During an ambush, Barker is shot. As he dies, his final words are "Oh, shit." A stunned Courcey is the only survivor. "I'm going home, Charlie," he tells an enemy sniper. At the fade out, the title card reads "1964"; *not* "The End."

In retrospect, GO TELL THE SPARTANS, which is about American innocence at the prelude to the Vietnam War, seems an even greater indictment of American naiveté at that turning point in world history. This telling film is brimful with ironies, such as Barker's confusion as to what a draftee like Courcey is doing in Vietnam when, at the time, the U.S. is only a military adviser. "You're a tourist," is the best Barker can make of the situation; not understanding that Courcey is one of hundreds of thousands of U.S. draftees who will soon flood into Vietnam.

Filmed in 31 days on a budget of less than $1,000,000 on locations in Valencia, California, GO TELL THE SPARTANS did not find an audience in 1978. It was a movie too much before its right time. It only grossed $3,000,000. In mid-1987, in the post-PLATOON wake, it was reissued, but by then it was considered derivative and was relegated quickly to the videocassette marketplace.

GOD IS MY CO-PILOT (Warner Bros., 1945) 90 mins.

Producer, Robert Buckner; director, Robert Florey; based on the book by Colonel Robert Lee Scott, Jr.; screenplay, Peter Milne, Abem Finkel; art director, John Hughes; set decorator, Jack McCaneghy; music, Franz Waxman; music director, Leo F. Forbstein; orchestrator, Jerome Moross; technical adviser, Colonel Robert Lee Scott, Jr.; assistant director, Les Guthrie; sound, Oliver S. Garretson; special effects, Roy Davidson, Edwin DuPar, Robert Burks; camera, Sid Hickox; editor, Folmer Blansted.

Dennis Morgan (Colonel Robert Lee Scott, Jr.); Dane Clark (Johnny Petach); Raymond Massey (Major General Claire Lee Chennault); Alan Hale ("Big Mike" Harrigan); Andrea King (Catherine Scott); John Ridgely (Tex Hill); Stanley Ridges (Colonel Meriam Coper); Craig Stevens (Ed Rector); Warren Douglas (Bob

Neale); Stephen Richards (Sergeant Baldridge); Charles Smith (Private Motley); Minor Watson (Colonel Caleb V. Haynes); Richard Loo (Tokyo Joe); Murray Alper (Sergeant Aaltonen); Bernie Sell (Gil Bright); Joel Allen (Lieutenant Doug Sharp); John Miles (Lieutenant "Alabama" Wilson); Paul Brooks (Lieutenant Jack Horner); Clarence Muse ("Prank"); William Forrest (Dr. Reynolds); Frank Tang (Chinese Captain); Philip Ahn (Japanese Announcer); Dan Dowling (Frank Schiel); Paul Fung (General Kitcheburo); Frances Chan (Specialty Dancer); Sanders Clark (British Officer Prisoner); Phyllis Adair (American Girl Prisoner); Dale Van Sickle, Tom Steele, Art Foster (American Pilots); Buddy Burroughs (Scott as a Boy); George Cleveland (Catherine's Father); Gigi Perreau (Robin Lee); Don McGuire, William Challee (A.V.G. Groundmen); Joel Friedkin (Newspaper Editor); James Flavin (Major); Colonel Robert Lee Scott, Jr. (Flying Double for Dennis Morgan).

Colonel Robert Lee Scott, Jr. wrote a best-selling book about his life-long love of flying and how, when at the age of 34 he was rejected for flight assignment by the military as being too old, he went to China to join the Flying Tigers. There he became "the one-man air force."

Warner Bros. turned this biography into a war adventure film with heavy religious overtones. In montage, Scott's (Dennis Morgan) life is recounted from his boyhood love of flying and his experimental jump from a barn roof using an umbrella for a parachute, to being a flying mail carrier, to his years at West Point, and then on to China. There he joins the illustrious Major General Claire Lee Chennault (Raymond Massey) and his Flying Tigers (actually the 23rd Fighter Group). Flying a P-40 (named *Old Exterminator*) he shoots down twelve Japanese planes (including, in the movie, enemy ace Tokyo Joe [Richard Loo]). This, in addition to his strafing attacks on Japanese troops on the Burma Road, makes him a hero. Because he survives so much danger, Scott comes to believe the words of missionary priest "Big Mike" Harrigan (Alan Hale): "Son, you're not up there alone. You have the greatest co-pilot in the world."

The film proved a commercial success, but was not favored by the critics. "Obviously Warner Brothers took the title of Colonel Robert L. Scott's war book . . . much more literally than the author did. . . . [The film] is heavily and often embarrassingly larded with piety" (Bosley Crowther, *New York Times*). James H. Farmer in *Celluloid Wings* (1984) recalls a 1978 interview with Scott in which the latter reflected how badly he felt after seeing a screening of GOD IS MY CO-PILOT in 1945: "And, man, I had to sit there and see that corny film in which so little is true. They made me have that malaria attack which never did happen . . . it's amazing how they make a movie!"

GOOD MORNING, VIETNAM (Buena Vista, 1987) Color 120 mins.

Producers, Mark Johnson, Larry Brezner; co-producers, Ben Moses, Harry Benn; director, Barry Levinson; screenplay, Mitch Markowitz; production designer, Roy Walker; art director, Steve Spence; set decorator, Tessa Davies; costumes, Keith Denny; music, Alex North; music consultant, Allan Mason; assistant directors, M. Mathis Johnson, Bill Westley; sound, Clive Winter; camera, Pete Sova; editor, Stu Linder.

Robin Williams (Adrian Cronauer); Forest Whitaker (Edward Garlick); Tung Thanh Tran (Tuan); Chintara Sukapatana (Trinh); Bruno Kirby (Lieutenant Steven Hauk); Robert Wuhl (Marty Lee Dreiwitz); J. T. Walsh (Sergeant Major Dickerson); Noble Willingham (General Taylor); Richard Edson (Private Abersold); Juney Smith (Phil McPherson); Richard Portnow (Dan "The Man" Levitan); Floyd Vivino (Eddie Kirk); Cu Ba Nguyen (Jimmy Wah).

"Those who confuse solemnity with seriousness, preferring carefully researched filmic treatises on the Vietnam War done from the vantage of the British Museum, might find this Buena Vista release flip, raw and not necessarily in lock-step with their own apprehensions of military stereotypes. Nevertheless, it's just plain funny, and [Robin] Williams' potshots rattle off faster than an M-16" (Duane Byrne, *The Hollywood Reporter*).

One of the more colorful arrivals to 1965 Vietnam is irreverent Airman Adrian Cronauer (Robin Williams), yanked to Saigon to help boost the morale of GIs who are fighting a "police action" no one understands. Cronauer's mentor is General Taylor (Noble Willingham) who spotted him in Crete as the lunatic radio disc jockey who did so much for team spirit. At once the battle lines are drawn at the Armed Forces Radio Station. Lieutenant Stephen Hauk (Bruno Kirby), a pompous nerd who thinks he understands "humor," immediately hates the iconoclastic, straight-shooting Cronauer; while the chunky black soldier Edward Garlick (Forest Whitaker) guides him through the ropes. Before long Cronauer's 6 A.M. radio stint (with his opening scream, "Go-oo-ooood Morning, Vietnam!") is the hit of the city and a joy to the disillusioned, confused troops. Nothing is sacred to this hip radio disc jockey with the machine-gun, manic delivery: military policy, the President, mom's apple pie. He tells it like it is, substituting real news for the station's typical "happy news." He banishes the Lawrence Welk and Mantovani records for the Beach Boys, Bob Dylan, and Martha and the Vandellas. It is not long before Sergeant Major Dickerson (J. T. Walsh) is maneuvering to have Cronauer silenced.

The story takes a serious turn when Cronauer falls in love with a local Vietnamese girl, Trinh (Chintara Sukapatana), aided and abetted in his romance by her opportunistic young brother Tuan (Tung Thanh Tran). Thanks to Dickerson's deliberate planning, Cronauer and Garlick are sent on a field mission which leads them into Viet Cong territory. Later Cronauer learns that he was saved because Tuan, a secret Viet Cong sympathizer, intervened. Cronauer is later ordered to leave Vietnam.

There were those who found structural flaws in GOOD MORNING, VIETNAM. "Instead of the disc jockey being the eyes and ears of the events around him, a barometer of the changes about to happen, Williams is a totally self-contained character, and despite numerous topical references, his comedy turns in on itself rather than opening on the scene outside. . . . At a time when the world is truly in transition, it is a bit shameful to reduce the events of Vietnam to a few good jokes" (*Daily Variety*). "When Cronauer is forced to confront the relative pettiness of his clashes with Army brass on a scale of napalm and civil war, the film owns up—he's shallow and he knows it. . . . There are more important questions than 'But is it funny?' Even in comedy" (*LA Reader*). "Robert Altman film of M*A*S*H [q.v.] and the subsequent TV series have forever shattered the confines of the service comedy, revealing the underlying absurdity of the military mind. At this point, anything less than the total anarchy of a DUCK SOUP renders this genre unsatisfying and more than a bit frivolous" (Richard Natale, *Movieline* magazine).

On the other side, *Time* magazine's Richard Shickel championed, "The film is the best military comedy since M*A*S*H disbanded. . . . Sometimes it is on the edge of hysteria. At others it can approach the fringe of sentiment. But wherever it stands, it is sure-footed and strong-minded—no easy laughs, no easy tears. . . . You may be all the way home before you realize you may have seen not just the comedy (and the comic performance) of the year, but just possibly the most insinuatingly truthful movie yet about Viet Nam." Michael Wilmington (*Los Angeles Times*) admitted the film had flaws (including the cheap shots of the plot, including a swishy Saigon bar owner who craves nude photos of Walter Brennan, and the trek to see a subtitled version of BEACH BLANKET BINGO), but acknowledged, "Williams kicks the movie up to the sublimely ridiculous, hot-wires it into realms of quick-witted chaos. He gives a fine, freezingly cheery hello and goodbye to the hell of war and the purgatory of radio."

The public thoroughly endorsed this cinematic showcase for the irrepressible stand-up comic. Robin Williams won a Golden Globe Award and was Oscar-nominated as Best Actor. The film grossed $119,555,151 in its first 22 weeks at the domestic box-office. Scriptwriter Mitch Markowitz, who only visited Vietnam *after* writing the screenplay, would later script a pilot for a projected TV series version of GOOD MORNING, VIETNAM. A sequel to the film is also in the "talking" stages in which the real-life Adrian Cronauer would return state-side for further misadventures.

THE GREAT ESCAPE (United Artists, 1963) Color 163 mins.

Producer/director, John Sturges; based on the book by Paul Brickhill; screenplay, James Clavell, W. R. Burnett; art director, Fernando Carrere; wardrobe, Bert Henrikson; makeup, Emile Lavigne; music, Elmer Bernstein; technical adviser, C. Wallace Floody; assistant director, Jack Reddish; sound, Harold Lewis;

Steve McQueen in THE GREAT ESCAPE (1963).

special effects, Paul Pollard; camera, Daniel L. Fapp; editor, Ferris Webster.

Steve McQueen ("Cooler King" Hilts); James Garner ("Scrounger" Hendley); Richard Attenborough (Squadron Leader Roger Bartlett ["Big X"]); James Donald (Senior Officer Ramsey); Charles Bronson (Danny Velinski); Donald Pleasence ("The Forger" Blythe); James Coburn ("The Manufacturer" Sedgwick); David McCallum (Ashley-Pitt); Gordon Jackson (MacDonald); John Leyton (Willie); Agnus Lennie ("The Mole" Ives); Nigel Stock (Cavendish); Jud Taylor (Goff); William Russell (Sorren); Robert Desmond ("The Tailor" Griffith); Tom Adams (Nimmo); Lawrence Montaigne (Haynes): Hannes Messemer (Von Luger); Robert Graf (Werner); Harry Riebauer (Strachwitz); Hans Reiser (Kuhn); Robert Freytag (Posen); Heinz Weiss (Kramer); Til Kiew (Frick); Ulrich Beiger (Preissen); George Mikell (Dietrich); Karl Otto Alberty (Steinach).

In 1942 Germany, captured Allied officers with a reputation for being incorrigible, are clustered in a Nazi prison camp (Stalag Luft Nord) that is considered escape proof. Nevertheless, the prisoners are determined to break free. Leading the plan for a mammoth escape (which would keep the Nazis on the hunt for months and draw their troops away from the front lines) are authoritarian British Squadron Leader Roger Bartlett (Richard Attenborough), known as "Big X," who has attempted many past breakouts and who is the engineer of the new great escape; Hendley (James Garner), the free-wheeling American with a genius for scrounging supplies; Danny Velinski (Charles Bronson), the Pole who will supervise the digging, but who suffers from severe claustrophobia; Blythe (Donald Pleasence), the forger needed to make passports and visas, who is going blind; and the non-conformist American Hilts (Steve McQueen), known as the "Cooler King" because he spends so much time in solitary confinement (where he bounces a baseball against the prison wall). Their elaborate scheme (and equally elaborate precautions) is to meticulously dig three tunnels—Tom, Dick, and Harry—in the hope that at least one of the paths will provide freedom for the 250 escapees. During a Fourth of July celebration, one of the tunnels ("Tom") is discovered by the Nazis, but the teams continue on the remaining two. Finally everything is prepared and the prisoners escape. They flee on foot, train, boat, and plane, with Hilts drawing the Germans on a sensational cross-country motorcycle chase before he crashes into a barbed wire fence and is apprehended. Some, such as Blythe and Ashley-Pitt (David McCallum) are killed, but a very few, including Velinski and Sedgwick (James Coburn), make it to the allied lines. To show their anger over what the escape has cost in manpower, the Germans execute fifty of the ex-escapees, including Big X and MacDonald (Gordon Jackson). Hendley and Hilts are returned to the stalag, with Hilts once again in solitary confinement. The sound of his baseball thumping against the walls indicates he is plotting another escape.

THE GREAT ESCAPE was based on the largely factual 1950 book by Paul Brickhill, who spent much of World War II in such a German prison camp.* Brickhill's book, which director John Sturges had long wanted to turn into a film, had inspired several interim prisoner-of-war escape films, such as THE WOODEN HORSE (1950) and THE COLDITZ STORY (1957), qq.v. These latter films, according to Adrian Turner in *Movies of the Sixties* (1983), ". . . consciously strove to create a microcosm of England behind barbed wire, where attitudes of class could maintain morale and discipline. The deprivations and dangers of incarceration were minimized to strengthen the point about British resilience and the known outcome of the war; eccentricity and xenophobia became patriotic attributes. . . ."

THE GREAT ESCAPE is a vastly different approach from such earlier downbeat prisoner-of-war pictures as STALAG 17 (1953), q.v., or such later somber entries as KING RAT (1965), q.v. Here is a rousing, action-filled, upbeat (if that is possible under the circumstances!) tale of servicemen determined in their united goal to escape. They are not only escaping for themselves, but because it was "the sworn duty of all officers to escape and to harass the enemy to the best of their ability." While the regurgitation of the minuscule tasks and tremendous care required to execute the escape becomes tedious viewing, the audience is always swept back into the 163-minute narrative by the impressively grand scale of the overall enterprise. And, of course, the film has a carefully crafted blend of tension, actions, stunts, and comedy relief with the focus swinging back and forth among its diverse cast of characters. And in the typical tradition of the early 1960s, it is oversized in star names, running length, widescreen, and a big story.

Thanks to its international star cast, and especially the presence of rising box-office superstar Steve McQueen, THE GREAT

---

*For a history of the (pre)production of this shot-in-Germany feature; such pre-shooting cast changes as Richard Attenborough replacing Richard Harris; and the stunts involved within the film, see: Steven Jay Rubin's *Combat Films: 1945-1970* (1980) and *The Films of Steve McQueen* (1984) by Casey St. Charnez.

ESCAPE earned $5,520,000 in theater rentals in the U.S. and Canada. Many establishment film critics endorsed the production. "A first-rate adventure film fascinating in its detail, suspenseful in its plot, stirring in its climax and excellent in performance" (Judith Crist, *New York Herald Tribune*). Twenty-five years later, a made-for-television movie sequel was shot in Yugoslavia: THE GREAT ESCAPE: THE FINAL CHAPTER, directed by Jud Taylor and starring Christopher Reeve.

THE GREEN BERETS (Warner Bros./Seven Arts, 1968) Color 141 mins.

Producer, Michael Wayne; directors, John Wayne, Ray Kellogg, (uncredited) Mervyn LeRoy; based on the novel by Robin Moore; screenplay, James Lee Barrett; production designer, Walter M. Simonds; set decorator, Ray Moyer; costumes, Jerry Alpert; makeup, Dave Grayson; music, Miklos Rozsa; second unit director, Cliff Lyons; assistant directors, Joe L. Cramer, Newt Arnold; Special Forces adviser, Jerold R. Dodds (Major), Fort Benning project officer, August Schomburg, Jr. (Captain); Defense Department project officer, William C. Byrns (Lieutenant Colonel); sound, Stanley Jones; special effects, Sass Bedig; camera, Winton C. Hoch; editor, Otho Lovering.

John Wayne (Colonel Mike Kirby); David Janssen (George Beckworth); Jim Hutton (Sergeant Petersen); Aldo Ray (Sergeant Muldoon); Raymond St. Jacques (Doc McGee); Bruce Cabot (Colonel Morgan); George Takei (Captain Nim); Luke Askew (Sergeant Provo); Jack Soo (Colonel Cai); Patrick Wayne (Lieutenant Jamison); Irene Tsu (Lin); Edward Faulkner (Captain MacDaniels); Jason Evers (Captain Coleman); Mike Henry (Sergeant Kowalski); Craig Jue (Hamchunk); Chuck Robertson (Sergeant Griffin); Eddy Donno (Sergeant Watson); Rudy Robins (Sergeant Parks); Richard "Cactus" Pryor (Collier); Bach Yen (Vietnamese Singer); Frank Koomen (Lieutenant Sachs); William Olds (General Phan Son Ti); Yodying Apibal (ARVN Soldier); Chuck Bail (Sergeant Lark); Vincent Cadiente (Viet Cong Soldier); William Shannon (Sergeant White).

"THE GREEN BERETS . . . was a Technicolored guts-and-glory parade of heroics in the jungles of Vietnam, though the setting might as easily have been Korea, the Pacific, or even the American mid-West at the time of Custer's last stand. That's how superficial it was. All the Yanks were untarnished heroes; the Viet Cong were savages to a man. No objective assessment of the situation was attempted. . . . A piece of blatant propaganda posing as entertainment. . . . " (Clive Hirschhorn, *The Warner Bros. Story*, 1979).

John Wayne and Ed Faulkner in THE GREEN BERETS (1968).

In the years between this film's release and his death in 1979, John "Duke" Wayne never publicly backed down from his stance that THE GREEN BERETS was his "objective" assessment of the U.S. involvement in Vietnam. He never once apologized for his hawkish stance, no matter what the latest revelations of the "true" story of America's Vietnam War, nor was he chastised by the furor of peaceniks who scorned this pro-war film.

THE GREEN BERETS is structured as an educational lesson for the viewer, a blood-and-guts brain-washing. As one military character says, "Let me put it in terms we can all understand." The student in the film is a cynical, middle-aged journalist named George Beckworth (David Janssen). His teacher is Colonel Mike Kirby (John Wayne) of the U.S. Special Forces. Beckworth's conversion to the right way of thinking forms the plot goal in THE GREEN BERETS.

"Hard to talk to anyone about this country [Vietnam] until they've been over and seen it." This taunt from right-winger Kirby is enough to bait liberal war correspondent Beckworth to accept the challenge. He arrives in Vietnam to chronicle Kirby's activities at a strike camp (named "Dodge City") situated in the heart of Viet

Cong territory near Da Nang. Among Kirby's men are: the good-hearted Sergeant Petersen (Jim Hutton), who later adopts Hamchunk (Craig Jue); the gruff military professional Sergeant Muldoon (Aldo Ray), who believes, "A soldier goes where he is told to go, fights where he is told to fight"; the sensitive black intellectual Sergeant McGee (Raymond St. Jacques), who insists the South Vietnamese "need us . . . and they want us"; the gung ho militarist Sergeant Provo (Luke Askew), who is concerned constantly with being remembered in an appropriate memorial when he falls in battle (and he does die, with Kirby respectfully naming a latrine after him!). Kirby and his men, joined by South Vietnamese soldiers and Montagnard tribesmen, lose "Dodge City" to the enemy but eventually retake the jungle base with the assistance of air support. With the help of slinky Lin (Irene Tsu), Kirby and Vietnamese Colonel Cai (Jack Soo) capture a senior enemy officer and escort him back to headquarters for questioning. Along the way Petersen is killed by a bamboo booby trap, which leaves it to Kirby to tell the re-orphaned Hamchunk that Petersen died to make it safe for all future Hamchunks "(You're what this war is all about!"). And Beckworth, whose anger at learning first-hand that the Viet Cong torture and rape civilians, not only joins in the fighting, but is converted totally to Kirby's political ideology. He promises to write about how he now feels for newspaper readers back home.

Critics then and today have had a journalistic romp in tearing apart THE GREEN BERETS, and especially in crucifying John Wayne (and his family—producer/brother Michael and featured player/son Patrick) for turning out this technically and artistically old-fashioned claptrap. "All the flaws of his aging physique are cruelly exposed by what would appear to be a pitiful attempt to recapture his youth: the rolling hips, the enormous, top-heavy frame . . . the craggy, weather-beaten featured topped by an implausible toupee. Age and costume apart, the role could have been patched together from a montage of his past appearances, so derivative is every last gesture; every drawling syllable, every quizzical arch of the eyebrow. There is something slightly indecent in . . . an old man playing a young man's game, one which many young men were no longer prepared to play" (Gilbert Adair, *Vietnam on Film* (1981).

Yet no matter how much one may criticize any aspect of THE GREEN BERETS, enough of the public flocked to see the controversial film and it earned a hefty $9,750,000 in theater rentals in the U.S. and Canada and remains a fixture of TV viewing today. The film's "The Ballad of the Green Berets" became, despite all, a popular song of the day.

GUADALCANAL DIARY (Twentieth Century-Fox, 1943) 93 mins.

Producer, Byron Foy; associate producer, Islin Auster; director, Lewis Seiler; based on the novel by Richard Tregaskis; adaptor, Jerry Cady; screenplay, Lamar Trotti; art directors, James Basevi, Leland Fuller; set decorators, Thomas Little, Fred J. Rode; music, David Buttolph; music director, Emil Newman; assistant director, Henry Weinberger; sound, Lorn Grigson, Harry M. Leonard; special effects, Fred Sersen; camera, Charles Clarke; editor, Fred Allen.

Preston Foster (Father Donnelly); Lloyd Nolan (Sergeant Hook Malone); William Bendix (Taxi Potts); Richard Conte (Captain Davis); Anthony Quinn (Private Jesus "Soose" Alvarez); Richard Jaeckel (Private Johnny "Chicken" Anderson); Roy Roberts (Captain Cross); Minor Watson (Colonel Grayson); Ralph Byrd (Ned Rowman); Lionel Stander (Butch); Reed Hadley (Correspondent); John Archer (Lieutenant Thurmond); Eddie Acuff (Tex); Robert Rose (Sammy); Miles Mander (Weatherby); Harry Carter (Dispatch Officer); Jack Luden (Major); Louis Hart (Lieutenant); Tom Dawson (Captain); Selmer Jackson (Colonel Thompson); Allen Jung (Japanese Officer); Paul Fung (Japanese Prisoner); Warren Ashe (Colonel Morton); Walter Fenner (Colonel Roper); Larry Thompson (Chaplain); Martin Black, Bob Ford, George Holmes, Russell Hoyt, Charles Lang, David Peter (Marines).

Paramount offered WAKE ISLAND (1942), q.v., MGM made BATAAN (1943), q.v., and Twentieth Century-Fox produced its major war film, GUADALCANAL DIARY. It depicted another bloody episode in the history of the Pacific Theater in World War II, where the combat took place on the beaches, in foxholes, and on jungle patrols. It was based on the well-received, factual account of the Gaudalcanal battle written by war correspondent Richard Tregaskis. Like the above-mentioned two films and more that followed, it established the tradition of the World War II combat film, focusing on an ethnically mixed group of soldiers who react to the physical and mental pressures of front-line warfare where survival is the name of the game.

Using a documentary, diary-like narrative, the film opens on Sunday, July 26, 1942 as a U.S. troop ship filled with Marines heads to the Solomon Islands in the South Pacific. Aboard are: avuncular Captain Davis (Richard Conte); veteran Sergeant Hook Malone (Lloyd Nolan); the Mexican American Private Jesus "Soose" Alvarez (Anthony Quinn), who has vengeance in his heart; new trooper Private Johnny "Chicken" Anderson (Richard Jaeckel);* accommodating Father Donnelly (Preston Foster), company clown Butch (Lionel Stander); and fast-talking Flatbush cab driver "Taxi" Potts (William Bendix) who loves two things, the Brooklyn Dodgers ball team and Betty Grable.

On Friday, August 7, 1942 the Guadalcanal landing takes place and the real battle starts. The Japanese are lodged in the dense jungle, hiding in trees and caves, and it requires treacherous hand-to-hand combat to win the terrain. ("The men behind the machine guns are fanatics; some are chained to the weapons. One by one they must be blasted from the earth that hides them.") The men know their mission, but more importantly they realize, like Sergeant Malone, that ". . . it's kill or be killed—besides they ain't people." These troops are everyday men who complain, sing war songs, pray, and, like Taxi Potts, have the infantryman's practical perspective: "I'm no hero. I'm just a guy. I'm out here because somebody had to come. I don't want no medals. I just want to get this thing over with and go back home. I'm just like everyone else and I don't like it." Having accomplished their objective against the devious enemy, who don't play by fair rules, the surviving troops (who are marching by a road sign pointing to Tokyo) are greeted by a new batch of soldiers.

While GUADALCANAL DIARY was lauded for its patriotic approach to recreating the jungle warfare of the prior year, there were those film reviewers who felt the film was not realistic enough, even by 1940s Hollywood standards. ". . . [Too] much footage is devoted to the gags of the marines—the wisecracks and stagey chatter which is familiar from previous films. And another is that the fighting is also comparatively routine [when not using documentary material], without any true indication of the tension of jungle warfare. And then, too, it seems too fortuitous that the four or five marines we stay with most enjoy a miraculous immunity from death—except for one, just at the end" (Bosley Crowther, *New York Times*).

In retrospect, Jay Hyams in *War Movies* (1984), judged GUADALCANAL DIARY "the most important wartime Holly-

---

*This was the film debut of 17-year-old former Twentieth Century-Fox mail boy, Richard Jaeckel of Long Beach, California. Like William Bendix, he would become a staple of Hollywood combat films; appearing in such genre entries as WING AND A PRAYER (1944), JUNGLE PATROL (1948), SANDS OF IWO JIMA (1949), ATTACK! (1955), THE GALLANT HOURS (1960), THE DIRTY DOZEN (1967), THE DEVIL'S BRIGADE (1968), and PACIFIC HELL (1978), and the short-lived teleseries "Super Carrier" (1988).

wood movie about the war in the Pacific. . . . The film is about the battle and the lessons the marines learned while adding a new verse to their hymn. It is also about the changes wrought on Americans by the experience of war. . . . The Marine Corps recognized the importance of the film and helped in its production. Their investment paid off; they set up recruiting stations near theaters showing the film and received more than twelve thousand new recruits."

GUNG HO! (Universal, 1943) 88 mins.*

Producer, Walter Wanger; director, Ray Enright; based on the account by Captain W. S. LeFrancois; screenplay, Lucien Hubbard; additional dialogue, Joseph Hoffman; art directors, John B. Goodman, Alexander Golitzen; set decorators, Russell A. Gausman, A. J. Gilmore; costumes, Vera West; music, Frank Skinner; music director, Hans J. Salter; assistant director, Fred Frank; technical adviser, Evans F. Carlson, U.S. Marine Corps; sound, B. Brown, Ed Wetzel; special effects, John P. Fulton; camera, Milton Krasner; special camera, John R. Fulton; editor, Milton Carruth.

Randolph Scott (Colonel Thorwold); Grace McDonald (Kathleen Corrigan); Alan Curtis (John Harbison); Noah Beery, Jr. (Kurt Richter); J. Carrol Naish (Lieutenant Cristoforos); David Bruce (Larry O'Ryan); Peter Coe (Kozzarowski); Robert Mitchum (Pigiron Matthews); Richard Lane (Captain Dunphy); Rod Cameron (Rube Tedrow); Sam Levene (Transport); Milburn Stone (Commander Blade); Harold Landon (Frankie Montana); John James (Buddy Andrews); Louis Jean Heydt (Lieutenant Roland Browning); Walter Sande (Gunner McBride); Harry Strang (Sergeant Jim Corrigan); Irving Bacon (Waiter); Joe Hayworth (Singing Marine); Carl Varnell (Marine on Submarine); Robert Kent (Submarine Officer); Chet Huntley (Narrator).

For the record, "Gung Ho" is the Chinese phrase for "working together." This film is based on the real life hit-and-go attack on Makin (an island in the Gilbert chain in the South Pacific) by U.S. Marine Corps officer Carlson and his Raiders. While 350 Japanese were killed, the raid cost the lives of over thirty Marines (some of whom were captured and beheaded) and led to the Japanese fortifying other, until then, unprotected islands. Second-in-command on the daring raid was Marine Corps Major James Roosevelt, son of the president.

As dramatically restructured from Captain W. S. LeFrancois' actual account to create an exciting film, GUNG HO traces

---

*Computer colorized version now available.

step-by-step how recruits for the highly-selective Second Marine Raider Battalion are chosen and trained for their objective, and led by Colonel Thorwold (Randolph Scott). Among his dedicated team are rugged Lieutenant Cristoforos (J. Carrol Naish); two half-brothers (David Bruce and Noah Beery, Jr.), who have a yen for the same blonde (Grace McDonald); and such diverse troopers as Transport (Sam Levene), Pigiron Matthews (Robert Mitchum) and Rube Tedrow (Rod Cameron). The motion picture follows their transportation to the Pacific and graphically shows how the men

Rod Cameron (right) in GUNG HO (1943).

sacrifice their lives to regain the island from the Japanese. Newspapers recorded the event as "Makin Taken."

While commending GUNG HO as exciting on the battlefield, but slow in the boot camp and fabricated romantic interludes, *Variety* quipped, ". . . dead Japs and live blondes don't mix."

THE GUNS OF NAVARONE (Columbia, 1961) Color 157 mins.

Producer, Carl Foreman; associate producers, Cecil F. Ford, Leon Becker; director, J. Lee Thompson; based on the novel *Guns of Navarone* by Alistair MacLean; screenplay, Foreman; production designer/art director, Geoffrey Drake; set decorator, Maurice Fowler; costumes, Monty Berman, Olga Lehman; makeup, Wally Schneiderman, Pamela Davies; music/music conductor, Dimitri Tiomkin; song, Paul Francis Webster and Alfred Perry; assistant director, Peter Yates; sound, John Cox, George Stephenson, Vivian C. Greenham; special effects, Bill Warrington, Wally Veevers; camera, Oswald Morris; additional camera, John Wilcox; editor, Alan Osbiston, Raymond Poulton, John Smith, Oswald Hafenichter.

Gregory Peck (Captain Mallory); David Niven (Corporal Miller); Anthony Quinn (Andrea Stavros); Stanley Baker (Chief Petty Officer Brown); James Darren (Spyros Pappadimos); Anthony Quayle (Major Franklin); Irene Papas (Maria Pappadimos); Gia Scala (Anna); James Robertson Justice (Jenson/Narrator); Richard Harris (Barnsby); Bryan Forbes (Cohn); Allan Cuthbertson (Baker); Michael Trubshawe (Weaver); Percy Herbert (Rogan); George Mikell (Sessler); Walter Gotell (Mussel); Norman Wooland (Group Captain); Albert Lieven (Commandant); Tutte Lemkow (Nicholai); Cleo Scouloudi (Bride); Nicholas Papakonstantinou (Patrol Boat Captain); Christopher Rhodes (German Gunnery Officer).

An Allied force in 1943 is trapped on the island of Kheros in the Aegean Sea. To escape, the troops must pass through a small channel controlled by two oversized German guns set deep in the rocks of Navarone. Because the guns cannot be hit by sea or air attack, an Allied sabotage team is dispatched to Navarone to destroy the guns. The commandos are led on the "suicide" mission by security officer Major Franklin (Anthony Quayle). The rest are: mountaineer Captain Mallory (Gregory Peck), demolition expert Corporal Miller (David Niven), Greek resistance fighter; Private Spyros Pappadimos (James Darren), who grew up in New York; and knife-wielding Chief Petty Officer Brown (Stanley Baker). Along the way, they lose their boat, Major Franklin is injured scaling the cliffs to reach Navarone, and they make connection with two partisans—Spyros' sister Maria (Irene Papas) and the tortured mute, Anna (Gia Scala). They are captured by the Nazis, but escape. After Maria shoots the group's spy, Anna, the explosives are set. Spyros and Brown die in an encounter with the enemy, but the rest escape. When the British destroyers come into view, the Nazis fire their mammoth guns at Navarone and they explode and crash into the sea.

Based on Alistair MacLean's best-selling novel of 1957, THE GUNS OF NAVARONE is a slick combination of film genres:

Gregory Peck, Stanley Baker, and David Niven in THE GUNS OF NAVARONE (1961).

combat, spy, and adventure. *Time* magazine labeled the film "the most enjoyable consignment of baloney in months." The *New York Times'* Bosley Crowther judged it a "big, robust action drama," and Paul V. Beckley in the *New York Herald Tribune* appraised it as "a good, bone-hard, manly military adventure." The film grossed $13,000,000 in domestic net rentals and was the top domestic grossing picture of the year. Its special effects won Academy Awards, and it was Oscar-nominated for Best Picture, Director and Screenplay. Sixteen years later a sequel of sorts, FORCE 10 FROM NAVARONE, q.v., would appear, and thereafter its profitable war/adventure motifs would be adapted by the RAMBO and MISSING IN ACTION series, both of them relating the motif to the perspective of the Vietnam War.

A GUY NAMED JOE (Metro-Goldwyn-Mayer, 1943) 118 mins.

Producer, Everett Riskin; director, Victor Fleming; story, Charles Sprague, David Boehm, Frederick H. Brennan; screenplay, Dalton Trumbo; art directors, Cedric Gibbons, Lyle Wheeler; set decorators, Edwin B. Willis, Ralph Hurst; music, Herbert Stothart; song, Roy Turk and Fred Ahlert; assistant director, Horace Hough; sound, Charles E. Wallace; special effects, A. Arnold Gillespie, Donald Jahraus, Warren Newcombe; camera, George Folsey, Karl Freund; editor, Frank Sullivan.

Spencer Tracy (Pete Sandidge); Irene Dunne (Dorinda Durston); Van Johnson (Ted Randall); Ward Bond (Al Yackey); James Gleason ("Nails" Kilpatrick); Lionel Barrymore (The General); Barry Nelson (Dick Rumney); Don DeFore ("Powerhouse" O'Rourke); Henry O'Neill (Colonel Hendricks); Addison Richards (Major Corbett); Charles Smith (Sanderson); Mary Elliott (Dance Hall Girl); Earl Schenck (Colonel Schenck); Maurice Murphy (Captain Robertson); Gertrude Hoffman (Old Woman); Mark Daniels (Lieutenant); William Bishop (Ray); Esther Williams (Ellen Bright); Eve Whitney (Powerhouse's Girl); Kay Williams (Girl at Bar); Walter Sande (Mess Sergeant); Gibson Gowland (Bartender); John Whitney, Kirk Alyn (Officers in Heaven); James Millican (Orderly); Ernest Severn (Davy); Edward Hardwicke (George); Raymond Severn (Cyril); Yvonne Severn (Elizabeth); Christopher Severn (Peter); John Frederick (Lieutenant); Frank Faylen, Phil Van Zandt (Majors); Marshall Reed, Blake Edwards (Flyers); Matt Willis (Lieutenant Hunter); Peter Cookson (Sergeant Hanson); Jacqueline White (Helen); Bill Arthur, John Bogden, Herbert Gunn, Bob Sully, Johnny Dunn, James Martin, Richard Woodruff, Ken Scott, Louis Hart, Fred Beckner (Cadets); Craig Flannigan, Melvin Nix, Earl Kent, Michael Owen (U.S. Lieuten-

Spencer Tracy, Irene Dunne, and Van Johnson in A GUY NAMED JOE (1943).

ants); Joan Thorsen, Leatrice Gilbert, Mary Ganley (Girls in Chinese Restaurant); Charles King. Jr. (Lieutenant Collins); Eddie Borden (Taxi Driver); Arthur Space (San Francisco Airport Captain); Alan Wilson (Sergeant in Jeep); Leslie Vincent (Sentry).

During World War II combat pilot Pete Sandidge (Spencer Tracy) wins acclaim for his reckless bravery. His foolhardy heroism inspires fellow pilots but worries his fiancée, Dorinda Durston (Irene Dunne), a ferry command pilot. Her fears are realized when Pete crashes his plane into an enemy aircraft carrier, dying a hero's death. In a special heaven for flyers, "The General" (Lionel Barrymore) dispatches Pete on a mission. He is to watch over fledgling pilots such as his bereaved Dorinda and newcomers like Ted Randall (Van Johnson). Returning to his old base, operated by "Nails" Kilpatrick (James Gleason), Pete carries on with his duties. He is perplexed, however, when Ted falls in love with Dorinda. Ted is assigned a dangerous bombing mission, but the night before he is scheduled to fly it, Dorinda, with Pete as her "co-pilot," borrows the plane. The ectoplasmic Pete and Dorinda carry out the mission successfully.*

For a war-weary public, satiated with grim death statistics, A GUY NAMED JOE was a refreshing alternative. Here fantasy, albeit with a religious overtone, can help win the war effort! The critics were well aware of MGM's astute box-office maneuver. *Newsweek* magazine reported, "As a war film, it combines excellent intentions and superb aerial combat shots with too much talk and an overcharge of sentiment. Call it a promising try that misses the boat but won't miss the box-office bull's eye." A GUY NAMED JOE earned $4,070,000 in distributors' domestic rentals, placing #8 on *Film Daily* newspaper's Ten Best pictures List for 1944 (the year of the film's general release). The film would be remade by director Stephen Spielberg in 1989 as ALWAYS, starring Richard Dreyfuss, Holly Hunter, John Goodman and Audrey Hepburn.

For the record, there is no character named "Joe" in A GUY NAMED JOE. As explained in the picture, "In the Army Air Corps, any fellow who is a right fellow is called 'Joe.' "

HALLS OF MONTEZUMA (Twentieth Century-Fox, 1950) Color 113 mins.

Producer, Robert Bassler; director, Lewis Milestone; screenplay, Michael Blankfort; art directors, Lyle Wheeler, Albert Hogstett; set decorators, Thomas Little, Bruce MacDonald; makeup, Ben Nye, Willard Buell, Thomas Tuttle; costumes, Charles Le Maire; music, Sol Kaplan; music director, Lionel Newman; technical adviser, Major George A. Gilliand (U.S. Marine Corps); assistant director, Nate Watt; sound, E. Clayton Ward, Harry M. Leonard; camera, Winston C. Hoch, Harry Jackson; special camera effects, Fred Sersen; editor, William Reynolds.

Richard Widmark (Lieutenant Anderson); Walter [Jack] Palance (Pigeon Lane); Reginald Gardiner (Sergeant Johnson); Robert Wagner (Coffman); Karl Malden (Doc); Richard Hylton (Corporal Conroy); Richard Boone (Lieutenant Colonel Gilfilan); Skip Homeier (Pretty Boy); Don Hicks (Lieutenant Butterfield); Jack Webb (Correspondent Dickerman); Bert Freed (Slattery); Neville Brand (Sergeant Zelenko); Martin Milner (Private Whitney); Philip Ahn (Nomura) Howard Chuman (Captain Makino); Frank Kum-

---

*The original conclusion for A GUY NAMED JOE has Dorinda dying while on the mission. Thereafter Ted returns to his former love, Ellen Bright (Esther Williams). Dorinda and Pete enter heaven together. MGM decided a happier finale was more appropriate commercially.

agai (Romea); Fred Coby (Captain McCreavy); Paul Lees (Captain Seaman); Jack Lee (Courier); Fred Dale (Pharmacist's Mate); Chris Drake (Frank); George Conrad (Corpsman); Harry McKim (Radioman); Bob McLean (Marine Guard); William Hawes (Paskowicz); Roger McGee (Davis); Clarke Stevens (Recruit); Helen Hatch (Aunt Emma); Michael Road (Ship's Captain); Rollin Moriyama (Fukado); Ralph Nagai (Willie); Marion Marshall (Nurse); Harry Carter (Bos'n Mate); Richard Allan (Private Stewart).

Lewis Milestone, who had directed such superior war films as ALL QUIET ON THE WESTERN FRONT (1930), THE STORY OF G.I. JOE (1945) and would later direct PORK CHOP HILL (1959), qq.v., was in charge of HALLS OF MONTEZUMA. "There's a fine patriotic note struck in the account of Marine heroism during the fierce South Pacific fighting of World War II, plus a generally smart commercial handling that gives it a favorable boxoffice outlook" (*Variety*).

As the Allies push across the Pacific during World War II, Marine Lieutenant Anderson (Richard Widmark) leads a patrol through Japanese-held terrain. His mission is to capture Japanese

HALLS OF MONTEZUMA (1950).

prisoners who can tell him where a deadly rocket site is located. Joining iron-handed but compassionate Anderson are such men as battle-experienced Slattery (Bert Freed) and Sergeant Zelenko (Neville Brand); punch drunk ex-boxer Pigeon Lane (Walter [Jack] Palance), raw recruits Coffman (Robert Wagner) and Pretty Boy (Skip Homeier). Their interpreter is the oddball Sergeant Johnson (Reginald Gardiner). It is Pretty Boy who goes berserk in battle and who has to be eliminated when he tries to kill the prisoners.

By now it was becoming almost standard practice to film such combat stories in color, making the depiction more vivid but removing it one further step from the reality of World War II black-and-white newsreels.

HAMBURGER HILL (Paramount, 1987) Color 110 mins.

Executive producers, Jerry Offsay, David Korda; producers, Marcia Nasatir, James Carabatsos; co-producer, Larry De Waay; director, John Irvin; screenplay, Carabatsos; production designer, Austen Spriggs; art director, Toto Castillo; wardrobe, David Murphy, Pense Libre; makeup, Cecille Bau, Neville Smallwood; music, Philip Glass; music editor, Michael Connell; assistant directors, Steve Harding, David Rose, Nik Korda, Soc Jose; stunt coordinator, Tip Tipping; military adviser, Command Sergeant Major Al Neal; Vietnamese adviser, Kieu Chinh; sound, David Hildyard, John Pitts; supervising sound editor, Les Wiggins; camera, Peter MacDonald; editor, Peter Tanner.

Third Squad, 1st Platoon: Anthony Barrile (Languilli); Michael Patrick Boatman (Motown); Don Cheadle (Washburn); Michael Dolan (Murphy); Don James (McDaniel); Dylan McDermott (Sergeant Frantz); M. A. Nickles (Galvan); Harry O'Reilly (Duffy); Daniel O'Shea (Gaigin); J. C. Palmore (Healy); Tim Quill (Beletsky); Tommy Swerdlow (Bienstock); Courtney B. Vance (Doc); Steven Weber (Sergeant Worcester); Tegan West (Lieutenant Eden); Kieu Chinh (Mama San); Doug Goodman (Lagunas); J. D. Van Sickle (Newsman).

In 1969 Vietnam the 3rd Squad, 1st Platoon of Bravo Company of the 101st Airborne Division is on bivouac, having sustained heavy losses battling at Ashau Valley. Some of the men use the opportunity to visit Mama San's (Kieu Chinh) whorehouse. Three black GIs—Doc (Courtney B. Vance), McDaniel (Don James), and Motown (Michael Patrick Boatman)—join the group and register their gripes against the white soldiers. ("They don't take niggers back at headquarters," says one. "Lighten up brother," one white soldier says to a black. "I'm not your brother," is the hostile retort. Another black observes cynically, "The smart white people go to college. The brothers are here because they can't afford the country club.") The Sergeants in charge, Frantz (Dylan McDermott) and Worcester (Steven Weber), tell the newcomers the enemy is tough and not to underestimate them. On May 10th the squad is back in the Ashau Valley and the losses increase, including McDaniel who is

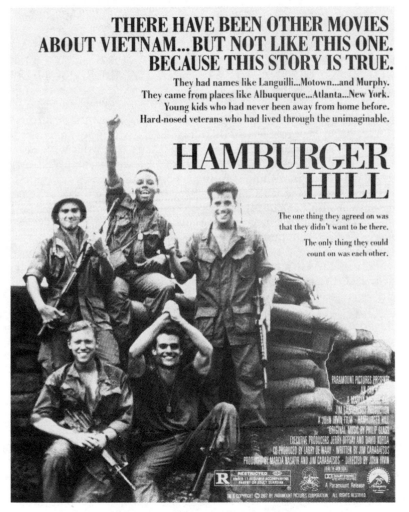

Advertisement for HAMBURGER HILL (1987).

killed by a sniper. By the next day the men are mounting an offensive to take Hill 937 in the face of heavy gunfire from the enemy. Although the men take a Viet Cong bunker, some of the Americans are mowed down by strafing from an American combat chopper. In the succeeding days, midst the rain and mud, more of 3rd Squad die, including Doc, who had reached the breaking point. By May 20th the hill is taken, but at a terrific loss of life. Among the few survivors are Beletsky, Washburn, and Sergeant Frantz. Hill 937, having been secured and renamed Hamburger Hill, is later abandoned. ("The war of hills and trails continued. The places and names forgotten except by those who were there.")

Sandwiched between such highly touted productions as PLA-TOON (1986), FULL METAL JACKET (1987) and GOOD MORNING, VIETNAM (1987), qq.v., HAMBURGER HILL never gained its rightful due. It only earned $5,750,000 in theater rentals in the U.S. and Canada.

It is a powerful film with a great deal to say about the absurdity of war, using memorable visuals and jarring, disturbing dialogue to zap across its message. There is the panorama of battle, with near mystical helicopters flying in and out of view, messengers from above delivering punishment to the enemy and rescuing comrades. There is the racial squabbling among the soldiers, where ethnic lines are drawn almost as sharply as the political ones between battle foes.

Events that have become de rigueur for combat films take on new meaning and punch in HAMBURGER HILL. There is a touching scene as the men greedily read the mail from home, and everyone listens to a tape one of the boys receives from his stateside girlfriend.("It must be very difficult for you over there and if you can't wait [to have sexual intercourse] I'll understand. I'm proud of you Joe. . . . I don't think it's fair that everyone back here is acting like nothing is going on.") There is the gut-rending sequence where some of the men survive a bloody encounter only to die at the hands of "friendly fire" from a misdirected U.S. helicopter. Later, an irritatingly dispassionate TV newsman rolls his video camera while demanding that the battle-fatigued men answer his asinine questions.

What do these men hope for? "Flush toilets, hot showers, pizza. I want a corn dog. I want some of that free love I'm always hearing about." One gripes that military life in the deadly tropics should be simpler: "How am I suppose to remember all this shit—panchos over your head, no half canteen . . . dogtags in your boots—orange pills once a week, whites daily. Don't ever walk on trails, burn the socks . . . the whole time I'm worried I might forget something." Another says, "All I want from anybody is to get their

ass wet in the grass with the rest of us. They don't have to like it, just show up." All one dying Marine asks for is, "Remember me."
". . . Unlike PLATOON, there's no subtext about Good and Evil, no Messiah figures either . . . this film is one of the more accomplished and compelling looks at soldiers living and dying in an insane struggle" (Joshua Mooney, *Movieline* magazine). "Its battle scenes have a raw, gritty power. . . . But its uncompromising indictment of the antiwar movement back home is much too simplistic and undercuts the film's tremendous momentum as a record of the combat soldiers' hellish ordeal. . . . This movie takes the blood and dirt and pain of Hamburger Hill and throws it in your face and your heart" (Jack Kroll, *Newsweek* magazine).

THE HANOI HILTON (Cannon, 1987) Color 123 mins.
Producers, Menahem Golan, Yoram Globus; director/ screenplay, Lionel Chetwynd; production designer, R. Clifford Searcy; art director, Carol Bosselman; set decorator, Ian Cramer; costume designer, Richard LaMotte; music, Jimmy Webb; assistant director, Bob Bender; sound, Gary Cunningham; camera, Mark Irwin; editor, Penelope Shaw.
Michael Moriarty (Lieutenant Commander Patrick Michael Williamson); Jeffrey Jones (Fischer); Paul Le Mat (Hubman); Stephen Davies (Miles); Lawrence Pressman (Cathcart); Aki Aleong (Cat); Gloria Carlin (Paula); John Diehl (Murphy); Rick Fitts (Turner); David Soul (Oldham); David Anthony Smith (Gregory); Ken Wright (Kennedy); Doug Savant (Ashby); John Vargas (Oliviera); Michael Russo (Fidel, the Cuban).
". . . Pic is a slanted view of traditional prison-camp sagas, injecting lots of hindsight and taking right-wing potshots that do a disservice to the very human drama of the subject" (*Variety*). "THE HANOI HILTON . . . is limited by sketchy characters and the absence of an absorbing plot. . . . The members of the vicious prison staff are Asian stereotypes you've seen in countless war movies . . . the movie's grimness isn't riveting" (*Los Angeles Times*).
The film traces a ten-year period from the autumn of 1964 onward, as U.S. pilots are shot down over North Vietnam and become prisoners-of-war kept in Hoa Lo Prison in Hanoi. The focus is on Lieutenant Commander Patrick Michael Williamson (Michael Moriarty), dogtag #2210771, as he does his best to make it through years of grueling torture, isolation, and deprivation at the hands of his captors, especially the sadistic Viet Cong officer nicknamed Fidel the Cuban (Michael Russo). New prisoners are brought into the compound as additional pilots are shot down over the years of the Vietnam War. As one of their brutalized number

says, "We die not so much for love of country, but of countrymen." Another suggests, "No matter what they do to us, we are Americans." Finally the "war" is over and the survivors are released, wondering if they endured all this for nothing. An epilogue states that of 3,400,000 American men and women who served in the Vietnam War, 58,135 never returned. Of the prisoners-of-war, 725 were repatriated, and 2,421 were unaccounted for.

HEARTBREAK RIDGE (Warner Bros., 1986) Color 128 mins.

Executive producer, Fritz Manes; producer/director, Clint Eastwood; screenplay, James Carabatsos; production designer, Edward Carfagno; set decorator, Robert Benton; costume supervisor, Glenn Wright; music, Lennie Niehaus; songs: Hal David, Paul Hampton, Sammy Fain, Paul Francis Webster, Eastwood, Sammy Cahn, Mario Van Peebles, Desmond Nakano; assistant directors, Paul Moen, L. Dean Jones, Jr., Michael Looney; stunt coordinator, Wayne Van Horn; sound, William Nelson, Alan Murray, Robert Henderson; special effects, Chuck Gaspar; camera, Jack N. Green; editor, Joel Cox.

Clint Eastwood (Gunnery Sergeant Thomas Highway); Marsha Mason (Aggie); Everett McGill (Major Powers); Moses Gunn (Sergeant Webster); Eileen Heckart (Little Mary); Bo Svenson (Roy Jennings); Boyd Gaines (Lieutenant Ring); Mario Van Peebles (Stitch Jones); Arlen Dean Snyder (Master Sergeant Choozoo); Vincent Irizarry (Fragetti); Ramon Franco (Aponte); Tom Villard (Profile); Mike Gomez (Quinones); Rodney Hill (Collins); Peter Koch ("Swede" Johanson); Richard Venture (Colonel Meyers); Peter Jason (Major Devin); J C. Quinn (Quartermaster Sergeant); Begona Plaza (Mrs. Aponte); John Eames (Judge Zane); Thom Sharp, Jack Gallagher (Emcees); John Hosteller (Reese); Holly Shelton-Foy (Sarita Dwayne); and: Nicholas Worth, Timothy Fall, Jon Pennell, Trish Garland, Dutch Mann, Darwyn Swalve, Christopher Lee Michael, Alex M. Bello, Steve Halsey, John Sasse, Rebecca Perle, Annie O'Donnell, Elizabeth Ruscio, Lloyd Nelson, Sergeant Major John H. Brewer, Michael Maurer, Tom Ellison.

Capitalizing on his status as the cinema's heir to John Wayne, filmmaker Clint Eastwood turned out HEARTBREAK RIDGE, a savvy depiction of a man who has made the military his family and now in middle age is being pushed aside by his loved one in favor of new, high-tech trappings and personnel.

Having won the Congressional Medal of Honor in the Korean War and served in Vietnam, aging Marine gunnery sergeant Thomas Highway (Clint Eastwood) realizes his days in the military are numbered. He is finally transferred, at his request, back to his old combat unit so he can end his military service where it began. On the way to base, he meets a would-be rock singer named Stitch Jones (Mario Van Peebles) who cheats and deserts him. At the base Major Powers (Everett McGill), the battalion commander, controls his unit by the book and regards Highway as an anachronism ("You ought to be sealed in a case labeled 'Break open only in case of war' "). More understanding is naive Lieutenant Ring (Boyd Gaines) and old friend Master Sergeant Choozoo (Arlen Dean Snyder), the latter always eager to recount old war experiences and extol Highway's past acts of heroism. Highway's duty is to whip the 2nd Reconnaissance Platoon into shape; his rival is the respected 1st Platoon headed by Sergeant Webster (Moses Gunn). Highway's men, including Stitch and the battling Swede Johanson (Peter Koch), learn the hard way that their trainer is much their superior in body and intellect, and in a showdown he can be more foul-mouthed than they. In the meantime, Highway tries to rekindle a romance with his bitter ex-wife Aggie (Marsha Mason), a cocktail waitress who is having an affair with her boss (Bo Svenson). Highway and his platoon are dispatched for Grenada where they join an invasion force rescuing American citizens. In the fighting, Profile (Tom Villard) is killed, while Highway disobeys Powers' order by successfully taking a strategic hill. Back at the base, Highway and Aggie reunite.

"Clint Eastwood's HEARTBREAK RIDGE uses an absolutely standard plot, and makes it special with its energy, its colorful characters, and its almost poetic vulgarity. We have seen this story in a hundred other movies, where the combat-hardened veteran, facing retirement, gets one last assignment to train a platoon of green kids and lead them into battle. But Eastwood . . . caresses the material as if he didn't know B movies have gone out of style" (Roger Ebert, *Movie Home Companion*, 1987).

Richard Combs observed in the British *Monthly Film Bulletin*, "Nothing fazed by the lack of a world war to show off all the skills so arduously won in training, it settles quite happily for the invasion of Grenada in 1983 as a showcase and presents it as a victory significant enough to square the account with Vietnam. . . . [It] reinforces the implicit perspective of the film that all the world is a Marine Corps training camp. . . ."

HEARTBREAK RIDGE was filmed in less than eight weeks and earned $21,600,000 in theater rentals in the U.S. and Canada. The Department of Defense withdrew its support of the film after seeing a completed print, objecting to the extensive profanity that was used.

HEARTS OF THE WORLD (Artcraft, 1918) 12 reels.
Director, D. W. Griffith; screenplay, M. Gaston de Tolignac,
Captain Victor Marier [both pseudonyms for Griffith]; music, Arlie
Elinor; camera, Billy Bitzer, Hendrik Sartow; editors, James Smith,
Rose Smith.

Adolphe Lestina (The Grandfather); Josephine Crowell (The
Mother); Lillian Gish (The Girl); Robert Harron (The Boy); Jack
Cosgrove (The Boy's Father); Kate Bruce (The Boy's Mother); Ben
Alexander (The Littlest Brother); Marion Emmons, Francis Marion
(The Boy's Other Brothers); Dorothy Gish (The Little Disturber);
Robert Anderson (Monsieur Cuckoo); George Fawcett (The Village
Carpenter); George Siegmann (Von Strohm); Fay Holderness (The
Innkeeper); L. Lowry (A Deaf and Blind Musician); Eugene Pouyet
(A Poilu); Anna May Walthall (A French Peasant Girl); Yvette
Duvoisin (A Refugee); Herbert Sutch (A French Major); Alphonse
Dufort (A Poilu); Jean Dumercier (A Poilu); Gustaon Riviere, Jules
Lemontier (The Stretcher Bearers); George Loyer (A Poilu);
George Nicholls (A German Sergeant); Mrs. Mary Gish (A Refugee
Mother); Mrs. Harron (Woman with Daughter); Jessie Harron (A
Refugee); Johnny Harron (Boy with Barrel); Mary Hay (A
Dancer); Noel Coward (Boy with Wheelbarrow); Erich von
Stroheim (A German Soldier); and: William Elliott.

The motion picture medium had already explored anti-war
themes in THE BATTLE CRY OF PEACE (1915), THE FALL OF
A NATION (1916), Thomas Ince's epic CIVILIZATION (1916),
and WAR BRIDES (1916) starring Alla Nazimova and Richard
Barthelmess. After the U.S. joined actively in World War I there were
such patriotic silent films as Mary Pickford's THE LITTLE AMERI-
CAN (1917), and the spy drama LEST WE FORGET (1918). Charles
Chaplin's comic-serious SHOULDER ARMS (1918), q.v., would
make its own telling statement on the war.

Then there was D. W. Griffith's HEARTS OF THE WORLD,
produced for Adolph Zukor's Artcraft Pictures which were released
by Famous Players-Lasky (Paramount). Filmed in France and England,* Griffith's story revolves around the son (Robert Harron) and
daughter (Lillian Gish) of two American painters living in France.
They are in love but when war is declared he joins the French army.
What follows is the protection of their French village from the

---

*D. W. Griffith had been invited by the British to go abroad and film a propaganda
production slanted to the glories of the war effort, a movie which would convince the
U.S. to join the fray. Even before his methodically-conceived production began
filming, America had entered the war. The film was produced under the auspices of
the British War Office. Griffith and his crew did some filming at the front in

Germans and the transformation of the girl (Lillian Gish) from a young, innocent girl into an adult who kills when the necessity arises. The elaborate production ran two and a half hours and was shown in two parts. Its premiere in April 1918 received great attention from the trade paper *Variety:* "... He makes his principal love story a fleshless skeleton upon which to hang a large number of brilliant war scenes. . . . Such things as depictions of a barrage, throwing of hand grenades, rifle grenades, shrapnel, firing of heavy artillery and so on, follow one another in such rapid succession that one cannot keep tabs on them." Kenneth MacGowan in *The New Republic* reported, "Here we have an art of pure emotion which can go beneath thought, beneath belief, beneath ideals, down to the brute fact of emotional psychology, and make a man or a woman who has hated war, all war, even this war, feel the surge of group emotion, group loyalty and group hate."

This very successful feature film had hardly been in release before the Armistice was becoming a reality. It had already been cut for general release after the major premiere runs, but it was further trimmed to suit the transitional peace period. By the end of 1918, HEARTS OF THE WORLD would gross over $500,000, indicating what a potent propaganda tool a war film could be.

HEAVEN KNOWS, MR. ALLISON (Twentieth Century-Fox, 1957) Color 107 mins.

Producers, Buddy Adler, Eugene Frenke; director, John Huston; based on the novel by Charles Shaw; screenplay, John Lee Mahin, Huston; costumes, Elizabeth Haffenden; music, Georges Auric; music conductor, Lambert Williamson; assistant director, Adrian Pryco-Jones; camera, Oswald Morris; editor, Russell Lloyd.

Deborah Kerr (Sister Angela); Robert Mitchum (Mr. Allison); Fusamoto Takasimi, Noboru Yoshida (Japanese Soldiers); and: Anna Sten, the Marines of Trinidad Base.

One of the tenets of war is that it throws together the unlikeliest of people, who in peace time would probably never meet, let alone interact on an intense level.

During World War II a Roman Catholic nun (Deborah Kerr) and a U.S. Marine (Robert Mitchum) find themselves trapped on a

---

France, but he found he could not get the "reality" he wanted and restaged many of the events for his picture on the Salisbury Plains in England. Regarding his inspection of the actual trench warfare, Griffith the romantic would say, "Viewed as drama the war is a disappointment. The dash and thrill of war of other days is missing." The film was promoted as "A Romance of the Great War" and "The Sweetest Love Story Ever Told."

small South Pacific island controlled by Japanese troops. While hiding from the enemy in a cave by day and foraging for food and supplies by night, the two contrasting personalities come to know each other. At first, the uneducated Allison is unaware that Sister Angela is a nun about to take her final vows—she is not wearing her nun's habit. He becomes infatuated with the quiet, dignified lady and one night after stealing a full ration of supplies right out from under the Japanese, he becomes somewhat drunk and makes

Robert Mitchum and Deborah Kerr in HEAVEN KNOWS, MR. ALLISON (1957).

advances to her. Afraid of her own feelings as much as she is of him, Sister Angela runs out into the jungle rain and becomes ill. Allison nurses her back to health, and the two come to an understanding and reach a mutual respect for each other now that he knows she is a nun. When U.S. troops begin their invasion of the isle, Allison must blow up enemy artillery so they cannot fire on American ships. In the effort he is badly wounded, but is saved by the medics. He and Sister Angela leave, each the better for their joint experiences.

The *New York Times'* Bosley Crowther rated this Cinema-
Scope and color production "stirring and entertaining." He did
note, "There are not many variations to be wrung from the
situation. However, the location is exciting . . . and it is drenched
with atmosphere. And the cast, while small, is excellent."

For her ingratiating performance, Deborah Kerr was Oscar-
nominated, as were John Huston and John Lee Mahin's screenplay
adaptation. The picture was lensed on the British West Indies' island
of Tobago and earned $4,200,000 in theater rentals in the U.S. and
Canada.

HELL BELOW (Metro-Goldwyn-Mayer, 1933) 105 mins.

Director, Jack Conway; based on the novel *Pigboats* by
Commander Edward Ellsberg; adaptors, Laird Doyle, Raymond
Schrock; dialogue, John Lee Mahin, John Meehan; technical
adviser, Lieutenant-Commander Morris D. Gilmore (U.S. Navy);
camera, Harold Rosson; editor, Hal C. Kern.

Robert Montgomery (Lieutenant Thomas Knowlton); Walter
Huston (Lieutenant-Commander Toler); Madge Evans (Joan
Toler); Jimmy Durante (Ptomaine); Eugene Pallette (MacDougal);
Robert Young (Lieutenant Brick Walters); Edwin Styles (Herbert
Standish); John Lee Mahin (Lieutenant Nelson); David Newell
(Lieutenant Radford); Sterling Holloway (Seaman Jenks); Charles
Irwin (Buck Teeth Sergeant); Henry Kolker (Admiral); Sid Saylor
(Chief Engineer Hendrickson); Maude Eburne (Admiral's Wife);
Paul Porcasi (Italian).

Life aboard a submarine is always filled with close encounters,
but when it is wartime and members of the crew are locked in heated
conflict with each other over what is right and wrong, everything
can get out of hand.

Submarine commander Toler (Walter Huston) is a rugged
disciplinarian whose sub has just completed successfully a special
wartime mission. When the vessel submerges suddenly to avoid
pursuing German destroyers, Lieutenant Brick Walters (Robert
Young) is left stranded on a lifeboat. Lieutenant Thomas Knowlton
(Robert Montgomery) cannot accept this sacrifice, especially since
he and Walters are buddies and because he adores Toler's daughter
(Madge Evans), who loves Walters. Against Toler's direct orders,
Knowlton fires torpedoes against the enemy, destroying some of
them, but not all. The Germans then drop depth charges filled with
deadly gas on the sub. Eight of the crew die, and Knowlton is later
dismissed from the service. To redeem himself, he returns to the
submarine and secretly takes it on a one-way mission destroying
enemy forces in the process.

HELL BELOW opened on Broadway in April 1933 with a steep (for that time) $2.00 a ticket admission price. The critics were not responsive. "Submarine warfare in the Adriatic, romance and broad comedy are curiously mingled. . . . The way in which it slips from farcical doings ashore to grim sights about a damaged United States submersible is decidedly jarring" (Mordaunt Hall, *New York Times*). A good deal of screen footage was allotted to MGM's resident clown, Jimmy Durante, who appeared as the cook Ptomaine, who not only fancies himself an amateur dentist but a boxer as well (leading to an encounter in the ring with a kangaroo).

Location filming for this major MGM production was done at Pearl Harbor and with the cooperation of the U.S. Navy.

HELL BENT FOR GLORY *see*: LAFAYETTE ESCADRILLE.

HELL IN KOREA (Distributors Corp. of America, 1957) 81 mins.

Producer, Anthony Squire; director, Julian Aymes; based on the novel by Max Catto; screenplay, Ian Dalrymple; music, Malcolm Arnold; camera, Freddie Francis; editor, Peter Hunt.

George Baker (Lieutenant Butler); Harry Andrews (Sergeant Payne); Stanley Baker (Corporal Ryker); Michael Medwin (Private Docker); Ronald Lewis (Private Wyatt); Stephen Boyd (Private Sims); Victor Maddern (Private Lindop); Harry Landis (Private Rabin); Robert Brown (Private O'Brien); Barry Lowe (Private Neill); Robert Shaw (Lance-Corporal Hodge); Charles Laurence (Private Kim); Eric Corrie (Private Matthews); David Morrell (Private Henson); Michael Caine (Private Lockyer); Percy Herbert (Private Moon).

Hollywood made most of the films based on the Korean War, but HELL IN KOREA was one of the few exceptions; it was made by the British.

After passing through a Korean village to be sure the enemy is not occupying it, a patrol of British soldiers find themselves isolated by the enemy. They take refuge in a hillside temple dominated by a statue of Buddha. Among the sixteen men are national service (draftee) soldiers and army regulars, the latter not sure if the former are up to the pressure. It is national service Lieutenant Butler (George Baker) who is convinced they are trapped, while Private Wyatt (Ronald Lewis) is the cowardly sort who has thrown away their radio when it became too heavy to carry. The Chinese Communists charge up the hillside, with the British withstanding the assault until their own planes begin bombing the temple. The Britishers, with the exception of the panicked Wyatt, escape during the bombing.

THEY DEPARTED AT 0600 HOURS
SOME WERE TOUGH AND SOME WERE SOFT...BUT BATTLE SCARRED HEROES ALL

...and they blended
their courage and
their cowardice to
fight an enemy for 72
nightmare hours!

A **dca** Release

with
"HELL IN KOREA"
RONALD LEWIS · STEPHEN BOYD
VICTOR MADDERN
Screenplay by IAN DALRYMPLE, ANTHONY SQUIRE and RONALD SPENCER
Produced by ANTHONY SQUIRE   Directed by JULIAN AMYES

Advertisement for HELL IN KOREA (1957).

While the film is unremarkable, it is filled with fine performances. It is also an opportunity to see the very young Stephen Boyd, Michael Caine, and Robert Shaw at work.

HELL IN KOREA was originally released in Great Britain by British Lion as A HILL IN KOREA (1956).

HELL IN THE PACIFIC (Cinerama Releasing, 1968) Color 103 mins.

Executive producers, Selig J. Seligman, Henry G. Saperstein; producer, Reuben Bercovitch; director, John Boorman; story, Bercovitch; screenplay, Alexander Jacobs, Eric Bercovici; art directors, Tony Pratt, Masao Yamazaki; set decorator, Makoto Kikuchi; makeup, Shigeo Kobayashi; technical adviser, Masaki Asukai; music, Lalo Schifrin; music editor, James Henrikson; assistant director, Hoichi Matsue; sound, Tooru Sakata; sound effects, Frank Warner; re-recording supervisor, Clem Portman; special effects, Joe Zomar, Kunishige Tanaka; camera, Conrad Hall; editor, Thomas Stanford; assistant editor, Neil Travis.

Lee Marvin (American Soldier); Toshiro Mifune (Japanese Soldier).

HELL IN THE PACIFIC reduces war to a minimal conflict—one man from each side fighting each another—in a microcosm of the larger conflict.

In World War II, an American (Lee Marvin) and a Japanese (Toshiro Mifune) soldier find themselves separated from their respective units during an encounter on a Pacific atoll. After a time, the two men become aware of one another, with the Japanese taking the American captive. The latter escapes and before long the situation is reversed. But the U.S. soldier lets his prisoner go and even joins with him later in a raft-building exercise. Eventually they reach an island chain where they find supplies among the war-torn debris. When the Japanese finds a copy of *Life* magazine showing the casualties inflicted on his people by the enemy, the peace is shattered. The deadly war game starts again.

As had been proven by other very small cast pictures, it is very difficult to keep a storyline moving properly or the situations fresh when there are so few people with whom the actors can interact. HELL IN THE PACIFIC had two forceful personalities to focus on, and the benefit of their opposing ideologies and contrasting cultures, but the film bogs down in fits of stagnation.

An alternative ending for the film, shown for some U.S. release engagements, has an explosion occurring, indicating that both men are killed. The film was shot on Koro and other Palau Islands of Micronesia.

HELL IS FOR HEROES (Paramount, 1962) 90 mins.

Producer, Henry Blanke; director, Don Siegel; based on the story "Separation Hill" by Robert Pirosh; screenplay, Pirosh, Richard Carr; art directors, Hal Pereira, Howard Richmond; set decorators, Sam Comer, Robert R. Benton; men's wardrobe, Wally Harton; makeup supervisor, Wally Westmore; makeup, William Morley, Bob Hickman; music, Leonard Rosenman; assistant directors, William McGarry, James Rosenberger, Jack Barry; technical adviser, William H. Harrigan, Jr. (Major, U.S. Army); sound, Philip Mitchell, John Wilkinson; special effects, Dick Webb; special camera effects, John P. Fulton; camera, Harold Lipstein; editor, Howard Smith.

Steve McQueen (Reese); Bobby Darin (Private Corby); Fess Parker (Sergeant Pike); Harry Guardino (Sergeant Larkin); Nick Adams (Homer); Bob Newhart (Private Driscoll); James Coburn (Henshaw); Mike Kellin (Kolinski); Joseph Hoover (Captain Loomis); Bill Mullikin (Private Cumberly); L. Q. Jones (Sergeant Frazer); Michele Montau (Monique); Don Haggerty (Captain Mace).

There are many factors which lead a person to commit heroic acts during wartime, one of them being an effort to redeem the individual's honor in his own eyes and those of others.

In the autumn of 1944, the Allies are fighting the Nazis at the Siegfried Line in Belgium. Rebellious, sullen Reese (Steve McQueen), a G.I. who has performed many heroic wartime deeds, loses his sergeant's stripes for drunkenness and is returned to his infantry squad. Embarrassed and resentful at being demoted, he is at odds with the other battle-weary men. The squad is ordered to hold a position adjacent to a German pillbox. They are told to remain there until replacements arrive and they use various ploys to fool the enemy into thinking they are a much larger, better equipped fighting unit. Reese perceives that the ruse will soon be discovered and, against orders, leads a raid against the pillbox. Not only does the charge fail, but he now faces court-martial. Rather than endure further disgrace, he creates a one-man assault, blowing up the German gun crew and himself. The Allies can now penetrate the Siegfried Line.

Iconoclastic, brooding Steve McQueen, a rebel with his own cause, would make several other combat films (including NEVER SO FEW, THE WAR LOVER, and THE GREAT ESCAPE, qq.v.), but it is the brutal HELL IS FOR HEROES which reveals the film star at his most charismatic—a rugged loner who cannot interact with his peers. He is the personification of the maxim: "The tough get going when the going gets tough." Among the cast of this exceptional film are Nick Adams and Bobby Darin, two Hollywood contemporaries of McQueen, also noted for their strong anti-establishment, aggressive behavior. Bob Newhart, "the buttoned-down comedian," made his screen debut in HELL IS FOR HEROES and is given a chance to do a variation of one of his famous nightclub monologues when he pretends to be many people talking on a walkie-talkie in order to fool the Germans. Directing the diverse cast (which also includes Fess Parker of "Davy Crockett" TV fame) is Don Siegel who gained a screen reputation for violent action picture. Few of his productions have been as vividly gory as HELL IS FOR HEROES.

Jeanine Basinger in *The World War II Combat Film* (1986) observes, "In its searing finale, Steve McQueen functions as a kind of human war machine. . . . His suicide/sacrifice demonstrates with dynamic image that only the McQueen character, the 'war hero,' understands what is wanted from men who fight our wars. They are to die, because that's what war asks of our young men. . . . At the end, the camera moves in on the pillbox, and the image is grained out, frozen, and changed to a newspaper image. Image becomes history. . . . One of the great war films."

The theatrical release version of HELL IS FOR HEROES contained a special prologue spoken by then President John F. Kennedy. It has been excised from television prints.

HELL TO ETERNITY (Allied Artists, 1960) 132 mins.

Producer, Irving H. Levin; director, Phil Karlson; story, Gil Doud; screenplay, Ted Sherdeman, Walter Roeber Schmidt; music, Leith Stevens; choreography, Roland Dupree; assistant director, Clark Paylow; special effects, Augie Lohman; camera, Burnett Guffey; editors, George White, Roy V. Livingston.

Jeffrey Hunter (Guy Gabaldon); David Janssen (Bill); Vic Damone (Pete); Patricia Owens (Sheila); Richard Eyer (Guy as a Boy); John Larch (Captain Schwabe); Miiko Taka (Ester); Sessue Hayakawa (General Matsui); Bill Williams (Leonard); Tsuru Aoki Hayakawa (Mother Une); Michi Kobi (Sono); George Shibata (Kaz); Reiko Sato (Famika); Richard Gardner (Sullivan); Bob Okazaki (Papa Une); George Matsui (George as a Boy); Nickey Blair (Semperi); George Takai (George).

HELL TO ETERNITY represents three favorite Hollywood ingredients: 1) be part of an already in vogue genre film cycle; 2) glamorize truth with fiction; 3) use, if at all possible, the word "hell" in the title—it's a guaranteed audience grabber.

Considering what was working against it, HELL TO ETER-

NITY is an amazingly forthright, sterling production. It stars one of Hollywood's most overlooked performers, Jeffrey Hunter, whose solid acting abilities always outshone his good looks. "This is the story of an immortal fighting man of World War II. Many who never even knew Guy Gabaldon are alive today because of him." Through flashbacks, the narrative focuses on young Guy (Richard Eyer) growing up in East Los Angeles during the Depression of the 1930s. When the homeless boy needs a refuge, his Japanese-American schoolmate takes him in as a member of his family, who then raise him. Pearl Harbor brings the U.S. into the war and the Nisei population of the West Coast is sent to relocation camps. The adult Gabaldon (Jeffrey Hunter) joins the Marines and with his military buddies (David Janssen, Vic Damone) prepares to be shipped overseas. In the bloody battle at Saipan, Gabaldon finds himself at odds with himself, struggling with his identity as an American or a Japanese (especially after the U.S. treatment of the Nisei). He proves heroic in battle and later captures General Matsui (Sessue Hayakawa). In conversations using fluent Japanese, he convinces the Japanese officer that it is his duty as a human being to let the soldiers and people of Saipan surrender. Matsui reluctantly orders his followers to surrender peacefully, but then commits hara-kiri. When Gabaldon returns to the Allied lines with his huge flock of prisoners, his fellow Marines are amazed.

"Was this not based on fact, it would be difficult to swallow. . . . Phil Karlson's direction is vigorous, most notably in the extremely realistic battle sequences (a pulsating beachhead and stimulating close contact shots). Much of this footage was shot on Okinawa, with military cooperation. It shows" (*Variety*).

HELLCATS OF THE NAVY (Columbia, 1957) Color 81 mins.

Producer, Charles H. Schneer; director, Nathan Juran; based on the book by Charles A. Lockwood (U.S. Navy, Retired) and Hans Christian Adamson (U.S. Air Force, Retired); screenplay, David Lang, Raymond Marcus; art director, Rudi Feld; music director, Mischa Bakaleinikoff; camera, Irving Lippman; editor, Jerome Thoms.

Ronald Reagan (Commander Casey Abbott); Nancy Davis (Helen Blair); Arthur Franz (Lieutenant Commander Don Landon); Robert Arthur (Freddy Warren); William Leslie (Lieutenant Paul Prentice); William Phillips (Carroll); Harry Lauter (Wes Barton); Joseph Turkel (Chick); Michael Garth (Charlie); Don Keefer (Jug); Selmer Jackson (Admiral Chester Nimitz); Maurice Manson (Admiral Charles A. Lockwood).

The most notable aspect of this formula war film is that it offers the only joint screen appearance of U.S. President Ronald Reagan and his actress wife/first lady.

The action is set in 1944 and focuses on the Sea of Japan—and the Tsushima Strait in particular—where the Navy must chart the Japanese mine fields so it can fight successfully against enemy shipping in the vicinity. Commander Casey Abbott (Ronald Reagan) not only must battle the enemy, but must deal with his hostile second-in-command (Arthur Franz). The latter is convinced that Abbott allowed a frogman (Harry Lauter) to be sacrificed more from personal feelings than as good military strategy. Helen Blair (Nancy Davis) is the nurse patiently waiting ashore for Abbott to marry her.

HELL'S ANGELS (United Artists, 1930) 135 mins.*

Producer, Howard Hughes; directors, Hughes, Marshall Neilan, Luther Reed; story, Neilan, Joseph Moncure March; screenplay, Harry Behn, Howard Estabrook, March; music, Hugo Riesenfeld; art directors, Julian Boone Fleming, Carroll Clark; assistant directors, Reginald Callow, William J. Scully, Frederick Fleck; dialogue director, James Whale; camera, Tony Gaudio, Harry Perry, E. Burton Steene, Elmer Dyer, Keck Wrigley, Dewey Rigley; editors, Douglas Biggs, Perry Hollingsworth, Frank Lawrence.

Ben Lyon (Monte Rutledge); James Hall (Roy Rutledge); Jean Harlow (Helen); John Darrow (Karl Arnstedt); Lucien Prival (Baron von Kranz); Frank Clarke (Lieutenant von Bruen); Roy Wilson (Baldy); Douglas Gilmore (Captain Redfield); Jane Winton (Baroness von Kranz); Evelyn Hall (Lady Randolph); W. B. Davidson (Staff Major); Wyndham Standing (Squadron Commander); Carl von Haartman (Zeppelin Commander); F. Shumann-Heink (First Officer); Lean Malena (Gretchen); Stephen Carr (Elliott); Hans Joby (Von Schleiben); Pat Somerset (Marryat); Marilyn Morgan (Girl Selling Kisses); William von Brinken (Von Richthofen); Harry Semels (Anarchist); Stewart Murphy, Ira Reed, Maurice "Loop the Loop" Murphy, Leo Nomis, Frank Tomick, Al Wilson, Roscoe Turner (Pilots).

Oxford University in pre-World War I days is a lark for devil-may-care American Monte Rutledge (Ben Lyon), but not so for his responsible brother Roy (James Hall). When war is declared, Roy enlists in the Royal Flying Corps and the dashing but cowardly Monte is lured into joining by accident. Meanwhile Monte remains

---

*Color sequences.

infatuated with beautiful, seductive Helen (Jean Harlow), who refuses to be faithful. She even lures Roy into an affair. Once in France, the two brothers encounter Helen at Lady Randolph's (Evelyn Hall) canteen and later they catch her in a relationship with yet another man. The brothers survive a mission to down a German zeppelin, but their co-fliers do not. Monte is accused of being a coward by the other officers. As a result, Roy and Monte volunteer for a dangerous mission behind enemy lines using a captured Gotha bomber. Their plane is captured by the Kaiser's force. Distraught Monte is willing to reveal the British position to the enemy and Roy is forced to shoot him in their cell. Because he will not give information to the Germans, Roy is executed in front of a firing squad. Later the 7th Brigade successfully attacks the Germans.

If any project was indicative of the lavish, obsessive, tunnel-vision behavior of Howard Hughes, "the eccentric billionaire," it is HELL'S ANGELS. Begun in 1926 to compete with Paramount's WINGS (1927), q.v., HELL'S ANGELS had a staggering production history. Directors (including uncredited Lewis Milestone) came and went, with Hughes finally supervising much of the filming himself. No sooner had the lavish production been completed and previewed than sound films came into prominence and Hughes, to protect his investment, reshot much of the footage in mid-1929. He replaced Swedish-accented Greta Nissen with virtual newcomer Jean Harlow and dubbed in sound effects for the aerial combat scenes, all the time ballyhooing this three-years-in-the-making project. When done he had spent $3,500,000 and had 2.5 million feet of film which was edited down to 135 minutes (and then further for general distribution). In the course of the filming, flyers Al Johnson and C. K. "Phil" Phillips and mechanic Phil Jones were killed and cameraman E. Burton Steene died of a stroke. Filming was accomplished at the Metropolitan Studios, Caddo Field in Van Nuys, Ryan Field in San Diego, March Field in Riverside, Oakland Airport, and Mines Field (now Los Angeles International Airport) in Inglewood. Other air fields were created at Chatsworth, Encino, and Santa Cruz. For the record, 87 planes (a fleet which cost a reputed $562,000 to acquire and recondition) and 137 pilots were used in the production, including Hughes himself, who would have a near brush with death flying one of the craft. A wide-screen process was used twice during HELL'S ANGELS and the ball scene at Lady Randolph's was filmed in Technicolor, with other special sequences being red tinted.

Critical response to HELL'S ANGELS was not surprising. In the air it was considered spectacularly breathtaking; especially the dogfights and the key two-reel sequence in which the mammoth

Zeppelin airship, guided by the German officer Karl Arnstedt (John Darrow), moves menacingly towards its bombing target: London's Trafalgar Square. On the ground HELL'S ANGELS was considered leaden, old-fashioned and barely serviceable. That is, except for sultry Jean Harlow as the wanton Helen. Her decolletage was as revealing as her spicy dialogue, especially her catchline which became famous: "Would you be shocked if I got into something more comfortable?"

HELL'S ANGELS' visual and technical feats would set the standards for all future films dealing with warfare in the air. In fact used and unused footage from the epic would appear in many other features of the 1930s including Hughes' own COCK OF THE AIR and SKY DEVILS, both released in 1932.

A HILL IN KOREA *see*: HELL IN KOREA.

HOME OF THE BRAVE (United Artists, 1949) 88 mins.

Producer, Stanley Kramer; associate producer, Robert Stillman; director, Mark Robson; based on the play by Arthur Laurents; screenplay, Carl Foreman; poem by Eva Merriam; art director, Rudolph Sternad; set decorator, Edward G. Boyle; makeup, Gus Norin; music/music director, Dimitri Tiomkin; assistant director, Ivan Volkman; dialogue director, Don Weis; sound, Jean Speak; special effects, J. R. Rabin; camera, Robert De Grasse; editor, Harry Gerstad.

Douglas Dick (Major Robinson); Steve Brodie (T. J.); Jeff Corey (Doctor); Lloyd Bridges (Finch); Frank Lovejoy (Mingo); James Edwards (Moss); Cliff Clark (Colonel).

Racial bigotry in the military service is nothing new, but HOME OF THE BRAVE was the first major Hollywood film to really capitalize on it. It was based on Arthur Laurents' 1945 play (which ran on Broadway for 69 performances), which had used anti-Semitism as its pivotal dramatic theme. Filmmaker Stanley Kramer thought that issue had been overexposed on the screen already and changed it to a study of blacks in the army. What emerged is a sensitive, if now dated, study of a man enduring more hell at the hands of his fellow soldiers than from the enemy.

A black soldier named Moss (James Edwards) is in a state of shock and paralysis, and the military psychiatrist (Jeff Corey) at the hospital base is determined to unravel the cause through narcosynthesis. Through flashbacks, the doctor pieces together Moss's shocking past. Moss and four other soldiers were on combat patrol against the Japanese on a South Pacific island. The others were: Major Robinson (Douglas Dick), the 26-year-old officer in charge;

Mingo (Frank Lovejoy), who had learned his wife had been unfaithful; Finch (Lloyd Bridges), a high school friend of Moss and his only buddy in the platoon; and T. J. (Steve Brodie) a bigot who endlessly harasses the sensitive Moss, who has spent a lifetime dealing with the epithet "nigger." Finally Moss is made to recall the pivotal trauma—Finch's death in action—and in so doing he is able now to recover completely. He and Mingo plan to open a bar together.

Made on a very tight budget and betraying its stage origins frequently, HOME OF THE BRAVE is nevertheless a pathmark film. It cost $511,000 to produce and earned $2,500,000 in domestic net box-office rentals.

HORNET'S NEST (United Artists, 1970) Color 110 mins.

Producer, Stanley S. Canter; director, Phil Karlson; story, S. S. Schweitzer, Stanley Colbert; screenplay, Schweitzer; art director, Arrigo Equini; set decorator, Andrea Fantacci; makeup, Telemaco Tilli; wardrobe coordinator, Annalisa Nasalli-Rocca; music/music director, Ennio Morricone; assistant director, Franco Cirinio; sound, David Hildyard; special effects, Paul Pollard; camera, Gabor Pogany; editor, J. Terry Williams.

Rock Hudson (Captain Turner); Sylva Koscina (Bianca); Mark Colleano (Aldo); Sergio Fantoni (von Hecht); Jacques Sernas (Major Taussig); Giacomo Rossi Stuart (Schwalberg); Mauro Gravina (Carlo); John Fordyce (Dino); Daniel Keller (Tekko); Daniel Dempsey (Giorgio); Joseph Cassuto (Franco); Tom Felleghi (Colonel Jannings); Andrea Bosic (General von Kleber); Bondy Esterhazy (General Dohrmann); Gerard Herter (Captain Kreuger); Hardy Stuart (Gunther); Marcello Turilli (Colonel Weede); Raphael Santos (Lieutenant with Taussig); Viti Caronia (Lieutenant at Village); Jacques Stany (Ehrlich); Bruno Marco Gobbi (Hermann); Alain Shammas, Amos Davoli (Sentries); Alessandro Jogan (Non-Commissioned Officer); Jean Valmont (Scarpi); Giancarlo Prete (Giulio); Mino Doro (Italian Doctor); Werner Hasselmann (General Lewis); Rod Dana (U.S. Colonel); John Lemma (Jumpmaster); Rick Petersen (Pilot); Fabrizio Tempio, Maurizio Tempio (Mario); Luisa Giacinti, Anna Giacinti (Maria); Vincenzo Danaro (Silvio); Amedeo Castracane, Ronald Colombaioni, Giancarlo Colombaioni, Valerio Colombaioni, Gaetano Danaro, Luigi Criscuolo, Giuseppe Coppola, Gaetano Colisano (Gang Members).

Rock Hudson had passed his box-office peak and this tattered international co-production did nothing to help re-establish him.

U.S. Army Captain Turner (Rock Hudson) is ordered to blow up a major Italian dam during World War II. He is injured when parachuting behind enemy lines and is assisted by a group of Italian orphans whose relatives were machine-gunned by the Nazis. Bianca (Sylva Koscina) is the German doctor who tends Turner and who is made to join the unusual commando squad. Unlike the storyline, the film ends with a big wallop.

Variety judged, "Instead of an offbeat war story, treatment would have been more effective as a low-key macabre tale of children alternating between juve pursuits and killing."

HOW I WON THE WAR (United Artists, 1967) Color 109 mins.

Producer, Richard Lester; associate producer, Denis O'Dell; director, Lester; based on the novel by Patrick Ryan; screenplay, Charles Wood; art directors, Philip Harrison, John Stoll; costume designer, Dinah Greet; music/music conductor, Ken Thorne; assistant director, Jose Lopez Rodero; sound, Les Hammond, Gerry Humphreys, Don Challis, Alan Pattillo; special effects, Eddie Fowlie; camera, David Watkin; editor, John Victor Smith.

Michael Crawford (right) in HOW I WON THE WAR (1967).

Michael Crawford (Lieutenant Ernest Goodbody); John Lennon (Gripweed); Roy Kinnear (Clapper); Lee Montague (Transom); Jack MacGowran (Juniper); Michael Hordern (Grapple); Jack Hedley (Melancholy Musketeer); Karl Michael Vogler (Oldebog); Ronald Lacey (Spool); James Cossins (Drogue); Ewan Hooper (Dooley); Alexander Knox (American General); Robert Hardy (British General); Sheila Hancock (Mr. Clapper's Friend); Charles Dyer (Flappy-Trousered Man); William Dysart (Paratrooper); Paul Daneman (Skipper); Peter Graves (Staff Officer); Jack May (Toby); Richard Pearson (Old Man at Alamein); Pauline Taylor (Woman in Desert); John Ronane (Operator); Norman Chappell (Soldier at Alamein); Bryan Pringle (Reporter); Fanny Carby (Mrs. Clapper); Dandy Nichols, Gretchen Franklin (Old Ladies); Jon Junkin (Large Child); John Trenaman (Driver); Mick Dillon, Kenneth Colley (Replacements).

It is often said that the bite of a satirist's pen is more lethal than the deadliest explosive. Such proved *not* to be the case with the British anti-war satire, HOW I WON THE WAR.

Smug World War II veteran Ernest Goodbody (Michael Crawford) recalls the "glories" of his military career. His varnished memories are anything but the truth. The badly-educated Goodbody is sadly equipped to lead the Third Troop of the Fourth Musketeers. Among his sorry lot of followers are: Clapper (Roy Kinnear), a beefy soldier concerned about his wife's infidelities; Gripweed (John Lennon), a soured Cockney; the buffoon Juniper (Jack MacGowran), who prefers to cavort in clown face; the cowardly Melancholy Musketeer (Jack Hedley), and Transom (Lee Montague), the only career soldier who vainly attempts to remedy Goodbody's assorted blunders. Goodbody and his motley crew are sent to North Africa to prepare for a cricket match for VIPs and soon a few of the men die in action. However, their ghosts (appearing in a distinctive color for each military engagement) return to perform their duties. As the troops move through France and on to Germany, the casualties (and ghosts) increase. At a bridge crossing the Rhine the humane Nazi commandant Oldebog (Karl Michael Vogler) captures Goodbody. The undaunted Goodbody is impressed by Oldebog, finding him "the first man I can really talk to," and learns that the German wants to sell the bridge to the Allies. Oldebog is run over by a tank controlled by Grapple (Michael Hordern) and soon, for Goodbody, the war is over. Returning to the present, he hosts a reunion for his men, but the only other attendee is Melancholy Musketeer, for no one else in the unit survived Goodbody's incompetent command.

At the time much was made of the fact that Richard Lester, who had directed the Beatles in A HARD DAY'S NIGHT (1964) and HELP! (1965), was here directing one of the singing quartet, John Lennon, in a solo appearance. HOW I WON THE WAR was a total box-office failure.

THE HUNTERS (Twentieth Century-Fox, 1958) Color 108 mins.

Producer/director, Dick Powell; based on the novel by James Salter; screenplay, Wendell Mayes; art directors, Lyle Wheeler, Maurice Ransford; set decorators, Walter M. Scott, Bertram C. Granger; executive wardrobe designer, Charles Le Maire; makeup, Ben Nye; music, Paul Sawtell; color consultant, Leonard Doss; second unit director, James C. Havens; assistant director, Ad Schaumer; technical advisers, Major Robert E. Wayne (U.S. Air Force), Captain Vernon L. Wright (U.S. Air Force); sound, E. Clayton Ward; Harry M. Leonard; special camera effects, L. B. Abbott; camera, Charles G. Clarke; aerial camera, Tom Tutwiler; editor, Stuart Gilmore.

Robert Mitchum (Major Cleve Saville); Robert Wagner (Lieutenant Ed Pell); Richard Egan (Colonel "Dutch" Imil); May Britt (Kristina Abbott); Lee Philips (Lieutenant Abbott); John Gabriel (Lieutenant Corona); Stacy Harris (Colonel Moncavage); Victor Sen Yung (Korean Farmer); Candace Lee (Korean Child); Jay Jostyn (Major Dart); Leon Lontoc (Casey Jones); Nobu McCarthy (Japanese Clerk); and: Ron Ely, Keye Luke, Captain Hugh Matheson.

Star Robert Mitchum and producer/director Dick Powell had teamed earlier for the resourceful World War II drama at sea, THE ENEMY BELOW (1957), q.v. Here they take to the sky in an intelligent study of combat men in the air, this time during the Korean War.

Major Cleve Saville (Robert Mitchum), a veteran of World War II combat, is known as "the iceman" because of his cool under fire. In January of 1952 he is stationed near the Yalu River in Korea, a demarcation point beyond which the flyers are not to pursue the Chinese "volunteers" who are flying Russian Migs. Among his younger cohorts in the air are stuffy Lieutenant Ed Pell (Robert Wagner) and Lieutenant Abbott (Lee Philips), the latter relying on drink to bolster his courage. Abbott's wife (May Britt) turns to Saville to put her husband back on the right path. In the process she and Saville begin a romance which leads them to meetings in Japan. On a crucial mission Abbott's plane is strafed by enemy fire and he parachutes into enemy terrain. Saville crash-lands his craft to come to the man's rescue, while Pell parachutes to join the Major. The two help the injured Abbott to survive and return to safety. During the course of the dangerous trek, both Pell and Abbott gain new perspectives of themselves and their military duty. Abbott's wife chooses to continue their marriage.

THE HUNTERS is well regarded for both its remarkable aerial footage shot in CinemaScope and color and for Mitchum's straightforward performance, which rises well above the hokum of the artifical love triangle.

I DUE NEMICI *see*: THE BEST OF ENEMIES.

IKE (Circle Films/ABC-TV, 5/3,4,6/79) Color 300 mins.

Executive producers, Melville Shavelson, Louis Rudolph; producer, Bill McCutchen; directors, Shavelson, Boris Sagal; based on the book *Past Forgetting* by Kay Summersby Morgan; teleplay, Shavelson; art directors, Ward Preston, Peter Murton; music, Fred Karlin; choreography, Marge Champion, Miriam Nelson; camera, Arch R. Daizell, Freddie Young; editors, John M. Woodcock, Kent Schafer, Bill Lenny.

Robert Duvall (General Dwight David Eisenhower); Lee Remick (Kay Summersby); Dana Andrews (General George C. Marshall); J. D. Cannon (General Walter Bedell Smith); Paul Gleason (Captain Ernest "Tex" Lee); Laurence Luckinbill (Major Richard Arnold); Darren McGavin (General George S. Patton); Wensley Pithey (Winston Churchill); Ian Richardson (Field Marshal Sir Bernard Montgomery); Stephen Roberts (President Franklin Delano Roosevelt); William Schallert (General Mark Clark); Wolfgang Preiss (Field Marshal Alfred Jodl); Bonnie Bartlett (Mamie Eisenhower); Charles H. Gray (General Lucian Truscott); Lowell Thomas (Himself); Vernon Dobtcheff (General Charles DeGaulle); Richard Herd (General Omar Bradley); K Callan (Mrs. Westerfield); Terry Alexander (General Arthur Tedder); Clifton Jones (Sergeant Hunt); Peter Hobbs (Admiral); Michael Mainick (General Strong); Vincent Marzello (Mickey McKeogh); Francis Matthews (Noel Coward); Patricia Michael (Gertrude Lawrence); Major Wiley (Sergeant Moaney); Jonathan Banks, Mitchell Group, Lloyd Alann (Sergeants); William Boyett (General Ward Hoffenberg); Anne Clements (Cockney Mum); Patrick Culliton (Young Lieutenant); David DeKeyser (Field Marshal Sir Alan Brooke); Clifford Earl (Lord Montbatten); Don Fellows (General Carl Spaatz); Lise Hilboldt (Jean Dixon); Ronald Leigh-Hunt (General Pagel); James Keane (Corporal); Julia MacKenzie (Sybil Bryan);

Richard McKenzie (Colonel Offenheim); Maurice Marsac (General Henri Giraud); Joe Unger (Private); Redmond Gleeson (Riley); Robert James (Captain Burns).

The focus of this gargantuan television mini-series steeped in period atmosphere was Dwight D. Eisenhower (Robert Duvall), the U. S. Army general who served as Allied Supreme Commander of the Sicily and Normandy invasions and for the remainder of the European phase of World War II. Since the elaborate production was based on a book by Kay Summersby (Lee Remick), Ike's driver during World War II, much screen time was devoted to their "relationship" as well as to Ike's (1890-1969) interaction with the other top brass. The multi-part program won five Emmy nominations. It later would be reedited to a four-hour version called IKE: THE WAR YEARS.

IKE: THE WAR YEARS see: IKE.

THE IMMORTAL SERGEANT (Twentieth Century-Fox, 1943) 91 mins.

Producer, Lamar Trotti; director, John Stahl; based on the novel by John Brophy; screenplay, Trotti; art directors, Richard Day, Maurice Ransford; set decorators, Thomas Little, Fred J. Rode; music, David Buttolph; music director, Alfred Newman; choreography, Arthur Appell; assistant director, Ad Schaumer; sound, W. D. Flick, Roger Heman; camera, Arthur Miller, Clyde De Vinna; editor, James B. Clark.

Henry Fonda (Corporal Colin Spence); Maureen O'Hara (Valentine); Thomas Mitchell (Sergeant Kelly); Allyn Joslyn (Cassidy); Reginald Gardiner (Benedict); Melville Cooper (Pilcher); Bramwell Fletcher (Symes); Morton Lowry (Cottrell); David Thursby (Bren Carrier Driver); Guy Kingsford (Lorry Driver); Bud Geary (Driver); Peter Lawford, Gordon Clark, John Whitney, John Meredith, Hans von Morhart, Henry Guttman, Frederick Giermann (Soldiers); Bob Mascagno, Italia DeNubila (Dance Specialty); Donald Stuart (Post Corporal); Eric Wilton (Headwaiter); Anthony Marsh (Assistant Post Corporal); Charles Irwin, James Craven (Non-Commissioned Men); Sam Waagenaar (German); John Banner (Officer); Wilson Benge (Waiter); Leslie Vincent (Runner).

Being timid and being a good soldier do not seem to go hand in hand, as THE IMMORTAL SERGEANT's plot shows.

Canadian Corporal Colin Spence is with the British Army in the Libyan desert, part of the North African campaign during

World War II. The unit is cut off from the main force and, with the coming of dawn, it seems likely the Axis troops will wipe them out. Spence is fearful that he does not have the courage to responsibly lead the men against the impossible odds. In a lengthy flashback, he recalls the pre-war years in London when he was a reporter and loved red-headed Valentine (Maureen O'Hara), and debonair war correspondent Benedict (Reginald Gardiner) was his rival for her love. Spence is too hesitant to ask Valentine to marry him. Thereafter he joins the military and the action returns to the near present. While fighting off a plane attack on their trucks, Sergeant Kelly (Thomas Mitchell) is wounded and many of the patrol are killed. The much older Sergeant, knowing he is dying, attempts to instill confidence in Spence with a very impassioned speech. Later Kelly shoots himself rather than burden the remaining men. Dawn comes. Spence is transformed, the encouraging words of the dead Sergeant now and forever in his ears and heart. He leads Cassidy (Allyn Joslyn), Cottrell (Morton Lowry), and Pilcher (Melville Cooper) against a German encampment, fighting the desert winds, sandstorm and the enemy all along the way. They blow up the depot and the light from the explosion leads the British to their rescue. Once recovered and having won the Distinguished Service Cross, Spence asks Valentine to marry him.

Because this was Hollywood's first feature film to deal with the fighting in North Africa, it was commercially very timely. Moreover, box-office star Henry Fonda was leaving films after THE IMMORTAL SERGEANT to serve in the Navy for the duration, so there was additional impetus for filmgoers to rush to this production. And, if these reasons were not sufficient for attracting filmgoers, there was extremely attractive Maureen O'Hara, not to mention the nightclub scene in which Bob Mascagno and Italia DeNubila perform a Latin American dance specialty number.

Discerning critics were scornful of Twentieth Century-Fox's cinematic manipulations. "The film's collaborators have tried to dramatize the simple sense of duty that pushes on the man in the ranks when common sense and even military honor would excuse his surrender to the enemy. . . . And they have not been content to let his action stand as his contribution to the success of the greater fight; they have paid him off with the Distinguished Service Cross, a lieutenancy, publicity and, of course, the girl. In short, Corporal Spence reaps a handsome profit—which seems to obscure his more important victory" (Theodore Strauss, *New York Times*). For years afterwards, Henry Fonda listed THE IMMORTAL SERGEANT among his least favorite films.

IN HARM'S WAY (Paramount, 1965) 165 mins.

Producer/director, Otto Preminger; based on the novel *Harm's Way* by James Bassett; screenplay, Wendell Mayes; production designer, Lyle Wheeler; associate art director, Al Roelofs; set decorators, Morris Hoffman, Richard Mansfield; costume coordinator, Hope Bryce; makeup, Del Armstrong, Web Overlander, David Grayson; music, Jerry Goldsmith; music editor, Richard Carruth; assistant directors, Daniel J. McCauley, Howard Joslin, Michael Daves; technical advisers: Colin J. Mackenzie (Captain, U.S. Navy, Retired), Project Officer Blake B. Booth (Captain, U.S. Navy); sound, Harold Lewis, Charles Grenzbach; sound effects editor, Don Hall, Jr.; special effects, Lawrence W. Butler; camera, Loyal Griggs; second unit camera, Philip Lothrop; special camera, Farciot Edouart; editors, George Tomasini, Hugh S. Fowler.

John Wayne (Captain Rockwell "Rock" Torrey); Kirk Douglas (Commander Paul Eddington); Patricia Neal (Lieutenant Maggie Haynes); Tom Tryon (Lieutenant William "Mac" McConnel); Paula Prentiss (Bev McConnel); Brandon De Wilde (Ensign Jeremiah "Jere" Torrey); Jill Haworth (Ensign Annalee Dorne); Dana Andrews (Admiral "Blackjack" Broderick); Stanley Holloway (Clayton Canfil); Burgess Meredith (Commander Egan Powell); Franchot Tone (CINCPAC I Admiral); Patrick O'Neal (Commander Neal O'Wynn); Carroll O'Connor (Lieutenant Commander Burke); Slim Pickens (Chief Petty Officer Culpepper); James Mitchum (Ensign Griggs); George Kennedy (Colonel Gregory); Bruce Cabot (Quartermaster Quoddy); Barbara Bouchet (Liz Eddington); Hugh O'Brian (Air Force Major); Tod Andrews (Captain Tuthill); Larry Hagman (Lieutenant [j.g] Cline); Stewart Moss (Ensign Balch); Richard Le Pore (Lieutenant [j.g.] Tom Agar); Chet Stratton (Ship's Doctor); Soo Young (Tearful Woman); Dort Clark (Boston); Phil Mattingly (PT Boat Skipper); Henry Fonda (CINCPAC Admiral).

The title of this film derives from John Paul Jones' statement, "I wish to have no connection with any ship that does not sail fast, for I intend to go in harm's way."

IN HARM'S WAY, as with most of Otto Preminger's post-1950s productions, is a bizarre carnival of overblown theatrics, controlled technical craftsmanship, and a point of view that sways alarmingly between vulgarly exploitive and stylized docudrama. That showman/ director Preminger chose to lens this expensive project in wide screen but in black and white is yet another aspect of his sense of "reality." He strives to give this film a realistic, unprettified look (which it has except for the obvious use of special effects models for battle scenes). However, at the same time he loads

John Wayne and Paula Prentiss in IN HARM'S WAY (1965).

the motion picture with so many star turns that they distract from the credibility level. With John "Duke" Wayne in the lead, there is no question that the film's point-of-view will be to treat war as a patriotic adventure, rather than the hellish and futile enterprise that it really is. For several critics, the fact that Wayne and many others in the cast are (almost) too old for their roles is another reflection on how contrived IN HARM'S WAY is. For others it is nature's subtle reminder that time was indeed moving on and that in 1965 World War II was already two decades old. The lines between truth and fiction were getting blurred.

An unprepared Pearl Harbor is attacked by the Japanese on December 7, 1941. Captain Rockwell "Rock" Torrey (John Wayne), along with his melancholy executive officer Commander Paul Eddington (Kirk Douglas), is on one of the few ships to survive the air attack. Torrey is ordered to lead his armada against the enemy. Wanting to save fuel, he disobeys regulations by not following the standard zig-zagging pattern. His cruiser is almost destroyed by enemy torpedo hits. For his actions he is disciplined and reassigned to desk command. He learns from nurse Maggie Haynes (Patricia Neal) that his ensign son Jere (Brandon De Wilde) is based on the island and is dating her nurse roommate Annalee (Jill Haworth). Torrey meets with Jere, whom he has not seen in the several years since divorcing Jere's mother. He finds that his son is a callow opportunist with allegiance to the conniving public relations Commander Neal O'Wynn (Patrick O'Neal). As the military recovers from the shock of Pearl Harbor, Torrey's value is reassessed and he is promoted to Rear Admiral. His task is to capture key islands, which indecisive Admiral "Blackjack" Broderick (Dana Andrews) has failed to do. Based on Gavabutu Island, Torrey enthusiastically launches his spearhead attack strategy and, against the odds, it proves successful. Jere is impressed by his father's accomplishments and asks to be transferred back to PT boat command. Meanwhile, Eddington, who has never recovered from the unfaithfulness of his wife (who died at Pearl Harbor), drunkenly rapes Annalee at a beach rendezvous. She in turn commits suicide and it is Torrey who must tell his son the bad news. To redeem himself, Eddington breaks orders and takes off in a reconnaissance plane to locate the approaching Japanese fleet. Eddington radios the size and position of the enemy force before being shot down. The two fleets engage in the first major sea battle of the Pacific war. Although the American force is basically destroyed, the confused Japanese depart the area through misjudgment of the situation. Operation Skyhook is a major success, but at the cost of many men and ships. Among the casualties, Torrey loses his leg in battle and Jere is killed. Torrey returns to base for recuperation under the loving care of Maggie. He looks forward to soon commanding a fresh task force against the Japanese.

Preminger cannot be faulted for his attention to minute detail in presenting the routine of naval life in wartime, or in his depiction of the attack on Pearl Harbor. It all has the ring of truth. But his cast is too often bigger than life. As if John Wayne's screen image was not already outsized enough, the script attempts to make him loom even larger. One character says, "We call him 'the rock.' He's all Navy and nothing but Navy." Oscar-winner Patricia Neal, who had co-starred with Wayne in the earlier and similar OPERATION PACIFIC (1951), q.v., was properly resolute as a Navy nurse, but her portrayal overemphasizes the unglamorous, duty-above-all aspect, and with her weather-beaten, world-weary look, she too emerges as a caricature. Kirk Douglas is saddled with an impossible role that makes no sense. At one moment he is brooding, the next he is announcing gleefully, "We've got ourselves another war . . . a gut-busting mother-loving Navy war!" The film's best performance is offered by Burgess Meredith as a genteel movie scriptwriter involved now in Naval politics. In the film's most intriguingly ironic moment, he muses whimsically, "I should be back in Hollywood sitting in front of a typewriter making this up for a movie."

IN LOVE AND WAR (Twentieth Century-Fox, 1958) Color 111 mins.

Producer, Jerry Wald; director, Philip Dunne; based on the novel *The Big War* by Anton Meyer; screenplay, Edward Anhalt; art directors, Lyle R. Wheeler, George W. Davis; set decorators, Walter M. Scott, Fay Babcock; costumes, Adele Palmer; music, Hugo Friedhofer; music conductor, Lionel Newman; orchestrator, Edward B. Powell; sound, E. Clayton Ward, Harry M. Leonard; camera, Leo Tover; editor, William Reynolds.

Robert Wagner (Frankie O'Neill); Dana Wynter (Sue Trumbell); Jeffrey Hunter (Nico Kantaylis); Hope Lange (Andrea Lenaine); Bradford Dillman (Alan Newcombe); Sheree North (Lorraine); France Nuyen (Kalai Ducanne); Mort Sahl (Danny Krieger); Steven Gant (Babe Ricarno); Harvey Stephens (Amory Newcombe); Paul Comi (Father Wallensack); Joe Di Reda (Capistron); Buck Class (Derek); Lili Valenty (Mrs. Kantaylis); Edith Barrett (Mrs. Lenaine); James Bell (Sidney Lenaine); Frank Murphy (Terrence); Mary Patton (Grace Scanlon); Murvyn Vye (Charles Scanlon); Edward "Tap" Canutt (Lieutenant D'Allesandro); Nelson Leigh (Lieutenant Colonel Herron); Veronica Cartwright (Allie O'Neill); Brian Corcoran (Bobby O'Neill).

Producer Jerry Wald had a penchant for using the Twentieth Century-Fox stock "star" company in multi-paired CinemaScope-lensed stories. Whether it was a musical (MARDI GRAS, 1958), a soap opera drama (NO DOWN PAYMENT, 1957) or a wartime drama (IN LOVE AND WAR), the narrative would be smartly grouped around at least three couples, balancing the screen time among them and their romances and problems, but never probing too deeply into characterization. It was a money-making formula.

Anton Meyer's novel of love and war during World War II was far better than this CinemaScope, color rendition. But the movie is more facile than it was given credit for at the time of release. (One critic quipped that the film ". . . will make the new generation see what their parents didn't live through during World War II.")

Meyer's theme—diluted but still adequately present in the film—is that wartime can have positive effects in the midst of its destructive chaos, especially in bringing men to a greater sense of their maturity. There is Frankie O'Neill (Robert Wagner), the smart-aleck coward who turns heroic in battle and finds love with warm, sensitive Andrea Lenaine (Hope Lange). Nico Kantaylis (Jeffrey Hunter) is the Greek-American ultra patriot who dies in battle for what he believes. Alan Newcombe (Bradford Dillman) is the sensitive intellectual who experiences the futility of war. It is he who abandons elegant Sue Trumbell (Dana Wynter) for the caring Hawaiian-French nurse (France Nuyen), ignoring the climate of bigotry regarding his "mixed" romance.

One of the reemerging trends of Hollywood war movies was to hire a nightclub comedian to appear as (in)appropriate comedy relief. It had been tried, with diminishing returns with Jimmy Durante in HELL BELOW (1933), q.v., and here it was Mort Sahl making his screen debut as the Jewish Marine, Danny Krieger. He is the nut who answers a walkie talkie in the midst of battle with, "Go-ood Mooor-ning, World War Two." Sound familiar?

IN WHICH WE SERVE (United Artists, 1942) 115 mins.

Producer, Noel Coward; associate producer, Anthony Havelock-Allan; directors, Coward, David Lean; screenplay/music, Coward; camera, Ronald Neame; editor, Lean.

Noel Coward (Captain Kinross); John Mills (Shorty Blake); Bernard Miles (Walter Hardy); Celia Johnson (Alix Kinross); Kay Walsh (Freda Lewis); Joyce Carey (Kath Hardy); Derek Elphinstone (Number One); Michael Wilding (Flags); Robert Sansom (Guns); Philip Friend (Torps); Ballard Berkeley (Engineer Commander); James Donald (Doctor); Chimmo Branson (Snotty); George Carney (Mr. Blake); Kathleen Harrison (Mrs. Blake); Penelope Dudley-Ward (Maureen Fenwick); Hubert Gregg (Pilot); Kenneth Carten (Submarine Lieutenant R.N.V.R.); Richard Attenborough (Young Stoker); Caven Watson (Brodie); Johnnie Schofield (Coxswain); John Boxer (Hollett); Daniel Massey (Bobby Kinross); Ann Stephens (Lavinia Kinross); Walter Fitzgerald (Colonel Lumsden); Leslie Dwyer (Parkinson); Dora Gregory (Mrs. Lemmon); Lionel Grose (Reynolds); Norma Pierce (Mrs. Satterthwaite); Jill Stephens (May Blake); Eileen Peel (Mrs. Farrell); Barbara Waring (Mrs. Macadoo); Kay Young (Barmaid); Everley Gregg (Nurse); Juliet Mills (Freda's Baby).

"Inspiring, expertly scripted war drama" (David Quinlan, *British Sound Films*, 1984). This was the superb British propaganda feature which combined patriotism with pathos under the sure hand of multi-talented Noel Coward and film editor turned director, David Lean. As with so many films produced in class-conscious

England, one of the chief tenets of any war picture from the British Isles was to show that, in time of crisis, the British could be very democratic, cutting across class lines. The high-caliber film would be very popular on both sides of the Atlantic. In the U.S., IN WHICH WE SERVE would be nominated for two Academy Awards (Best Picture, Original Screenplay), with Noel Coward given a special Academy Award citation for "outstanding production achievement." It was chosen the Best Picture of the Year by the New York Film Critics, and reportedly grossed twice its $1,000,000 production costs in America alone.

It is 1941 and the British destroyer HMS *Torrin* returns to port for repairs, having participated in the Dunkirk evacuation and sea encounters with the enemy. Later in May 1941 at the Battle of Crete, the *Torrin*, commanded still by Captain Kinross (Noel Coward), is bombed and sinks in the Mediterranean. The captain and his remaining men cling to a rubber raft, recalling their dear ones at home, and coping with enemy dive bombers who strafe them. Many of the survivors reach safety, but their task is not done. Kinross says farewell to each of them as they depart, not to home but to serve on other vessels. "There will always be other ships and men to sail in them. It is these men—in peace or war—to whom we owe so much. . . . In spite of changing values in a changing world, they give to us their countrymen, eternal and indomitable pride. God bless our ships and all who sail in them."

What makes this enduring classic so engrossing is the expertness of the ensemble cast, from top officers (Noel Coward, Michael Wilding) to non-commissioned officers (Bernard Miles) and the novice seamen (John Mills, Richard Attenborough). The homefront scenes are filled with typical British understatement and stiff-upper lips, and especially noteworthy are the warm performances of Celia Johnson and Joyce Carey as Coward's and Bernard Miles' wives respectively. The structural unity is provided by Coward having us experience a dramatic unity: the time span from the completion to the destruction of the HMS *Torrin*.

IN WHICH WE SERVE almost did not come into being. One high-ranking British official thought the submitted storyline for the film was offensive to the war effort—showing a British ship to be fallible and sinking. However, when reminded about the fate of the destroyer HMS *Kelly* (upon which Coward based his story), his objection evaporated.

IN WHICH WE SERVE was released in England in September 1942 by British Lion. The bulk of its American distribution came in 1943.

INCHON (Metro-Goldwyn-Mayer/United Artists, 1981) Color
140 mins.
   Producer, Mitsuharu Ishii; director, Terence Young; story,
Robin Moore, Paul Savage; screenplay, Moore; music, Jerry
Goldsmith; special adviser on Korean matters, Sun Myung Moon;
camera, Bruce Surtees.
   Laurence Olivier (General Douglas MacArthur); Jacqueline
Bisset (Barbara Hallsworth); Ben Gazzara (Major Frank
Hallsworth); Toshiro Mifune (Saito-San); Richard Roundtree (Ser-
geant August Henderson); David Janssen (David Feld); Nam Goon
Won (Park); Gabriele Ferzett (Turkish Brigadier); Rex Reed (Long-
fellow); Sabine Sun (Marguerite); Dorothy James (Jean Mac-
Arthur); Karen Kahn (Lim); Lydia Lei (Mila); James Callahan
(General Almond); Rion Morgan (Pipe Journalist); Anthony
Dawson (General Collins); Peter Burton (Admiral Sherman); John
Pochna (Lieutenant Alexander Haig); William Dupree (Turkish
Sergeant); Grace Chan (Au Cheu); Nak Hoon Lee (Jimmy); Kwang
Nam Yang (President Rhee); Il Woong (North Korean Commis-
sar); Mickey Knox (Admiral Doyle); and: The Little Angels.
   "INCHON is the worst movie ever made. . . . Actually,
INCHON isn't really a film, it's a grotesque footnote in movie
history" (Jack Kroll, *Newsweek* magazine).
   INCHON ranks as one of the most outlandish non-epics of
recent decades. The $46,000,000 project was co-financed by a
Japanese newspaper publisher (Mitsuharu Ishii) and by Reverend
Sun Myung Moon of the Unification Church. The latter's participation was only belatedly made known and created great embarrassment for everyone concerned. The film starred a badly cast and even
more abysmally made-up Laurence Olivier as General Douglas
MacArthur; his sole reason for performing in the mishmash was his
$1.25 million salary. The war film went months and millions of
dollars in over-production and when finally released was so badly
received that it quickly faded from view, even in its abbreviated
105-minute version. It was an odd choice for movie critic Rex
Reed's comeback screen vehicle, he having been lambasted for his
non-performance in Mae West's MYRA BRECKINRIDGE (1970).
He plays the art critic turned war correspondent. David Janssen is
on hand as the archetypical cynical journalist, and Jacqueline Bisset
is a women's libber, the self-oriented wife of stodgy Major Frank
Hallsworth (Ben Gazzara), who finds romance among the locals in
the countryside. Toshiro Mifune is wasted as Saito-San, the father of
the girl with whom Gazzara dallies. And to round out the clichés
there is Richard Roundtree as the black macho Sergeant August
Henderson.

Oh yes, there are lots of war scenes of explosions, explosions, and more explosions. And something about General Douglas MacArthur's landing at Inchon with United Nations troops during the Korean War in 1950.

IS PARIS BURNING? (Paramount, 1966) 173 mins.*
Presenter, Ray Stark; producer, Paul Graetz; director, Rene Clement; based on the book by Larry Collins, Dominique Lapierre; screenplay, Gore Vidal, Francis Ford Coppola, Jean Aurenche, Pierre Bost, Claude Brule; additional dialogue for French scenes, Marcel Moussy; additional dialogue for German scenes, Beate von Molo; art director, Willy Holt; set decorator, Roger Wolper; costumes, Jean Zay, Pierre Nourry; makeup, Michel Derulle, Aida Carange; music, Maurice Jarrey; second unit director, Andre Smagghe; assistant directors, Yves Boisset, Michael Wynn; sound, William Sivel, Antoine Petitjean; camera, Marcel Grignon; second unit camera, Jean Tournier; editor, Robert Lawrence.

Jean-Paul Belmondo (Morandat); Charles Boyer (Monod); Leslie Caron (Francoise Labe); Jean-Pierre Cassel (Lieutenant Henri Karcher); George Chakiris (G.I. in Tank); Claude Dauphin (Lebel); Alain Delon (General Jacques Chaban-Delmas); Kirk Douglas (General George Patton); Glenn Ford (General Omar Bradley); Gert Frobe (General Dietrich von Choltitz); Daniel Gelin (Yves Bayet); E. G. Marshall (Intelligence Officer Powell); Yves Montand (Marcel Bizien); Anthony Perkins (Sergeant Warren); Claude Rich (General Jacques Leclerc); Simone Signoret (Cafe Proprietress); Robert Stack (General Edwin Sibert); Jean-Louis Trintignant (Serge); Pierre Vaneck (Major Roger Gallois); Marie Versini (Claire); Skip Ward (G.I. with Warren); Orson Welles (Consul Raoul Nordling); Bruno Cremer (Colonel Rol); Suzy Delair (A Parisienne); Pierre Dux (Parodi); Billy Frick (Adolf Hitler); Harry Meyen (von Arnim); Hannes Messemer (Jodl); Michel Piccoli (Pisani); Sacha Pitoeff (Joliot-Curie); Wolfgang Preiss (Ebernach); Michel Berger (Chief of Explosives); Gehrard Borman (von Choltitz's Secretary); Georges Claisse (Intern with Monod); Germaine de France (Old Woman); Doc Ericson (Jeep Driver); Michel Etcheverry (Luizet); Pascal Fardoulis (Gilet); Bernard Fresson (Liaison Agent); Ernst Fritz Furbringer (von Boineburg); Clara Gansard (Wife of Colonel Rol); Rol Gauffin (Consul Nordling's Secretary); Georges Geret (Commandant George); Michel Gonzales (Jacques); Konrad Georg (von Model);

---

*Color sequences.

Claus Holm (Huhm); Jean-Pierre Honore (Alain Perpezat); Peter Jacob (General Burgdorf); Catherine Kamenka (Diane); Billy Kearns (Patton Aide); Joelle Latour (Young Girl with Warren); Michel Lonsdale (Debu-Bridel); Roger Lumont ("Jade Amicol"); Maria Machado (Stella); Aime de March (Roland Pre); Felix Marten (Landrieu); Paloma Matta (The Bride); Pierre Mirat (Cafe Proprietor); Harold Momm (Colonel Jay); Georges Montant (Doctor); Russ Moro (Lieutenant with Warren); Del Negro (Officer with Chaban-Delmas); Jean Negroni (Villon); Alain Pommier (Franjoux); Georges Poujouly (Landrieux); Michel Puterflam (Laffont); Christian Rode (Blache); Serge Rousseau (Colonel Fabien); Michel Sales (Gallois' Friend); Wolfgang Saure (Hegel); Georges Staquel (Captain Dronne); Otto Stern (Wagenknecht); Henia Suchar (Prefecture Switchboard Operator); Toni Taffin (Bernard Labe); Pierre Tamin (Maurannes); Jean Valmont (Bazooka); Jo Warfield (Major with Chaban-Delmas); Joachim Westhoss (German Officer with Claire); Jean-Pierre Zola (Corporal Mayer); and: Karl Otto Alberty, Joachim Hansen, Gunter Meisner, Albert Remyu, Helmut Schneider.

The 1965 book *Is Paris Burning?* proved unwieldy when translated to the screen: it emerged as a pictorially vivid, but factually distorted and confused recreation of August 1944 when the French capital was almost burned to the ground by *Der Fuehrer*'s troops. Director Rene Clement uses a semi-documentary style to effectively blend actual newsreel/combat footage with new material, but the star-heavy vehicle proved a mishmash of cameo vignettes. None of these mini-stories add up to a cohesive whole. Part of the problem is an over-ambitious endeavor to depict simultaneously the French, the American, and German points of view. The film was a box-office failure.

In August 1944 Hitler (Billy Frick) places General Dietrich von Choltitz (Gert Frobe) in charge of Paris. Von Choltitz is told to burn the city to the ground if the Germans cannot hold it. Much of the city is already under the control of the Free French, led by General Jacques Chaban-Delmas (Alain Delon). Chaban-Delmas fears the local Communists will turn Paris into a bloodbath and he hopes Swedish consul Raoul Nordling (Orson Welles) can gain the release of Bernard Labe (Toni Taffin), an influential politician, who it is anticipated can control the Communist faction. Nordling fails and Labe is shot. Meanwhile, the Allies who have been awaiting marching orders into Paris, instead decide to push on to the Rhine. The Free French send Major Roger Gallois (Pierre Vaneck) to persuade the Allied top command that at least one military unit must liberate Paris if Germany is to surrender the city peacefully and with honor. Meanwhile Von Choltitz procrastinates about following Hitler's repeated, hysterical orders to burn Paris. Nordling is a key in convincing Von Choltitz that if he does not destroy the treasure-filled, historical city, his name will become immortal. On August 25, 1944, Paris is liberated. Von Choltitz is imprisoned and General Charles de Gaulle and his troops return to the city.

After the Paris opening of PARIS BRULE-T-IL?, with a running time of 173 minutes, it was subsequently cut to 135 minutes, and all scenes featuring E. G. Marshall as an Intelligence Officer, plus others, were deleted.

Producer Paul Graetz died shortly after filming of this massive undertaking was completed and Von Choltitz died a few days before the film was released.

ISLAND ESCAPE *see*: NO MAN IS AN ISLAND.

JOURNEY'S END (Tiffany, 1930) 130 mins.

Producer, George Pearson; director, James Whale; based on the play by R. C. Sherriff; screenplay, Joseph Moncure March, V. Gareth Tundrey; art director, Harvey Libbert; sound, Buddy Myers; camera, Benjamin Kline; editor, Claude Berkeley.

Colin Clive (Captain Denis Stanhope); Ian MacLaren (Lieutenant Osborne); David Manners (Second Lieutenant James Raleigh); Billy Bevan (Second Lieutenant Trotter); Anthony Bushell (Second Lieutenant Hibbert); Robert Adair (Captain Hardy); Charles Gerrard (Private Mason); Tom Whiteley (Sergeant Major); Jack Pitcairn (Colonel); Warner Klinger (German Prisoner).

Today JOURNEY'S END is considered an interesting curio which suffers from primitive early sound equipment, stagy theatrics, and too much high-toned British resolve. In its day, it was ranked an impressive translation of a major London and Broadway hit. "From the first flash of trench life to the last flicker of a candle flame in a dug-out . . . JOURNEY'S END is an absorbing piece of work. James Whale . . . has availed himself of the scope of the camera and the microphone, and under his knowledgeable guidance the interpolated scenes of the climactic raid, which are left to the imagination in the play, are intensely vivid. They are undoubtedly far better than any other glimpses of warfare that have come to the screen" (Mordaunt Hall, *New York Times*).

On the Western Front of World War I, British Captain Denis Stanhope (Colin Clive), who has won the Military Cross for bravery in battle, is cracking under the strain of three years of fighting and uses liquor as a salve. It is left to Lieutenant Osborne (Ian MacLaren), the philosophical second-in-command known as

"Uncle," to keep newcomer Second Lieutenant James Raleigh (David Manners) from realizing that his hero, Stanhope, is at the breaking point. Although Stanhope is enamored with Raleigh's sister, he finds Raleigh's optimism irritating and cannot cope with his blind loyalty. Stanhope turns to the cowardly Second Lieutenant Hibbert (Anthony Bushell) to confide his fears and concerns. After Osborne calms the anxious Raleigh by reciting from "Alice in Wonderland" and talking of the good things of British home life, they go on a dangerous raid on the German trenches. Osborne and others die. Later it is Raleigh's own death which ends his conflicts with the paranoid, heavy-drinking Stanhope. Grief stricken Stanhope, now more alone than ever, steels himself to face the next rounds of battle.

When JOURNEY'S END debuted on Broadway at the Gaiety Theatre on April 8, 1930, the lengthy 130-minute picture (with an intermission) was shown on a twice per day schedule with a (for then high) $2.00 admission top. Much comparison was made between the film version and the still running Broadway stage edition. *Variety* reported, ". . . The picture delivered the same powerful grip as an epic of war brought from stage to screen intact in all its sardonic grimness and bitter protest. . . . One detail is improved. Picture opens with a night scene, force of British Tommies moving up through a shell torn town toward the first line trench. . . . First rate bit of pictorial atmosphere and it gets the action moving quickly."

JUMP INTO HELL (Warner Bros, 1955) 92 mins.

Producer, David Weisbart; director, David Butler; screenplay, Irving Wallace; art director, Stanley Fleischer; music, David Buttolph; camera, J. Peverell Marley; editor, Irene Morra.

Jack [Jacques] Sernas (Captain Guy Bertrand); Kurt Kasznar (Captain Jean Callaux); Arnold Moss (The General); Peter Van Eyck (Lieutenant Heinrich Heldman); Marcel Dalio (Sergeant Taite); Norman Dupont (Lieutenant Andre Maupin); Lawrence Dobkin (Major Maurice Bonet); Pat Blake (Gizele Bonet); Irene Montwill (Jacqueline); Alberto Morin (Major Riviere); Maurice Marsac (Captain LeRoy); Louis Mercier (Captain Darbley); Peter Bourne (Lieutenant Robert); Roger Valmy (Lamoreaux); Lisa Montell (Jacqueline); George Chan (Thai); Jack Scott (Dejean); Harold Dyrenforth (Plandrin); Leon Lontoc (Pharm).

Long before Vietnam became America's military and moral dilemma, the country was known as Indo-China and the French were paying dearly for their past imperialism with an arduous battle against the Communists.

JUMP INTO HELL, with a script by Irving Wallace, is an ungripping fiction concerning four commandoes (Jacques Sernas, Kurt Kasznar, Peter Van Eyck and Norman Dupont) who are parachuted into Indo-China at the request of the desperate commander at Dien Bien Phu. Through flashback, the reasons for each of the quartet volunteering for the dangerous mission are shown. Not even the interpolated use of newsreel footage made this story feel real.

In actuality the battle at Dien Bien Phu (located on the North Vietnam/Laos border) was between 16,000 French troops (as well as those Vietnamese, Cambodians, and Laotians fighting on their side) and the 60,000 troops under the command of Viet Minh General Vo Nguyen Giap. The battle lasted from March 13, 1954 to May 7, 1954, when the French stronghold was overrun. As a direct result of this major defeat, France agreed to the independence of Vietnam at the Geneva Conference that year.

JUNGLE FIGHTERS *see*: THE LONG AND THE SHORT AND THE TALL.

KELLY'S HEROES (Metro-Goldwyn-Mayer, 1970) 145 mins.
Producers, Gabriel Katzka, Sidney Beckerman; associate producer, Irving Leonard; director, Brian G. Hutton; screenplay, Troy Kennedy Martin; production designer/art director, Jonathan Barry; set decorator, Mike Ford; wardrobe, Anna Maria Fea; makeup, Trevor Crole-Rees; music, Lalo Schifrin; songs: Schifrin and Curb, Schifrin and Gene Lees; technical adviser, Alexander Gerry; stunt coordinator, Alf Joint; Yugoslav assistant directors, John Chulay, Stevo Petrovic; sound, Cyril Swern, Harry W. Tetrick; sound editor, Jonathan Bates; special effects, Karli Baumgartner; camera, Gabriel Figueroa; second unit camera, H. A. R. Thornson; editor, John Jympson.
Clint Eastwood (Lieutenant Kelly); Telly Savalas (Big Joe); Don Rickles (Crapgame); Donald Sutherland (Oddball); Carroll O'Connor (General Colt); Hal Buckley (Maitland); Stuart Margolin (Little Joe); Fred Pearlman (Mitchell); Tom Troupe (Job); Gavin MacLeod (Moriarty); Gene Collins (Babra); Perry Lopez (Petchuko); Dick Balduzzi (Fisher); [Harry] Dean Stanton (Willard); Richard Davalos (Gutkowski); Len Lesser (Bellamy); Jeff Morris (Cowboy); Michael Clark (Grace); George Fargo (Penn); Dee Pollock (Jonesy); Shepherd Sanders (Turk); Frank J. Garlotta, Sandy Kevin, Phil Adams (Tank Commanders); Read Morgan (ADC Driver); David Hurst (Colonel Dankhopf); Robert McNamara (Roach); James McHale (Guest); Ross Elliott (Booker);

Tom Signorelli (Bonsor); George Savalas (Mulligan); John G. Heller (German Lieutenant); Karl Otto Alberty (German Tank Commander); Hugo De Vernier (French Mayor); Harry Goines (Supply Sergeant); David Gross (German Captain); Donald Waugh (Roamer); Vincent Maracecchi (Old Man in Town).

Not every combat movie focuses on bravery versus cowardice, or pro- versus anti-war philosophies. Some deal with other aspects of human nature, such as man's greed for money. KELLY'S HEROES is just such a rare excursion, gussied up in an adventure/ combat motif and filled with the stereotyped personae of such war

Stuart Margolin (rear left) and Telly Savalas in KELLY'S HEROES (1970).

films, including such genre staples as Telly Savalas and Carroll O'Connor. The addition of stern-lipped Clint Eastwood insured the picture's box-office success.

In the midst of a World War II sortie in Europe, a GI squad captures a German general who, while drunk, informs Kelly (Clint Eastwood) that his mission is to deliver $16 million worth of gold to a top-secret German treasury in France. Back at headquarters Kelly learns that the company has a three-day pass and he figures that is just enough time to strike behind enemy lines, steal the gold, secrete it, and after the war divide the proceeds.

Top sergeant Big Joe (Telly Savalas) is against the harebrained scheme but when he realizes his men are insistent, he agrees, although reluctantly. Crapgame (Don Rickles), an imaginative hustler who knows how to get what is needed, is enlisted, as is the beatnik drug-taking philosopher Oddball (Donald Sutherland), the peculiar lead officer of a Sherman tank squad. Soon Kelly has created his own money hit squad. As they move through enemy lines, the little army scores several remarkable victories which reach the attention of General Colt (Carroll O'Connor), who thinks the men are overzealous patriots tired of dumb generals hampering Allied victories. He schemes to turn their activities into a personal success and plans to rendezvous with them at Claremont, coincidentally the site of the hidden gold. Kelly's unorthodox heroes reach Claremont, having suffered several casualties. They now have a dual obstacle. On one side of town General Colt has established headquarters; on the other a dedicated Panzer tank commander is protecting the gold-laden bank vault. Kelly bribes the Panzer leader into taking a share of the gold. Meanwhile Colt is mistaken for General Eisenhower and is received warmly by the French populace. With the celebration diverting attention, Kelly and his men cart away their fortune. On the bank's wall they leave a message, "Kilroy was here. Up yours baby."

Enough of the public endorsed the film to generate a respectable $5,350,000 in theater rentals in the U.S. and Canada. Nevertheless, more demanding film critics were unimpressed. "By punctuating his film with continual bombings and skirmishes, director Brian Hutton has assured himself of a wide-awake audience, even though the war theme is tiresome. Those who want action will find plenty of it here" (Ann Guarino, *New York Daily News*). "It's obvious that dumb-dumb venality, with lack of taste and/or wit and an opportunity to use the Yugoslav army at cut-rate prices, motivated the making of KELLY'S HEROES . . ." (Judith Crist, *New York* magazine).

From the opening theme song ("Burning Bridges") on, it is
hard to take KELLY'S HEROES seriously. And action director
Brian Hutton does not want the audience to! There is bullying
stand-up comic Don Rickles as the wise-mouthed whiz of the
supply depot, who is outrageously and deliberately out of place in
this war film. His constant whining, delivered with staccato
intensity, keeps everyone on his toes. There certainly must have
been soldiers as drugged out as the music-loving Oddball, but
Donald Sutherland gives the spaced-out G.I. tank commander an
exaggerated fantastic edge that turns warfare into a "fun" game. As
for Carroll O'Connor's bombastic, egotistic General Colt—God
help the U.S. army. Finally there is the confrontation between
Kelly's heroes and the Panzer tank. It is a satiric showdown played
to the hilt, with western music accompanying this fight-to-the-
finish à la Eastwood's own spaghetti western hit, THE GOOD,
THE BAD, AND THE UGLY (1967).

KING RAT (Columbia, 1965) 134 mins.

Producer, James Woolf; associate producer, Marvin Miller;
director, Bryan Forbes; based on the novel by James Clavell;
screenplay, Forbes; art director, Robert Smith; set decorator, Frank
Tuttle; makeup supervisor, Ben Lane; men's costumes, Ed Ware;
music/music conductor, John Barry; assistant directors, Russell
Saunders, Bob Templeton, C. M. Florance; sound supervisor,
Charles J. Rice; special effects, John Burke; camera, Burnett
Guffey; editor, Walter Thompson.

The American Hut: George Segal (Corporal King); Patrick
O'Neal (Max); Todd Armstrong (Tex); Sammy Reese (Kurt);
Joseph Turkel (Dino); Michael Stroka (Miller); William Fawcett
(Steimetz); Dick Johnson (Pop).

Hut 16: James Fox (Flight Lieutenant Marlowe); Denholm
Elliott (Lieutenant Colonel Denholm Larkin); Leonard Rossiter
(Major McCoy); John Standing (Captain Daven); Hamilton Dyce
(Chaplain Drinkwater); Wright King (Brough); John Ronane (Cap-
tain Hawkins); Geoffrey Bayldon (Squadron Leader Vexley); John
Levingston (Myner); John Barclay (Spence); David Frankham
(Cox).

The Provost Staff: Tom Courtenay (Lieutenant Grey); David
Haviland (Masters); Roy Dean (Peterson).

The Senior Officers: John Mills (Colonel Smedley-Taylor);
Gerald Sim (Colonel Jones); Alan Webb (Colonel Brant); John
Merivale (Foster); John Warburton (Commandant).

The Hospital Staff: James Donald (Dr. Kennedy); Hedley
Mattingly (Dr. Prodhomme); Michael Lees (Stephens).

The Australians: Reg Lye (Tinkerbell); John Orchard (Private Gurble); Laurence Conroy (Townsend); Arthur Malet (Blakely); Edward Ashley (Prouty); Richard Dawson (Weaver).

The Japanese: Dale Ishimoto (Yoshima); Teru Shimada (Japanese General); Louis Neervort (Torusumi).

Others: George Pelling (Major Barry); and: Anthony Faramus.

James Clavell's effective novel *King Rat* (1963), based on his own World War II war experiences, provided the basis for this stark

Advertisement for KING RAT (1965).

prisoner-of-war study which fared poorly with the public due to its downbeat theme and excessive running time (134 minutes). KING RAT revolves around man's baser nature, which comes frequently to the fore when he is struggling for survival.

In the last months of World War II at the Japanese over-crowded Changi prisoner-of-war camp near Singapore, things are going badly for the Allied captives. Most of them are physically and mentally emaciated. Of these 10,000 American, Australian and British prisoners, most outrank U.S. Corporal King (George Segal) in seniority. However, opportunistic King, a conniving wheeler-dealer, heads a black market operation offering bare essentials to the others. He even breeds rodents to sell as food to his starved comrades. Cold-blooded King's prime opponent is the stern pro-vost, Lieutenant Grey (Tom Courtenay), who believes the former is an immoral bastard. Grey's goal is to catch the corrupt King in black market activity and then have him punished. Occasionally the cynical King appears to be performing a kindly act, such as providing black market antibiotics for Flight Lieutenant Marlowe (James Fox) when his arm becomes badly infected after being crushed by a falling tree while he is out on a wood detail. But there is an ulterior purpose. Marlowe can speak Malaysian and therefore can barter with the prison guards. On the other hand, Marlowe accepts King for what he is and what he can accomplish. Marlowe thus is the only officer in the prison camp who can view King objectively, with neither friendship nor fear as a motive. Just as Grey has the goods on King, the war ends and the sadistic King, stripped of his special status, is just another man among the men. King and Marlowe, once thought of by others as friends, go their different ways, for Marlowe now reject King's bid of friendship. King leaves Changi Prison in his own state of shock.

"[Bryan] Forbes' sharp writing and direction eventually work against the overall effect. In the overlong 134 minutes there is a tendency to pile on the raw incidents, effect of which, in view of the early character definition, is not to advance the plot but seems shock for shock's sake" (*Variety*).

The elaborate prison compound was created for on-location filming at Thousand Oaks, California.

LAFAYETTE ESCADRILLE (Warner Bros., 1958) 93 mins.

Producer/director, William A. Wellman; based on the story "C'est La Guerre" by Wellman; screenplay, A. S. Fleischman; production designer, Donald A. Petes; art director, John Beckman; set decorator, Ralph Hurst; music, Leonard Rosenman; costumes,

Marjorie Best; makeup, Gordon Bau; sound, John Kean; camera, William Clothier; editor, Owen Marks.

Tab Hunter (Thad Walker); Etchika Choureau (Renee Beaulieu); William Wellman, Jr. (Bill Wellman/Narrator); Jody McCrea (Tom Hitchcock); Dennis Devine (Red Scanlon); Marcel Dalio (Drillmaster); David Janssen ("Duke" Sinclaire); Paul Fix (U.S. General); Veola Vonn (The Madam); Will Hutchins (Dave Putnam); Clint Eastwood (George Moseley); Bob Hover (Dave Judd); Tom Laughlin (Arthur Blumenthal); Brett Halsey (Frank Baylies); Henry Nakamura

Etchika Choureau and Tab Hunter in LAFAYETTE ESCADRILLE (1958).

(Jimmy); Maurice Marsac (Sergeant Parris); Raymond Bailey (Mr. Walker); George Nardelli (Concierge).

"A bad picture is like a frightful birthmark on your face—it never leaves you, first run, second run, reruns, TV prime time, late time, lousy time; it's always there for people to stare at unbelievingly or turn away from or, worse still, turn off, or should that be better still? It's your eternal badge of embarrassment" (William A. Wellman, *A Short Time for Insanity*, 1977).

For many, including Wellman himself, it was painfully hard to accept that the acclaimed director of WINGS (1927), THE STORY

OF G.I. JOE (1945), and BATTLEGROUND (1949), qq.v., could be responsible for the puerile LAFAYETTE ESCADRILLE. But then the Oscar winner had helmed the previous year's DARBY'S RANGERS (1957), q.v.

Wellman had long nurtured the idea of filming a story of the air corps which he himself had joined in World War I. But he had thought in terms of a nostalgic love story with war as a background; movie mogul Jack L. Warner thought in terms of a mini-war epic with then hot box-office attraction Tab Hunter in the lead. The artistic clashes led to the cinematic no-man's land that became LAFAYETTE ESCADRILLE.

Having suffered through a bad childhood due to an overly disciplinarian father, Thad Walker (Tab Hunter) rushes off to Paris where he joins the French Foreign Legion along with such soon-to-be-pals as Bill Wellman (Bill Wellman, Jr.), Tom Hitchcock (Jody McCrea), and "Duke" Sinclaire (David Janssen). The idealistic Thad falls in love with a prostitute (Etchika Choureau) and eventually marries her. Meanwhile, Walker, who deals poorly with authority, strikes the company Drillmaster (Marcel Dalio) and is imprisoned. His pals arrange his escape and once the U.S. has entered World War I, he is allowed to join the Lafayette Escadrille, the American Flying Corps. Here he proves himself in aerial battle.

Besides the contingent of second-generation Hollywood actors, LAFAYETTE ESCADRILLE featured such future stars as Clint Eastwood (as a pilot who has no dialogue) and Tom Laughlin who for a time in the late 1960s would be the Hollywood whiz kid because of his hit series of "Billy Jack" features.

British release title: HELL BENT FOR GLORY.

THE LAST GRENADE (Cinerama, 1970) Color 94 mins.

Presenter, Dimitri De Grunwald; producer, Josef Shaftel; associate producer, Rene Dupont; director, Gordon Flemyng; based on the novel *The Order of Major Grigsby* by John Sherlock; screenplay, Kenneth Ware, James Mitchell, Sherlock; art director, Anthony Pratt; set decorator, Terence Morgan, II; makeup, Wally Schneiderman; costumes, Beatrice Dawson; music, John Dankworth; special effects, Pat Moore; camera, Alan Hume; editors, Ernest Hosler, Ann Chegwidden.

Stanley Baker (Major Harry Grigsby); Alex Cord (Kip Thompson); Honor Blackman (Katherine Whiteley); Richard Attenborough (General Charles Whiteley); Ray Brooks (Lieutenant David Coulson); Rafer Johnson (Joe Jackson); Andrew Keir (Gordon MacKenzie); Julian Glover (Andy Royal); John Thaw (Terry Mitchell); Philip Latham (Adams); Neil Wilson (Wilson);

Gerald Sim (Dr. Griffiths); A. J. Brown (Governor); Pamela Stanley (Governor's Wife); Kenji Takaki (Te Ching); Paul Dawkins (Commissioner Doyle).

In the post-1960s cinema where filmmakers were seeking "new" wars to mine for box-office dollars, the theme of the mercenary at war became a recurring film subject. At first tied to unnamed wars in Third World countries, it would find a natural extension in the 1980s in revisionist stories dealing with Vietnam (e.g. the RAMBO and MISSING IN ACTION, qq.v., series). THE LAST GRENADE's claim to cinematic fame was being advertised on a huge Times Square, New York billboard.

In the Congo, sullen Major Harry Grigsby (Stanley Baker) and his mercenaries are attacked by a squad headed by inhuman Kip Thompson (Alex Cord), a former pal of Grigsby's, now hired by the opposition. Grigsby is severely wounded and returns to London to regain his health. There he is approached by a government official who asks him to go to Hong Kong and continue his fight with Thompson, who is now fighting for the Chinese Communists. Grigsby agrees but once in action his commandos are badly defeated by Thompson and the wounded Grigsby is taken prisoner. He escapes and while hospitalized meets Katherine Whiteley (Honor Blackman), the wife of Grigsby's liaison (Richard Attenborough). They fall in love and she plans to divorce her husband and marry Grigsby. Thompson arranges Katherine's death in an auto accident and in the final battle, Grigsby is killed. Before he dies he heaves a hand grenade which ends Thompson's life.

"What could have been a reasonably good actioner. . . has been badly marred by a flat predictability in plot, intrusion of an inept and, at times ludicrously irrelevant romance and some quite dreadful dialog" (*Variety*).

LAWRENCE OF ARABIA (Columbia, 1962) Color 222 mins.

Producers, Sam Spiegel, David Lean; director, Lean; based on the life and writings of T. E. Lawrence; screenplay, Robert Bolt, (uncredited) Michael Milson; production designer, John Box; art director, John Stoll, set decorator, Dario Simoni; music, Maurice Jarre; music arranger, Gerard Schurmann; music coordinator, Morris Stoloff; music conductor, Adrian Boult; assistant director, Roy Stevens; sound, Winston Ryder, John Cox; camera, Freddie A. Young; second unit camera, Skeets Kelly, Nicholas Roeg, Peter Newbrook; editor, Anne V. Coates.

Peter O'Toole (T. E. Lawrence); Alec Guinness (Prince Feisal); Anthony Quinn (Sheik Auda Abu Tayi); Jack Hawkins (General Allenby); Jose Ferrer (Turkish Bey); Anthony Quayle

(Colonel Harry Brighton); Claude Rains (Mr. Dryden); Arthur Kennedy (Jackson Bentley); Donald Wolfit (General Murray); Omar Sharif (Sherif Ali ibn el Kharish); I. S. Johar (Gasim); Gamil Ratib (Majid); Michel Ray (Farraj); Zia Mohyeddin (Tafas); John Dimech (Daud); Howard Marion Crawford (Medical Officer); Jack Gwillim (Club Secretary); Hugh Miller (R.A.M.C Colonel); Kenneth Fortescue (Allenby's Aide); Stuart Saunders (Regimental Sergeant-Major); Fernando Sancho (Turkish Sergeant); Henry Oscar (Reciter); Norman Rossington (Corporal Jenkins); John Ruddock (Elder Harith); M. Cher Kaoui, Mohammed Habachi.

"Authentic desert locations, a stellar cast and an intriguing subject combine to put this into the blockbuster league" (*Variety*).

While LAWRENCE OF ARABIA is best known as the multi-Academy Award-winning* adventure epic with the gorgeous cinematography, haunting music, and the archetypical fantasy hero engaged in noble deeds, it does treat of warfare; this time desert battles during World War I.

Opening with the motorcycle accident (suicide?) death of T. E. Lawrence (Peter O'Toole) in Dorset, England on May 19, 1935, the story flashes back to 1916. The British are supporting the Arabs in their rebellion against the Turkish-German combine of World War I. Dryden (Claude Rains) of the Arab Bureau asks the introspective and complicated Lawrence to study the Arab revolt at first hand. Agreeing to the task, he persuades Prince Feisal (Alec Guinness) to loan him 50 men to cross the Nefud Desert. Along the way he meets Sherif Ali ibn el Kharish (Omar Sharif) who joins his group. When one of his men is missing, Lawrence has the band return to the desert to rescue him, all of which adds to his reputation as a heroic leader. Soon Sheikh Auda Abu Tayi (Anthony Quinn) joins Lawrence's contingent, and they assault successfully the Turkish port of Agaba. Later Lawrence must order the execution of the man he saved in the desert, for he has killed one of Auda Abu Tayi's followers. In Cairo British General Allenby (Jack Hawkins) provides Lawrence with the needed support to carry on more warfare. His desert victories are reported internationally by American war correspondent Jackson Bentley (Arthur Kennedy). Surviving Turkish capture and torture, Lawrence is directed by General Allenby to attack Damascus. The bloody battle leaves the British and Arabs

---

*LAWRENCE OF ARABIA claimed seven Oscars: Best Picture, Director, Cinematography, Art Direction, Music Score, Sound, and Film Editing. Peter O'Toole and Omar Sharif were Oscar-nominated (for Best Actor), as was the Screenplay.

victorious, but once in possession of the city, the fragmented authority threatens to ruin what is left of Damascus. The idealistic Lawrence departs leaving Allenby and Feisal to work out a settlement. He returns to an anonymous life in England.

One of the most beautifully filmed movies ever, this engrossing war/adventure epic, which cost $15,000,000 and took three years to produce, earned $16,700,000 in theater rentals in the U.S. and Canada alone. In 1989 a restored version of LAWRENCE OF ARABIA, adding back a few deleted bridging sequences and remastered with high tech stereo sound, was issued theatrically.

THE LEGION OF THE CONDEMNED (Paramount, 1928) 74 mins.

Presenters, Adolph Zukor, Jesse L. Lasky; associate producer, E. Lloyd Sheldon; director, William A. Wellman; story, John Monk Saunders; screenplay, Saunders, Jean De Limur; titles, George Marion, Jr.; assistant director, Richard Johnston; camera, Henry Gerrard; supervising editor, Sheldon; editor, Alyson Shaffer.

Gary Cooper (Gale Price); Fay Wray (Christine Charteris); Barry Norton (Byron Dashwood); Lane Chandler (Charles Holabird); Francis McDonald (Gonzolo Vasquez); Voya George (Robert Montagnal); Freeman Wood (Richard De Witt); E. H. Calvert (Commandant); Albert Conti (Von Hohendorff); Charlot Bird (Celeste); Toto Guette (Mechanic).

Using a lot of footage from his Academy Award-winning WINGS, director William A. Wellman elevated that film's Gary Cooper to star status in THE LEGION OF THE CONDEMNED.

Gale Price (Gary Cooper) is one of the reckless young men who join the French flying escadrille for a variety of causes: boredom, escape from sordid pasts, desire for adventure. This elite group is known as "The Legion of the Condemned," for its members face sure death on their dangerous flying missions. Price joins the legion because, months before when he was a reporter, he had loved Christine Charteris (Fay Wray) and had been aghast to find her cavorting with a German baron (Albert Conti). Only now, as he is about to take a spy on an assignment behind enemy lines, does he learn that his new passenger is Christine. He drops her behind enemy lines, but she is captured. Before she can be executed Gale rescues her and they are reunited.

The *New York Post* acknowledged that the somewhat melancholy film ". . . has its tense moments, with a far-fetched and romantic plot." This film inaugurated the new screen love team of

Cooper and Wray, which failed to register with audiences, even in such further pairings as THE FIRST KISS (1928) and THE TEXAN (1930).

LETTER FROM KOREA *see*: A YANK IN KOREA.

LILAC TIME (First National, 1928) 100 mins.
        Presenter, John McCormick; producer/director, George Fitzmaurice; based on the play by Jane Cowl and Jane Murfin, and the book by Guy Fowler; adaptor, Willis Goldbeck; screenplay, Carey Wilson; titles, George Marion; art director, Horace Jackson; music, Nathaniel Shilkret; song, Shilkret and L. Wolfe Gilbert; assistant director, Cullen Tate; technical flight commander, Dick Grace; technical expert, Captain L. J. Scott; French military expert, Captain Robert De Couedic (26th Blue Devils); ordnance expert, Harry Redmond; camera, Sidney Hickox; aerial camera, Alvin Knechtel; editor, Al Hall.
        Colleen Moore (Jeannine [Jeannie] Berthelot); Gary Cooper (Captain Philip Blythe); Burr McIntosh (General Blythe); George Cooper (Mechanic's Helper); Cleve Moore (Captain Russell); Kathryn McGuire (Lady Iris Rankin); Eugenie Besserer (Madame Berthelot); Emile Chautard (Mayor); Jack Stone (The Infant); Edward Dillon (Mike the Mechanic); Dick Grace, Stuart Knox, Harlan Hilton, Richard Jarvis, Bob Blair, Frank Baker, Clement Phillips, Jack Ponder, Dan Dowling (Aviators); Nelson McDowell (French Drummer); Philo McCullough (German Officer); Arthur Lake (Dying Officer).
        First National Pictures advertised the sentimental LILAC TIME as "A lavish spectacle of beauty and thrills." It was based on the 1917 play by Jane Cowl and Jane Murfin and was released in both silent and sounds-effects versions.
        Several young men of the Royal Air Corps are billeted at the widow Berthelot's (Eugenie Besserer) farm in France, near their airfield. The widow's perky daughter Jeannine becomes the Corps' mascot. When the latest one housed there dies in World War I action, Captain Philip Blythe (Gary Cooper) is sent as a replacement. He crashes his plane when landing rather than hurt Jeannine, who is in his path. At first their relationship is as pals, then amused friends, and finally they fall in love. When the flyers go on a deadly mission, Jeannine promises to wait for Blythe. While he is facing death in the air, the farm is being bombarded by the Germans. Later, his plane crash-lands near the farm and he is sent to the local hospital. Blythe's unresponsive father (Burr McIntosh) tells Jeannine that his son is dead. The heartbroken Jeannine sends lilacs

("their" flower) to his hospital room. As she heads home young Blythe notices the flowers, and crawling to the window, spots Jeannine. He calls her back.

For some, LILAC TIME is memorable for its romantic theme song ("I Dream of Lilac Time"); for others, it is the wonderful display of the comedic talents of Colleen Moore; and there are those who relish the romance of bouncy Miss Moore and the young, handsome Gary Cooper. As a war adventure, LILAC TIME benefits from superb aerial footage. These were filmed using the hilly countryside between San Juan Capistrano and Santa Ana, California. Stunt pilot Frank Baker was killed during production.

THE LION HAS WINGS (United Artists, 1939) 76 mins.

Producer, Alexander Korda; directors, Michael Powell, Brian Desmond Hurst, Adrian Brunel; story, Ian Dalrymple; screenplay, Adrian Brunel, E. V. H. Emmett; production designer, Vincent Korda; music, Richard Addinsell; music director, Muir Mathieson; camera, Harry Stradling; editors, Henry Cornelius, Charles Frend.

Merle Oberon (Mrs. Richardson); Ralph Richardson (Wing Commander Richardson); June Duprez (June); Robert Douglas (Briefing Officer); Anthony Bushell (Pilot); Derrick de Marney (Bill); Brian Worth (Bobby); Austin Trevor (Schulemburg); Ivan Brandt (Officer); G. H. Mulcaster (Controller); Herbert Lomas (Holveg); Milton Rosmer (Head of Observer Corps); Robert Rendel (Chief of Air Staff); Archibald Batty (Air Officer); Lowell Thomas (Narrator);* and: Ronald Adam, Charles Carson, Gerald Case, Carl Jaffe, Ian Fleming, John Longden, Miles Malleson, Bernard Miles, John Penrose, John Robinson, Ronald Shiner, Torin Thatcher, Frank Tickle.

With war a reality for Britain, this super-patriotic documentary/feature was released in November 1939. It was filmed in twelve days, completed in five weeks, and produced on a budget of £30,000. It was sponsored by the newly-formed Ministry of Information and was received far more enthusiastically abroad than on the homefront. (It is reported that a pirated print reached Hitler and he was angered by the righteous we'll-pull-through tone of the British.)

The propaganda message of THE LION HAS WINGS was a display of the power of the Royal Air Force, that their Kiel Canal raid on the Germans was typical of what the enemy could expect, and that the tight little island could and would hold off any Luftwaffe attacks. Producer Alexander Korda used film clips from

---

*E. V. H. Emmett (Narrator in British release version).

FIRE OVER ENGLAND (1937) to parallel England's past strength against the Spanish Armada, and juxtaposed newsreel clips of a haranguing Adolf Hitler and his goose-stepping troops with contrasting shots of the British monarch (King George VI) and the more sedate, civilized Britishers on the homefront.

LION OF THE DESERT (United Film, 1981) Color 162 mins. Producer/director, Moustapha Akkad; screenplay, H. A. L. Craig; production designers, Mario Garbuglia, Syd Cain; art directors, Giorgio Desideri, Maurice Cain, Bob Bell; costumes, Orietta Nasallirocca, Piero Cicoletti, Hassan Ben Dardaf; music, Maurice Jarre; special effects, Kit West; camera, Jack Hildyard; editor, John Shirley.

Anthony Quinn (Omar Mukhtar); Oliver Reed (General Rodolfo Graziani); Rod Steiger (Benito Mussolini); John Gielgud (Sharif El Gariani); Irene Papas (Mabrouka); Raf Vallone (Diodiece); Gastone Moschin (Major Tornelli); Stefano Patrizi (Lieutenant Sandrini); Sky Dumont (Prince Amadeo); Robert Brown (Al-Fadeel); Eleonora Stathopoulou (Ali's Mother); Andrew Keir (Salme); Adolfo Lastretti (Colonel Sarsani); Pietro Gerlini (Barillo); George Sweeney (Captain Biagi); Mario Feliciani (Lobitto); Claudio Gora (President of Court); Massimiliano Baratta (Capture Captain); Franco Fantasia (General Graziani's Aide); Rodolfo Bigotti (Ismail); Ihab Werfali (Ali); Gianfranco Barra (Sentry); Mark Colleano (Infantry Corporal); Scott Fensome (Machine Gun Sergeant); Aisha Hussein (Aisha); Mukhtar Aswad (Collaborator); Pietro Tordi (Field Marshal); Takis Emmanuel (Bu-Matari); and: Victor Baring, Loris Bazoki, Pietro Brambilla, Luciano Catenacci, Lino Capolicchio, Filippo Degaro, Alec Mango, Ewen Solon.

This super-lavish war epic was produced in 1979 on a $35,000,000 + budget, financed largely by Libya's dictator general Muammar Gaddafi. It presents a blatant militarist approach to the 1911-1931 struggle of Omar Mukhtar (Anthony Quinn), a Bedouin leader who conducted guerrilla warfare against the invading Italians. "Film's many large-scale battle scenes include two ingenious ambushes where Mukhtar succeeds in beating the better-equipped Italian forces. . . . Much of the battle footage is impersonal with blood-packs exploding in anonymous soldiers of both armies. What's missing is the excitement and tension of men in battle whom the audience has come to know and care about" (*Variety*).

General Rodolfo Graziani (Oliver Reed) is the Italian military commander sent by Benito Mussolini (Rod Steiger) to subdue the Libyan population, bringing with him innovative tanks for desert warfare. Those he cannot subdue, he hangs; others he herds into barbed wire concentration camps; at all junctures he machine guns anyone in his way, even innocent civilians. The elder Libyan teacher and freedom fighter Mukhtar is captured eventually. When he will not submit to Graziani's will, he is tried and hung. But the tribesmen of Libya refuse to admit defeat.

The propaganda (both historical and a deliberate parallel to Palestine in the late twentieth century) to one side, LION OF THE DESERT offers a powerful panorama of partisan warriors combatting technologically superior invaders.

THE LONG AND THE SHORT AND THE TALL (Continental Distributing, 1961) 102 mins.

Executive producer, Hal Mason; producer, Michael Balcon; director, Leslie Norman; based on the play by Willis Hall; screenplay, Wolf Mankowitz; additional dialogue, Willis Hall; art directors, Terence Verity, Jim Morahan; makeup, L. V. Clark; music director, Stanley Black; assistant directors, Frederic Goode, Michael Profit, Bill Cartlidge; technical adviser, Jack Hetherington; sound, Charles Crafford, H. L. Bird, Len Shilton; special effects, George Blackwell; camera, Erwin Hiller; editor, Gordon Stone.

Richard Todd (Sergeant Mitchem); Laurence Harvey (Private Bamforth); Richard Harris (Corporal Johnstone); Ronald Fraser (Lance-Corporal MacLeish); John Meillon (Private Smith); David McCallum (Private Whitaker); John Rees (Private Evans); Kenji Takaki (Tojo).

"At a distance, enemy soldiers are targets; close up, they are men, and killing them is not so very easy. This truism of war, used to great effect in the antiwar films of World War I, appears in films about other wars" (Jay Hyams, *War Movies*, 1984).

In the Burma jungle of World War II, a seven-man British patrol headed by bumbling Sergeant Mitchem (Richard Todd) captures a Japanese scout named Tojo (Kenji Takaki). The men, including second-in-command Corporal Johnstone (Richard Harris), intend to kill the prisoner, but Mitchem believes he must be taken to headquarters for questioning. Private Bamforth (Laurence Harvey), one of those who thinks Tojo should die, is told to guard the man. It is not long before the two become friends. Later, the patrol is cut off from escape by a rockslide. Frustrated by these events and learning that Tojo has been guilty of looting, Private Whitaker (David McCallum) kills him. The gunfire brings Japanese troops into the vicinity and soon only Johnstone and Whitaker are left alive. The Japanese take them prisoner and when they discover Whitaker has Tojo's water canteen, Johnstone and Whitaker are the ones whom this patrol intends to shoot.

A.k.a. JUNGLE FIGHTERS.

THE LONG DAY'S DYING (Paramount, 1968) Color 93 mins.
Executive producer, Michael Deeley; producers, Harry Fine,
Peter Collinson; director, Collinson; based on the novel by Alan
White; adaptors, Deeley, Peter Yates; screenplay, Charles Wood;
art directors, Disley Jones, Michael Knight; wardrobe supervisor,
Eddie Boyce; makeup, Bob Lawrence; technical adviser, John
Williams (R.S. M.); assistant directors, Michael Dryhurst, Michael
Guest; special effects, Pat Moore; camera, Brian Probyn; editor,
John Trumper.

David Hemmings (John); Tom Bell (Tom); Tony Beckley
(Cliff); Alan Dobie (Helmut).

"One of those pictures that go on the assumption that if you
avow your sensibility early enough as tough antiwar, and if you
dismember your characters incessantly, an eye at a time, with mud,
and gore and blood vomiting, you can make the same picture the
prowar people have been making all along and find an audience
warmed by its humanism" (*New York Times*).

Three British parachutists are separated from their regiment.
They seek refuge in a bombed-out house while awaiting their
sergeant. The group consists of the well-educated John (David
Hemmings), a pacifist but proud of his military training; Tom (Tom
Bell), the eldest, who is a by-the-books man; and Cliff (Tony
Beckley), a sadistic jingoist. They capture a German officer, Helmut
(Alan Dobie), whose life they spare. Later they find their sergeant
dead with his throat cut. In a battle with a German search party,
Cliff and the German patrol are killed. As the three survivors reach
the British lines, the British open fire and Tom dies. Distraught
John kills Helmut before he is shot accidentally by his own side.

THE LONGEST DAY (Twentieth Century-Fox, 1962) 180 mins.
Producer, Darryl F. Zanuck; associate producer/coordinator
of battle episodes, Elmo Williams; director, American exteriors,
Andrew Marton; director of the British exteriors, Ken Annakin;
director of the German episodes, Bernhard Wicke; director of the
Ste. Mère-Eglise episodes, Gerd Oswald; based on the book *The
Longest Day: June 6, 1944* by Cornelius Ryan; screenplay, Ryan;
additional episodes, Romain Gary, James Jones, David Pursall,
Jack Seddon; art directors, Ted Haworth, Leon Barsacq, Vincent
Korda; set decorator, Gabriel Bechir; music/music conductor,
Maurice Jarre; music arranger, Mitch Miller; theme song, Paul
Anka; assistant directors, Bernard Farrel, Tom Pevsner, Louis
Pitzele, Gerard Renateau, Henri Sokal; military consultants: Gun-

THE LONGEST DAY (1962).

ther Blumentritt (General); James M. Gavin (Lieutenant General); John Howard (Major); Philippe Kieffer (Captain de Fregate); Pierre Koenig (General d'Armée); Helmuth Lang (Captain); Earl of Lovat, Frederick Morgan (General); Max Pemsel (Lieutenant General); Werner Pluskat (Major); Josef Priller (Colonel); Lucie Maria Rommel, Friedrich Ruge (Vice Admiral); technical advisers: Jean Barral (Commandant); Roger Bligh (Lieutenant Colonel); Willard L. Bushy (Commander); Hubert Deschard (Commandant); A. J. Hillebrand (Lieutenant Colonel); James R. Johnson (Colonel); Fernand Prevost (Captain); E. C. Peake (Lieutenant Commander); Albert Saby (Colonel); Joseph B. Seay (Colonel); John Crewdson (Captain); sound, Jo de Bretagne, Jacques Maumont, William Sivel; optical effects, Jean Fouchet; special effects, Karl Helmer, Karl Baumgartner, Augie Lohman, Robert MacDonald, Alex Weldon; camera, Jean Bourgoin, Walter Wottitz, Henri Persin; helicopter camera, Guy Tabary; editor, Samuel E. Beetley.

   The Americans: John Wayne (Colonel Benjamin Vandervoort); Robert Mitchum (Brigadier General Norman Cota); Henry Fonda (Brigadier General Theodore Roosevelt, Jr.); Robert Ryan (Brigadier General James Gavin); Rod Steiger (Destroyer Commander); Robert Wagner, Paul Anka, Fabian, Tommy Sands (U.S. Rangers);

Richard Beymer (Schultz); Mel Ferrer (General Haines); Jeffrey Hunter (Sergeant Fuller); Sal Mineo (Private Martini); Roddy McDowall (Private Morris); Stuart Whitman (Lieutenant Sheen); Eddie Albert (Colonel Newton); Edmond O'Brien (General Raymond O. Barton); Red Buttons (Private Steele); Tom Tryon (Lieutenant Wilson); Alexander Knox (General Bedell Smith); Ray Danton (Captain Frank); Henry Grace (General Dwight D. Eisenhower); Mark Damon (Private Harris); Steve Forrest (Captain Harding); John Crawford (Colonel Caffey); Ron Randell (Joe Williams); Nicholas Stuart (General Omar Bradley); John Mellon (Rear Admiral Alan G. Kirk); Fred Durr (Major of the Rangers); George Segal (Commando Going Up the Cliff); Peter Helm (Young G.I.).

The British: Richard Burton, Donald Houston, Leslie Phillips (Royal Air Force Pilots); Kenneth More (Captain Maud); Peter Lawford (Lord Lovat); Richard Todd (Major Howard); Leo Genn (General Parker); John Gregson (Padre); Sean Connery (Private Flanagan); Jack Hedley (Briefing Man); Michael Medwin (Private Watney); Norman Rossington (Private Clough); John Robinson (Admiral Ramsay); Patrick Barr (Captain Stagg); Trevor Reid (General Montgomery); Richard Wattis (British Soldier); Louis Mounier (Air Chief Marshal Sir Arthur William Tedder); Sian Phillips (Wren); Howard Mario Crawford (Doctor).

The French: Irina Demick (Janine); Bourvil (Mayor); Jena-Louise Barrault (Father Roulland); Christian Marquand (Kieffer); Arletty (Madame Barrault); Madeleine Renaud (Mother Superior); Georges Riviere (Sergeant Montlaur); Georges Wilson (Renaud); Jean Servais (Admiral Jaujard); Fernand Ledoux (Louis); Maurice Poli (Jean); and: Daniel Gelin, Francoise Rosay.

The Germans: Curt Jurgens (General Blumentritt); Werner Hinz (Marshal Rommel); Paul Hartmann (Marshal Rundstedt); Peter Van Eyck (Lieutenant Colonel Ocker); Gert Frobe (Sergeant Kaffeeklatsch); Hans Christian Blech (Major Pluskat); Wolfgang Preiss (General Pemsel); Heinz Reinckle (Colonel Priller); Richard Munch (General Marcks); Ernst Schroder (General Salmuth); Kurt Meisel (During); Wolfgang Lukschy (General Alfred Jodl); Eugene Deckers (German Soldier); Heinz Spitzner (Lieutenant Colonel Hellmuth Meyer); Robert Freytag (Meyer's Aide); Til Kiwe (Captain Hellmuth Lang); Wolfgang Buttner (Major General Dr. Hans Spiedel); Ruth Hausmeister (Frau Rommel); Michael Hinz (Manfred Rommel); Paul Roth (Colonel Schiller); Harmut Rock (Sergeant Bergsdorf); Karl John (Luftwaffe General); Dietmar Schoenherr (Luftwaffe Major); Riner Penkert (Lieutenant Fritz

Theen); Kurt Pecher (German Commander); Serge Tolstoy (German Officer).

One of the cinema's most spectacular combat films opens with a shot of a turned-over battle helmet on a beach, and a title card states it is now the fifth year of World War II in France. Then German General Rommel (Werner Hinz), standing on the shoreline looking out toward England addresses his subordinates: ". . . Beyond that peaceful horizon, a monster waits. A coiled spring of men. Ships and planes straining to be released against us. But not a single Allied soldier shall reach the shore. Whenever or wherever the invasion may come gentlemen, I shall destroy the enemy there . . . at the water's edge. The first twenty-four hours of the invasion will be decisive. For the Allies, as well as the Germans. It will be the longest day. . . ."

In reassembling the look, the impact, and the enormous number of people involved in D-Day, the 6th of June, 1944, Darryl F. Zanuck's task was enormous. His financially troubled studio, Twentieth Century-Fox was suffering through the perilous CLEO-PATRA, being lensed in Italy and was bobbing in and out of solvency. That the veteran filmmaker succeeded in gaining the financial capital ($10 million), organizing the almost insurmountable logistics, and hiring such a star-studded cast—and succeeding—is amazing indeed.* The film would earn $17,600,000 in theater rentals in the U.S. and Canada alone and earn two Academy Awards (Cinematography, Special Effects), as well as an Oscar nomination (Editing).

As the basis for this three-hour war history lesson, Zanuck utilized Cornelius Ryan's 1959 book, which depicts meticulously all aspects and sides of the impact of the Allies' European invasion. To give the motion picture its authentic look it was decided to shoot in black and white, while using the studio's widescreen CinemaScope process for added dimension. Zanuck astutely knew that filmgoers demanded sugar coating to make the project financially successful, so he packed the production with stars; not only Hollywood favorites but luminaries from the international film scene, which would make the movie appealing to foreign markets. Since this was a (semi)documentary, the story would be told from the American, British, French and German points of view, with dialogue carried on in native language (with subtitles when necessary).

---

*In *Combat Films: 1945-1970* (1981), Stephen Jay Rubin provides an extensive history of the making of this complex motion picture.

General Dwight D. Eisenhower (Henry Grace) determines the allied invasion of Europe will be on June 6th, 1944. The German High Command is convinced the invasion will be from Dover, but certainly not in the present inclement weather. The Luftwaffe is scattered on various duty assignments and Hitler had taken a sleeping pill and has given orders not to be disturbed. The French Resistance is alerted for the gigantic invasion and in preparation begins blowing up ammunition trains and bridges, and cutting telegraph wires. Dummy parachute figures (loaded with distracting firecrackers) are dropped on the confused German troops. Glider infantrymen are landed near the Orne River Bridge, a key site. At dawn of June 6th, 150,000 troops from thousands of ships land at the Normandy beachheads of Juno, Omaha, and Utah. A paratrooper division is machine gunned when they overshoot their destination. The French commandos capture the coastal town of Oistreham while the American Rangers scale the cliffs of Point-du-Hoc, despite the tremendous losses due to machine gunning from the enemy. At Omaha Beach the Allies are almost stymied by the Nazis who are holding fast at a cement wall, preventing the invading troops from advancing. Brigadier General Norman Cota (Robert Mitchum) urges his men onward and Sergeant Fuller (Jeffrey Hunter) places a dynamite charge, blasting a clear path (and himself) from the beach. By nightfall, the Allies are entrenched on the continent.

While viewers are frequently entrapped into playing "Which star is on screen now?", there are many engrossing cameo performances. Henry Fonda shines as Brigadier General Theodore Roosevelt, Jr., who, despite an arthritic leg, wants to lead his men in the landing assault; Robert Ryan as Brigadier General James Gavin, helping to plan the strategy; and Richard Todd as a British commando leader parachuting into enemy territory. Less can be said for the in-and-out appearances of the pop singers and actors hired to draw young moviegoers to THE LONGEST DAY: Frankie Avalon in the food line, Sal Mineo gambling in a crap game, or Paul Anka (who wrote the film's theme song) and Tommy Sands as U.S. Rangers. One of the few female roles in the film is played by Irina Demick, Zanuck's then companion, as a curvacious French resistance worker. There is a flamboyant appearance by Peter Lawford as the more flamboyant real life Lord Lovat, who, wearing kilts and with members of his unit playing the bagpipes, participated in the D-Day assault. And, of course, among the star power is John Wayne as Colonel Benjamin Vandervoort, a bolstering force of the gargantuan invasion. He is the leader who tells his high-level group in a pre-invasion briefing, "Your assignment tonight is strategic.

Don't give them a break. Send them to hell!'' When he breaks his leg during the invasion but continues to walk on it, he earns the greater admiration of his troops (whom he has admonished to use their compasses!). He tells them, "Well God willing, we'll do what we came here to do."

If any moments stand out* in this lengthy, incident-jammed film, they are the following: the harrowing sequence in which the 82nd Airborne paratroopers miss their landing mark and drift helplessly into a barrage of German machine gunners. Most are killed and only because his chute catches in a church steeple and he plays dead does Private Steele (Red Buttons) survive the massacre. There is also the rousing speech that Robert Mitchum's Brigadier General Norman Cota delivers on the Normandy beaches. He barks at Colonel Newton (Eddie Albert), "Do you think we brought them in here to let part of them die and the rest turn tail? Hell, no! We're not leaving. We're going to get up that hill! Only two kinds of people are going to stay on the beach— those that are dead and those who are going to die!'' Also there is the moment when Curt Jurgens, in a sympathetic turn as General Blumentritt, voices, "I wonder sometimes what side God is on." Perhaps most affecting of all is Richard Burton as an RAF Pilot. Lying wounded and filled with pain-killing morphine, he points out ironically to a D-Day invasion soldier named Schultz (Richard Beymer), "I'm crippled, he's dead,

---

*With a film of this length and catering to popular taste as it does, clichés probably were unavoidable. They abound in the production:

Colonel Vandervoort (John Wayne) proclaims, " We're on the threshold of the most crucial day of our times."

RAF Pilot (Richard Burton) to a peer, "You mean he's bought it?" And later in the conversation with another pilot about the hazards of their flying duties: "The thing that has always worried me about being one of the few is that we get fewer."

And still further on, he says to his fellow pilot: "I have a feeling it's on for tonight."

Destroyer Commander (Rod Steiger): "You want to know something? It gives me goose pimples just to be part of it."

A German high commander admits ominously, "An invasion of Normandy would be against all military logic . . . it would really be against all logic."

General Barton (Edmond O'Brien) to Brigadier General Roosevelt (Henry Fonda): "You're important to this operation. We can't have you knocked off the first day."

Sarcastic Brigadier General Cota (Robert Mitchum) to a scared soldier, "Don't you think you should go get your rifle? You'll surely need it before this day is over."

And not to be overlooked, Colonel Vandervoort (John Wayne) acknowledges, "It's a hell of a war!"

you're lost. I suppose it's always like that in war." In its way, it is a summation of this enormous feature film.

THE LONGEST HUNDRED MILES (NBC-TV, 1/21/67) Color 100 mins.

Producer, Jack Leewood; director, Don Weis; story, Hennie Leon; adaptor, Paul Mason; teleplay, Winston Miller; music, Franz Waxman; music supervisor, Stanley Wilson; camera, Ray Flin; editor, Richard G. Wray.

Doug McClure (Corporal Steve Bennett); Katharine Ross (Laura Huntington); Ricardo Montalban (Father Sanchez); Ronald Remy (Miguel); Helen Thompson (Lupe); Berting Labra (Pedro); Loaki Bay (Paz); Vilma Santos (Maria); Danilo Jurado (Vincente); Debra Gaza (Teresa); Juan Marcelo (Jose); Danny Tariuam (Chico); Tommy Bismark (Coro); Victor Vematsu (Hiko).

One of the earliest of the made-for-television movies is set in the Philippines in World War II as Bataan falls to the Japanese. An American GI (Doug McClure), an army nurse (Katharine Ross), a priest (Ricardo Montalban) and a bus full of native children flee the invaders. There is no comparison between this lightweight entry and such theatrical motion pictures as John Wayne's BACK TO BATAAN (1945), q.v.

A.k.a. ESCAPE FROM BATAAN.

LOST COMMAND (Columbia, 1966) Color 129 mins.

Producer, Mark Robson; associate producer, John R. Sloan; director, Robson; based on the novel *Les Centurions* [The Centurions] by Jean Lartéguy; screenplay, Nelson Giddings; art director, John Stroll; set decorator, Vernon Dixon; costumes, Tanine Autre; makeup, Harold Fletcher, Francisco Puyol; music, Franz Waxman; orchestrator, Leonid Raab; French military adviser, Rene Lepage (Commandant); Spanish military adviser, Antonio Sanz Ridruejo; assistant directors, Jose Ochoa, John Quested, Jonathan Benson; camera, sound, Wally Milner, Jack Haynes; sound editor, Alfred Cox; special effects, Manuel Baquero, Kit West; Robert Surtess; editor, Dorothy Spencer.

Anthony Quinn (Lieutenant-Colonel Pierre Raspeguy); Alain Delon (Captain Philippe Esclavier); George Segal (Lieutenant Ben Mahidi); Michele Morgan (Countess de Clairefons); Maurice Ronet (Captain Boisfeuras); Claudia Cardinale (Aicha); Gregoire Aslan (Ben Saad); Jean Servais (General Melies); Maurice Saffati (Lieutenant Merle); Jean-Claude Bercq (Lieutenant Orsini); Syl Lamont (Sergeant Verte); Jacques Marin (Mayor); Jean Paul Moulinot (De Guyot); Andres Monreal (Ahmed); Gordon Heath (Dia); Simona

Doug McClure in THE LONGEST HUNDRED MILES (1967).

Anthony Quinn and Maurice Ronet in LOST COMMAND (1966).

(Spainsky); Rene Havard (Ferdinand); Armand Mestral (Administration Officer); Burt Kwouk (Viet Officer); Al Mulock (Paratrooper Mugnier); Marie Burke (Raspeguy's Mother); Aldo Sambrell (Ibrahim); Jorge Rigaud (Priest); Roberto Robles (Manuel); Emilio Carrer (Mahidi's Father); Carmen Tarrazo (Mahidi's Mother); Howard Hagen (Helicopter Pilot); Mario de Barros (Geoffrin); Walter Kelly (Major M. P.); Robert Sutton (Yusseff); Simon Benzaken (Arab Customer); Hector Quiroga (Bakhti); Felix de Pomes (Aged Speaker).

Following the French defeat at Dien Bien Phu, Indochina in 1954, Lieutenant Colonel Pierre Raspeguy's (Anthony Quinn) paratroop command returns to France. The power-hungry Raspeguy, who has gained rank through the attrition of top command in the Indochina war, persuades the Countess de Clairefons (Michele Morgan), the widow of one of his officers killed in action, to use her influence to arrange for his transfer to Algeria. She agrees to marry him if he becomes a general. Raspeguy and two of his former officers, Philippe Esclavier (Alain Delon) and Boisfeuras (Maurice Ronet), train the new regiment into a capable fighting squad. They learn that the Arab Ben Mahidi (George Segal), another one of Raspeguy's men, has joined the Algerian terrorist network against the French. Meanwhile, Esclavier and Aicha (Claudia Cardinale) have been having an affair, he not knowing she is Ben Mahidi's terrorist sister. Later, the overly sensitive Esclavier forces her to reveal her brother's hiding place, and Ben Mahidi is killed along with his men when the brutal Boisfeuras and his Frenchmen storm the terrorists' headquarters. A few days later Raspeguy receives his promotion to general with the proud Countess watching. The disillusioned Esclavier has left the army and the Algerian terrorists continue their struggle against the French.

Based on a 1960 French novel that had a good deal to say about French colonialism in Indochina and Algeria, LOST COMMAND emerged as one of those diluted international co-productions that tries to be all things to all people. Anthony Quinn is sterling as the low-born professional soldier who manipulates everything to serve his career, but George Segal is badly miscast as the Algerian-born Lieutenant whose homeland loyalties outweigh his army ties. The clashing of the French troops with the Algerian underground barely scrapes the surface of how desperate and cruel the struggle was on both sides.

THE LOST PATROL (RKO, 1934) 74 mins.

Executive producer, Merian C. Cooper; associate producer, Cliff Reid; director, John Ford; based on the novel *Patrol* by Philip MacDonald; screenplay, Dudley Nichols, Garrett Fort; art directors, Van Nest Polglase, Sidney Ullman; music, Max Steiner; sound, Glen Portman; camera, Harold Wenstrom; editor, Paul Weatherwax.

Victor McLaglen (The Sergeant); Boris Karloff (Sanders); Wallace Ford (Morelli); Reginald Denny (George Brown); J. M. Kerrigan (Quincannon); Billy Bevan (Herbert Hale); Alan Hale (Cook); Brandon Hurst (Bell); Douglas Walton (Pearson); Sammy Stein (Abelson); Howard Wilson (Aviator); Neville Clark (Lieutenant Hawkins); Paul Hanson (Jock Mackay); and: Francis Ford.

Often the best genre films are deceptively simple in their structure. Such is THE LOST PATROL, filmed in two weeks in the Yuma, Arizona desert by John Ford in his first production for RKO. It is based on a Philip MacDonald novel which had previously been made into a 1929 British silent film starring Cyril McLaglen, in the role that his more famous brother Victor would make more famous.

In the midst of World War I, in 1917 Mesopotamia, a small cavalry patrol of British soldiers makes its way across the desert. Only its leading officer knows their objective, their destination, or even where they are. When he is shot by Arab snipers, the Sergeant (Victor McLaglen) takes charge of the twelve survivors. He is a resourceful professional who, like the others, realizes that the odds against them surviving are tremendous. They have seemingly unbeatable adversaries: the hidden Arabs, the brutal desert weather, and thirst and hunger. The men pick their way to an oasis, but before long their ranks are diminished further by the Arabs, who later steal their horses. Soon only the Sergeant and two others are left alive: Morelli (Wallace Ford), who regards himself a bad luck Jonah; and Sanders (Boris Karloff), a religious fanatic who has become mentally unhinged. A British pilot (Howard Wilson) spots them in the desert and lands. Refusing to heed their warnings to beware the invisible Arabs, he strides towards the oasis and is shot dead. Sanders, carrying a makeshift cross, runs, half mad, into the

Victor McLaglen and Wallace Ford in THE LOST PATROL (1934).

desert (dressed in John the Baptist-like rags), raving at the unseen enemy, and is killed. And so is Morelli who rushes after him. Left alone, the Sergeant buries all of his men, and from his own dug grave, begins firing at the attacking Arabs with a machine gun taken from the plane. He survives the encounter and is still alive when British relief troops appear on the scene.

THE LOST PATROL benefits from its economic production values, with the hidden enemy more frightening than had they been visible. The unrelenting desert heat and winds of the location filming give added grit to the narrative as one by one the soldiers are picked off by the Arabs. So much of what is unique in THE LOST PATROL would become standard fare in later combat films: the ethnically representative troopers, the doomed men being decimated one by one, and the patriotic leader giving his men a decent burial and even digging his own grave (much of this latter scene would be duplicated by Robert Taylor in MGM's BATAAN, 1943, q.v.). THE LOST PATROL would be directly remade as the Western film, BAD LANDS (1939), and would be the basis for the Humphrey Bogart combat feature, SAHARA (1943). Countless other filmmakers would borrow from THE LOST PATROL for years to come.

Ironically, THE LOST PATROL was not thought remarkable by some mainstream critics of the day. "The present production is highly effective from a photographic standpoint, but the incidents are often strained. . . . It is a pity that the dialogue is too forced and often far from natural in the circumstances, even granted that several of the men desired to set an example by showing their coolness" (Mordaunt Hall, *New York Times*). "Its appeal is directed mostly to men, with the cast all male and the locale of the story entirely in the desert, yet women whose tastes are often an enigma may find something about it they like" (*Variety*). The film did place sixth on the National Board of Review's "Ten Best" list for the year.

Max Steiner's score for THE LOST PATROL would be nominated for an Academy Award.

MacARTHUR (Universal, 1977) Color 128 mins.

Executive producers, Richard Zanuck, David Brown; producer, Frank McCarthy; director, Joseph Sargent; screenplay, Hal Barwood, Matthew Robbins; production designer, John J. Lloyd; set decorator, Hal Gausman; makeup, Jim McCoy, Frank McCoy; stunt coordinator, Joe Canutt; music, Jerry Goldsmith; assistant directors, Scott Maitland, Donald E. Zepfel; sound, Don Sharpless, Robert L. Hoyt; special effects, Albert Whitlock; camera, Mario Tosi; editor, George Jay Nicholson.

Ivan Bonar (left) and Gregory Peck in MacARTHUR (1977).

Gregory Peck (General Douglas MacArthur); Ed Flanders (President Harry S Truman); Dan O'Herlihy (President Franklin D. Roosevelt); Ivan Bonar (General Sutherland); Ward Costello (General George Marshall); Nicholas Coster (Colonel Huff); Marj Dusay (Mrs. MacArthur); Art Fleming (The Secretary); Russell D. Johnson (Admiral King); Sandy Kenyon (General Wainwright); Robert Mandan (Representative Martin); Allan Miller (Colonel Diller); Dick O'Neill (Colonel Whitney); Addison Powell (Admiral Chester Nimitz); Tom Rosqui (General Sampson); G. D. Spradlin (General Eickelberger); Kenneth Tobey (Admiral "Bull" Halsey); Gary Walberg (General Walker); Lane Allan (General Marquat); Barry Coe (TV Reporter); Everett Cooper (General Krueger); Charles Cyphers (General Harding); Manuel De Pina (Prettyman); Jesse Dizon (Castro); Warde Donovan (General Shepherd); John Fujioka (Emperor Hirohito); Jerry Holland (Aide); Philip Kenneally (Admiral Douyle); John McKee (Admiral Leahy); Walter O. Miles (General Kenney); Gerald S. Peters (General Blamey);

Eugene Peterson (General Collins); Beulah Quo (Al Cheu); Alex
Rodine (General Derevyanko); Yuki Shimoda (Prime Minister
Shidehara); Fred Stuthman (General Bradley); Harvey Vernon
(Admiral Sherman); William Wellman, Jr. (Lieutenant Buckley).
It is 1962 and the setting is the chief mess hall at the United
States Military Academy at West Point. The speaker is 82-year-old
General Douglas MacArthur (Gregory Peck),* delivering an ad-
dress at his alma mater to the newest graduating class of cadets.
"Duty - honor - country. Those three hallowed words reverently
dictate what you ought to be, what you can be, what you will be.
. . ." As he continues his famous farewell speech, the narrative
flashes back to 1942 when he was Supreme Commander of Allied
Forces in the Southwest Pacific. It traces from the Allied evacuation
of Corregidor in the Philippines (where he voices the famous
promise, "I shall return"), to the Battle at Leyte (1944) where the
Allies do return, to the official surrender of the Japanese aboard the
battleship USS *Missouri* in Tokyo Bay. The chronicle follows
General MacArthur's landing at Inchon with United Nations Forces
during the Korean War (1950), and his subsequent dismissal for
insubordination by President Harry S Truman (Ed Flanders) and
triumphant return to the U.S., and his "Old soldiers never die"
address to Congress. The film returns to the present as MacArthur
concludes his farewell address to the cadets. Two years later the old
general will be dead.

Because Frank McCarthy had also produced the highly acclaimed PATTON (1970), q.v., the critics (and public) made the
inevitable comparisons between these two biographical films. "Unlike PATTON, which was loaded with emotional and physical
action highlights, MacARTHUR is a far more introspective and
introverted story," *Variety* insisted, adding "It's not a back-handed
compliment to say that MacARTHUR is as good a film as could be
made, considering the truly appalling egomania of its subject. . . ."
Vincent Canby (*New York Times*) decided that although ". . . its
subject is not as colorful as PATTON" and it "covers too much
ground too quickly," nevertheless "MacARTHUR comes in a close
second." Jack Kroll (*Newsweek* magazine) judged that Mac-
ARTHUR ". . . doesn't have the flair and panache of PATTON but
in many ways it cuts deeper and churns up more food for thought.

---

*Others who have played General MacArthur on the screen include: Robert Barrat
(THEY WERE EXPENDABLE, 1945 and AN AMERICAN GUERRILLA IN
THE PHILIPPINES, 1950), Dayton Lummis (THE COURT MARTIAL OF
BILLY MITCHELL, 1955), and Laurence Olivier (INCHON, 1982).

. . . MacARTHUR is hardly a brilliant film, but it has a certain dogged integrity, and the figure of MacArthur as hero and bogeyman remains a crucial one. . . ." Far less enthusiastic was *New York Daily News'* Kathleen Carroll who complained, "Unlike the snappy, smartly executed PATTON, MacARTHUR is so stiff-necked and generally undistinguished that it leaves one wishing that Hollywood had allowed its old soldier to fade away quietly. . . ." And finally, Judith Crist (*Saturday Review of Literature* magazine) offered, "A lack of feeling—more specifically a lack of viewpoint—appears to be the hallmark of MacARTHUR. . . ."

MacARTHUR had been planned as a three-hour feature but was cut to 144 minutes and then to 128 minutes for its official release. Because of its overly rapid covering (too often on the backlot) of so many historical events, frequently there is little insight into the egocentric General and how he handled the pressures of war and politics. As for handsome leading man turned character-star Gregory Peck, he is so encased in makeup, costume, and posturing that it is difficult to perceive how his MacArthur feels about his tremendous power and control over lives in both the Second World War and Korea.

MacArthur would earn $8,298,075 in theater rentals in the U.S. and Canada.

A.k.a. MacARTHUR THE REBEL GENERAL.

MacARTHUR THE REBEL GENERAL *see*: MacARTHUR.

THE McKENZIE BREAK (United Artists, 1970) Color 108 mins.

Producer, Arthur Gardner, Jules Levy; director, Lamont Johnson; based on the novel *The Bowmanville Break* by Sidney Shelley; screenplay, William Norton; production designer, Frank White; set decorator, Keith Liddiard; costumes, Tiny Nicholls; makeup, Alan Brownie; music, Riz Ortolani; assistant director, Roger Good; sound, Laurie Clarkson; special effects, Thomas "Knobby" Clark; camera, Michael Reed; editor, Tom Rolf.

Brian Keith (Captain Jack Connor); Helmut Griem (Schluetter); Ian Hendry (Major Perry); Jack Watson (General Kerr); Patrick O'Connell (Sergeant Major Cox); Horst Janson (Neuchl); Alexander Allerson (Von Sperrie); John Abineri (Kranz); Constantin De Goguel (Lieutenant Hall); Tom Kempinski (Schmidt); Eric Allan (Hochbauer); Caroline Mortimer (Sergeant Bell); Mary Larkin (Corporal Watt); Gregg Palmer (Berger); Michael Sheard (Unger); Ingo Mogendorf (Fullgrabe); Franz von Norde (Dichter); Desmond Perry (Accomplice); Jim Mooney (Guard Foss); Vernon Hayden (Scottish Dispatcher); Maura Keely (Scots Lassie); Noel

Purcell (Ferry Captain); Paul Murphy (Weber); Frank Hayden (Holtz); Paddy Robinson (Pilot); Brendan Mathews, Robert Somerset, Des Keogh (Guards); Barry Cassin (Guard Jones); Denis Latimer (Lieutenant Everett); Conor Evans (Orderly Joss); Stephen Good (Paisley); Emmet Bergin (Orderly Johnston); John Kavanagh (Police Inspector); Joe Pilkington (Police Communications Sergeant); Dave Kelly (Adjutant); Mark Mulholland (Skipper); Martin Demsey (Colonel); Alec Doran (Police Official).

Most English-language war films deal with *Allied* prisoners-of-war. THE McKENZIE BREAK, a rare exception, focuses on Axis captives held at Camp McKenzie in Scotland during World War II, detailing the structured Nazi society within the compound. Tough British Captain Jack Connor (Brian Keith), an ex-crime reporter, is installed at the camp to keep tabs on the prisoners and learns that the rebelling wards are planning an escape. U-boat commander Schluetter (Helmut Griem) is in charge of the breakout and his men are digging a tunnel which will allow 28 submarine crewmen to escape. Connor forces ineffectual Major Perry (Ian Hendry) to let

Helmut Griem and Brian Keith in THE McKENZIE BREAK (1970).

the "Jerries" continue their scheme, as Connor intends capturing the German sub scheduled to pick up the escapees. However, Schluetter outwits his pursuer, and although he and two others are captured, the rest make their getaway.

Based on a 1968 novel and filmed in Ireland, THE McKENZIE BREAK received scant attention when released on double bills. It was a shame for it was a well-conceived and well-acted feature with an intriguing plot premise. Its dismissal was a far cry from the hugely receptive greeting given the studio's earlier THE GREAT ESCAPE (1963), q.v.

MALTA STORY (United Artists, 1954) 98 mins.

Producer, Peter De Sarigny; director, Brian Desmond Hurst; screenplay, William Fairchild, Nigel Balchin; music, William Alwyn; camera, Robert Krasker; editor, Michael Gordon.

Alec Guinness (Peter Ross); Jack Hawkins (Air Officer); Anthony Steel (Bartlett); Muriel Pavlow (Maria); Flora Robson (Melita); Renee Asherson (Joan); Ralph Truman (Banks); Reginald Tate (Payne); Hugh Burden (Eden); Ronald Adam (Control Operator); Nigel Stock (Guiseppe); Harold Siddons (Matthews); Colin Loudan (O'Connor); Edward Chaffers (Stripey); Stuart Burge (Paolo).

Two of England's best actors, who would reteam in THE BRIDGE ON THE RIVER KWAI (1957), q.v., joined forces for this documentary-style drama of the World War II defense of Malta.

Because the island of Malta is strategically situated between Italy and North Africa, the British used it as a jumping off point to attack German convoys carrying supplies to General Rommel's Afrika Korps. The Germans attacked this base from the air for well over two years, receiving as many casualties as they inflicted.

En route to Egypt, camera reconnaissance pilot Peter Ross (Alex Guinness) has his plane blown up and is stranded in Malta. While disobeying orders on a fact-gathering flight he uncovers the Germans' plan to unleash gliders from Italy to attack Malta. The Air Officer (Jack Hawkins) in charge of Malta is nearly helpless, as supply planes are destroyed by the enemy and the Malta base faces starvation and further assaults. Finally sufficient Spitfires arrive to help take the offensive, and the German convoy is bombed.

Actual World War II newsreel footage was interpolated into this well-regarded feature, which can only be faulted for its obtrusive love subplot between a Maltese (Muriel Pavlow) and a forthright Britisher (Anthony Steel).

THE MALTA STORY was originally released in Great Britain

by General Film Distributors in 1953 with a 103-minute running time.

THE MAN FROM WYOMING (Paramount, 1930) 71 mins.
Director, Rowland V. Lee; story, Joseph Moncure March, Lew Lipton; screenplay, Albert Shelby Le Vino; sound, Eugene Merritt; camera, Harry Fischbeck; editor, Robert Bassler.
Gary Cooper (Jim Baker); June Collyer (Patricia Hunter); Regis Toomey (Jersey); Morgan Farley (Lieutenant Lee); E. H. Calvert (Major General Hunter); Mary Foy (Inspector); Emile Chautard (French Mayor); Edgar Deering (Sergeant); William B. Davidson (Major); Ben Hall (Orderly); and: Hall Parker.

This film proves to be a preposterous piece of claptrap thrown together to take advantage of Gary Cooper's rising box-office status. Its depiction of life in the trenches was cavalier at best.

Jim Baker (Gary Cooper) and his pal Jersey (Regis Toomey) leave their bridge construction jobs in Wyoming to join the Army during World War I. They are shipped to France with the Engineers Corp. At the front lines Baker meets former society girl Patricia Hunter (June Collyer), an ambulance driver who has abandoned her duty. Baker is forced to arrest her, but later marries her. He returns to active duty and is reported killed in action. When Pat learns the news she moves to Nice, where she leads a wild life. Baker, who had not died but had been injured in action, is sent to Nice to recover and is disgusted to see what his wife has become. He returns yet again to the front, with Pat now in pursuit. After the Armistice, the two are reunited.

MANILA CALLING (Twentieth Century-Fox, 1942) 81 mins.
Producer, Sol M. Wurtzel; director Herbert I. Leeks; screenplay, John Larkin; art directors, Richard Day, Lewis Creber; music directors, Cyril J. Mockridge, Emil Newman; camera, Lucien Andriot; editor, Alfred Day.
Lloyd Nolan (Lucky Matthews); Carole Landis (Edna Fraser); Cornel Wilde (Jeff Bailey); James Gleason (Tom O'Rourke); Martin Kosleck (Heller); Ralph Byrd (Corbett); Charles Tannen (Fillmore); Ted [Michael] North (Jamison); Elisha Cook, Jr. (Gillman); Harold Huber (Santoro); Lester Matthews (Wayne Ralston); Louis Jean Heydt (Watson); Victor Sen Yung (Amando); Angel Cruz, Carlos Carrido, Rudy Robles (Moro Soldiers); Ken Christy (Logan); Leonard Strong (Japanese Officer); Richard Loo, Charles Steven (Filipinos); Ted Hecht (Japanese Announcer).

When the Japanese invade Mindanao in the Philippines, cynical Lucky Matthews (Lloyd Nolan) takes charge of a group of Americans as they make a desperate last stand from a high ground position against the enemy. Among those helping the woman-soured Matthews are: wise-cracking sidekick Tom O'Rourke (James Gleason), entertainer Edna Fraser (Carole Landis) and army officer Jeff Bailey (Cornel Wilde), who is a telephone engineer. It is Bailey who rigs a short-wave radio to alert the outside world of their valiant last stand.

This was another of those pictures that borrowed its dramatic premise from THE LOST PATROL (1934), q.v., but to less advantage. The *New York Times'* Thomas M. Pryor criticized the filmmakers: "They have simply made use of the clichés which require (a) that one man go berserk from the strain, (b) that one man try to escape at the expense of the others, and (c) that the tight-lipped hero has a heart-breaking story locked in his memory somewhere." The *Times'* reviewer also noted, "Assuredly, war is accompanied by a great deal of noise, and in that respect the producer, Sol Wurtzel, has gone all-out for realism . . . he has filled his film with loud reports, concussions, flame and explosion. Machine guns chatter violently and at length. Actors grow hoarse shouting at each other above the uproar."

Years later Cornel Wilde would say of MANILA CALLING, "I hated the film and remember as little as possible about it."

MARINE RAIDERS (RKO, 1944) 91 mins.

Producer, Robert Fellows; director, Harold Schuster; story, Martin Rackin, Warren Duff; screenplay, Duff; art directors, Albert D'Agostino, Walter E. Keller; set decorators, Darrell Silvera, Harley Miller; music, Roy Webb; music director, Constantin Bakaleinikoff; assistant director, Edward Killy; sound, James S. Thomson; special effects, Vernon L. Walker; camera, Nicholas Musuraca; editor, Philip Martin, Jr.

Pat O'Brien (Major Steve Lochard); Robert Ryan (Captain Dan Craig); Ruth Hussey (Ellen Foster); Frank McHugh (Sergeant Louis Leary); Barton MacLane (Sergeant Maguire); Richard Martin (Jimmy); Edmund Glover (Miller); Russell Wade (Tony Hewitt); Robert Andersen (Lieutenant Harrigan); Michael St. Angel (Lieutenant Sherwood); Martha MacVickers [Vickers] (Sally); Harry Brown (Cook); Sammy Stein (Sergeant); Edward Fielding (General Slayton); William Forrest (Colonel Carter); Richard Davies (Instructor); Jimmy Jordan (Jackson); Chris Drake (Orderly); Mike Kilian (Shoe Gag Soldier); Patrick O'Moore (Doctor); Patricia Cameron (Nurse); Robert Dane (Lieutenant, Junior Grade); Selmer

Jackson (Colonel Douglas); James Leong (Japanese Officer); Bert Moorhouse (Ship's Captain); James Hamilton, Jack Reeves, Melvin Mix, James Damore, Glenn Vernon, Blake Edwards, Carl Kent, Don Dillaway (Marines); Eddie Acuff (Marine Veteran); Laurie Shermoen (Communications Corps); George Ford (Flyer); Barry Macollum (Inn Keeper); Daun Kennedy (Model); Mike Lally (Conductor); Isabel O'Madigan (Newswoman).

In the 1930s Pat O'Brien had made raucous service comedies with his pal James Cagney at Warner Bros. Ten years later and in the midst of World War II, he and Robert Ryan (who had appeared

Center: Audrey Manners, Pat O'Brien, Ruth Hussey, and Robert Ryan in MARINE RAIDERS (1944).

together in BOMBARDIER, 1943, q.v.) were reteamed for RKO's patriotic salute to the Marine Corps. It combined a decent balance of action, the training of new recruits, and 1940s-style screen romance.

Major Steve Lochard (Pat O'Brien) and Captain Dan Craig (Robert Ryan) of the First Marine Raider battalion survive the defeat at Guadalcanal in 1942. While in Australia to recuperate from the battle, Craig falls in love with sympathetic Ellen Foster (Ruth Hussey). Lochard, believing his pal's best interests lie in returning to the U.S. to train new Marines, has him ordered back to Camp Elliott in California. This causes a rupture in their friendship. Later, after being reunited, they head back to the Pacific to attack a Japanese-held island. En route, they stop at Australia where Craig and Ellen wed, with avuncular Lochard giving his blessings. The para-Marines led by Craig and the traditional landing force headed by Lochard combat the entrenched Japanese.

No rah-rah service comedy/combat film would be complete without the comic relief of the camp cook (Frank McHugh) or the presence of the ever heckling sergeant (Barton MacLane). Made with the full cooperation of various military branches, actual government newsreel footage of attacks on Guadalcanal and other islands were interpolated into the scenario.

MARINES, LET'S GO! (Twentieth Century-Fox, 1961) Color 103 mins.

Producer/director/story, Raoul Walsh; screenplay, John Twist; art directors, Jack Martin Smith, Alfred Ybarra; makeup, Ben Nye; music, Irving Gertz; song, Mike Phillips and George Watson; orchestrator, Edward B. Powell; assistant director, Milton Carter; technical adviser, Jacob G. Goldberg (Coöp U.S. Marine Corps); sound, Bernard Freericks, Warren B. Delaplain; camera, Lucien Ballard; editor, Robert Simpson.

Tom Tryon (Skip Roth); David Hedison (David Chatfield); Tom Reese (McCaffrey); Linda Hutchins (Grace Blake); William Tyler (Russ Waller); Barbara Stuart (Ina Baxter); David Brandon (Newt Levells); Steve Baylor (Chase); Peter Miller (Hawkins); Adoree Evans (Ellen Hawkins); Hideo Inamura (Pete Kono); Vince Williams (Hank Dyer); Fumiyo Fujimoto (Song Do); Henry Okawa (Yoshida).

While genre filmmaker Raoul Walsh is highly appreciated for his WHAT PRICE GLORY? (1926) and OBJECTIVE, BURMA! (1945) and acknowledged for his less resourceful DESPERATE JOURNEY (1942) and FIGHTER SQUADRON (1948), all discussed in this book, he is sympathized with for his heavy-handed, puerile MARINES, LETS GO!

Having survived bloody combat duty during the Korean War, a group of U.S. Marines go on furlough in Yokosuka, Japan. They include: Bostonian David Chatfield (David Hedison), who plans to marry native girl Song Do (Fumiyo Fujimoto); intellectual Skip Roth, tagged "the brain"; and heavy-drinking "Let's Go" McCaffrey (Tom Reese), who has a grudge against David for his snobbishness. Whether in a bath house, a nightclub or en route, the trio have (mis)adventures as they intermingle with an assortment of

American and Japanese women. Trouble-maker McCaffrey is about to be court-martialed for brawling when orders come through that the Marines are needed again at the front lines—the Chinese Communists have gone on the offensive again. Chatfield and Song Do are captured by the Chinese but are saved. On the battlefield, McCaffrey is mortally wounded and, after making amends with Chatfield, dies.

Edward F. Dolan, Jr. in *Hollywood Goes to War* (1985) brands this as "what may well be the worst film made about the Korean War."

M*A*S*H (Twentieth Century-Fox, 1970) Color 116 mins.

Producer, Ingo Preminger; associate producer, Leon Ericksen; director, Robert Altman; based on the novel by Richard Hooker [Dr. H. Richard Homberg, William Heinz]; screenplay, Ring Lardner, Jr.; art directors, Jack Martin Smith, Arthur Lonergan; set decorators, Walter M. Scott, Stuart A. Reiss; makeup, Dan Striepeke, Lester Berns; music, Johnny Mandel; orchestrator, Herbert Spencer; song, Mike Altman and Mandel; assistant director, Ray Taylor, Jr.; medical adviser, David Sachs; sound, Bernard Freericks, John Stack; special effects, L. B. Abbott, Art Cruickshank; camera, Harold E. Stine; editor, Danford B. Greene.

Donald Sutherland (Hawkeye Pierce); Elliott Gould (Trapper John McIntyre); Tom Skerritt (Duke Forrest); Sally Kellerman (Major Margaret "Hot Lips" O'Houlihan); Robert Duvall (Major Frank Burns); Jo Ann Pflug (Lieutenant Hot Dish); Rene Auberjonois (Dago Red); Roger Bowen (Colonel Henry Blake); Gary Burghoff (Corporal Radar O'Reilly); David Arkin (Sergeant Major Vollmer); Fred Williamson (Spearchucker Jones); Michael Murphy (Me Lay); Kim Atwood (Ho-Jon); Tim Brown (Corporal Judson); Indus Arthur (Lieutenant Leslie); John Schuck (Painless Pole); Ken Prymus (Private First Class Seidman); Dawn Damon (Captain Scorch); Carl Gottlieb (Ugly John); Tamara Horrocks (Captain Knocko); G. Wood (General Hammond); Bobby Troup (Sergeant Gorman); Bud Cort (Private Boone); Danny Goldman (Captain Murrhardt); Corey Fischer (Captain Bandini); J. B. Douglas (Colonel Douglas); Yoko Young (Japanese Servant); Tom Brown, Buck Buchanan, Jack Concannon, Ben Davidson, John Myers, Fran Tarkenton, Nolan Smith, Howard Williams, Tom Woodeschick (Football Players).

Freewheeling U.S. Army surgeons Hawkeye Pierce (Donald Sutherland) and Duke Forrest (Tom Skerritt) are reassigned to the 4077th Mobile Army Surgical Hospital near the front during the Korean War. These two anti-establishment figures are at odds immediately with the righteous Major Frank Burns (Robert Duvall), with whom they share a tent, and Corporal Radar O'Reilly (Gary Burghoff), who administers the camp on behalf of the disorganized, often absent Colonel Henry Blake (Roger Bowen). Hawkeye and Duke make a target of the Army-loving Burns and are soon joined by Trapper John McIntyre (Elliott Gould) who finds Burns' handling of hospital procedures sloppy. Another new arrival is Major Margaret O'Houlihan (Sally Kellerman), a striking blonde in charge of the nurses who makes Burns her ally.

Margaret and Burns spark a passionate romance which is charted for the entire camp when Radar, now an enthusiastic follower of the new doctors, places a microphone under Burns' bed and records his night of passionate romance with Margaret. Margaret is dubbed "Hot Lips" but refuses to be bested by the anti-authoritarians; straight-laced Burns is removed from the unit in a straitjacket. When Painless Pole (John Schuck), the hospital's dentist and noted lover, suspects himself of homosexual tendencies

Robert Duvall, Sally Kellerman, Elliott Gould, and Timothy Brown in M*A*S*H (1970).

he decides on suicide. The staff arranges his "Last Supper" and encourages the married Lieutenant Hot Dish (Jo Ann Pflug), with whom Hawkeye is having an affair, to couple with Painless, thus proving to Painless that he is still very masculine. At another juncture the group performs clinical testing to determine if Hot Lips is *really* a natural blonde. They rig the outdoor shower so one of the walls will collapse and all the onlookers can judge for themselves when the unsuspecting nurse is caught naked. When Trapper John is ordered to Japan to operate on a V.I.P.'s son, Hawkeye joins him, and after the surgery they play a bizarre round of golf. Back at the hospital, General Hammond (G. Wood) arrives to investigate Hot Lips' complaints. He soon challenges Hawkeye's men to a football game against his own team. With $5,000 at stake, the M*A*S*H unit stops at nothing to win the madcap game, including using a professional ball player and sedatives. Before long Hawkeye and Duke are ordered back to the States.

If BATTLE CIRCUS (1953), q.v., had been an undistinguished study of Army medics during the Korean War, the wacky M*A*S*H was just what the doctors ordered. It was iconoclastic in its far-out approach, mingling outrageous black humor with the goriness of war (as seen in the surgical tents). Hollywood was not yet ready to discuss the humiliating Vietnam War on its own terms, but it could reflect on that embarrassment in the guise of the safely-in-the-past Korean War. The public was massively enthusiastic. The film earned $36,720,000 in theater rentals in the U.S. and Canada and was Oscar-nominated for Best Picture, Direction, Supporting Actress (Sally Kellerman), and Editing, and won an Academy Award for Ring Lardner, Jr.'s screenplay adaptation of the 1968 novel. It won the Grand Prize at the Cannes Film Festival in 1970 and was named Best Film of 1970 by the National Society of Film Critics.

M*A*S*H makes its own vivid anti-war statements with unrelenting, uncompromising views of torn, bleeding bodies in the hospital surgery. Having acknowledged this grim aftermath of warfare, it postures that war is insane, pointless, and horrific, while the crazy shenanigans of the irrepressible staff are presented as normal behavior. The zany humor is constantly dark and the jokes perpetrated are often cruel, but the viewer is made not to much mind. The balmy announcements over the P.A. system are punctuations to the nuttiness of the irrepressible unit who want nothing more than to be jobless and have this war over.

The M*A*S*H saga would continue. There would be a 251-episode teleseries starring Alan Alda, Wayne Rogers, MacLean Stevenson, Loretta Swit, David Ogden Stiers, and Henry "Harry"

Morgan which debuted 9/17/72 (with only Gary Burghoff from the original film repeating his screen role), and two spin-off series: the successful "Trapper John, M.D." with Pernell Roberts and the short-lived "Aftermash," which follows the further adventures of Dr. Sherman Potter (Henry Morgan), Maxwell Klinger (Jamie Farr) and Father Francis Mulcahy (William Christopher).

MEN IN WAR (United Artists, 1957) 104 mins.

Producer, Sidney Harmon; director, Anthony Mann; based on the novel *Day Without End* (*Combat*) by Van Van Praag; screenplay, Philip Yordan; production designer, Lewis Jacobs; art director, Frank Sylos; costumes, Norman Marten; makeup, Layne Britton; music, Elmer Bernstein; assistant director, Leon Chooluck; special effects, Jack Erickson, Lee Zavitz; sound, Jack Solomon; sound effects editor, Henry Adams; special camera effects, Jack Rabin, Lewis DeWitt; camera, Ernest Haller; editor, Richard C. Meyer.

Robert Ryan (Lieutenant Benson); Aldo Ray (Sergeant Montana); Robert Keith (Colonel); Philip Pine (Riordan); Vic Morrow (Zwickley); Nehemiah Persoff (Lewis); James Edwards (Killian); L. Q. Jones (Sam Davis); Adam Kennedy (Maslow); Scott Marlowe (Meredith); Walter Kelley (Ackerman); Race Gentry (Haines); Robert Normand (Christensen); Anthony Ray (Penelli); Michael Miller (Lynch); Victor Sen Yung (Korean Sniper).

"A two-fisted account of what happens to an infantry platoon in the late Korean battling . . . with a general air of excitement, tension and action. . . . Where the film does stand out over the usual

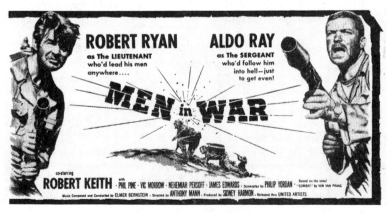

Advertisement for MEN IN WAR (1957).

warpic is in its intelligent use of music. Elmer Bernstein composed and conducted the score, never trying to compete with the sounds of battle and thereby heightening the effect of many scenes" (*Variety*). In the midst of the Korean War, combat-fatigued Lieutenant Benson (Robert Ryan) has one objective—to get the surviving members of his platoon back to battalion headquarters. When his weapons vehicle is destroyed, he commandeers a jeep driven by Sergeant Montana (Aldo Ray) of another unit. Benson is immediately at odds with war-loving Montana, who is determined to shepherd his shell-shocked colonel (Robert Keith) to the base hospital. The unlikely trio fight their way back to Benson's platoon only to find that the Chinese Communists now control the hill (#465) and only one other GI survives. Facing insurmountable odds, the men make their valiant last stand.

The film is low-budget and compact, but Robert Ryan especially, as the grizzled, blurry-eyed fighter tormented by war's horrors, makes this a memorable enterprise. As the film's opening title card states, "Tell me the story of the foot soldier and I will tell you the story of all wars."

MEN OF THE FIGHTING LADY (Metro-Goldwyn-Mayer, 1954) Color 79 mins.

Producer, Henry Berman; director, Andrew Marton; based on the stories "The Forgotten Heroes of Korea" by James A. Michener and "The Case of the Blind Pilot" by Commander Harry A. Burns; screenplay, Art Cohn; art director, Cedric Gibbons; technical adviser, Commander Paul N. Gray (U.S. Navy); music, Miklos Rozsa; assistant director, Joel Freeman; camera, George Folsey; editor, Gene Ruggiero.

Van Johnson (Lieutenant [j.g.] Howard Thayer); Walter Pidgeon (Commander Kent Dowling); Louis Calhern (James A. Michener); Dewey Martin (Ensign Kenneth Schechter); Keenan Wynn (Lieutenant Commander Ted Dodson); Frank Lovejoy (Lieutenant Commander Paul Grayson); Robert Horton (Ensign Neil Conovan); Bert Freed (Lieutenant [j.g.] Andrew Szymanski); Lewis Martin (Commander Michael Coughlin); George Cooper (Cyril Roberts); Dick Simmons (Lieutenant Wayne Kimbrell); Chris Warfield (Pilot White); Steve Rowland (Pilot Johnson); Ed Tracy (Pilot Brown); Paul Smith (Ensign Dispatcher); John Rosser (Officer); Ronald Lisa (Replacement); Teddy Infuhr (Szymanski's Son); Sarah Selby (Mrs. Szymanski); Jerry Mathers, Ronald Stafford, Joseph "Bucko" Stafford (Dodson's Sons); Ann Baker (Mary Reynolds); Jonathan Hale (Announcer); Dorothy Patrick (Mrs. Dodson).

MGM had produced several sterling films dealing with World War II (including: BATAAN in 1943, THIRTY SECONDS OVER TOKYO in 1944, THEY WERE EXPENDABLE IN 1945, COMMAND DECISION in 1948, BATTLEGROUND in 1949 and GO FOR BROKE in 1951; qq.v.). When it came to depicting the unpopular Korean War, the best it could muster was BATTLE CIRCUS (1953), q.v., and MEN OF THE FIGHTING LADY. By the time of the latter's release the inconclusive Korean police action had faded away in an inconclusive truce.

Much of MEN OF THE FIGHTING LADY is a photographed record of take-offs and landings aboard a massive U.S. aircraft carrier stationed off the Korean coast during the war. Aboard are freckle-faced Lieutenant Howard Thayer (Van Johnson); veteran flight surgeon Kent Dowling (Walter Pidgeon); Lieutenant Commander Paul Grayson (Frank Lovejoy), who insists that low-flying missions will do in the enemy; comical maintenance officer Andrew Szymanski (Bert Freed), and such ensigns as Kenneth Schechter (Dewey Martin) and Neil Conovan (Robert Horton). Chronicling the men's activities is James A. Michener (Louis Calhern), one of the real-life contributing authors to the scenario. The highlight of this film is Thayer's dramatic talking down of combat-blinded Schechter.

Lensed in Ansco color and full of the usual Metro-Goldwyn-Mayer polish, MEN OF THE FIGHTING LADY lacks that needed point of view or zest. To be noted is Jerry "Leave It to Beaver" Mathers playing one of Lieutenant Commander Ted Dawson's (Keenan Wynn) young sons.

MERRILL'S MARAUDERS (Warner Bros., 1962) Color 98 mins.

Producer, Milton Sperling; director, Samuel Fuller; based on the book *The Marauders* by Charlton Ogburn, Jr.; screenplay, Sperling, Fuller; music, Howard Jackson; assistant director, William Kissel; makeup, Gordon Bau; technical adviser, Samuel Wilson (Lieutenant Colonel); sound, Francis M. Stahl; special effects, Ralph Ayres; camera, William Clotheri; second unit camera, Higino J. Fallorina; editor, Folmar Blangsted.

Jeff Chandler (Brigadier General Frank D. Merrill); Ty Hardin (Lieutenant Lee Stockton); Peter Brown (Bullseye); Andrew Duggan (Major George "Doc" Nemeny); Will Hutchins (Chowhound); Claude Akins (Sergeant Kolowiez); Luz Valdez (Burmese Girl); John Hoyt (General Joseph W. Stilwell); Charles Briggs (Muley); Chuck Hayward, Chuck Roberson (Officers); Jack Williams (Medic); Chuck Hicks (Corporal Doskis); Vaughan Wilson (Lieutenant Colonel Bannister); Pancho Magalona (Taggy).

Ty Hardin, Charles Briggs, and Claude Akins in MERRRILL'S MARAUDERS (1962).

Warner Bros. had received much unfavorable reaction overseas from OBJECTIVE, BURMA! (1945), q.v., with its overzealous depiction of Errol Flynn and Americans soldiers winning World War II single-handedly. Much more gritty and realistic was Samuel Fuller's similar study of the 5307th Composite Group of American infantrymen. Led by colorful Brigadier General Frank D. Merrill (Jeff Chandler), Merrill's Marauders fought guerrilla warfare deep behind Japanese lines in World War II Burma. Merrill would command Operation Galahad, the Chinese-American effort to free up the Burma road for directing supplies into China. Born in 1903, Merrill would die in 1955.

In 1944 Merrill's 3,000 exhausted soldiers are detailed to capture a railway yard, an enemy arsenal, and a strategic gun emplacement. The well-trained troops badly need rest but Merrill's newest objective is to march them 500 miles to Myitkyina to prevent Japanese and German armies from joining forces in India. Merrill collapses in action, but from his stretcher pushes his men onward. When he becomes unconscious, sensitive Lieutenant Lee Stockton

(Ty Hardin) stirs the bone-weary men forward. Merrill revives later to discover new troops and supplies landing at Myitkyina, the airfield liberated by his men.

As in all of Samuel Fuller's graphic combat features* the tight budget forces the innovative director to make his action compact, his relatively small casts to work extra hard, and the movie to gain ironic twists by juxtaposing violent and quiet scenes. He never allows the viewer to be lulled into complacency.

Variety complimented the visual compositions of MERRILL'S MARAUDERS: "The battle sequences can compare with any seen on the screen. Considering the small number of troops available, Fuller creates an amazing impression of large scale maneuvers. . . . [In the railroad station invasion sequence] Fuller uses an overhead shot that gives the approach the feeling of a beautifully choreographed ballet, a labyrinth leading to unknown dangers, then they're through and the camera draws back for a full-screen shot of the entire railroad yard, littered with the dead as far as the eye can see. This is one of the best visual impressions of carnage since the Atlanta sequence in GONE WITH THE WIND."

MERRILL'S MARAUDERS proved to be the most successful commercially of all of Fuller's war films to date. This production would be released after the untimely death of actor Jeff Chandler. Much of the location shooting was accomplished in the Philippines.

MERRY CHRISTMAS, MR. LAWRENCE (Universal, 1983) Color 124 mins.

Executive producers, Mastato Hara, Eiko Oshima, Geoffrey Nethercott, Terry Glinwood; producer, Jeremy Thomas; associate producers, Joyce Herlihy, Larry Parr; director, Nagisa Oshima; based on the novel *The Seed and the Sower* (and the stories "A Bar of Shadow" and "The Sword and the Doll") by Laurens Van Der Post; screenplay, Nagisa Oshima, Paul Mayersberg; production designer, Shigemasa Toda; art director, Andrew Sanders; set decorator, Masaru Arakawa; makeup supervisor, Anthony Clavet; wardrobe supervisor, Christine West; music, Ryuichi Sakamoto; song, Stephen McCurdy; interpreter, Didi Dickson; sound, Mike Westgate; sound effects, Akira Houma; camera, Toichiro Narushima; editor, Tomoyo Oshima.

David Bowie (Major Jack "Straffer" Celliers); Tom Conti (Colonel John Lawrence); Ryuichi Sakamoto (Captain Yonoi); Takeshi (Sergeant Gengo Hara); Jack Thompson (Group Captain

---

*Fuller's war films include: THE STEEL HELMET (1951), FIXED BAYONETS (1951), CHINA GATE (1957) and THE BIG RED ONE (1981), qq.v.

Hicksley); Johnny Okura (Kanemoto); Alistair Browning (De Jong); James Malcolm (Celliers' Brother); Chris Brown (Jack Celliers at Age 12); Yuya Uchida (Commandant of Military Prison); Ryunosuke Kaneda (Colonel Fujimura, President of the Court); Takashi Naito (Lieutenant Iwata); Tamio Ishikura (Prosecutor); Rokko Toura (Interpreter); Kan Mikami (Captain Ito); Yuji Honma (PFC Yajima); Daisuke Iijima (Corporal Ueki); Hideo Murota (New Camp Commandant); Barry Dorking (Chief Doctor); Geoff Clendon (Australian Doctor); Grant Bridger (POW Officer); Ian Miller (English Guard); Richard Adams, Geoff Allen, Michael Baxter-Lax, Marc Berg, Marcus Campbell, Colin Francis, Richard Hensby, Richard Hoare, Martin Ibbertson, Rob Jayne, Richard Mils, Mark Penrose, Arthur Ranford, Steve Smith, Stephen Taylor, Richard Zimmerman (POWs); Don Stevens (Pastor).

When a Korean guard, Kanemoto (Johnny Okura), sexually assaults a Dutch prisoner (Alistair Browning) at a Japanese prisoner-of-war camp in 1942 Java, Sergeant Gengo Hara (Takeshi) orders the man to commit hara-kiri. The Japanese-speaking British Colonel John Lawrence (Tom Conti), who acts as interpreter between captors and captives, protests. The camp's youthful commandant, Captain Yonoi (Ryuichi Sakamoto), postpones making a decision until he returns from Batavia and the military trial of accused spy Major Jack "Straffer" Celliers (David Bowie). The latter arouses Yonoi's sympathies and he has him sent to his prisoner camp. Meanwhile, Yonoi insists on knowing who the weapons experts are among the prisoners. Lawrence refuses to respond, but Group Captain Hicksley (Jack Thompson) questions his loyalties to them. Hicksley also knows that Yonoi would like to replace him as prisoner commander with Celliers. Kanemoto's execution occurs and the prisoners rebel. Celliers and Lawrence escape, but they are captured and put in the stockade. As a goodwill gesture at Christmas, a drunken Hara releases them. Hicksley is sentenced to die for still refusing to name his weapons expert. A desperate Celliers diverts attention by walking up to Yonoi and kissing him on both cheeks. Yonoi collapses in shame. Celliers' death is ordered by the new commandant (Hideo Murota). In 1946 Lawrence visits Hara, a condemned war criminal, and relates how Yonoi, also recently executed, gave him a lock of hair from Celliers' head to be dedicated at his ancestral shrine in Japan.

This ambitious and complex study of contrasting cultures and intermingling relationships is most noted for the presence of rock star David Bowie as the guilt-ridden Celliers. In flashback it is revealed that as a young man Celliers allowed his classmates to humiliate his hunchbacked, younger brother, and the traumatic event so affected him that Celliers never sang again. This is the first English-language picture by Japanese filmmaker Nagisa Oshima. It is at once brutal, intellectual and full of oblique references. The parallel relationships between Colonel Lawrence and the sadistic but honor-bound Sergeant Hara on one hand, and the more subtle (filled with sexual undertones) interaction of the defiant Celliers and the empathetic Captain Yonoi on the other hand, form the structure of this intricate picture.

MERRY CHRISTMAS, MR. LAWRENCE was not a success in the U.S.

MIDWAY (Universal, 1976) Color 132 mins.

Producer, Walter Mirisch; director, Jack Smight; screenplay, Donald S. Sanford; art director, Walter Tyler; set decorator, John Dwyer; music, John Williams; technical adviser, Vice Admiral Bernard M. Strean (U.S. Navy, Retired); assistant director, Jerome Siegel; special effects, Jack McMaster; sound, Robert Martin, Leonard Peterson; camera, Harry Stradling, Jr.; editors, Robert Swink, Frank J. Urioste.

Charlton Heston (Captain Matt Garth); Henry Fonda (Admiral Chester W. Nimitz); James Coburn (Captain Vinton Maddox); Glenn Ford (Rear Admiral Raymond A. Spruance); Hal Holbrook (Commander Joseph Rochefort); Toshiro Mifune (Admiral Isoroku Yamamoto); Robert Mitchum (Admiral William F. Halsey); Cliff Robertson (Commander Carl Jessop); Robert Wagner (Lieutenant Commander Ernest L. Blake); Robert Webber (Rear Admiral Frank J. "Jack" Fletcher); Ed Nelson (Admiral Harry Pearson); James Shigeta (Vice Admiral Chuichi Nagumo); Christina Kokubo (Haruko Sakura); Monte Markham (Commander Max Leslie); Biff McGuire (Captain Miles Browning); Kevin Dobson (Ensign George Gahy); Christopher George (Lieutenant Commander C. Wade McClusky); Glenn Corbett (Lieutenant Commander John Waldron); Gregory Walcott (Captain Elliott Buckmaster); Edward Albert (Lieutenant Tom Garth); Dabney Coleman (Captain Murray Arnold); Conrad Yarma (Admiral Nobutake Kondo); Dale Ishimoto (Vice Admiral Moshiro Hosogaya); Larry Csonka (Commander Delaney); Dennis Rucker (Ensign Mansen); and: Phillip R. Allen, Erik Estrada, John Fujioka, Kurt Grayson, James Ingersoll, Robert Ito, Steve Kanaly, Lloyd Kino, Clyde Kusatsu, David Mackln, Pat Morita, Kip Niven, Bennett Ohta, Ken Pennell, Michael Richardson, Richard Sarradet, Sab Shimono.

"The June, 1942 sea-air battle off Midway Island was a turning point in World War II. However, the melee of combat was the usual hysterical jumble of noise, explosion and violent death. MIDWAY

tries to combine both aspects but succumbs to the confusion"
(*Variety*).

MIDWAY is overstuffed with patriotic good intentions; a big
name cast doing stiff cameos as ponderous historical figures;
platitudinous dialogue lifted from the mouths of famous military
leaders; cost-cutting special effects miniatures substituting for
reconstructed naval encounters;* and the then gimmicky Sensurround system (a noise-effect blaster that simulated miniature earth-
quake-like vibrations in the theater). MIDWAY earned an astonish-
ing (considering its mediocrity) $21,610,435 in theater rentals in the
U.S. and Canada, thanks largely to its Sensurround process.

By cross-cutting back and forth between the American battle
fleet and the invading Japanese armada, MIDWAY traces the events
leading up to and during the decisive, milestone naval engagement.
To give "dimension" to the cardboard theatrics as cameo guest stars
parade by, there is the personal story of the son (Edward Albert) of
stalwart but grim-faced Captain Matt Garth (Charlton Heston),
who wants to marry a Japanese-American Hawaiian girl (Christina
Kokubo), much against Naval regulations. Every time audiences fell
asleep keeping score of the stock footage, miniatures, dubbed
dialogue, and atrocious performances, they were jolted awake by
the vibrating Sensurround.

Many of the major military personages presented in MIDWAY
had been interpreted on screen before and to much better affect.

MISSING IN ACTION (Cannon, 1984) Color 101 mins.

Executive producer, Lance Hool; producers, Menahem Golan,
Yoram Globus; associate producer, Avi Kleinberger; co-associate
producer, Ken Metcalfe; director, Joseph Zito; based on characters
created by Arthur Silver, Larry Levinson, Steve Bing; story, John
Crowther, Hool; screenplay, James Bruner; art director, Ladi
Wilheim; set decorator, Celso de la Cruz; costume designer, Nancy
Cone; music, Jay Chattaway; assistant director, Gidi Amir; stunt
coordinator, Aaron Norris; sound, Donald Santos; sound effects
editors, Jerry Ross, Ed Callahan, Richard Candib, Ira Spiegel, Fred
Wasser; special effects, Danilo Dominguez; camera, Joao Fernandez; editors, Joel Goodman, Daniel Loewenthal.

Chuck Norris (Colonel James Braddock); M. Emmett Walsh
(Tuck); David Tress (Senator); Lenore Kasdorf (Ann); James Hong
(General Tran); Ernie Ortega (Colonel Vinh); Pierrino Mascarino
(Jacques); E. Erich Anderson (Masucci); Joseph Carberry (Carter);

---

*MIDWAY is one of several films to utilize footage from TORA! TORA! TORA!
(1970), q.v., as well as material from DESTINATION TOKYO (1944), q.v.

Avi Kleinberger (Dalton); Willy Williams (Randall); Ric Segreto (G.I.); Bella Flores (Madame Pearl); Gil Arceo, Roger Dantes (Vietnamese Businessmen); Sabatini Fernandez (Dinh); Renato Morado (Mike); Jim Crumrine (Gibson); Jeff Mason (Barnes); Stephen Barbers (Moore); Nam Moore (Translator); Kim Marriner, Deanna Crowe (Newscasters); Jesse Cuneta (Street Hawker); Juliet Lee (Bar Girl); Joonee Gamboa (Bartender); Augusto Victa (Tran's Aide); Protacio Dee (Yang); Omar Camar, Jack Perez (Bouncers); Dar Benjamin (Stunt Double).

MISSING IN ACTION II: THE BEGINNING (Cannon, 1985) Color 96 mins.

Producers, Menahem Golan, Yoram Globus; associate producer, Christopher Pearce; director, Lance Hool; screenplay, Arthur Silver, Larry Levinson, Steve Bing; production designer, Michael Baugh; set decorator, David Varod; costume supervisor, Poppy Cannon; makeup, Mony Mansano; music, Brian May; music editor, Michael Linn; stunt co-ordinator, Aaron Norris; second unit director, Thomas Moore; assistant directors, Joe Ochoa, Terry Buchinski, Steven Kossover; special effects, Dick Parker, Joseph Quinlivan; supervising sound editor, Robert A. Fitzgerald, Jr.; sound effects editors, Tracey Smith, Peter Combs; camera, Jorge Stahl; second unit camera, Ernie C. Reed; editors, Mark Conte, Marcus Manton.

Chuck Norris (Colonel James Braddock); Soon-Teck Oh (Colonel Yin); Steven Williams (Captain David Nester); Bennett Ohta (Colonel Ho); Cosie Costa (Lieutenant Anthony Mazilli); Joe Michael Terry (Corporal Lawrence Opelka); John Wesley (Master Sergeant Ernest Franklin); David Chung (Dou Chou); Professor Toru Tanaka (Lao); John Otrin (Soldier); Christopher Cary (Clive Emerson); Joseph Hieu (Guard); Dean Ferrandini (Kittle); Pierre Issot (Francois); Mischa Hausserman (Kelly); Randon Lo, Andrea Lowe, Nancy Martin, Michiyo Tanaka (Hookers); Dar Benjamin (Stunt Double).

"I was one of those patriotic, gung-ho guys who believed that when your government calls you to go to war, you go, no matter what. . . . My feelings have changed a lot since then, and I don't believe in political wars at all. . . . Vietnam was a war we shouldn't have been in, and I wish I'd believed that at the time. A lot of men are dead and a lot of men are suffering for the rest of their lives." (Chuck Norris in an interview with Jonathan Gold, *LA Weekly*, January 22, 1988.)

FIRST BLOOD (1982) and RAMBO: FIRST BLOOD II (1985), qq.v., spawned karate champ Chuck Norris' MISSING IN

ACTION series and other less potent imitators. Arguments raged back and forth as to whether the films were spurious exercises in violence or actually anti-war statements, or whether the movies truly provided a deep vicarious remedy for filmgoers needing to relive the Vietnam defeat in the context of military one-upmanship, or, still again, whether there was any intrinsic merit to the highly exaggerated on-screen heroics which seemed to equate the quantity of gore and mutilated bodies with the depth of artistic integrity. Meanwhile, both the RAMBO and the MISSING IN ACTION series proved to be mega moneymakers.

Seven years after the Vietnam War has "ended" American Colonel James Braddock (Chuck Norris) and several fellow servicemen escape their Viet Cong captors. Braddock becomes an ardent campaigner on behalf of the MIAs (missing in action) whom he insists are still in enemy hands. He is part of the American investigating team in Ho Chi Minh City (a.k.a. Saigon), but his opponents, led by General Tran (James Hong), do their best to discredit him. Braddock forces Tran at knife point to tell him where the MIAs are imprisoned. In Bangkok Braddock and ex-army pal Tuck (M. Emmett Walsh) join forces to penetrate the Vietnamese jungle. They are pursued by Colonel Vinh (Ernie Ortega), who had been Braddock's captor, and Vinh is killed. They follow the MIAs on their assault raft and free four of the Americans. Tuck dies in the skirmish, but Braddock and the others are rescued and return to Ho Chi Minh City to prove his point.

The makers of MISSING IN ACTION were so sure their concoction would be a box-office bonanza (it earned $10,000,000 in theater rentals in the U.S. and Canada) that while shooting the first in production, they also lensed a second MISSING IN ACTION II: THE BEGINNING, which is a prequel. (It was originally planned to release the two films in reverse order from what actually was done.)

MISSING IN ACTION II: THE BEGINNING tells how Braddock came to be in a Vietnam War MIA prisoner-of-war camp and how he and a few others escaped. In 1972 during a reconnaissance mission, Braddock and four other Americans leave their crippled helicopter and are captured by the Viet Cong. They are held prisoners by sadistic Colonel Yin (Soon-Teck Oh). The brutal Yin promises to release the men *if* Braddock will confess to alleged war crimes. A French drug smuggler (Pierre Issot) alerts Braddock that Australian photographer Clive Emerson (Christopher Cary) is scouting the area for evidence of MIAs. When Emerson appears on the scene, Yin kills him, as he does the malaria-ridden Master Sergeant Ernest Franklin (John Wesley). Braddock and Lieutenant

Anthony Mazilli (Cosie Costa) escape into the jungle and join Corporal Lawrence Opelka (Joe Michael Terry) who escaped earlier. Later Mazilli is recaptured. Captain David Nester (Steven Williams) dies to save Mazilli and Braddock kills Yin in a man-to-man martial arts struggle that ends with the commandant blown up with explosives. The Americans flee in Issot's helicopter.

Despite bad reviews, endless comparisons to Sylvester Stallone's RAMBO films and to the other MISSING IN ACTION picture, Norris' new entry did all right, earning $4,217,312 in theater rentals in the U.S. and Canada. Audiences evidentially thrived on seeing a gasoline-soaked man ignited, another person having his brain blown out in slow motion, etc. It led to BRAD-DOCK: MISSING IN ACTION III, q.v., which continued the on-screen saga of gross mayhem, gratuitous violence, laughable cartoon heroics, and the in-game of keeping score of the body count per sub-genre production.

MR. WINKLE GOES TO WAR (Columbia, 1944) 80 mins.

Producer, Jack Moss; director, Alfred E. Green; based on the novel by Theodore Pratt; screenplay, Waldo Salt, George Corey, Louis Solomon; art directors, Lionel Banks, Rudolph Sternad; set decorator, George Montgomery; Army technical adviser, Lieutenant Robert Albaugh; music, Carmen Dragon, Paul Sawtell; music director, Morris W. Stoloff; assistant director, Earl Bellamy; sound, Lambert Day; camera, Joseph Walker; editor, Richard Fantl.

Edward G. Robinson (Wilbert George Winkle); Ruth Warrick (Amy Winkle); Ted Donaldson (Barry); Bob Haymes (Jack Petti-grew); Richard Lane (Sergeant "Alphabet"); Robert Armstrong (Joe Tinker); Richard Gaines (Ralph Wescott); Walter Baldwin (Plummer); Art Smith (McDavid); Ann Shoemaker (Martha Petti-grew); Paul Stanton (A. B. Simkins); Buddy Yarus (Johnson); William Forrest, Warren Ashe (Captains); Bernardine Hayes (Gladys); Jeff Donnell (Hostess); Howard Freeman (Mayor); Nancy Evans, Ann Loos (Girls); Larry Thompson (Military Police); James Flavin, Fred Kohler, Jr. (Sergeants); Robert Mitchum (Corporal); Fred Lord, Cecil Ballerino, Ted Holley (Draftees); Ben Taggart, Sam Flint, Nelson Leigh, Forbes Murray, Ernest Hilliard, Herbert Heyes (Doctors); Emmett Vogan (Barber); Tommy Cook (Kid); Hugh Beaumont (Range Officer).

War is not always for the young, and the modestly produced MR. WINKLE GOES TO WAR proves it. In 1942 when the U.S. is drafting men up to age 45, middle-aged bank clerk Wilbert George Winkle (Edward G. Robinson) is sick of his job and has opened a fix-it shop, much to the disgust of his wife (Ruth Warrick). When 44-year-old Winkle is drafted he is startled that he passes the army physical and even more amazed that he endures basic training. He and his neighbor's son Jack Pettigrew (Bob Haymes), Sergeant "Alphabet" (Richard Lane), and Joe Tinker (Robert Armstrong) find themselves stationed in the South Pacific on the edge of action. Winkle is repairing a bulldozer when the enemy attacks and he plows the Japanese under in their foxhole. The wounded Winkle recuperates in an army hospital and receives an honorable discharge, with honors heaped on him. The unassuming man returns home where he is reconciled with his wife.

It was part of Hollywood's conceit during World War II that filmgoers would enjoy seeing screen gangsters in patriotic roles. So the screen's former LITTE CAESAR became a celluloid hero. The critics were not impressed. "If you can take Edward G. Robinson as a very mouse of a man, hen-pecked beyond endurance and virtually subsisting on a diet of pills, then you may find modest entertainment in MR. WINKLE GOES TO WAR" (Bosley Crowther, *New York Times*).

MURPHY'S WAR (Paramount, 1971) Color 106 mins.

Producer, Michael Deeley; director, Peter Yates; based on the novel by Max Catto; screenplay, Stirling Silliphant; production designer, Disley Jones; makeup, Basil Newall; music, John Barry, Ken Thorne; music director, Barry; stunt coordinator, Frank Tallman; assistant director, Bert Batt; sound, Robin Gregory; special effects, Alan Barnard; camera, Douglas Slocombe; editors, Frank P. Keller, John Glen.

Peter O'Toole (Murphy); Sian Phillips (Dr. Hayden); Philippe Noiret (Louis Brezan); Horst Janson (Kapitan Lauchs); John Hailam (Lieutenant Ellis); Ingo Mogendorf (Lieutenant Voght).

Wartime conflict is usually envisioned as between two or more opposing groups. MURPHY'S WAR details how *one* (!) man confronts the enemy and wages his own private war.

Murphy is a ship's aviation mechanic aboard an armed British merchantman vessel sunk off the coast of Venezuela by a German U-boat in the closing months of World War II. He is rescued by a French oil engineer named Brezan (Philippe Noiret), who lives on a barge, and is nursed to health by a Quaker missionary nurse (Sian Phillips). When a wrecked plane comes into his grasp, Murphy, the mad Irishman, repairs it and plans to use it to blow up the German submarine which has become beached along the Orinoco River. Even after the armistice is declared he continues his driven efforts to destroy the U-boat. He finally does so by using Brezan's barge and an unexploded German torpedo. His mission succeeds at the cost of his own life.

There is a lot of borrowing from the much superior THE AFRICAN QUEEN (1951) in this bizarre war drama, but it quickly develops into a peculiar study of a man turned mad by war, who cannot curb his (insane) desire for revenge, even when the war is over. While O'Toole and his real-life wife (Sian Phillips) were praised for their screen portrayals, there were many (including those filmgoers that viewed this offbeat picture) who felt very uncomfortable about its deranged anti-hero.

MYSTERY SUBMARINE (Universal, 1963) 92 mins.

Producer, Bertram Ostrer; director, C. M. Pennington-Richards; based on the play by Jon Manchip White; screenplay, Hugh Woodhouse, White, Ostrer; art director, Charles Bishop; makeup, Phil Leakey; music, Clifton Parker; music director, John Hollingsworth; assistant directors, Colin Brewer, Scott Wodehouse, Barry Langley; sound, George Stephenson, Bob Jones; dubbing editor, Jim Sibley; special effects, Wally Veevers; camera, Stanley Pavey; editor, Bill Lewthwaite.

Edward Judd (Lieutenant Commander Tarlton); James Robertson-Justice (Rear-Admiral Rainbird); Laurence Payne (Lieutenant Seaton); Joachim Fuchsberger (Commander Scheffler); Arthur O'Sullivan (Mike Fitzgerald); Albert Lieven (Captain Neymarck); Robert Flemying (Vice-Admiral Sir James Carver); Richard Carpenter (Lieutenant Haskins); Richard Thorp (Lieutenant Chatterton); Jeremy Hawk (Admiral Saintsbury); Robert Brown (Coxwain Drage); Frederick Jaeger (Lieutenant Henze); George Mikell (Lieutenant Remer); Peter Myers (Telegraphist Packshaw); Leslie Randall (Leading Seaman Donnithorne); Ewen Solon (Lieutenant Winner); Fulton Mackaw (Leading Torpedoman McKerrow); Gerard Heinz (German Admiral); Hamilton Deck (Commander Sivewright); Peter Stanwick (Lieutenant Lyncker); Peter Zander (Lieutenant John); Sean Kelly (Lieutenant Heilborn); Dennis Edwards (Lieutenant Neumann); Keigh Anderson (German Radio Operator); Brandon Brady (Pilot of *Catalina*); John Chappell (Bomb Aimer); Desmond Davies (Radar Operator); Nigel Green (Chief ERA Lovejoy); Ray Smith (Signalman Lewis); Anthony Wickert (ERA Barnes); David Glover (P.O. Telegrapher Hubbard); Hedger Wallace (Stoker Thompson); Michael Ritterman (Lieutenant Commander Torgau); Graeme Bruce (Lieutenant Schliemann); Dixon Adams (Lieutenant Anstey); Norman Johns

(German ASDIC Operator); Declan Mulhooland (Duty Chef); Fred Wilson (Sailor); William Semour (Leading Seaman Grant); Derek Smek (Leading Seaman Boydell); Dusty Hood (Leading Seaman Fuller); Henry Kaufman (Stoker Mechanic Parham).

This little-seen World War II drama was based on Jon Manchip White's stage play. The British Navy captures a German submarine, complete with codebook and log, and after refurbishing, sends it to join other Nazi U-boats. Lieutenant Commander Tarlton (Edward Judd) is in charge and his U-153 must battle the Nazi wolfpack when his ploy is discovered. A British frigate rescues the U-153's crew and is amazed to discover that the prisoners are British.

"The film is more or less competent of its extremely hackneyed kind. . . . C. M. Pennington-Richards' direction is blandly anonymous" (British *Monthly Film Bulletin*).

THE NAKED AND THE DEAD (Warner Bros., 1958) Color 131 mins.

Producer, Paul Gregory; director, Raoul Walsh; based on the novel by Norman Mailer; screenplay, Denis Sanders, Terry Sanders; art directors, Ted Haworth; set decorator, William L. Kuehl; wardrobe supervisor, Oscar Rodriguez; makeup supervisor, Allan Snyder; music/music director, Bernard Herrmann; assistant director, Russ Saunders; sound, Robert B. Lee; camera, Joseph LaShelle; editor, Arthur P. Schmidt.

Aldo Ray (Sergeant Croft); Cliff Robertson (Lieutenant Hearn); Raymond Massey (General Cummings); Lili St. Cyr (Lily); Barbara Nichols (Mildred); William Campbell (Brown); Richard Jaeckel (Gallagher); James Best (Ridges); Joey Bishop (Roth); Jerry Paris (Goldstein); Robert Gist (Red); L. Q. Jones (Wilson); Casey Adams (Dalieson); John Berardino (Mantelli); Edward McNally (Conn); Greg Roman (Minetta); Henry Amargo (Martinez).

"Considering the gutsy material. . . . [the] film bears little more than surface resemblance to the hard hitting (and foul-mouthed) Norman Mailer novel of the same title. It catches neither the spirit nor the intent of the original yarn and thus THE NAKED AND THE DEAD becomes just another war picture, weighed with some tedious dialog sporadically lifted from the book, but becoming tense and exciting in extremely well-photographed action sequences" (*Variety*).

"The abundance of expletives, which made the [721-page] book so notorious for its time, were deleted, together with the author's acute observation of men under stress. Instead, types instantly recognizable from a plethora of World War II movies infiltrated the

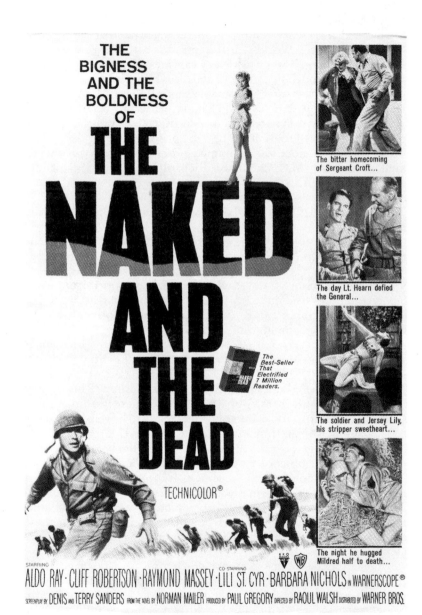

Advertisement for THE NAKED AND THE DEAD (1958).

narrative, and the novel's blazing originality and immediacy was reduced to an elaborate cliché" (Clive Hirschhorn, *The Warner Bros. Story*, 1979).

Norman Mailer's 1948 best seller was one of those screen projects begun at the dying RKO Studio in the mid-late 1950s, but released by another company. Like so many other hopefully incisive combat films of the time, such as BATTLE CRY (1955), IN LOVE AND WAR (1958) and THE PROUD AND PROFANE (1958), qq.v., the filmmakers relied too much on "titillating" sex and romance for substance rather than a perceptive study of the effect of warfare. It was a sad commentary that the most exploitable item in this "major" production was the brief appearance of exotic burlesque queen Lili St. Cyr doing a mild striptease in a Honolulu nightclub.

In the Pacific Theatre of World War II, manipulative U.S. General Cummings (Raymond Massey) is taking the offensive on a Japanese-held jungle island. It is this authoritarian's belief that the men must hate him if he is to instill the will of survival in them. One of his units, commanded by sadistic Sergeant Croft (Aldo Ray), pushes into the dense jungle. When the primitive Croft is killed by the Japanese, the liberal Lieutenant Hearn (Clift Robertson), a former playboy and Cummings' aide, takes charge of the doomed men. He survives the bloody foray to prove his theory that, contrary to Cummings' anti-human philosophy, "the spirit in man is godlike, eternal, indestructible."

For too much of this lengthy exercise the key characters are symbolic robots stiffly acting out contrived situations. (The flashback scenes used to open up the drama and to explain the ethnic stereotype characters' behaviors are generally embarrassments.) Those who had never read Mailer's evocative psychological study could never understand from this sparse picturization what all the fuss had been about when THE NAKED AND THE DEAD was first published. This film did nothing to enhance the diminishing reputation of veteran filmmaker Raoul Walsh who would slip down several more notches in estimation with his MARINES, LETS GO! (1961), q.v.

THE NELSON TOUCH *see*: CORVETTE K-225.

NINE MEN (United Artists, 1943) 68 mins.
    Associate producer, Charles Crichton; director, Harry Watt; story, Gerald Kersh; screenplay, Watt; art director, Duncan Sutherland; music, John Greenwood; camera, Roy Kellino; supervising editor, Sidney Cole; editor, Charles Crichton.

Jack Lambert (Sergeant Jack Watson); Gordon Jackson (Young 'Un); Frederick Piper (Banger Hill); Grant Sutherland (Jock Scott); Bill Blewett (Bill Parker); Eric Micklewood ("Booky" Lee); John Varley ("Dusty" Johnstone); Jack Horsman (Joe Harvey); Richard Wilkinson (John Crawford); Giulio Finzi (Italian Mechanic); and: Trevor Evans.

In the same year that Hollywood produced SAHARA, q.v., borrowing its premise from THE LOST PATROL (1934) and from a 1930s Russian film (THE THIRTEEN), England turned out the similarly structured NINE MEN. The action narrative is framed by new recruits being told the account of nine valiant British army men (of varying backgrounds and social classes) who are stranded in the North African desert, and how, when their commanding officer dies, Scottish Sergeant Watson (Jack Lambert) takes charge. Struggling to reach the safety of a decaying tomb, they hold out against the unseen enemy killers for a full day before rescuers finally appear.

NINE MEN was filmed in North Wales at Margam Sands for a cost of £20,000 pounds.

NO MAN IS AN ISLAND (Universal, 1962) Color 114 mins.

Producers, John Monks, Jr, Richard Goldstone; co-producer, Rolf Bayer; associate producers, Robert E. Lewis, Albert R. Joseph; directors, Monks, Goldstone; based on the wartime experiences of George R. Tweed (U.S. Navy); screenplay, Monks, Goldstone; art director, Benjamin Resella; music/song, Restie Umali; sound, Joseph Keener, Harry M. Leonard, Blandino Aquin, Tommy Santos; special effects, Robert R. Joseph; camera, Carl Kayser; additional camera, Mars Rasca; editor, Basil Wrangell.

Jeffrey Hunter (George Ray Tweed); Marshall Thompson ("Sonn" Sonnenberg); Barbara Perez ("Joe" Cruz); Ronald Remy (Chico Torres); Paul Edwards, Jr. (Al Turney); Rolf Bayer (Chief Schultz); Vicente Liwanag (Vicente); Fred Harris II (Roy Lund); Lamberto V. Avellana (Mr. Shimoda); Amparo (Chicay); Custodio (Mrs. Nakamura); Antonio de la Mogueis (Florecito); Vic Silayan (Major Hondo); Bert La Fortesa (Commander Oto Harada); Eddie Infante (Sus Quintagua); Nardo Ramos (Tumon); Rosa Mia (Primera Quintagua); Mike Anzures (Santos); Joseph de Cordova (Father Pangolin); Mario Barri (Limtiago); Stevie Joseph (Tommy Tanaka); Ding Tello (Japanese Sergeant Major); Burt Olivar (Antonio Cruz); Veronica Palicleo (Josefa Cruz); and: Bruno Punzalan, Nena Ledesma, Segundo Veloria.

The amazing but true life adventures of U.S. Navy radioman George Ray Tweed (Jeffrey Hunter) served as the broad basis for

Jeffrey Hunter in NO MAN IS AN ISLAND (1962).

this serviceable action film filmed in the Philippines. He was one of 555 American servicemen cornered on Guam when it came under Japanese control on December 10, 1941 (the first U.S. territory captured in World War II). During the 31 months until Guam was retaken (July 21, 1944) he hid in the hills and avoided capture. When the U.S. Navy began bombarding the shore during its pre-invasion Tweed signalled the ships with flags (mirrors in the film) and was picked up. His information on the island and enemy positions helped in the victory.

Two major elements defused the potential impact of NO MAN IS AN ISLAND: 1) producers/directors/scenarists John Monks, Jr. and Richard Goldstone were not sufficiently adept in providing this actionful slice-of-life biography with the needed zip, tightness and unadulterated authenticity, and 2) Jeffrey Hunter had just starred as the Christ in Nicholas Ray's highly exploited THE KING OF KINGS (1962) and that image—for worse, not better—stuck in viewers' and critics' minds.

For the record, Barbara Perez plays "Joe" Cruz, the hero's fictionalized romantic interest in the story, and the real-life George Ray Tweed received $6,027 in back pay after his Navy rescue. British release title: ISLAND ESCAPE.

NONE BUT THE BRAVE (Warner Bros., 1965) Color 105 mins.

Executive producer, Howard W. Koch; producers, Frank Sinatra, Kikumaru Okuda; associate producer, William H. Daniels; director, Frank Sinatra; story, Okuda; screenplay, John Twist, Katsuya Suzaki; art director, LeRoy Deane; art adviser, Haruyoshi Oshita; set decorator, George James Hopkins; makeup supervisor, Gordon Bau; music, Johnny Williams; music supervisor/music conductor, Morris Stoloff; Japanese music adviser, Kenjiro Hiorse; assistant directors, David Salven, Mitsushige Tsurushima; technical adviser, Kazuo Inoue; sound, Stanley Jones; camera, Harold Lipstein; editor, Sam O'Steen.

The Americans: Frank Sinatra (Chief Pharmacist's Mate Maloney); Clint Walker (Captain Dennis Bourke); Tommy Sands (Second Lieutenant Blair); Brad Dexter (Sergeant Bleeker); Tony Bill (Air Crewman Keller); Sammy Jackson (Corporal Craddock); Richard Bakalyan (Corporal Ruffino); Rafer Johnson (Private Johnson); Jimmy Griffin (Private Dexter); Christopher Dark (Private "Searcy); Don Dorrell (Private Hoxie); Phil Crosby (Private Magee); John Howard Young (Private Waller); Roger Ewing (Private Swensholm); Richard Sinatra (Private Roth); and: Laraine Stephens.

The Japanese: Tatsuya Mihashi (Lieutenant Kuroki); Takeshi Kato (Sergeant Tamura); Homare Suguro (Lance Corporal Hirano); Kenjo Sahara (Corporal Fuji Moto); Masahiko Tanimura (Private Ando); Toru Ibuki (Private Arikawa); Ryucho Shunputei (Private Okuda); Hisao Dazai (Private Tokumaru); Susumu Kurobe (Private Goro); Takashi Inagaki (Private Ishii); Kenichi Hata (Private Sato).

Crooner Frank Sinatra's antidote to male menopause was starring in a series of war movies in the late 1950s through the mid-1960s. This entry is not as cartoonish as NEVER SO FEW (1959), q.v., nor as "entertaining" as VON RYAN'S EXPRESS (1965), q.v.

A Japanese patrol without benefit of radio equipment is isolated on a remote South Pacific island during World War II. A planeload of American marines crashes on the isle and since the GIs' radio is damaged, they too are isolated. When the two groups discover one another, fighting erupts; the Japanese are led by Lieutenant Kuroki (Tatsuya Mihashi) and the Marines are supervised by Captain Dennis Bourke (Clint Walker). It is the Japanese who command a vital fresh water spring. When one of the Nipponese is wounded, Kuroki agrees to let Bourke's men have access to the water *if* Chief Pharmacist's Mate Maloney (Frank Sinatra) tends to the wounded soldier. Maloney has to amputate the man's leg, which saves his life, and a truce is formed between the two sides. The agreement is that when and if either side can ever rejoin the war effort, the truce is over. The Americans repair their radio and are advised that a U.S. warship is fast approaching. Kuroki refuses Bourke's suggestion that the Japanese surrender. The ship appears and the battling starts again. Soon all the Japanese are dead and only five of the Marines—including Bourke and Maloney—survive. Bourke takes Kuroki's journals which he has promised to have delivered someday to the man's widow.

When this slick production, the first in Sinatra's new Warner Bros. pact, was announced it was highly touted as being the first American-Japanese co-production and one that would objectively tell its combat story from both sides' point of view. It was also announced that Sinatra would not only produce and co-star in the film, but would be making his directorial debut. Before all was said and done on this less than stellar motion picture, Sinatra and the film had gained additional, unexpected publicity.

On Sunday, May 10, 1964 during a break in filming on Kauai, Hawaii, Sinatra was swimming in the ocean in front of his rented house. The clan was on the beach and with him in the ocean was executive producer Howard Koch's wife Ruth. Suddenly those on the beach realized that the two swimmers were drowning in the rough water. Actor Brad Dexter raced into the ocean and saved them. For his daring, he was made part of Sinatra's inner circle—for a time. The worldwide publicity the rescue generated did more to insure audience interest in NONE BUT THE BRAVE than anything that appeared on-screen.

It was the intent of NONE BUT THE BRAVE to balance the story with parallel characters in each of the opposing military groups. The casting directors must have favored the Japanese, for they far outshone their American counterparts in this very unoriginal presentation. Sinatra was his saloon singer self, Clint Walker was as wooden as ever, and Sinatra's then son-in-law, pop singer Tommy Sands, was ineffectual. (Sinatra's relative Richard was nondescript in a brief role.)

Japanese release title: YUSHA NOMI.

THE NUN AND THE SERGEANT (United Artists, 1962) 73 mins.

Producer, Eugene Franke; associate producer, Harold N.

Even; director, Franklin Adreon; screenplay, Don Cerveris; art director, Bob Kinoshita; costumes, Marjorie Corso; makeup, Carlie Taylor; music, Jerry Fielding; special effects, Norman Breedlove; camera, Paul Ivano; editor, John Hoffman, Carl Mahakian.

Robert Webber (Sergeant McGrath); Anna Sten (Nun); Leo Gordon (Dockman); Hari Rhodes (Hall); Robert Easton (Nupert); Dale Ishimoto (Pak); Linda Wong (Bob Soon); Linda Ho (Soon Cha); Tod Windsor (Nevins); Valentin De Vargas (Rivas); Kenny Miller (Quill); Norman Du Pont (Mossback); Roger Torrey (Turnbridge); Gregori F. Kris (Johnson); Caroline Kido (Myung Hee); King Moody (Pollard); Yashi (Kil Cha); Anna Shin (Ok-Cha).

Before THE DIRTY DOZEN (1967), q.v., appeared on the scene, there was THE NUN AND THE SERGEANT, which used a very similar plot premise. During the Korean War Marine Sergeant McGrath (Robert Webber) is ordered on a suicide mission. Rather than waste worthwhile fighting men, he picks a mixed crew from the brig. They are parachuted behind enemy lines where they encounter a wounded nun (Anna Sten) and a busload of Korean schoolgirls. Concerned that she might reveal their position to the enemy, McGrath has her and the girls travel with his squad. In the face of all the obstacles everyone comes to respect McGrath; all except Dockman (Leo Gordon), who attempts to rape one of the girls. Later, McGrath allows the girls to take the ailing nun to a nearby village for medical attention while he and the men embark on their fateful mission.

OBJECTIVE, BURMA! (Warner Bros., 1945) 142 mins.

Producer, Jerry Wald; director, Raoul Walsh; story, Alvah Bessie; screenplay, Ranald MacDougall, Lester Cole; art director, Ted Smith; set decorator, Jack McConaghy; makeup, Perc Westmore; assistant director, Elmer Decker; music, Franz Waxman; orchestrator, Leonid Raab; technical adviser, Major Charles S. Galbraith (U.S. Army Parachute Troops); dialogue director, John Maxwell; sound, C. A. Riggs; special effects, Edwin DuPar; camera, James Wong Howe; editor, George Amy.

Errol Flynn (Major Nelson); James Brown (Sergeant Treacy); William Prince (Lieutenant Jacobs); George Tobias (Gabby Gordon); Henry Hull (Mark Williams); Warner Anderson (Colonel Carter); John Alvin (Hogan); Mark Stevens (Lieutenant Barker); Richard Erdman (Nebraska Hooper); Anthony Caruso (Miggleori); Hugh Beaumont (Captain Hennessey); John Whitney (Negulesco); Joel Allen (Brophy); George Tyne (Soapy); Rodric Redwing (Sergeant Chattu); William Hudson (Hollis); Asit Koomar

(Ghurka); Lester Matthews (Major Fitzpatrick); John Sheridan (Co-Pilot); Carlyle Blackwell, Jr. (Pilot); Kit Carson, Neil Carter, Helmert Ellingwood, Shephard Houghton, Peter Kooy, Harlan Miller (Paratroopers); Erville Anderson (General Joseph W. Stilwell).

Several ingredients make OBJECTIVE, BURMA! a superior combat film. There is a specifically defined mission with a very clearly stated objective. There is a realistic approximation of the steamy, insect-infested jungle where the stalking action occurs. And the cast, including Warner Bros. superstar Errol Flynn and the studio stock company, is guided by an expert director (Raoul Walsh) who carefully mixes the pacing with fluid camera work and a balance of the expected with the unexpected. There are *no* flashbacks to artificially introduce women and romance into this taut tale, although the battle-weary, frightened men often think about and discuss the opposite sex.

Much of the plotline of OBJECTIVE, BURMA! is based on the wartime exploits of U.S. Army Lieutenant General Joseph W. Stilwell, who was Commander in Chief of the China/Burma/India Theater. It was he and his men who retreated 140 miles through the Burmese jungle in 1942 just steps ahead of the advancing Japanese. (In 1944 he would beat the Japanese in Burma.) There are also aspects of the military life of U.S. Army Brigadier General Frank D. Merrill who, with his 5307th Composite Group ("Merrill's Marauders"), waged guerrilla warfare against the Japanese in Burma. (MERRILL'S MARAUDERS would be the subject of a 1962 Warner Bros. film, q.v., starring Jeff Chandler.)

Major Nelson (Errol Flynn) heads a task force of 50 American parachutists who, under the orders of General Joseph W. "Vinegar Joe" Stilwell (Erville Anderson), are dropping behind enemy lines in Burma. Their task is to blast a Japanese radar post. Among Nelson's command are: good friend Lieutenant Jacobs (William Prince), nervous newcomer Miggleori (Anthony Caruso), midwesterner Nebraska Hooper (Richard Erdman), American Indian Sergeant Chattu (Rodric Redwing), and talkative Gabby Gordon (George Tobias). The one civilian in the squad is weathered reporter Mark Williams (Henry Hull), who is chronicling this brave leap to glory. Once landed, Nelson and his unit struggle through the jungle and the swamps and successfully blow up their objective. But then their real difficulties begin. The Japanese are alerted to the Americans' presence and prevent them from making a successful rendezvous with their rescue planes. To reach the new pick-up point, Nelson and his men must tramp 150 miles through the jungle! He divides his squad in two, with Jacobs heading the other group.

Japanese snipers lurk everywhere, decimating the ranks of the Marines. At a native village Flynn's team comes on the grisly remains of Jacobs' team, slaughtered and mutilated by the enemy. Nelson is unable to have the dead buried properly because he and his men must flee immediately from the unrelenting Japanese. Finally, using a signal mirror, Nelson contacts the plane piloted by Lieutenant Barker (Mark Stevens) and establishes a new rendezvous point. Meanwhile Nelson's exhausted, nearly-beaten men dig in and fight off the advancing Japanese with grenades, machines guns and hand-to-hand combat. Among those killed during the night are newsman Williams and the young Hollis (William Hudson). The sound of planes overhead proves to be from American aircraft and soon hundreds of G.I. paratroopers are dropping from the skies. Colonel Carter (Warner Anderson) greets Nelson and congratulates him on completing the mission. Dropping a bunch of dogtags into his commander's hand, he says, "Here's what it cost. Not much to send home. A handful of Americans." Nelson and his 11 fellow survivors are ordered out of the combat zone.

Released in the year World War II would come to a close, OBJECTIVE, BURMA! was enormously popular with filmgoers and critics.* It was nominated for three Academy Awards: Screenplay, Scoring, Editing. There is no denying that director Walsh created a near masterpiece of non-stop action and that star Flynn eschewed most of his swashbuckling mannerisms for this patriotic flagwaver. There was understandably hardly a contemporary critic who chastised Warner Bros. for its overzealous depiction of the Japanese as "slanty-eyed devils" and "monkeys" who are always "swarming like locusts" and "squirming" through the jungle. When Major Nelson and reporter Mark Williams come across the Japanese atrocities, the horrified, angered Williams shouts out, "I thought I'd seen or read about everything one man can do to another, from the torture chambers of the middle ages to the gang wars and lynchings of today. But this—this is different. This was done in cold blood by people who claim to be civilized. Civilized! They're degenerate, immoral idiots. Stinking little savages. Wipe them out, I say. Wipe them off the face of the earth. Wipe them off the face of the earth." This passage says everything about what Americans were taught to

---

*One of those critics who expected more from OBJECTIVE, BURMA! was James Agee. Writing in *The Nation*, he lectured, "However good they may be, known actors in this sort of semi-documentary film inevitably blunt the edge of your best hopes and intentions. If you are forced to use actors, known or unknown, at least put them, and yourself, and everyone else involved in making the movie, through an inch-by-inch study of the faces and postures and total images of actual warfare, as they appear in record fims of the war."

feel about the Japanese in the 1940s. It is ironic to note that just a few decades later these hated Japanese would successfully invade the U.S. with high technology and even higher financing.

One of the most telling speeches in the film is spoken by Negulesco (John Whitney) when he finds young Hollis' body after the final Japanese assault on Nelson's survivors. As he gives Major Nelson the dead man's dogtag, he says, "So much for Mrs. Hollis' nine months of pain and twenty years of hope." Hollis' death is part of the price of war.

When OBJECTIVE, BURMA! opened in England the British press and public were immediately and immensely furious with its depiction of the Americans as the "sole" fighters in the Burmese war. So intense was public reaction that the film had to be withdrawn from distribution there. In 1952 it was reissued successfully in England, this time with a special prologue depicting newsreel scenes of British and other Allied troops participating in the Burmese Campaigns.

OH! WHAT A LOVELY WAR (Paramount, 1969) Color 132 mins.

Producers, Brian Duffy, Richard Attenborough; associate producer, Mack Davidson; director, Attenborough; based on the play by Charles Chilton; screenplay, Len Deighton; production designer, Don Ashton; art director, Harry White; set decorator, Peter James; main titles, Raymond Hawkey; costume designer, Anthony Mendleson; makeup supervisor, Stuart Freeborn; song orchestrator/incidental music/ music conductor, Alfred Ralston; choreography, Eleanor Fazan; assistant director, Claude Watson; military adviser, Douglas Campbell (Major-General); sound editors, Don Challis, Brian Holland; special sound effects, Peter Handford; camera, Gerry Turpin; editor, Kevin Connor.

Ralph Richardson (Sir Edward Grey); Meriel Forbes (Lady Grey); Wensley Pithey (Archduke Franz Ferdinand); Ruth Kettlewell (Duchess Sophie); Ian Holm (President Poincaré); John Gielgud (Count Berchtold); Kenneth More (Kaiser Wilhelm II); John Clements (General von Moltke); Paul Daneman (Tsar Nicholas II); Pamela Abbott (Tsarina); Stella Courtney (Poincaré's Lady); Kathleen Helme (Berchtold's Lady); Ruth Gower (Von Moltke's Lady); Elizabeth Craven (Kaiserin); Joe Melia (The Photographer); Anthony Morton (Italian Military Attaché); Steve Plytas (Turkish Military Attaché); Jack Hawkins (Emperor Franz Josef); John Hussey (Soldier on Balcony); Kim Smith (Dickie Smith); Mary Wimbush (Mary Smith); Paul Shelley (Jack Smith); Wendy Allnutt (Flo Smith); John Rae (Grandpa Smith); Kathleen Wileman (Emma

Smith at Age 4); Corin Redgrave (Bertie Smith); Malcolm McFee (Freddie Smith); Colin Farrell (Harry Smith); Maurice Roeves (George Smith); Angela Thorne (Betty Smith); John Mills (Field Marshal Sir Douglas Haig); Julia Wright (His Secretary); Jean-Pierre Cassel (French Colonel); David Scheuer (French Soldier); Michael Wolf (German Officer); Jeremy Child (Wealthy Young Man); Ambrose Coghill (His Father); Penny Allen (Solo Chorus Girl); Sheila Cox, Sue Robinson, Hermione Farthingale, Joyce Franlin, Carole Gray, Dinny Jones, Delia Linden (Chorus Girls); Maggie Smith (Music Hall Star); David Lodge (Recruiting Sergeant); Michael Redgrave (General Sir Henry Wilson); Laurence Olivier (Field Marshal Sir John French); Peter Gilmore (Private Burgess); Derek Newark (Shooting Gallery Proprietor); Richard Howard (Young Soldier at Mons); John Trigger (Officer at Station); Ron Pember (Corporal at Station); Juliet Mills, Nanette Newman (Nurses at Station); Susannah York (Eleanor); Dirk Bogarde (Stephen); Norman Jones, Andrew Robertson, Angus Lennie, Brian Tipping (Scottish Soldiers); Ben Howard (Private Garbett); Christian Doermer (Fritz); Tony Vogel (German Soldier); Paul Hansard (German Officer); John Woodnutt (British Officer); Tony Thawnton (Officer on Telephone); Frank Coda, Kim Grant, Richard Loring, Tom Marshall (Soldiers in "Goodbyee"); Annie Bee, Valerie Smith, Isabelle Metcalfe, Jenny Morgan (Girlfriends in "Goodbyee"); Cecil Parker (Sir John); Zeph Gladstone (His Chauffeuse); Stanley McGeagh, Stanley Lebor (Soldiers in Gassed Trench); Robert Flemyng (Staff Officer in Gassed Trench); Thorley Walters, Norman Shelley (Staff Officers in Ballroom); Isabel Dean (Sir John French's Lady); Guy Middleton (General Sir William Robertson); Natasha Parry (His Lady); Cecilia Darby (Sir Henry Wilson's Lady); Phyllis Calvert (Lady Haig); Raymond S. Edwards (Staff Officer in Ballroom); Freddie Ascott ("Whizzbang" Soldier); Edward Fox, Geoffrey Davies, Anthony Ainley (Aides); Pippa Steele, Elisabeth Murray (Scoreboard Girls); Christian Thorogood, Paddy Joyce, John Dunhill, John Owens, P. G. Stephens (Irish Soldiers): Vanessa Redgrave (Sylvia Pankhurst); Clifford Mollison, Dorothy Reynolds, Harry Locke, George Ghent, Bette Vivian (Hecklers); Michael Bates (Drunken Lance Corporal); Charles Farrell (Policeman); Pia Colombo (Estaminel Singer); Vincent Ball (Australian Soldier); Gerald Sim (Chaplain); Maurice Arthur (Soldier Singer in Church Parade); Richard Davis (Sergeant in Burial Party); Arthur White (Sergeant in Dugout); Christopher Cabot (Soldier in Shell Hole); Linda Joyce, Mary Yeomans (Other Scoreboard Girls); Fanny Carby, Christine Noonan, Marianne Stone (Mill Girls); Charlotte Attenborough (Emma Smith at Age 8);

Joanne Browne (Singer); Frank Forsyth (Woodrow Wilson); John Gabriel (Nikolai Lenin).

Oh! What a Lovely War, based on a radio program of 1914-1918 songs, boasted 507 performances in its 1963 British stage run. When the musical entertainment, reached Broadway in December 1964, its run was only 125 performances. This should have alerted the producers of the film version that this satirical musical salute to the trials and tribulations of World War I might be too insular for global box-office success.

OH! WHAT A LOVELY WAR is framed as a highly stylized music hall interpretation of World War I through biting songs and telling quotes from the period. It gets underway at Brighton, England with an electric sign flashing the start of the First World War. British General Sir Douglas Haig (John Mills) is the ringmaster of this song and dance sideshow and the Smith family soon buy their tickets. Several of the Smith menfolk enlist: Harry (Colin Farrell), Jack (Paul Shelley), Bertie (Corin Redgrave) and George (Maurice Roeves). In the course of the war they are sacrificed on the battlefields. There is a giant cricket scoreboard which keeps tally of the war dead. The socially elegant Stephen (Dirk Bogarde) and Eleanor (Susannah York) vow to boycott German wine as their war effort. By war's end, with nine million dead, five of the Smith boys are buried on a hillside where the female members of the clan are seen picnicking.

This very full film, with its loving recreation of a bygone era, is a wonderful who's who of British acting royalty, with the likes of Laurence Olivier, Michael Redgrave, John Gielgud, and John Clements portraying archetypical genteel warlords and warmongering politicians who pontificate (and sing!) from the safe sidelines while the troopers do the trooping. There are 35 songs and song bits. Perhaps the most effective selection is Maggie Smith and chorus line performing "We Don't Want To Lose You." The film was 144 minutes when it opened in England; sixty minutes already cut. It was highly praised in its English distribution and the public there cared enough to see the film. In its disappointing U.S. release it would be chopped to 132 minutes, but it made little impact with filmgoers more focused on the then current Vietnam War. This was Richard Attenborough's first film directorial credit.

ONE MINUTE TO ZERO (RKO, 1952) 106 mins.

Producer, Edmund Grainger; director, Tay Garnett; screenplay, Milton Krims, William Wister Haines; art directors, Albert S. D'Agostinio, Jack Okey; set decorators, Darrell Silvera, John Sturtevant; music, Victor Young; English lyrics for Korean-

Japanese song, Norman Bennett; music director, C. Bakaleinikoff; camera, William E. Snyder; editor Sherman Todd.

Robert Mitchum (Colonel Steve Janowski); Ann Blyth (Linda Day); William Talman (Colonel Johnny Parker); Charles McGraw (Sergeant Baker); Margaret Sheridan (Mary Parker); Robert Gist (Major Carter); Richard Egan (Captain Ralston); Eduard Franz (Dr. Gustav Engstrand); Robert Osterloh (Major Davis); Lalo Rios (Chico Mendoza); Roy Roberts (General Thomas); Wally Cassell (Private Means); Larry Stewart (Private Weiss); Alvin Greenman (Private Lane, the Cook); Tom Irish (Sergeant Cook); Maurice Marsac (M. F. Villon); Dorothy Granger, Karen Hale (Nurses); Kay Christopher (Mrs. Stuart); Wallace Russell (Pilot Norton); Stuart Whitman (Officer); Hazel Sunny Boyne, Louise Saraydar, Mari Leon (Bystanders); Owen Song (Interpreter); Monya Andre (French United Nations Woman); John Mallory (Soldier).

RKO spent $2,181,000 to produce this unperceptive formula study of the Korean War. Colonel Steve Janowski (Robert Mitchum) is one of those American officers involved in the United Nations police action to prevent the Chinese Communists from pushing south below Korea's 38th parallel. He is a self-made military man who is tough enough to order mortar fire directed on civilians because enemy soldiers lurk in their midst. Linda Day (Ann Blyth—replacing Claudette Colbert) is the war widow working for the United Nations who brings warmth to Janowski's grim life. (In fact they even get to harmonize "Tell Me, Golden Moon.") Newsreel combat footage was integrated into the mundane storyline.

ONE OF OUR AIRCRAFT IS MISSING (United Artists, 1942) 90 mins.

Producers/directors/screenplay, Michael Powell, Emeric Pressburger; art director, David Rawnsley; camera, Roland Neame; editor, David Lean.

Godfrey Tearle (Sir George Corbett); Eric Portman (Tom Earnshaw); Hugh Williams (Frank Shelley); Bernard Miles (Geoff Hickman); Hugh Burden (John Glyn Haggard); Emrys Jones (Bob Ashley); Googie Withers (Jo de Vries); Pamela Brown (Else Meertens); Joyce Redman (Jet von Dieren); Hay Petrie (Burgomeister); Arnold Marle (Pieter Sluys); Robert Helpmann (De Jong); Peter Ustinov (Priest); Alec Clunes (Organist); Roland Culver (Naval Officer); Stewart Rome (Commander); David Evans, John Salew (Sentries); William D'Arcy (Officer); David Ward, Robert Duncan (Airmen); Selma Van Dias (Burgomeister's Wife); Hector Abbas (Driver); James Carson (Louis); Bill Akkerman (Willem);

Peter Schenke (Hendrik); Valerie Moon (Jannie); Robert Beatty (Hopkins); Joan Akkerman (Maartje); Michael Powell (Dispatching Officer).

ONE OF OUR AIRCRAFT IS MISSING is deliberately (slowly) paced, low-keyed, and uses that semi-documentary approach so favored by the British in their 1940s war films.

A squadron of British fighter planes attacks Stuttgart. All return safely to base except a Wellington bomber. That plane, without crew, eventually comes flying over the North Sea, and explodes into a pylon. What happened to its leader (Eric Portman) and its crew (Godfrey Tearle, Hugh Williams, Bernard Miles, Hugh Burden, Emrys Jones) is the basis of this well-executed film. The men had bailed out over Holland when their plane was damaged and they land in occupied territory. Passed from friendly person to person, including a priest (Peter Ustinov), the men return safely to England. Before long they are airborne again—their new target is Berlin.

To give the production a more realistic atmosphere, no forced romantic interlude was introduced into the story nor was music

(Front row): Pamela Brown, Hugh Williams, Joyce Redman; (rear row): Robert Helpmann, Peter Ustinov, and Bernard Miles in ONE OF OUR AIRCRAFT IS MISSING (1942).

used as an emotional tool. The Royal Netherlands government in exile provided authentication of the Dutch backdrop.

ONE OF OUR AIRCRAFT IS MISSING was originally released in Great Britain in April 1942 by Anglo-American with a 100-minute running time. Filmmaker Michael Powell appears briefly as a dispatching officer.

OPERATION PACIFIC (Warner Bros., 1951) 111 mins.

Producer, Louis F. Edelman; director/screenplay, George Waggner; art director, Leo K. Kuter; music, Max Steiner; camera, Bert Glennon; editor, Alan Crosland, Jr.

John Wayne (Lieutenant Commander "Duke" Gifford); Patricia Neal (Mary Stuart); Ward Bond ("Pop" Perry); Scott Forbes (Larry); Philip Carey (Bob Perry); Paul Picerni (Jonesy); William [Bill] Campbell (The Talker); Kathryn Givney (Commander Steele); Vincent Forte (Soundman); Martin Milner (Caldwell); Cliff Clark (Comsubpac); Jack Pennick (The Chief); Virginia Brissac (Sister Anne); Lewis Martin (Squad Commander); Louis Mosconi

James Flavin and John Wayne in OPERATION PACIFIC (1951).

(Radarman); Carleton Young (Captain McAllister); Gordon Gebert (Tommy Kirby); Steve Flagg (Lieutenant Jorgenson); Brett King (Lieutenant Ernie Stark); Dick Wessell (Mess Sergeant); Gail Davis (Virginia Blithe); Milburn Stone (Ground Control Officer); Sam Edwards (Junior); Gayle Kellogg (Herbie); and: Keith Larsen, Mack Williams.

During World War II in the Pacific, the submarine USS *Thunderfish* picks up Lieutenant Commander "Duke" Gifford (John Wayne) who has escaped from the Japanese-held island with a baby. The infant reminds Gifford of the child (who died in infancy) born to him and his now ex-wife Mary Stuart (Patricia Neal), an Army nurse. After surviving skirmishes with enemy cruisers the *Thunderfish* returns to base and he finds that Mary is dating Navy pilot Bob Perry (Philip Carey), the younger brother of "Pop" Perry (Ward Bond). Mary still has great feelings for Gifford but refuses to give in to sentiment, especially since she bitterly resents Gifford leaving her alone to cope with her grief. Back at sea the *Thunderfish* is damaged and wounded "Pop" Perry, on topside, orders the craft to submerge, even though it means he will drown. Gifford follows the order and not only feels guilty for his actions but is blamed by Bob Perry for his brother's death. Later the crew of the *Thunderfish* is successful in combat, shooting off torpedoes at enemy craft and rescuing downed pilots, including Bob Perry. Gifford and his men are proclaimed heroes and he and Mary are reunited.

Because of the marquee power of John Wayne and the promotional effort of Warner Bros., the over-long OPERATION PACIFIC was a money-earner. However, *Variety* noted, ". . . It's the standard motion picture conception of heroics, seemingly more fiction than fact, although well-founded on World War II incidents in the Pacific."

OPERATION PACIFIC mixed borrowed footage from the studio's DESTINATION TOKYO (1944) with new footage shot on location in Honolulu. John Wayne and Patricia Neal would reteam fourteen years later in similar roles for Otto Preminger's IN HARM'S WAY (1965), q.v.

OVERLORD (EMI, 1975) 85 mins.

Producer, James Quinn; director, Stuart Cooper; screenplay, Cooper, Christopher Hudson; music, Paul Glass; camera, John Alcott; editor, Jonathan Gili.

Brian Stirner (Tom); Davyd Harries (Jack); Nicholas Ball (Arthur); Julie Neesam (Girl); Sam Sewell (Trained Soldier).

OVERLORD is a little known anti-war film directed by

American-born Stuart Cooper. Filmed in black-and-white, this understated British production was entered in the 1975 Berlin Film Festival. *Variety* complimented the film, which uses flashbacks and flashforwards, for its ". . . understated, unheroic feel, bringing home the tragedy of war even more strongly by his [Cooper] muted buildup of one man's fate without sensationalizing or, for that matter, preaching, no mean achievement."

In World War II England Tom (Brian Stirner) is inducted into military service. Between the span of his brief training period and his death during the D-Day invasion of France, he has a brief romantic interlude. She (Julie Neesam) is both his first and last girl.

PARIS BRULE-T-IL? *see:* IS PARIS BURNING?

THE PASSWORD IS COURAGE (Metro-Goldwyn-Mayer, 1962) 116 mins.

Producers, Andrew L. Stone, Virginia Stone; associate producer, Sydney Streeter; director, Andrew L. Stone; based on the book by John Castle; screenplay, Andrew L. Stone; art director, Wilfred Arnold; wardrobe, Larry Stewart; music, Derek New; assistant director, George Pollard; technical adviser, Charles Coward; recording supervisor, A. W. Watkins; special effects, Bill Warrington; camera, Davis Boulton; supervising editor, Virginia Stone; editor, Noreen Ackland.

Dirk Bogarde (Sergeant Major Charles Coward); Maria Perschy (Irena); Alfred Lynch (Corporal Billy Pope); Nigel Stock (Cole); Reginald Beckwith (Unterofficer); Richard Marner (Schmidt); Ed Devereaux (Aussie); Lewis Flander (Pringle); George Mikell (Necke); Richard Carpenter (Robinson); Margaret Whiting (French Farm Woman); Olaf Pooley (German Doctor); Ferdy Mayne (German Officer); Colin Blakely (German Goon); Michael Mellinger (Feldwebal); and: Bernard Archard, Mark Eden, Tommy Elliott, John Gardiner, Philo Hauser, Douglas Livingstone, Howard Pays, George Pravda, Bernard Proctor.

The husband-and-wife filmmaking team of Andrew and Virginia Stone were better known for their taut suspense films rather than this type of dramatic biography based on John Castle's 1955 book.

As he is being marched to a World War II German prisoner-of-war camp, British Sergeant Major Charles Coward (Dirk Bogarde) escapes by feigning to be one of a group of wounded German soldiers. He is hospitalized and given the Iron Cross medal before the truth is discovered. No sooner is he at a prison camp than he starts planning a tunnel escape. He wrangles a pass into a nearby

Maria Perschy and Dirk Bogarde in THE PASSWORD IS COURAGE (1962).

town where he meets with Irena (Maria Perschy), a member of the Polish underground. She provides him with maps and other information. Back at the camp he finishes the tunnel and, with his friend Corporal Billy Pope (Alfred Lynch), escapes. However, they are recaptured in Vienna and sent to the I.G. Farben plant at Auschwitz, where they do their best for the doomed Jewish concentration camp victims. As the war almost ends, Coward and Pope "borrow" a fire engine and drive to freedom through enemy territory.

Although based on true facts about the ironically named Charles Coward who made seven escape attempts, the switch in mood from the nearly comedic to the deadly serious disturbed some viewers.

PATHS OF GLORY (United Artists, 1957) 86 mins.
    Producer, James B. Harris; director, Stanley Kubrick; based on the novel by Humphrey Cobb; screenplay, Kubrick, Calder Willingham, Jim Thompson; art director, Ludwig Reiber; music, Gerald Fried; camera, George Krause; editor, Eva Kroll.

Kirk Douglas (Colonel Dax); Ralph Meeker (Corporal Paris); Adolphe Menjou (General Broulard); George Macready (General Mireau); Wayne Morris (Lieutenant Roget); Richard Anderson (Major Saint-Auban); Joseph Turkel (Private Arnaud); Timothy Carey (Private Ferol); Peter Capell (Colonel Judge); Susanne Christian (German Girl); Bert Freed (Sergeant Boulanger); Kem Dibbs (Private LeJeune); Harold Benedict (Captain Nichols); Emile Meyer (Priest); John Stein (Captain Rousseau); Frederic Bell (Shell-Shocked Soldier).

"We're fighting a war, Dax, a war we've got to win. Those men didn't fight and they were shot." These words spoken by crafty General Broulard (Adolphe Menjou) to righteous Colonel Dax (Kirk Douglas) are at the heart of Stanley Kubrick's trenchant anti-military and anti-war film, PATHS OF GLORY.

It is 1916 on the Western Front and World War I has been in progress for two years. Pressured by politicians and the press for a notable victory, suave General Broulard arrives at General Mireau's (George Macready) headquarters—an idyllic, peaceful chateau—and demands that the French troops take the apparently impregnable Ant Hill from the Germans. When Mireau suggests this is impossible, Broulard indicates that a victory would mean a quick promotion for the pompous Mireau. The latter quickly agrees to the offensive and visits the ragged 701st Regiment commanded by Colonel Dax, who in peacetime had been a criminal lawyer. After summarily reviewing the bewildered troops in the muddy trenches and slapping a sergeant (Bert Freed) who comes to the defense of a shell-shocked soldier (Frederic Bell) whom Mireau has rebuked, Mireau informs Dax of the new battle strategy. Dax contends that the mission is suicidal; Mireau retorts that losses are part of victory. Finally the compassionate Dax agrees to lead his men on this deadly task rather than have a new officer, unfamiliar with the soldiers, substituted in his place. On a reconnaissance patrol that night through no-man's-land, drunken and cowardly Lieutenant Roget (Wayne Morris) is responsible for the death of Private LeJeune (Kem Dibbs), and Corporal Paris (Ralph Meeker) has witnessed this disgusting situation. However, Paris understands military politics and remains silent. The next dawn Dax leads the attack and the casualties are enormous as they head to and through no-man's land. Mireau spots through his telescope that an entire French unit has not advanced according to plan and demands that battery commander Captain Rousseau (John Stein) open fire on the men. ("If those little sweethearts won't face German bullets, they'll face French ones!") Rousseau refuses unless Mireau will place the order in writing. Meanwhile Dax's attack is a complete failure. To save face, Mireau

Kirk Douglas in PATHS OF GLORY (1957).

places the entire regiment under collective arrest and decides to try one section of each company for cowardice and mutiny. Eventually, through Dax's manipulations and General Broulard's intervention, it is agreed that three men will be picked at random to stand trial and Dax will be their defense counsel. The mock trial is held in the chateau's Grand Ballroom but it is a travesty. No records of the proceedings are kept; no witnesses are allowed. The three defendants, the radical Private Arnaud (Joseph Turkel), the dim-witted Private Ferol (Timothy Carey) and Corporal Paris (selected "at random" by Lieutenant Roget), are found guilty and sentenced to death. Later, Dax learns from Captain Rousseau of Mireau's unfilled order against his own troops and confronts the suave, unruffled Broulard at the chateau where he is hosting an elegant dinner party. At first Broulard thinks Dax merely wants to discredit his superior and win his post, but then, understanding bits of the truth but admitting none of it, he insists that the executions must go through as scheduled. He also suggests that Mireau's action will be investigated by a court of inquiry. The next morning, with the remorseful Roget forced by Dax to head the firing squad, the three prisoners, including stretcher-carried Arnaud, are shot. Dax wanders, distraught, into a cafe where a German girl (Susanne Christian) is entertaining the troops. At first Dax is angered that his men can so soon forget their three comrades, but then he understands that they are reaching out for sanity—something normal—in a crazy, deadly world. A sergeant arrives to inform Dax that his men must move up to the front lines again. He asks the sergeant to give the men a few more moments of relaxation.

PATHS OF GLORY is filled with superior performances, especially by Kirk Douglas, George Macready and Adolphe Menjou. The depiction of trench warfare is horrifically grim and reportedly accurate. The horror of combat is all-encompassing—complete with the faceless, unseen enemy, the constant tension, the dirt, and everywhere the smells and sounds of death. But most frightening of all, in the midst of this senseless war, is the manipulating of the self-interested, uninformed, and duplistic military brass. When Colonel Dax realizes how expendable their lives are to their own hypocritical superior officers, he is aghast. "There are times when I'm ashamed to be a member of the human race, and this is one such occasion," Dax hisses at the convened court of complacent military leaders.

The meticulous PATHS OF GLORY was filmed in black-and-white in Puchiem, Germany (near Munich) for $900,000. It remains one of the most realistic (First World) War films, with its biting indictment of war in general and the military in particular. It was evolved by Kirk Douglas' production company, based on Humphrey Cobb's 1934 novel, which was itself based on an actual incident. At the time of release it was banned from screenings at U.S. military bases and is still banned today in France. The wife (Susanne Christian) of the film's director (Stanley Kubrick) played the German cafe singer.

Although the highly-praised PATHS OF GLORY won no Academy Awards (not *even* a nomination), Douglas and Kubrick (who also co-wrote the script for PATHS OF GLORY) would join for the elaborate, highly intelligent spectacle of the rebelling Roman slave, SPARTACUS (1960), which cost more than ten times what PATHS OF GLORY had. Kubrick, considered the "wunderkind" of post-World War II Hollywood, would turn out the caustic anti-war satire DR. STRANGELOVE (1964) and in 1987 create his latest anti-war statement set in Vietnam, FULL METAL JACKET, q.v.

PATTON (Twentieth Century-Fox, 1970) Color 170 mins.

Producer, Frank McCarthy; associate producer, Frank Caffey; director, Franklin J. Schaffner; based on the books *Patton: Ordeal and Triumph* by Ladislas Farago and *A Soldier's Story* by Omar N. Bradley; story/screenplay, Francis Ford Coppola, Edmund H. North; art directors, Urie McCleary, Gil Parrondo; set decorators, Antonio Mateos, Pierre-Louis Thevenet; makeup, Del Acevedo; music, Jerry Goldsmith; orchestrator, Arthur Morton; assistant directors, Eli Dunn, Jose Lopez Rodero; technical advisers, Paul D. Harkins (General), Glover S. Johns, Jr. (Colonel); senior military adviser, Omar N. Bradley (General); Spanish military adviser, Martin Pozuelo (Lieutenant Colonel); action coordinator, Joe Canutt; sound supervisor, James Corcoran; mechanical effects, Alex Weldon; special camera effects, L. B. Abbott, Art Cruickshank; camera, Fred Koenekamp; second unit camera, Clifford Stine, Cecilio Paniagua; editor, Hugh S. Fowler.

George C. Scott (General George Smith Patton, Jr.); Karl Malden (General Omar N. Bradley); Michael Bates (Field Marshal Sir Bernard Law Montgomery); Edward Binns (Major General Walter Bedell Smith); Lawrence Dobkin (Colonel Gaston Bell); John Doucette (Major General Lucian K. Truscott); James Edwards (Sergeant William George Meeks); Frank Latimore (Lieutenant Colonel Henry Davenport); Richard Munch (Colonel General Alfred Jodl); Morgan Paull (Captain Richard N. Jenson); Siegfried Rauch (Captain Oskar Steiger); Paul Stevens (Lieutenant Colonel Charles R. Codman); Michael Strong (Brigadier General Hobart Carver); Karl Michael Vogler (Field Marshal Erwin Rommel);

Stephen Young (Captain Chester B. Hansen); Peter Barkworth (Colonel John Welkin); John Barrie (Air Vice-Marshal Sir Arthur Coningham); David Bauer (Lieutenant General Harry Buford); Tim Considine (Soldier Who Gets Slapped); Albert Dumortier (Moroccan Minister); Gerald Flood (Air Chief Marshal Sir Arthur Tedder); Jack Gwillim (General Sir Harold Alexander); David Healy (Clergyman); Bill Hickman (General Patton's Driver); Sandy Kevin (Correspondent); Carey Loftin (General Bradley's Driver); Alan MacNaughtan (British Briefing Officer); Lionel Murton (Third Army Chaplain); Clint Ritchie (Tank Captain); Douglas Wilmer (Major General Francis de Guingand); Patrick J. Zurica (First Lieutenant Alexander Stiller); Lowell Thomas (Narrator); Abraxas Aaran (Willy the Dog).

"I want you to remember that no bastard ever won a war by dying for his country. He won it by making the other poor dumb bastard die for his country." In this flabbergasting opening speech of PATTON, the amazing militarist General George Smith Patton, Jr. (George C. Scott) establishes immediately his unorthodox philosophy of warfare.

"Men," he informs the assembled troops from the podium with its backdrop of a huge American flag, "all this stuff you've heard about America not wanting to fight, wanting to stay out of the war is a lot of horse dung. Americans traditionally love to fight. All real Americans love the sting of battle. Americans love a winner and will not tolerate a loser. Americans play to win all the time . . . the very thought of losing is hateful to Americans."

By this early point there is no doubt how this supreme egoist, who loves war and thrives on command power, will react to any given situation. His goal is victory and his men are the expendable means. "Now, an army is a team. It lives, fights and sleeps as a team. This individuality stuff is a bunch of crap. The bilious bastards who wrote that stuff about individuality for the *Saturday Evening Post* don't know anything about real battle."

The iconoclastic Patton, impeccably outfitted, concludes his dynamic pep rally with, "By God I actually pity those poor bastards we're going up against, by God I do. We're not going to just shoot them, we're going to cut out their living guts and use them to grease the treads of our tanks. We're going to murder those lousy Hun bastards by the bushel."

In 1943 U.S. General Omar N. Bradley (Karl Malden) turns to General Patton after German Field Marshal Erwin Rommel's (Karl Michael Vogler) Afrika Korps defeats the American tanks at the Kasserine Pass in Tunisia. Patton, who endlessly studies military history and the Bible, beats Rommel's forces at El Guettar, leading to Allied victory in North Africa. (The Germans say of the victor, "Patton is a romantic warrior lost in contemporary times.") "Blood and Guts" Patton is assigned to push into Sicily with the 7th Army by capturing Palermo, but it is British Field Marshal Montgomery (Michael Bates)—his prime rival—who leads the attack while Patton's men must "merely" protect the flank of the British. Angered by this turn of events, Patton takes it on his own to take Messina; all of which causes more dissension with Montgomery.

While visiting a field hospital, Patton speaks to a G.I. patient (Tim Considine), asking what ails him. " It's my nerves, sir. I can't stand the shelling," he admits, breaking into tears. The mercurial Patton becomes enraged. "Hell, you're just a God damned coward. We have a yellow bastard sitting here crying in front of these brave men who have been wounded in battle. Shut up!" He interrupts his tirade to slap the man, and then yells at the shocked staff, "Don't admit this yellow bastard! We won't have sons of bitches who are afraid to fight stinking up this place of honor." Turning back to the battle-fatigued youth he pronounces, "You're going back to the front, my friend. You may get shot or you may get killed, but you're going to the fighting; either that, or I'm going to stand you up in front of the firing squad." As he strides out of the room, he adds, almost hysterically, "Get him out of here! Send him up to the front! . . . I won't have cowards in my army."

Allied Commander Dwight D. Eisenhower calls this highly publicized incident "despicable" and Patton is shunted to the side lines. Eisenhower demands that Patton make a full apology to everyone involved, and he does so graciously. Patton is disheartened when the recently elevated Bradley uses him as a decoy in the Mediterranean in the Allies' planned D-Day invasion of Europe. Finally he is given command of the 3rd Army and during the Battle of the Bulge Patton and his men push through Normandy to rescue the 101st Airborne at Bastogne. Next Patton's troops sweep through to Czechoslovakia. At this juncture the high command demands that he allow Montgomery's men and the Russian troops to claim final victory against the Nazis. The war in Europe is over, but General MacArthur indicates that he does not need Patton in his part of the Pacific Theater of War. In a press interview Patton makes damaging remarks about the so-called ally, Russia, and is again removed from command.

Peace is here and Patton does not know how to handle it. Bradley suggests, "I have a feeling from now on just being a good soldier won't mean a thing. I'm afraid we're going to have to be diplomats . . . administrators . . . you name it." "God help us," Patton sighs. There are intimations that future wars will be fought "with no heroes, no generals." This is all too much for Patton, who feels, "There's only one proper way for a professional soldier to die. That's from the last bullet of the last battle of the last war." (In actuality Patton will die in December 1945 as the result of an automobile "accident" which some still insist to this day was the result of an assassination plot.)

While infantrymen in combat are a definite aspect of this superb film, it is the controversial military genius, Patton, who is the film's focal point. This is warfare viewed from on top, where a general can one moment be boastfully delighted with his troops ("God, God, I'm proud of these men") and the next be slapping a soldier with complete disregard for the man's emotional scars. This is a man born for war ("All I want to do is to command an army in combat"), of whom his superior says, "You do this job because you love it!" Bombastic and full of bravado, Patton thrives in his military domain. Beneath the surface of this strong screen biography is the subtext question: If there were no war, would such a man create one for his own personal needs?

As Steven Jay Rubin states in *Combat Films: 1945-1970* (1980), "PATTON became a mirror through which warring doves and hawks viewed the confirmation of their own deeply emotional beliefs. To the former, General Patton was the Antichrist, who symbolized the gutsy brand of militarism that had led to the Vietnam debacle. And yet, as an audience, they found it difficult to criticize a film that was so overtly honest. It would be the key to the film's success, for there was no need to embellish or disparage the character of Patton; the paradox of his makeup was obvious from the beginning."

PATTON had been a pet project of retired Brigadier General Frank McCarthy since 1951,* but it would be nearly twenty years before the film would become a reality for Darryl Zanuck, who wanted this film, along with the same year's TORA! TORA! TORA!, q.v., to be a coda to his earliest war epic THE LONGEST DAY (1962), q.v. PATTON proved a critical and commercial hit. It would earn a remarkable $28,100,000 in theater rentals in the U.S. and Canada and would receive Academy Awards for Best Picture, Best Actor (George C. Scott—who refused to accept the award), Screenplay, Art Direction, Sound, and Editing, with Oscar nominations for Cinematography, Score, and Special Visual Effects.

PATTON co-scripter Francis Ford Coppola would go on to conceive his own massive reaction to war in APOCALYPSE NOW

---

*See Rubin's essay on the (pre)-production of PATTON in *Combat Pictures: 1945-1970*.

(1979), q.v. Producer Frank McCarthy would later turn to another equally amazing, if terrifying, World War II general in Mac-ARTHUR (1977), q.v. And eighteen years after the mega hit, George C. Scott would return to the role of the larger-than life Patton* in THE LAST DAYS OF PATTON (CBS-TV, 9/14/86), a telefeature co-starring Eva Marie Saint as his wife Beatrice, Richard Dysart as General Dwight D. Eisenhower, and Murray Hamilton as his military buddy, General Hobart "Hap" Gay. The 150-minute production focused on the final post-war months (May to December 1945) of the general's life.

PILOT NO. 5 (Metro-Goldwyn-Mayer, 1943) 70 mins.

Producer, B. P. Fineman; director, George Sidney; screenplay, David Hertz; art directors, Cedric Gibbons, Howard Campbell; set decorator, Edwin Willis, Glen Barner; music, Lennie Hayton; assistant director, Sanford Roth; sound, J. S. Burnbridge, James Z. Flaster; special effects, A. Arnold Gillespie, Don Jahraus; camera, Paul C. Vogel; editor, George White.

Franchot Tone (George Braynor Collins); Marsha Hunt (Freddie); Gene Kelly (Vito S. Allesandro); Van Johnson (Everett Arnold); Alan Baxter (Winston Davis); Dick Simmons (Henry Willoughby Clavens); Steven Geray (Major Eichel); Howard Freeman (Hank Durbin); Frank Ferguson (Tully); William Tannen (American Soldier); Carl Saxe (Dutch Boy); Peter Lawford (Englishman); Jack Gardner (Mechanic); Sara Haden (Landlady); James Davis, Cliff Danielson (Military Police); Hobart Cavanaugh (Boat Owner); William Halligan (Bartender); Kay Medford (Secretary); Eddie Acuff, Billy Wayne (Cameramen); Betty Jaynes, Marilyn Maxwell, Jacqueline White, Marie Windsor (Party Girls); William Bishop, Leigh Sterling (Cadets); John Dilson (Defense Instructor); Harry Semels (Barber); Ava Gardner (Girl); Frank Puglia (Nikota); Edward Fielding (Dean Barrett).

What makes a man fulfill his patriotic duty? This is the key to this glib and glossy "B" film churned out by MGM with a very personable cast.

During World War II, U.S. pilot George Braynor Collins (Franchot Tone) volunteers for a desperate mission in the South Pacific. After his takeoff the other flyers wonder what led him to take on this deadly risk. His pal, Vito S. Allesandro (Gene Kelly),

---

*Other actors who have portrayed Patton onscreen are: John Larch in MIRACLE OF THE WHITE STALLIONS (1963), Kirk Douglas in IS PARIS BURNING? (1966), George Kennedy in BRASS TARGET (1978), and Darren McGavin in IKE (1979—telefeature).

Dick Simmons, Gene Kelly, Steven Geray, Alan Baxter, and Van Johnson in
PILOT NO. 5 (1943).

knows the reasons and in a lengthy flashback recalls the details.
Collins had been a crusading young attorney who only learned
belatedly that the southern state governor (Howard Freeman) he
once idolized and worked for was nothing more than a would-be
fascist. He exposes the man at the expense of his own career. Collins
joins the Air Corps to continue his battle against the fascists.
Coming back to the present, he is seen crashing his plane onto a
Japanese aircraft carrier in order to destroy the carrier.

PLATOON (Orion, 1986) Color 111 mins.

Executive producers, John Daly, Derek Gibson; producer,
Arnold Kopelson; co-producer, A. Kitman Ho; director/
screenplay, Oliver Stone; production designer, Bruno Rubeo; art
directors, Rodel Cruz, Doris Sherman Williams; set decorator, Roy
Lachica; wardrobe supervisor, Wynn Arenas; special makeup effects, Gordon J. Smith; title designer, Dan Perri; music, Georges
Delerue; technical military advisers, Captain Dale Dye (U.S.
Marine Corps, Retired); Stanley White (U.S. Marine Corps, Retired); Kathryn Clayton, Mark K. Ebenhoch, Robert M. Galotti,

Jr.; stunt coordinator, Gil Arceo; assistant directors, H. Gordon Boos, Gerry Toomey, Pepito Diaz, Evan Kopelson; sound, Simon Kaye, Taffy Haines; sound re-recording, John "Doc" Wilkinson, Richard Rogers, Charles "Bud" Grenzbach; supervising sound editor, Gordon Daniel; sound editors, David Campling, Greg Dillon, James J. Klinger, Tony Palk; camera, Robert Richardson; second unit camera, Tom Sigel; editors, Claire Simpson, Tom Finan.

Tom Berenger (Sergeant Barnes); Willem Dafoe (Sergeant Elias); Charlie Sheen (Chris Taylor); Forest Whitaker (Big Harold); Francesco Quinn (Rhah); John C. McGinley (Sergeant O'Neill); Richard Edson (Sal); Kevin Dillon (Bunny); Reggie Johnson (Junior); Keith David (King); Johnny Depp (Lerner); David Neidorf (Tex); Mark Moses (Lieutenant Wolfe); Chris Pedersen (Crawford); Corkey Ford (Manny); Corey Glover (Francis); Bob Orwig (Gardner); Tony Todd (Warren); Kevin Eshelman (Morehouse); James Terry McIlvain (Ace); J. Adam Glover (Sanderson); Ivan Kane (Tony); Paul Sanchez (Doc); Dale Dye (Captain Harris); Peter Hicks (Parker); Basile Achara (Flash); Steve Barredo (Fu Sheng);

Tom Berenger (center) in PLATOON (1987).

Chris Castillejo (Rodriguez); Andrew B. Clark (Tubbs); Bernardo Manalili (Village Chief); Than Rogers (Village Chief's Wife); Li Thi Van (Village Chief's Daughter); Clarisa Ortacio (Old Woman); Romy Sevilla (One-Legged Man); Mathew Westfall (Terrified Soldier); Nick Nickelson, Warren McLean (Mechanized Soldiers); Li Mai Thao (Rape Victim); Ron Barracks (Medic).

Because several other Vietnam War films so quickly followed the trendsetting PLATOON, the reasons why this Oscar-winning feature film, with its sharp insight into the ways war tears down a man's psyche, was such a dramatic revelation to filmgoers were obscured. PLATOON provides a very real cast of characters caught up in a no-holds-barred depiction of the inferno of futility known as the Vietnam War. It was the first major English-language film to reach out to the hearts of viewers with its gutsy, honest approach to how badly and confusing it felt being part of the war in Vietnam.

PLATOON opens with a quotation from Ecclesiastes: "Rejoice, O Young Men in Youth," and is dedicated to the men who fought and died in Vietnam.

Vietnam—September 1967. Men are seen being disgorged from the bowels of a U.S. bomber transport. Filled body bags cover the ground. Nineteen-year-old Chris Taylor (Charlie Sheen) is a college dropout who volunteered for one year's military duty. He is now part of Bravo Company, 25th Infantry, somewhere near the Cambodian border. Soon Chris is wounded on a night patrol in the jungle, while others are killed. Later, another two are blown up by a bomb and Manny (Corkey Ford) is found impaled on a tree. It is battle-hardened, psychopathic Sergeant Barnes (Tom Berenger) who leads the men into a Vietnamese village where the natives are rounded up. Chris makes one of the Vietnamese "dance" to the tune of his bullets, and Bunny (Kevin Dillon) smashes in the man's head with his rifle. The vicious Barnes nonchalantly shoots the village chief's wife (Than Rogers) when she becomes hysterical. Sensitive Sergeant Elias (Willem Dafoe), who has retained his humanity despite the horrors of war, intends to report Barnes' atrocity. They torch the village and Chris prevents some soldiers from raping a native girl. Once back at camp, the soldiers are divided into two factions: those supporting Elias and those loyal to Barnes. The next day the platoon is ambushed by the Viet Cong and Lieutenant Wolfe's (Mark Moses) faulty information to the artillery support costs the lives of some of his men. Barnes shoots the isolated Elias; he insists to Chris that the man is dead from enemy fire and there is no point trying to confirm that. However, later, Chris spots Elias being murdered by the enemy. Back at the camp Chris attacks the savage, stoic Barnes, but to no avail. Once more on patrol near the

Cambodian border, the 25th is attacked by the 101st North Vietnamese Army and suffers severe casualties. Chris and Barnes have a final confrontation which is interrupted by an air strike. Chris shoots and kills the badly wounded Barnes: his revenge has been accomplished. The American position is reaffirmed and the wounded Chris is airlifted out by helicopter.

PLATOON was shot in 54 days in the Philippines on a $6,500,000 budget. It had long been a project Vietnam veteran Oliver Stone wanted to make. "I saw combat at the ground level. I saw people die. I killed. I almost was killed. Almost immediately I realized that combat is totally random. It has nothing to do with heroism. Cowardice and heroism are the same emotion—fear—expressed differently. And life is a matter of luck. Two soldiers are standing two feet apart. One gets killed, the other lives."

Stone's PLATOON succeeds on many emotional and intellectual levels, incisively showing the Vietnam War from the soldier's (the "grunt's") point of view. The men are frightened at times, there is interracial squabbling, they rely sometimes on drugs and drink to forget the hell they are in. And somehow some of them manage to survive, much to their own amazement. (One soldier says bewilderingly, "The shit's getting way out of hand!" Another decides, "Just make it out of here. All the rest of your life is gravy . . . every day is gravy.") The visuals of war are eerily realistic.

One accepts Stone's artificial device of the symbolic good and evil as represented by Barnes and Elias, although the latter comes out with some overly discerning, poetic remarks. ("I love this place at night. The stars. There's no right, no wrong in them. They're just there.") However, by having Chris the off-screen narrator, the film falters. It distances the audience from the extremely poignant story, just as the narrator (played by Charlie Sheen's actor father Martin) did in APOCALYPSE NOW (1979), q.v. We are lectured at by the pontificating, precocious Chris.

At one point the too perceptive Chris says, "Nobody cares about the new guys. The unwritten rule is, a new guy's life isn't worth as much because he hasn't put his time in and they say if you're going to get it in Nam it's better to get it in the first few weeks. The logic being you don't suffer that much."

Later he observes, "Most of them got nothing, but they're fighting for our society. They're called grunts cause they can take it." And he admits, "I don't know what's right or wrong any more."

Finally, at the film's end he realizes, "We did not fight the enemy, we fought ourselves and the enemy was in us. The war is over for me now, but it will always be there for the rest of my days.

... But those of us who did make it have an obligation to build again to teach to others what we know and to try with what's left of our lives to find a goodness and meaning to this life."

The much heralded, much-analyzed* PLATOON would win four Academy Awards: Best Picture, Director, Film Editing, and Sound. It grossed over $140,000,000 in its first several months at the box-office. Its delayed videocassette release** (due to a highly-publicized lawsuit between two distributors) extended consumer interest in this sensitive and articulate war film. When PLATOON continued to earn box-office dollars and to engender a continuing raft of imitators, it was announced in April 1987 that a PLATOON sequel was in the planning stages, with Oliver Stone scheduled to write the script.

PORK CHOP HILL (United Artists, 1959) 97 mins.

Producer, Sy Bartlett; director, Lewis Milestone; story, S. L. A. Marshall; screenplay, James R. Webb; production designer, Micholai Remisoff; set decorator, Edward G. Boyler; costumes, Eddie Armand; music/music conductor, Leonard Rosenman; technical adviser, Captain Joseph G. Clemons, Jr.; camera, Sam Leavitt; editor, George Boemler.

Gregory Peck (Lieutenant Joseph G. Clemons, Jr.); Harry Guardino (Forstman); Rip Torn (Lieutenant Russell); George Peppard (Fedderson); James Edwards (Corporal Jurgens); Bob Steele (Kern); Woody Strode (Franklin); George Shibita (Lieutenant O'Hashi); Norman Fell (Sergeant Coleman); Robert Blake (Velie); Biff Elliot (Bowen); Barry Atwater (Davis); Michael Garth (S-2

---

*Karate champ/actor Chuck Norris, who made a Vietnam War film trilogy, the MISSING IN ACTION series, reacted adversely to PLATOON: "If I was a Vietnam vet who'd put my life on the line over there, and then went to see PLATOON—with those scenes of G.I.'s tormenting villagers and raping young girls—I'd be furious. . . . PLATOON insinuates that it is about all platoons. Well, you can talk to a thousand veterans and a lot of them will say, 'That's not the way it was.' " Actress Jane Fonda, who was labeled by some as "Hanoi Jane" for her strong anti-war feelings in the 1970s and for her trip to North Vietnam, said of PLATOON, "A movie like this helps to insure that will never happen again. . . . What PLATOON does—better than I've ever seen before—is to show what it was like being there. What those men went through."

**A crassly commercial special introduction was provided for PLATOON's videocassette release. It features Chrysler Corp. president Lee Iacocca solemnly intoning in front of a Chrysler jeep, "The film PLATOON is a memorial not to war, but to all the men and women who fought in a time and in a place no one really understood. Who knew only one thing . . . they were called and they went. That in the truest sense is the spirit of America. The more we understand it, the more we honor those who kept it alive."

Officer); Ken Lynch (General Trudeau); Paul Comi (Sergeant Kreucheberg); Abel Fernandez (McKinley); Lou Gallio (P.I. Officer); Cliff Ketchum (Corporal Payne); Martin Landau (Marshall); Bert Remson (Lieutenant Cummings); Kevin Hagen (Corporal Kissell); Dean Stanton (MacFarland); Leonard Graves (Lieutenant Cook); Sylvester Lamont (Sergeant Kuzmick); Gavin McCloud (Saxon); John Alderman (Lieutenant Waldorf); John McKee (Olds); Charles Aidman (Harrold); Chuck Hayward (Chalmers); Buzz Martin (Radio Operator); Robert Williams (Soldier Runner); Bill Wellman, Jr. (Iron Man); Viraj Amonsin (Chinese Broadcaster); Barry Maguire (Lieutenant Attridge).

In 1953 Korea the peace talks drag on and the United Nations police action continues pointlessly. U.S. Army Lieutenant Joseph G. Clemons, Jr. (Gregory Peck) is advised by his superior that his men must assault a fortified but tactically unimportant hill position held by the North Koreans and Chinese Communist troops. "Remember this," Clemons is told, "you've got a hundred and thirty-five men, all of them thinking of the peace talks at Panmunjon. It's a cinch they won't want to die in what may be the last battle. . . ."

Gregory Peck (left) and Paul Comi (right) in PORK CHOP HILL (1959).

Clemons is no foolhardy hero, but an intelligent veteran soldier who cares for his men's welfare, and wants to live himself. He understands that their mission to regain control of this worthless bit of terrain—Pork Chop Hill—is a futile exercise. At best it may have symbolic value at the peace negotiations. But he appreciates fully that his duty as a soldier is to follow orders. Clemons and King Company dig in on the hillside and prepare to battle to the finish. The bloody battle wears on with a see-sawing balance of power, and all the while the Chinese Reds have loudspeakers blasting away in English that this attack and all the casualties are pointless. Finally, the remnants of King Company take the hilltop position and are supported by late-arriving reinforcements. Twenty-five of their number, including Clemons, have survived. But now, with the truce announced, the hill is no longer of value. It has become a part of the no-man's land between the two sides. The film concludes with a narrator explaining, "Victory is a fragile thing, and history does not linger long in our time. But those who fought there know what they did. . . . Millions live in freedom today because of what they did."

"Hollywood has come a long way to be able to make war films such as PORK CHOP HILL, a grim, utterly realistic story that drives home both the irony of war and the courage men can summon to die in a cause which they don't understand. . . . As war pictures go, this one makes most of the rest look pale" (*Variety*). With the real life Clemons serving as technical advisor, PORK CHOP HILL presents the man as a "born leader," a person filled with resolve to do his job but still human enough to have doubts. There is the usual gathering of ethnic stereotypes, including a Japanese American lieutenant (George Shibita) and two blacks (James Edwards and Woody Strode). It is Strode's Franklin who attempts to desert in the face of fire, and when he later meets up with Clemons, the infantryman spits out his rationale, "I don't want to die for Korea. What do I care about this stinking hill? You oughtta see where I live back home. I sure ain't sure I'd die for that. . . ."

Lewis Milestone had directed ALL QUIET ON THE WESTERN FRONT (1930), q.v., about World War I, and A WALK IN THE SUN (1945), q.v., about World War II. With PORK CHOP HILL he provided an equally impressive celluloid testament to the Korean War. "Among all war films it is unusual for an utter lack of bombast, mawkishness, or the customary misunderstanding of the circumstances of infantry action. . . . For Milestone this film marks a trilogy. . . . In terms of pure military authenticity I should say this one tops them all . . ." (Paul V. Beckley, *New York Herald Tribune*).

PORK CHOP HILL was the first project of Melville Productions, owned by producer Sy Bartlett and star Gregory Peck. For the record, the film's title refers to the shape of the hotly contested hill.

PRIDE OF THE MARINES (Warner Bros., 1945) 119 mins.

Producer, Jerry Wald; director, Delmer Daves; story, Roger Butterfield; screenplay, Albert Maltz, Marvin Borowsky; art director, Leo Kuter; set decorator, Walter F. Tilford; music, Franz Waxman; music director, Leo F. Forbstein; orchestrator, Leonard Raab; technical advisers, Major Louis Aronson (U.S. Marine Corps), Major Gordon Warner (U.S. Marine Corps, Retired); assistant director, Art Lusker; sound, Stanley Jones; special effects, L. Robert Burgs; camera, Peverell Marley; editor, Owen Marks.

John Garfield (Al Schmid); Eleanor Parker (Ruth Hartley); Dane Clark (Lee Diamond); John Ridgely (Jim Merchant); Rosemary De Camp (Virginia Pfeiffer); Ann Doran (Ella Merchant); Warren Douglas (Kebabian); Don McGuire (Irish); Tom D'Andrea

Eleanor Parker and John Garfield in PRIDE OF THE MARINES (1945).

(Tom); Rory Mallinson (Doctor); Stephen Richards (Ainslee); Anthony Caruso (Johnny Rivers); Moroni Olsen (Captain Burroughs); Dave Willock (Red); John Sheridan (Second Marine); John Miles (Lieutenant); John Compton (Corporal); Lennie Bremen (Lenny); Michael Brown (Corpsman).

Many films* would focus on the effects of war on returning servicemen, but the optimistic PRIDE OF THE MARINES devotes much of its early footage to depicting what makes a patriotic man heroic in battle. The film opens with Philadelphia blue-collar worker Al Schmid romancing and marrying Ruth Hartley (Eleanor Parker). When Pearl Harbor comes, he believes it is his patriotic duty to enlist in the Marines. On Guadalcanal, when his machine gun crew buddies are killed in harrowing combat, he takes over their gun and fires away at the advancing Japanese. He kills many of them before an exploding grenade blinds him. He returns home a hero. The remainder of this feature details how the sightless Schmid rebels at adjusting to his special civilian life and how through the love and encouragement of his wife he regains his faith and dignity.

"Although the war scenes are about the finest that have appeared in a Hollywood production, there is a sensitive probing of human experiences in most of the sequences which gives the work a certain timeless quality. . . . Thanks to a remarkably realistic treatment, the motion picture has over-all conviction" (Howard Barnes, *New York Herald Tribune*).

PRIDE OF THE MARINES was Oscar-nominated for Best Screenplay and it provided rebel star John Garfield with his best screen characterization (based on the real-life Al Schmid). The film did extremely well at the box-office.

British release title: Forever In Love.

PRISONER OF WAR (Metro-Goldwyn-Mayer, 1954) 80 mins.

Producer, Henry Berman; director, Andrew Marton; screenplay, Allen Rivkin; art directors, Cedric Gibbons, Malcolm Brown; music, Jeff Alexander; camera, Robert Planck; editor, James Newcom.

Ronald Reagan (Web Sloane); Steve Forrest (Corporal Joseph Robert Stanton); Dewey Martin (Jesse Treadmun); Oscar Homolka

---

* e.g: THE BEST YEARS OF OUR LIVES (1946), CROSSFIRE (1947), HOME OF THE BRAVE (1948), q.v., HOMECOMING (1949), THE MEN (1950), BRIGHT VICTORY (1951), THE RACK (1956), THE MANCHURIAN CANDIDATE (1962), GORDON'S WAR (1971), WELCOME HOME, SOLDIER BOYS (1972), ROLLING THUNDER (1977), COMING HOME (1978), THE DEER HUNTER (1978), q.v.

(Colonel Nikita I. Biroshilov); Robert Horton (Francis Aloysius Belney); Paul Stewart (Captain Jack Hodges); Henry [Harry] Morgan (Major O. D. Halle); Stephen Bekassy (Lieutenant Georgi M. Robovnik); Leonard Strong (Colonel Kim Doo Yi); Darryl Hickman (Merton Tollivar); Ralph Ahn, Weaver Levy (Red Guards); Rollin Moriyama (Captain Lang Hyun Choi); Ike Jones (Benjamin Julesberg); Clarence Lung (MVD Officer); Jerry Paris (Alex Horstrom); John Lupton (Lieutenant Peter Reilly); Stuart Whitman (Captain); Bob Ellis (Alan H. Rolfe); Lewis Martin (General); Otis Greene (David Carey); Lalo Rios (Sachez Rivero); Lester C. Hoyle (Emanuel Hazard); Roy Boyle (Donald C. Jackwood); Leon Tyler (Jacob Allen Lorfield); Edo Mita (Red Doctor); Peter Hansen (Captain Fred Osborne).

"This is a grim film account of the atrocities practiced on prisoners of war by North Koreans. While the incidents are well-documented in actual records by returning POWs, the presentation here is uninspired so there's little shock value or credibility to carry the picture" (*Variety*).

Man may require greater heroics as a war prisoner than on the battlefield. To verify the truth of p.o.w. brutalities, Web Sloane

Steve Forrest, Ronald Reagan, Dewey Martin, Robert Horton, and Darryl Hickman in PRISONER OF WAR (1954).

(Ronald Reagan) parachutes behind North Korean lines and becomes one of the G.I. prisoners at a Chinese Communist prison camp. There he witnesses at first hand the beatings, tortures, killings, and brainwashing instigated by the captors.

PT 109 (Warner Bros., 1963) 140 mins.

Personal supervisor, Jack L. Warner; producer, Bryan Foy; director, Leslie H. Martinson; based on the book, *PT 109, John F. Kennedy in World War II*; adaptors, Howard Sheehan, Vincent X. Flaherty; screenplay, Richard L. Breen; second unit director, Russell Saunders; assistant directors, William Kissel, Russell Saunders, Jack Cunningham, C. M. Florance; art director, Leo K. Kuter; set decorator, John P. Austin; costumes, Alexis Davidoff; makeup, Gordon Bau, Norman Pringle; music, William Lava, David Buttolph; orchestrators, David Strech, Carl Brandt, Gus Levene; technical adviser, J. E. Gibbon (Captain); dialogue director, Lew Gallo; sound, Francis M. Stahl; special effects, Ralph Webb; camera, Robert Surtees; second unit camera, Mark Davis; editor, Folmar Blangsted.

Cliff Robertson (Lieutenant [j.g..] John F. Kennedy); Ty Hardin (Ensign Leonard J. Thom); James Gregory (Commander C. R. Ritchie); Robert Culp (Ensign "Barney" Ross); Grant Williams (Lieutenant Alvin Cluster); Lew Gallo (Yeoman Rogers); Errol John (Benjamin Kevu); Michael Pate (Lieutenant Reginald Evans); Robert Blake ("Bucky" Harris); William Douglas (Gerald E. Zinser); Biff Elliott (Edgar F. Mauer); Norman Fell (Edmund Drewitch); Sam Gilman (Raymond Starkey); Clyde Howdy (Leon Drawdy); Buzz Martin (Maurice Kowal); James McCallion (Patrick McMahon); Evan McCord (Harold Marney); Sammy Reese (Andrew Kirksey); Glenn Sipes (William Johnston); John Ward (John Maguire); David Whorf (Raymond Albert).

There was tremendous pre-production ballyhoo when Warner Bros. announced that it planned to film Robert J. Donovan's 1961 book about John Fitzgerald Kennedy (1917-1963), the incumbent thirty-fifth U.S. president. Kennedy made three demands of studio head Jack L. Warner: 1) he must have personal approval of the actor chosen to depict him; 2) his proceeds from the film be distributed to the crew and/or surviving families of PT 109, and 3) the motion picture be as accurate as possible.

PT (plywood torpedo) boats were lightly armed crafts utilized by the U.S. Navy in World War II. British engineer Hubert Scott-Paine designed them to use speed as their prime defense. The PT boat insignia (a mosquito sitting astride a torpedo) was drawn by Walt Disney. According to Don McCombs and Fred L. Worth

Cliff Robertson in PT 109 (1963).

(*World War II: Strange and Fascinating Facts*, 1983), "The Navy attitude toward PT crews in World War II was that if someone graduated from Navy boot camp and was incapable of recognizing various knots, they were assigned to PT boats. If the PT's were sent out on patrol and did not return, the Navy then knew where the enemy was located."

In the early days of World War II, Lieutenant (j.g.) John F. Kennedy (Cliff Robertson), having commanded PT 101, assumes charge of PT 109 in the Solomon Islands. He and his crew rescue a Marine patrol bottled on Choiseul. Their goal is reached, but the boat runs out of fuel and must be towed back to base. On August 2, 1943, PT 109 is split in two by the Japanese destroyer *Amagiri*. Two of the crew are killed. The only hope for survival is to swim to a nearby island, with Kennedy having to tow one of his badly burned men. They are marooned on Plum Pudding and Olasana Islands with no communication equipment to make contact with the military, so Kennedy writes a message on a coconut which natives take to Rendova. Eventually Kennedy is delivered safely to an Australian vessel which in turn rescues his men. Although he is eligible now for transfer stateside, Kennedy chooses to command another PT boat (PT 59).

This antiseptic production was so concerned with being reverential and inoffensive that its pacing and character delineations suffered badly. Most of the crew emerge as war film clichés, including comic relief Biff Elliott as Edgar F. Mauer, the inventive unit cook. Robertson's performance as the future President is solemn (almost glum). Too much of the storyline treats war as a near lark and extreme bravery as a casual course of events.

THE PURPLE HEART (Twentieth Century-Fox, 1944) 99 mins.

Producer, Darryl F. Zanuck; director, Lewis Milestone; story, Melville Crossman [Darryl F. Zanuck]; screenplay, Jerry Cady; art directors, James Basevi, Lewis Creber; set decorators, Thomas Little, Walter M. Scott; music, Alfred Newman; assistant director, Artie Jacobson; sound, Alfred Bruzlin; special camera effects, Fred Sersen; camera, Arthur Miller; editor, Douglas Biggs.

Dana Andrews (Captain Harvey Ross); Richard Conte (Lieutenant Canelli); Farley Granger (Sergeant Clinton); Kevin O'Shea (Potoski); Donald Barry (Lieutenant Vincent); Trudy Marshall (Mrs. Ross); Sam Levene (Lieutenant Wayne Greenbaum); Charles Russell (Lieutenant Bayforth); John Craven (Sergeant Stoner); Tala Birell (Johanna); Richard Loo (General Ito Mitsubi); Peter Chong (Judge Toyama); Gregory Gaye (Voshensky); Torben Meyer (Kappel); Kurt Katch (Kruger); Martin Garralaga (Siva); Erwin Kalser

(Schleswig); Igor Dolgoruki (Boris Evenik); Alex Papana (Ludovescu); H. T. Tsiang (Yuen Chiu Ling); Key Chang (Admiral Yamagichi); Allen Jung (Sakai); Wing Foo (Police Captain); Paul Fung (Court Clerk); Joseph Kim (Procurator); Luke Chan (Court Stenographer); Beal Wong (Toma Nogato); Marshall Thompson (Morrison); Lee Tung-Foo (Third Judge); Spencer Chan, Leon Lontoc, Roque Espiritu, Harold Fong, Bruce Wong, Johnny Dong (Naval Aides); James Leong, Eddie Lee, Pete Katchenaro, Angel Cruz (Army Aides); Philip Ahn (Sburo Goto); Clarence Lung (Japanese Lieutenant); Benson Fong (Moy Ling); Nestor Paiva (Francisco De Los Santos).

"You started this war. You wanted it, and now you're going to get it, and it won't be finished until your dirty little empire is wiped off the face of the earth!" This statement by one of the doomed heroes of THE PURPLE HEART reflects the degree of war hysteria that existed and was necessary for a soldier not only to fight

Dana Andrews and Richard Loo in THE PURPLE HEART (1944).

and endure in battle but to suffer capture, torture, and death as bravely as possible.

On April 18, 1942 sixteen B-25 bomber planes were launched from the USS *Hornet* for the "Tokyo Raid." Led by Lieutenant Colonel James H. Doolittle, the American planes dropped sixteen tons of bombs on Japanese cities and then headed for the Chinese-controlled territory of China. Because they ran out of fuel, many of the planes crash-landed in the Japanese-held part of China. Eight of the captured flyers were found guilty of war crimes. Five were given life prison terms; the other three were beheaded on October 10, 1942. It was not until April 23, 1943 any of this information was released to the public, with President Franklin D. Roosevelt terming the Japanese actions "inhuman and depraved." Among the films which depicted aspects of this raid were THIRTY SECONDS OVER TOKYO (1944), q.v., DESTINATION TOKYO (1945), and the highly inflammatory THE PURPLE HEART. It was a personal project of Twentieth Century-Fox studio head Darryl F. Zanuck, who conceived the storyline under his pseudonym, Melville Crossman. It was his intention that this film be "almost documentary in its honesty" and he insisted, "We don't want any business such as fliers chalking up the names of the victims, etc. No mock heroics." He underscored that the film would have a racist, patriotic point of view when he told his staff on this film, "Everyone knows Japs are fanatics."

The prologue title card to THE PURPLE HEART reads: "Out of the dark mists of the Orient have come no details of the actual fate of the heroic American aviators forced to earth in the bombing of Tokyo. Perhaps those details will never be known. The Japanese Government, in mingled hate and fear, announced only that some were executed. This picture, therefore, is the author's conception of what may well have happened, based on unofficial reports."

Eight downed American pilots from the Doolittle mission have been betrayed by Yuen Chiu Ling (H. T. Tsiang), the Japanese-controlled Chinese governor of Kunlin Province in China. They are now on trial not as prisoners of war, but for alleged war crimes (bombing schools, churches, etc.). The goal of the kangaroo trial, headed by Judge Toyama (Peter Chong) of the Black Dragon Society, is to force the men to reveal where their raid originated*. In the course of the proceedings, the prisoners are gruesomely tortured. Before the hearings are over, all of the Americans, except

---

*It would be President Roosevelt in one of his radio fireside chats to the public who would announce that Doolittle's morale-boosting raid had emanated from "Shangri-la" (that mythical kingdom of James Hilton's *Lost Horizon*).

Captain Harvey Ross (Dana Andrews) and Lieutenant Wayne Greenbaum (Sam Levene), are mutilated, crippled victims. By the time of their sentence, Ling's son (Benson Fong) has shot his father in court for being a collaborationist and is himself arrested, and the sadistic General Mitsubi (Richard Loo), who supervised the physical and mental torture of the prisoners, has committed hara-kiri in the courtroom because the Americans will not reveal the wanted information. As their death sentence is announced, Captain Ross says, "You can kill us, all of us, or part of us. But if you think that's going to put the fear of God into the United States of America and stop them from sending other fliers to bomb you, you're wrong— dead wrong." The prisoners are led down a long courthouse corridor to meet their fate.

Unquestionably one of the most patriotic films made about gallant Americans acting bravely in harrowing circumstances, only a few reviewers of the day perceived that the effect of THE PURPLE HEART ". . . is to narrow and solidify hatred of a group of people into hatred of a whole people" (Manny Farber, *New Republic* magazine).

The title of this film refers to the U.S. military decoration awarded to soldiers for wounds sustained in action against the enemy.

PURSUIT OF THE GRAF SPEE (Rank Film Distributors, 1957) 106 mins.

Executive producer, Earl St. John; producers, Michael Powell, Emeric Pressburger; associate producer, Sydney Streeter; directors/ screenplay, Powell, Pressburger; art director, Hein Heckroth; music, Brian Easdale; music director, Frederic Lewis; camera, Christopher Chills; editor, Reginald Mills.

John Gregson (Captain Bell); Anthony Quayle (Commodore Harwood); Peter Finch (Captain Hans Langsdorff); Jack Gwillim (Captain Parry); Bernard Lee (Captain Dove); Lionel Murton (Mike Fowler); Anthony Bushell (Mr. Millington-Drake); Michael Goodliffe (Captain McCall); Patrick MacNee (Lieutenant Commander); John Chandos (Dr. Oangmann); Douglas Wilmer (Mr. Desmoulins); William Squire (Ray Martin); Roger Delgado (Captain Varela); Andrew Cruickshank (Captain Stubs); Christopher Lee (Manola); Edward Atlenza (Pop); April Olrich (Dolores).

This film was unusual in its objective and sympathetic presentation of the humane and respectful Captain Hans Langsdorff (1890-1939), the German admiral in command of the pocket battleship, *Graf Spee*. When the famed *Graf Spee* is attacked by three British cruisers in the Battle of the Plate River (December

1939), Langsdorff (Peter Finch) maneuvers his ship into the neutral harbor of Montevideo, Uruguay. When he is forced by a series of complex diplomatic moves to leave there, he scuttles the ship rather than be bested by the British. On December 19, 1939 he committed suicide. The defeat of the Graf Spee was regarded as Great Britain's first major naval victory in World War II.

Variety praised the film for its opening battle scenes, but added, ". . . Despite its impressive technical achievements, it's lacking in human, emotional and dramatic qualities . . . the players are almost secondary to the ships themselves."

Filmed in Technicolor and widescreen VistaVision, the film was released originally in Great Britain as BATTLE OF RIVER PLATE by the Rank Organization with a running time of 119 minutes. When it opened in England in late 1956 it was the selection for the Royal Command film gala.

RAID ON ROMMEL (Universal, 1971) Color 99 mins.

Producer, Harry Tatelman; director, Henry Hathaway; screenplay, Richard Bluel; art directors, Alexander Golitzen, Henry Bumsted; set decorator, Robert C. Bradford; music, Hal Mooney; special effects, Albert J. Whitlock; camera, Earl Rath; editor, Gene Palmer.

Richard Burton (Captain Alec Foster); John Colicos (Sergeant Major Al MacKenzie); Clinton Greyn (Major Tarkington, the Medical Officer); Wolfgang Preiss (General Erwin Rommel); Danielle De Metz (Vivi); Karl Otto Alberty (Captain Heinz Schroeder); Christopher Cary (Conscientious Objector); John Orchard (Garth); Brook Williams (Sergeant Joe Reilly); Greg Mullavey (Private Peter Brown); Ben Wright (Admiral); Michael Sevareid (Corporal Bill Wembley); Chris Anders (Tank Sergeant).

Richard Burton had starred in the solidly made THE DESERT RATS (1953), q.v., dealing with the Allied attacks on Field Marshal Rommel's Afrika Korps in World War II. He was on hand once again for the derivative RAID ON ROMMEL, which had its genesis in left-over footage from the studio's earlier and far better TOBRUK (1967), q.v. Many insisted that Burton had good cause to sleepwalk through this low-budget contrivance.

British Intelligence officer Captain Alec Foster (Richard Burton) must make contact with fellow commandos planted behind enemy lines. Their (impossible) mission is to detonate the large artillery at Tobruk before the British fleet arrives in the harbor. Among those involved are decorative Vivi (Danielle De Metz), an Italian army camp follower, and Major Tarkington (Clinton Greyn), the medical officer. It is the latter who encounters the very civilized General Rommel (Wolfgang Preiss), with whom he has a bizarre, erudite discussion on a rare early 1900s stamp.

RAMBO: FIRST BLOOD, PART II (Tri-Star, 1985) Color 95 mins.

Executive producers, Mario Kassar, Andrew Vajna; producer, Buzz Feitshans; associate producer, Mel Dellar; director, George P. Cosmatos; based on the story by Kevin Jarre and characters created by David Morrell; screenplay, Sylvester Stallone, James Cameron; production designer, Bill Kenney; art directors, Roy Barnes, Agustin Ituarte Salazar; set decorators, Sig Tingloff, William Skinner; costumes, Tom Bronson; makeup, Leonard Engleman; music, Jerry Goldsmith; helicopter unit director, Peter MacDonald; assistant directors, Fred Rollin, Patrick Kinney, Mario Cisneros Rivera; stunt coordinators, Richard Farnsworth, Loren Janes; sound, Rob Young; supervising sound editor, Frederick J. Brown; sound editors, Michele Sharp, Denis Horta; camera, Jack Cardiff; helicopter unit camera, Peter MacDonald; editors, Mark Goldblatt, Mark Helfrich.

Sylvester Stallone (John Rambo); Richard Crenna (Colonel Trautman); Charles Napier (Murdock); Steven Berkoff (Podovsky); Julia Nickson (Co Bao); George Kee Cheung (Tay); Andy Wood (Banks); Martin Kove (Ericson); William Ghent (Vinh); Vojo Goric

Sylvester Stallone and Julia Nickson in RAMBO: FIRST BLOOD, PART II (1985).

(Yushin); Dana Lee (Kinh); Baoan Coleman (Gunboat Captain); Steve Williams (Lifer); Don Collins, Christopher Grant, Alain Hocquenghem, William Rothlein, John Sterlini (Prisoners of War); Tony Munafo (Prison Guard); Tom Gehrke (Russian Pilot).

In 1982 Sylvester Stallone deviated from his ROCKY, the boxer hit film series, to make FIRST BLOOD, the tale of a near mute Vietnam War Green Beret veteran* who leads small town police and the military on an explosive obstacle course in the rugged American northwest. The cartoonish adventure grossed $23,000,000 in domestic net box-office rentals and went on to become an international success and a staple of the home video cassette marketplace. Once again Stallone proved he had a sharp eye for what would "fly" with filmgoers. No one, except perhaps Stallone, was prepared for the tremendous reception the sequel would engender; earning $78,919,250 just in theater rentals in the U.S. and Canada alone.

FIRST BLOOD ends its onscreen orgy of blood and violence with the cinema's prime fighting machine sobbing (and mumbling) rhetorically to Colonel Traubman (Richard Crenna). He asks why Vietnam soldiers returned to America only to face scorn from their fellow countrymen and to find their heroism in action had become an embarrassment to U.S. politicians. A sub-statement of this and the other RAMBO films is: how does/can a man trained by his government to be an impersonal fighting machine in time of war re-adapt to peacetime living?

In RAMBO: FIRST BLOOD, PART II John Rambo (Sylvester Stallone) asks, "Sir, do we get to win this time?" And indeed in RAMBO and all its ilk, including Chuck Norris' MISSING IN ACTION trilogy, q.v., the answer is yes. RAMBO would evoke tremendous excitement among psychologists and film critics, all vying to explain how and why this film is the prize illustration of how best to channel a public catharsis into a mega-hit motion picture. RAMBO: FIRST BLOOD, PART II provided a way for Americans to make "sense" out of the senseless Vietnam War. It took a 34-year-old superstar from New York's Hell's Kitchen, noted more for his muscles than intellect, to provide these answers.

---

*Ted Kotcheff, who directed FIRST BLOOD, would say, "I certainly never saw [FIRST BLOOD] as any kind of celebration of jingoism. I saw it as a cry from the veteran. . . . John Rambo was like a machine that couldn't stop its engine. He was this Frankenstein monster we had created in Vietnam and then brought home." Obviously Sylvester Stallone had his own interpretation of his legendary screen hero and the next two "Rambo" installments depicted the hero fighter as a deeply philosophizing, self-motivated soul.

Colonel Trautman (Richard Crenna) gains the release of Vietnam veteran John Rambo (Sylvester Stallone) who has been jailed for his guerrilla warfare against the police of a small Northwestern town. In exchange for his freedom, Rambo must undertake a covert mission to Vietnam to determine the validity of reports that the Viet Cong are still holding as prisoners Americans reported as missing-in-action (MIAs) during the Vietnam War. If he succeeds he will receive a full pardon; if he doesn't. . . .

From his Thailand base where he is briefed by American intelligence officer Marshall Murdock (Charles Napier), Rambo parachutes into Vietnam and moves upriver on a boat with Co Bao (Julia Nickson), his Vietnamese guide. Rambo's order are to find evidence, of the photographic sort, about the MIAs. However, he rescues one of the men and starts the trek down river. They outmaneuver an attack from a Viet Cong patrol boat. While Co Bao disappears into the jungle, Murdock aborts the mission and the rescue helicopters because he has learned that Rambo actually has an MIA with him. (It is now revealed that the Washington political bureacracy wanted the mission to show no MIAs existed.) Rambo is captured and the Viet Cong's Russian advisers (Steven Berkoff, Vojo Goric) supervise his torturous interrogation. Co Bao appears at the camp disguised as a whore and helps Rambo to escape. Along the way he single-handedly inflicts tremendous casualties on the enemy. After Co Bao's death in combat, Rambo gains control of a helicopter, returns to the prison camp and rescues the surviving MIAs. After overwhelming a Russian copter, he and the prisoners reach the Thailand base safely. Rambo warns the duplicitous Murdock that if he does not institute an immediate search for other MIAs, Rambo will personally come after him. To punctuate his threat, he empties his M-60 gun into the walls and ceiling of their meeting room.

Even at the hysterical heights of any of the major twentieth-century wars, no filmmaker would have dared (or gotten away with) such blatant jingoism as RAMBO. This film is full of outlandish heroics, overwhelming success by a one-man army, and enough mayhem to decimate a small country. The plot contrivances make any attempts at combat realism ludicrous. But none of that matters, obviously, to most viewers. For Stallone's bloody vengeance is both a mission of mercy and a battle cry of love. As the sensitive at-heart Rambo informs Trautman, "I want what every guy who came here [to Vietnam] to spill his guts wants; for our country to love us as much as we loved it."

Amidst tremendous production problems and rising expenses,

RAMBO III was completed in early 1988 for release in mid-year. Set in Afghanistan and dealing with Rambo's (Sylvester Stallone) single-handed rescue of Colonel Trautman (Richard Crenna), the new $60,000,000+ epic had a very rocky time at the box-office, where it was consistently outshone by another sequel from another late twentieth-century folk hero, Paul Hogan's CROCODILE DUNDEE II. The message and lure of John Rambo had finally worn thin.

REACH FOR THE SKY (Rank Film Distributor, 1957) 123 mins.

Producer, Daniel M. Angel; associate producer, Anthony Nelson-Keys; director, Lewis Gilbert; based on the book *Story of Douglas Bader* by Paul Brickhill; screenplay, Gilbert, Vernon Harris; art director, Bernard Robinson; music, John Addison; music director, Muir Mathieson; camera, Jack Asher; editor, John Shirley.

Kenneth More (Douglas Bader); Muriel Pavlow (Thelma Bader); Lyndon Brook (Johnny Sanderson); Lee Patterson (Stan Turner); Alexander Knox (Mr. Joyce); Dorothy Alison (Nurse Brace); Michael Warre (Harry Day); Sydney Tafler (Robert Desoutter); Howard Marion Crawford ("Woody" Woodhall); Jack Watling (Peel); Nigel Green (Streatfield); Anne Leon (Sister Thornhill); Ronald Adam (Air Vice Marshal Leigh-Mallory); Charles Carson (Air Chief Marshal Sir Hugh Dowding); Basil Appleby (Crowley-Milling); Eddie Byrne (Sergeant Mills); Beverly Brooks (Sally); Michael Ripper (Warrant Officer); Derek Blomfield (Civilian Pilot); Avice Landone (Mrs. Bader); Erich Pohlmann (Adjutant of Prison Camp); Michael Gough (Flying Instructor); and: Michael Balfour, Michel Clement, Anton Diffring, Sam Kydd, Harry Locke, Clive Revill, Philip Stainton.

The British creators of REACH FOR THE SKY did not have to fabricate any events for this amazing story—they were all real! It is based on the 1954 book by Paul Brickhill, a fellow pilot.

The facts are: British flyer Douglas Bader (1910-1982) lost both legs in a 1931 plane crash. With the use of artificial limbs he learned to fly again and at the start of Word War II managed to be taken back into the R.A.F. (which was desperately short of qualified pilots). In the course of the war he is credited with 22.5 aircrafts destroyed. On August 9, 1941 his plane crashed and he was captured by the Germans. He engineered three escape attempts and was placed by the Nazis thereafter in the "impregnable" Colditz Castle prison for difficult prisoners.

Kenneth More shines as the pilot with a charmed life, who not only wins the respect of his fellow pilots during aerial combat, but so confounds the Germans with his courage and resiliency that they honor him with admiration.

RED BALL EXPRESS (Universal, 1952) 83 mins.

Producer, Aaron Rosenberg; director, Budd Boetticher; story, Marcel Klauber, Billy Grady, Jr.; screenplay, John Michael Hayes; art directors, Bernard Herzbrun, Richard H. Riedel; music director, Joseph Gershenson; camera, Maury Gertsman; editor, Edward Curtiss.

Jeff Chandler (Lieutenant Chick Campbell); Alex Nicol (Sergeant Ernest Kalleck); Charles Drake (Private Ronald Partridge); Judith Braun (Joyce McClellan); Hugh O'Brian (Private Wilson); Jacqueline Duval (Antoinette DuBois); Jack Kelly (Private John Heyman); Cindy Garner (Kitty Walsh); Sidney Poitier (Corporal Andrew Robertson); Howard Petrie (General Gordon); Bubber Johnson (Private Taffy Smith); Robert Davis (Private Dave McCord); John Hudson (Sergeant Max); Frank Chase (Higgins); John Pickard (Major); Palmer Lee [Gregg Palmer] (Tank Lieutenant); and: Jack Warden, Richard Garland, Harry Lauter, Tommy Long, Arthur Space, Robert Karnes, Eugene Borden, Yola D'Avril, Sid Clute, Emmett Smith, Nan Boardman.

During its four months of existence in the fall of 1944, the Red Ball Express (Army transportation unit) was charged with moving 410,000+ tons of needed supplies to the Allied army as it swept inland from Normandy during World War II.

Lieutenant Chick Campbell (Jeff Chandler) of the Red Ball Express must get needed fuel to General George Patton for his tank command before the cut-off unit is destroyed in its French campaign. Making his non-stop task more difficult are disgruntled Sergeant Ernest Kalleck (Alex Nicol) and Corporal Andrew Robertson (Sidney Poitier). The latter feels he and the other blacks in the unit are subjected to too much discrimination.

This production-line movie is filled with lame clichés. It exploited a real-life situation (the black soldiers of the Red Ball Express who were commanded by white officers) by using rising film actor Sidney Poitier as a foil for Universal's contract leading man, Jeff Chandler. The latter is so lacking in artifice that he gives the film a badly needed shot of credibility.

On October 5, 1973, "Roll Out," a CBS-TV sitcom series debuted, dealing with the lives of the men of the 5050th Trucking Company, the Red Ball Express of World War II. It featured Stu Gilliam, Hilly Hicks, Mel Stewart and Ed Begley, Jr. The short-lived series was off the air by January 4, 1974.

THE RED BARON *see*: VON RICHTHOFEN AND BROWN.

THE RELUCTANT HEROES (ABC-TV, 11/23/71) Color 78 mins.

Executive producer, Aaron Spelling; producer, Robert Mirisch; associate producer, Shelley Hull; director, Robert Day; teleplay, Herman Hoffman, Ernest Frankel; art director, Paul Sylos; costumes, Robert Harris; music, Frank DeVol; assistant director, Lou Place; sound effects, Gene Elliot; camera, Arch R. Dalzell; editor, Art Seid.

Ken Berry (Lieutenant Parnell Murphy); Cameron Mitchell (Sergeant Marion Bryce); Warren Oates (Corporal Leroy Sprague); Don Marshall (Private Carver LeMoyne); Jim Hutton (Corporal Bill Lukens); Trini Lopez (Private Sam Rivera); Ralph Meeker (Captain Luke Danvers); Richard Young (Private Golden); Michael St. George (Corporal Bates); Soon-Teck Oh (Korean Officer).

A very low-energy, low-budget telefeature set in Korea during the War. An ex-seminarian, Lieutenant Parnell Murphy (Ken Berry), the unit's historian, is roped into a mission by cigar-chomping Sergeant Marion Bryce (Cameron Mitchell). It is egghead Murphy, using battle strategies he recalls from the history books, who saves his squad from extinction on Hill 656. The film is filled with clichés about "goons" and "gooks" and such maxims as "When the brass start sweet talkin' you, stand by for a ramming."

RETREAT, HELL! (Warner Bros., 1952) 95 mins.

Producer, Milton Sperling; director, Joseph H. Lewis; story, Sperling; screenplay, Sperling, Ted Sherdeman; art director, Edward Carrere; music, William Lava; camera, Warren Lynch; editor, Folmar Blangsted.

Frank Lovejoy (Colonel Steve Corbett); Richard Carlson (Captain Paul Hanson); Rusty [Russ] Tamblyn (Jimmy McDermid); Anita Louise (Ruth Hanson); Ned Young (Sergeant Novak); Lamont Johnson (Captain "Tink" O'Grady); Robert Ellis ("Shorty" Devine); Paul Smith (Andy Smith); Peter Ortiz (Major Knox); Dorothy Patrick (Eve O'Grady); Mort Thompson (Captain Kyser); Joseph Keane (Lieutenant Ortiz).

Steve Corbett (Frank Lovejoy) is the gung ho Marine commander in Korea who insists (paraphrasing real life Major General Oliver P. Smith) during the military withdrawal from the Chosin Reservoir, "Retreat, hell! We're not retreating, we're just advancing in a different direction."

At the start of the Korean conflict in 1950, the Marines are in desperate need of retraining their World War II veterans for the new war. Among those called back to active duty is Paul Hanson (Richard Carlson) who, along with company commander Steve Corbett, supervises the transformation of the men into a battle-ready unit at Camp Pendleton. In Korea the First Marine Division lands at Inchon and from this beachhead fights to recapture Seoul. They move northward, but are pushed back by the Chinese Communists. Yet they never lose their fighting spirit.

RETREAT, HELL! combines newsreel footage with studio sets and presents the expected military types: the rugged but understanding colonel (Frank Lovejoy), the civilian (Richard Carlson) who must readjust to military life and command, the battle-hungry sergeant (Ned Young), reserve officer Captain "Tink" O'Grady (Lamont Johnson), and the Marine newcomer (Russ Tamblyn), anxious to prove himself heroic in combat. Real-life Marine hero Peter Ortiz appears as Major Knox.

THE ROAD TO GLORY (Twentieth Century-Fox, 1936) 95 mins.

Producer, Darryl F. Zanuck; associate producer, Nunnally Johnson; director, Howard Hawks; based on the French motion picture, LES CROIX DES BOIS [Wooden Crosses] and the novel by Roland Dorgeles; screenplay, Joel Sayre, William Faulkner, (uncredited) Johnson; art director, Hans Peters; set decorator, Thomas Little; costumes, Gwen Wakeling; music director, Louis Silvers; camera, Gregg Toland; editor, Edward Curtiss.

Fredric March (Lieutenant Michel Denet); Warner Baxter (Captain Paul LaRoche); Lionel Barrymore (Papa LaRoche); June Lang (Monique); Gregory Ratoff (Bouffiou); Victor Kilian (Regnier); Paul Stanton (Relief Captain); John Qualen (Duflous); Julius Tannen (Lieutenant Tannen); Theodore von Eltz (Major); Paul Fix (Rigaud); Leonid Kinskey (Ledoux); Jacques Lory (Courier); Jacques Vanaire (Doctor); Edythe Raynore (Nurse); George Warrington (Old Soldier); Louis Mercier (Soldier).

"Soldiers of France, you are now members of the Fifth Company, Second Battalion of the 39th Regiment of the Line. . . . Since 1914, it's been fighting on this front. Its record of valor has not yet been damaged. I do not expect any man or any platoon or even an entire company to add stature to that record, but I do and will require that no man in it detract from that record."

This is the standard indoctrination speech offered by battle-fatigued Captain Paul LaRoche (Warner Baxter) as each batch of new soldiers is processed through his unit and sent to the front line trenches to fight (and mostly die). His compassion for his men and his weariness with the toils of war lead him to a diet of aspirin and

Warner Baxter in THE ROAD TO GLORY (1936).

cognac. Soon two newcomers join his ever-changing group: the young officer, Lieutenant Michael Denet (Fredric March), and LaRoche's elderly father (Lionel Barrymore), a veteran of the Franco-Prussian War of 1870 and a man who talks endlessly of his courage. It is idealistic Denet who falls into an affair with Monique (June Lang), the nurse whom LaRoche loves and to whom he promises, "I'll come back—I always come back. I'm eternal." It is also Denet who is horrified by LaRoche's sternness, even coldness, in sending so many men to their deaths. Papa LaRoche should be too old for combat, but so many Frenchmen have been slaughtered by the Germans in this First World War that any walking gun fodder is welcome. In one of the senseless assaults, Papa LaRoche panics and causes the death of one of his comrades. Later, Captain LaRoche is blinded by a head wound and having discovered that Monique and Denet are lovers, feels life holds nothing further. With repentant Papa LaRoche acting as his eyes, LaRoche and his father embark on a suicide mission and die in action. Back at headquarters, Denet, now realizing why LaRoche had to be so callous on the surface, takes charge of the men and soon is swilling aspirin and cognac, and giving the same tired speech to the new recruits as LaRoche had.

As in the earlier THE DAWN PATROL (1930), q.v., the endless generational cycles of life and death continue, with all men destined to follow the ironic "road to glory" and death as long as wars are fought. Why men follow that path is never questioned, as is seen in Denet's statement, "Men always have died in wars and probably always will. For what reason we do not know."

THE ROAD TO GLORY was an expensive concoction made to take advantage of the battle footage and storyline conceived for the French film, LES CROIX DES BOIS (1932), which had gained international acclaim. Warner Baxter was still Twentieth Century-Fox's premier leading man as Lionel Barrymore, on loanout, was MGM's major character star. But they could not make this well-intentioned film a box-office success. America was just emerging from the Great Depression and had not yet become involved with the budding World War II in Europe. This film was considered too morose and cynical by fun-seeking filmgoers.

A.k.a.: WOODEN CROSSES, ZERO HOUR.

ROMMEL—DESERT FOX *see*: THE DESERT FOX.

A RUMOR OF WAR (CBS-TV, 9/24-25/80) Color 200 mins.

Executive producers, Charles Fries, Dick Berg; producer, David Manson; associate producer, Allan Marcil; director, Richard

T. Heffron; based on the book by Philip Caputo; teleplay, John Sacret Young; art director, Herman Zimmerman; music, Michael Gross; camera, Jorge Stahl, Jr., Stevan Larner; editors, Michael Eliot, Thomas Fries, Scott C. Eyler.

Brad Davis (Phil Caputo); Keith Carradine (Lieutenant Murph McCoy); Michael O'Keefe (Walter Cohen); Richard Bradford (General Merle Rupert); Brian Dennehy (Sergeant Ned Coleman); John Friedrich (Corporal Pascarella); Perry Lang (Woodward); Steve Forrest (Colonel Atherton); Christopher Mitchum (Captain Peterson); Stacy Keach (Major Ball); Dan Shor (Manhole); Lane Smith (Sergeant William Holgren); Nicolas Woodeson (Corporal Kazmarak); Gail Young (Carol); Phillip R. Allen (Colonel Perry); Michael Cavanaugh (Captain Lake); Mickey Ellerbee (Corporal Mackey); Bobby Elliott (Sullivan); Larry Fishburne (Lightbulb); Redmond Gleeson (Sergeant Furth); Edward Grover (Coker); Gavan O'Herlihy (Stanton); Christopher Allport (Van Cott); Jeff Daniels (Chaplain); John Herzfeld (Drill Instructor); Stephen Keep (Angry Major); Helaine Lembeck (Lisa Modesta); Sandy McPeak (Joe Caputo); Chris Mulkey (Radio Man); Enrique Novi (Jose Romirez); Sean Thomas Roche (Hodkins); Steven Rothblatt (Zirpoli); Al Ruscio (Uncle Al); Koko Tani (Simone); Thu Thuy (Le Dung's Wife); Marion Yue (Hoa); David Chow (Mayor of Dansang); Eunice Christopher (Mrs. Caputo); Oliver Chung (Le Dung); Alex Daniels (Stasek); John Diehl (D T); John Ferrand (Sergeant Whittaker); Ken Foree (MP): Karen Kondazian (Mrs. Modesta); Lynn Kazue Kuratomi (Yip Yap); Joe Lowry (Winslow); David Manson, Scott Sebastian (Reporters); Scott Mulhern (Priest); Qui Van Ngo (ARVN Interrogator); Rodney Saulsberry (Sergeant Wehr); Stewart Wolinski (Doctor).

With the Vietnam War accepted as a commercial subject—thanks to such films as THE DEER HUNTER (1978), q.v., and COMING HOME (1978)—television turned increasingly to the topic. This expensively produced two-part mini-series telefilm is based on Philip Caputo's Pulitzer Prize-winning book of his Vietnam experiences. It traces his (Brad Davis) transformation from carefree college boy to avid Marine, to a toughened, embittered combat veteran who faces a court-martial for alleged atrocities in a Vietnamese village. Lieutenant Murphy McCoy (Keith Carradine) and Walter Cohen (Michael O'Keefe) are his buddies.

RUN SILENT, RUN DEEP (United Artists, 1958) 93 mins.

Producer, Harold Hecht; associate producer, William Schorr; director, Robert Wise; based on the novel by Commander Edward L. Beach; screenplay, John Gay; art director, Edward Carrere;

music, Franz Waxman; technical adviser, Beach; special effects, A. Arnold Gillespie; camera, Russell Harlan; editor, George Boemler.

Clark Gable (Commander Richardson); Burt Lancaster (Lieutenant Jim Bledsoe); Jack Warden (Mueller); Brad Dexter (Cartwright); Don Rickles (Ruby); Nick Cravat (Russo); Joe Maross (Kohler); Mary LaRoche (Laura Richardson); Eddie Foy, III (Larto); Rudy Bond (Cullen); H. M. Wynant (Hendrix); John Bryant (Beckman); Ken Lynch (Frank); Joel Fluellen (Bragg); Jimmie Bates (Jessie); John Gibson (Captain Blunt).

Commander Richardson (Clark Gable) has lost one submarine in the Bungo Straits near Japan in 1942 and, full of obsessive revenge, is assigned to captain another sub, the USS *Nerka*. Before the enemy can be dealt with, tight-lipped Richardson must cope with his unfriendly new crew. Steely-eyed executive officer Jim Bledsoe (Burt Lancaster) insists that the command should have gone to him, and he and his surly subordinates (including a wise-cracking Don Rickles) make life exceedingly rough for the older seaman, especially when the latter puts them through endless rigorous drills. Eventually they return to the site of Richardson's earlier defeat and this time they sink the targeted enemy vessel.

If HELL BELOW (1933), DESTINATION TOKYO (1944), and SUBMARINE COMMAND (1951), qq.v., had not already set, explored and saturated the idiom for submarine warfare films, then the spate of late 1950s films on the subject did (PURSUIT OF THE GRAF SPEE, 1957, THE ENEMY BELOW, 1958, TORPEDO RUN, 1958, and UP PERISCOPE,1959, qq.v.). What gave RUN SILENT, RUN DEEP its modest box-office appeal was the combination of two he-man screen stars squared off for a CAINE MUTINY-type combat, with no way to avoid one another aboard the claustrophobic submarine. Their personal battle of wills in the midst of the tensions of wartime survival, and not the traditional "up periscope," "take her down," etc., gives this film substance and pacing. This was one of the several motion pictures produced by Lancaster's production company.

SAHARA (Columbia, 1943) 97 mins.

Producer, Harry Joe Brown; director, Zoltan Korda; based on the story by Philip MacDonald and an episode from the Russian film, THE THIRTEEN; screenplay, John Howard Lawson, Korda; art directors, Lionel Banks, Eugene Lourie; set decorator, William Kiernan; music, Miklos Rozsa; music director, Morris W. Stoloff; assistant director, Abby Berlin; sound, Lodge Cuningham; John Livadary; camera, Rudolf Mate; editor, Charles Nelson.

Humphrey Bogart (Sergeant Joe Gunn); Bruce Bennett (Waco

Hoyt); Lloyd Bridges (Fred Clarkson); Rex Ingram (Sergeant Tambul); J. Carrol Naish (Giuseppe); Dan Duryea (Jimmy Doyle); Richard Nugent (Captain Jason Halliday); Patrick O'Moore (Ozzie Bates); Louis Mercier (Jean Leroux); Carl Harbord (Marty Williams); Guy Kingsford (Peter Stegman); Kurt Kreuger (Captain Von Schletow); John Wengraf (Major Von Falken); Hans Schumm (Sergeant Krause); Frank Lackteen (Arab Guide); Frederic Worlock (Radio Newscaster's Voice).

After a defeat in the see-saw battle between the Allies and Field Marshal Rommel's Afrika Korps in 1942, an American M-3 tank crew attached to the British Eighth Army is cut off by the advancing Germans. Crossing the Libyan Desert in "Lulubelle" to reattach with their command, Sergeant Joe Gunn (Humphrey Bogart) and his crew—machine gunner Waco Hoyt (Bruce Bennett) and radio man Jimmy Doyle (Dan Duryea)—pick up several passengers. There are five Allied stragglers—including Irish-born South African, Dr. Jason Halliday (Richard Nugent), and Australian soldier, Fred Clarkson (Lloyd Bridges)—plus a Free French soldier named Jean Leroux (Louis Mercier), and a British Sudanese sergeant (Rex Ingram) with his English-speaking Italian prisoner (J. Carrol Naish). They shoot down an attacking Messerschmitt plane and capture its arrogant, racist German pilot (Kurt Kreuger). The Italian leads them to a promised well, but it is dry. The Sudanese takes them to an old mosque where there is some water, although the well is nearly dry. While there they are overtaken by a pursuing German motorized battalion. They learn from a captured German scout that the 500 Germans also need water. Gunn decides to stand off the enemy. The Germans slowly demolish the group, until only Gunn and Ozzie Bates (Patrick O'Moore), one of the British soldiers, are still alive. At this point the thirst-crazed Germans surrender, begging for water. A German shell has ironically hit the well and now there is water for all. News arrives of the Allied victory at El Alamein.

There is much in this film to illustrate the official Allied position during World War II. The American Sergeant Gunn plays by the rules, refusing to shoot the dangerous German pilot prisoner because it is not the right thing to do to a prisoner-of-war. (The Nazi flyer will later stab the Italian and seek to betray the group; and the pursuing Germans shoot the Frenchman Leroux in the back.) Here the Nazis are the villains while the Italians, represented by simplistic Giuseppe, are depicted as misguided people who at heart do not endorse Hitler's, let alone Mussolini's, inhumane aggressions. (Giuseppe says, ". . . Are my eyes blind that I must fall to my knees to worship a maniac who has made of my country a concentration camp? Who has made of my people slaves?. . . . It's because of a man like him that God, my God, created hell!") And blacks (the Sudanese Tambul) are treated by the Allies as equals: here Tambul not only leads the tank crew to a water supply, but is the heroic soul who in the billowing desert sands kills the escaping Aryan pilot bare-handed before German snipers end his life.

SAHARA was based on incidents in the Soviet film, THE THIRTEEN (1937), and the plot structure of THE LOST PA-TROL (1934), q.v. Unlike the latter film it is a more optimistic study, showing two of the protagonists surviving the onslaught. There is the same amalgam of representative ethnics bonded together by a common goal—survival against the elements and the pursuing enemy. Unlike THE LOST PATROL, which was a structured unit of men under the same military discipline, here a variety of Allies (and captured enemies) must homogenize to live. At first the M-3 tank is their safety shelter; then it is the decaying mosque. Always there are the brutally hot desert sun and the pounding winds, and never far behind, the advancing Germans (in the air, in their tanks, and on foot).

With former screen tough guy Humphrey Bogart in the lead and tight direction by Zoltan Korda, this patriotic action film was an extremely popular release. It was nominated for three Academy Awards: Best Supporting Actor (J. Carrol Naish), Cinematography, and Sound Recording.

SALERNO BEACHHEAD *see*: A WALK IN THE SUN.

SANDS OF IWO JIMA (Republic, 1949) 110 mins.*
    Executive producer, Herbert J. Yates; associate producer, Edmund Grainger; director, Allan Dwan; story, Harry Brown; screenplay, Brown, James Edward Grant; art director, James Sullivan; set decorators, John McCarthy, Jr., Otto Siegel; costumes, Adele Palmer; makeup, Bob Mark, Vern Murdock; music/music director, Victor Young; assistant director, Nate Barrager; sound, T. A. Carman, Howard Wilson; special effects, Howard Lydecker, Theodore Lydecker, Jack Coffe; camera, Reggie Lanning; editor, Richard L. Van Enger.
    John Wayne (Sergeant John M. Stryker); John Agar (Private First Class Peter Conway); Adele Mara (Allison Bromley); Forrest Tucker (Private First Class Al Thomas); Wally Cassell (Private First

---

*Computerized color version now available.

Class Benny Ragazzi); James Brown (Private First Class Charlie Bass); Richard Webb (Private First Class "Handsome Dan" Shipley); Arthur Franz (Corporal Robert Dunne/Narrator); Julie Bishop (Mary); James Holden (Private First Class Soames); Peter Coe (Private First Class George Hellenopolis); Richard Jaeckel (Private First Class Frank Flynn); Bill Murphy (Private First Class Eddie Flynn); George Tyne (Private First Class Harris); Hal Fieberling [Hal Baylor] (Private "Ski" Choynski); John McGuire (Captain Joyce); Martin Milner (Private Mike McHugh); Leonard Gumley (Private Sid Stein); William Self (Private L. D. Fowler, Jr.); Dick Wessel (Grenade Instructor); I. Stanford Jolley (Forrestal); David Clarke (Wounded Marine); Gil Herman (Lieutenant Baker); Dick Jones (Scared Marine); Don Haggerty (Colonel); Bruce Edwards (Marine); Dorothy Ford (Tall Girl); and: John Whitney (Lieutenant Thompson); Colonel D. M. Shoup (U.S. Marine Corps); Lieutenant Colonel H. P. Crowe (U.S. Marine Corps); Captain Harold G. Schrier (U.S. Marine Corps); Private First Class

John Wayne and John Agar in SANDS OF IWO JIMA (1949).

Rene A. Gagnon, Private First Class Ira H. Hayes, PM Third Class John H. Bradley (Themselves).

As the viewer is informed at the start of SANDS OF IWO JIMA, "This is the story of a squad of Marines—a rifle squad. I'm Corporal Robert Dunne [Arthur Franz], a member of that squad. We were at Guadalcanal. When that island was declared secure we were pulled out for rest, refitting, replacements, retraining. The Marine Corps is long on training and retraining and re. . . . Let that go!"

At New Zealand's Camp Packakariki (near Wellington) in 1943 a U.S. Marines squad is being rigorously trained, in short order, by tough Sergeant John M. Stryker, who constantly barks at his men, "Saddle up! Saddle up!"* Private First Class Charlie Bass (James Brown) and Corporal Dunne have served with the seasoned Stryker before and understand the reasons for his extremely strict regimentation. The others, especially Private First Class Peter Conway (John Agar), have their doubts about this loner taskmaster ("who's got the regulations tattooed on his back"). Stryker had served under Conway's colonel father and has nothing but praise for this hero who died at Guadalcanal. Such praise rubs Conway the wrong way for he had always been browbeaten by his dad for being a "no guts intellect" and doesn't want to continue the martial Marine Corps tradition when he has his own child. (He insists, "Instead I'll try to make him intelligent. Instead of a Marine Corps emblem, I'll give him a set of Shakespeare.")

The Marines are sent to Tarawa and Red Beach 3, where they engage in fierce combat with the Japanese who are dug in there. It is up to Stryker and his leathernecks to finish the task started by naval gunning and B-24 bombers. In the midst of battle, Stryker heroically throws a satchel full of bombs, blowing up a strategic Japanese bunker. During the battle many Marines die, including Hellenopolis (Peter Coe), because Private First Class Al Thomas (Forrest Tucker) stopped for coffee and did not return with needed ammunition in time. Conway wants to rescue the dying Bass, who is screaming for Stryker to help him, but Stryker will not allow it. It would give away their position to the enemy.

Tarawa is finally taken and the squad is given a brief leave in Hawaii. There Stryker meets a prostitute (Julie Bishop) and, through talking with her and seeing her infant child, gains a new

---

*Stryker advises his men, "You gotta learn right and you gotta learn fast. . . . You're gonna move like one man and think like one man. If you don't, you'll be dead. . . . You joined the Marines because you wanted to fight. Well you're gonna get your chance and I'm here to see that you know how and if I can't teach you one way, I'll teach you another. But I'm gonna get the job done."

perspective on life, almost forgetting his rotten marriage and that he has not seen his son in years.

On the volcanic island of Iwo Jima the fighting is the most desperate and violent yet. It is Conway, now with a new slant on military life and duty, who joins with Stryker and Private First Class Benny Ragazzi (Wally Cassell) in a strategic assault on the Japanese. The attack leads to the end of Japanese control of the island. Stryker is shot dead by a Japanese while he relaxes with a cigarette after having just told a fellow Marine, "I never felt so good in my life." Conway kills the sniper, and after reading aloud Stryker's unfinished letter to his son, the now battle-toughened Conway promises to name his recently-born son after his celebrated father. Conway barks at the men, "Okay. Saddle up! Let's get back to the war!" The Marines raise the American flag on Mount Suribachi and victory is proclaimed.

SANDS OF IWO JIMA is a rugged action picture dedicated to the U.S. Marine Corps ("whose exploits and valor have left a lasting impression on the world and in the hearts of their countrymen"). Its mixture of newsreel footage and restaged brutal battle scenes is gripping in its protracted violence. There are interludes of romance (Conway and the blonde Allison [Adele Mara] he weds), tenderness (Stryker with the prostitute and her baby), and camaraderie (the men on leave in Hawaii, and a relaxed Stryker having a drink with Bass). There is the familiar rebellious officer (Thomas) who is made contrite by combat and death; there is the Jewish recruit (Leonard Gumley); and the two scrapping brothers (Richard Jaeckel and Bill Murphy) from Philadelphia. There are the senior and junior military men (Stryker and Conway): one who lives by the book and blood and guts; the other who learns that intellectual discussions will not stop the enemy from killing you. And as in most structured war films, there is the death of a commanding officer (Stryker), with his one-time adversary (Conway) now recast in his mold and taking over the mantle of leadership in battle. There is talk of macho service pride ("I'm gonna ride ya till ya can't stand up and when you can, you'll be Marines!"); philosophizing about the meaning of combat ("That's war—trading real estate for men"); and analysis of the burden of command ("We make a mistake and some guy don't walk away—forevermore he don't walk away.")

The *New York Times*' Thomas M. Pryor endorsed this film: "There is so much savage realism in SANDS OF IWO JIMA, so much that reflects the true glory of the Marine Corps' contribution to victory in the Pacific that the film has undeniable moments of greatness." *Variety*, more prone to hyperbole, enthused, ". . .

SANDS OF IWO JIMA wraps up all the familiar war pix formulas into a star-spangled ear-shattering entertainment package that's bound to have sock mass appeal." John Wayne's performance as the very human hero of this film did much to make this Republic Pictures' production a financial success. For his dominating characterization he was Oscar-nominated as Best Actor. The film earned a very solid $5,000,000 in theater rentals in the U.S. and Canada, an amount that would have been higher had a more major studio released the project.

THE SEA CHASE (Warner Bros., 1955) 117 mins.

Producer/director, John Farrow; based on the novel by Andrew Geer; screenplay, James Warner Bellah, John Twist; art director, Franz Bachelin; set decorator, William Wallace; costumes, Moss Mabry; makeup, Gordon Bau; music, Roy Webb; orchestrators, Maurice de Packh, Leonid Raab; assistant directors, Emmett Emerson, Russell Llewellyn; sound, Francis J. Scheid; camera, William Clothier; editor, William Ziegler.

John Wayne (Captain Karl Erlich); Lana Turner (Elsa Keller); Lyle Bettger (Krichner); David Farrar (Commander Napier); Tab Hunter (Cadet Wesser); James Arness (Schlieter); Wilton Graff (Hepke); Richard Davalos (Cadet Walter Stemme); John Qualen (Chief Schmidt); Paul Fix (Max Heinz); Luis Van Rooten (Matz); Peter Whitney (Bachman); Alan Hale, Jr. (Wentz); Lowell Gilmore (Captain Evans); John Doucette (Bo'sun); Alan Lee (Brounck); Claude Akins (Winkler); Adam Williams (Kruger); Gil Perkins (Baldhead); Fred Stromsoe (Mueller); John Indrisano, James Lilburn, Joey Ray, Tony Travers (Sub Lieutenants); Cameron Grant (Kruse); Gavin Muir (Officer-of-the-Watch); Gloria Dea, Lucita, Josephine Para (Spanish Girls); Isabel Dwan, Renata Huy, Theresa Tudor (Frauleins); John Sheffield (Patron in Dining Room); Anthony Eustrel (British High Official); Tudor Owen (Trawler Survivor); Jean de Briac (French Governor); Patrick O'Moore (Warship Officer); and: Gilbert Perkins, Gail Robinson.

THE SEA CHASE is one of those glossy CinemaScope, color diversions of the mid-1950s that tried to be many things to many people. It was an inept translation of a well-received novel. A badly miscast John Wayne appears as a humane German merchant marine captain who is heading to Valparaiso from Sydney, Australia at the outbreak of World War II. Also on board is an exotic German lady (Lana Turner!) of dubious virtue and loyalties. The German ship is pursued by British Commander Napier (David Farrar) of the HMS *Rockhampton*. Eventually the British sink the German ship. Any attempts at reality are strictly accidental. But because John Wayne, Lana Turner and widescreen films were in vogue, this cinematic jumble earned an impressive $6,000,000 in theater rentals in the U.S. and Canada.

SEA OF SAND *see*: DESERT PATROL.

THE SEA SHALL NOT HAVE THEM (United Artists, 1955) 91 mins.

Producer, Daniel M. Angel; director, Lewis Gilbert; based on the novel by John Harris; screenplay, Gilbert, Vernon Harris; art director, Bernard Robinson; music, Malcolm Arnold; music director, Muir Mathieson; special effects, Cliff Richardson; camera, Stephen Dade; editor, Russell Lloyd.

Michael Redgrave (Air Commodore Waltby); Dirk Bogarde (Flight Sergeant Mackay); Anthony Steel (Flying Officer Treherne); Nigel Patrick (Flight Sergeant Slingsby); Bonar Colleano (Sergeant Kirby); James Kenney (Corporal Skinner); Sydney Tafler (Captain Robb); Ian Whittaker (Air Crewman Milliken); George Rose (Tebbitt); Victor Maddern (Gus Westover); Michael Ripper (Botterill); Glyn Houston (Knox); Jack Taylor (Robinson); Michael Balfour (Dray); Paul Carpenter (Lieutenant Pat Boyle); Eddie Byrne (Porter); Anton Diffring (German Pilot); Rachel Kempson (Mrs. Waltby); Joan Sims (Mrs. Tebbitt); Ann Gudrun (Kirby's Fiancée); Griffith Jones (Group Commander Todd); Jack Watling (Flight Officer Harding); Guy Middleton (Squadron Leader Scott); and: Nigel Green, Moultrie Kelsall, Jack Lambert.

In the fall of 1944 the crew of a British Hudson plane is forced down into the North Sea after a dogfight with an enemy aircraft. Among the downed men is Air Commodore Waltby (Michael Redgrave) who has just returned from enemy-held territory with secret documents the English need. The British rescue team is hampered by bad weather and the men must stay afloat and alive on the inflatable dinghy for two days and a night. They are finally saved off the coast of Belgium, with enemy artillery bursting all around the dinghy. Others on the boat enduring the elements and staving off the Germans are: Flight Sergeant Mackay (Dirk Bogarde), Flying Officer Treherne (Anthony Steel), Sergeant Kirby (Bonar Colleano), and Flight Sergeant Slingsby (Nigel Patrick).

THE SEA SHALL NOT HAVE THEM is "a war picture whose more than competent execution atones for its less than competent script" (London *News Chronicle*).

THE SECRET INVASION (United Artists, 1964) 95 mins.

Producer, Gene Corman; director, Roger Corman; story/

screenplay, R. Wright Campbell; art director, John Murray; set decorator, Ian Love; makeup, Sandra James; wardrobe, Sharon Compton; assistant director, Charles Griffith; music, Hugo Friedhofer; sound, Dale Knight; special effects, George Blackwell; camera, Arthur E. Arling; editor, Ronald Sinclair.

Stewart Granger (Major Richard Mace); Raf Vallone (Roberto Rocca); Mickey Rooney (Terrence Scanlon); Edd Byrnes (Simon Fell); Henry Silva (John Durrell); Mia Massini (Mila); William Campbell (Jean Saval); Helmo Kindermann (German Fortress Commandant); Enzo Fiermonte (General Quadri); Peter Coe (Marko); Nan Morris (Stephana); Helmut Schneider (German Captain); Giulio Marchetti (Italian Officer); Nicholas Rend (Captain of Fishing Boat); Craig March (Petar); Todd Williams (Partisan Leader); Charles Brent (Monk); Richard Johns (Wireless Operator); Kurt Bricker (German Naval Lieutenant); Katrina Rozan (Peasant Woman).

"SECRET INVASION, a war drama, has action—almost unceasingly . . . . [The filmmakers] have evidently made an excellent study of previous films that dealt with war, prison, heroism and patriotism, as there are some familiar scenes in their bloody tale. Luckily, they all seem quite at home" (*Variety*).

THE SECRET INVASION was filmed on location in Yugoslavia and predated MGM's more elaborately produced THE DIRTY DOZEN, q.v., by three years. In World War II Cairo, British Intelligence selects several hardened convicts to undertake a dangerous mission in return for their pardons. The five are: the murderer John Durrell (Henry Silva), ex-crime syndicate head Roberto Rocca (Raf Vallone), demolition expert Terrence Scanlon (Mickey Rooney), Simon Fell (Edd Byrnes), the forger, and art thief Jean Saval (William Campbell). Major Richard Mace (Stewart Granger) heads this commando group to free Italian General Quadri (Enzo Fiermonte) from a Dubrovnik prison so that he can lead his own troops against the Nazis. Along the way, Fell, Scanlon and Saval are killed, and Mace finds out that the kidnapped general is a Nazi substitute. The imposter is made to speak to his Italian troops and Durrell, costumed as a Nazi, kills the imitation general. This action helps persuade the Italians to turn against the Nazis. The mission is completed but only Rocca, of the convicts, has survived.

SERGEANT YORK (Warner Bros., 1941) 134 mins.*

Producers, Jesse L. Lasky, Hal B. Wallis; director, Howard

---

*Computerized color version now available.

Hawks; based on the books *War Diary of Sergeant York* by Sam K. Cowan, *Sergeant York and His People* by Cowan, *Sergeant York—Last of the Long Hunters* by Tom Skeyhill; screenplay, Abem Finkel, Harry Chandlee, Howard Koch, John Huston; art director, John Hughes; set director, Fred MacLean; makeup, Perc Westmore; music, Max Steiner; music director, Leo F. Forbstein; technical adviser, Donoho Hall, Paul Walters (Captain, F.A.R.); William Yettes; camera, Sol Polito, (war sequences) Arthur Edeson; editor, William Holmes.

Gary Cooper (Alvin Cullum York); Walter Brennan (Pastor Rosier Pile); Joan Leslie (Gracie Williams); George Tobias (Michael T. "Pusher" Ross); Stanley Ridges (Major Buxton); Margaret Wycherly (Mother York); Ward Bond (Ike Botkin); Noah Beery, Jr. (Buck Lipscomb); June Lockhart (Rose York); Dickie Moore (George York); Clem Bevans (Zeke); Howard Da Silva (Lem); Charles Trowbridge (Cordell Hull); Harvey Stephens (Captain Danforth); David Bruce (Bert Thomas); Charles [Carl] Esmond (German Major); Joseph Sawyer (Sergeant Early); Pat Flaherty (Sergeant Harry Parsons) Robert Porterfield (Zeb Andrews); Erville Alderson (Nate Tomkins); Joseph Girard (General John Pershing); Frank Wilcox (Sergeant); Donald Douglas (Captain Tillman); Lane Chandler (Corporal Savage); Frank Marlowe (Beardsley); Jack Pennick (Corporal Cutting); James Anderson (Eb); Guy Wilkerson (Tom); Tully Marshall (Uncle Lige); Lee "Lasses" White (Luke, the Target Keeper); Jane Isbell (Gracie's Sister); Frank Orth (Drummer); Arthur Aylesworth (Marten, the Bartender); Lucia Carroll, Rita La Roy, Kay Sutton (Saloon Girls); Elisha Cook, Jr. (Piano Player); William Haade (Card Player); Jody Gilbert (Fat Woman); Victor Kilian (Andrews); Frank Faylen, Murray Alper (Butt Boys); Gaylord "Steve" Pendleton, Charles Drake (Scorers); Theodore Von Eltz (Prison Camp Commander); Roland Drew (Officer); Russell Hicks (General); Jean Del Val (Marshal Foch); Selmer Jackson (General Duncan); Creighton Hale (AP Man); George Irving (Harrison); Ed Keane (Oscar of the Waldorf); Gig Young (Soldier); and: Kit Guard, Si Jenks, Ray Teal.

"Sergeant York and I had quite a few things in common even before I played him on the screen. We both were raised in the mountains—Tennessee for him, Montana for me—and learned to ride and shoot as a natural part of growing up. SERGEANT YORK won me an Academy Award, but that's not why it's my favorite. I liked the role because of the background of the picture, and because I was portraying a good, sound American character" (Gary Cooper).

Alvin Cullum York* (1887-1964) is scarcely remembered today, but in his time the World War I hero ("the greatest civilian soldier of all time") was a famous symbol of American patriotism, an example of such dredged up by this slick motion picture for U.S. moviegoers as the country prepared to enter World War II. This film did its part in persuading Americans that they must fight in this new war. (Interestingly enough co-producer Jesse L. Lasky would say, "I wish to emphasize that this is in no sense a war picture. It is a story Americans had to be told today.")

Lanky Alvin C. York (Gary Cooper) is a rugged, sharp-shooting farmer living in the Three Forks area of the Tennessee Valley. He has his own brand of religion and when drafted into World War I the backwoodsman lists himself as a conscientious objector. It is compassionate Major Buxton (Stanley Ridges) who hands him an American history book which teaches York that sometimes violence is required to insure freedom for everyone. (He finds scripture in the Bible which justifies his new belief: "Therefore render unto Caesar the things that are Caesar's, and unto God the things that are God's.") He goes to France as part of the American Expeditionary Forces, assigned to Company G, 328th Infantry, 82nd Division. During the battle of the Argonne Forest Sergeant York witnesses one of his pals killed by the Germans. This leads the angry Tennesseean on October 8, 1918 to kill twenty-five of the enemy and to capture 132 prisoners single-handedly (using the same turkey-gobble-calling marksmanship he employed back home). He later tells his superior officers he did what he did to save lives. "I'm as much agin killin' as ever, but when I heard them machine guns . . . well, them guns was killin' hundreds, maybe thousands, and there weren't nothin' anybody could do but to stop them guns. That's what I done." As a result General John Pershing (Joseph Girard) terms York a hero and this leads to his receiving an assortment of medals: the Congressional Medal of Honor, the Croix de Guerre, the Medaille Militaire, the Distinguished Service Cross. He refuses after the war to endorse products with his name. Instead he returns to his family and friends in Three Forks. He is greeted by, among others, his beloved Miss Gracie (Joan Leslie), who takes him to a new bottom land farm and farmhouse donated to him by the

---

*Filmmakers had been attempting for years to make a motion picture of York's amazing story, but it was not until Cooper was suggested to play him that York agreed to the film version. An additional proviso was that York be able to supervise every detail of the production.

people of Tennessee. "The Lord sure do move in mysterious ways," he confesses modestly.

Although the obvious studio sets for the too idyllic Tennessee sequences were criticized by many, as were the southern "drawls" of some players (in particular, Joan Leslie* as his religious young girlfriend, Gracie), there is much to commend within this lengthy, timely film biography. Under director Howard Hawks' guidance, it remains fixed on target to present the inner conflict of the once boisterous York who has grave misgivings about killing another person. Among the procession of people shaping York's life are: York's tough widowed mother (Margaret Wycherly), who loves her brood of children and knows how unmerciful life can be; Pastor Rosier Pile (Walter Brennan), who runs the local general store and who guides York in his religious faith; the conniving landowner, Zeb Andrews (Robert Porterfield); "Pusher" Ross (George Tobias), a former New York City subway guard who tells York about big-town life.

When SERGEANT YORK had its dual premiere on Broadway (July 3, 1941), the Astor Theatre boasted a four-story-high likeness of Cooper (as York) in which thousands of multi-colored bulbs showed York changing from a hillbilly hunter to a soldier with rifle. There was a tickertape parade down Broadway with Cooper and the real-life Alvin York riding in front of the procession. Among those attending the premiere were General John Pershing, Eleanor Roosevelt, *Time* magazine publisher Henry Luce, presidential nominee Wendell Willkie, and General Lewis B. Hershey (director of the selective service). The film proved to be the top moneymaker of the year, earning $6,100,000 in theater rentals in the U.S. and Canada. Gary Cooper won an Oscar for Best Actor, as did the Editing; and there were Oscar nominations for: Best Picture, Supporting Actor (Walter Brennan), Supporting Actress (Margaret Wycherly), Direction, Original Screenplay, Cinematography, Interior Design, Sound, and Scoring.

SHE GOES TO WAR (United Artists, 1929) 87 mins.

Associate producers, Victor Halperin, Edward R. Halperin; director, Henry King; based on the story by Rupert Hughes; adaptor, Mme. Fred De Gresac; screenplay, Howard Estabrook; dialogue/titles, John Monk Saunders; art directors, Albert

---

*Director Hawks wanted a voluptuous Daisy Mae type actress for the role of "Miss Gracie" and even considered Jane Russell for the part. However, co-producer Hal B. Wallis chose 16-year-old studio contractee Joan Leslie for the key assignment.

Eleanor Boardman in SHE GOES TO WAR (1929).

D'Agostino, Robert M. Haas; songs, Harry Akst; camera, John Fulton, Tony Gaudio; editor, Lloyd Nosler.

Eleanor Boardman (Joan Morant); John Holland (Tom Pike); Edmund Burns (Reggie Van Ruyper); Alma Rubens (Rosie); Al St. John (Bill); Glen Walters (Katie); Margaret Seddon (Tom's Mother); Yola D'Avril (Yvette); Evelyn Hall (Joan's Aunt); Augustino Borgato (Major); Dina Smirnova (Joan's Maid); Yvonne Starke (Major's Wife); Eulalie Jensen (Matron of Canteen); Captain H. M. Zier (Major); Edward Chandler (Top Sergeant); Ann Warrington (Hostess); Gretchen Hartman, Florence Wix (Knitting Ladies).

SHE GOES TO WAR is an unusual blend of trench warfare, romance, and comedy. It is also one of the few 1920s films from Hollywood to deal with World War I in any (partially) serious sense. Made at a time when the film industry was switching to sound productions, it contains 10% talking/singing interludes, with comedy bits and songs by Alma Rubens as one of the heroine's co-workers in the war effort at the front.

Smalltown socialite Joan Morant (Eleanor Boardman) is excited about the advent of World War I, as it presents so many unique opportunities for her. Through her congressman uncle she obtains a posting overseas. In France she encounters two former hometowners: garage owner Tom Pike (John Holland), too frazzled by combat duty to care about romancing her; and playboy Reggie Van Ruyper (Edmund Burns), now a supply sergeant with all the comforts of home, who finds Joan charming. When Reggie is ordered to the front and becomes drunk, Joan, who has been learning about the realities of war, takes his place. She serves bravely at the front under her commander, Tom. They later renew their romance.

The *New York Times* (Mordaunt Hall), among others, was unimpressed by this mongrel picture: "Neither the singing nor the few words of dialogues are of much help. . . . Mr. King has achieved no small success with his fighting scenes, but toward the end the idea of the Germans rolling metal barrels of oil down an incline and exploding them is spectacular without being convincing. It gives the director an opportunity to show tanks forging their way through the flaming area, which is impressive, but subsequently, on seeing the gunners firing shells from the tanks, one realizes the impossibility of this moviesque hazard."

SHELL SHOCK (Parade Releasing Organization, 1964) 94 mins.

Presenters, Riley Jackson, Robert Patrick; producer, Charles Beach Dickerson; director, John Hayes; screenplay, Randy Fields, Hayes; art director/music, Jaime Mendoza-Nava; sound, Frank

Murphy; special effects, Ross Hahn, Sam Altonian; camera, Vilis Lapenieks; editor, Thomas Conrad.

Beach Dickerson (Rance); Carl Crow (Johnny Wade); Frank Leo (Gil Evans); Pamela Grey (Maria); Bill Guhl (Sergeant Wrigley); Max Huber (Major); Dolores Faith (American Girl); and: Martin Brady, Roland Roberts, Bill Roblin.

An artistic mishmash which, in its inept way, still depicts the conflicting loyalties and desires created by wartime in a combat zone.

In 1943 Italy decorated World War II GI Johnny Wade (Carl Crow) is suffering from shell shock. His sergeant, Rance (Beach Dickerson), claims the man is pretending, but Wade's hometown buddy, Gil Evans (Frank Leo), arranges for Wade to have medical attention. Rance, jealous of Wade's medal, persuades him to escape and plans to kill him while he is A.W.O.L. Rance, Evans and Sergeant Wrigley (Bill Guhl) go after Wade as they also make their way to the American lines. Wrigley is killed by the enemy and an Italian girl (Pamela Grey) they meet mistakes Rance for a German and kills him. An American patrol finds the survivors and Johnny recovers from his shell shock.

SHIPS WITH WINGS (United Artists, 1942) 89 mins.

Producer, Michael Balcon; associate producer, S. C. Balcon; director, Sergei Nolbandov; screenplay, Patrick Kirwan, Austin Melford, Diana Morgan, Nolbandov; art director, Wilfred Shingleton; music, Geoffrey Wright; songs, Morgan; technical adviser, Lieutenant Commander J. Reid (Royal Navy); camera, Mutz Greenbuzam, Wilkie Cooper; editor, Robert Hamer.

John Clements (Lieutenant Dick Stacey); Leslie Banks (Admiral Wetherby); Jane Baxter (Celia Wetherby); Ann Todd (Kay Gordon); Basil Sydney (Captain Fairfax); Edward Chapman (Papadopulous); Hugh Williams (Wagner); Frank Pettingell (Fields); Michael Wilding (Lieutenant Grant); Michael Rennie (Lieutenant Peter Maxwell); Frank Cellier (General Scarappa); Cecil Parker (Air Marshal); John Stuart (Commander Hood); Morland Graham (Chief Petty Officer Marsden); Charles Victor (MacDermott); Hugh Burden (Lieutenant Wetherby); John Laurie (Lieutenant Commander Reid); and: Betty Marsden, George Merritt, Elizabeth Pengally, Graham Penley, Charles Russell.

This very contrived outing was filled with wild melodramatics, untidy plot contrivances, too much unsophisticated model work, and was considered anachronistic by its release date.

In 1936 dashing young pilot Lieutenant Dick Stacey (John Clements) is in love with pretty Jane Baxter (Celia Wetherby). To impress her, he takes up a plane without permission. When it crashes, the passenger, Jane's brother, is killed. Stacey is court-martialed and thrown out of the service. He becomes the pilot of a one-man airline on the Greek island of Palmos. When the Germans overrun the area at the start of World War II and plant mines to destroy the aircraft carrier HMS *Ark Royal* and her planes, Stacey sets out to warn the ship's commander. In the ensuing naval and air battles all seems lost for the British. However, Stacey has gained permission to take up a plane from the *Ark Royal* and manages to crash it into a German dam which explodes and stops the enemy offensive. The HMS *Ark Royal* is saved. Having noted Stacey's victory and death, two stiff-lipped *Ark Royal* officers discuss Stacey's amazing regeneration:

> "I knew he wouldn't come back."
>
> "I think he'd have preferred it that way," says the other.

In combat death, Stacey has made amends to the service, to his country, and to his lost love.

United Artists had released the Ealing Studios' SHIPS WITH WINGS in December 1941 in England with a 140-minute running time. By then the 23,000-ton HMS *Ark Royal* had been sunk (November 14, 1941) by a German submarine. The film almost did not get its domestic release. Prime Minister Winston Churchill was against the film because it depicted the Fleet Air Arm as almost defeated (and only saved by wild heroics). Churchill thought it would cause "alarm and despondency" in the British ranks. After much arbitration, SHIPS WITH WINGS was distributed at home and in an abbreviated version abroad.

SHOULDER ARMS (First National, 1918) 36 mins.
    Director/screenplay, Charles Chaplin.
    Charles Chaplin (Recruit); Edna Purviance (French Girl); Sydney Chaplin (Sergeant/Kaiser); Jack Wilson (German Crown Prince); Henry Bergman (Fat German Sergeant/Field Marshal von Hindenburg); Albert Austin (American Soldier/German Soldier/Kaiser's Chauffeur); Tom Wilson (Training Camp Sergeant); John Rand, Park Jones (American Soldiers); Loyal Underwood (Small German Officer); W. G. Wagner, J. T. Powell, W. Herron, W. Cross, G. E. Marygold (Motorcyclists); C. L. Dice, G. A. Godfrey, L. A. Blaisdell, W. E. Allen, J. H. Warne (Motorcyclists, Alternate Group); Roscoe Ward, Ed Hunt, M. J. Donovan, E. B. Johnson, Fred Graham, Louis Orr, Al Blake, Ray Hanford, Cliff Brouwer, Claude McAtee, F. S. Colby, Jack Shalford, Joe Van

Meter, Guy Eakins, Jack Willis, Charles Cole, T. Madden (American/German Soldiers); Harry Goldman, Jack Willis, Mark Faber, E. H. Devere, Fred Everman, A. North, Charles Knuske, O. E. Haskins, Tom Hawley, W. E. Graham, James Griffin, W. A. Hackett, E. Brucker, J. H. Shewry, Sam Lewis, R. B. McKenzie, K. Herlinger, A. J. Hartwell (People on Street).

On first thought it would seem incongruous that Charlie Chaplin, the King of Comedy, could turn out a war film that is tasteful, pertinent, and realistic. However, he understood perfectly that tragedy and comedy are close relatives and often interchangeable.

This relatively short silent film features a new recruit (Charlie Chaplin) at the front lines in World War I France. Life in the trenches is terrible: there's the unseen enemy sniping away at the men, the rain and mud, the terrible food, the mice and lice, and the horrible homesickness. The new recruit deals with these obstacles in an amazingly inventive way, with the resultant comedy never far from wishful reality. When an overripe limburger cheese reaches him, he heaves it over to the enemy, using it as a gas bomb. He carries a mousetrap in his back pack to deal with trench vermin. He lights his cigarette with a passing bullet, and when settling down for the night, blows out a candle as it floats by in the trench waters. When he receives no mail from home, he stops by a guard who is reading a letter and vicariously shares all the emotions the other doughboy is undergoing. Later he finds himself camouflaged as a tree in no-man's land, scuttling out of range of the cross fire, and before the silent comedy has concluded, he has captured a trio of high-ranking enemies: the Kaiser, the Crown Prince, and von Hindenburg. He awakens from this boastful dream to discover he is back in boot camp, having fallen asleep after a rugged training workout.*

The press was enthusiastic about the new Chaplin picture. "He is even more enjoyable than one is likely to anticipate because he abandons some of the tricks of former comedies and introduces new properties into his horseplay" (*New York Times*). "SHOULDER ARMS includes much more action than generally found in a Chaplin comedy. . . . Had Chaplin held back the subject until after victory

---

*Originally SHOULDER ARMS was to have been a three-sectioned story, with Chaplin the father of three children and suffering from a shrewish wife. He would endure the indignities of the army physical and have his (mis)adventures at the front, and then in the third part he would be toasted by European nobility celebrating his capture of the Kaiser. At the finale he would awake in training camp. During production in the summer of 1918 Chaplin would discard the bulk of the storyline and refilm the story into its final form.

it would have been even a bigger comedy, although one must still laugh heartily notwithstanding what the subject matter forces into memory, but it's never mournful fun" (*Variety*). The film proved to be a large financial hit for Chaplin.

In David Robinson's *Chaplin* (1985) the author notes, "When Chaplin reissued SHOULDER ARMS more than half a century later, he proudly prefaced it with "actuality shots of the war, to show how well his set-builders had done."

THE SILENT ENEMY (Universal, 1959) 92 mins.

Producer, Bertram Ostrer; director, William Fairchild; based on the book *Commander Crabb* by Marshall Pugh; screenplay, Fairchild; art director, Bill Andrews; music, William Alwyn; music director, Muir Mathieson; special effects, Wally Veevers; camera, Otto Heller; underwater camera, Egil Woxholt; editor, Alan Osbiston.

Laurence Harvey (Lieutenant Lionel Crabb); Dawn Addams (Third Officer Jill Masters); Michael Craig (Leading Seaman Knowles); John Clements (The Admiral); Sidney James (Chief Petty Officer Thorpe); Alec McCowen (Able Seaman Morgan); Nigel Stock (Able Seaman Fraser); Ian Whittaker (Ordinary Seaman Thomas); Arnold Foa (Tomolino); Gianna Maria Canale (Conchita); Massimo Serato (Forzelli); Giacomo Rossi Stuart (Rosati); Carlo Justini (Fellini); Raymond Young (Celloni); Howard Marion Crawford (Wing Commander); Cyril Shaps (Miguel); Lee Montague (Miguel's Mate); Terence Longdon (Lieutenant Bailey); Alan Webb (British Consul); John Moffatt (Driver Volunteer); Sydney King (Cruiser Captain); Peter Welch (Helmsman); Murray Kash (Tattooed Sailor); Yvonne Warren (Spanish Girl); Ewen Solon (Willowdale Captain); Brian Oulton (Holford); and: Michael Brill, Laurence Brooks, Desmond Jordan, Sydney King, John Lee, David Lodge, Ian McNaughton, Hugh Moxey, Derren Nesbitt, Yvonne Romain, Harold Siddons, Tom Watson, Peter Welsh, Jerome Willis.

Real-life World War II adventures continued to provide ample fodder for British filmmakers.

Lieutenant Crabb (Laurence Harvey) is assigned to Gibraltar in 1941. His task is to combat the Italian frogmen who are successfully attacking shipping in the area by planting bombs on the hulls of the vessels. He and equally anti-authority co-diver Knowles (Michael Craig), without permission, discover the enemy is based in an interned Italian ship in Spain. Crabb et al. destroy this base of operations before the Italians can blow up the British convoy

Laurence Harvey in THE SILENT ENEMY (1959).

headed for the North African invasion. For his courage in and out of the line of duty, Crabb is awarded the George Medal.

Without overplaying the heroics, THE SILENT ENEMY is an exciting display of a special underwater arm of the Allied forces. Laurence Harvey, who would soon become an increasingly mannered staple of Hollywood productions, effectively underplays his role as the real-life maverick whose enthusiasm for his patriotic task leads him to adopt unorthodox methods in order to succeed.

THE SILENT ENEMY was originally released in Great Britain by Independent Films Distributors in March 1958 with a 112-minute running time.

SINK THE BISMARCK! (Twentieth Century-Fox, 1960) 97 mins.

Producer, John Brabourne; director, Lewis Gilbert; based on the book by C. S. Forester; screenplay, Edmund H. North; music, Clifton Parker; music director, Muir Mathieson; special effects, Howard Lydecker, Bill Harrington; camera, Christopher Challis; editor, Peter Hunt.

Kenneth More (Captain Jonathan Shepard); Dana Wynter (Anne Davis); Carl Mohner (Captain Ernst Lindemann); Laurence Naismith (First Sea Lord); Geoffrey Keen (A.C.N.S.); Karel Stepanek (Admiral Gunther Lutjens); Michael Hordern (Com-

The crew of SINK THE BISMARCK! (1960).

mander on *King George*); Maurice Denham (Commander Richards); Michael Goodliffe (Captain Banister); Edmund Knight (Captain on *Prince of Wales*); Jack Watling (Signals Officer); Jack Gwillan (Captain on *King George*); Mark Dignam (Captain on *Ark Royal*); Ernest Clark (Captain on *Suffolk*); John Horsley (Captain on *Sheffield*); Peter Burton (Captain on First Destroyer); John Stuart (Captain on *Hood*); Walter Hudd (Admiral on *Hood*); Sidney Tafler (Workman); and Ed Morrow.

What distinguishes SINK THE BISMARCK! from so many other war films is its three-pronged story focus. The viewer participates in the British high command's strategy sessions which cross-cut with the actual naval encounter presented from both the British and German naval officers' points of view. What results is a "fine, authentic account of Britain's search-and-destroy mission against the German battleship Bismarck" (*TV Guide*).

The Germans launch the *Bismarck* in 1939. It is their premier battleship, displacing 42,000 tons of water. The action jumps ahead to May 1941 and the British learn that the *Bismarck* has broken out of the British blockade and can now attack Atlantic convoys at will. At the underground British Admiralty office, Captain Jonathan Shepard (Kenneth More) resolutely begins a deadly earnest war game to stop the Germans on the high seas. The *Bismarck*, commanded by Admiral Gunther Lutjens (Karel Stepanek) and Captain Ernst Lindemann (Carl Mohner), wins the first round by sinking the prime British vessel, HMS *Hood*. This defeat causes British Prime Minister Churchill to order the mammoth enemy vessel sunk at any cost! Moving his models into battle position across a large map in the war room, Shepard then sends the aircraft carrier *Ark Royal* after the *Bismarck*, and the latter is damaged. This allows the British to dispatch the *King George V* and the *Rodney* which, in the major naval battle of May 27, 1941, sink the unsinkable *Bismarck*, with the stupefied Lutjens and Lindemann going down with their invincible ship.

To give added, personal dimension to this effectively detailed study of World War II naval warfare, Captain Shepard must put aside his personal grief over his wife who has been killed in an air raid and concern for his son who is a gunner aboard the *Ark Royal*. Assisting him in the war room is W.R.N.S. Anne Davis (Dana Wynter). Shepard is convincingly presented as a tireless strategist, determined to outmaneuver his opponents in "a most interesting chess game." The film carefully mixes newsreel footage, model miniatures in studio tanks, and new footage to reconstruct the war scenes.

633 SQUADRON (United Artists, 1964) Color 94 mins.
Executive producer, Lewis J. Rachnil; producer, Cecil F. Ford; director, Walter E. Grauman; based on the novel by Frederick E. Smith; screenplay, James Clavell, Howard Koch; production designer, Michael Stringer; music, Ron Goodwin; stunt coordinator, John Crewdson; second unit director, Roy Stevens; sound, John Bramail, J. B. Smith; special effects, Tom Howard; camera, Edward Scaife; aerial camera, John Wilcox; editor, Bert Bates.

Cliff Robertson (Wing Commander Roy Grant); George Chakiris (Lieutenant Erik Bergman); Maria Perschy (Hilde Bergman); Harry Andrews (Air Marshal Davis); Donald Houston (Wing Commander Tom Barrett); Michael Goodliffe (Squadron Leader Bill Adams); John Meillon (Flight Lieutenant Gillibrand); John Bonney (Flight Lieutenant Scott); Angus Lennie (Flight Lieutenant Hoppy Hopkinson); Scot Finch (Flight Lieutenant Bissel); Barbara Archer (Rosie, the Barmaid); Julian Sherrier (Flight Lieutenant Singh); Suzan Farmer (Mary, the WAF Sergeant); John Church (Flight Lieutenant Evans); Jeremy Wagg (Flight Lieutenant Reynolds); Johnny Briggs (Flight Lieutenant Jones); Sean Kelly (Flight Lieutenant Nigel); Edward Brayshaw (Flight Lieutenant Greiner); Arnold Locke (Kearns); Peter Kriss (Flight Lieutenant Milner); Geoffrey Frederick (Flight Lieutenant Frank); Richard Shaw (Johansen); Anne Ridley (SS Woman); Cavan Malone (Ericsen); Drewe Henley (Thor); John Dray (Henrik); Chris Williams (Goth).

633 SQUADRON is an unconvincing mixture of aerial daring, espionage melodrama, and a poor script equalled by unsubtle acting. It was filmed in England. *Variety* reported: ". . . [It] contains some of the most rip-roaring aerial action photography ever recorded on celluloid. Unfortunately, this technical prowess is not matched by the drama it adorns." Oscar-winning George Chakiris was not believable as the dashing Norwegian resistance fighter who breaks under torture; attractive Maria Perschy was equally unconvincing as his sister who loves the RAF hero; and stern-faced Cliff Robertson was obviously not at home in the role of the bold, cocky pilot.

The British are told of a major German V-2 fuel manufacturing plant in Norway. The only way to destroy the target is to bomb the cliff above the plant. Wing Commander Roy Grant's (Cliff Robertson) 633 squadron of Mosquito aircraft is assigned the dangerous mission. Unknown to the English, the Nazis have tortured information from underground leader Erik Bergman (George Chakiris) and are prepared for the attackers. The entire flying squadron is destroyed, but the final bomb dropped hits the target. The only survivors are Canadian Grant and his navigator.

Director Walter Grauman had served in the Mediterranean Theatre in World War II with the Twelfth Air Force. As a B-25 pilot he participated in 56 combat missions and won the Distinguished Flying Cross.

THE SIXTH OF JUNE *see*: D-DAY, THE SIXTH OF JUNE.

SO PROUDLY WE HAIL (Paramount, 1943) 126 mins.

Producer/director, Mark Sandrich; screenplay, Allan Scott; art directors, Hans Dreier, Earl Hedrick; set decorator, Stephen Seymour; makeup, Wally Westmore; music, Miklos Rozsa; song, Edward Hayman and Rozsa; technical advisers: First Lieutenant Eunice Hatchitt, Colonel Thomas W. Doyle; special effects, Gordon Jennings, Farciot Edouart, George Dutton; assistant director, Joe Youngerman; sound, Harold Lewis, Walter Oberst; camera, Charles Lang; editor, Ellsworth Hoagland.

Barbara Britton, Paulette Goddard, and Claudette Colbert in SO PROUDLY WE HAIL (1943).

Claudette Colbert (Lieutenant Janet Davidson); Paulette God-dard (Lieutenant Joan O'Doul); Veronica Lake (Lieutenant Olivia D'Arcy); George Reeves (Lieutenant John Summers); Barbara Britton (Lieutenant Rosemary Larson); Walter Abel (Chaplain); Sonny Tufts (Kansas); Mary Servoss (Captain "Ma" McGregor); Ted Hecht (Dr. Jose Bardia); John Litel (Dr. Harrison); Dr. Hugh Ho Chang (Ling Chee); Mary Treen (Lieutenant Sadie Schwartz); Kitty Kelly (Lieutenant Ethel Armstrong); Helen Lund (Lieutenant Elsie Bollenbacher); Lorna Gray (Lieutenant Tony Dacolli); Dorothy Adams (Lieutenant Irma Emerson); Ann Doran (Lieuten-ant Betty Peterson); Jean Willes (Lieutenant Carol Johnson); Lynn Walker (Lieutenant Fay Leonard); Joan Tours (Lieutenant Margaret Stevenson); Jan Wiley (Lieutenant Lynne Hopkins); Mimi Doyle, Julia Faye, Hazel Keener, Frances Morris (Nurses); James Bell (Colonel White); Dick Hogan (Flight Lieutenant Archie McGre-gor); Bill Goodwin (Captain O'Rourke); James Flavin (Captain O'Brien); Byron Foulger (Mr. Larson); Elsa Janssen (Mrs. Larson); Richard Crane (Georgie Larson); Boyd Davis (Colonel Mason); Will Wright (Colonel Clark); James Millican (Young Ensign); Damian O'Flynn (Young Doctor); Roy Gordon (Ship's Captain); Jack Luden (Steward); Larry Strang (Major Arthur); Edward Dew (Captain Lawrence); Yvonne De Carlo (Girl); William Forrest (Major at San Francisco Dock); Amparo Antenercruz, Linda Brent, Isabel Cooper (Filipino Nurses); Victor Kilian, Jr. (Corporal); Edward Earle, Byron Shores (Doctors); Hugh Prosser (Captain); Charles Lester (Soldier).

"I realize that a good deal of sincerity, emotion, and desire to honor went into it, and I have no desire to laugh at that; but it is impossible to accept the result, except in a kind of fascination. This is probably the most deadly-accurate picture that will ever be made of what war looks like through the lenses of a housewives'-magazine romance. . . . Some reviewers who grant that the story itself is painful feel that the picture is redeemed by the deep sincerity of the players and by the powerful realism of the war scenes. But it seems to me that the most sincere thing Paramount's young women did was to alter their make-up . . ." (James Agee, *The Nation* magazine).

The narrative opens* in Australia and then follows a group of Army nurses who are sailing back to America on a troop ship.

---

*The opening title cards of SO PROUDLY WE HAIL state: "Out of the black horror and tragedy of Bataan came a light—the light of a miracle! Eight American girls—Army nurses—had been delivered from that holocaust. The story that

Sitting on deck in a trance-like state is nurse Lieutenant Janet Davidson (Claudette Colbert), staring blankly out at sea. Dr. Harrison (John Litel) asks the others to tell him about Janet's wartime trauma. Flashback: it is 1941 and a group of American nurses is leaving San Francisco, headed for Hawaii. When the Japanese attack Pearl Harbor their ship is diverted to Bataan to tend the mounting casualties. Captain "Ma" McGregor (Mary Servoss) is their leader, but it is Janet to whom the others looks for inspiration and guidance. She is the intensely dedicated nurse who understands their serious mission. "Time is short. There's no time to waste it on personal things. We've got a job and a responsibility." It had been Janet who counseled wise-cracking, man-chasing Lieutenant Joan O'Doul (Paulette Goddard) against letting romance interfere with her vital job, but it is Janet who falls in love with Lieutenant John Summers (George Reeves) and who, against regulations but with Ma's permission, marries the man. (She falls asleep on their one-night honeymoon, exhausted from her hospital duties.) As the Marines set up a holding action against the Japanese on Bataan during the retreat to Corregidor, Lieutenant Olivia D'Arcy (Veronica Lake), who has never gotten over seeing her fiancé die in the Pearl Harbor attack, sacrifices herself to save the others. With a grenade inside her blouse, she walks out into a midst of Japanese soldiers and explodes herself and the enemy. Meanwhile, at Corregidor ("the Gibraltar of the Pacific") Janet learns her husband has been lost in combat in Mindanao, where he was sent to locate quinine. The film returns to the present, once again aboard the ship bound back to the United States. Janet is still in a near catatonic state. But Dr. Harrison reads to her a letter written by her dead husband: "This is a not a people's war because civilians also get killed. It's the people's war because they have taken it over and are going to win it and end it with a purpose—to live like men with dignity, in freedom. . . . This is our war now, and this time it will be our peace." Enclosed in the letter is a deed to a small farm. Janet brightens, for she knows now she has a new duty and a reason for living—to go home, make things grow, and renourish life. As the finale music plays, the troop ship sails under the Golden Gate Bridge into a bright new day. A superimposed poster urges women to volunteer for the nurses corp.

SO PROUDLY WE HAIL was and is a crucial motion picture on many levels. It was one of the few major Hollywood produc-

---

follows is inspired by their courage, devotion and sacrifice, and is based on the records of the U.S. Army Nursing Corps. We dedicate this picture to them and to their comrades still somewhere in the Philippines and to nurses everywhere."

tions, besides CRY HAVOC (1943), q.v., to present the story of women in war. And it did so in many traditional terms, usually reserved for male combat films. There is the all-knowing parent figure (Mary Servoss); the sex-chasing subordinate (Paulette Goddard) who insists, "I don't know who said the flesh was weak; I find it very strong," and lucks out by finding a naive, but sincere midwestern ex-footballer (Sonny Tufts) who truly loves her; the green newcomer (Barbara Britton); the comic (Mary Treen); the embittered soul (Veronica Lake), who finds peace through sacrificial death; and the heroine (Claudette Colbert) who is punished for ignoring duty for romance. As in all efficient war films, SO PROUDLY WE HAIL is full of patriotic speeches about duty to country and about the barbarism of the insidious enemy who blithely strafe Red Cross hospitals, cruelly kill civilians, and generally play unfair. There is also sacrifice and death in combat. Ma McGregor has lost her husband in the war and now her son dies in action; Olivia's boyfriend from St. Louis died at Pearl Harbor and she gives her life on the warfront; Janet's husband is missing in action in the Bataan retreat; and many of the nurses die at the hands of the Japanese.

What makes SO PROUDLY WE HAIL unique is how it deals with women at war. They are engaged in constant life-and-death situations and, like male soldiers, they need to divert themselves. For them, a solace is to constantly fret about their wardrobe: the big fuss made over Joan's coveted black lace negligee in one of the shipboard party scenes; the insistence that Janet wear a blouse and skirt at her wedding; the nurses' realization that their white uniforms make them sitting targets in the Bataan jungle; the arrival in the mail for Rosemary Larson (Barbara Britton) of a stylish, feminine hat that reminds the nurses of what they left behind at home. They are hardworking, efficient professionals who think about or act on romance *without* the usual hesitancy and shyness of civilian women; and they face the great dangers (rape, torture, death) to women in war with resolute calmness. They can be as determined as any man to gain revenge. (Olivia says, "I'm going to kill Japs. Every blood-stained one I can get my hands on. They must be punished and I'm going to punish them.") In what must be one of the most memorable scenes of any World War II film, Olivia does an inversion of the usual—she invites the enemy to physically assault her, even removing her helmet to make herself more alluring. The exploding grenade completes the situation reversal. In *The World War II Combat Film* (1986), Jeanine Basinger observes, "Perhaps more than any other variation of the woman's film, SO

PROUDLY WE HAIL demonstrates how two genres can merge."

SO PROUDLY WE HAIL was enormously popular despite the damning praise of the critics* and received four Oscar nominations: Best Actress (Paulette Goddard), Screenplay, Cinematography, and Special Effects. The film was a revelation to filmgoers who saw Veronica Lake, of the famous "peekaboo" hairdo, with a new short hair style, and the film marked the screen introduction of Sonny Tufts who would enjoy a brief vogue in the mid-1940s and then suffer years of "Sonny Tufts? . . . Who is Sonny Tufts?" At the time of production much was made of the on-set contretemps between Paramount's three top female stars. Forty-three years later, the inept WOMEN OF VALOR (CBS-TV, 11/23/86) would try unsuccessfully to recreate the formula established in SO PROUDLY WE HAIL. Starring Susan Sarandon, Kristy McNichol, and Alberta Watson, this shot-in-the-Philippines telefeature dealt with American army nurses incarcerated in Japanese prisoner-of-war camps on Bataan.

SONS O'GUNS (Warner Bros., 1936) 82 mins.

Producer, Harry Joe Brown; director, Lloyd Bacon; based on the play by Fred Thompson, Jack Donahue; screenplay, Jerry Wald, Julius J. Epstein; songs, Al Dubin and Harry Warren; music director, Leo F. Forbstein; choreography, Bobby Connolly; camera, Sol Polito; editor, James Gibbons.

Joe E. Brown (Jimmy Canfield); Joan Blondell (Yvonne); Beverly Roberts (Mary Harper); Winifred Shaw (Bernice Pearce); Eric Blore (Hobson—Canfield's Butler); G. P. Huntley, Jr. (Captain Archibald Ponsonby-Falcke); Joseph King (Colonel Harper); David Worth (Arthur Travers); Craig Reynolds (Lieutenant Burton); Robert Barrat (Pierre); Michael Mark (Carl); Frank Mitchell (Ritter); Bert Roach (Vogel); Hans Joby (Fritz); Mischa Auer, Otto Fries (German Spies); Bill Dagwell, Leo Sulky, Don Turner, Max Wagner (Soldiers); James Eagles (Young Soldier); Milton Kibbee, Allen Matthews (Military Policemen);

---

*"The basic fault in this picture is that it sets up the illusion of place but fails to maintain it with the illusion of genuine people there. And so we behold the horror of Bataan through a transparency, through the studiously disheveled glamour of the Misses Colbert, Goddard and Lake" (Bosley Crowther, New York Times). "The three leading ladies are so comely even in coveralls that despite all the realistic shooting, they spend most of their time fighting a woman's war" (Time magazine).

Robert A'Dair, Olaf Hytten (Sentries); Pat Flaherty, Sol Gorss, Henry Otho (Apaches).

This film was one of wide-mouthed comedian Joe E. Brown's lesser comedy/musical vehicles. He is vaudevillian Jimmy Canfield who finds himself enlisted by error in the war and fighting the Krauts during World War I. Singlehanded, he goes over the trench tops, captures an entire German regiment and is awarded the Croix de Guerre by the French. On the distaff side Joan Blondell is the French girl Yvonne; Beverly Roberts is Mary Harper, the object of Brown's affection; and specialty performer Wini Shaw appears as the quasi-vamp Bernice Pearce who headlines one of the film's too few production numbers, "Arms of an Army Man."

The 1929 stage musical had been planned for a long time as a screen project for Al Jolson.

STALAG 17 (Paramount, 1953) 119 mins.

Producer, Billy Wilder; associate producer, William Schorr; director, Wilder; based on the play by Donald Bevan, Edmund Trezinski; screenplay, Wilder, Edwin Blum; art directors, Hal Pereira, Franz Bachelin; set decorators, Sam Comer, Ray Mayer; makeup, Wally Westmore; music, Franz Waxman; sound, Harold Lewis, Gene Garvin; special camera effects, Gordon Jennings; camera, Ernest Laszlo; editors, Doane Harrison, George Tomasini.

William Holden (Sefton); Don Taylor (Lieutenant Dunbar); Otto Preminger (Oberst Von Scherbach); Robert Strauss ("Animal" Stosh); Harvey Lembeck (Harry); Richard Erdman (Hoffy); Peter Graves (Price); Neville Brand (Duke); Sig Ruman (Schultz); Michael Moore (Manfredi); Peter Baldwin (Johnson); Robinson Stone (Joey); Robert Shawley (Blondie); William Pierson (Marko); Gil Stratton, Jr. (Cookie); Jay Lawrence (Bagradian); Erwin Kalser (Geneva Man); Edmund Trezinski (Triz); Harold D. Maresch, Carl Forcht (German Lieutenants); Alex J. Wells, Bob Templeton, Paul T. Salata (Prisoners with Beards); Jerry Singer (The Crutch); Ross Bagdasarian, Richard Porter Beedle, Ralph Jarvis Caston, William McLean, John Mitchum, Robin Morse, Harry Reardon, James R. Scott, Bill Sheehan, Warren Sortomme (Prisoners of War); Janice Carroll, Yvette Eaton, Alla Gursky, Olga Lebedeff, Mara Sondakoff (Russian Women Prisoners); Ross Gould (German Orderly); Mike Bush (Dancer); Joe Ploski (German Guard Volley); Max Willenz (German Lieutenant Supervisor); Peter Leeds (Barracks #1 Prisoner of War); and: Robert Beckham, Donald Cameron, James Dabney, Jr., Ralph Gaston, Jerry Gerber, Russell Grower, Svetlana McLee, Audrey Strauss, Lyda Vashkulat.

A decade before THE GREAT ESCAPE (1963) and KING RAT (1965), qq.v., STALAG 17 set the tone for studies of World War II prisoner-of-war films. Life was hell at the battlefront but it was equally gruelling in incarceration: deprivation, humiliation, numbing boredom, torture, death, and everything made worse when there is a traitor in your midst.

Based on the hit Broadway play,* STALAG 17 is set in a German prisoner-of-war camp filled with captured American military and run by the autocratic Oberst Von Scherbach (Otto Preminger). Two G.I.s attempt a well-conceived escape and their bullet-riddled bodies are found the next morning. With this failure the captives realize that there is an informer in their midst. The logical suspect is the loner Sefton (William Holden), a grasping opportunist who stages games (of chance) and (rat) races and makes home-made liquor to gain cash, cigarettes, food, etc. for himself. He trades some of his black market goods with the Nazi guards and uses his goods to gain favors with women prisoners in a nearby barracks. Among Sefton's comic stooges are Stosh (Robert Strauss) and Harry (Harvey Lembeck); his chief adversaries are the suspicious, quick-to-anger Duke (Neville Brand) and the disgusted barracks chief, Hoffy (Richard Erdman). When an American Air Corps flyer, Lieutenant Dunbar (Don Taylor), is brought into camp, Von Scherbach is determined to learn how he managed to destroy a German ammunition train while being escorted to Stalag 17. Dunbar is questioned and tortured but does not yield his secret. Meanwhile, Duke and his cohorts badly beat up Sefton, insisting that this creep is the enemy in their midst. Yet it is the bedridden Sefton who later hears Price (Peter Graves) conversing with Schultz (Sig Ruman) and who comes to the realization that Price is the spy. The men plan to ferret Dunbar out of camp before the Nazis remove him to another location to be tried as a saboteur. When Price volunteers to lead Dunbar to freedom, Sefton exposes him and finally makes the others understand that the man is really a German agent. Sefton agrees to take Price's place, reasoning that Dunbar's well-to-do parents back in the States will reward him for his efforts. Price has tin cans tied to him and is thrown out into the yard where the Germans shoot him, thinking he is an escaping prisoner. Sefton and Price make their prison break.

---

*The Broadway production opened on May 8, 1951 and was a hit. It ran for 472 performances. It was produced and directed by Jose Ferrer and starred John Ericson, Robert Strauss, Harvey Lembeck, Frank Campanella, Eric Fleming, and Frank Maxwell.

As a reflection of reality and to soften the drama of a hero-heel, there is much boisterous comedy in STALAG 17, supplied mainly by Robert Strauss and Harvey Lembeck from the Broadway cast. Much of the humor stems from the men lusting after the women prisoners, the men making do in their state of deprivation, and the sarcasm they volley back and forth at each other regarding each other's intelligence, virility, and resourcefulness. The butt of the contempt and jokes is the camp commandant and his not-so-loyal, corrupt guards, especially Schultz. It is in opposition to the official enemy (when not stewing about Sefton's manipulations) that the prisoners devote their full resources: scheming to embarrass the captors, dreaming of escaping, and hoping for Allied victory and their release.

". . . The movie emerges as the finest comedy drama out of Hollywood this year. Raucous and tense, heartless and sentimental, always fast-paced, it has already been assigned by critics to places on their lists of the year's best ten movies" (*Life* magazine). "A lusty comedy-melodrama, loaded with bold, masculine humor and as much of the original's uninhibited earthiness as good taste and the Production code will permit" (*Variety*).

There was a built-in movie audience for STALAG 17 given word-of-mouth news about the Broadway original. With top Hollywood star William Holden cast against type, as he had also been with director Billy Wilder's earlier SUNSET BOULEVARD (1950), the movie's success was insured. The film grossed several million dollars in its first months of release. Holden won an Academy Award and the picture was Oscar-nominated for Best Supporting Actor (Robert Strauss) and Direction. Much acting praise went to producer/director/actor Otto Preminger for his restrained performance as the overbearing Nazi. Among the cast was the play's co-author, Edmund Trezinski. A spinoff of STALAG 17—played entirely for laughs—was the long-running tele-series, "Hogan's Heroes" (1965-1971), starring Bob Crane, Werner Klemperer, and John Banner.

STAND BY FOR ACTION (Metro-Goldwyn-Mayer, 1942) 109 mins.

Producers, Robert Z. Leonard, Orville O. Dull; director, Leonard; based on the story by Captain Harvey Haislip (U.S. Navy), R. C. Sherriff, and suggested by the story "A Cargo of Innocence" by Laurence Kirk; screenplay, George Bruce, John L. Balderston, Herman J. Mankiewicz; art director, Cedric Gibbons; music, Lennie Hayton; special effects, A. Arnold Gillespie, Don Jahraus; camera, Charles Rosher; editor, George Boemler.

Robert Taylor (Lieutenant Gregg Masterson); Charles Laughton (Rear Admiral Stephen Thomas); Brian Donlevy (Lieutenant Commander Martin J. Roberts); Walter Brennan (Chief Yeoman Henry Johnson); Marilyn Maxwell (Audrey Carr); Henry O'Neill (Commander Stone, Marine Corps); Marta Linden (Mary Collins); Chill Wills (Chief Boatswain's Mate Jenks); Douglass Dumbrille (Captain Ludlow); Richard Quine (Ensign Lindsay); William Tannen (Flag Lieutenant Dudley); Douglas Fowley (Ensign Martin); Tim Ryan (Lieutenant Tim Ryan); Dick Simmons (Lieutenant Royce); Byron Foulger (Pharmacist Mate "Doc" Miller); Hobart Cavanaugh (Carpenter's Mate "Chips"); Inez Cooper (Susan Garrison); Ben Welden (Chief Quartermaster Rankin); Harry Fleischman (Chief Signalman).

When World War II breaks out, the U.S. Navy takes not only old World War I vessels out of mothballs, but admirals as well. Rotund Rear Admiral Stephen Thomas (Charles Laughton) wants sea duty and not a desk job at the San Francisco Naval Base. This means his handsome Harvard playboy aide, Lieutenant Gregg Masterman (Robert Taylor), will have to take the war seriously, especially when he is placed under the direct command of rigorous Lieutenant Commander Martin J. Roberts (Brian Donlevy). While escorting a convoy in choppy waters, Roberts' destroyer picks up survivors from a torpedoed boat, including women and babies. Later Roberts engineers a plan to save the convoy from the Japanese, who are attacking by air and sea. He leads his ship against the enemy battleship and when he is injured, Masterman carries out his military strategies successfully. Rear Admiral Thomas is aboard the convoy flagship and congratulates the men on their success, with everyone scheduled to undertake further wartime missions.

Good looking Robert Taylor (who replaced British Robert Donat in the lead role) is very cardboard-like in his performance and Charles Laughton is too unrestrained as the crusty old admiral. However, the much-underrated Brian Donlevy is vigorous as the self-made naval officer, and best of all is Walter Brennan as a civilian ship caretaker who is recruited as chief yeoman. As with most MGM productions, everything is polished, from the script to the props.

British release title: CARGO OF INNOCENTS.

THE STEEL BAYONET (United Artists, 1958) 84 mins.

Producer/director, Michael Carreras; screenplay, Howard Clewes; art director, Ted Marshall; music, Leonard Salzedo; music director, John Hollingsworth; camera, John Asher; editor, Bill Lenny.

Leo Genn (Major Gerrard); Kieron Moore (Captain Mead); Michael Medwin (Lieutenant Vernon); Robert Brown (Sergeant Major Gill); Michael Ripper (Private Middleditch); John Paul (Lieutenant Colonel Derry); Shay Gorman (Sergeant Gates); Tom Bowman (Sergeant Nicholls); Bernard Horsfall (Private Livingstone); John Watson (Corporal Bean); Arthur Lovegrove (Jarvis); Percy Herbert (Clark); Paddy Joyce (Ames); Jack Stewart (Wentworth); David Crowley (Harris); Barry Lowe (Ferguson); Michael Dear ("Tweedie"); Ian Whittaker (Wilson); Michael Balfour (Thomas); Raymond Francis (General); Anthony Warren (Wounded German); Rolf Carston (German Non-Commissioned Officer); Gerard Green (German Company Commander); Wolf Frees (German Staff Officer); Jeremy Longhurst (German Sniper); David Ritch (Mahomet); Abdul Noor (Arab); Victor Platt (Sentry); John Trevor (Captain).

British-based Hammer Films would have far more success with its horror film series than with such lower-case productions as THE STEEL BAYONET, turned out for United Artists release.

In 1943 Tunis the battle-worn Company C, headed by Major Gerrard (Leo Genn), attempts to hold an abandoned farmhouse against enemy attack from Rommel's Afrika Korps. The British receive five new recruits headed by the belligerent Lieutenant Vernon (Michael Medwin). When the Germans call up tank support, the cause is lost. The farm is overrun and only Lieutenant Vernon escapes.

Variety categorized it as "earnest, but inept," and blamed producer/director Michael Carreras, ". . . who has not been able to extract much out of the tight-lipped, loose-drawn characters. . . ."

THE STEEL CLAW (Warner Bros., 1961) Color 96 mins.

Producer/director, George Montgomery; screenplay, Montgomery, Ferde Grofe, Jr., Malvin Wald; music/music director, Harry Zimmerman; camera, Manuel Rojas; editor, Jack Murray.

George Montgomery (Captain John Larsen); Charito Luna (Lolita); Mario Barri (Santana); Paul Sorensen (Frank Powers); Amelia De La Rama (Christina); Carmen Austin (Rosa); Ben Perez (Dolph Rodriguez); John MacGloan (Commander); Joe Sison (Himself); Pedro Faustino (Father); Oscar Keesee, Jr. (Child); Al Wyatt (Sergeant).

Filmmaker George Montgomery, who at one time or another has been a Twentieth Century-Fox leading man, married to Dinah

Shore, and designed furniture, spent much of the 1960s creating action films in the Philippines. Because of a drunken accident, Marine Captain John Larsen (George Montgomery) loses his right hand. He is to be discharged from the service, but instead manages to join a rescue party sent to locate a Marine general the Japanese are holding for ransom. When the mission is halted by enemy attack, Larsen undertakes the trek himself, now joined by Filipino guerrillas who want the ransom money. Larsen creates a steel hook to substitute for his missing hand. The rescue attempt is successful, but on the trip back to safety Larsen discovers that the real general has died and the man he has saved is Frank Powers (Paul Sorensen), a cowardly sergeant who took the deceased's identity hoping to get better treatment from the enemy. Later, in a Japanese raid, Powers dies. The survivors disguise themselves as members of a sea-going funeral party and reach a naval rescue vessel. Larsen and the wounded native Lolita (Charito Luna), his lover, get aboard while the guerrillas return ashore to continue fighting the Japanese.

The final verdict on this effort: contrived, clichéd, and cheaply-produced.

THE STEEL HELMET (Lippert, 1951) 84 mins.

Executive producer, Robert Lippert; producer, Samuel Fuller; associate producer, William Berke; director/screenplay, Fuller; art director, Theobald Holsopple; set decorator, Clarence Steenson; costumes, Alfred Berke; makeup, George Bruce; music, Paul Dunlap; assistant director, John F. Murphy; sound, William Lynch; special effects, Ben Southland, Ray Mercer; camera, Ernest W. Miller; editor, Philip Cahn.

Gene Evans (Sergeant Zack); Robert Hutton (Private "Conchie" Bronte); Richard Loo (Sergeant "Buddhahead" Tanaka); Steve Brodie (Lieutenant Driscoll); James Edwards (Corporal "Medic" Thompson); Sid Melton (Joe, the G.I.); Richard Monahan (Private Baldy); William Chun ("Short Round"); Harold Fong (The Red, a North Korean Major); Neyle Morrow (GI); Lynn Stallmaster (Second Lieutenant).

Controversial filmmaker Samuel Fuller (born: 1911 in Worcester, Massachusetts) served in World War II with the 1st Infantry Division (in North Africa and Europe), winning the Bronze Star, the Silver Star, and the Purple Heart. His harrowing real-life experiences provided the grist for several well-regarded war films, including two released in 1951: FIXED BAYONETS, q.v., and the earlier THE STEEL HELMET. Both dealt with an innovative subject for Hollywood, the still-being-fought Korean War. THE STEEL HELMET was filmed in two weeks for less than $175,000.* Like FIXED BAYONETS, released far later in 1951, Fuller's panorama of men in war is raw, gritty, and uncompromisingly realistic. His depiction has none of the glamor of a Tyrone Power in CRASH DIVE (1943), q.v., or an Errol Flynn in OBJECTIVE, BURMA! (1945), q.v., but shows the grime of the ordinary infantryman. Nevertheless, Fuller's viewpoint is to treat such men heroically. His movies are a celebration of the dogfaces in battle.

The film opens in the battle zone of South Korea with the by now famous shot of a steel helmet. Soon the rough, ready, and resourceful Sergeant Zack (Gene Evans) pops into view. He alone has survived the machine-gunning of bound American prisoners by the Chinese Communists. His hands are untied by an American slang-speaking Korean boy whom the sergeant names "Short Round"** (William Chun). He would prefer to be rid of the boy, but the youth insists on tagging along with the wounded man. On the way back to his lines, they meet a black medic (James Edwards), the sole survivor of another unit, who joins with them. Before long they cross paths with a green infantry platoon. It includes a conscientious objector (Robert Hutton) from World War II, who had a change of heart when the Korean War came along, and a Nisei veteran (Richard Loo) of World War II. The disparate group sets up an observation outpost in a Buddhist temple where they hold a captured North Korean major (Harold Fong). The English-speaking major attempts to play each of his captors against the others, trying to ally either the minorities or the racist others with him. Later, a sniper kills "Short Round" and the gruff Zack, who had become very attached to the youth, shoots his unarmed prisoner in anger. The North Korean troops advance, attempting to overrun the temple. As suddenly as it started, the confrontation ends. A new GI squad arrives and finds only Zack, the medic, the Nisei and a fourth alive. "What kind of an outfit is this?" the newcomer asks. "U.S. infantry," Zack shoots back. The film ends with a closing title card: "There is no end to this story."

---

*Working on a very restricted budget and a quick shooting schedule, Fuller confined most of his action to the one set (the Buddha temple), and to give his soundstage-bound production atmosphere he shrouded the outside in fog and mist. Fuller used combat footage to depict artillery barrages.

**Steven Spielberg in INDIANA JONES AND THE TEMPLE OF DOOM (1984) would name the hero's faithful little friend "Short Round."

THE STEEL HELMET is peopled with soldiers trying to survive in the midst of war. There is Lieutenant Driscoll (Steve Brodie), who did everything he could previously to stay out of combat. For cigar-chomping Zack, his protection is an icy-cold exterior which allows no human warmth to escape, except momentarily for "Short Round." This is a war where it is difficult to tell friend from foe. When asked how to separate a North from a South Korean, Zack explains, "If he is running with you, he's a South Korean. If he's running after you, he's a North Korean." The men's sense of being is always in confusion; they always seem to be going in circles. One admits, "That's how it is all the time. No one knows where we are but the enemy." And, most importantly, the individual human life is depicted as having no value in war. As Zack views it, ". . . A dead man is a dead man, and nobody cares." In short, man must be a machine in war to survive; when he uses his emotions he will end up dead. (E.g., when a G.I. insists upon removing a dead soldier's dogtag he is killed by the booby-trapped body.)

THE STEEL HELMET is filled with symbolism (the oversized Buddha statue) and packed with representative minorities. When asked why he is now fighting in the Korean War, the one-time conscientious objector explains, "If a man lives in a house that's endangered and wants to keep on living in it, he fights to defend it." The Nisei is quick to identify his heritage: "I'm not a dirty Jap rat. I'm an American." The black medic (who today would be called an "Uncle Tom") is ready to accept that integration in America will not happen overnight. And in its own bid for propaganda, the dying North Korean officer has a change of heart, renouncing Communism and embracing his ancestral heritage of Buddhism.

One of the growing themes in this and other motion pictures about the Korean War is G.I.s grumbling about being called back into service so soon after the end of World War II. If there were good reasons to fight in the last war, these "grunts" cannot fathom what the reasons are for this United Nations police action in South Korea and why the United States must supply the "policemen."

Although released by a non-major studio (Lippert Pictures), THE STEEL HELMET did not go unnoticed. "It pinpoints the Korean fighting in a grim, hardhitting tale that is excellently told. . . . Timely exploitation values are supplied in a story that makes no bid for obvious sensationalism, yet has it" (*Variety*). ". . . THE STEEL HELMET has some surprisingly good points. . . . [Fuller] has sidestepped the romantic war clichés and has taken a distinctly melancholy and dismal view of the business at hand . . ." (Bosley Crowther, *New York Times*).

THE STORY OF DR. WASSELL (Paramount, 1944) Color 140 mins.

Producer, Cecil B. DeMille; associate producer, Sidney Biddell; director, DeMille; based on the story by Dr. Corydon M. Wassell and the story by James Hilton; screenplay, Alan LeMay, Charles Bennett, Hilton; art directors, Hans Dreier, Roland Anderson; set decorator, George Sawley; costumes, Natalie Visart; music, Victor Young; assistant directors, Eddie Salven, Oscar Rudolph; second unit director, Arthur Rosson; Technicolor consultants, Natalie Kalmus, William Snyder; technical consultant, Commander Corydon M. Wassell; technical supervisor, Captain Fred F. Ellis (B.M.M.); sound, Hugo Grenzbach; special effects, Farciot Edouart, W. Wallace Kelley, Gordon Jennings; camera, Victor Milner; editor, Anne Bauchens.

Gary Cooper (Dr. Corydon M. Wassell); Laraine Day (Madeleine Day); Signe Hasso (Bettina); Carol Thurston (Tremartini); Dennis O'Keefe (Benjamin "Hoppy" Hopkins); Carl Esmond (Lieutenant Dirk Van Daal); Stanley Ridges (Commander William B. Goggins); Renny McElvoy (Joe Leinwerber); Elliott Reid (William Anderson); Melvin Francis (Himself); Joel Allen (Robert Kraus); Paul Kelly (Murdock); Oliver Thorndike (Alabam); James Milican (Robert Elroy Whaley); Mike Kilian (Thomas Borghetti); Philip Ahn (Ping); Doodles Weaver (Harold Hunter); Barbara Britton (Ruth); Ludwig Donath (Dr. Vranken); Richard Loo (Dr. Wei); Davison Clark (Dr. Holmes); Si Jenks (The *Arkansas* Mailman); Morton Lowry (Lieutenant Bainbridge); Richard Nugent (Captain Carruthers); Lester Matthews (Dr. Wayne); Victor Varconi (Captain Ryk); George Macready (Captain Blaen); Edward Fielding (Admiral Hart); Harvey Stephens (Captain in Charge of Evacuation); Frank Wilcox (Captain's Aide for Evacuation); Minor Watson (Australian Rear Admiral); Edmund MacDonald (Rear Admiral's Aide); William Severn (Little English Boy); Edith Barrett (Mother of Little English Boy); Catherine Craig (Mrs. Wayne); Frank Puglia (Javanese Temple Guide); Irving Bacon (Missionary); Ottola Nesmith (Missionary's Wife); Sybil Merritt, Yvonne De Carlo (Javanese Girls); Maria Loreedo (Fat Javanese Girl); Loretta Luiz (Pretty Javanese Girl); Luke Chan (Chinese Coolie, the Boatman); Oie Chan (Chinese Coolie's Wife); Yu Feng Sung (Chinese Priest); Moy Ming (Chinese Tea Vendor); Hugh Beaumont (Admiral Hart's Aide); Roy Gordon (Commander, U.S. Navy); Ferdinand Schumann (Ensign Watch Officer, U.S. Navy); Charles Trowbridge, Gus Glassmire (Captains, U.S. Navy—Surabaya); Edward Earle, Allan Ray (Officer, U.S. Navy—Surabaya); Anthony Caruso (Pharmacist's Mate); Sven Hugo Borg

(Dutch Guard); Frank Lackteen (Javanese Conductor); Fred Kohler, Jr. (Bosun's Mate during Evacuation); Jack Luden (Captain Carruther's Driver); George Eldredge (Damage Control Officer, U.S. Navy); Forbes Murray (Captain, U.S. Navy—Australia); Mary Currier (English Woman); John Mylong (Joyful Passenger); Ann Doran (Praying Woman); Stanley Price (Sobbing Man); Carla Boehm, Marion de Sydow, Maxine Fife, Ameda Lambert, Phyllis Perry (Women Evacuees); Gloria Dea, Forrest Dickson, Geraldine Fisette (Javanese Nurses); Eric Alden, Richard Barrett, John Benson, Carlyle Blackwell, John Bogden, George Bronson, Edgar Caldwell, Tony Cirillo, James Cornell, James Courtney, Clint Dorrington, Reynold DuPont, Edward Howard, Henry Kraft, Buddy Messinger, Robert Wilbur (U.S. Sailors); Jack Norton (Passenger along Companionway); Mike Lally (Civilian); Sam Flint, Milton Kibbee, Frances Morris, Hazel Keener, Cecil Weston (Passengers—Janssens); Frank Elliott (English Doctor); Joe Dominguez, Roque Espiritu, Rodric Redwing (Javanese Orderlies); Russ Clark (Chief Petty Officer—Marblehead); Julia Faye (Anne, the Dutch Nurse); Sarah Edwards, Ron Randell (Passengers); and: Griff Barnett, Lane Chandler, Isabel Cooper, Douglas Fowley, Isabel Lamal, Elmo Lincoln, Miles Mander.

"It actually happened—that is the point! Even with the elaborate trimmings of a Cecil DeMille production, we never lose sight of the fact that the heroics are real. It is this particular point that gives heart and stability to a picture that, at times, seems almost too ornate for the saga of a great doctor who refused to abandon fifteen desperately injured seamen of Uncle Sam's Navy and literally went through hell to bring them back home" (Louella O. Parsons, *Los Angeles Examiner*).

Dr. Corydon M. Wassell (Gary Cooper) from Arkansas becomes a medical missionary in China where he meets a young nurse (Laraine Day). Although they are in love, fate and the changing political climate pull them apart. When World War II is declared, Wassell joins the U.S. Navy and is sent to Java, where he is placed in charge of evacuating marines injured in the battle of Macassar. When the Japanese bomb Java, Wassell insures that the wounded are evacuated. He remains behind with the most seriously injured, whom he takes through the jungle, helped by British and Dutch soldiers on the islands. When they reach Australia he is proclaimed a hero.

Producer/director Cecil B. DeMille was among the many who heard President Franklin D. Roosevelt's fireside chat in 1942 when he described the courageous sixty-year-old Dr. Wassell. DeMille decided to film the story and, utilizing interviews with the real-life

Wassell, he and his scripting team (including James Hilton) put together this elaborate retelling which includes Javanese dancing girls (including Yvonne De Carlo), two leading ladies (Laraine Day and Signe Hasso), and every wartime cliché DeMille could insert into this 140-minute color drama which did not see release until mid-1944, coincidentally opening on D-Day, the 6th of June. Wassell's salary was donated to the Navy Relief Fund. Melvin Francis, one of the men who lived through the evacuation, played himself in the film. Mexican locations served for most of the jungle sequences.

As was true with most DeMille extravaganzas, the critics* hated the film and the public flocked to it. THE STORY OF DR. WASSELL was Oscar-nominated for its photographic and sound Special Effects.

THE STORY OF G.I. JOE (United Artists, 1945) 109 mins.

Producer, Lester Cowan; associate producer, David Hall; director, William A. Wellman; based on the books *Here Is Your War* and *Brave Men* by Ernie Pyle; screenplay, Leopold Atlas, Guy Endore, Philip Stevenson; art directors, James Sullivan, David Hall; set decorator, Edward G. Boyle; music, Ann Ronell, Louise Applebaum; song, Jack Lawrence and Ronell; music director, Louis Forbes; technical advisers: Lieutenant Colonel Roy A. Murray, Jr., Lieutenant Colonel Edward H. Coffey, Lieutenant Colonel Robert Miller, Major Walter Nye, Captain Milton M. Thornton, Captain Charles Shunstrom; sound, Frank McWhorter; camera, Russell Metty; supervising editor, Otho Lovering; editor, Albrecht Joseph.

Burgess Meredith (Ernie Pyle); Robert Mitchum (Lieutenant Walker); Freddie Steele (Sergeant Warnicki); Wally Cassell (Private Dondaro); Jimmy Lloyd (Private Spencer); Jack Reilly (Private Murphy); Bill Murphy (Private Mew); William Self (Cookie Henderson); Dick Rich (Sergeant at Showers); Billy Benedict (Whitey); Tito Renaldo (Lopez); Michael Browne (Sergeant); Yolanda Lacca

---

*"[THE STORY OF DR. WASSELL] whips the story, in every foot, into a nacreous foam of lies whose speciousness is only the more painful because Mr. DeMille is so obviously free from any desire to alter the truth except for what he considers to be its own advantage. All the more touching, and terrifying, is the fact that Dr. Wassell himself thinks that the picture, with a few trifling exceptions, is true and good" (James Agee, *The Nation* magazine). ". . . It is blood, sweat and tears built up to spectacle in the familiar De Mille 'epic' style. . . . De Mille has screened a fiction which is as garish as the spires of Hollywood. He has telescoped fact with wildest fancy in the most flamboyantly melodramatic way. And he has messed up a simple human story with the cheapest kind of comedy and romance" (Bosley Crowther, *New York Times*).

(Amelia); Dorothy Coonan (Nurse); Hal Boyle, Chris Cunningham, Sergeant Jack Foisie, Lucien Hubbard, George Lait, Robert Landry, Robert Reuben, Clete Roberts, Don Whitehead (Themselves—War Correspondents).

Perhaps the best of all World War II combat films is the unpretentious THE STORY OF G.I. JOE. General Dwight D. Eisenhower termed it "the greatest war picture I've ever seen." It was directed by William A. Wellman, the man responsible for the Academy Award-winning WINGS (1927), q.v., who would go on to create BATTLEGROUND (1949), q.v.

This intimate study of muddied foot soldiers on the front lines facing "their baptism of fire" has the same qualities of integrity and simplicity that made war correspondent Ernie Pyle's (1900-1945) writings so popular during the war. He wrote about the common man—full of foibles—in commonplace situations, not about famous generals in big battles. Pyle reported about men fighting fear and fatigue and enduring combat not for the glory of it, but because it is a job that must be done. The flavor of Pyle's writing director Wellman translated to the screen in his own clearcut style in which scenes, as in life, end abruptly, and actions are not always tied together.

The semi-documentary film opens in Africa as novice war correspondent Ernie Pyle (Burgess Meredith) comes upon the green members of Company C of the 18th Infantry, about to head off for the Faid Pass in the desert. He joins the Americans headed by Lieutenant Walker (Robert Mitchum) and follows them as they fight in 1943 through Sicily into Italy and on to Rome in June 1944. The squadron participates in the controversial bombing of the monastery at Monte Cassino and the pitched combat with the Germans. By the time the surviving members are marching on to Rome, Walker—now a captain— has died and tough Sergeant Warnicki (Freddie Steele) has cracked under the strain. The film ends with Ernie Pyle's voiceover, "This is our war. We will carry it with us from one battleground to another. In the end we will win. I hope we can rejoice in our victory. . . . As for those beneath the wooden crosses we can only murmur, 'Thanks, pal, thanks.' "

There is no plot as such in this stark and grim motion picture. The viewer sees this slice of everyday war through the eyes and ears of unobtrusive Ernie Pyle. His point of view and offscreen commentary provide our perception of the doughboys as they fade in and out of sight, some never to be seen again, for they have died. Nothing is told in grand strokes, not even the unrelenting combat which often occurs among village ruins or mud-filled roadways. Then the camera pushes on, hopping from building to building as the soldiers proceed street by street against the enemy, always felt but rarely seen. The men fight, wish, grumble, die, and are silently replaced. They rejoice over a mascot dog named A-rab and later celebrate a bleak, cold Christmas in the war-torn valley near Cassino. They see the irony of using a bombed-out church as a battleground. Sergeant Warnicki spends most of the war trying to find a phonograph player so that he can hear a recording of his new-born son, and later falls victim to battle fatigue; sex-starved Private Dondaro (Wally Cassell) is always pursuing "les femmes" or digging latrines; Private "Wingless" Murphy (Jack Reilly) complains about being too tall to be a pilot and is killed shortly after his wedding to an army nurse. And most central of all there is the restrained, stoic Lieutenant Walker who grows in stature as he becomes the experienced front-line soldier who is made a captain. It is he who says, "If only we could create something good out of all this energy, all these men." He is the laconic soul who protects his men as best he can and who has the painful duty of writing their kin when they fall in action. When the strong and capable Walker dies of unknown causes and his body is brought down unceremoniously on a donkey's back, the shocked men bid their farewells and march on to Rome.

Although THE STORY OF G.I. JOE did not premiere until after the end of World War II, it still had great relevancy and power. The *New York Times'* Thomas M. Pryor praised it as a "hard-hitting, penetrating drama" that is "truly inspired" and "humorous, poignant and tragic, an earnestly human reflection of a stern life and the dignity of man." James Agee (*The Nation* magazine) lauded, "William Wellman and the others who are responsible for STORY OF G.I. JOE obviously did not regard their job as an ordinary one. They undertook a great subject. It is clear that they undertook it in a determination to handle it honestly and to make a masterpiece. A wonderful amount of their achievement measures up to their intention. . . . Many things in the film itself move me to tears. . . ."

THE STORY OF G.I. JOE was Oscar-nominated for Best Supporting Actor (Robert Mitchum), Screenplay, Song, and Scoring. Pulitzer Prize-winning Ernie Pyle selected Burgess Meredith to play him in this film. Pyle lived only to see the film's rough cut, for by the time the picture was ready for distribution he had returned to covering the action in the Pacific. He was killed by a Japanese machine gunner on Ie Shima (off Okinawa) on April 18, 1945. Several other experienced war correspondents were used as technical advisers as well as appearing in the film and later promoting the project to the public. A hundred and fifty veterans of the Italian warfront were cast as extras in the film; they later went off to fight in the Pacific Theater. To flesh out the combat scenes with realism,

director Wellman utilized Signal Corps footage of the North African and Italian campaigns, especially John Huston's documentary THE BATTLE OF SAN PIETRO (1945). As Clayton R. Koppes and Gregory D. Black assess in *Hollywood Goes to War* (1987), "THE STORY OF G.I. JOE, which began as a salute to the common soldier, became also a tribute to the writer who understood them best."
A.k.a. WAR CORRESPONDENT, G.I. JOE.

SUBMARINE COMMAND (Paramount, 1951) 87 mins.

Producer, Joseph Sistrom; director, John Farrow; story/screenplay, Jonathan Latimer; art directors, Hal Pereira, Henry Bumstead; set decorators, Sam Comer, Ross Dowd; makeup, Wally Westmore; technical adviser, Rear Admiral T. M. Dykers (U.S. Navy, Retired); music, David Buttolph; assistant director, William Coleman; sound, Harry Lindgren, Gene Garvin; special camera effects, Gordon Jennings, Harry Barndollar; camera, Lionel Lindon; process camera, Farciot Edouart; editor, Eda Warren.

William Holden (Commander White); Nancy Olson (Carol White); William Bendix (C. P. Boyer); Don Taylor (Lieutenant Commander Peter Morris); Arthur Franz (Lieutenant Carlson); Darryl Hickman (Ensign Wheelwright); Peggy Webber (Mrs. Alice Rice); Moroni Olsen (Rear Admiral Joshua Rice); Jack Gregson (Commander Rice); Jack Kelly (Lieutenant Barton); Don Dunning (Quartermaster Perkins); Jerry Paris (Sergeant Gentry); Charles Meredith (Admiral Tobias); Philip Van Zandt (Gavin); Gordon Polk (Ralph); Walter Reed (Chief O'Flynn); Noel Neill (Mrs. Sue Carlson); John V. Close, Fred Zendar (Frogmen); George Wallace (Chief Herb Bixby); Richard Berggren (Clem); Harold Fong (Korean Officer); Jerry James (Man).

Within hours of the end of World War II, executive officer White (William Holden) makes a fateful decision. Japanese planes are attacking the USS *Tiger Shark* and White orders the submarine to submerge, even though it means the injured skipper and quartermaster on deck will drown. White is tormented by his action, especially when chief torpedoman C. P. Boyer (William Bendix) says he did the wrong thing. Years pass and White's marriage to Carol (Nancy Olson) is floundering. The Korean War breaks out and both the *Tiger Shark* and White are called back into service. In war maneuvers off the coast of Korea, White regains his self-respect. He also learns that Carol is expecting a baby.

Psychologically it was a tough job equating the Korean War with World War II; and it was even tougher fleshing out this moderate production with its contrived storyline. This was the fourth and final screen teaming of William Holden and Nancy Olson. It has been much reported that Holden and co-star Don Taylor spent much of the off-production time on SUBMARINE COMMAND as freewheeling drinking buddies getting into all sorts of mischief on and off the studio sets.

SUBMARINE RAIDER (Columbia, 1942) 65 mins.

Producer, Wallace MacDonald; director, Lew Landers; screenplay, Aubrey Wisberg; camera, Franz F. Planer; editor, William Lyon.

John Howard (Chris Warren); Marguerite Chapman (Sue Curry); Bruce Bennett (First Officer Russell); Warren Ashe (Bill Warren); Eileen O'Hearn (Vera Lane); Nino Pipitone (Captain Yamanada); Philip Ahn (First Officer Kawahami); Larry Parks (Sparksie); Rudy Robles (Steward Seffi); Roger Clark (Grant Duncan); Forrest Tucker (Pulaski); Eddie Laughton (Shannon); Stanley Brown (Levy); Jack Shay (Oleson); Gary Breckner (Brick Brandon).

Forrest Tucker, John Howard, Marguerite Chapman and Bruce Bennett in SUBMARINE RAIDER (1942).

This was one of those quickly-produced, cheap exploitation items which attempted to be topical and relevant, but ended up being mostly dated and comical. When the American yacht she is on is sunk by Japanese, Sue Curry (Marguerite Chapman) is rescued by a U.S. submarine commanded by Chris Warren (John Howard). Warren tries in vain to warn the base about the impending enemy attack. Later he engages a Japanese aircraft carrier in battle and with well-aimed torpedoes sinks the craft.

SUBMARINE SEAHAWK (American International, 1959) 83 mins.

Producer, Alex Gordon; director, Spencer Gordon Bennet; screenplay, Lou Rusoff, Owen Harris; music, Alexander Laszlo; camera, Gilbert Warrenton; editor, Ronald Sinclair.

John Bentley (Paul Turner); Brett Halsey (David Shore); Wayne Heffley (Dean Stoker); Steve Mitchell (Andy Flowers); Henry McCann (Ellis); Frank Gerstle (Captain Boardman); Paul Maxwell (Bill Hallohan); Jan Brooks (Ellen Turner); Mabel Rea (Maisie); Leon Tyler (Ed); Nicky Blair (Sam); Hal Bogart, Don Fenwick (Radio Operators); Frank Watkins (Sonar Operator); Marilyn Hanold (Nancy); Dolores Domasin (Waitress); Robin Priest (Medic); Frank Ray (Shore Patrol); Brian Wood (Courier); Alan Aric, Ted Fish, Howard Hampton, Scott Peters, Vince Williams (Sailors).

"SUBMARINE SEAHAWK is most effective when it sticks to the tension-building sequences of the sub stalking the enemy. . . . It's been done before, but it's still engrossing. The production weakens when it gets ashore or when it explores some of the human relationships of the crew-members" (*Variety*).

Novice commander Paul Turner (John Bentley) takes charge of the USS *Seahawk* during World War II. His sub is assigned to patrol duty in the Pacific. His crew is disgruntled when book-smart Turner refuses to attack the enemy, not understanding that he is waiting for bigger prey. Eventually he is redeemed with his men when they attack the Japanese fleet.

This low-budget entry, which utilized a great deal of stock footage, was paired in release with another AIP World War II-set quickie, PARATROOP COMMAND.

SUBMARINE X-1 (United Artists, 1969) Color 89 mins.

Executive producer, Irving Temaner; producer, John C. Champion; associate producer, Ted Lloyd; director, William Graham; story, Champion, Edmund H. North; screenplay, Donald S.

Advertisement for SUBMARINE X-1 (1969).

Sanford, Guy Elmes; art director, Bill Andrews; wardrobe, John Briggs; makeup, George Blackler; music, Ron Goodwin; assistant director, Anthony Waye; sound mixer, Cyril Swern; special effects, Bowie Films; camera, Paul Beeson; editor, John S. Smith.

James Caan (Lieutenant Commander John Bolton); Rupert Davies (Vice Admiral Redmayne); David Sumner (Lieutenant Davies); William Dysart (Lieutenant Gogan); Norman Bowler (Sub-Lieutenant Pennington); Brian Grellis (Chief Petty Officer Barquist); Paul Young (Leading Seaman Quentin); John Kellard (Sub-Lieutenant Willis); Kenneth Farrington (Chief Petty Officer Knowles); George Roubicek (Redmayne's Flag Officer); Keith Alexander (Sub-Lieutenant); Carl Rigg (Chief Petty Officer Kennedy); Nicholas Tate (Leading Seaman on X-1); Steve Kirby (Leading Seaman on X-2); Dennis Mayers (Sub-Lieutenant on X-1); Keith Alexander (Sub-Lieutenant on X-3); Diana Beevers (W.R.N.S. Officer); Paul Hansard (Commander Steiner); Hans De Vries (German Lieutenant); Richard Steele (Captain in Redmayne's Office); Desmond Jordan (Naval Doctor); George Pravda (Captain Erlich).

In 1943 Canadian commander John Bolton (James Caan) loses most of his crew and his submarine in an attack on the German warship *Lindendorf*. Bolton is cleared of any misconduct and is assigned a new mission by Vice Admiral Redmayne (Rupert Davies). He is ordered to train three four-man crews to use miniature submarines against the *Lindendorf*, which is making repairs in a Norwegian fjord. Before the enemy vessel is blown up, Bolton must (re)gain the respect of his crews and cope with the loss of more men.

This modest film was shot in 1967 but not released until 1969, and then on the bottom half of double-bill programs. It was lensed in Scotland (at Loch Ness) and at Boreham Wood Studios in London.

SUICIDE RUN *see*: TOO LATE THE HERO.

SUICIDE SQUADRON (Republic, 1942) 83 mins
Producer, William Sistrom; director, Brian Desmond Hurst; story/screenplay, Shaun Terence Young; art director, John Bryan; music, Richard Addinsell; music director, Muir Mathieson; camera, Georges Perinal; editor, Alan Jaggs.

Anton Walbrook (Stefan Radetzky); Sally Gray (Carole Peters); Derrick de Marney (Mike Carroll); Kenneth Kent (De Guise); Percy Parsons (Bill Peters); H. H. Roberts (Physician); Cecil Parker

(Specialist); Guy Middleton (Shorty); John Laurie (British Commander); Frederick Valk (Polish Commander).

Perhaps the best-remembered item of this British feature film is the "Warsaw Concerto"* composed by Richard Addinsell. "The film's emotive force as propaganda was deepened by the constant resort to music, the rich bravura combination of art and warfare playing the audience's dual response to the heroism and the culture of Poland" (Roger Manvell, *Films and the Second World War*, 1974).

Polish pianist Stefan Radetsky (Anton Walbrook) forsakes music for flight training when Poland is forced to fight the Nazis during World War II. He is among those who escape the overrun country and comes to the United States in 1938. There he plays concerts (for Polish relief organizations) and reaffirms his romance with American journalist Carole Peters (Sally Gray). They marry, and in 1940 he joins the Free Polish Squadron in England, much against her wishes. During the Battle of Britain his plane crashes and his nerves and musical skill fail him. Through the love of his returning wife, he becomes whole again.

This film was released originally in Great Britain by RKO Radio British as DANGEROUS MOONLIGHT with a 90-minute running time. *Variety* was quick to point up the film's technical flaws and virtues, "Sound is remarkably poor; ear has to strain the early footage. Photography of Georges Perinal captured exquisitely the pianissimo mood of soft-lighted interiors; air stuff is also tops from his department."

TARGET ZERO (Warner Bros., 1955) 92 mins.

Producer, David Weisbart; director, Harmon Jones; based on the story "Bug Out" by James Warner Bellah; screenplay, Sam Rolfe; art director, Leo K. Kuter; set decorator, G. W. Bernstsen; costumes, Moss Mabry; music, David Buttolph; camera, Edwin DuPar; editor, Clarence Kolster.

Richard Conte (Lieutenant Tom Flagler); Peggie Castle (Ann Galloway); Charles Bronson (Sergeant Vince Gaspari); Richard Stapley (Sergeant David Kensemmit); L. Q. Jones (Private Felix Zimbalist); Chuck Connors (Private Moose); John Alderson (Corporal Devon Enouch); Terence De Marney (Private Harry Fontenoy); John Dennis (Private First Class George); Angela Loo (Sue); Abel Fernandez (Private Geronimo); Richard Park (Private Ma Koo Sung); Don Oreck (Private Stacey Zorbados); Strother

---

*A recording by Louis Kentner and the London Symphony Orchestra, conducted by Muir Mathieson, became very popular at the time.

Martin (Dan O'Hirons); Aaron Spelling (Strangler); George Chan (Priest); Joby Baker (Soldier); Leo K. Kuter (Colonel); Hal Sheiner (Marine Officer).

With the Korean War already history, more filmmakers were turning to that international conflict as a background for war yarns. This one was a formula outing with the standard array of stereotypes. The modestly-conceived film was shot at the army base at Fort Carson, Colorado. Any seasoned filmgoer could tell by the lackluster ad campaign that Warner Bros. was stretching for copy to promote this unremarkable entry in the once again oversaturated war film cycle. "The Story of the Glory of the Fighting G.I.!. . . A Tight-Lipped Hero—a Red-Lipped Girl—and Only One Desperate Way Out!. . . . When a Thousand Guns Zeroed in on a Hell-Hill They Called 'Sullivan's Muscle'—and a 'Pick-Up Army' of Ten Proud Men Packed the Wallop that Blasted Them Out!. . . . ON TARGET! IT'S A BULLS-EYE IN SCREEN-BLASTING ENTERTAINMENT!"

Peggie Castle and Richard Conte in TARGET ZERO (1955).

Lieutenant Tom Flagler (Richard Conte) and his surviving patrol members are returning to safety, but when they reach the appointed ridge (known as "Sullivan's Muscle") they find the company has been decimated and only a single telephone line to the Command Post remains intact. Along the way career soldier Flagler and the others are joined by stranded United Nations biochemist Ann Galloway (Peggie Castle)—with whom he has a romance—and by a tank filled with three feisty Britishers, including Sergeant David Kensemmit (Richard Stapley) who hasn't much use for the Yankees. At the ridge the units hold off the enemy and develop an esprit de corps. Eventually the counter-attacking UN forces rescue them. And Ann lets Flagler know she is in love with him.

THEY WERE EXPENDABLE (Metro-Goldwyn-Mayer, 1945) 135 mins.*

Producer, John Ford; associate producer, Cliff Reid; directors, Ford, (uncredited) Robert Montgomery; based on the book by William L. White; screenplay, Frank W. Wead; art directors, Cedric Gibbons, Malcolm F. Brown; set decorators, Edwin B. Willis, Ralph S. Hurst; music, Herbert Stothart; song, Earl Brent and Stothart; assistant director, Edward O'Fearna; second unit director, James Havens; sound, Douglas Shearer; special sound effects, Michael Steinore; special camera effects, A. Arnold Gillespie, Donald Jahraus, R. A. MacDonald; camera, Joseph H. August; editors, Frank E. Hull, Douglass Biggs.

Robert Montgomery (Lieutenant John Brickley); John Wayne (Lieutenant [j.g.] "Rusty" Ryan); Donna Reed (Second Lieutenant Sandy Davyss); Jack Holt (General Martin); Ward Bond ("Boots" Mulcahey, Chief Bosun's Mate); Marshall Thompson (Ensign "Snake" Gardner); Paul Langton (Ensign Andy Andrews); Leon Ames (Major James Morton); Arthur Walsh (Seaman Jones, First Class); Donald Curtis (Lieutenant [j.g.] "Shorty" Long); Cameron Mitchell (Ensign George Cross); Jeff York (Ensign "Lefty" Tony Aiken); Murray Alper ("Slug" Mahan, T.M. First Class); Harry Tenbrook ("Cookie" Squarehead Larsen, Second Class); Jack Pennick ("Doc" the Storekeeper); Alex Havier (Benny Lacoco, Steward Third Class); Charles Trowbridge (Admiral Blackwell); Bruce Kellogg (Lieutenant Elder Tompkins, M.M. Second Class); Louis Jean Heydt (Captain Ohio Carter); Russell Simpson (Dad Knowland); Vernon Steele (Army Doctor at Corregidor); Trina Lowe (Gardner's Girl Friend); Bill Barnum, Dan Borzage, Larry Dods, Art Foster, Duke Green, Del Hill, Michael Kirby, Stubby

---

*Computer colorized version now available.

Kruger, Ted Lundigan, William Neff, Major Frank Pershing, Robert Shelby Randall, Joey Ray, Phil Schumacher (Boat Crew Members); Frank McGrath (Slim); Sammy Stein (Sammy); Blake Edwards (Gunner); Stephen Barclay, Franklin Parker, Ernest Seftig (Navy Officers); Robert Emmett O'Connor (Bartender at Silver Dollar); Leslie Sketchley (Marine Orderly); Philip Ahn (Army Orderly); Pacita Tod-Tod (Filipino Girl Singer); Robert Homans (Bartender at Manila Hotel); William B. Davidson (Hotel Manager); Jack Cheatham (Commander); Forbes Murray (Navy Captain); Emmett Vogan (Captain, Navy Doctor); Sherry Hall (Marine Major); Alan Bridge (Lieutenant Colonel); Jack Luden (Naval Air Captain); Jon Gilbreath (Submarine Commander); Marjorie Davies, Eve March (Nurses); George Bruggerman, James Carlisle, Tony Carson, Charles Calhoun, Bruce Carruthers, Gary Delmar, Frank Donahue, Karl Miller, Len Stanford, Reginald Simpson, Dutch Schlickenmeyer, Jack Lorenz, Brad Towne, Leonard Mellin, Dan Quigg, Clifford Ruthjen, Dick Karl, Jack Lee, Wedgewood Norwell, Dick Thorne, Leonard Fisher, John Roy, Michael Kostrick, Jimmy Magrill, George Magrill, Sam Simone, Paul Kruger, Jack Semple, Roy Thomas, Bob Thom, Larry Steers (Personnel in Admiral's Office); Betty Blythe, Jane Crowley, Almeda Fowler, Leota Lorraine, Eleanor Vogel (Officers' Wives); Charles Murray, Jr. (Jeep Driver); Margaret Morton (Bartender's Wife); George Economides, Michael Economides, Nino Pipitone, Jr., Roque Yberra, Jr. (Bartender's Children); Ralph Soncuya (Filipino Orderly); Vincent Isla (Filipino Schoolteacher); Max Ong (Mayor of Cebu); William Neff (Submarine Skipper); Jim Farley (Mate); Ernest Dominguez, Henry Mirelez (Filipino Boys); Lee Tung Fo (Bartender); Max Ong (Filipino); Tom Tyler (Captain of Airport); Bill Wilkerson (Sergeant Smith); John Carlyle (Lieutenant James); Mary Jane French (Lost Nurse); Patrick Davis (Pilot); Fred Beckner, Jack Carrington, Roger Cole, Bill Donahue, Frank Eldridge, Jon Eppers, Charles Ferguson, Bill Nind, Don Lewis, Kermit Maynard, Jack Ross, Brent Shugar, Robert Strong, Jack Trent, Russell Warner (Officers at Airport); William [Merrill] McCormick (Wounded Officer at Airport); Jack Mower (Officer).

William L. White's 1942 best-selling book *They Were Expendable* was based on the wartime heroics of U.S. Naval officer John Duncan Bulkeley who was the commander of Torpedo Boat Squadron 3, the initial Navy unit to engage the Japanese in the Philippines. It was Bulkeley who commanded PT 41 which evacuated General Douglas MacArthur and his family from Corregidor to Mindanao in 1942. Later, during D-Day operations at Normandy he headed Torpedo Boat Squadron 2. For his wartime services,

Bulkeley was awarded: the Congressional Medal of Honor, the Navy Cross, the Army Distinguished Service Cross, the Silver Star, the Legion of Merit, and the Purple Heart. The title of White's book derived from a young Naval Lieutenant telling him, "In a war, anything can be expendable—money or gasoline or equipment or, most usually, men."

To direct the film version of White's book, MGM and the U.S. Navy selected veteran moviemaker John Ford who had been in the U.S. Navy since the fall of 1941 and who, as a commander in its photographic unit, created such remarkable documentaries as the Oscar-winning THE BATTLE OF MIDWAY (1942) and DECEMBER SEVENTH (1943). Ford had personally met and become friendly with Bulkeley. When feisty Ford broke his leg a few weeks before completing this project, Robert Montgomery, who was starring as the screen counterpart of Bulkeley, took over as director. During World War II, MGM contract star Montgomery had served as, among other capacities, a PT boat commander (in Panama, at Gaudalcanal, and in the Marshall Islands) and later as an operations

Ward Bond, Robert Montgomery, and Donald Curtis in THEY WERE EX-PENDABLE (1945).

officer and lieutenant commander aboard a destroyer. As one of the first to enter the captured port of Cherbourg, he received a Bronze Star and later was given the French Legion of Honor for having been an ambulance driver with the American Field Services in France in 1940. John Wayne appears as the counterpart of Bulkeley's second-in-command, the real-life Lieutenant Robert Balling Kelly.

The film opens with a title card caption from director Ford, "I speak for the thousands of silent lips forever stilled among the jungles and in the deep waters of the Pacific which marked the way." Lieutenant John Brickley (Robert Montgomery) and Lieutenant (j.g.) "Rusty" Ryan (John Wayne) are in charge of a PT boat squadron in Manila Bay. The Navy regards these high-powered craft (which carry machine guns and torpedoes) as play toys. However, all that changes after the Japanese attack Pearl Harbor on December 7, 1941 and the value of these small boats becomes more apparent. Brickley saves his mini-fleet from destruction by moving it out into open waters and soon they are encountering the enemy on the high seas. In one such night-time engagement Ryan receives a hand wound which becomes badly infected and he is ordered to sick bay at Corregidor. Ryan is a difficult patient who bridles at hospital regimentation, especially that of army nurse 2nd Lieutenant Sandy Davyss (Donna Reed). However, the rambunctious Ryan and the dedicated Sandy soon fall in love, but they each have more important duties to handle and their romance must be put on hold for the duration.

The casualties are mounting and the medical unit is worn down tending these men who are part of the doomed holding action against the Japanese. Later Admiral Blackwell (Charles Trowbridge) informs Brickley, "Listen son. You and I are professionals. If the manager says 'Sacrifice,' we lay down a bunt, and let somebody else hit the home runs. Our job is to lay down that sacrifice. That's what we were trained for and that's what we'll do." Brickley understands the suicidal task at hand.

Combatting the Japanese on their desperate holding sorties is costly, and Brickley sees his crews and boats diminished by terrible losses. By now it is acknowledged that the Americans must retreat from Bataan and Corregidor, with the high-level officers removed by PT boats and later flown to Australia. Among those Brickley and Ryan's remaining PT boats carry to safety is General Douglas MacArthur (Robert Barrat) and his family. Once on Mindanao, General Martin (Jack Holt) employs the PT boats to combat Japanese supply ships. In an attack to torpedo an enemy cruiser, the men succeed but both Brickley and Ryan lose their PT boats. The two beached officers, along with two of their ensigns (Marshall

Thompson, Cameron Mitchell), are ordered to fly on to Australia and organize a new PT boat squadron. The remainder of their men, including the injured "Boots" Mulcahey (Ward Bond), remain behind to hold off the advancing enemy as best they can. Ryan would rather stay with the men to the hopeless finish, but Brickley reminds him that they have a greater duty to perform.

Although World War II was over by the time of its release in November 1945, THEY WERE EXPENDABLE was still considered a timely, patriotic salute. Even more, it was regarded as a major war picture which fully captured not only the prowess of the brave PT boat crews in perilous action, but demonstrated that in the chaos of defeat (the retreat from the Philippines) there could still be glory. A great deal of praise was given to Ford (and Montgomery) for creating such an eloquently vivid, slam-bang array of naval battle scenes with the tiny PT boats and their death-defying crews as the heroes. The highlight of the film is the proud General MacArthur leaving the Philippines but determined to return and defeat the enemy. For many viewers this near-mystical appearance of Mac-Arthur ranks as one of Hollywood's finest on-screen moments. As in all contemporary World War II films, the men are shown respectful of rank, a brotherhood of soldiers knowing their ultimate duty, and ready to sacrifice themselves willingly for the greater good. Through it all they maintain both a sense of humor and an iron will that would seem fictitious were not so much of it true. As Roger Manvell states in *Films and The Second World War* (1974), "No American film reflects more profoundly the age-old tradition of war than THEY WERE EXPENDABLE."

The critics were quick to endorse THEY WERE EXPENDA-BLE. "This is one of the fine war movies and a stirring reminder of American gallantry in the early days of disaster. . . . The acting is first-rate throughout, but the film is at its documentary best in action, whether the sea-going gadflies are nipping at a Kuma-class cruiser or, in the blackest day of the campaign, whisking General MacArthur to his historic rendezvous off Mindanao . . ." (*Newsweek* magazine). Perhaps Bosley Crowther summed it best in his *New York Times* column when he selected this film as one of the ten best of the year: "An exciting and nostalgic story of Navy men who fought the tiny PT-boats in the rear-guard action around the Philippines in the first months of the war. Played stoutly and with plenty of rugged sentiment by Robert Montgomery, John Wayne, Ward Bond, Donna Reed and a solid cast."

THEY WERE EXPENDABLE was Academy Award-nominated for Sound and Special Effects.

THEY WERE NOT DIVIDED (United Artists/Rank Film Distributor, 1951) 91 mins.

Producer, Herbert Smith; director/screenplay, Terence Young; music, Lambert Williamson; music director, Muir Mathieson; sound, W. H. Liudop, G. I. McCallum; camera, Harry Waxman; editors, Ralph Kemplen, Vera Campbell.

Edward Underdown (Philip); Ralph Clanton (David); Helen Cherry (Wilhelmina); Stella Andrews (Jane); Michael Brennan (Smoke O'Connor); Michael Trubshawe (Major Bushy Noble); John Wynn (45 Jones); Desmond Llewellyn (77 Jones); Rufus Cruickshank (Sergeant Dean); Estelle Brody (Correspondent); Christopher Lee (Lewis); R.S.M. Brittain (Regimental Sergeant Major); and: Robert Ayres, Peter Burton, Anthony Dawson, Rupert Gerard, Ian Murray, Charles Perry.

A miniature history of World War II from Dunkirk to the battle at Ardennes as seen through the eyes of Englishman Philip (Edward Underdown), American David (Ralph Clanton) and an Irishman named Smoke O'Connor (Michael Brennan): all are members of the British Armoured Guard. David marries an English girl (Stella Andrews) while on one of his leaves and later in the climactic battle is wounded by a mortar shell. His long-standing buddy Philip stays by his side and they die together. As David Quinlan determined in *British Sound Films* (1984), "Rambling but popular film with good battle scenes and a sense of comradeship." *Variety* pointed out, "At almost every corner, the British troops seem to catch up with the Americans, and this ingenuous approach is too blatantly designed to make the film more palatable to U.S. tastes."

THEY WERE NOT DIVIDED was released originally in Great Britain by General Film Distributors in 1950 with a 102-minute running time.

THEY WHO DARE (British Lion, 1954) Color 100 mins.

Producers, Maxwell Setton, Aubrey Baring; director, Lewis Milestone; screenplay, Robert Westerby; art director, Don Ashton; music, Robert Gill; camera, Wilkie Cooper; editor, V. Sagovsky.

Dirk Bogarde (Lieutenant Graham); Denholm Elliott (Sergeant Corcoran); Akim Tamiroff (Captain George One); Gerard Oury (Captain George Two); Eric Pohlmann (Captain Papadopoulos); Alec Mango (Patroklis); Kay Callard (Nightclub Singer); Russell Enoch [William Russell] (Lieutenant Poole); Lisa Gastoni (George Two's Girl Friend); Sam Kydd (Marine Boyd); Peter Burton (Marine Barrett); David Peel (Sergeant Evans); Michael Mellinger (Toplis); Anthea Leigh (Marika); Eileen Way (Greek Woman).

The British Eighth Army is launching its attack at El Alamein in North Africa during World War II. If the offensive is to succeed, a nagging squadron of German aircrafts must be put out of commission. A commando unit of ten, headed by Lieutenant Graham (Dirk Bogarde), is assigned to blow up two airbases on the island of Rhodes. The overland raid is successful, but a tactical error on Graham's part leads to the capture of most of his unit. Only he and Sergeant Corcoran (Denholm Elliott) make it safely to an awaiting submarine.

For American director Lewis Milestone, who had created several classic war films, this off-the-cuff, claptrap production was an unhappy experience. Dirk Bogarde claimed that most of the picture was filmed without a usable script, and said, "I wouldn't want to work that way again. But I trusted Milestone." The London *Sunday Dispatch* would report of this film, "Dirk Bogarde spends most of his time apologizing to his crew for the mistakes he makes. Nobody apologized for the script."

THEY WHO DARE was released originally in Great Britain in 1953 by British Lion with a 107-minute running time.

THE THIN RED LINE (Allied Artists, 1964) 99 mins.

Executive producers, Lester A. Sansom, Bernard Glasser; producer, Sidney Harmon; director, Andrew Marton; based on the novel by James Jones; art director, Jose Alguero; wardrobe, Charles Simminger; makeup, Emilio Puyol; music/music conductor, Malcolm Arnold; assistant director, Jose Maria Ochoa; sound, Ronald Brown, Maurice Askew; sound editor, Kurt Hernfeld; special effects, Ron Ballanger, Pat Carr; camera, Manuel Berenguer; editor, Derek Parsons.

Keir Dullea (Private Doll); Jack Warden (First Sergeant Welsh); James Philbrook (Colonel Tall); Ray Daley (Captain Stone); Bob Kanter (Fife); Merlyn Yordan (Judy Doll); Kieron Moore (Lieutenant Band); Jim Gillen (Captain Gaff); Steve Rowland (Private Mazzi); Stephen Levy (Staff Sergeant Stack); Mark Johnson (Medic); and: Bill Barrett, Bill Christmas, John Clarke, Joe Collins, Harold Core, Francis Deale, Thomas Entwhistle, Evaristo Falco, Thomas Freeman, Jack Gaskins, Howard Hagen, Edward King, Frank Koomen, Gonzalo Largo, Gary Lasdun, Ted Macauley, Stan Nelson, Jeffrey O'Kelly, Solomon Silva, Charles Stalnaker, Russ Stoddard, Graham Sumner, Ben Tatar.

Having examined the manner and attitudes of American soldiers as the U.S. entered World War II (in *From Here to Eternity*) and how a returning GI reacts to civilian life (in *Some Came Running*), James Jones turned to combat blood lust in *The Thin Red*

Jack Warden and Keir Dullea in THE THIN RED LINE (1964).

Line (1962), which became as a film a complex, but poorly received, psychological study. "In its attempt at deeper insight into the mental and emotional stresses that govern men's behavior at the front . . . [THE THIN RED LINE] lacks the necessary motivational clarity and dramatic eloquence to attract the attention of the more discerning picturegoer" (*Variety*).

Young Private Doll (Keir Dullea) is among those marines disembarking at Guadalcanal in 1942. Bent on surviving, he steals a pistol to insure his safety. Almost immediately this intense youth is at odds with free-wheeling First Sergeant Welsh (Jack Warden), a battle-worn veteran who ruthlessly pushes his men onward. Already his immediate enemy, Welsh is there to scoff when Doll must cope with his feelings at killing his first enemy. By the next day, filled with new resolve, Doll wipes out an enemy machine-gun post. Welsh refuses to acknowledge the newcomer's bravery, labeling it the act of a man who kills for pleasure. Their mutual antagonism continues, even when they are a combat team. Soon only a small group from the unit survives and they must capture a cliffside, all the time worrying about the Japanese hidden in the many caves there. Doll scales the cliff and the others follow. At the crucial moment, Welsh throws himself in front of the private to shield him from Japanese gunfire. Welsh dies in Doll's arms and the fighting continues.

James Jones was among several writers-to-be who served in the taking of Guadalcanal. Others include: William Manchester, James Michener, and Leon Uris.

THIRTY SECONDS OVER TOKYO (Metro-Goldwyn-Mayer, 1944) 138 mins.

Producer, Sam Zimbalist; director, Mervyn LeRoy; based on the book by Captain Ted W. Lawson, Robert Considine; screenplay, Dalton Trumbo; art directors, Cedric Gibbons, Paul Groesse; set decorators, Edwin B. Willis, Ralph S. Hurst; music, Herbert Stothart; songs: Art Fitch, Kay Fitch and Bert Lowe; Dorothy Terris, Paul Whiteman, and Ferde Grofe; assistant director, Wally Worsley; technical advisers, Lawson, Major Dean Davenport; sound, Douglas Shearer, John F. Dullam; special camera effects, A. Arnold Gillespie, Warren Newcombe, Donald Jahraus; camera, Harold Rosson, Robert Surtees; editor, Frank Sullivan.

Spencer Tracy (Lieutenant Colonel James H. Doolittle); Van Johnson (Captain Ted W. Lawson); Robert Walker (David Thatcher); Phyllis Thaxter (Ellen Jones Lawson); Tim Murdock (Dean Davenport); Scott McKay (Davey Jones); Gordon McDonald (Bob Clever); Don DeFore (Charles McClure); Robert Mitchum (Bob Gray); John R. Reilly (Shorty Manch); Horace [Stephen] McNally (Doc White); Donald Curtis (Lieutenant Randall); Louis Jean Heydt (Lieutenant Miller); William Phillips (Don Smith); Douglas Cowan (Brick Holstrom); Paul Langton (Captain Ski York); Leon Ames (Lieutenant Jurika); Moroni Olsen (General); Benson Fong (Young Chung); Dr. Hsin Kung Chuan Chi (Old Chung); Hazel Brooks, Myrna Dell, Peggy Maley, Elaine Shepard, Kay Williams (Girls in Officers' Club); Dorothy Ruth Morris (Jane); Ann Shoemaker (Mrs. Parker); Alan Napier (Mr. Parker); Wah Lee (Foo Ling); Ching Wah Lee (Guerrilla Charlie); Jacqueline White (Emmy York); Jack McClendon (Dick Joyce); John Kellogg (Pilot); Peter Varney (Spike Henderson); Steve Brodie (Military Policeman); Morris Ankrum (Captain Halsey); Selena Royle (Mrs. Jones); Harry Hayden (Judge); Blake Edwards (Second Officer); Will Walls (Hoss Wyler); Jay Norris (Hallmark); Robert Bice (Jig White); Bill Williams (Bud Felton); Wally Cassell (Sailor).

On April 18, 1942 U.S. Army Air Force Lieutenant Colonel James H. Doolittle led a daring attack of sixteen B-25 bombers on Tokyo and other Japanese industrial cities. It was launched from the aircraft carrier USS *Hornet*, a new procedure for that time. Because they were spotted by the enemy, the squadron left ahead of schedule, causing repercussions at the tail end of the top secret mission. Having dropped their bombs, the planes flew on to China where most of the craft ran out of fuel and crash-landed in Japanese-held territory. Three of the eight flyers captured were executed in October 1942; the others were given life prison sentences. Captain Ted W. Lawson, one of the escaping pilots, wrote a best-seller (with Robert Considine) in 1943 detailing the raid. He was the flyer who named his plane Ruptured Duck and it carried the insignia of Donald Duck on crutches. Because of injuries suffered when his plane crashed, his legs were amputated. The blow-by-blow account of this morale-boosting raid served as the basis for THIRTY SECONDS OVER TOKYO.*

Captain Ted W. Lawson (Van Johnson) learns he is to join in the surprise attack on Japan in retaliation for the Japanese raid on Pearl Harbor. Lieutenant Colonel James H. Doolittle (Spencer Tracy) visits the flyers and explains their dangerous task. He requests that any man who feels he does not wish to risk his life in so perilous an objective drop out without fear of ridicule. None do. He tells the men, "This is going to be the toughest training you have ever had. You'll have the same crew all the way through, and the same ship. And the man or the ship that fails will be dropped. You're going to do things with a B-25 that you thought were impossible." After the ten weeks of intensive training, sixteen B-25 twin-engined Mitchell bombers are launched from the pitching USS *Hornet* on that April 1942 morning. Flying low over Japan to take the enemy by surprise, the attack is a success. Some planes reach safety, others are destroyed or crash in enemy territory. Lawson's craft, the *Ruptured Duck*, crashes off the China coast. Lawson and his crew make their way inland but Lawson's injuries result in the amputation of the lower part of one of his legs. With the help of fellow crewmen, especially mechanic/gunner David Thatcher (Robert Walker), and the Chinese people themselves, Lawson is returned safely to Allied lines. He is reunited with Doolittle, who commends his bravery. In the joy of seeing his wife Ellen (Phyllis Thaxter), Lawson jumps up from his wheelchair, forgetting his

---

* Other films to utilize the Doolittle raid for their storyline were DESTINATION TOKYO (1944) and THE PURPLE HEART (1944), qq.v.

amputation. He collapses to the floor, but she is there to comfort him. "Tell me honey," he asks her as she cradles him in her arms. "How come you're so cute?" She replies, "I had to be, to get such a good looking fella."

THIRTY SECONDS OVER TOKYO had more than its share of production problems.* It had taken a year after the Doolittle raid for the information about the spectacular event to be declassified by the U.S. Government, allowing Lawson to publish his true-life account in May 1943. When MGM acquired the screen rights to his book, Lawson was hired by MGM as a special technical adviser on the picture. However, before filming got underway, he was recalled to duty as a liaison officer and based in Santiago, Chile. Dean Davenport, his *Ruptured Duck* co-pilot, replaced him as consultant. MGM intended to make the production authentic and wanted to use real names. Another studio offered Doolittle and his wife $250,000 if they would deny MGM the rights to their name in this picture. The Doolittles declined the offer. Spencer Tracy, who had just completed two films with war themes (A GUY NAMED JOE, q.v., and THE SEVENTH CROSS), initially against appearing in this picture, was especially fearful of portraying such an acclaimed hero (Doolittle had been awarded the Congressional Medal of Honor and promoted to Brigadier General). When the producers received approval from Doolittle's wife that Tracy was a fine choice to play her husband, the Oscar-winning star agreed to his cameo assignment. There were more delays in starting production due to wartime priorities and restrictions. After filming did get underway—with location work at air fields in Florida, Los Angeles and San Francisco—relative screen newcomer Van Johnson was involved in a near fatal motorcycle accident. It was touch-and-go whether he would survive, let alone be able to return to filming. MGM wanted to replace him, but Tracy insisted the production shoot around Johnson until the actor recuperated sufficiently. (Johnson's tell-tale accident scars are visible on-screen.)

THIRTY SECONDS OVER TOKYO was well rewarded for its painstaking depiction of this dramatic air raid attack. The critics heartily endorsed the film. "As the re-created picture of one of our boldest blows in this war and as a drama of personal heroism, it is nigh the best yet made in Hollywood. . . . All of the production involving planes and technical action is so fine that the film has the tough and literal quality of an Air Force documentary" (Bosley Crowther, *New York Times*). "One of Hollywood's finest war

---

*For a detailed account of the trials and tribulations of filming THIRTY SECONDS OVER TOKYO, see *Celluloid Wings* (1984) by James H. Farmer.

films to date" (*Newsweek* magazine). THIRTY SECONDS OVER TOKYO placed eighth in the National Board of Review's Ten Best Pictures. It won an Academy Award for Best Special Effects and was Oscar-nominated for its Cinematography. The film would gross $4,500,000 in theater rentals in the U.S. and Canada alone, making it the top drawing combat feature film of the World War II era.

THUNDER ACROSS THE PACIFIC *see:* WILD BLUE YONDER.

A TIME TO LOVE AND A TIME TO DIE (Universal, 1958) Color 133 mins.

Producer, Robert Arthur; director, Douglas Sirk; based on the novel by Erich Maria Remarque; screenplay, Orin Jannings; art directors, Alexander Golitzen, Alfred Sweeney; set decorator, Russell A. Gausman; costumes, Bill Thomas; music, Miklos Rozsa; special effects, Clifford Stine, "Whitey" McMahan; camera, Russell Metty; editor, Ted J. Kent.

John Gavin (Ernest Graeber); Lilo Pulver (Elizabeth Kruse); Jock Mahoney (Immerman); Don DeFore (Boettcher); Keenan Wynn (Reuter); Erich Maria Remarque (Pohlmann); Dieter Borsche (Captain Rahe); Barbara Rutting (Woman Guerrilla); Thayer David (Oscar Binding); Charles Regnier (Joseph); Dorothea Wieck (Frau Lieser); Kurt Meisel (Heini); Agnes Windeck (Frau Witte); Clancy Cooper (Sauer); John Van Dreelen (Political Officer); Klaus Kinski (Gestapo Lieutenant); Alice Treff (Frau Langer); Alexander Engel (Warden); Dana J. Hutton [Jim Hutton] (Hirschland); Wolf Harnisch (Sergeant Muecke); Karl-Ludwig Lindt (Dr. Karl Fresenburg); Lisa Helwig (Frau Kleinert).

Twenty-eighty years after producing the screen version of Erich Maria Remarque's ALL QUIET ON THE WESTERN FRONT, q.v., Universal released A TIME TO LOVE AND A TIME TO DIE, based on Remarque's novel of German soldiers and civilians engulfed in World War II. Despite its on-location CinemaScope filming in Germany, two attractive if generally unknown leads (John Gavin, Lilo Pulver), and a well-publicized guest appearance by Remarque himself (as a suspect school teacher), the film lacks a biting point of view. In attempting to translate Remarque's novel to the screen, the German idiom becomes American slang; what is poignant and telling in print emerges as distended, plodding sequences on camera. On the written page Remarque's book is a panorama of the "real" Germans and how they felt and reacted in and to World War II; on the big screen it is a tale of romance Hollywood-style with occasional forays into combat and stereotyped cameos of "representative" German feelings during the Third Reich.

German soldier Ernest Graeber (John Gavin) is on the Russian front in 1944 as the Nazis slowly realize they are losing the war. On furlough, he returns home to his small village and marries Elizabeth Kruse (Lilo Pulver). Their honeymoon is spent in the midst of a bombed-out building and they mingle with a war-torn cross-section of German civilians, politicians, and ranking party officials. Back on the Russian front, Graeber receives a letter from his wife telling him he will be a father. He is killed that day in battle.

TO HELL AND BACK (Universal, 1955) Color 106 mins.

Producer, Aaron Rosenberg; director, Jesse Hibbs; based on the book by Audie Murphy; screenplay, Gil Doud; art directors, Alexander Golitzen, Robert Clatworthy; music director, Joseph Gershenson; camera, Maury Gertsman; editor, Edward Curtiss.

Audie Murphy (Himself); Marshall Thompson (Johnson); Jack Kelly (Kerrigan); Charles Drake (Brandon); Paul Picerni (Valentino); Gregg Palmer (Lieutenant Manning); David Janssen (Lieutenant Lee); Richard Castle (Kovak); Paul Langton (Colonel Howe); Bruce Cowling (Captain Marks); Julian Upton (Steiner); Denver Pyle (Thompson); Felix Noriego (Swope); Art Aragon (Sanchez); Brett Halsey (Saunders); Tommy Hart (Klasky); Anthony Garcen (Lieutenant Burns); Gordon Gebert (Audie as a Boy); Mary Field (Mrs. Murphy); Howard Wright (Mr. Houston); Edna Holland (Mrs. Houston); Anabel Shaw (Helen); Susan Kohner (Maria); Maria Costi (Julia); Didi Ramati (Carla); Barbara James (Cleopatra); Joey Costaretta (Vincenti); Rand Brooks (Lieutenant Harris); Nan Boardman (Maria's Mother); Henry Kulky (Stack); John Pickard (Military Police); Ashley Cowan (Scottish Soldier); Don Kennedy (Marine Recruit Sergeant); Ralph Sanford (Chief Petty Officer); Howard Price (Truck Driver); Alexander Campbell (Rector); Rankin Mansfield (Dr. Snyder); Madge Meredith (Corinne); Mort Mills (Soldier); John Bryant (Jim).

Audie Murphy (1924-1971) was officially the most decorated World War II soldier, having been awarded the Congressional Medal of Honor in addition to twenty-seven other medals. He was credited with capturing or killing 240+ German soldiers. After the war he was brought to Hollywood, and the good-looking boyish hero became a film star, mostly in grade B Westerns. He married and divorced another budding and tragic film star (Wanda Hendrix) who never overcame her agonized love for him. His home studio,

Universal Pictures, made this feature film based on Murphy's best-selling autobiography. In its folk-hero way, much in the style of SERGEANT YORK (1941), q.v., TO HELL AND BACK depicts an unassuming farm boy who, at an early age, takes to war as his patriotic duty and along the way becomes a shy hero. The film accounts for few of the tremulous psychological motives that made him battle-crazed or the after-effects of his war experiences which created his private hell. TO HELL AND BACK would earn an impressive $5,799,852 in theater rentals in the U.S. and Canada.

TO HELL AND BACK opens in the early 1940s in Texas, where Audie Murphy (himself) and his family barely survive day to day on their farmland. When his mother (Mary Field) dies, the children are shifted to various homes and sharpshooter Audie, barely eighteen, joins the Army. By 1943 Audie is one of many replacements in Company B, 15th Infantry Regiment, Third Division, 7th Army and serves with the unit in Tunisia, Italy, France, Germany, and Austria. By war's end he is one of two soldiers left in the original unit and has risen from Private First Class to company commander. Along the way he has lost most of his fellow infantrymen pals and has shared a few tender moments with an Italian girl (Susan Kohner) in Naples.

With Murphy serving as the film's technical adviser as well as starring in his own amazing-but-true account, TO HELL AND BACK has a built-in authenticity which cannot be faulted. Anytime a stereotype platoon member appears or a clichéd combat scene occurs, the viewer is forced by Murphy's presence to remember that this is (supposedly) all real. The black-and-white, CinemaScope film depicts Murphy as a frightened youth who is turned into a fighting machine by the horrors of war, his anger at seeing buddies die in action, and his basic survival instinct. At heart, the film—as did his life—asks the questions: Can man be sane and survive war?, and if one survives war, can he be sane?

TO THE SHORES OF HELL (Crown International, 1966) Color 82 mins.

Executive producer, Robert Patrick; producer, Will Zens; associate producer, Richard Bertea; director, Zens; screenplay, Zens, Robert McFadden; wardrobe, Lillias Haddock; music, William Schaefer; sound, Robert Sands; special effects, Harry Woolman; camera, Leif Rise; editor, Michael David.

Marshall Thompson (Major Greg Donahue); Kiva Lawrence (Mary); Richard Jordahl (Father Jacques Bourget); Robert Dornan (Dr. Gary Donahue); Jeff Pearl (Mic Phin); Richard Arlen (Brigadier General F. W. Ramgate); Dick O'Neill (Major Fred Howard); Freeman Lusk (Captain Lusk); Bill Bierd (Sergeant Bill Gabreski); Marvin Yim (Major Toang).

This film was one more of those lower-case action films that utilized the Vietnam War as a backdrop for its all-too-standard activity. Richard Arlen, who starred in WINGS (1927), q.v., has a brief guest starring role as Brigadier General F. W. Ramgate.

Marine Major Greg Donahue (Marshall Thompson) lands at Da Nang in Vietnam with his unit. His brother, Dr. Gary Donahue (Robert Dornan), is being held by the Viet Cong to treat their wounded. Along with Sergeant Bill Gabreski (Bill Bierd), Vietnamese Mic Phin (Jeff Pearl) and a French priest (Richard Jordahl), Donahue sets out on the rescue mission. By the end of the mission only Donahue and his freed brother are alive; they are saved by a Marine rescue helicopter. The Vietnamese are left to bury their own.

TOBRUK (Universal, 1967) Color 109 mins.

Producer, Gene Corman; in charge of production, Edward Muhl; director, Arthur Hiller; screenplay, Leo V. Gordon; art directors, Alexander Golitzen, Henry Bumstead; set decorators, John McCarthy, Oliver Emert; makeup, Bud Westmore; music, Bronislaw Kaper; music supervisor, Joseph Gershenson; technical adviser, L. J. Loughran (Colonel, Royal Australian Infantry, Retired); assistant directors, Terence Nelson, John Anderson, Jr.; sound, Waldon O. Watson, Lyle Cain; matte supervisor, Albert Whitlock; camera, Russell Harlan; aerial camera, Nelson Tyler; editor, Robert C. Jones.

Rock Hudson (Major Donald Craig); George Peppard (Captain Kurt Bergman); Nigel Green (Colonel John Harker); Guy Stockwell (Lieutenant Max Mohnfeld); Jack Watson (Sergeant Major Tyne); Percy Herbert (Dolan); Norman Rossington (Alfie); Liam Redmond (Henry Portman); Heidy Hunt (Cheryl Portman); Leo Gordon (Sergeant King); Robert Wolders (Corporal Bruckner); Anthony Ashdown (Lieutenant Boyden); Curt Lowens (German Colonel); Rico Cattani (Corporal Stuhler); Peter Coe (Tuareg Chieftain); Lawrence Montaigne (Italian Officer); Robert Hoy (British Corporal); Phil Adams (S.I.G. Bocker); Ronnie Rondel (S.I.G. Schell).

One of Rock Hudson's last financially successful feature films, this expensively-mounted, rousing action film is set in the Libyan Desert of 1942.

No sooner is Major Donald Craig (Rock Hudson) of the British North African Army rescued by (German-born) Palestinian Jews from the Vichy French than he is taken to Colonel John Harker (Nigel Green). With his knowledge of the area he is "requested" to lead a dangerous raid on the Nazi fuel dumps at the seaport of Tobruk. The scheme revolves around the Jews, led by Captain Kurt Bergman (George Peppard), pretending to be German soldiers marshalling British prisoners across the desert. They encounter German and Italian tank units, down an Allied plane to conceal their identity, and corral two Nazi spies who later escape. Despite Craig and Harker's distrust (and anti-Semitic feelings) toward Bergman, they succeed in exploding the fuel bunkers. Of the 83 who started the mission, only four survive, and Lieutenant Max Mohnfeld (Guy Stockwell) has been exposed as the spy in their midst.

Variety would acknowledge that the film has ". . . plenty of guts and suspense to hold the action buff." Portions of TOBRUK's explosive finale would be reused for Universal's rehash of the same decisive battle in RAID ON TOBRUK (1971), q.v., starring Richard Burton.

TOO LATE THE HERO (Cinerama Releasing, 1970) Color 133 mins.

Producer, Robert Aldrich; associate producer, Walter Blake; director, Aldrich; story, Aldrich, Robert Sherman; screenplay, Aldrich, Lukas Heller; art director, James Dowell Vance; set decorator, John W. Brown; main title, Richard Kuhn; wardrobe supervisor, Charles James; makeup, William Turner, Jack Stone; music, Gerald Fried; music editor, William Saracino; assistant directors, Grayson Rogers, Malcolm Harding; second unit director, Oscar Rudolph; second unit assistant director, Francisco MacLang; technical advisers, Robert C. Lefever (Captain), Takashi Ohashi; dialogue supervisor, Sherman; recording supervisor, Franklin Milton; sound effects, Milo Lory; special effects, Henry Millar, Jr.; camera, Joseph Biroc; editor, Michael Luciano; montage editor, Albert Malpas; associate editor, Joseph Harrison.

Michael Caine (Private Tosh Hearne); Cliff Robertson (Lieutenant Sam Lawson); Henry Fonda (Captain John G. Nolan); Ian Bannen (Private Thornton); Harry Andrews (Lieutenant Colonel Thompson); Denholm Elliott (Captain Hornsby); Ronald Fraser (Private Campbell); Lance Percival (Corporal McLean); Percy Herbert (Sergeant Johnstone); Michael Parsons (Private Rafferty); Harvey Jason (Signalman Scott); William Beckley (Private Currie); Don Knight (Private Connolly); Sean MacDuff (Private Rogers); Martin Horsey (Private Griffiths); Roger Newman (Private Riddle); Ken Takakura (Major Yamaguchi); Sam Kydd (Sergeant-Major); Patrick Jordan (Soldier); and: Frank Webb.

Cliff Robertson in TOO LATE THE HERO (1970).

Despite the combination of a high-powered cast, a seasoned genre director, and plenty of jungle combat action, this was not a hit film. The movie's advertising slogan depicted a dead soldier emblazoned with the slogan, "It's a dying business!"

In World War II, lackadaisical U.S. Naval Lieutenant Sam Lawson (Cliff Robertson) is placed in charge of a suicide mission by British commandos to wipe out a Japanese observation point on a New Hebrides island. This outpost is being used to transmit radio information for attacks on the Allied fleet. Lawson, who speaks Japanese fluently, embarks with the ineffectual Captain Hornsby (Denholm Elliott) and the others. Three of their number die in a Japanese ambush and both Lawson and the cynical Private Tosh Hearne (Michael Caine) wonder if Hornsby can complete the task. Hornsby shows his mettle and is killed destroying the radio shack (while Lawson cowers in the bush), and the surviving five push through the jungle ahead of the pursuing Japanese. Japanese commander Major Yamaguchi (Ken Takakura) offers leniency to the commandos if they surrender. Private Campbell (Ronald Fraser) and two others do so, but Campbell is killed by his captors for having desecrated a dead Japanese soldier to steal a ring. Later Hearne and Lawson ambush Yamaguchi and, at the British lines, make a dash across the open ground. Hearne alone survives and details Lawson's "bravery" in action.

Variety was among the many unimpressed by the results: ". . . [TOO LATE THE HERO] is more protein than protest, more roughage than revolt, and more meal than meaning. . . . Call it uninspired, or vacillating, or self-consciously commercial; and any [or] all descriptions fit." There were many who felt that producer/director/co-scripter Robert Aldrich used the cynicism-steeped plotline as a lame excuse for gratuitous mayhem as the commando unit is whittled down graphically to its final survivor.

A.k.a. SUICIDE RUN.

TOO YOUNG THE HERO (CBS-TV, 3/27/88) Color 100 mins.

Executive producers, Pierre Cossette, Alan Landsburg, Joan Barnett; producer, Buzz Kulik; associate producer, Diane Schroder; director, Kulik; based on the manuscript by Calvin Graham and Gary Thomas; teleplay, David J. Kinghorn; production designer, Norm Baron; music, Steve Dorff; sound, Jennifer McCauley; camera, Don Burgess; editor, Les Green.

Ricky Schroder (Calvin Graham); John De Vries (Captain Gatch); Debra Mooney (Calvin's Mother); Thomas Mills Wood (Davy Cluff); John Linton (Scotty); Rick Warner (Holbrook); Mary Louise Parker (Pearl); Christopher Yore (Frank Graham);

Advertisement for TOO YOUNG THE HERO (1988).

Christopher Curry (Laslo); Markus Flanagan (Sparky); Ron Shelley (Cracker); Terry Loughlin (Necker); Thomas McGovern (Turkel); Carl Mueller (Lieutenant Sargent Shriver); Jimmy Wiggins (Cleon); Christopher De Oni (Avila); Mert Hatfield (Harry); James Eric (Pratt).

The true-life account of America's "Baby Vet" of World War II.

On August 12, 1942 Calvin Graham (Ricky Schroder), a twelve-year-old from a broken home in Houston, Texas, enlists in the Navy using phony documents. He passes from boot camp in San Diego to sea duty as a brave gunner aboard the battleship USS *South Dakota,* which sees combat action in the South Pacific. Then his true age is discovered. ("You're just a child, a boy," his superior officer says. "I'm a sailor," Graham replies.) He is ordered to be demobilized at home. By an ironic error he is listed as A.W.O.L. and ends up in a military jail, victimized by the guards and fellow prisoners. Through his sister Pearl (Mary Louise Parker), he is released on April 5, 1943.

Actor Ricky Schroder, who had grown up on screen, offers a sincere performance in this based-on-true-facts account of a child who becomes a hero in combat, only to have red tape turn everything sour. (The real life Calvin Graham was finally restored his Bronze Star and Purple Heart medals and honorable discharge in 1978, but he has yet to be re-granted his military service pension.) When Calvin Graham says, "The navy's all I have, sir. This ship is the only real home I've had," it rings with dramatic intensity, even if a similar scene had been played out in AN OFFICER AND A GENTLEMAN (1982) by Richard Gere.

This highly-publicized telefeature met with viewer endorsement even if critics carped about the production's hackneyed flashback gimmicks and the storyline structure, "His internment and suffering at the hands of the marine guards is an indictment; the flashbacks are a celebration of courage, of youthful exuberance and of a boy's battle over homelessness. The two approaches don't jibe" (*Daily Variety*).

TORA! TORA! TORA! (Twentieth Century-Fox, 1970) Color 143 mins.

Producer, Elmo Williams; *U.S. production credits*: director, Richard Fleischer; based on the book by Gordon W. Prange and the book *The Broken Seal* by Ladislas Farago; screenplay, Larry Forrester; art directors, Jack Martin Smith, Richard Day; set decorators, Walter M. Scott, Norman Rockett; wardrobe supervisor, Courtney Halsam; makeup supervisor, Dan Stripeke; music,

Jerry Goldsmith; orchestrator, Arthur Morton; second unit director, Ray Kellogg; assistant directors, David Hall, Elliott Schick; technical advisers: Arthur P. Wildern (Lieutenant Colonel, Retired), George Watkins (Captain, U.S. Navy), Jack Canary (DOD Project Officer/Naval Coordinator), E. P. Stafford (Commander, U.S. Navy, Retired); sound, James Corcoran, Murray Spivack, Douglas O. Williams, Ted Soderberg, Herman Lewis; special camera effects, L. B. Abbott, Art Cruickshank; mechanical effects, A. D. Flowers; camera, Charles F. Wheeler; editors, James E. Newcom, Pembroke J. Herring.

Japanese production credits: associate producers for Japanese sequences, Otto Lang, Masayuki Takagi, Keinosuke Kubo; directors of Japanese sequences, Toshio Masuda, Kinji Fukasaku; screenplay, Hideo Oguni, Ryuzo Kikushima; art directors, Yoshiro Muraki, Taizo Kawashima; assistant director, Hiroshi Nagai; technical advisers, Kameo Sonakawa, Kuranoshuke Isoda, Shizuo Takada, Tsuyoshi Saka; sound, Shin Watarai; camera for Japanese sequences, Shinsaku Himeda, Masamichi Sato, Osami Furuya; editor, Inoue Chikaya.

Martin Balsam (Admiral Husband E. Kimmel); So Yamamura (Admiral Isoroku Yamamoto); Jason Robards (General Walter C. Short); Joseph Cotten (Henry L. Stimson); Tatsuya Mihashi (Commander Minoru Genda); E. G. Marshall (Lieutenant Colonel Rufus S. Bratton); Takahiro Tamura (Lieutenant Commander Fuchida); James Whitmore (Admiral William F. Halsey); Eijiro Tono (Admiral Chuichi Nagumo); Wesley Addy (Lieutenant Commander Alvin D. Kramer); Shogo Shimada (Ambassador Kichisaburo Nomura); Frank Aletter (Lieutenant Commander Thomas); Koreya Senda (Prince Fumimaro Konoye); Leon Ames (Frank Knox); Junya Usami (Admiral Zengo Yoshida); Richard Anderson (Captain John Earle); Kazuo Kitamura (Foreign Minister Yosuke Matsuoka); Keith Andes (General George C. Marshall); Edward Andrews (Admiral Harold R. Stark); Neville Brand (Lieutenant Kaminsky); Leora Dana (Mrs. Kramer); Asao Uchida (General Hideki Tojo); George Macready (Cordell Hull); Norman Alden (Major Truman Landon); Walter Brooke (Captain Theodore S. Wilkinson); Rick Cooper (Lieutenant George Welch); Elven Havard (Doris Miller); June Dayton (Miss Ray Cave); Jeff Donnell (Cornelia the Aviatrix); Richard Erdman (Colonel Edward F. French); Jerry Fogel (Lieutenant Commander William W. Outerbridge); Shunichi Nakamura (Kameto Kurojima); Carl Reindel (Lieutenant Kenneth Taylor); Edmon Ryan (Rear Admiral Patrick N. L. Bellinger); Hisao Toake (Saburo Kurusu); and: Sosumu Fujita, Toshio Hosokawa, Kazuko

Ichiwa, Hank Jones, Karl Lukas, Ron Masak, Bonitaro Miyake, Kan Nihonyanagi, Ichiro Reuzaki.

Filmmaker virtuoso Darryl F. Zanuck, who had produced a rash of highly regarded combat epics* at Twentieth Century-Fox, conceived TORA! TORA! TORA! as his moviemaking swansong. It was a revisionist's approach to what "really" happened on December 7, 1941, the "Day of Infamy." To provide his $25,000,000 production with an objective point of view, the motion picture was an American-Japanese co-production, a feat as remarkable as the events leading up to the sneak attack on Pearl Harbor. Zanuck would explain in a print advertisement for TORA! TORA! TORA! that his reason for producing the film was " . . . to arouse the American public to the necessity for preparedness in this acute missile age when a sneak attack could occur at any moment." Unlike PATTON, Twentieth Century-Fox's other study of World War II released that year, TORA! TORA! TORA!, at 143 minutes, was considered lumbering and a bore** until the actual attack is presented in the post-intermission 65-minute segment. And then the meticulous reproduction of aerial assaults becomes a never-ending loop of strafing, exploding bombs, and continuous devastation. For many filmgoers—as the media were quick to pinpoint—the resourceful Japanese pilots, ritualistically committed to death beforehand and jubilant in their conquest afterwards, are the film's heroes, not the disorganized and unprepared Americans.

For its intricate weaving of the facts from both the American and Japanese points of view, TORA! TORA! TORA! relies on the 1969 book, *Tora! Tora! Tora!* by Gordon W. Prange, and Ladislas Farago's *The Broken Seal* (1967). While U.S. Secretary of State Cordell Hull (George Macready) and Secretary of War Henry L. Stimson (Joseph Cotten) debate the relevance of breaking diplomatic relations with Japan after it signs an alliance with Germany in 1941, Japanese Admiral Isoroku Yamamoto (So Yamamura) deter-

---

*Twentieth Century-Fox released such well-regarded combat films as: CRASH DIVE (1943), GUADALCANAL DIARY (1943), THE IMMORTAL SERGEANT (1943), THE PURPLE HEART (1944), WING AND A PRAYER (1944), A WALK IN THE SUN (1945), TWELVE O'CLOCK HIGH (1949), AN AMERICAN GUERRILLA IN THE PHILIPPINES (1950), FIXED BAYONETS (1951), THE FROGMEN (1951), THE DESERT FOX (1951), HALLS OF MONTEZUMA (1951), THE ENEMY BELOW (1957), THE HUNTERS (1958), THE LONGEST DAY (1962), qq.v.

**One of the bizarre highlights in the film is the almost comic moment where bewildered aviatrix Cornelia (Jeff Donnell) finds herself accidentally caught in the aerial assault on Pearl Harbor.

mines that U.S. Naval operations at Pearl Harbor must be destroyed if Japanese expansion in the Pacific is to occur.

A cacophony of misjudgments and errors on both sides, combined with the Japanese tactical expertise, leads to the successful Pearl Harbor raid. General Walter C. Short (Jason Robards), U.S. ground forces commander at Pearl Harbor, who fears saboteurs more than invaders, orders all U.S. military planes set in the middle of the field runways. The base's new radar system is useless since the operators do not understand its workings. Although Army intelligence and the War Department warn the command at Pearl Harbor that the Japanese appear to be mounting an attack on Hawaii, preparations are only half-hearted. Because Army Chief of Staff George C. Marshall (Keith Andes) is busy horseback riding, a decoded message detailing that Japanese Admiral Chuichi Nagumo (Eijiro Tono) and his fleet of six aircraft carriers are on their way to Pearl Harbor, does not reach Marshall in time. The Japanese plan to have Ambassador Kichisaburo Nomura (Shogo Shimada) deliver an ultimatum to Hull in Washington, D.C. at a strategic moment. Their strategy is to push the U.S. into breaking off diplomatic relations with Japan so that the Pearl Harbor bombing will seem a military answer to the U.S. stance. But Nomura does not receive his orders in time because of a Japanese Embassy error. His delivery of the Emperor's demands occurs at the same time as the bombing. In the Pacific, Yamamoto appreciates the success of his daring raid, but knows that a long, deadly war lies ahead.

TORA! TORA! TORA! won an Academy Award for its spectacular Special Visual Effects and was Oscar-nominated for Art Direction/Set Decoration, Sound, Cinematography, and Editing. Understandably the film did far better commercially in Japan than in the United States. Footage from TORA! TORA! TORA! would be used in MIDWAY (1976) and MacARTHUR (1977), qq.v. The film earned $14,530,000 in theater rentals in the U.S. and Canada, which, considering the production costs and efforts, was not remarkable.

TORPEDO ALLEY (Allied Artists, 1953) 84 mins.

Producer, Lindsley Parsons; director, Lew Landers; screenplay, Sam Roeca, Warren Douglas; art director, David Milton; camera, William Sickner; editor, W. Donn Hayes.

Mark Stevens (Bingham); Dorothy Malone (Susan); Charles Winninger (Peabody); Bill Williams (Graham); Douglas Kennedy (Gates); James Millican (Heywood); Bill Henry (Instructor); James Seay (Skipper); Robert Rose (Anniston); John Alvin (Professor); Carleton Young (Psychiatrist); Ralph Sanford (Hedley); Ralph

Reed (Lookout); Carl Christian (Happy); John Close (Turk); and: Richard Garland, Keith Larson, Ross Thompson, William Schallert.

A minor-key combat film dealing with yet another guilt-ridden serviceman doing his duty on a wartime submarine. Stock footage was amply utilized to mesh with the manufactured naval combat scenes.

Pilot Bingham (Mark Stevens) loses his plane and two crewmen near the end of World War II. He cannot adjust to civilian life and turns to the submarine service. While training at the Navy's sub base at New London, Connecticut, he falls in love with naval nurse Susan (Dorothy Malone), who happens to be the girl friend of submarine officer Gates (Douglas Kennedy), the man responsible for rescuing him in that flight crash years ago. Bingham and Gates see action off the Korean coast during the Korean War.

TORPEDO RUN (Metro-Goldwyn-Mayer, 1958) Color 98 mins.

Producer, Edmund Grainger; director, Joseph Pevney; based on stories by Richard Sale; screenplay, Sale, William Wister Haines; art directors, Willam A. Horning, Malcolm Brown; special effects,

L. Q. Jones, Glenn Ford, and Ernest Borgnine in TORPEDO RUN (1958).

A. Arnold Gillespie, Harold Humbrock; camera, George J. Folsey; editor, Gene Ruggiero.

Glenn Ford (Lieutenant Commander Barney Doyle); Ernest Borgnine (Lieutenant Archer Sloan); Diane Brewster (Jane Doyle); Dean Jones (Lieutenant Jake "Fuzz" Foley); L. Q. Jones ("Hash" Benson); Philip Ober (Admiral Samuel Setton); Richard Carlyle (Commander Don Adams); Fredd Wayne (Orville "Goldy" Goldstein); Don Keefer (Ensign Ron Milligan); Robert Hardy (Lieutenant Redley); Paul Picerni (Lieutenant Burl Fisher).

The late 1950s saw a rash of submarine warfare films, and one of the more worthy entries was MGM's CinemaScope color entry, TORPEDO RUN. It benefitted from firm acting by Glenn Ford, the wonderfully resilient presence of Ernest Borgnine (in a William Bendix-type assignment), and the presence of combat genre veteran, L. Q. Jones. The screenplay was co-authored by William Wister Haines, the scenarist of such entries as COMMAND DECISION (1948) and ONE MINUTE TO ZERO (1952), qq.v. *Variety* was among those who complemented the innovative lighting by cinematographer George J. Folsey which gave the settings more dimension and contrast.

Earlier in World War II Lieutenant Commander Barney Doyle (Glenn Ford) made a tactical error. He had been stalking a Japanese aircraft carrier which was using a transport filled with American prisoners as a cover. The torpedoes from Doyle's sub sank the transport, not the targeted carrier. Aboard the downed vessel were Doyle's wife and daughter. He becomes obsessed with sinking the enemy carrier and drives his already pressured crew to the straining point, with only self-sacrificing pal Lieutenant Archer Sloan (Ernest Borgnine) to smooth the way. Eventually they sink the Japanese carrier, but in the process the sub is badly damaged. The crew makes its narrow escape by using Momsen lungs.

TORPEDO RUN was Oscar-nominated for its Special Effects.

TWELVE O'CLOCK HIGH (Twentieth Century-Fox, 1949) 132 mins.

Producer, Darryl F. Zanuck; director, Henry King; based on the novel by Sy Bartlett and Beirne Lay, Jr.; screenplay, Bartlett, Lay; art directors, Lyle R. Wheeler, Maurice Ransford; set decorators, Thomas Little, Bruce MacDonald; makeup, Ben Nye, Roy Stork; music/music director, Alfred Newman; orchestrator, Edward Powell; technical advisers, Colonel John H. De Rusay, Major Johnny McKee; assistant director, F. E. Johnston; sound, William D. Flick, Roger Heman; camera, Leon Shamroy; editor, Barbara McLean.

Advertisement for TWELVE O'CLOCK HIGH (1949).

Gregory Peck (General Frank Savage); Hugh Marlowe (Lieutenant Colonel Ben Gately); Gary Merrill (Colonel Keith Davenport); Dean Jagger (Major Harvey Stovall); Millard Mitchell (General Pritchard); Robert Arthur (Sergeant McIllhenny); Paul Stewart (Captain "Doc" Kaiser); John Kellogg (Major Cobb); Robert Patten (Lieutenant Bishop); Lee MacGregor (Lieutenant Zimmerman); Sam Edwards (Birdwell); Roger Anderson (Interrogation Officer); John Zilly (Sergeant Ernie); William Short (Lieutenant Pettinghill); Richard Anderson (Lieutenant McKessen); Lawrence Dobkin (Captain Twombley); Kenneth Tobey (Sentry); John McKee (Operations Officer); Campbell Copelin (Mr. Britton); Don Guadagno (Dwight); Peter Ortiz (Weather Observer); Steve Clark (Clerk in Antique Shop); Joyce McKenzie (Nurse); Don Hicks (Lieutenant Wilison); Ray Hyke (Bartender); Harry Lauter (Radio Officer); Leslie Denison (RAF Officer); Russ Conway (Operations Officer); Pat Whyte (Clerk); Paul Mantz (Stunt Flyer).

In today's world, where dedication is a suspect word, it is

difficult for some viewers to accept the overzealous behavior of Army Air Force General Frank Savage (Gregory Peck) in 1949's TWELVE O'CLOCK HIGH. Not only is this military martinet following in the celluloid tradition of THE DAWN PATROL (1930, 1938), and COMMAND DECISION (1948), qq.v., but Savage is based on fact: events in the wartime command of World War II Army Air Force General A. Armstrong, who guided the first U.S. daylight precision bombing raids against the Germans. It had been Armstrong himself who related the facts of his command and past nervous breakdown to two wartime subordinates, Sy Bartlett and Beirne Lay, Jr. They had turned this into a novel which Twentieth Century-Fox acquired for filming.* What resulted is one of the most striking films of any era about the burden of warfare at the top—the overwhelming strain of command on an "iron tail" general. He accomplishes the rehabilitation of his squadron but at the price of a complete nervous breakdown. Here is heroism off the pedestal, the quiet, personal version.

In 1949 London American attorney Harvey Stovall (Dean Jagger) stops at an antique shop and buys a battered mug. It sets him to reminiscing and he visits Archbury Field where he walks through the weed-covered grounds of what had been an American Army Air Force base. Flashback: it is the fall of 1942 and the 918th Bomb Group is under the command of Colonel Keith Davenport (Gary Merrill), whose growing compassion for his men has faulted his judgment. General Pritchard (Millard Mitchell) replaces him with stern General Frank Savage (Gregory Peck), who sets about whipping his demoralized, exhausted men into shape. His discipline is thorough and no one is spared, especially not executive officer Lieutenant Colonel Ben Gately (Hugh Marlowe), who is later demoted and humiliated publicly. It is not long before the pilots of the 918th request transfers. But Savage has a purpose: to increase the unit's discipline, which will not only insure better combat results on their B-17 bombing flights, but will ultimately save more men's lives. No one understands this better than wry Major Harvey Stovall, a World War I retread who makes the transfer requests evaporate; General Pritchard, who brought Savage in to effect the needed transformation; and sympathetic flight surgeon, Captain "Doc" Kaiser (Paul Stewart). These people help Savage remain the iron man who bullies his men into success and (sometimes) survival.

---

*For a history of the (pre)production of TWELVE O'CLOCK HIGH and its eventual filming at Eglin Air Force Base near Fort Walton, Florida and at Ozark Field near Dothan, Alabama, see Steve Jay Rubin's *Combat Films: 1945-1970* (1980).

Savage's severe, seemingly brutal tactics have positive results. His now well-trained crews have better morale. They succeed in more of their missions using his low-flying daytime precision bombing methods, and less of their number die. On one of the successful target raids Savage disobeys orders by refusing to turn back. On this daring flight, several of his ground crew, including the methodical Stovall, the Doc, and the chaplain, have snuck aboard so that for once they can be a true part of the flight squadron. Soon the 918th has orders to bomb Wilhelmshaven and is finally able to hit the enemy on its home ground. But the personal price is high for Savage. Like Davenport, he has gotten too close to the men and has himself flown too many missions. Those nearest him realize that Savage is cracking under the strain, but he has been so successful with the unit that he is allowed to continue in charge, often bolstered by his long-time friend, Davenport. Finally it is all too much and Savage, suffering a nervous breakdown, is unable to make it into the cockpit of his B-17. He is led from the field in a catatonic state of near immobility and speechlessness. Gately, the playboy pilot-turned-hero, takes over the latest mission and is successful. The cycle goes on.

Not all of TWELVE O'CLOCK HIGH (the title refers to military slang for a plane being directly overhead its target—usually another plane!) is ground-bound. There are fine combat scenes in the air, a technically superb blending of Allied and German newsreel footage, new aerial cinematography, and soundstage special effects.

Twentieth Century-Fox promoted this high-caliber film with such catchlines as "THE WORLD STANDS STILL AT 12 O'CLOCK HIGH. . . . TIME FOR HIGH ADVENTURE!" Other promotional copy read: "OUT OF THE SUN . . . WHERE DANGER WAITED! OUT OF THE THUNDER AND THE NIGHT . . . THAT SOUNDED THE HIGH FURY OF BATTLE . . . COMES THE STAR-SPANGLED STORY OF THE HE-ROIC 8TH AIR FORCE!" And perhaps most telling of all, was the catchphrase, "WHEN MEN ARE STRIPPED TO RAW EMO-TIONS . . . AS THEIR WOMEN NEVER KNEW THEM! . . . AS THE WORLD WILL NEVER FORGET THEM! " The critics responded enthusiastically to this study of military brass under wartime crisis. ". . . There hasn't yet been . . . [a war picture] from Hollywood which could compare in rugged realism and punch to TWELVE O'CLOCK HIGH, a top-flight drama . . ." (Bosley Crowther, *New York Times*). Regarding the inevitable comparison to the earlier COMMAND DECISION, Crowther added they were not really similar, pointing out about TWELVE O'CLOCK HIGH: ". . . not only is the situation which confronts the hero in this film on a tactical, personnel [*sic*] level—not on the level of command—but it is a situation that compels his weight to be thrown at his subordinates, and not at the 'brass.' " *Variety* enthused, "It is a topflight drama, polished and performed to the nth degree. . . . The trade paper, however, did note that ". . . all war pictures are beginning to be stamped with a familiarity that cries for a new character and story setup."

TWELVE O'CLOCK HIGH won two Academy Awards: Best Supporting Actor (Dean Jagger) and Sound; it was Oscar-nominated for Best Picture and Best Actor (Gregory Peck).

UNCOMMON VALOR (Paramount, 1983) Color 105 mins.

Producers, John Milus, Buzz Geitshans; associate producers, Burton Elias, Wings Hauser; director, Ted Kotcheff; screenplay, Joe Gayton; production designer, James L. Schoppe; art director, Jack G. Taylor, Jr.; set decorators, John H. Anderson, George Gaines; music, James Horner; assistant director, Craig Huston; camera, Stephen H. Burum, Ric Waite; editor, Mark Melnick.

Gene Hackman (Colonel Jason Rhodes); Robert Stack (Hugh MacGregor); Fred Ward (Wilkes); Reb Brown (Blaster); Randall "Tex" Cobb (Sailor); Patrick Swayze (Scott); Harold Sylvester (Johnson); Tim Thomerson (Charts); Alice Lau [Lau Nga Lai] (Lai Fun); Kwan Hi Lim (Jiang); Gail Strickland (Mrs. Helen Rhodes); Kelly Yunkermann (Paul MacGregor); Todd Allen (Frank Rhodes); Jeremy Kemp (Ferryman); Jane Kaczmarek (Mrs. Wilkes); Gloria Strock (Mrs. MacGregor); Constance Forslund (Mrs. Charts); Charles Aidman (Senator Hastings); Debi Parker (Mai Ling); Jan Triska (Gericault); James Edgcomb (CIA Agent); Ken Farmer (Jail Guard); Tad Horino (Mr. Ky); Michael Dudikoff (Blaster's Assistant); Bruce Paul Barbour (Helicopter Pilot); Jerry Supiran (Frank at Age Nine); Juan Fernandez (Orderly); Darwyn Carson (Secretary); Emmett Dennis, III (Medic); Charles Faust, David Austin (GIs); Le Tuan (Guard); Don Mantooh, Laurence Neber, Steven Solberg (POWs); Justin Bayly, Kevin Brando, Brett Johnson, Marcello Krakoff, Angela Lee, Barret Oliver (Kids); David Dangler, Nancy Linari (Reporters); William S. Hamilton, Napoleon Hendrix, Chip Lally, Michael P. May, Tom Rands, Larry Charles White (American Soldiers).

Current global politics have made it untenable for most people to celebrate contemporary warfare in traditional patriotic ways. Therefore an increasing number of trendy filmmakers have attempted to follow the suit of the hugely popular RAMBO, q.v., and MISSING IN ACTION, q.v., series. Their on-screen ploy is to mix adventure, action and combat film formulas with thinly disguised mercenaries/patriots/soldiers-of-fortune as the heroes. No longer is it nationalism which inspires the leading characters. Now the motivations have become private goals: freeing fellow soldiers/relatives still held as prisoners-of-war after the war is over; seeking a catharsis for physical/mental anguish caused by the former enemy; attempting to capitalize financially on the plight of others by becoming part of a commando team for pay. To help insure a ready audience, these moviemakers paint an oblique patriotic veneer over the storyline. And somewhere along the line in this new breed of film a guerrilla task force member will utter that understandable, but now suspect, rhetorical question, "Do we win this time?"

Retired U.S. Army colonel Jason Rhodes (Gene Hackman) is convinced that his son Frank, a Marine listed as missing-in-action (MIA) during the Vietnam War eleven years earlier, is still alive—a captive somewhere in southeast Asia. The American military brass and politicians refuse to investigate his theories. However, industrialist Hugh MacGregor (Robert Stack), whose own son is an MIA, finances Rhodes' expensive, seemingly foolhardy rescue mission. The forceful Rhodes persuades Frank's one-time Marine buddies— Blaster (Reb Brown), Charts (Tim Thomerson), Johnson (Harold Sylvester), Sailor (Randall "Tex" Cobb), and Wilkes (Fred Ward)— to participate in this dangerous mission. At the Texas training camp (a scaled-down reproduction of the targeted Laotian camp) they meet Scott (Patrick Swayze) and learn that this rebellious young ex-GI has a father who is an MIA. Their mission is almost aborted by American secret service agents who alert Thai forces of Rhodes' coming. When their supplies are intercepted by the Thai, Rhodes rearms his squad through blackmarketeer and drug dealer Jiang (Kwan Hi Lim) and his two daughters, Mai Ling (Debi Parker) and Lai Fun (Alice Lau). En route to the p.o.w. work camp Mai Ling is killed. The ground squad, headed by Wilkes and Blaster, attacks and frees the prisoners. Rhodes' delayed helicopter team arrives to complete the rescue. Blaster and the wounded Sailor (who explodes himself and several of the enemy) die. One of the rescued Americans is MacGregor's son, who tells Rhodes that Frank died of an illness while a prisoner.

What gives UNCOMMON VALOR its substance is Academy Award winner Gene Hackman as the driven father determined to rescue his son at any cost and any risk. What makes his mission more noble is that he is willing to join the rescue squad himself. His gutsiness overcomes the clichés of his stereotyped task force role. The pathetic look on his face when he learns that his reason for being (his son's rescue) no longer exists, sticks in the mind. It goes almost without saying that in this breed of film, military strategy is outweighed by plot loopholes and the structural rule of thumb is always: when in doubt, kill off a character or treat the viewer to another spectacular bomb explosion.

Ted Kotcheff, who directed Sylvester Stallone's FIRST BLOOD (1982)—the first RAMBO film—was in charge of this above par subgenre entry. UNCOMMON VALOR was considered very topical since about its time of release it was made known that a similar privately-financed American plan existed to free p.o.w.s from camps in Southeast Asia. The film earned a solid $13,000,000 in theater rentals in the U.S. and Canada.

British release title: UNCOMMON VALOUR.

UNCOMMON VALOUR *see*: UNCOMMON VALOR.

UNDER TEN FLAGS (Paramount, 1960) 92 mins.

Producer, Dino De Laurentiis; director, Duilio Coletti; based on the diaries of Bernhard Rogge; screenplay, Vittoriano Petrilli, Coletti, Ulrich Moh, William Douglas-Home; art director, Mario Garbuglia; costumes, Piero Cheradi; music, Nino Rota; camera, Aldo Tonti; editor, Jerry Webb.

Van Heflin (Captain Reger); Charles Laughton (Admiral Russell); Mylene Demongeot (Zizi); John Ericson (Krueger); Liam Redmond (Windsor); Alex Nicol (Knoche); Gregoire Aslan (Master of Abdullah); Cecil Parker (Colonel Howard); Eleonora Rossi-Drago (Sara); Gian Maria Volonte (Braun); Philo Hauser (Clown); Dieter Eppler (Dr. Hartmann); Ralph Truman (Admiral Benson); Peter Carsten (Lieutenant Mohr); Folco Lulli (Paco).

In World War II, Ship 16, or HSK II, was the code name for the German auxiliary cruiser *Atlantis*. Under Captain Bernhard Rogge this commerce raider plied the Atlantic and Indian Oceans, disguising itself as other types of vessels and sinking Allied merchant ships. From March 1940 to its sinking (November 22, 1941) by the HMS *Devonshire*, it sank twenty-two Allied ships. After the war Rogge's diaries of his amazing exploits were published and led Italian producer Dino De Laurentiis to manufacture this expensive production.

Nazi Captain Reger (Van Heflin) is in charge of a German merchant raider ship, *Atlantis*, during World War II. Its task is to lure Allied vessels within target range, and then destroy them. To accomplish his goal, Reger has an amazing array of tricks: repainting the ship, disguising his crew as female passengers promenading on deck, erecting phony smokestacks, hoisting neutral flags—whatever it requires to bring British merchant ships within range. Crafty Reger is a humanitarian, and, unlike his unyielding subordinate Krueger (John Ericson), he feels obliged to rescue survivors from the waters. In the meantime, Admiral Russell (Charles Laughton) is charged with hunting and destroying Reger's ship. His task is made easier by Knoche (Alex Nicol), an American spy who steals into German headquarters in Paris and photographs their secret codes. It provides the British with the key to locating and destroying Reger's ship. The target is destroyed but Reger survives.

For many, the highlight of this well-mounted battle of wits was Van Heflin's interpretation of the resourceful, philosophical Reger, while Charles Laughton's unrestrained hamming as his opponent made the latter's cause unsympathetic. Because pro-Allied audiences could not deal well with a pro-German stance, the movie was a box-office misfire. Blonde Mylene Demongeot, a Gallic fad star(let) of the late 1950s and early 1960s, was visually stunning as the shapely French prisoner aboard Reger's ship.

UP FROM THE BEACH (Twentieth Century-Fox, 1965) 98 mins.

Producer, Christian Ferry; director, Robert Parrish; based on the book *Epitaph for an Enemy* by George Barr; screenplay, Howard Clewes; additional dialogue, Stanley Mann,* production designer, Albert Rajau; art director, Willy Holt; music/music conductor, Edgar Cosma; assistant directors, Michel Wyn, George Gradzenczyk, Andre Frederick; sound, Max Olivier; special effects, George Iaconelli, Karl Baumgartner, Daniel Braunschweig; camera, Walter Wottitz; editor, Samuel E. Beetley.

Cliff Robertson (Sergeant Edward Baxter); Red Buttons (Private First Class Harry Devine); Irina Demick (Lili Rolland): Marius Goring (German Commandant); Slim Pickens (Artillery Colonel); James Robertson-Justice (British Beachmaster); Broderick Crawford (U.S. Military Police Major); George Chamarat (Mayor); Francoise Rosay (Lili's Grandmother); Raymond Bussieres (Dupre); Fernand Ledoux (Barrelmaker); Louise Chevalier (Marie); Germaine Delbat (Seamstress); Paula Dehelly (Widow Clarisse); Gabriel Gobin (Trombonist); Charles Bouillaud (French Horn Player); Georges Adet (Drummer); Pierre Moncorbier (Field-Keeper); Nicole Chollet (Post Office Clerk); Raoul Marco (Cobbler); Charlotte Eizlini (Cobbler's Wife); Pierval (Grocer); Renee Gardes (Grocer's Wife); Paul Maxwell (U.S. Corporal Evans); Ken Wayne (U.S. Private First Class Solly); Brian Davies (U.S. Private First Class Dinbo); Robert Hoffmann (S.S. Captain); Michael

---

*In contrast to the on-screen credits, studio fact sheets list Stanley Mann and Claude Brule as scenarists, with Howard Clewes as adaptor.

Munzer (S.S. Sergeant); Henri Kuhn (S.S. Corporal); Jean-Claude Berva (Resistance Fighter); Bibi Morat (Picot); Frawley Becker (Grocer's Assistant); Roy Stephens (Colonel's Driver); Jo Warfield (Medic Driver); Rod Calvert (Other Medic); Alexandre Grecq (German Pilot); Tracy Wynn (Soldier in Truck); Billy Kearns (Colonel in Bunker); Thomas Farnsworth (Major in Bunker).

". . . UP FROM THE BEACH is a moderately-paced, reasonably successful attempt to humanize post-D-Day operations by focussing on a small group caught in a sidepocket of the action. Generally good performances by cast of lesser names are underplayed against properly drab backdrop of impending death" (*Variety*).

Twentieth Century-Fox borrowed footage from its own THE LONGEST DAY (1962), q.v., and interweaved it into this road company version of that great combat epic. However, grim-faced Cliff Robertson, ever-smiley Red Buttons, busty Irina Demick, and compassionate Marius Goring were not sufficiently engaging enough to draw in audiences.

On the day following D-Day, Sergeant Edward Baxter (Cliff Robertson) and his squadron kill the German soldiers holding French civilians hostage at Verville. The thoughtful German town commandant (Marius Goring) is left alive, and among the freed French are resistance worker Lili Rolland (Irina Demick), who loves the Nazi officer. Meanwhile the villagers ironically become a political pawn between the joint U.S./British forces, who cannot coordinate evacuating the villagers to England, and the Germans who continue to shell Verville. The commandant dies in a booby trap explosion. Once the bombardment stops, the townspeople rejoice in their new freedom and Baxter and his men leave to join the troops heading to the front.

UP PERISCOPE (Warner Bros., 1959) Color 111 mins.

Producer, Aubrey Schenck; director, Gordon Douglas; based on the novel by Robb White; screenplay, Richard Landau; art director, Jack T. Collis; music, Ray Heindorf; camera, Carl Guthrie; editor, John F. Schreyer.

James Garner (Ken); Edmond O'Brien (Stevenson); Andra Martin (Sally); Alan Hale, Jr. (Malone); Carleton Carpenter (Carney); Frank Gifford (Mount); William Leslie (Doherty); Richard Bakalyan (Peck); Edward [Edd] Byrnes (Ash); Sean Garrison (Floyd); Henry Kulky (York); George Crise (Murphy); and: Warren Oates.

"Maverick" teleseries star James Garner had proven in DARBY'S RANGERS (1958), q.v., that he was big-screen leading man material and in UP PERISCOPE he showed a wry comic flair that he would exploit to even better results in his later career. WARNER BROS. spent a $1,000,000 + to make this widescreen, color production visually appealing. It wisely added Edmond O'Brien to the cast as the martinet submarine chief.

World War II submarine commander Stevenson (Edmond O'Brien) plays everything too much by the rule book and finds demolition expert/frogman Ken (James Garner) too flippant and disrespectful of military protocol. These difficulties lead to a clash during their special assignment, infiltrating a Japanese-held Pacific island to steal a special code book. The crew misunderstands Stevenson's fixation on duty and wonders, along with the audience, if the sub skipper will wait for Ken to accomplish his hit-and-run assignment before he orders "Full speed ahead!" The absurd finale finds the vessel returning to Pearl Harbor and the crew's adoring spouses and girlfriends waiting dockside.

The crew includes a young Warren Oates; Alan Hale, Jr., attempting to handle the type of boisterous, jolly role his father made so famous at Warner Bros. in the 1930s-1940s; Sean Garrison, who almost made a mark as a Universal contractee in the early 1960s; and ex-MGM contract song-and-dancer Carleton Carpenter, who seemed lost without Debbie Reynolds to join him in a duet of "Aba Dabba Honeymoon."

THE VALIANT (United Artists, 1962) 100 mins.

Producer, Jon Penington; directors, Roy [Ward] Baker, Giorgio Capitani; based on the play *L'Equipage au Complet* by Robert Mallet; screenplay, Willis Hall, Keith Waterhouse, Capitani, Caprino; art director, Arthur Lawson; music director, Christopher Whelan; special effects, Wally Veevers; camera, Wilkie Cooper; underwater camera, Egil Woxholt; editor, John Pomeroy.

John Mills (Captain Morgan); Ettore Manni (Luigi Durand de la Penne); Roberto Risso (Emilio Bianchi); Robert Shaw (Lieutenant Field); Liam Redmond (Surgeon Commander Reilly); Ralph Michael (Commander Clark); Colin Douglas (Chief Gunner's Mate); Dinsdale Landen (Norris); John Meillon (Bedford); Moray Watson (Turnbull); Charles Houston (Medical Orderly); Gordon Rollings (Payne); Laurence Naismith (Admiral); Patrick Barr (Reverend Ellis); and: Leonardo Cortese.

Too much of this British/Italian co-production shows its theatrical origins (a French play from 1957) and the story emerges stage-bound. None of it is helped by John Mills' constipated performance as tense Captain Morgan.

In December 1941 the HMS *Valiant* and HMS *Queen Eliza-*

beth are the only two battleships available to the British Fleet in the Mediterranean. They both are stationed in Alexandria Harbor. Two Italian frogmen, Luigi Durand de la Penne (Ettore Manni) and Emilio Bianchi (Roberto Risso) are captured near the *Valiant* and it is uncertain whether they have placed mines on the hull of the ship and if so where, and when the mines will explode. Morgan, forced to evacuate most of his crew, remains aboard with the prisoners and a few others. The bomb explodes and does great damage and the British hide from Italian reconnaisance planes while needed repairs are made.

THE VICTORS (Columbia, 1963) 175 mins.

Producer, Carl Foreman; associate producer, Harold Buck; director, Foreman; based on the book *The Human Kind: a Sequence* by Alexander Baron; screenplay, Foreman; production designer, Geoffrey Drake; art director, Maurice Fowler; prologue and title designer, Saul Bass; wardrobe designer, Olga Lehmann; wardrobe supervisor, Elsa Fennell; makeup, Ernest Gasser, Wally Schneiderman; music/music conductor, Sol Kaplan; orchestrator, Wally Scott; songs: Kaplan and Freddy Douglas; Kaplan, Douglass and Howard Greenfield; Jack Keller, Greenfield and Gerry Goffin; assistant director, Eric Rattray; technical adviser, Nils Runelundquist (Captain); sound, Buster Ambler, Bob Jones; sound editor, Winston Ryder; special effects, Cliff Richardson, Wally Veevers; camera, Christopher Challis; editor, Alan Osbiston; assistant editor, Joan Morduch; dialogue editor, Don Deacon.

Vince Edwards (Baker); Albert Finney (Russian Soldier); George Hamilton (Corporal Trower); Melina Mercouri (Magda); Jeanne Moreau (Frenchwoman); George Peppard (Corporal Chase); Maurice Ronet (French Lieutenant Cohn); Rosanna Schiaffino (Maria); Romy Schneider (Regine); Elke Sommer (Helga); Eli Wallach (Sergeant Craig); Michael Callan (Eldridge); Peter Fonda (Weaver); Jim Mitchum (Grogan); Senta Berger (Trudi); Joel Flateau (Jean-Pierre); Albert Lieven (Herr Metzger); Mervyn Johns (Dennis); Tutte Lemkow (Sikh Soldier); Peter Vaughan (Policeman); George Roubicek, George Mikell (Russian Sentries); Alf Kjellin (Priest); Alan Barnes (Tom); John Rogers (Young British Soldier); Marianne Deeming (Frau Metzger); Patrick Jordan (Tank Sergeant); Elizabeth Erey (Young French Girl); Milo Sperber (Concentration Camp Prisoner); Malya Nappi (Barmaid); Vanda Godsell (Nurse); Bee Duffell (Joan); James Chase (Condemned Soldier); Tom Busby, Larry Caringi, Charles De Temple, Graydon Gould, Ian Hughes, Anthony McBride, Riggs O'Hara, Al Waxman (The Squad); and: Peter Arne, Veite Bethke,

John Crawford, Sean Kelly, Mickey Knox, Colin Maitland, Russ Titus, Tony Wallace.

Three decades later it is extremely hard to fathom what all the fuss was about this film. In its day, this was one of Hollywood's most highly touted movies. Those who rejected roles in this in-love-and-war extravaganza shouted artistic integrity; those who were hired were accused of selling out; and those actors overlooked in its casting war pretended it all did not matter. This was "the" big-budget epic geared to make somnambulist Vince Edwards of TV's "Ben Casey" a mooo-vie star, and producer/director/scenarist Carl Foreman hired a bevy of internationally famous film actresses to flesh out the jaded romantic distractions from the grim storyline. At times, viewing the badly performed hokum now seems more unendurable than the ugly path of war the film depicted.

In World War II, Sergeant Craig (Eli Wallach) and the younger Corporal Trower (George Hamilton) and Corporal Chase (George Peppard) are among the GI infantrymen sent to combat duty in Italy after training in England. After gaining control of an objective, G.I. Baker (Vince Edwards) romances Maria (Rosanna Schiaffino), who wonders what has happened to her soldier husband. The foot soldiers reach France after D-Day and Craig shares an evening with a distraught Frenchwoman (Jeanne Moreau). Black marketeer Magda (Melina Mercouri) vainly tries to persuade Chase to join her in her illegal dealings, but he returns to his duty and is wounded in action. Later, in Belgium, Trower is jilted by nightclub performer/prostitute Regine (Romy Schneider). When the war in Europe is over, the battle-weary men have fared badly: Craig is hospitalized with grave facial wounds; Chase is still suffering from his leg wound; and Trower, hiding out in Berlin's Russian zone, realizes grasping Helga (Elke Sommer) is merely an opportunist. He and a drunken Russian soldier (Albert Finney) have a pointless argument because they cannot understand one another and both end up dead.

With its (unstructured) vignettes of horrors on the battlefield, in the bedroom, and in the barracks, THE VICTORS attempts to be an ironic depiction of war's stupidity and how it mangles men's bodies and tears at women's souls. There are scenes of racial squabbling among the troops, a G.I. (Chris Mitchum) cruelly shoots a dog, a little French boy propositions soldiers, a deserter is executed on Christmas eve by a firing squad; and every woman portrayed has been corrupted by the war. Many characters appear and disappear, never to return again (especially after Columbia Pictures ordered the picture re-edited and tightened); the interpolated newsreel footage of the homefront to give an atmospheric perspective is a clichéd misfire. Most sadly, cinema veteran Carl

Foreman (who co-scripted several war films including THE BRIDGE ON THE RIVER KWAI, 1957, q.v.) thought he was creating a strong anti-war masterpiece out of Alexander Baron's 1953 novel.

VON RICHTHOFEN AND BROWN (United Artists, 1971) Color 97 mins.

Producer, Gene Corman; director, Roger Corman; screenplay, John Corrington, Joyce Corrington; art director, Jim Murakami; set decorator, Maureen Roche; costumes, Charles Guerin, Dymphna McKenna; makeup, Toni Delaney; music, Hugo Friedhofer; assistant director, Jake Wright; special effects, Peter Dawson; camera, Michael Reed, Peter Allwork, Peter Pechowski, Seamus Corcoran; editors, George Van Noy, Alan Collins.

John Philip Law (Baron Manfred von Richthofen); Don Stroud (Roy Brown); Barry Primus (Hermann Goering); Peter Masterson (Major Oswald Boelcke); Robert Latourneaux (Ernst Udet); George Armitage (Wolff); Steve McHattie (Voss); Brian Foley

Advertisement for VON RICHTHOFEN AND BROWN (1971).

(Lothar von Richthofen); David Osterhout (Holzapfel); Clint Kimbrough (Major Von Hoeppner); Gordon Phillips (Cargonico); Peadar Lamb (German Staff Major); Seamus Forde (Kaiser); Karen Huston (Ilse); Ferdy Mayne (Father Richthofen); Maureen Cusack (Mother Richthofen); Fred Johnson (Jeweler); Hurd Hatfield (Anthony Fokker); Vernon Hayden (Trackl); Michael Fahey (Richthofen at Age 3); Corin Redgrave (Major Lance Hawker); Tom Adams (Owen); David Weston (Murphy); Brian Sturdivant (May); Des Nealon (British Intelligence officer); John Flanagan (Thompson); Lorraine Rainier (Girl in Woods); Robert Walsh (Richthofen at Age 13).

For any viewer who has seen either version of THE DAWN PATROL (1930, 1938), qq.v., the ludicrous VON RICHTHOFEN AND BROWN is an expensive joke. Evidently the filmmaking brother team, Gene and Roger Corman, did not profit from Twentieth Century-Fox's fiasco with THE BLUE MAX (1966), q.v., which also depicted World War I in the air.

Arrogant young Baron Manfred von Richthofen (John Philip Law) joins the German air force during World War I. Major Oswald Boelcke (Peter Masterson) is the fighter squadron leader, and among the other flyers is boastful egotist Hermann Goering (Barry Primus). Von Richthofen quickly proves himself in the air and when Boelcke dies in a dogfight, von Richthofen is made the new commander. One of his few acts is to paint his plane a bright red, which leads to the combat ace being nicknamed "The Red Baron." On the other side, Canadian wheat farmer Roy Brown (Don Stroud) joins the British as they fight the Germans in the air. Ungenteel Brown thinks it ludicrous that his co-flyers behave so gentlemanly to the enemy. On one daring raid led by Brown, the Allies destroy several parked German planes, but before they can return to base, von Richthofen and Goering—in new fast planes designed by Anthony Fokker (Hurd Hatfield)—retaliate on the British base, killing several nurses in the process. As the war nears an end, there is a movement in Germany to have von Richthofen use his hero status as a politician, but he is too hot-blooded and vain for such peaceful activities. Once more in the air, he duels with Brown and is killed. His red plane (following historical legend) lands on it own.

Since it boasts wonderfully staged aerial sequences it is a shame that so much of VON RICHTHOFEN AND BROWN is spoiled by bad acting, sloppy dubbing, poor scripting, and inept direction. Obviously the Cormans intended this visually colorful production to be an expensive (over $1,000,000) tribute to the gallant and reckless World War I fighter pilots, in particular the legendary (and near mythical) title figures.

A.k.a.: THE RED BARON.

VON RYAN'S EXPRESS (Twentieth Century-Fox, 1965) Color 117 mins.

Producer, Saul David; director, Mark Robson; based on the book by David Westheimer; screenplay, Wendell Mayes, Joseph Landon; art directors, Jack Martin Smith, Hilyard Brown; set decorators, Walter M. Scott, Raphael Bretton; makeup, Ben Nye, Roy Stork; wardrobe, Mickey Sherrard; music, Jerry Goldsmith; orchestrator, Gould Morton; assistant director, Eli Dunn; sound, Carlton W. Faulkner, Elmer Raguse; special camera effects, L. B. Abbott, Emil Kosa, Jr.; camera, William H. Daniels; second unit camera, Harold Lipstein; editor, Dorothy Spencer.

Frank Sinatra (Colonel Joseph L. Ryan); Trevor Howard (Major Eric Fincham); Raffaella Carra (Gabriella); Brad Dexter (Sergeant Bostick); Sergio Fantoni (Captain Oriani); John Leyton (Orde); Edward Mulhare (Constanzo); Wolfgang Preiss (Major von Klemment); James Brolin (Private Ames); John Van Dreelen (Colonel Gortz); Adolfo Celi (Battaglia); Vito Scotti (Italian Train Engineere); Richard Bakalyan (Corporal Giannini); Michael Goodliffe (Captain Stein); Michael St. Clair (Sergeant Dunbar); Ivan Triesault (Von Kleist); Jacques Stanislavski, Gino Gottarelli (Gortz's Aides); John Day, Buzz Henry, James Sikking, Al Wyatt (American Soldiers); Eric Micklewood (Ransom); John Mitory (Oriani's Aide); Benito Prezia (Italian Corporal); Dominick Delgarde (Italian Soldier); Barry Ford (Ransom's Batman); Peter Hellman (Pilot); Michael Romanoff (Italian Nobleman); Walter Linden (German Captain); Bard Stevens (German Sergeant); Ernesto Melinari (Italian Tailor); Bob Rosen (Prisoner of War Who Opens Sweatbox).

Most prisoner-of-war movies films rightly deal with torture, deprivation, bravery, corruption, and death. It was an affirmative change of pace when THE GREAT ESCAPE (1963), q.v., added humor and high adventure to the standard ingredients. Taking note of its box-office success, entrepreneurial Frank Sinatra turned David Westheimer's 1964 novel into a hit motion picture for himself. VON RYAN'S EXPRESS took the p.o.w. premise one step further, turning it into an exciting adventure/escape film. Because Sinatra was its star, there was a built-in levity that neither his serious performance nor his character's fate could dampen.

British Major Eric Fincham (Trevor Howard) heads the Allied prisoners in an Italian prisoner-of-war-camp in 1943. When American pilot Colonel Joseph L. Ryan (Frank Sinatra) arrives, Fincham is forced reluctantly to defer to this higher-ranking officer. The men

Frank Sinatra and Trevor Howard in VON RYAN'S EXPRESS (1965).

find Ryan an arrogant and tough taskmaster and tag him "Von Ryan," especially when he seems to side too often with the Italian captors. Their attitude changes when he endures torture to obtain improved living conditions for them. The war is now lost for the Italians and they willingly help the prisoners in their latest mass escape attempt. After misadventures which lead to their recapture, the 400 men gain control of a freight train carrying them into Germany and redirect it across Italy and on to Switzerland. The Nazis catch on to the scheme and come in fast pursuit by plane and train, whittling away at the escapees. En route, Ryan shoots Gabriella (Raffaella Carra) after he learns she is a collaborationist. While most of his men reach safety, Ryan is machine-gunned just as they cross over into Switzerland.

WAKE ISLAND (Paramount, 1942) 78 mins.

Producer, Joseph Sistrom; director, John Farrow; based on the records of the U.S. Marine Corps; screenplay, W. R. Burnett, Frank Butler; art directors, Hans Dreier, Earl Hedrick; set decorator, Bertram Granger; makeup, Wally Westmore; music, David Buttolph; second unit director, Hal Walker; sound, Philip Wisdom, John Cope; camera, Theodor Sparkuhl, William C. Mellor; aerial camera, Elmer Dyer, Wallace Kelley; second unit camera, Harry Hallenberger; special camera effects, Gordon Jennings; process camera, Farciot Edouart; editors, LeRoy Stone, Frank Bracht.

Brian Donlevy (Major Geoffrey "Artillery" Caton); MacDonald Carey (Lieutenant Bruce Cameron); Robert Preston (Joe Doyle); William Bendix (Aloysius K. "Smacksie" Randall); Albert Dekker (Shad McClosky); Walter Abel (Commander Roberts); Mikhail Rasumny (Probenzky); Don Castle (Private Cunkel); Rod Cameron (Captain Pete Lewis): Bill Goodwin (Sergeant); Barbara Britton (Sally Cameron); Damian O'Flynn (Captain Patrick); Frank Albertson (Johnny Rudd); Philip Terry (Private Warren); Philip Van Zandt (Corporal Gus Goebbels); Keith Richards (Sparks Wilcox); Willard Robertson (Colonel Cameron); Marvin Jones (Tommy); Jack Chapin (Squeaky Simpkins); Rudy Robles (Triunfo); John Sheehan (Pete Hogan); Charles Trowbridge (George Nielson); Mary Thomas (Cynthia Caton); Mary Field (Miss Pringle); Richard Loo (Mr. Saburo Kurusu); Earle "Tex" Harris ("Tex" Hannigan); Hillary Brooke, Patty McCarty (Girls at Inn); William Forrest (Major Johnson); Jack Mulhall (Dr. Parkman); Ivan Miller (Colonel); Hugh Beaumont (Captain); Edward Earle (Commander); James Brown (Wounded Marine); Angel Cruz (Rodrigo); Anthony Nace (Captain Gordon); Hollis Bane [Mike

Ragan] (First Lieutenant); Alan Hale, Jr. (Sight Setter); Frank Faylen (Marine Who Finds Skipper the Dog).

Soon after the Japanese surprise attack on Pearl Harbor in December 1941 came headlines revealing that G.I.-held Wake Island (which is 4,254 miles from San Francisco) had fallen to the enemy. It was a major American setback in World War II (followed by similar ones at Bataan and Corregidor). However, this military last stand at Wake Island was heralded for the heroism of the 385 outnumbered American soldiers who died fighting instead of surrendering to the Japanese. Only months after the tragedy Paramount released its Oscar-nominated WAKE ISLAND. It was dedicated to the brave Marines there who ". . . fought savagely to the death because in dying they gave eternal life to the ideas for which they died."*

As with so many later World War II features, WAKE ISLAND opens in the shadows of pre-December 7, 1941 when the Marine Corps** had already established a military base there. The smilingly polite, bespectacled Japanese envoy (Richard Loo) and his fellow diplomats arrive on their way to "peace" talks in Washington and are hosted by the Marine hierarchy at a very civilized dinner. Among the people on the island are newly-arrived, square-jawed Marine Major Geoffrey "Artillery" Caton (Brian Donlevy), now the tough head of the compound; his former college football rival, boisterous construction engineer head Shad McClosky (Albert Dekker); two brawling Quirt-Flagg-type G.I.s, Joe Doyle (Robert Preston) and wise-cracking Brooklynite Aloysius K. "Smacksie" Randall (William Bendix), the latter having doubts about reenlisting in the service because he intends to marry his girlfriend Myrtle back home and start a chicken ranch; fatherly Commander Roberts (Walter Abel); and young pilot Lieutenant Bruce Cameron (Mac-Donald Carey) who has just married his sweetheart (Barbara Britton). Suddenly war is declared and the Japanese send a squadron of planes to attack Wake Island, causing severe damage and losses. Then the enemy dispatches more planes for a "mop up" action and also orders a flotilla of battleships to invade Wake Island. Major

---

* The prologue links the Wake Island holding action to the past: "America and Americans have long been used to victory but the great names of her military history—Valley Forge—Custer's Last Stand—The Long Batallion—represent the dark hours."

**The film focuses on the exploits of Marine Fighting Squadron 211 of the Marine Aircraft Group 21 and the Wake Detachment of the 1st Defense Battalion, U.S. Marine Corps.

Caton is told by the enemy to surrender, and he responds with a come-and-get-us. The men dig into the trenches awaiting the invasion, knowing that their shore batteries can hardly dent the massive offensive. Cameron flies on a suicide mission to avenge his wife's death (she was killed at Pearl Harbor), hitting the off-shore ship bombarding the island. He is successful and his plane returns to the airfield. But he is found dead in the cockpit. A nighttime burial of his remains is done, with Caton reading the service by flashlight. The Marines know they cannot survive the onslaught, but they are determined to go out fighting. Caton tells his men, "Don't fire until you can see the whites of their eyes," and soon the Japanese are overrunning the island. The remaining Marines, except for Captain Lewis who has been sent back to Honolulu to teach Marines the Japanese tactics, die in slit trench skirmishes. The final title card reads, "These Marines fought a great fight. They wrote history. But this is not the end. There are other leathernecks, other fighting Americans. One hundred and forty million of them whose blood and sweat and fury will exact a just and terrible vengeance."

If today WAKE ISLAND seems riddled with clichés, it is only because it was *the* trend-setting feature film which established the war film formula everyone in Hollywood would use thereafter. Under John Farrow's direction, it set the path to be followed. The patriotic soldiers never question their duty or dying; they know their objective, no matter the personal price. There is the tough commanding officer who really has a heart-of-gold; there is the inevitable soldier hailing from Brooklyn, U.S.A. (a role William Bendix would make his own and replay a number of times thereafter); the dog Skipper who has a litter of pups and becomes the soldiers' mascot; brawling-carousing friendly enemies, here in a double presentation: the military commander (Brian Donlevy) versus the civilian (Albert Dekker) and the two Marine infantrymen (Robert Preston versus William Bendix). On tap is the brave soldier (MacDonald Carey) who has a double reason for sacrificing himself in battle. The enemy is depicted as gloating and inhumane (gunning down opponents in the back, shooting soldiers parachuting from exploding planes, killing civilians, etc.). Throughout the film there is much reminiscing about the good things of life back home in the States; of the women (mothers/sweethearts/wives) and children left behind; of sporting events. There is constant philosophizing about duty, heroism, and winning.* And there is the climactic last stand,

---

*Major Caton tries to console the embittered widower Cameron: "Memories are funny things. They mold a man. From the time a man can remember, his main memories are those given to him by women. Mothers, sisters, sweethearts, his wife, even those women he might like to forget, even they give him memories that

showing trapped men (here the flighting leathernecks) resolved to die, even if in glorious defeat.

Filmed with the cooperation of the Marine Corps and shot at the Salton Sea area of the California desert, WAKE ISLAND did its best to avoid standing Hollywood conventions and to depict the reality of the then raging war. As *Newsweek* magazine assessed, it was "Hollywood's first intelligent, honest, and completely success-ful attempt to dramatize the deeds of an American force on a fighting front." The *New York Times'* Bosley Crowther realized, "the story of Wake Island needed no dramatic dressing up." He added, "And here is a film for which its makers deserve a sincere salute. . . . It might be a literal document of the manner in which the Wake detachment of Marines fought and died in the finest tradition. . . . Paramount has tactfully resisted all the obvious temptations to beat the drum. It has made a realistic picture about heroes who do not pose as such." WAKE ISLAND was an enormous money-maker** and was nominated for four Academy Awards: Best Picture, Director, Supporting Actor (William Bendix), Screenplay.

A WALK IN THE SUN (Twentieth Century-Fox, 1945) 117 mins.

Producer/director, Lewis Milestone; story, Harry Brown; screenplay, Robert Rossen; art director, Max Bertisch; music, Frederic Efrem Rich; songs, Millard Lampell and Earl Robinson; technical adviser, Colonel Thomas D. Drake; assistant director, Maurice Suess; camera, Russell Harlan; editor, Duncan Mansfield.

Dana Andrews (Sergeant Tyne); Richard Conte (Private Ri-vera); John Ireland (Private Windy Craven); George Tyne (Private Friedman); Lloyd Bridges (Sergeant Ward); Sterling Holloway (Private McWilliams); Herbert Rudley (Sergeant Porter); Norman Lloyd (Private Archimbeau); Steve Brodie (Private Judson); Huntz

---

might help sometimes. . . . You are like me now—a man with a memory. But we are not alone. In this war wherever they've dropped a stick of bombs they've made thousands like us . . . men without wives, without children, without a single thing they've ever loved or held dear. And for those men there is a job to do. To fight, to fight with guns and bayonets and tanks and ships and planes. . . . Fight to destroy destruction. We've got to destroy destruction. That's our job Bruce."

**In *Hollywood Goes to War* (1987), Clayton R. Koppes and Gregory D. Black trace the effect of WAKE ISLAND on the public in 1942 and the cooperation/reaction of the U.S. Office of War Information. They note that in mid-1945, the New York office of OWI Overseas was unwilling to export a film to Asia which showed an American defeat at the hands of the Japanese. "WAKE ISLAND was a film for 1942. Three years later it seemed like ancient history. The battle scenes were unrealistic, as were the preachments in the trenches about fighting for democracy. . . . The battle scenes had a sanitized quality that made war seem more like a big football game than a mortal encounter."

Hall (Private Carraway); James Cardwell (Sergeant Hoskins); Chris Drake (Private Rankin); Richard Benedict (Private Tranella); George Offerman, Jr. (Private Tinker); Danny Desmond (Private Trasker); Victor Cutler (Private Cousins); Anthony Dante (Giorgio); Harry Cline (Corporal Kramer); Jay Norris (Private James); Al Hammer (Private Johnson); Don Summers (Private Dugan); Malcolm O'Guinn (Private Phelps); Grant Maiben (Private Smith); John Kellogg (Private Riddle); Dick Daniels (Private Long); Matt Willis (Sergeant Halverson); George Turner (Reconnaissance); Robert Lowell (Lieutenant Rande); Burgess Meredith (Narrator).

A platoon of American infantrymen takes "a little walk in the warm Italian sun." It is definitely not as simple as it sounds. It is World War II Italy and these men are part of the bloody assault on Salerno. They tumble from a landing boat onto the beachhead early one morning. Already they have lost their lieutenant and one sergeant. Sergeant Tyne (Dana Andrews) takes command eventually as they attempt to complete their objective: to capture a farmhouse and destroy a bridge some six miles away. En route, German planes strafe them, a Nazi armored car battles them, and two Italian soldiers willingly surrender. Always there is war in the background, with the sounds and look of exploding shells everywhere. Private McWilliams (Sterling Holloway) complains, "We've got a grandstand seat, only we can't see nothing. That's the trouble with war, you can't see nothing! You have to find them by ear." By the hot, bright noon one group has pushed through a farm field and another has skirted around by the river and has taken the German-held farmhouse. However, the modest victory is at a great loss to the original 53 men. Their goal accomplished, they plan to move on. As Private Rivera (Richard Conte) sees it, "Everything in the army is simple. You live or you die."

A WALK IN THE SUN is structured with deceptive simplicity. There is an opening and closing ballad (with chorus lines interjected throughout the film) telling of "the men of that fighting platoon" and "the job that they done." There is a focus on ordinary men doing "ordinary" things during a typical day's battling. These men are part of the Texas Infantry (even though the focal figures are from every place in the U.S. but Texas). There is nervous Sergeant Tyne (Dana Andrews) from Providence, Rhode Island, the man who dislikes travel and who rises quietly to the occasion by leading the group after Sergeant Porter (Herbert Rudley) cracks under the strain; Italian-American Private Rivera (Richard Conte), the machine gunner who adores opera and who hopes to marry an attractive woman and have lots of children; the minister's son, Private Windy Craven (John Ireland) from Ohio, who likes to walk by himself and think and who is always composing letters to his sister Frances which he never writes; Private Archimbeau (Norman Lloyd), the talkative unit scout who has a dim view of man's future; the man-of-the-earth, the farmer Sergeant Ward (Lloyd Bridges); Southerner Private McWilliams (Sterling Holloway), the slow-witted first aid man; Private Tranella (Richard Benedict) from Brooklyn; New York City-born Private Friedman (George Tyne), a lathe operator and amateur boxer; the too rigid Sergeant Porter (Herbert Rudley), who cannot cope any more with war's pressures. Through the voice-over narration by Burgess Meredith, through abrupt vignettes, through their interaction as a fast-diminishing platoon, and the ever present off-screen balladeers, the viewer learns about these men who seek no glory in battle, only survival. They are battle-fatigued and have no idea when or where it will end, for they are (and they realize it) insignificant pawns in the deadly big game planned by generals. (But this being 1945, they do not complain about what series of events transformed them from American civilians to foot soldiers in a strange land fighting an enemy they always feel but rarely see.)

While A WALK IN THE SUN avoids the over-zealous patriotic speeches which filled so many war films, it is full of philosophizing about the meaning of life, the lack of meaning in life, and the tangible versus intangible goals each of the men covets. Whenever the artiness of this stylized film is bogging down in talkiness, the realities of war hit the viewer square in the face. There is the brutal loss of men in the pre-dawn landing at Salerno and, of course, the mini-combats along the way to the farmhouse. At their objective the climactic assault finds the men showing their mettle in action. With their objective taken, they enjoy a momentary reward: rest and reflection. Windy starts yet another letter home, "We just blew a bridge and took a farmhouse. It was easy. Terribly easy." The film concludes with the surviving men trooping out of the farmhouse and past the camera's eye for a final inspection.

Lewis Milestone, who had directed the unforgettable ALL QUIET ON THE WESTERN FRONT (1930), q.v., had independently produced and directed A WALK IN THE SUN, based on ex-Private Harry Brown's best-selling novel of 1944. When he required distribution financing* he turned to Twentieth Century-Fox. Because the studio had so little control over the film's making, company head Darryl F. Zanuck was of two minds about the project. By the time of its release, World War II was over. Zanuck

---

*For details of the (pre)production of A WALK IN THE SUN see Steven Jay Rubin's *Combat Films: 1945-1970* (1980).

assumed America was tired of war-themed films and A WALK IN THE SUN was not budgeted for a big promotional push. (The film's advertising slogan read, "The picture that captures the heart of our time—for all time!")

A WALK IN THE SUN was disappointing commercially, but it proved to be a film that would not die. It was one of the first major films to be released to television and remains a staple on the airwaves today. A computer-colorized videocassette version is planned. When the film was finally released theatrically in England in 1951 (retitled SALERNO BEACHHEAD) on a double-bill, it received enthusiastic reviews from the critics. Its innovative narration ballad technique led the way for such later films as HIGH NOON (1952). And its director Lewis Milestone would go on to direct another classic combat study, PORK CHOP HILL (1959), q.v.

British release title: SALERNO BEACHHEAD.

WAR CORRESPONDENT *see*: THE STORY OF G.I. JOE.

WAR HUNT (United Artists, 1962) 81 mins.
Producer, Terry Sanders; director, Denis Sanders; screenplay, Stanford Whitmore; art director, Edgar Lansbury; title designer, Vance Johnson; music, Bud Shank; assistant director, Jack Bohrer; sound, Roy Meadows; camera, Ted McCord; title camera, Terry Sanders; editors, John Hoffman, Edward Dutko.

John Saxon (Private Raymond Endore); Robert Redford (Private Roy Loomis); Charles Aidman (Captain Wallace Pratt); Sydney Pollack (Sergeant Van Horn); Gavin MacLeod (Private Crotty); Tommy Matsuda (Charlie); Tom Skerritt (Corporal Showalter); Tony Ray (Private Fresno).

This low-budget, intellectual film is best remembered for introducing Robert Redford to motion picture audiences. It was filmed in fifteen days and was the start of a working relationship between director-to-be Sydney Pollack (here as the Sergeant) and Redford.

Fighting in the Korean War has taken its toll on Private Raymond Endore (John Saxon). This loner has become a psychopathic killer who enjoys killing for killing's sake. Each night he ritualistically darkens his face, creeps into enemy territory, murders a Chinese Communist with his knife and then performs an Indian war dance over the body. Endore's only friend is Charlie (Tommy Matsuda), an eight-year-old Korean war orphan who hero worships his benefactor. It is Private Roy Loomis (Robert Redford), a new replacement, who challenges Endore's influence over the boy. When the cease-fire is announced and Loomis notices Endore still embarking on his nightly ritual, he and Captain Wallace Pratt (Charles Aidman) track Endore. They find the demented Endore and faithful Charlie in a bunker and when Endore attacks them, Pratt shoots him. The distraught Charlie runs off.

"With a little more character penetration and a little less melodramatic spit and polish, it might have been a small classic of its genre" (Variety). Despite the obtrusive symbolism, there is a remarkable atmospheric quality to this film.

THE WAR LOVER (Columbia, 1962) 105 mins.

Producer, Arthur Hornblow, Jr.; director, Philip Leacock; based on the novel by John Hersey; screenplay, Howard Koch; art director, Bill Andrews; set decorator, Andrew Low; costume designer, Julie Harris; wardrobe supervisor, Elsa Fennell; makeup, George Parthleton; music, Richard Addinsell; music conductor, Muir Mathieson; assistant directors, Basil Rayburn, Timothy Burrill, John Danischewsky; technical advisers, Robert F. Spence (Lieutenant Colonel); William Tesla (Lieutenant Colonel, U.S. Air Force); sound, John Cox; sound editor, Christopher Lancaster; special effects, Wally Veevers, Ted Samuels; camera, Bob Huke; aerial camera, Ron Taylor, Skeets Kelly; editor, Gordon Hales; assistant editors, Geoffrey Fry, Roy Benson.

Steve McQueen (Buzz Rickson); Robert Wagner (Ed Bolland); Shirley Ann Field (Daphne Caldwell); Gary Cockrell (Lynch); Michael Crawford (Junior Sailen); Billy Edwards (Brindt); Chuck Julian (Lamb); Robert Easton (Handown); Al Waxman (Prien); Tom Busby (Farr); George Sperdakos (Bragliani); Bob Kanter (Haverstraw); Jerry Stovin (Emmett); Edward Bishop (Vogt); Richard Leech (Murika); Bernard Braden (Randall); Sean Kelly (Woodman); Charles De Temple (Braddock); Neil McCallum (Sully); Viera (Singer); Justine Lord (Street Girl); Louise Dunn (Hazel); Arthur Hewlett (Vicar).

It was hard to believe that John Hersey's well-received World War II novel (1959) could be converted into such an obnoxiously juvenile motion picture, filled with such embarrassing performances, ridiculous dialogue, and clichéd situations. Not even Steve McQueen's ingratiating smiles, bravado, or athletic prowess could make the "symbolic" proceedings credible. It was a shame because Hersey had a poignant message to tell: that for some, war is an incredibly pleasurable game, all the more exciting because it is deadly dangerous. As Hersey's novel details, such a war lover is incapable of meaningful personal relationships of any sort. Little of the author's humanitarian point of view came across in the film.

Buzz Rickson (Steve McQueen) and Ed Bolland (Robert Wagner) are among the many American pilots based in World War II England. While Ed is more serious and hates killing in the name of peace, Buzz is the opposite—reckless, daring in the air, and thriving on the life-and-death dogfights. He considers himself indestructible: "When you come up with a bomb big enough to blow up Rickson, you can blow up the world!" Both men meet Britisher Daphne Caldwell (Shirley Ann Field) and she later decides it is Ed she loves, especially since the overly macho Buzz refuses to let down his defenses with her. On one of their Flying Fortress missions, their plane, "The Body," is hit. Ed and the others parachute to safety, but Buzz refuses to leave the controls of his beloved plane. Wounded and knowing he faces death, he remains on board as his plane smacks into the Dover cliffs.

As with so many faulted air war films, THE WAR LOVER is best in the skies, when the flyers in their B-29 bombers are making air raids over enemy territory.

WARKILL (Universal, 1968) Color 100 mins.

Executive producer, Demetrio Tuason; producer, Ferde Grofe, Jr.; associate producer, Stanford Tischler; director/screenplay, Grofe; music, Gene Kauer, Douglas Lackey; assistant director, Ricardo Velasco; sound, Demetrio Carrianga; special effects, Enrique Ledesma; camera, Remegio Young; editor, Philip Innes.

George Montgomery (Colonel John Hannegan); Tom Drake (Phil Sutton); Conrad Parham (Pedring); Eddie Infante (Dr. Fernandez); Henry Duval (Willy); Paul Edwards, Jr. (Mike Harris); Bruno Punzalan (Major Hashiri); David Michael (Sergeant Johnson); Joaquin Fajardo (Max); Bert La Fortesa (Dr. Namura); Claude Wilson (U.S. Major); and: Ken Loring.

That combat heroes sometimes have clay feet is the thrust of WARKILL, another of the U.S./Philippines productions turned out by prolific George Montgomery. This time a major studio, Universal Pictures, distributed the action feature made in 1967. As usual in such movies, the body count is far higher than the caliber of performances or dubbing.

Near the end of World War II American newspaperman Phil Sutton (Tom Drake) arrives in the Philippines. Having written several books about heroic U.S. Colonel John Hannegan (George Montgomery) who is leading Filipino guerrillas against the remaining Japanese army, he hopes to meet the celebrated man. To his disgust he discovers that Hannegan is a blood-thirsty killer who shows his captives no mercy. Meanwhile, Japanese Major Hashiri (Bruno Punzalan) is doing his best to destroy a hospital base, and

Hannegan and his squad, with Sutton joining in the fight, make a stand against the enemy. Just before victory is theirs, Hannegan is killed. Sutton determines to keep Hannegan's less savory qualities secret.

WE DIVE AT DAWN (General Film Distributors, 1943) 98 mins.

Producer, Edward Black; director, Anthony Asquith; screenplay, J. B. Williams, Val Valentine, (uncredited) Frank Launder; art director, W. Murton; music director, Louis Levy; camera, Jack Cox; editor, R. E. Dearing.

Eric Portman (James Hobson); John Mills (Lieutenant Freddie Taylor); Reginald Purdell (Chief Petty Officer Dicky Dabbs); Niall MacGinnis (Petty Officer Mike Corrigan); Joan Hopkins (Ethel Dabbs); Josephine Wilson (Alice Hobson); Louis Bradfield (Lieutenant Brace); Ronald Millar (Lieutenant Johnson); Jack Watling (Lieutenant Gordon); Caven Watson (Chief Petty Officer Duncan); Leslie Weston (Tug Wilson); Norman Williams (Canada); Lionel Grose (Spud); Beatrice Varley (Mrs. Dabbs); Frederick Burtwell (Sidney Biggs); Marie Ault (Mrs. Metcalfe); John Salew (Drake); Philip Friend (Humphries); David Peel (Oxford); Philip Godfrey (Flunkey); Robert Wilton (Pincher); and: Franklin Bennett, George Cross, Kenneth Evans, Molly Johnson, Bryan Powley, John Redmond, Charles Russell, Gerik Schjelderup, Johnnie Schofield, John Slater, Joan Sterndale, Merle Tottenham.

Britisher John Mills, who has enhanced so many films, and several combat films in particular, is the resolute focal figure of WE DIVE AT DAWN, yet another fine World War II English film in the tradition of Noel Coward's IN WHICH WE SERVE (1942), q.v. It too salutes the individual heroics of men teamed together in battle.

Lieutenant Taylor (John Mills) is in charge of HMS *Sea Tiger*, the British submarine ordered to sink a German battleship before it leaves Bremerhaven. Finding their target has already passed through the Kiel Canal, Taylor skirts through the rough seas and minefields of the Baltic to meet the prey at the other end of the canal. In the midst of torpedoing the battleship, the *Sea Tiger* is damaged by depth charges and loses most of its oil supply. Seaman Hobson (Eric Portman) is the knowledgeable mariner who suggests that they ferret out a German fuel tanker based at a Danish port. Despite the odds they succeed and head homeward. When they return to England they learn that they were successful in blowing up the enemy ship, and Hobson finds that his skittish wife (Josephine Wilson) has decided not to end their marriage.

WEEKEND WAR (Columbia Pictures-TV/ABC-TV, 2/1/88) Color 100 mins.

Executive producers, Pal Pompian, Gil Atamian; producer, Pompian; co-producer, Gregory Widen; associate producers, Peter Rich, Rhonda Bloom; director, Steven H. Stern; story, Dennis Hackin, Steven Hackin; teleplay, Dennis Hackin, Steven Hackin, Widen; music, Brad Fiedel; sound, Charles Knight, Antonio Betancourt; camera, King Baggot; editor, Barrett Taylor.

Stephen Collins (John Deason); Evan Mirand (Dulcy); Daniel Stern (David Garfield); James B. Tolkan (Colonel Alex Thompson); Charles Haid (Sergeant Kupjack); Scott Paulin (Rudd); Michael Beach (Wiley); Charles Kimbrough (Priest); and: Victor Mhica, Kidany Lugo Santiago, Christine Healy, Judith Baldwin, Bruce Daniel Diker, Cucho Viera, Gisselle Ortiz, Orvil Miller, Jose Perez Meijer, Henry Gonzalez, Jose Maldonaldo, Leonard Fleites, Marian Pabon, Sandra Torres Marrero, Orestes Alexander, Lourdes Moran, Jose M. Torres.

Fitfully entertaining and sporadically perceptive, WEEKEND WAR is a lightweight attempt at making thought-provoking innuendoes about contemporary American politics. It is obvious that the teleplay's authors have seen their quota of combat films, for they introduce a wide range of clichés and stereotypes into the proceedings, including the brawling/funning pals (Evan Mirand, Michael Beach), the heroic priest (Charles Kimbrough) and the young boy (Kidany Lugo Santiago) as mascot. The all-revealing promotional slogan was: "They thought two weeks in the National Guard was going to be a vacation. Instead, it's become a war."

An engineering unit of California National Guardsmen is sent to Honduras for two weeks of "easy" summer duty—to restore an airstrip. Once there a U.S. government representative (Scott Paulin) convinces their commanding officer (James B. Tolkan) that a bridge near the border must be repaired. Soon the men are being attacked and killed by guerrilla forces, which could belong to any one of several political factions. Thankfully, Sergeant Kupjack (Charles Haid) has had combat experience (two tours of duty in Vietnam).

WHAT PRICE GLORY? (Fox, 1926) 120 minutes.

Presenter, William Fox; director, Raoul Walsh; based on the play by Maxwell Anderson, Laurence Stallings; screenplay, James T. O'Donohoe; titles, Malcolm Stuart Boylan; assistant director, Daniel Keefe; music score, Erno Rapee; camera, Barney McGill, John Marta, John Smith.

Victor McLaglen (Captain Flagg); Edmund Lowe (Sergeant Quirt); Dolores Del Rio (Charmaine); William V. Mong (Cognac

Pete); Phyllis Haver (Hilda of China); Elena Jurado (Carmen); Leslie Fenton (Lieutenant Moore); August Tollaire (French Mayor); Barry Norton (Private Lewisohn); Sammy Cohen (Private Lipinsky); Ted McNamara (Private Kiper); Mathilde Comont (Camille the Cook); Pat Rooney (Mulcahy).

WHAT PRICE GLORY? (Twentieth Century-Fox, 1952) Color 111 mins.

Producer, Sol C. Siegel; director, John Ford; based on the play by Maxwell Anderson, Laurence Stallings; screenplay, Phoebe Ephron, Henry Ephron; art director, Lyle R. Wheeler; set decorators, George W. Davis, Thomas Little, Stuart A. Reiss; music, Alfred Newman; orchestrator, Edward Powell; songs, Jay Livingston and Ray Evans; Technicolor consultant, Leonard Doss; sound, Winston Leverett, Roger Heman; camera, Joseph MacDonald; editor, Dorothy Spencer.

James Cagney (Captain Flagg); Corinne Calvet (Charmaine); Dan Dailey (Sergeant Quirt); William Demarest (Corporal Kiper); Craig Hill (Lieutenant Aldrich); Robert Wagner (Lewisohn); Marisa Pavan (Nicole Bouchard); Casey Adams (Lieutenant Moore); James Gleason (General Cokely); Wally Vernon (Lipinsky); Henry Letondal (Cognac Pete); Fred Libby (Lieutenant Schmidt); Ray Hyke (Mulcahy); Paul Fix (Gowdy); James Lilburn (Young Soldier); Henry Morgan (Morgan); Dan Borzage (Gilbert); Bill Henry (Holsen); Henry Kulky (Company Cook); Jack Pennick (Ferguson); Ann Codee (Nun); Stanley Johnson (Lieutenant Cunningham); Luis Alberni (The Great Uncle); Barry Norton (Priest); Torben Meyer (Mayor); Alfred Zeisler (English Colonel); George Braggerman (English Lieutenant); Sean McClory (Lieutenant Austin); Scott Forbes (Lieutenant Bennett); Charles Fitzsimons (Captain Wickham); Louis Mercier (Bouchard); Mickey Simpson (Military Police); and: Olga Andre, Tom Tyler.

On September 3, 1924, WHAT PRICE GLORY? opened on Broadway at the Plymouth Theatre. This trendsetting World War I drama* by Maxwell Anderson and Laurence Stalling is regarded as the pioneer American play to deal with the topic of war in unromanticized terms. The basic storyline conflict is between Captain Flagg and Sergeant Quirt, two rough-and-tumble profes-

---

*One of the most intriguing revivals of the play was in 1948-1949 when John Ford directed a West Coast production starring Ward Bond as Captain Flagg, Pat O'Brien as Sergeant Quirt, with Maureen O'Hara as Charmaine and a supporting cast which included: John Wayne, Gregory Peck, William Lundigan, and Wallace Ford. Proceeds went to raising money for the Military Order of the Purple Heart.

sional servicemen who, in World War I France, vie for the favors of French tart Charmaine. That episode aside, they return to the battlefront trenches, with fast-talking Quirt (whose trademark is "sez you") shouting the famous tag line, "Hey Flagg, wait for baby!" It was lauded for being ". . . so true, so alive, so salty, and so richly satisfying" (Alexander Woollcott, *New York Sun*) and enjoyed a run of 435 performances.

On the screen, WHAT PRICE GLORY? became Fox Films' profitable answer to MGM's smash hit, THE BIG PARADE (1925), q.v., which was written by WHAT PRICE GLORY?'s co-author, Laurence Stallings. "It's a picture that has everything except an out and out love story of the calibre of the one that there was in THE BIG PARADE," *Variety* enthused. "But where it lacks in that it certainly does make up in sex stuff and comedy. . . . Comedy that will appeal to the veriest lowbrow and still click with those who have no hair at all."

WHAT PRICE GLORY? traces the brawling, rough-mouthed Captain Flagg (Victor McLaglen) and virile, robust Sergeant Quirt (Edmund Lowe) as they caper through China and the Philippines, and especially as they vie for favors from a Shanghai prostitute (Phyllis Haver). In France the two Marines meet the passionate and beautiful Charmaine (Dolores Del Rio) in a little village. She has no qualms about romancing both men. It's touch-and-go between Flagg and Quirt over this free-loving young woman, but after Flagg learns that she really cares for Quirt, he defers to his pal. The two buddies leave to go back to the front and the muddy trench fighting. By their second return from the front, Quirt, having been wounded, is hospitalized (leading to his pajama-clad love scenes with Charmaine). When their unit is called back to the front, Flagg forgets about his leave and joins them. The still-recuperating Quirt rushes after his comrade. Charmaine understands that her two men probably will not return this time from fighting the Germans; their luck has run out.

As this was a silent film, it mattered little to audiences that the French Charmaine was played by a gorgeous Mexican actress (Dolores Del Rio). What appealed to filmgoers was the careful blend of romance, battle scenes, and risqué good humor. For moviegoers able to read lips, many of the leading men's mouthed profanities (not translated by the title cards) were a revelation. The *New York Times'* Mordaunt Hall observed that "war is stripped of its glamour. . . ." He also reported, "There are some very realistic fighting scenes . . . with cannon booming. Very [*sic*] lights tearing through the air and poison gas being wafted from the enemy lines. . . . The 'Trench of Death,' a short scene, is one of the tragic notes. Here a

Victor McLaglen, Dolores Del Rio, and Edmund Lowe in WHAT PRICE GLORY? (1926).

whole line of men is buried through the explosion of a mine and after the disaster the bayonet points are beheld sticking up through the earth."

Having succeeded so well (over $2,000,000) with the raw comedy, rich romance, and realistic combat of WHAT PRICE GLORY? Fox was not about to abandon Flagg and Quirt, no matter how the Broadway play had "ended." Flagg (McLaglen) and Quirt (Lowe) would appear in future screen brawls: THE COCK-EYED WORLD (1929), WOMEN OF ALL NATIONS (1931), and HOT PEPPER (1933). These two actors would be re-teamed for further non-Flagg and Quirt adventures in CALL OUT THE MARINES (1942).

Then, in the midst of the Korean War, Twentieth Century-Fox had the misguided notion of remaking* WHAT PRICE GLORY? as a Technicolor anti-war salute, with two (ex)-song-and-dance men as the sparring leads: James Cagney and Dan Dailey. "The total result is deplorable, which is shocking when you see the name of John Ford as director" (*New York Post*). Overweight, snarling James Cagney especially was too old for the role, and with Ford pushing too hard with visual images to instill meaning into an already forgotten war, it made 1952 filmgoers wonder what all the fuss had been about the original play and film. Only Corinne Calvert as the new talk of Bar-Le-Duc made a vivid (bosomy) impression as the innkeeper's pulchritudinous daughter with a penchant for singing.

WHEELS OF TERROR (Panorama Film International, 1987) Color 101 mins.

Producers, Just Betzer, Benni Korzen; line producers, Korzen, Milos Antic; director, Gordon Hessler; based on the novel by Sven Hassel; screenplay, Nelson Gidding; production designer, Vladistav Lasic; music, Ole Hoyer; camera, George Nikolic; editor, Bob Gordon.

David Carradine (Colonel von Weisshagen); Don W. Moffett (Captain von Barring); Keith Szarabajka ("Old Man"); Bruce Davison (Porta); Jay O. Sanders (Tiny); David Patrick Kelly (The Legionnaire); Slavko Stimac (Sven); Andrija Maricic (Stege); Boris Kommenic (Bauer); Bane Vidakovic (Muller); Oliver Reed (The

---

*In *The Hollywood Professionals, Volume I* (1973), Kingsley Canham compares the two versions: ". . . Walsh's heroes were like two bulls in a china shop, but then Walsh was concerned with their adventures while Ford uses their escapades and reactions to develop his point about the behaviour patterns of men in war, with the girl representing a civilising influence on their anarchic, aggressive natures."

General); Irene Prosen (The Madam); and: Svetlana, Gordana Les, Lidija Pieill, Annie Korzen.

The Allies were not the only ones to use "Dirty Dozen" attack squads in World War II. According to WHEELS OF TERROR, based on Sven Hassel's best-selling novel, the Nazis recruited such members from its Penal Regiments—a collection of confirmed criminals and political/religious dissenters. Their mission (im)possible is to explode a Soviet ammunition train on the Russian Eastern front of 1943.

If imitation is the sincerest form of flattery then WHEELS OF TERROR is deeply indebted to Robert Aldrich's THE DIRTY DOZEN (1967), q.v., and its sequels, as well as to Clint Eastwood's KELLY'S HEROES (1969), q.v. The stock characters comprising the hit squad are guided by kindly Captain von Barring (Don W. Moffett) and the sinister Colonel von Weisshagen (David Carradine), and tormented by the ruthless General (Oliver Reed). They enjoy partying at the whorehouse run by the Madam (Irene Prosen) and thrive on the pulsating action of their commando raid. The focal trio of characters are the ironically named Tiny (Jay O'Sanders), the Legionnaire (David Patrick Kelly), and the slighty crazy Porta (Bruce Davison). A sidelight of the film shows the men here, like the "Dirty Dozen" crew, undertaking their tough assignment not for the glory of the homeland, but for personal reasons, none of which have to do with the glories of the Fuehrer or the Third Reich.

Variety reported of this actioner, "Screenplay and production occasionally lean towards the crude, but most of the way plot and character delineations as well as the playing in all roles are clean-cut and convincing. Bloodshed and brutality and the awful noise of battle (latter complemented by even louder soundtrack music) is kept reasonably in check."

WILD BLUE YONDER (Republic, 1952) 98 mins.

Producer, Herbert J. Yates; director, Allan Dwan; story, Andrew Geer, Charles Grayson; screenplay, Richard Tregaskis; art director, James Sullivan; set decorators, John McCarthy, Jr., Charles Thompson; costumes, Adele Palmer; music, Victor Young; songs: Robert Crawford; Young and Ned Washington; Young and Dwan; Charles R. Green; special effects, Ellis F. Thackery, Howard Lydecker, Theodore Lydecker; camera, Reggie Lanning; editor, Richard L. Van Enger.

Wendell Corey (Captain Harold Calvert); Vera Ralston (Lieutenant Helen Landers); Forrest Tucker (Major Tom West); Phil Harris (Sergeant Hank Stack); Walter Brennan (Major General Wolfe); William Ching (Lieutenant Ted Cranshaw); Ruth Donnelly

(Major Ida Winton); Harry Carey, Jr. (Sergeant Shaker Schuker); Penny Edwards (Connie Hudson); Wally Cassell (Sergeant Pulaski); James Brown (Sergeant Pop Davis); Richard Erdman (Corporal Frenchy); Philip Pine (Sergeant Tony); Martin Kilburn (Peanuts); Hal Baylor (Sergeant Eric Nelson); Joe Brown, Jr. (Sergeant O'Hara); Jack Kelly (Lieutenant Jessup); Bob Beban (Sergeant Barney Killion); Peter Coe (Sergeant Pollio); Hall Bartlett (Lieutenant Jorman); William Witney (General Curtis E. LeMay); David Sharpe (Sergeant "Red" Irwin); Paul Livermore (Sergeant Harker); Jay Silverheels (Benders); Glen Vernon (Crew Man); Joel Allen (Chaplain Goodrich); Don Garner (George); Gayle Kellogg (Pilot); Gil Herman, Freeman Lusk, Reed Hadley (Commanding Officers); Richard Avonde (Joe Wurtzel); Robert Karnes (Co-Pilot); Kathleen Freeman (Nurse Baxter); Ray Hyke, Jim Leighton (Lieutenants); John Hart, Robert Kent, Paul McGuire (Generals); Amy Iwanabe (Tokyo Rose's Voice); Andy Brennan (Orderly); Bob Morgan (Engineer Schiller); Steve Wayne (Sergeant); Stan Holbrook (Bombardier); Myron Healey, Jack Sherman (Tower Voices).

Hollywood had by no means exhausted the possibilities of exploiting World War II on screen, and Republic Pictures' head Herbert J. Yates was definitely not through promoting his protegée/wife-to-be Vera Ralston, the former ice skating star. If John Wayne had not abhorred working with Czechoslovakian-born Ms. Ralston, he would certainly have been cast in the role which went to Wendell Corey.

There are feeble attempts within WILD BLUE YONDER to carry on the celluloid traditions of nurses in combat found in SO PROUDLY WE HAIL (1943) and CRY HAVOC (1943), qq.v. Lieutenant Helen Landers (Vera Ralston) is one of the nurses, under the command of motherly but tough Major Ida Winton (Ruth Donnelly), serving in the front lines of the Pacific Theatre of World War II. She knows her professional duty but cannot help being attracted to both Captain Harold Calvert (Wendell Corey) and Major Tom West (Forrest Tucker). These two Army Air Force flyers are better piloting B-29 Superfortress planes than courting exotic, accented Helen. On a major raid against a Japanese target, the mission is successful, but West is fatally wounded. It leaves the path clear for Calvert and Helen.

One of the strange anomalies of WILD BLUE YONDER, directed by the veteran, patient Allan Dwan, is the jarring introduction of musical (!) interludes within this contrived war drama. At one point Sergeant Hank Stack (played by Phil Harris) breaks into a rendition of his hit record, "The Thing," and later warbles "The Heavy Bomber Song," while Lieutenant Ted Cranshaw (William Ching) sings "The Man Behind the Armor-Plated Desk." Obviously passing a physical wasn't the only requirement for this branch of the military service.

In a world of entertainment increasingly dominated by television, WILD BLUE YONDER did not fare well commercially in relation to its hefty production costs. The cast is filled with veteran Republic Pictures' action performers (David Sharpe, John Hart); the offspring of famous performers (Andy Brennan, Joe Brown Jr.); and even a future filmmaker (Hall Bartlett) who in the late 1980s would become a best-selling novelist.

British release title: THUNDER ACROSS THE PACIFIC.

WING AND A PRAYER (Twentieth Century-Fox, 1944) 97 mins.

Producers, William A. Bacher, Walter Morosco; director, Henry Hathaway; screenplay, Jerome Cady; art directors, Lyle Wheeler, Lewis Creber; set decorators, Thomas Little, Fred J. Rode; music, Hugo Friedhofer; music director, Emil Newman; assistant director, Henry Weinberger; sound, Alfred Bruzlin; special camera effects, Fred Sersen; camera, Glen MacWilliams; editor, Watson Webb.

Don Ameche (Bingo Harper); Dana Andrews (Edward Moulton); William Eythe (Oscar Scott); Charles Bickford (Captain Waddell); Sir Cedric Hardwicke (Admiral); Kevin O'Shea (Cookie Cunningham); Richard Jaeckel (Beezy Bessemer); Henry "Harry" Morgan (Malcolm Brainard); Richard Crane (Ensign Gus Chisholm); Glenn Langan (Executive Officer); Renny McEvoy (Ensign Cliff Hale); Bob Bailey (Paducah Holloway); Reed Hadley (Commander O'Donnell); George Mathews (Dooley); B. S. Pully (Flat Top); Dave Willock (Hans Jacobson); Murray Alper (Benny O'Neill); Charles Lang (Ensign Chuck White); Irving Bacon (Scissors); John Miles (Ensign "Lovebug" Markham); Joseph Haworth (Murphy); Charles B. Smith (Alfalfa); Ray Teal (Executive Officer); Charles Trowbridge (Medical Officer); John Kelly (Lew); Larry Thompson (Sam Cooper); Billy Lechner (Anti-Aircraft Gunner); Jerry Shane (Foley); Robert Condon, Blake Edwards, Frank Ferry, Mike Kilian, William Manning, Mel Schubert (Pilots); Carl Knowles (Marine Orderly); John Kellogg (Assistant Air Officer); Eddie Acuff, Irving Bacon, Eddie Friedman, Frank Marlowe (Sailors); Chet Brandenburg, Jimmy Dodd, Robin Short, Jay Ward (Mail Orderlies); Raymond Roe (Gunner); Stanley Andrews (Marine General); Van Anthony, Selmer Jackson,

Frank McLure, Jack Mower, Edward Van Sloan, Charles Waldron, Pierre Watkin, Crane Whitley, Frederic Worlock, and Matt McHugh.

The decisive battle of Midway (June 4-6, 1942) was the turning point in naval warfare in the Pacific Theater, allowing the U.S. to turn from a defensive to an offensive position now that the Japanese carriers were no longer an overwhelming threat. The battle was primarily one of air attack, rather than artillery, with the Japanese (whose ships greatly outnumbered the Americans) losing four carriers (*Akagi, Hiryu, Kaga, Soryu*) and the U.S. losing the USS *Yorktown*. Events leading up to this naval encounter form the basis of WING AND A PRAYER (the title of a very popular World War II song).

The focal figures in WING AND A PRAYER are squadron commander Edward Moulton (Dana Andrews), feisty flight commander Bingo Harper (Don Ameche), who must hide his deep regard for his men, and Oscar Scott (William Eythe), a movie star and now courageous serviceman. Their ship, commanded by Captain Waddell (Charles Bickford), is the aircraft carrier "X" which has top secret orders to create diversionary tactics to mislead the enemy about the true whereabouts of the U.S. fleet. The day-to-day routine of the men aboard the carrier, as they grow restless with being decoys, is well-depicted (director Henry Hathaway did research aboard an aircraft carrier), even to Harper's tough and unpopular (with the men) decision not to radio their location to a ship's pilot who has lost his course, for fear of alerting the enemy to their position.

For the record, there is a scene of the men aboard the carrier watching a print of Betty Grable and Alice Faye in TIN PAN ALLEY (1940).

WINGS (Paramount, 1927) 139 minutes.

Producer, Lucien Hubbard; director, William A. Wellman; story, John Monk Saunders; screenplay, Hope Loring, Louis D. Lighton; titles Julian Johnson; assistant director, Norman Z. McLeod; supervisors of flying sequences, S. C. Campbell, Ted Parson, Carl von Hartmann, James A. Healy; music score, J. S. Zamecnik; song, Zamecnik and Ballad MacDonald; engineering effects, Roy Pomeroy; camera, Harry Perry; additional camera, E. Burton Steene, Cliff Blackston, Russell Harland, Bert Baldridge, Frank Cotner, Fraxon M. Dean, Ray Olsen, Herman Schoop, L. Guy Wilky, Al Williams; editor, Lucien Hubbard.

Clara Bow (Mary Preston); Charles "Buddy" Rogers (Jack

Powell); Richard Arlen (David Armstrong); Jobyna Ralston (Sylvia Lewis); Gary Cooper (Cadet White); Arlette Marchal (Celeste); El Brendel (Patrick O'Brien); Gunboat Smith (The Sergeant); Richard Tucker (Air Commander); Julia Swayne Gordon (Mrs. Armstrong); Henry B. Walthall (Mr. Armstrong); George Irving (Mr. Powell); Hedda Hopper (Mrs. Powell); Nigel De Brulier (Peasant); Roscoe Karns (Lieutenant Cameron); James Pierce (Military Police); Carl von Hartmann (German Officer); Tommy Carr, Dick Grace, Rod Rogers (Aviators); Charles Barton (Doughboy Hit by Ambulance); Margery Chapin Wellman (Peasant Woman); Gloria Wellman (Peasant Child); William Wellman (Doughboy).

If other studios' THE BIG PARADE (1925) and WHAT PRICE GLORY? (1927), qq.v., could celebrate the doughboy infantryman in World War I, then Paramount intended to cash in on the war film cycle, but with an additional twist. It would be an epic study of the gallant First World War fighting men of the sky. At a cost of approximately $2,000,000, with the full cooperation of the U.S. War Department,* and on-location filming at Kelly Field near San Antonio, Texas, the massively extravagant WINGS was directed by William A. Wellman. He had been a member of the Lafayette Escadrille in World War I. John Monk Saunders, who wrote the story of WINGS, had been a former journalist and served as second lieutenant flyer in the First World War. Their war experiences lent authenticity to the film. To execute some of the extraordinary stunts employed in WINGS, skilled stunt pilot Dick Grace was hired. All the aerial sequences were staged live, with no process photography used for the magnificently captured dogfights.

WINGS opens with a statement by Charles A. Lindbergh, who said of American flyers in World War I, ". . . Feats were performed and deeds accomplished which were far greater than any peace accomplishments of aviation." The film is dedicated "To those young warriors of the sky, whose wings are folded about them forever. . . ."

---

*The War Department provided men, planes, ammunition, tanks, field equipment, etc., with the proviso that it have full approval rights over the final production. Not only did the War Department intend to use the completed film to generate public interest, support, and recruitment in the Flying Corps, but it actually used the filmmaking as a training ground for its pilots. Among the flyers and technical advisers on WINGS who went on to noteworthy military careers were: General Hoyt S. Vanderberg (commander of the Ninth Army Air Force in World War II) and Lieutenant General Frank M. Andrews (he had been selected to command all American forces in Europe in World War II, but died in an aircrash in Iceland in 1943 and General Dwight D. Eisenhower replaced him).

Both Jack Powell (Charles "Buddy" Rogers) and David Armstrong (Richard Arlen) love Sylvia Lewis (Jobyna Ralston). During World War I the young men join the Army Air Corps and go off to basic training together. ("The first steps on the road to glory—no thrills . . . no glamour; and as exciting as going back to school!") Before long the two become good friends. Meanwhile they experience their first sense of mortality. Hardened veteran pilot Cadet White (Gary Cooper) stops by their tent before going up on a training exercise. Between bites of a candy bar he advises, "When your time comes, you're going to get it." Seconds later his plane crashes and he is dead. Soon Powell and Armstrong are in France where they learn that Mary Preston (Clara Bow)—who has always loved Powell—is at the front, having joined the Women's Motor Corps. The two men prove themselves in combat, are awarded medals, and given a Paris furlough. When all leaves are cancelled, Mary insures that the drunken Powell gets back to base on time but at the cost of sacrificing her reputation and she is sent home. Later, Armstrong is shot down over enemy territory and a German aviator tells the Americans that Armstrong is dead. The angered Powell wants revenge and takes up a plane, bombing and machine-gunning any German targets in sight. Meanwhile, Armstrong has escaped from the Germans, stolen one of their planes, and is flying back to Allied lines. When Powell spots this German plane he shoots it down, not knowing who its pilot is. Powell lands, hoping to cut the insignia from the plane, and finds the dying Armstrong at a nearby French farmhouse. Armstrong dies in his arms. While sorting through his friend's possessions, Powell learns that it was his friend whom Sylvia loved best. This knowledge disillusions Powell further. After the war Powell is back home, still brokenhearted over his buddy's death. Mary restores his confidence. Powell goes to his late friend's parents, begging their forgiveness. Mrs. Armstrong (Julia Swayne Gordon) comforts the young man, insisting that she forgives him. After all, she explains, "It was war." As Mary and Powell sit in her back yard planning their lives together, they see a shooting star. The memory of their dead young friend will be with them forever.

To insure that WINGS would not miss any angle to lure in the public, several sequences were shot in the gimmicky Magnascope widescreen process. The film contains elements to appeal to all tastes. There is an expansive recreation of the horrendous battle at St. Mihiel. The aerial sequences are so real and majestic that they stand on their own. There is filmdom's "It" girl in the lead role with two very popular young actors (Richard Arlen, Charles "Buddy"

Rogers) playing opposite her. There is a relative newcomer (Gary
Cooper) who would make a tremendous impact on audiences and go
on to stardom and an Academy Award. WINGS celebrates the
glories of war, particularly the reckless yet gallant men of the sky. In
the pitched trench warfare scenes, in the death of Cadet White and
David Armstrong it makes its own commentary about the waste
of war.

WINGS would win the first Academy Award for Best Picture,
as well as an Oscar for Best Engineering Effects. It was a huge
moneymaker both in its silent version and a year later when it was
reissued with sound effects. (Five years later Paramount would issue
a crisp videocassette version of WINGS.) Footage from WINGS
would be utilized by Paramount Pictures and other studios for years
to come, while director William Wellman, scenarist John Monk
Saunders, and star-to-be Gary Cooper would also participate in
several other combat films.

WINGS OVER THE PACIFIC (Monogram, 1943) 59 mins.

Producer, Lindsley Parsons; director, Phil Rosen; screenplay,
George Wallace Sayre; music director, Edward J. Kay; camera,
Mack Stengler; editor, Carl Pierson.

Inez Cooper (Nona Butler); Edward Norris (Allan); Montagu
Love (Jim Butler); Robert Armstrong (Pieter, the Dutch Trader);
Henry Guttman (Kurt); Ernie Adams (Harry); Santini Pauiloa
(Island Chief); John Roth (Taro); Alex Havier (Japanese Officer);
George Kamel, James Lono, Hawksha Paia (Natives).

The minor league, poverty row film studios could not afford to
produce elaborate combat studies, let alone pay for appropriate
stock footage. Mostly, when they attempted to depict the glories of
men in war, the battles became skirmishes talked about (but not
seen), conflicts between single representatives of opposing armies
(rather than massive confrontations), and to make up for the paucity
of battle action visuals, there was always the tried-and-true romantic triangle formula.

Jim Butler (Montagu Love) is a U.S. World War I veteran who
has had enough of war. He and his daughter Nona (Inez Cooper)
live on a remote Pacific island, avoiding all contact with the raging
World War II. Then all hell breaks loose. U.S. Naval pilot Allan
(Edward Norris) and German fighter pilot Kurt (Henry Guttman)
crash-land on the isle after a nasty dogfight. Kurt quickly spots the
natural reservoirs of oil and alerts the Japanese to invade. And. . . .

A decade earlier, co-star Robert Armstrong had sailed for a

magical island with an oversized gorilla; in WINGS OVER THE PACIFIC he is the Dutch trader who cares for Nona and freedom.

WOODEN CROSSES *see*: THE ROAD TO GLORY.

THE WOODEN HORSE (British Lion, 1951) 101 mins.

Producer, Ian Dalrymple; director, Jack Lee; based on the book by Eric Williams; screenplay, Williams; production designer, William Kellner; music, Clifton Parker; music director, Muir Mathieson; camera, G. Pennington-Richards; editors, John Seabourne, Sr., Peter Seabourne.

Leo Genn (Peter); David Tomlinson (Phil); Anthony Steele (John); David Greene (Bennett); Peter Burton (Nigel); Patrick Waddington (Senior British Officer); Michael Goodliffe (Robbie); Anthony Dawson (Pomfret); Bryan Forbes (Paul); Franz Schafheitlein (Commandant); Hans Meyer (Charles); Jacques Brunius (Andre); Peter Finch (The Australian); Dan Cunningham (David); Russell Waters ("Wings" Cameron); Ralph Ward (Adjutant); Her-

Leo Genn (second from left) in THE WOODEN HORSE (1951).

bert Kilitz (Camp Guard); Lis Lovert (Kamma); Helge Ericksen (Sigmund); Walter Hertner (German Policeman); Meinhart Maur (Hotel Proprietor); Walter Gotell (The Follower); and: Philip Dale, Johannes Johanson, Bill Travers.

What happens to men on the fighting front creates tremendous dramatic opportunities for dissecting the essence of the human spirit. In the same vein, the plight and resourcefulness of prisoners-of-war has long provided much the same occasion for focusing on a wide range of individuals caught in a common wartime cause (survival). How soldiers react to such internment is a never-ending fascination to filmmakers.

One of the earliest post-World War II examples of the genre was THE CAPTIVE HEART (1946), a British-produced film by Basil Dearden shot at Marlag Nord, a former German p.o.w. compound near Hamburg. Then came the publication of Paul Brickhill's remembrances, *The Great Escape* (1950) which would not be turned into a hit motion picture until 1963. In the meantime, there was THE WOODEN HORSE, one of the more energetic English entries in the sub-genre.

At Stalag Luft III in 1943 Germany, enterprising British prisoners Peter (Leo Genn) and Phil (David Tomlinson) devise an ingenious escape scheme. They build a box-shaped exercise horse which is lugged out to the prison compound yard daily. While other prisoners vault over its structure, one to two prisoners are inside, busily digging a tunnel. Eventually John (Anthony Steel) joins the escape plan. After several near-detections by the Germans, the trio break to freedom late one night. Peter and John are sped along their way together, thanks to the French and Danish underground. In Sweden they meet up with Bennett (David Greene), who has also made it to freedom.

The film was so successful that it set the pattern for many such films to come. One of the joys of this and other British productions of the 1940s and 1950s is the tremendous ensemble playing by the cast. There are rarely any "star turns," each performer acting as their real-life counterparts would have done—as a member of a team with a common goal.

A YANK IN INDO-CHINA (Columbia, 1952) 67 mins.

Producer, Sam Katzman; director, Wallace A. Grissell; screenplay, Samuel Newman; art director, Paul Palmentola; music director, Ross DiMaggio; camera, William Whitley; editor, Aaron Stell.

John Archer (Mulvancy); Douglas Dick (Clint Marshall); Jean Willes (Cleo); Maura Murphy (Ellen Philips); Hayward Soo Hoo (Jake); Don Harvey (Swede Philips); Harold Fong (Captain Sung);

Rory Mallinson (Professor Johnson); Leonard Penn (Colonel Sabien); Kamtong (Major Leo Kay); Pierre Watkin (Kingston); Peter Chang (General Wang).

In the years before the French abandoned Indo-China, that country seemed an exotic locale for Hollywood to situate action pictures. Moreover, it was geographically and politically remote, and it allowed a fresh battlefield for the West to fight its newest foes —the Communists.

Mulvancy (John Archer) and Clint Marshall (Douglas Dick) operate an air freight service in Indo-China. One of their extracurricular activities is destroying cargo belonging to the Reds. With Cleo (Jean Willes) and mother-to-be Ellen Philips (Maura Murphy) in tow, they flee from the enemy through the jungle. The United Nations force provide the support for Mulvancy and Marshall to explode the enemy base.

No one at the time realized it, but this helter-skelter Sam Katzman budget movie was setting the path for such later action/ combat film series as RAMBO and MISSING IN ACTION, qq.v. It was a follow-up to Katzman's earlier A YANK IN KOREA, *infra.*

British release title: HIDDEN SECRET.

A YANK IN KOREA (Columbia, 1951) 73 mins.

Producer, Sam Katzman; director, Lew Landers; story, Leo Lieberman; screenplay, William Sackheim; art director, Paul Palmentola; set decorator, Sidney Clifford; music director, Ross DiMaggio; assistant director, Leonard Katzman; sound, John Westmoreland; camera, William Whitley; editor, Edwin Bryant.

Lon McCallister (Andy Smith); William "Bill" Phillips (Sergeant Kirby); Brett King (Milo Pagano); Larry Stewart (Sollie Kaplan); William Tannen (Lieutenant Lewis); Tommy Farrell (Jinx Hamilton); Norman Wayne (Stan Howser); Rusty Wescoatt (Sergeant Hutton); William Haade (Corporal Jawolski); Sunny Vickers (Peggy Cole); Richard Paxton (Powers): Ralph Hodges (Randy Smith); Richard Gould (Junior).

Lon McCallister gained a following in the 1940s for his screen interpretations of wholesome farmboys (as in HOME IN INDIANA, 1944). His career was on the downslide by the time of this modest production tossed out by quickie filmmaker Sam Katzman. To everyone's amazement its topicality gave the movie unexpected box-office strength.

With the Korean War (and stock footage) as the backdrop, A YANK IN KOREA details the transformation of newly married

Andy Smith (Lon McCallister) who becomes part of the overseas police action and finds himself by daring deeds on the battlefront (destroying a munitions dump, etc.). Along the way his carelessness nearly kills his fellow GIs, which does nothing for their accepting him into their number.

British release title: LETTER FROM KOREA.

A YANK IN THE R.A.F. (Twentieth Century-Fox, 1941) 98 mins.

Producer, Darryl F. Zanuck; director, Henry King; story, Melville Crossman [Zanuck]; screenplay, Darrel Ware, Karl Tunberg; art directors, Richard Day, James Basevi; set decorator, Thomas Little; costumes, Travis Banton; music director, Alfred Newman; songs, Leo Robin and Ralph Rainger; special effects, Fred Sersen; camera, Leon Shamroy, Ronald Neame; editor, Barbara McLean.

Tyrone Power (Tim Baker); Betty Grable (Carol Brown); John Sutton (Wing Commander Morley); Reginald Gardiner (Roger Pillby); Donald Stuart (Corporal Harry Baker); John Wilde (Graves); Richard Fraser (Thorndyke); Morton Lowry (Squadron Leader); Ralph Byrd (Al Bennett); Denis Green (Redmond); Bruce Lester (Richardson); Gilchrist Stuart (Wales); Lester Matthews (Group Captain); Stuart Robertson (Intelligence Officer); Frederic Worlock (Canadian Major); Ethel Griffies (Mrs. Fitzhugh); Claud Allister, Guy Kingsford (Officers); John Rogers (Chauffeur); John Hartley (Co-Pilot); Eric Lonsdale (Radio Man); Alphonse Martell (Headwaiter); Lynne Roberts (Nurse at Boat); Fortunio Bonanova (Headwaiter at Regency); Gladys Cooper (Mrs. Pillby); Denis Hoey (Intelligence Officer); James Craven (Instructor); Gavin Muir (Wing Commander); Lillian Porter (Chorus Girl); G. P. Huntley, Jr. (Radio Operator); Forrester Harvey (Cubby); Gil Perkins (Sergeant); Charles Irwin (Uniformed Man); John Meredith (Cadet); Howard Davis (Air Raid Warden); Patrick O'Hearn (Navigator); Leslie Denison (Group Commander); Kurt Kreuger, Otto Reichow (German Pilots); Hans Von Morhart (German Sergeant); Bobbie Hale (Cab Driver); Hans Schumm (German Soldier); Crauford Kent (Group Captain); Maureen Roden-Ryan (Barmaid).

If one must go to war and risk death for country, there is some compensation if Betty Grable is the girl who loves you.

Twentieth Century-Fox yanked shapely singing star Grable away from her Technicolor musicals and assigned her to this patriotic flagwaver with Tyrone Power as her leading man. It was one of the major pre-World War II films showing Americans fighting with the British R.A.F. in the days before Pearl Harbor brought the U.S. officially into the war.

Cocky American pilot (Tim Baker) ferries bomber planes from Canada to England. In London (during an air raid) he encounters Texas entertainer Carol Brown (Betty Grable), an old flame. To impress her and win her affections he joins the R.A.F., but his arrogant ways and flippancy about the British war effort anger his co-flyers. Meanwhile Carol, who is a volunteer nurse, is romancing Wing Commander Morley (John Sutton). When Baker's pal, Roger Pillby (Reginald Gardiner), is killed during a bombing mission, Baker awakens to the seriousness of war. He and Morley are among those providing air support for the British evacuation at Dunkirk. Their plane is shot down and they make their way through German lines. When they return to England Carol realizes that Baker is a hero and admits she loves him.

A YANK IN THE R.A.F., filmed in black-and-white (as an economy measure and to prove it was "serious" entertainment), uses chunks of newsreel footage for its combat scenes, with some restaging of the Dunkirk event integrated into the mix. Grable sings "Hi-Ya Love" and "Another Little Dream Won't Do Us Any Harm" in the nightclub interludes. In the original script the hero dies at Dunkirk, but the British government, which cooperated in making this picture, requested storyline changes for morale purposes. A YANK IN THE R.A.F. was extremely popular and at one point it was rumored that Twentieth Century-Fox would produce a sequel. (It never was made.)

A YANK IN VIET-NAM (Allied Artists, 1964) 80 mins.

Producer, Wray Davis; director, Marshall Thompson; story, Jack Lewis; screenplay, Jane Wardell, Lewis; art director, Frank Holquist; set decorator, Ronald Witort; costumes, Rynol Dahlman; music/music director, Richard LaSalle; special effects, Crisanto Hilario; camera, Emmanuel Rojas; editors, Basil Wrangell, Orven Schanzer.

Marshall Thompson (Major Benson); Enrique Magalona (Andre); Mario Barri (Houng); Kieu Chinh (Herself); Urban Drew (Colonel Haggerty); Donald Seely (Kastens); Hoang Vinh Loc (Chau); My Tin (Quon); Rene Laporte (Father Francois); Doan Chau Mau (Colonel Thai); Pham Phuoc Chi (Kim); Nam Chau (Dr. The); Kieu Nanh (Madame The); Le Van (Viet Cong Leader); Nam Luong (Cung).

Former MGM contract player Marshall Thompson turned director/ actor in A YANK IN VIET-NAM. It was shot on location in Vietnam and is one of the few American-financed pictures of the decade to focus on this bloody war turf. It made no impact on the public and became lower-bill fodder all too soon. In retrospect it seems more telling than it was when released.

Major Benson (Marshall Thompson) is among the Marines stationed in South Vietnam. The Viet Cong capture him when his helicopter crashes. He is saved by a rescue squad which is out to recover Dr. The (Nam Chau) from the enemy. Benson falls in love with the doctor's daughter (Kieu Chinh) and they make it back to friendly lines thanks to the intervention of Marine paratroopers.

There is plenty of jungle guerrilla warfare, which is the raison d'être for this rather choppily edited film. But, said *Variety*, it is ". . . undistinguished as screen literature and devoid of revealing insight into the nature of that conflict. . . ."

A.k.a.: THE YEAR OF THE TIGER.

A YANK ON THE BURMA ROAD (Metro-Goldwyn-Mayer, 1942) 65 mins.

Producer, Samuel Marx; director, George B. Seitz; screenplay, Gordon Kahn, Hugo Butler, David Lang; camera, Lester White; editor, Gene Ruggiero.

Laraine Day (Gail Farwood); Barry Nelson (Joe Tracey); Stuart Crawford (Tom Farwood); Keye Luke (Kim How); Victor Sen Yung (Wing); Philip Ahn (Dr. Franklin); Knox Manning (Radio Announcer); Matthew Boulton (Rangoon Aide de Camp).

Americans and much of the world may have been caught by surprise by the Japanese attack on Pearl Harbor in December 1941, but MGM evidently was not. This "B" film was in distribution by late January 1942.

Pugnacious New York taxi driver Joe Tracey (Barry Nelson) becomes a publicized hero when he captures two wanted gunmen. His notoriety leads to a Chinese delegation hiring him to lead a truck convoy of medical supplies along the Burma Road to Chungking. Gail Farwood (Laraine Day) is the lady without a passport searching for her aviator spouse (Stuart Crawford). Before the climactic sortie with the Japanese, Tracey had elevated himself from opportunist to patriot.

The film may be short on budget, credibility, and sharp performances, but it had a timely pro-involvement, nationalistic message to tell. It was a true forerunner of the America-going-to-war pictures and hinted at what would happen once troops (and front line nurses) got into the heat of battle (i.e., they would become better people for the harrowing experience).

THE YEAR OF THE TIGER *see*: A YANK IN VIET-NAM.

YESTERDAY'S ENEMY (Columbia, 1959) 95 mins.
Producer, Michael Carreras; director, Val Guest; based on the teleplay by Peter R. Newman; screenplay, Newman; art directors, Bernard Robinson, Don Mingaye; camera, Arthur Grant; editors, James Needs, Alfred Cox;
Stanley Baker (Captain Langford): Guy Rolfe (Padre); Leo McKern (Max); Gordon Jackson (Sergeant MacKenzie); David Oxley (Doctor); Richard Pasco (Second Lieutenant Hastings); Russell Waters (Brigadier); Philip Ahn (Yamazaki); Bryan Forbes (Dawson); Wolf [Wolfe] Morris (Informer); David Lodge (Perkins); Percy Herbert (Wilson); Edwina Carroll (Suni); Barry Lowe (Turner); Alan Keith (Bendish); Howard Williams (Davies): Timothy Bateson (Simpson); Arthur Lovegrove (Patrick); Donald Churchill (Elliott); Nicholas Brady (Orderly); Barry Steele (Brown).
There is nothing pretty about this grisly war tale. It examines the thesis that in wartime ordinary rules of decency are usually (or must be?) outweighed by expediency. Hard as these decisions are, they are more difficult if the responsible officer in charge has strong moral scruples. And is there anyone more moral-bound than a repressed, battle-weary, by-the-books English officer?
In 1942 Burma Captain Langford (Stanley Baker) is trying to get his remaining unit members back to headquarters. Along the way they exterminate those defending a seemingly unimportant village and Langford's suspicions are aroused when he notes there is a high-ranking Japanese officer among the dead, as well as a suspicious field map. Tautly-strung Langford demands to know what is behind these two discoveries and tortures a captive and kills two civilian hostages to get the answers. (His troopers are aghast at his inhumane actions.) Before long, the situation has reversed. Langford and the now fewer survivors of his squad are the prisoners of the advancing enemy, and the Japanese do as he would have done: kill him when he will not talk and execute his men.
YESTERDAY'S ENEMY was not widely seen, coming at the wrong end of a cyclical war film craze. However, it was one of the better pictures made by the British Hammer Films and boasts a strong cast. "One of the film's best features is that the soldiers all seem to act, think and invariably talk like soldiers and not actors and so the smell of fear, blood, mud and sweat communicates itself to the audience" (*Variety*).

THE YOUNG INVADERS *see*: DARBY'S RANGERS.

THE YOUNG LIONS (Twentieth Century-Fox, 1958) 167 mins.
Producer, Al Lichtman; director, Edward Dmytryk; based on the novel by Irwin Shaw; screenplay, Edward Anhalt; art directors, Lyle R. Wheeler, Addison Hehr; set decorators, Walter M. Scott, Stuart A. Reiss; costumes, Adele Balkan, Charles LeMaire; make-up, Ben Nye; music, Hugo Friedhofer; music director, Lionel Newman; special effects, L. B. Abbott; camera, Joe MacDonald; editor, Dorothy Spencer.

Marlon Brando (Christian Diestl); Montgomery Clift (Noah Ackerman); Dean Martin (Michael Whiteacre); Hope Lange (Hope Plowman); Barbara Rush (Margaret Freemantle); May Britt (Gretchen Hardenberg); Maximilian Schell (Captain Hardenberg); Dora Doll (Simone); Lee Van Cleef (Sergeant Rickett); Liliane Montevecchi (Francoise); Parley Baer (Brant); Arthur Franz (Lieutenant Green); Hal Baylor (Private Burnecker); Richard Gardner (Private Cowley); Herbert Rudley (Captain Colclough); John Alderson (Corporal Kraus); Sam Gilman (Private Faber); L. Q. Jones (Private Donnelly); Julian Burton (Private Brailsford); Vaughn Taylor (John Plowman); Gene Roth (Cafe Manager); Stephen Bekassy (German Major); Ivan Triesault (German Colonel); Clive Morgan (British Colonel); Ashley Cowan (Maier); Paul Comi (Private Abbott); Michael Pataki (Private Hagstrom); John Gabriel (Burna); Kendall Scott (Emerson); Stan Kambler (Acaro); Robert Ellenstein (Rabbi); Jeffrey Sayre (Drunk); Kurt Katch (Camp Commandant); Milton Frome (Physician); Otto Reichow (Bavarian); Robert Burton (Colonel Mead); Harvey Stephens (General Rockland); Anne Stebbins (Brunette); Mary Pierce (Young French Girl); Ann Codee (French Woman); Christian Pasques (French Boy); Doris Wiss (Nurse); Alfred Tonkel (German Waiter); John Banner (Burgermeister); Norbert Schiller (Civilian); Henry Rowland (Sergeant); David Dabov, Art Reichle (Soldiers); Wade Cagle (Lieutenant Emerson); Lee Winter (Private First Class); Nicholas King (Medic); Harry Ellerbe (Draft Board Chairman); Craig Karr (Draft Board Secretary); Michael Smith (Draft Board Member); Voltaire Perkins (Druggist); Ann Daniels (Hatcheck Girl); Alberto Morin (Bartender); George Meader (Milkman); Joan Douglas (Maid); Ed Rickard (Mailman); and: Joe Brooks, Hubert Kerns, Ann Paige.

THE YOUNG LIONS is one of those lavish motion pictures that equate production costs and screen running time with craft and artistic value. It received tremendous publicity during its pre-production casting wars and its in-progress feuding and fussing by its method-acting leads: Marlon Brando and Montgomery Clift. To everyone's surprise (including his own), the film's most unaffected performance is turned in by Dean Martin, until then more famous as the cinema's one-time singing straight man to clowning Jerry Lewis. It was shot in widescreen CinemaScope and in black-and-white.

Based on Irwin Shaw's best-selling novel about war's corruption of the soul and the body, the storyline focuses on three disparate, focal characters—one Nazi and two G.I.s. The narrative opens in 1938 at an Alpine ski resort. Young German ski instructor Christian Diestl (Marlon Brando) favors the policies of Adolf Hitler and the Third Reich because he wants a better way for Germany. He insists to wealthy American tourist Margaret Freemantle (Barbara Rush) that he is not a Nazi. Soon war is declared and Diestl is among the Germans taking Paris; he is assigned there to arch-Nazi Captain Hardenberg (Maximilian Schell). Back home, Margaret's fiancé, Broadway producer/entertainer Michael Whiteacre (Dean Martin), cannot alter his draft status. At the draft center he meets shy store clerk Noah Ackerman (Montgomery Clift) and invites him to a cocktail party at Margaret's; there Ackerman meets Vermont-born Hope Plowman (Hope Lange). Soon Ackerman and Hope marry. Meanwhile Diestl performs his duties as a member of the occupying force in Paris, where he starts to question the glories of the Nazi regime and its determined leaders. When he begins an affair with Hardenberg's already promiscuous wife Gretchen (May Britt) he is further disillusioned.

Back in America, Ackerman, who is anxious to fight, and Whiteacre, who fears he may be a coward at heart, join the army. During basic training the intellectual Ackerman is harassed by the anti-Semitic tactics of his fellow servicemen, and in a fight he is badly beaten by four roughshod soldiers. He later deserts, but is caught. While he is in the brig his pregnant wife visits him and he decides to return to his unit. There he is finally accepted and the sadistic Captain Colclough (Herbert Rudley) is court-martialed.

In North Africa, with Rommel's elite Africa Korps, the cold-hearted Hardenberg remains the efficient soldier following brutal orders, but Diestl's growing sense of humanity gets in his way. In one episode he is ordered to kill a wounded British soldier and when he refuses, the angered Hardenberg does it. To escape the advancing Allies, Hardenberg and Diestl flee on motorcycle and when a land mine explodes under them, Hardenberg is gravely injured. When Diestl visits Hardenberg at the hospital, the officer asks for a bayonet to put a fellow patient out of his misery. Later, in bomb-scarred Berlin, Diesel learns from a disinterested Gretchen that her husband killed himself with a bayonet. He returns to Paris where he attempts to find new hope through the love of the French woman Francoise (Liliane Montevecchi), but eventually he leaves her to return to duty because, he says, "I am a German soldier."

In London Whiteacre, who has maneuvered a Special Services assignment, begins to question the propriety of his being safe from combat while others are fighting the real war. Margaret urges him to test himself in battle and he rejoins his unit now battling in Normandy. On the French battlefront he re-encounters Ackerman, who has proven himself courageous in combat. The two are part of the Allied forces which liberate a concentration camp; the same camp which Diestl has earlier visited and left in total revulsion. In the woods, as Ackerman and Whiteacre talk, a German soldier bursts upon the scene. Thinking he plans to attack, Whiteacre shoots him. It is Diestl who falls dead. The two Americans survive the war and return to America safely.

A good deal of the bite and irony of Irwin Shaw's novel was deleted or distorted in the final release version of THE YOUNG LIONS. Most critics made only token acknowledgment of the picture's strong anti-war message. They preferred to heap praise on the highly stylized performance of Marlon Brando, who dyed his hair blonde and adopted a Teutonic accent for this film. Having portrayed the neurotic underdog in several previous movies, Clift's interpretation of the victimized Noah Ackerman was less liked. Great attention went to Dean Martin for his full-bodied performance and to Maximilian Schell for his portrait of an unrelenting Nazi follower. THE YOUNG LIONS received Oscar nominations for; Cinematography, Sound, and Scoring. In particular, Hugo Friedhofer's score does a great deal to enhance a production which suffers from an episodic storyline and a focus on ideological discussion by spokespeople in set pieces rather than actual men in actual battles. THE YOUNG LIONS earned $4,480,000 in theater rentals in the U.S. and Canada, which was very decent by late 1950s standards.

THE YOUNG WARRIORS (Universal, 1967) Color 93 mins.

Producer, Gordon Kay; director, John Peyser; based on the novel *The Beardless Warriors* by Richard Matheson; screenplay, Matheson; art directors, Alexander Golitzen, Alfred Ybarra; set decorators, John McCarthy, Ralph Sylos; makeup, Bud Westmore; assistant director, Joseph Kenny; technical adviser, H. L. Covington; sound, Waldon O. Watson, Clarence Self; camera, Loyal Griggs; editor, Russell F. Schoengarth.

James Drury (Sergeant Cooley); Steve Carlson (Private Hacker); Jonathan Daly (Private Guthrie); Robert Pine (Private

Foley); Jeff Scott (Private Lippincott); Michael Stanwood (Private Riley); Johnny Alladin (Private Harris); Hank Jones (Private Fairchild); Tom Nolan (Private Tremont); Norman Fell (Sergeant Wadley); Buck Young (Private Schumacher) Kent McWhirter (The Lieutenant); and: Jon Drury, Buck Kartalian, Morgan Jones, Noam Pitlik, George Sawaya.

Hollywood took a step back with this overblown, synthetic attempt to revive the World War II combat drama.

In 1944 Europe* battle-worn Sergeant Cooley (James Drury) is assigned a fresh batch of inexperienced recruits—his "young warriors." The attention focuses on Private Hacker (Steve Carlson), a loner who develops a thirst for killing the enemy, even when they try to surrender. Hacker and Cooley are in agreement about nothing, but later it is Hacker who drags the wounded Cooley to safety during an assault on a German position. When Cooley returns to the U.S., Hacker becomes the unit sergeant. He is the tough veteran who indoctrinates the next batch of green infantrymen into the rites of war.

THE YOUNG WARRIORS was properly slapped down when released. *Variety* lambasted it for ". . . a screenplay ridden with just about every possible cliché and a cast that is collectively damp behind the ears. . . ." The only good aspects of this movie are its visual production values.

YUSHA NOMI *see*: NONE BUT THE BRAVE.

ZERO HOUR *see*: THE ROAD TO GLORY.

---

*The film opens with the statement: "This is a story of young men in war. It takes place in Europe during World War II. It could be any army . . . any place . . . any time."

GREAT COMBAT PICTURES: FILMOGRAPHY

ABOUT WORLD WAR I:

ACES HIGH (1976)
ALL QUIET ON THE WESTERN FRONT (1930)
ALL QUIET ON THE WESTERN FRONT (1979-TV)
BEHIND THE FRONT (1926)
BEYOND VICTORY (1931)
THE BIG PARADE (1925)
THE BLUE MAX (1966)
BORN FOR GLORY [FOR EVER ENGLAND] (1935)
CRIMSON ROMANCE (1934)
THE DAWN PATROL [FLIGHT COMMANDER] (1930)
DAWN PATROL (1938)
A DOG OF THE REGIMENT (1927)
DOUGH BOYS [FORWARD MARCH] (1930)
THE EAGLE AND THE HAWK (1933)
THE FIGHTING 69TH (1939)
THE FLIGHT COMMANDER *see*: THE DAWN PATROL
    (1930)
FOR EVER ENGLAND *see*: BORN FOR GLORY
FORWARD MARCH *see*: DOUGH BOYS
THE FOUR HORSEMEN OF THE APOCALYPSE (1921)
GALLIPOLI (1981)
HEARTS OF THE WORLD (1918)
HELL BELOW (1933)
HELL BENT FOR GLORY *see*: LAFAYETTE ESCADRILLE
HELL'S ANGELS (1930)
JOURNEY'S END (1930)
LAFAYETTE ESCADRILLE [HELL BENT FOR GLORY]
    (1958)
LAWRENCE OF ARABIA (1962)
THE LEGION OF THE CONDEMNED (1928)

LILAC TIME (1928)
THE LOST PATROL (1934)
THE MAN FROM WYOMING (1930)
OH! WHAT A LOVELY WAR! (1969)
PATHS OF GLORY (1957)
THE RED BARON *see*: VON RICHTHOFEN AND BROWN
THE ROAD TO GLORY [WOODEN CROSSES; ZERO
   HOUR] (1937)
SERGEANT YORK (1941)
SHE GOES TO WAR (1929)
SHOULDER ARMS (1918)
SONS O'GUNS (1936)
A TIME TO LOVE AND A TIME TO DIE (1958)
VON RICHTHOFEN AND BROWN [THE RED BARON]
   (1971)
WHAT PRICE GLORY? (1926)
WHAT PRICE GLORY? (1952)
WINGS (1926)
WOODEN CROSSES *see*: THE ROAD TO GLORY
ZERO HOUR *see*: THE ROAD TO GLORY

ABOUT WORLD WAR II:

ABOVE AND BEYOND (1952)
ABOVE US THE WAVES (1955)
ACTION IN THE NORTH ATLANTIC (1943)
AIR FORCE (1943)
ALBERT, R.N. (1953)
AMBUSH BAY (1966)
AN AMERICAN GUERRILLA IN THE PHILIPPINES (1950)
THE AMERICANIZATION OF EMILY [EMILY] (1964)
ANGELS ONE FIVE (1952)
ANZIO [BATTLE FOR ANZIO] (1968)
ATTACK! (1956)
ATTACK ON THE IRON COAST (1968)
AWAY ALL BOATS (1956)
BACK TO BATAAN (1945)
BATTLE CRY (1955)
BATTLE FOR ANZIO *see*: ANZIO

THE BATTLE OF BRITAIN (1969)
BATTLE OF RIVER PLATE *see*: PURSUIT OF THE GRAF SPEE
BATTLE OF THE BULGE (1965)
BATTLE OF THE CORAL SEA (1959)
BATTLE STATIONS (1956)
BATTLEGROUND (1949)
BEACH RED (1967)
THE BEST OF ENEMIES [I DUE NEMICI] (1961)
BETWEEN HEAVEN AND HELL (1956)
THE BIG RED ONE (1981)
BOMBARDIER (1943)
BREAKOUT [DANGER WITHIN] (1959)
BREAKTHROUGH (1950)
THE BRIDGE AT REMAGEN (1969)
THE BRIDGE ON THE RIVER KWAI (1957)
A BRIDGE TOO FAR (1976)
THE CAINE MUTINY (1954)
THE CAMP ON BLOOD ISLAND (1958)
CAPTAIN OF THE CLOUDS (1942)
CARGO OF INNOCENTS *see*: STAND BY FOR ACTION
CASTLE KEEP (1969)
CATCH-22 (1970)
COCKLESHELL HEROES (1955)
THE COLDITZ STORY (1955)
COMMAND DECISION (1948)
CONVOY (1940)
CORREGIDOR (1943)
CORVETTE K-225 [THE NELSON TOUCH] (1943)
CRASH DIVE (1943)
CROSS OF IRON (1977)
THE CRUEL SEA (1954)
CRY HAVOC (1943)
D-DAY, THE SIXTH OF JUNE [THE SIXTH OF JUNE] (1956)
THE DAM BUSTERS (1955)
DANGER WITHIN *see*: BREAKOUT
DANGEROUS MOONLIGHT *see*: SUICIDE SQUADRON
DARBY'S RANGERS [THE YOUNG INVADERS] (1958)
THE DEEP SIX (1958)
THE DESERT FOX [ROMMEL—DESERT FOX] (1951)

DESERT PATROL [SEA OF SAND] (1962)
THE DESERT RATS (1953)
DESPERATE JOURNEY (1942)
DESTINATION GOBI (1953)
DESTINATION TOKYO (1944)
THE DEVIL'S BRIGADE (1968)
THE DIRTY DOZEN (1967)
THE DIRTY DOZEN: DANKO'S MISSION: THE SERIES
  (1988-TV)
DIRTY DOZEN: THE DEADLY MISSION (1987-TV)
THE DIRTY DOZEN: THE FATAL MISSION (1988-TV)
DIRTY DOZEN: THE NEXT MISSION (1985-TV)
DUNKIRK (1958)
EAGLE SQUADRON (1942)
EMILY *see:* THE AMERICANIZATION OF EMILY
THE ENEMY BELOW (1957)
ENOLA GAY (1981-TV)
ESCAPE FROM BATAAN *see:* THE LONGEST HUNDRED
  MILES
ESCAPE TO MINDANAO (1968-TV)
FIGHTER ATTACK (1953)
FIGHTER SQUADRON (1948)
THE FIGHTING SEABEES (1944)
FIRST TO FIGHT (1967)
FLYING FORTRESS (1942)
FLYING LEATHERNECKS (1951)
FORCE OF ARMS (1951)
FORCE 10 FROM NAVARONE (1978)
FOREVER IN LOVE *see:* PRIDE OF THE MARINES
THE FOUR HORSEMEN OF THE APOCALYPSE (1962)
THE FROGMEN (1951)
G.I. JOE *see:* THE STORY OF G.I. JOE
THE GALLANT HOURS (1960)
GO FOR BROKE! (1951)
GOD IS MY CO-PILOT (1945)
THE GREAT ESCAPE (1963)
GUADALCANAL DAIRY (1943)
GUNG HO! (1943)
THE GUNS OF NAVARONE (1961)

A GUY NAMED JOE (1943)
HALLS OF MONTEZUMA (1950)
HEAVEN KNOWS, MR. ALLISON (1957)
HELL IN THE PACIFIC (1968)
HELL IS FOR HEROES (1962)
HELL TO ETERNITY (1960)
HELLCATS OF THE NAVY (1957)
HOME OF THE BRAVE (1949)
HORNET'S NEST (1970)
HOW I WON THE WAR (1967)
I DUE NEMICI *see*: THE BEST OF ENEMIES
IKE [IKE: THE WAR YEARS] (1978-TV)
IKE: THE WAR YEARS *see*: IKE
THE IMMORTAL SERGEANT (1943)
IN HARM'S WAY (1965)
IN LOVE AND WAR (1958)
IN WHICH WE SERVE (1942)
IS PARIS BURNING? [PARIS BRULE-T-IL?] (1966)
ISLAND ESCAPE *see*: NO MAN IS AN ISLAND
JUNGLE FIGHTERS *see*: THE LONG AND THE SHORT
    AND THE TALL
KELLY'S HEROES(1969)
KING RAT (1965)
THE LION HAS WINGS (1939)
LION OF THE DESERT (1981)
THE LONG AND THE SHORT AND THE TALL [JUNGLE
    FIGHTERS] (1961)
THE LONG DAY'S DYING (1968)
THE LONGEST DAY (1962)
THE LONGEST HUNDRED MILES [ESCAPE FROM
    BATAAN] (1967)
MacARTHUR [MacARTHUR, THE REBEL GENERAL] (1977)
MacARTHUR, THE REBEL GENERAL *see*: MacARTHUR
THE McKENZIE BREAK (1970)
THE MALTA STORY (1954)
MANILA CALLING (1942)
MARINE RAIDERS (1944)
MERRILL'S MARAUDERS (1962)
MERRY CHRISTMAS, MR. LAWRENCE (1983)

MIDWAY (1976)
MR. WINKLE GOES TO WAR (1944)
MURPHY'S WAR (1971)
MYSTERY SUBMARINE (1963)
THE NAKED AND THE DEAD (1958)
THE NELSON TOUCH *see*: CORVETTE K-225
NINE MEN (1943)
NO MAN IS AN ISLAND [ISLAND ESCAPE] (1962)
NONE BUT THE BRAVE [YUSHA NOMI] (1965)
THE NUN AND THE SERGEANT (1962)
OBJECTIVE, BURMA! (1945)
ONE OF OUR AIRCRAFT IS MISSING (1942)
OVERLORD (1975)
PARIS BRULE-T-IL? *see*: IS PARIS BURNING?
THE PASSWORD IS COURAGE (1962)
PATTON (1970)
PILOT NO. 5 (1943)
PRIDE OF THE MARINES [FOREVER IN LOVE] (1945)
PT 109 (1963)
THE PURPLE HEART (1944)
PURSUIT OF THE GRAF SPEE [BATTLE OF RIVER PLATE]
    1957)
RAID ON ROMMEL (1971)
REACH FOR THE SKY (1956)
RED BALL EXPRESS (1952)
ROMMEL—DESERT FOX *see*: THE DESERT FOX
RUN SILENT, RUN DEEP (1958)
SAHARA (1943)
SALERNO BEACHHEAD *see*: A WALK IN THE SUN
SANDS OF IWO JIMA (1949)
THE SEA CHASE (1955)
SEA OF SAND *see*: DESERT PATROL
THE SEA SHALL NOT HAVE THEM (1954)
THE SECRET INVASION (1964)
SHELL SHOCK (1964)
SHIPS WITH WINGS (1942)
THE SILENT ENEMY (1958)
SINK THE BISMARCK! (1960)
633 SQUADRON (1964)
THE SIXTH OF JUNE *see*: D-DAY, THE SIXTH OF JUNE

SO PROUDLY WE HAIL (1943)
STALAG 17 (1953)
STAND BY FOR ACTION [CARGO OF INNOCENTS] (1942)
THE STEEL BAYONET (1958)
THE STEEL CLAW (1961)
THE STORY OF DR. WASSELL (1944)
THE STORY OF G.I. JOE [G.I. JOE; WAR
   CORRESPONDENT] (1945)
SUBMARINE RAIDER (1942)
SUBMARINE X-1 (1969)
SUICIDE RUN *see*: TOO LATE THE HERO
SUICIDE SQUADRON [DANGEROUS MOONLIGHT]
   (1942)
THEY WERE EXPENDABLE (1945)
THEY WERE NOT DIVIDED (1950)
THEY WHO DARE (1954)
THE THIN RED LINE (1964)
THIRTY SECONDS OVER TOKYO (1944)
THUNDER ACROSS THE PACIFIC *see*: WILD BLUE
   YONDER
TO HELL AND BACK (1955)
TOBRUK (1966)
TOO LATE THE HERO [SUICIDE RUN] (1970)
TOO YOUNG THE HERO (1988-TV)
TORA! TORA! TORA! (1970)
TORPEDO ALLEY (1952)
TORPEDO RUN (1958)
TWELVE O'CLOCK HIGH (1949)
UNDER TEN FLAGS (1960)
UP FROM THE BEACH (1965)
UP PERISCOPE (1959)
THE VALIANT (1962)
THE VICTORS (1963)
VON RYAN'S EXPRESS (1965)
WAKE ISLAND (1942)
A WALK IN THE SUN [SALERNO BEACHHEAD] (1945)
WAR CORRESPONDENT *see*: THE STORY OF G.I. JOE
THE WAR LOVER (1962)
WARKILL (1968)
WE DIVE AT DAWN (1943)

WHEELS OF TERROR (1987)
WILD BLUE YONDER [THUNDER ACROSS THE PACIFIC]
  (1952)
WING AND A PRAYER (1944)
WINGS OVER THE PACIFIC (1943)
THE WOODEN HORSE (1951)
A YANK IN THE R.A.F. (1941)
A YANK ON THE BURMA ROAD (1942)
YESTERDAY'S ENEMY (1959)
THE YOUNG INVADERS see: DARBY'S RANGERS
THE YOUNG LIONS (1958)
THE YOUNG WARRIORS (1967)
YUSHA NOMI see: NONE BUT THE BRAVE

ABOUT THE KOREAN WAR:

ALL THE YOUNG MEN (1960)
BATTLE CIRCUS (1953)
BATTLE HYMN (1956)
BATTLE TAXI (1955)
BATTLE ZONE (1952)
THE BRIDGES AT TOKO-RI (1954)
FIXED BAYONETS! (1951)
HELL IN KOREA [A HILL IN KOREA] (1957)
A HILL IN KOREA see: HELL IN KOREA
THE HUNTERS (1958)
INCHON (1981)
LETTER FROM KOREA see: A YANK IN KOREA
MARINES, LET'S GO (1961)
M*A*S*H (1970)
MEN IN WAR (1957)
MEN OF THE FIGHTING LADY (1954)
ONE MINUTE TO ZERO (1951)
PORK CHOP HILL (1959)
PRISONER OF WAR (1954)
THE RELUCTANT HEROES (1971-TV)
RETREAT, HELL! (1952)
THE STEEL HELMET (1951)
TARGET ZERO (1955)

WAR HUNT (1962)
A YANK IN KOREA [LETTER FROM KOREA] (1951)

ABOUT THE INDO-CHINA/VIETNAM WAR:

APOCALYPSE NOW (1979)
THE BOYS IN COMPANY C (1978)
BRADDOCK: MISSING IN ACTION III (1988)
CHINA GATE (1957)
THE DEER HUNTER (1978)
EYE OF THE EAGLE (1986)
FLY AWAY HOME (1981-TV)
FULL METAL JACKET (1987)
GO TELL THE SPARTANS (1978)
GOOD MORNING, VIETNAM (1987)
THE GREEN BERETS (1968)
HAMBURGER HILL (1987)
THE HANOI HILTON (1987)
HIDDEN SECRET *see*: A YANK IN INDO-CHINA
JUMP INTO HELL (1955)
LOST COMMAND (1966)
MISSING IN ACTION (1984)
MISSING IN ACTION II: THE BEGINNING (1985)
PLATOON (1986)
RAMBO: FIRST BLOOD, PART II (1985)
A RUMOR OF WAR (1980-TV)
TO THE SHORES OF HELL (1966)
UNCOMMON VALOR [UNCOMMON VALOUR] (1983)
UNCOMMON VALOUR *see*: UNCOMMON VALOR
A YANK IN INDO-CHINA [HIDDEN SECRET] (1952)
A YANK IN VIET-NAM [THE YEAR OF THE TIGER]
    (1964)
THE YEAR OF THE TIGER *see*: A YANK IN VIET-NAM

ABOUT OTHER WAR ACTIONS:

CAST A GIANT SHADOW (1966)
THE CHALLENGE (1970-TV)

CHE! (1969)
HEARTBREAK RIDGE (1984)
THE LAST GRENADE (1970)
WEEKEND WAR (1988-TV)

COMBAT PROGRAMS ON TELEVISION*

Compiled by Vincent Terrace

THE BLACK SHEEP SQUADRON (a.k.a. BAA BAA BLACK SHEEP). 9/21/76 to 9/1/78, NBC. With: Robert Conrad, Dana Elcar, Simon Oakland, John Larroquette, Dirk Blocker, Robert Ginty.

CALL TO GLORY. 8/13/84 to 2/12/85, ABC. With: Craig T. Nelson, Cindy Pickett, Elizabeth Shue, Kathleen Lloyd, David Hollander.

CAMPO 44 (pilot). 9/9/67, NBC. With: Jim Dawson, Dino Fazio, Fred Smoot.

THE CASE AGAINST PAUL RYKER (pilot, aired on "The Bob Hope Chrysler Theater"; basis for "Court-Martial" series). 10/10, 10/17/63, NBC. With: Lee Marvin, Bradford Dillman, Vera Miles, Peter Graves.

CATCH-22 (pilot). 5/21/73, ABC. With: Richard Dreyfuss, Dana Elcar, Stewart Moss.

CHINA BEACH. 4/26/88 (premiere), ABC. With: Dana Delany, Chloe Webb, Marg Helgenberger, Nan Woods.

CITIZEN SOLDIER (a.k.a. THE BIG ATTACK). 1957, syndicated. With: actual servicemen.

COMBAT. 10/2/62 to 8/29/67, ABC. With: Rick Jason, Vic Morrow, Jack Hogan, Shecky Greene.

COMBAT SERGEANT. 6/29/56 to 9/27/56, ABC. With: Michael Thomas, Mara Corday, Cliff Clark.

---

*As with this book's entries on theatrical feature films and telefeatures dealing with twentieth-century combat, this listing of combat television series and pilots does *not* include those shows which are primarily documentaries, espionage tales, service (training) comedies/dramas, civilians on the homefront.

CONVOY. 9/17/65 to 12/10/65, NBC. With: John Gavin, John Larch, Linden Chiles.

COURT-MARTIAL. 4/8/66 to 9/2/66, ABC. With: Peter Graves, Bradford Dillman, Diene Clare.

THE DIRTY DOZEN: THE SERIES. 4/30/88 to 8/21/88, Fox Network. With: Ben Murphy, Tom Tenney, John Slattery, John Di Aquino.

THE FIGHTING NIGHTINGALES (pilot). 1/16/78, CBS. With: Adrienne Barbeau, Ken Mars, Erica Yohn, Stephanie Faracy.

THE FLIERS (pilot; aired on "The Bob Hope Chrysler Theater"). 2/5/65, NBC. With: John Cassavetes, Carol Lynley, Chester Morris.

FOR LOVE AND HONOR. 9/23/83 to 1/15/84, NBC. With: Cliff Potts, Shelley Smith, Rachel Ticotin, Yaphet Kotto.

THE GALLANT MEN. 10/5/62 to 9/14/63, ABC. With: James Reynolds, Robert McQueeney, Roger Davis, Richard X. Slattery.

The G.I.s (pilot). 7/29/80, CBS. With: Ken Gilman, Jonathan Banks, Gregg Berger, Lorry Goldman.

THE GYPSY WARRIORS (pilot). 7/29/80, CBS. With: James Whitmore, Jr., Tom Selleck, Lina Raymond, Kenneth Tigar.

HOGAN'S HEROES. 9/17/65 to 7/4/71, CBS. With: Bob Crane, Werner Klemperer, John Banner, Richard Dawson.

McHALE'S NAVY. 9/11/62 to 8/30/66, ABC. With: Ernest Borgnine, Tim Conway, Joe Flynn, Carl Ballantine, Gavin MacLeod.

M*A*S*H. 9/17/72 to 9/19/83, CBS. With: Alan Alda, Wayne Rogers, Loretta Swit, Larry Linville, Harry Morgan, McLean Stevenson, Jamie Farr.

NAVY LOG. 9/20/55 to 9/25/56, CBS; 10/17/56 to 9/25/58, ABC. With: guest players such as: Beverly Garland, Robert Montgomery, Clint Eastwood, Steve Brodie, Ernest Borgnine.

OFF WE GO (pilot). 9/5/66, CBS. With: Michael Burns, Dick Foran, Dick Curtis, Ann Jillian.

PURSUE AND DESTROY (pilot). 8/14/66, ABC. With: Van Williams, Paul Comi, David Thorpe, Dee Pollock.

THE RAT PATROL. 9/12/66 to 9/16/68, ABC. With: Christopher George, Justin Tarr, Gary Raymond, Hans Gudegast [Eric Braeden].

ROLL OUT. 10/5/73 to 1/4/74, CBS. With: Stu Gilliam, Hilly Hicks, Mel Stewart, Ed Begley, Jr., Garrett Morris.

THE SIX O'CLOCK FOLLIES. 4/24/80 to 4/26/80, NBC. With: Joby Baker, Aarika Wells, A. C. Weary, Randall Carver.

SKYFIGHTERS (pilot). 8/59. Non-network. With: Joe Maross, Brian Kelly, Lisa Gaye.

SNAFU (pilot). 8/23/76, NBC. With: Tony Roberts, James Cromwell, Kip Niven, Jay Leno.

SOMEWHERE IN ITALY . . . COMPANY B (pilot). 8/21/66, ABC. With: Robert Reed, Harold J. Stone, Barbara Shelley.

SUPER CARRIER. 3/6/88 to 5/14/88, ABC. With: Richard Jaeckel, Robert Hooks, Ken Oland, Marie Windsor.

TENKO. 1986, syndicated. With: Louise Jamison, Ann Bell, Renee Asherson, Stephanie Beachman, Patricia Lawrence, Stephanie Cole.

VIETNAM WAR STORY (pilot). 8/7/87, Home Box Office. With: Tom Frindley, Eriq LaSalle, Nicholas Cascone.

ABOUT THE AUTHOR

JAMES ROBERT PARISH, Studio City, California-based direct marketing consultant and free-lance writer, was born in Cambridge, Massachusetts. He attended the University of Pennsylvania and graduated Phi Beta Kappa with a degree in English. A graduate of the University of Pennsylvania Law School, he is a member of the New York Bar. As president of Entertainment Copyright Research Co., Inc. he headed a major researching facility for the film and television industries. Later he was a film reviewer-interviewer for *Motion Picture Daily* and *Variety* trade newspapers. He is the author of more than 75 volumes, including: *The Fox Girls, Good Dames, The Slapstick Queens, The RKO Gals, The Tough Guys, The Jeanette MacDonald Story, The Elvis Presley Scrapbook, The Hollywood Beauties,* and *Black Action Pictures From Hollywood.* Among those he has co-written are: *The MGM Stock Company, The Debonairs, Liza!, Hollywood Character Actors, The Hollywood Reliables, The Funsters, The Best of MGM,* and his ongoing series, *Complete Actors Television Credits,* with Vincent Terrace. With Michael R. Pitts, he has co-written such tomes as *Hollywood on Hollywood, The Great Western Pictures* (base and companion volumes), *The Great Gangster Pictures* (base and companion volumes), *The Great Spy Pictures* (base and companion volumes), and *The Great Science Fiction Pictures* (base and companion volumes). Mr. Parish's entertainment reference collection is archived at Kent State University Library in Kent, Ohio.